THE US

WAR MACHINE

An encyclopedia of American military equipment and strategy

THE US WAR MACHINE

An encyclopedia of American military equipment and strategy

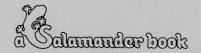

a Salamander book

Published by Crown Publishers, Inc.
NEW YORK

A Salamander Book

First published in 1983 in the United States by Crown Publishers Inc., One Park Avenue, New York, New York 10016, United States of America.

All rights reserved. Except for use in a review, no part of this book may be utilized or reproduced, in any form or by any means, electronic or mechanical, including photocopying, recording or by any information storage and retrieval system, without the permission in writing from the publisher.

First published in the United Kingdom in 1983 by Salamander Books Limited.

© Salamander Books Ltd. 1983 Salamander House, 27 Old Gloucester Street, London WC1N 3AF, United Kingdom.

ISBN O-517-54984-0

All correspondence concerning the content of this volume should be addressed to Salamander Books Ltd.

This book is not to be sold outside the United States of America and Canada.

Published in Canada by General Publishing Company Ltd.

Library of Congress Cataloging in Publication Data

Main entry under title:

The US war machine.
   "A Salamander book."
   Includes index.
   1.   United States—Armed Forces.   2.   United States—Military policy.   3.   Munitions—United States.
I. Bonds, Ray.   II. Dornan, James E.
UA23.U79 1983   355'.00973   82-22124
ISBN 0-517-54984-0 (pbk.)

Credits

Editor: Ray Bonds

Designer: Philip Gorton

Filmset: SX Composing Ltd., and Modern Text Typesetting Ltd.

Color reproduction: Rodney Howe Ltd.

Printed in Belgium by Henri Proost & Cie, Turnhout.

Editor's Acknowledgements

In the process of preparing this unique volume for publication I have been fortunate in having received the help and advice of so many people and organizations that it is impossible to acknowledge them all individually here. But I do thank them all for their assistance and their patience in the face of my persistent requests for information and illustrations. In particular, while co-ordinating the efforts of all concerned, I have been extremely grateful to have been able to call upon the unstinting energy and great depth of knowledge of United States (and worldwide) military/political affairs exercised by the consultant, the late Dr.James E. Dornan, Jr. With his guidance, an authoritative team of commentators was forged together whose contributions,combined with those of British technical specialists, will I am sure become standard works of reference (and food for thought). Dr. Dornan died tragically in January 1979. Each of the US Services has been extremely helpful, and I accordingly thank the offices of information of the Department of Defense, The Army, Navy, Air Force and Marine Corps, The Defense Intelligence Agency and other government organizations and agencies in the United States and in Europe.

I sincerely thank *Air Force Magazine* and *Army* for their cooperation in allowing us to reproduce or use as references some of their tables, diagrams and charts, and thank also all of the manufacturers of weapons and systems for making available many excellent photographs and useful information.

Ray Bonds

Contents

The Consultant

The original edition of this book was based on a concept of the late Dr. James E. Dornan, Jr., who was Associate Professor and Chairman of the Department of Politics at the Catholic University of America, and Senior Political Scientist at the Strategic Studies Center of Stanford Research Institute International, Washington D.C. He received a B.A. (magna cum laude) from LeMoyne College and the Ph.D. from the Johns Hopkins Univeristy, both in Political Science. He also taught at Johns Hopkins University, lectured at numerous colleges and universities, and contributed articles to many professional journals, including *Political Science Reviewer*, the *Journal of Politics*, *Armed Forces Journal*, *Intercollegiate Review* (of which he was contributing editor), *Modern Age*, *Sea Power* and *Brassey's Annual*. He also contributed chapters to many books and monographs, including Salamander's *The Soviet War Machine*, and was the editor and co-author of the forthcoming volume, *US National Security Policy in the Decade Ahead* (Crane Russak). Dr. Dornan received research grants from NATO and the Earheart Foundation for the study of US–NATO military policy, and made study-visits to and attended conferences in both Europe and Asia a number of times in recent years. He was also a contributing editor of the *Journal of International Relations* and a member of the Editorial Board of *Orbis*, the Journal of the Foreign Policy Research Institute, University of Pennsylvania.

The Authors

Dr. William R. Van Cleave is Professor of International Relations and Director of the Defense and Strategic Studies Program at the University of Southern California. He is a Consultant to the Office of the Secretary of Defense; was a member of the "B Team" (Presidential Panel to Review National Intelligence on USSR, 1976–77); was Special Assistant, Strategic Policy, NSC Affairs, and SALT, Office of the Secretary of Defense (ASD/ISA, 1969–71); was a member of the US Delegation to the Strategic Arms Limitation Talks (SALT) 1969–1971. Dr. Van Cleave is also a consultant to the Central Intelligence Agency, the US Energy Research and Development Agency and to many non-Government research institutes and agencies. He has contributed to very many professional journals

Dr Ray S. Cline is a Senior Associate of the Center for Strategic and International Studies, Georgetown University. Before assuming this position in 1974 Dr. Cline served for more than 30 years in several US Government agencies. He was Deputy Director for Intelligence in the Central Intelligence Agency (1962–66) and Director of the Bureau of Intelligence and Research in the Department of State (1969–73), a position equivalent to Assistant Secretary of State. Dr.Cline holds A.B., M.A. and Ph.D. degrees from Harvard University; he also studied at Balliol College, Oxford University, as a Henry Prize Fellow, and later was a member of the Society of Fellows at Harvard. Dr. Cline is author of *Washington Command Post* US Army in World War II, a book on US military planning during World War II which is a standard reference; *Policy Without Intelligence*, *Foreign Policy* No. 17; *Secrets, Spies and Scholars: A Blueprint of the Essential CIA* (which has appeared under other titles in updated form); and *World Power Assessment*.

John M. Collins is Senior Specialist in National Defense, US Library of Congress. He received a B.A. from the University of Kansas City, and an M.A. from Clark University, Massachusetts. His military education has taken in the Army Command and General Staff College, the Armed Forces Staff College, Industrial College of the Armed Forces and the National War College. Having enlisted as a private in the US Army in 1942, he retired as a colonel in 1972. Mr Collins has specialized in joint/combined contingency planning, with particular attention to NATO Europe, the Middle East, Southeast Asia and Cuba, was Director, Military Strategy Studies, and Chief, Strategic Research Group, at the National War College.He is the author of several books and official documents.

Christopher F. Foss is Editor of the periodical *Jane's Defence Review*, and of *Jane's World Armoured Fighting Vehicles*, author of two Jane's pocketbooks on modern AFV's and towed artillery, besides contributing annually to *Jane's Weapons Systems* and to *Infantry Weapons*. He is former weapons correspondent to *Defence* magazine, and contributor to many professional journals.

Stephen P. Gibert is Professor of Government and Director of the National Security Studies Program at Georgetown University, Washington D.C. Dr. Gibert has served as an advisor to the Asia Foundation and the Government of the Union of Burma, and has been a visiting Professor at the University of Rangoon and the US Naval War College. He has contributed a number of articles on foreign policy and international security affairs to leading professional journals and is co-author of the book, *Arms for the Third World: Soviet Military Aid Diplomacy*. His most recent work is *Soviet Images of America*.

Bill Gunston is an advisor to several major aviation companies. He is a noted writer on aviation and technical affairs, being former technical editor of *Flight International*, and technology editor of *Science Journal*. He is a contributor to *Jane's All The World's Aircraft*

and to many authoritative international military journals. Mr. Gunston is author of many Salamander military reference books.

John Jordan has contributed numerous technical articles on ships of the US Navy, the Soviet Navy and the NATO navies to defense journals which include *Navy International, Warship* and *Defence*. He was a consultant to the Soviet section of the 1980–81 edition of *Jane's Fighting Ships*. He is co-author of Salamander's *The Balance of Military Power*, and author of Salamander's *Illustrated Guide to the Soviet Navy* and *Illustrated Guide to the US Navy*.

Dr. Lawrence J. Korb is Assistant Secretary of Defense (Manpower, Reserve Affairs and Logistics). He was formerly Professor of Management, US Naval War College, and Adjunct Scholar of the American Enterprise Institute for federal budgetary analysis and national security policy. He served as consultant to the Office of the Secretary of Defense, the National Security Council and the Office of Education. He is the author of *The Joint Chiefs of Staff: The First Twenty Years; The Price of Preparedness, The FY 1978–82 Defense Program;* and has co-authored *Public Claims on US Output: Federal Budget Options for the Last half of the Decade.*

Doug Richardson is a defense journalist specializing in the fields of aviation, guided missiles and electronics. Currently Editor of *Defence Materiel,* he was formerly Defense Editor of *Flight International,* and Editor of *Military Technology and Economics.* He was co-author of the Salamander books *The Balance of Military Power* and *The Illustrated Encyclopedia of Modern Warplanes.*

Bruce F. Powers is a Senior Fellow at the Strategic Concepts Development Center of the National Defense University, Washington, D.C. He has also been at the RAND Corporation, the Institute for Defense Analyses, and the Center for Naval Analyses. His early career alternated between studies in Washington and one year assignments with admirals who were in command of fleets. He holds degrees in Operational Research (Illinois Institute of Technology), Physical Chemistry (University of Chicago), and Chemistry (University of Illinois).

Lt. Col. David K. Riggs is an instructor in the Department of Joint and Combined operations of the US Army Command and General Staff College. A graduate of the US Military Academy with an M.A. in International Studies from the University of Geneva, he has served in Korea, Vietnam and Europe. Recent assignments include the faculty of the US Military Academy, the staff of the Assistant Secretary of Defense for International Security Affairs and command of a tank battalion.

Alan Ned Sabrosky (Ph.D., University of Michigan) is Senior Fellow in Political-Military Studies at The Center for Strategic and International Stdies, Washington, D.C.; Professorial Lecturer in Government and Adjunct Professor of National Security Studies at Georgetown University; and Lecturer in Political Science at the University of Pennsylvania. A specialist in international security affairs and civil-military relations, he has taught at the US Military Academy at West Point and lectured widely at public and private defense-related institutions, including the US National War College, the Inter-American Defense College, the NATO Defense College, and the International Institute for Strategic Studies. His published work includes *Great Power Games* (1982), *Military Manpower and Military Power* (1980), *Defense Manpower Policy: A Critical Reappraisal* (1978), and *Blue-Collar Soldiers.*

Lt. Col. Donald B. Vought, USA (Ret.) retired from service with the US Army after 23 years of service which included three years with NATO, one year in Vietnam and one year in Iran as advisor to the Imperial Armor School. He was for seven years on the faculty of the US Army Command and General Staff College at Fort Leavenworth, Kansas, where he specialized in low-intensity warfare, intercultural communications and the study of national development as a multidisciplinary phenomenon. He is a graduate of Norwich University with M.A.s in Political Science (University of Louisville) and International Relations (Boston University). Lt. Col. Vought has been a frequent contributor to professional conferences and publications

Russell F. Weigley is professor of history at Temple University, Philadelphia. He has taught also at the University of Pennsylvania, Drexel University, and Dartmouth College, and in 1973–74 he was US Army Visiting Professor of Military History Research at the US Army Military History Institute and the Army War College. He is president of the Pennsylvania Historical Association and has been president of the American Military Institute. His books include *Towards an American Army: Military Thought from Washington to Marshall; History of the United States Army;* and *The American Way of War: A History of United States Military Strategy and Policy.*

Roy A. Werner is Corporate Director, Policy Research, of Northrop Corporation. He was formerly Principal Deputy Assistant Secretary of the Army, and was on the staff of the US Senate Foreign Relations Committee. He has previously served as a Foreign Affairs Officer in the US Federal Energy Administration. He has been Task Force Director and Associate Director, Programs, White House Conference on Youth, consultant to Senator Philip Hart, Legislative Assistant to Senator John Glenn, an analyst at the Office of the Secretary of the Army, and Secretary (Executive Director), Oxford University Strategic Studies Group.

Foreword

by General Richard G. Stilwell,
US Army (Ret.), former Commander,
Eighth Army and United Nations
Command, Korea

Throughout the last decade and a half, the foreign and defense policies of the United States have been the subject of deepening controversy. And since policies and power are closely interrelated, the primary focus of debate has been the posture of the American military establishment. Issues of deterrent and war fighting concepts, of force structure and force balance, of tactical doctrine, of weaponry, of deployments, readiness and staying power have all come under intense scrutiny and critique. While the great bulk of analyses and commentary has originated in American circles and been addressed to the domestic body politics, interest in these vital matters has been international in scope. The debates have commanded high and sustained attention among the allies of the United States, within much of the balance of the free world and in the People's Republic of China. The reason needs no elaboration. In varying degrees, all of these nations are dependent on the will and ability of the United States—and principally through the medium of its armed forces—to help them deal with extant and perceived future threats to their security and well-being. Hence the timeliness and importance of this comprehensive and objective profile of the American military machine.

As detailed in the pages of this volume, the United States armed forces are impressive for their size, power, and versatility. Their reach is global. They possess the means for, and are geared to conduct, military operations throughout the entire spectrum of conflict from strategic nuclear exchange to high intensity conventional combat to sub-limited warfare to projection of power in support of political initiative. Backing these forces are enormous demographic resources, unsurpassed industrial capability and a pre-eminent scientific base. In the aggregate, these formidable strengths are proof positive that the United States is a military superpower. However, these strengths alone do not gauge the adequacy of the defense posture of the nation or, pertinently, of the free

world. That assessment involves consideration of numerous other factors, some quantifiable and some not. Principal among these factors are the range and nature of missions assigned and the capabilities of potential adversaries.

In the years since World War II the United States military establishment has shouldered responsibilities of unprecedented magnitude and diversity. Its supreme mission—akin to that of the armed forces of any nation which acts responsibly—is to protect the American people, institutions and territory from direct and indirect attack. Beyond that, it is tasked with the contingent defense of Western Europe, Japan and numerous other nations pursuant to multi-lateral and bi-lateral security arrangements to which the United States is party; all of these commitments, incidentally, involve extensive preparations for the orchestration of US and allied forces under varying coalition modes. Moreover, since the United States exercises leadership of what is, in essence, a maritime alliance its military establishment bears primary responsibility for ensuring that member states have uninterrupted use of international waters and air space and access to markets, raw materials and energy sources. Overall, those armed forces have had the generic task of preventing the threat of use of naked military force—particularly nuclear—for purpose of political or economic coercion of the nations of the free world community. Though this complex of missions has generated exceedingly heavy demands and the United States military resources have been spread correspondingly thin, the record of the last twenty years and more has been quite creditable. All major tasks have been successfully discharged. Vietnam, of course, was a conspicuous failure, albeit one due, in the main, to collapse of national will rather than inadequate military performance. In any case, past achievements are not a harbinger of the future. For one thing, the United States and her allies were spared multiple concurrent crises. For another, the United States enjoyed, for most of the period, both actual and perceived superiority in the strategic nuclear dimension, reasonably assured command of the seas and a decided edge in capability to project force to areas outside the Eurasian land mass. These favorable differentials counterbalanced weaknesses in other segments of the overall defense posture. However, these differentials are not likely to persist, given the prodigious Soviet efforts to overcome the United States' lead in precisely these areas.

To be sure, the lengthening shadow cast by the Soviet military machine is not the only threat that needs to be reckoned with. But it is certainly the most ominous. The last ten years have been witness to extraordinary increases in Soviet nuclear and conventional forces. As the build-up continues unabated all evidence points to Soviet intent to achieve dominance in every dimension of military power. Though prepared for the eventuality of armed conflict at any level and at any time, the Soviets have studied Clausewitz with consummate care. They thus aspire to advance, step by step, toward world hegemony employing every strategem short of unambiguous war. By consequence, the principal role of the Soviet armed forces is to undergird political and economical moves to disrupt the free world alliance system, sap the vitality of the free enterprise area and isolate the United States and China. Thus, the Soviet armed forces constitute a many faceted threat.

Over two centuries, the US military has been tested, retested, and never found wanting, but its supreme challenge lies ahead. With the quantitative military balance (not only in the ground components, where Soviet advantages have been long standing, but in nuclear, naval and air dimensions as well, given the respective military trend lines) decidedly adverse and with the former qualitative edge increasingly in doubt, we can assume a favorable outcome in the event of war only by superior concepts, tactics and leadership. We are desperately in need of a strategy —not only for war-fighting, but for winning without war.

For the first time since the War of Independence, the United States forces are destined to be the under-dog. These predictable developments are cause for concern but they by no means portend unfavorable outcomes either in war or in military confrontation in crisis scenarios short of war. In the long history of warfare numerical advantage has rarely been the decisive factor. Nor have perceptions of relative power in crisis situations been primarily shaped by size alone. Most frequently, the major determinents of favorable issue—in campaign or in confrontation— have been superior strategy, tactical concepts, leadership, audacity and discipline. Naturally the United States and its allies cannot afford to let the quantitative gap widen appreciably more or, worse yet, accept technological inferiority. As an example, the Soviets must not be permitted to attain a politically exploitable superiority in strategic nuclear systems. Nor can the Soviets be allowed to inhibit free world projection of power or untrammelled use of the high seas. But, in the last analysis, the United States armed forces will measure up to their manifold tasks to the extent —and only to the extent—that they are able to devise the better strategy and carry out that strategy with unexcelled professionalism.

The History of the US Armed Forces

Russell F. Weigley, Professor of History at Temple University, Philadelphia; past-president, American Military Institute.

The famous martial pageantry of the US Military Academy at West Point is that of a bygone era. The close-order drill of the Corps of Cadets has its roots in the discipline taught by Baron von Steuben to General George Washington's Continental Army at Valley Forge in 1778, and beyond that in the necessity of eighteenth-century armies to maneuver on the battlefield as though the soldiers were automatons on parade, to maintain the line in the face of the enemy's volley firing and bayonet charge. The cadets' gray uniforms memorialize Winfield Scott's and Eleazar Wheelock Ripley's brigades of United States Regulars who charged the British at Chippewa and Lundy's Lane in Upper Canada in 1814, the first battles in which American troops were able to hold their own against approximately equal numbers of British veterans in stand-up combat throughout the battle. Scott's and Ripley's men happened to be clothed in gray, because the quartermaster had run out of regulation United States Army blue.

For the United States, the perpetuating of ancient military memories and rituals is much more paradoxical than it is for other nations such as Britain, because for Great Britain the remote past is for the most part the nation's militarily prominent past. For the United States, in contrast, as General Maxwell D. Taylor remarked in a West Point commencement address in 1963 in the very midst of the antique pageantry, it is only since World War II that the nation has assuredly attained a special eminence among the military powers of the world. It did so with abrupt suddenness. Through most of the American past, the United States was in military tutelage to Europe, almost in a colonial relationship militarily. Since 1945, military officers from all countries friendly to the United States have attended military schools in America; but until the abrupt change of World War II, Americans learned their military lessons from Europe.

The principal reason for this history of recent and rapid transition from military obscurity to military prominence is simply that until World War I, or at least until the American War with Spain in 1898, the United States was an isolated power not participating in world military events or the world diplomacy of the military great powers. The oceans, not American ships or forts, were the source of American security. The American army was less an army of the European type than a constabulary for the patrolling of the Indian country in the West. By European standards, the American armed forces are almost armed forces without a history— which is no doubt one reason why Americans cling all the more tightly to the thin historical military tradition that does exist, as in the West Point parades.

After so rapid a rise to first-rank power, the American forces in the twentieth century have displayed a sensitivity about their status as newcomers. For a century, from the close of the 1775–1783 and 1812–1815 conflicts with Great Britain until World War I, the military forces of United States did not have to test themselves against any first-rate foreign foe. Under these circumstances, General John J. Pershing, the commander of the 1917–1918 American Expedi-

tionary Forces, was exceedingly conscious that his army was meeting first-division opponents on the first modern occasion, and that he must take care to make a good impression from the very beginning, for the sake of his own army's morale as well as to uphold America's weight in Allied councils. Many American soldiers themselves had come to doubt, as Lieutenant Colonel James S. Pettit had put it in a prize-winning essay in the *Journal* of the United States Military Service Institution in 1906, whether the American democracy could "maintain an organization or discipline comparable to that of little Japan", let alone the Continental powers.

General Pershing himself sufficiently doubted American readiness for European military competition that, if he had been able to have his way, he would have put every American division through nearly a year-long training regimen in France under French and British instructors, as he did the 1st Division, before committing his troops to the front in carefully planned set-piece battles, as he did with the 1st Division in a small offensive at Cantigny on May 28, 1918. The great German offensives of 1918 washed away Pershing's painstaking plans, obliging him to commit his troops to battle with much less preparation than he would have liked. Their performance was considerably better than their own officers anticipated, but sensitivity to the feeling — and reality — of being newcomers lingered on. In their final campaign of the war, the Meuse–Argonne Offensive of September 26–November 11, 1918, American troops were still suffering the disproportionately high casualties that fall to soldiers who are not battle-wise and battle-wary.

As late as World War II, the US Navy still displayed an acute and no doubt excessive consciousness of the fact that it was the only great navy that had never fought a full-scale fleet action. Because the Navy had no Tsushima and no Jutland in its past, in the Pacific Ocean war in 1941–1945 it pursued a super-Jutland—a grand, climactic battle against the Japanese fleet—with zeal beyond the boundaries of strategic good sense. The pursuit almost produced disaster when Admiral William F. Halsey followed a Japanese decoy fleet and thus exposed the Philippine Islands invasion force at Leyte Gulf to the main Japanese fleet in October, 1944. Fortunately, by this time the skill as well as the bravery of the crews of the smaller and older American warships guarding the invasion beaches was enough to discourage Japanese admirals who enjoyed material superiority.

The recency of America's emergence as a world military power has shaped the American armed forces also in matters more profound than an acute sensitivity about the thinness of the country's past military tradition. Having fought few wars against major foreign powers, at least until the recent past, Americans still tend to regard foreign war as an extraordinary occasion. Their military history combines with the national ideology, which is derived from the liberalism of the eighteenth and nineteenth centuries, to assure them that war is an abnormal state of affairs, that it can be accounted for only in terms of an uncommon eruption of evil into the world, and that the appropriate response is to extirpate the evil by means of an

In comparison with human history the life-span of the United States is but the blink of an eyelid. But these two centuries have seen the US involved in military actions of every kind. Gettysburg, 1-3 July 1864 (below) is remembered for its intensity of casualties, among other things, whereas the favorite heroic image is the raising of the Old Glory over Iwo Jima on 26 March 1944 by four Marines, subject of the Marine Corps Memorial at Arlington (far left). Controversy reached its peak in the "involvement" in Southeast Asia, though it was muted in 1965 when the F-4B Phantom of Navy squadron VF-21 dropped its bombs on the Viet Cong (left).

all-out military assault upon it. Thus the American propensity for demanding "unconditional surrender" of their country's enemies in war. To the argument that Americans may have grown more sophisticated in the use of military force to serve their national interests during their exercise of world power since 1945, it is necessary to respond with partial agreement, but also to point to the popular dissatisfaction in America during both the Korean and the Vietnam wars over the fact that in those conflicts military force was applied in limited, measured dosage, not hurled all-out against the enemy to compel his complete capitulation.

Indeed, the American tendency to regard war as demanding unlimited force in pursuit of the unlimited subjugation of the enemy has still deeper roots than those provided by inexperience in world affairs and by the national ideology, with still deeper consequences in shaping the American armed forces. Though American wars against European military powers have been few, the American past includes much experience of war with the North American Indians—almost continuous experience from 1607 to 1890. The military struggles against the Indians were of course the first wars fought in their new homes by Europeans who emigrated to the New World, the first wars to form a distinctive part of the American national memory.

From a very early juncture, the Indian wars took a different line of development from that which warfare in Europe was following in the seventeenth and eighteenth centuries. European war was becoming limited war, an enterprise of statecraft waged for dynastic, boundary, and colonial advantages but not for the very survival of the major states, in an era when monarchs recognized their common European and monarchical interests as well as their mutual rivalry and thus did not seek to eliminate each other altogether. In the same era, between

the Peace of Westphalia in 1648 and the onset of the French Revolution, when European war developed strict limitations, war in America grew decidedly unlimited. War in America became war for survival.

As early as 1643, for example, the Pequot War between the Connecticut and Massachusetts settlements on the one hand and the Pequot tribe on the other ended in the white men's complete destruction of the Pequots as an identifiable tribe. In King Philip's War, fought by a confederation of Wampanoags, Narragansetts, Nipmucks, and Abenaki under a chieftain the English called King Philip against the New England colonies in 1675–1676, the Indians in turn came dangerously close to throwing the still-youthful New England settlements back into the sea. The Americans' experience of war against the Indians became an experience of war aimed at total results, the extermination of the enemy as a military power, even as a society. Because the wars were frequently fought by what a later generation would call guerrilla methods, and since the Indians did not observe European rules for the conduct of the fighting, the wars aimed at total results seemed often to be waged with total ferocity.

In the War of the American Revolution, the Americans again displayed the conviction nourished by their Indian wars that only total solutions would suffice. First the Indians had to be removed completely from the neighborhood of the white Americans' settlements; then the French had to decamp from North America; now it was the British whose presence could in no way be endured. Not satisfied to expel the British from those colonies that had spontaneously risen in rebellion, the American rebels promptly in 1775 mounted expeditions to drive the British from Canada, which had not joined the rebellion. Though the conquest of

Canada proved beyond the rebels' strength, the idea of again attempting it persisted throughout the war.

Furthermore, the American desire for total solutions made itself felt once more in the new Treaty of Paris of 1783, ending the War of the Revolution, just as it had shaped the older Treaty of Paris of 1763. Having tried and failed to conquer Canada, the new United States could hardly demand its cession. But the presumptuousness of the infant Republic was considerable nevertheless. With only the most tenuous of military claims to the vast area extending west from the Appalachian Mountains to the Mississippi River, and with the British still in effective control of much of the area, the United States insisted that the British should not only recognize the independence of the thirteen rebellious colonies, but should cede to them the whole trans-Appalachian region. Once again furthermore, the American preference for unlimited solutions to the issues of war converged with a British desire to placate —this time to wean the United States from its 1778 alliance with France by means of British generosity. The United States received the Mississippi River as its western frontier.

It might be argued that the limitations of American military power during the Republic's early years soon curbed the tendency to seek total results from war. In the War of 1812–1815 with Great Britain, after all, the United States eventually settled for a peace reverting to the status quo ante bellum. In the War with Mexico in 1846–1848, the Yankees did not totally exterminate Mexican military power or sov-

Below: A stylized yet possibly truthful painting (by Chappel, 1828-87) of the Wyoming massacre of July 1778, one of a series in which settlers in the Susquehanna valley were murdered by Tories and Indians.

ereignty, but rather made do with the limited territorial acquisitions of the former Republic of Texas plus everything west from Texas to the Pacific Ocean—present New Mexico, Arizona, Utah, Nevada, and California, along with parts of Colorado and Wyoming (which might lead to the exclamation, "Some limits!"). But caution is necessary in ascribing even to the early, and militarily weak, American Republic any limited conception of the proper results of war. Though the actual peace terms of the War of 1812 were modest, they had been preceded by plenty of American talk about the annexation of all of Canada; it was not the will that was lacking, but the means. In regard to Mexico in 1848, by which time American military means were more ample, President James K. Polk rushed through the Senate a peace treaty negotiated by an emissary whom he had already repudiated before the terms were arranged, in part because the President thought he must hurry lest public sentiment for the annexation of all of Mexico get out of hand.

Nor did the military power of the American Republic remain at all feeble for very long. As early as the War with Mexico, the United States had the military capacity to conquer another American republic having to travel thousands of miles from the economic and population centers of the United States in order to do so. By the 1860s, the United States could mobilize against a domestic rebellion, taking the form of the secession of eleven of its southern states, great armies and navies that made it by 1865 the foremost military nation in the world—for a brief moment at least, until, characteristically, with the extermination of the evils that had caused the war the country hastily demobilized.

Meanwhile, for four years the American Civil War pitted armies of hundreds of thousands against each other in an arena that was continental in extent—one of the major wars of world history, and even though viewed legalistically it involved "only" a domestic rebellion, by far the greatest American war until World War II, and thus a war that confirmed American conceptions about the nature of war and military power all the way to World War II, at the least. Once more, the United States sought a total resolution of all the issues of the war, particularly the total extermination of all of the rebellious Southern Confederacy's pretensions to sovereignty. If this absolute result was largely implicit in the fact that the contest originated in a rebellion, nevertheless American preconceptions about war made the Union government all the more ready to assume, without examining the issue, that the outcome could be nothing else but total elimination of the enemy as a political and military force. Furthermore, the means of pursuing this end still more explicitly reflected the combination of American military experience in the Indian wars and the plenitude of United States military power by the 1860s. The means of securing the Confederacy's unconditional surrender was to be the total destruction of the Confederate armies.

When U. S. Grant moved from triumphs in the western theater of war to become Commanding General of all the Armies of the United States at the beginning of 1864, he instructed each of the commanders of major army groups and field armies under him that their objective was the destruction of the enemy armies contending against them. Thus to Major General George G. Meade, commanding the Army of the Potomac, the principal Union army in the eastern theater, Grant wrote: "Lee's army will be your objective point. Wherever Lee goes, there you will go also." To Major General William Tecumseh Sherman, commanding a group of three Union armies in the West, Grant gave similar instructions to grasp in battle and destroy the Confederate forces led by General Joseph E. Johnston. When the Confederates formed a new army later in the year to operate in the Shenandoah Valley of Virginia, Grant again similarly told the War Department: ". . . I want Sheridan put in command of all the troops in the field, with instructions to put himself south of the enemy and follow him to the death. Wherever the enemy goes let our troops go also."

Sherman advancing out of the western theater toward the Atlantic coast and Major General

Philip Sheridan in the Shenandoah carried still further the totalization of the means by which total submission was to be imposed upon the enemy. With Grant's advice and encouragement, Sherman and Sheridan attempted to destroy not only the enemy armies, but also the Confederacy's economic ability to sustain the war, and the will of the southern people to persevere in the war. Grant instructed Sheridan: "If the war is to last another year, we want the Shenandoah Valley to remain a barren waste." Sherman's avowed purpose was not only to deprive the Confederacy of economic resources, but to break the morale of the people by terrorizing them: ". . . we are not only fighting hostile armies," he wrote, "but a hostile people, and must make old and young, rich and poor, feel the hard hand of war, as well as the organized armies."

After the utter destruction of the Confederate armies and the ruination of the Confederate economy produced the desired complete abandonment of Confederate claims to sovereignty, the United States returned with renewed vigor to fight the last of the wars against the Indians and rid the continental domain of Indian military power—and any vital Indian culture— once and for all. As the attitudes formed from the beginning of the Indian wars helped lead the United States to conduct the Civil War as a total war, so the experience of the Civil War diluted any humane compunctions that hitherto restrained the United States Army in dealing with the Indians. Specifically, the Army now applied the strategy of Sherman and Sheridan to the Indian wars, aiming its blows not only at the Indians' fighting power but at their fragile economy and their ability to maintain any existence at all independent of the white men.

An American historical tradition at least as strong as the compulsion to pursue war to total

13

victory—the fear of entanglement in Europe—served to keep the war with Spain in 1898 a relatively limited conflict. The Americans were content to destroy all the remnants of the Spanish Empire in the western hemisphere and the Pacific, without carrying the war to Spain itself. In World War I, the American participation came too late and was relatively too small for the American attitudes toward war to have much impact on the peace. Indeed, American emotional involvement was limited enough that President Woodrow Wilson could appear especially generous in his peacemaking policies toward Germany. At that, Wilson did not necessarily reflect American public opinion, and General Pershing was probably closer to the views of most of his countrymen in his urging that the Allies should punish Germany by marching all the way to Berlin.

In World War II, the United States participated much longer and made a much larger contribution to the eventual Allied victory, with a consequently larger impact on the shape of the war and the peace terms that followed it. The United States emerged from the war at its

Right: American "doughboys" in World War I made up in spirit for their lack of experience. This is the 43rd Balloon Company USA on the march near Bertrance Farm shortly before the Armistice.

Below: In World War II American industrial might was crucial to Allied victory. Here, supplies and troops pour onto Normandy beaches just after D-Day, supporting the ousting of German forces from France.

military high tide, unquestionably the greatest military power in the world of 1945. The war was a climax of American military history also in the sense that the American past fitted the United States so well to wage its part in it. Adolf Hitler's Nazi regime and its partners and accessories in international crime appeared throughout the Allied world to be enemies so villainous that there could be almost universal agreement on the American prescription of "unconditional surrender" as the only appropriate peace terms for such a crew. If a characteristically American peace of total victory over altogether submissive enemies won assent as the objective of all the Allies, then a characteristically American military strategy became a suitable means of pursuing the objective, though on this point agreement proved less universal.

Nevertheless, the American strategists persuaded their somewhat reluctant British partners that the principal Anglo-American military effort of the war in Europe must be a cross-Channel invasion of Europe, to take on the German armies in western Europe not where they were weak but where their strength was greatest, to confront the enemy's strength and annihilate it in the manner of U. S. Grant facing Robert E. Lee. The American emphasis on the simultaneous strategy of the Combined Bomber Offensive against Germany meanwhile echoed Sherman's and Sheridan's extension of Grant's strategy of annihilation from the enemy armed forces to the enemy economy. In the Pacific Ocean war, the US Navy similarly sought to annihilate the principal enemy armed force in the theater of war, in this instance the Japanese battle fleet, drawing on the strategic precepts not only of the American Civil War but of the Navy's own great strategic

thinker, the turn-of-the-century American prophet of sea power, Rear Admiral Alfred Thayer Mahan. From the air, the Americans wracked Japan not only with a bomber offensive comparable to the one waged against Germany, but eventually with the weapon representing the apotheosis of the Sherman-Sheridan manner of war. Meanwhile the tremendous wealth of the United States, as developed in the mid-twentieth century, and its large population, afforded it ample resources to wage a war seeking unconditional surrender through unconditional means. So well did the circumstances of World War II fit American capacities and methods in the waging of war, that it was with this war that the United States became abruptly transformed from pupil to tutor in its relations with most of the other military powers.

It will have become apparent by now, furthermore, that however recent the emergence of the United States as a major actor on the world military stage, the Americans historically have not been altogether a peaceful, unmilitary people. Yet they have also drawn from their history strong prejudices regarding the military. The Americans, like the British, have usually been loath to apply military conscription in peacetime. The desire to escape compulsory military service was among the motives that propelled many of their immigrant ancestors to the New World. The United States also inherited from its British antecedents the British suspicion of standing, professional military forces. When the victors of the American Revolution wrote the United States Constitution in 1787, the military dictatorship of Cromwell was recent enough to be a vivid part of their historical memories, and still more recently Great Britain's threat to maintain a large standing army in her American colonies

had reacted upon inherited fears of military usurpation of power to serve as one of the major causes of the Revolution. Therefore the United States Constitution contains elaborate safeguards against military despotism, such as guarantees of the existence of armed citizens' militias in the various states to offset the federal military forces, and division of control over the federal military between the President and Congress.

At that, fear that the Constitution went too far toward encouraging a powerful military helped make its ratification a near thing, and throughout the nineteenth century Americans persisted in viewing the small Regular Army acting as a constabulary on the Indian frontier as though it were a potential praetorian guard that might bar the doors of Congress and create an emperor.

Thus the Americans have waged war zestfully when war has engulfed them; but in addition to regarding war as an abnormal condition, they have distrusted the professional soldiers whom they need to lead them in war. One effect of a widespread civilian distrust of the military has been a reciprocated distrust of American society, politics, and even democracy, on the part of the professional soldiers. The American army's leading writer and intellectual in the nineteenth century, Brevet Major General Emory Upton, capitalized upon his Civil War record of heroism to spread through the army after the war a gospel of military reforms along German lines to im-

Below: The US Army is back in the Philippines and a 37mm anti-tank gun of the 129th Regiment, 37th Division, opens up on Japanese positions on the west wall of the Intramuros, Manila.

prove the efficiency of the army, coupled with a pessimism that democratic America would ever reorganize its military in the proper German manner, or that therefore the United States could ever compete militarily with the great powers. Upton's doleful influence was a principal ingredient in the self-doubt already alluded to as part of the American forces' belated plunge into the mainstream of military history.

The means on which Americans have historically preferred to rely to reconcile their distrust of professional soldiers and standing armies with their penchant for ferocity in war has been some form of people's army. Before the Revolution, every British colony had maintained a citizens' militia of part-time soldiers, who left their plows and workshops to take up muskets whenever they were needed for defense against the Indians and the French. The Continental Army of the Revolution sprang forth from these citizens' militias, and the Continental Army's eventual success against the British army, despite the military deficiencies of the Continentals' militia origins, lent substance to the belief of the writers of the Constitution that state militias could fend off the potential military tyranny of a federal army. The citizens' militias maintained by the states indeed gave each of the member states of the American Union enough military power of its own, and thus a large enough measure of sovereignty, that the states had the capacity to go to war against one another in 1861. The Southern Confederacy began life with an army already in being, because it had the militia forces of the seceded states. Just as the colonial militia had formed the core of the Continental Army in the Revolution, so now in the Civil War it was the militia forces of the states—not the Regular Army, so tiny as to be insignificant —around which both the Union and the Confederate armies took shape.

With such a military tradition as this, it is not remarkable that well into the twentieth century opponents of Emory Upton's ideas of reforming the American military on the German model argued for reorganization upon the Swiss model instead. The latter would have reduced the professional cadre to the slimmest of skeletons and made almost the whole of the American army a citizens' militia. Paradoxically in view of the historic American dislike of conscription, the means of recruitment for this democratized army would have been universal military training.

Taking on the military responsibilities of a great power ruled out, if nothing else did, America's emulating the Swiss army. Nevertheless, we have now surveyed a complex of deeply engrained American attitudes toward the military and war, all of which enhance the difficulties of maintaining American armed forces suitable to the responsibilities of the United States in the late 20th century. The introduction in 1945 of nuclear weapons made the absolute destruction of both enemy armed forces and enemy resources and population all too literally possible. Despite the nation's past military history, Americans still nourish a sense of guilt over having dropped two atomic bombs on Japanese cities; American military power had to be used henceforth with uncharacteristic limitations and restraint.

Yet the Korean and Vietnam wars indicate how quickly the American public become impatient with a restrained application of military power—with a so-called "no win" war—and these wars cast doubt on the future availability of limited war as a tool of American statecraft. The historic American suspicion of the military remains alive, furthermore, to aggravate public discontent whenever the United States attempts to use military force as an instrument of policy.

Because few Americans trust the military in any event, during an unpopular limited war the military can be equally accused of bloodthirsty militarism for waging the war at all, and of pusillanimity for not waging it in the historic American mode with all available means employed! During the Vietnam crisis, the American military were thus assailed at home from right and left simultaneously, and much of the public apparently believed both lines of criticism simultaneously, however contradictory they were. Meanwhile, with the United States since World War II maintaining by far the largest peacetime armed forces in its history —about two million men and women even after the close of the Vietnam War—and at immense cost, traditional fears of military influence upon government have been aroused as never since the eighteenth century. Occasionally the old fear of a military *coup d'état*—Oliver Cromwell updated—surfaces again, as in the novel *Seven Days in May*.

More realistically, the fear is that military forces so consistently large and expensive, with much of the economy at least partially dependent on their remaining large, have created a military-industrial complex whose influence on national policy is everywhere and inescapable. There is also public apprehension that having immense military power at their disposal will make Presidents excessively willing to seek a military route out of every otherwise intractable international crisis—though what happened at home during the Korean and Vietnam wars should have considerably undercut this ground for concern.

Altogether, the persistent American sus-

Below: In the closing stages of the Pacific war every ounce of firepower was needed to reduce fanatical defenders of even small islands and atolls.

icion of the military and its place in American life did much to end conscription and cause the United States to revert in 1974 to all-volunteer armed forces. The issue of conscription is by no means resolved. Draft registration, though not a call-up to active service, was reinstated in 1980. While the registration system is being contested in the courts, the armed forces and defense analysts continue to question the quality of recruits joining the volunteer forces and look forward with trepidation to the early 1990s, when the number of 18-year-olds will be only about three-fourths what it was in 1978. Whether the United States can fulfil worldwide military responsibilities for an indefinite period without a draft seems extremely dubious.

These unsettling and destabilizing historical tendencies and conditions affecting the American war machine ought to be pondered by all those states and those millions of the world's people who rely on American military power as the principal counterweight to the might of the Soviet Union. With the Americans carrying the military leadership of the non-Communist world, a still relatively inexperienced military hand is at the throttle, and one not accustomed to measured, patient applications of military force adjusted to complex situations. Furthermore, the American military have to contend

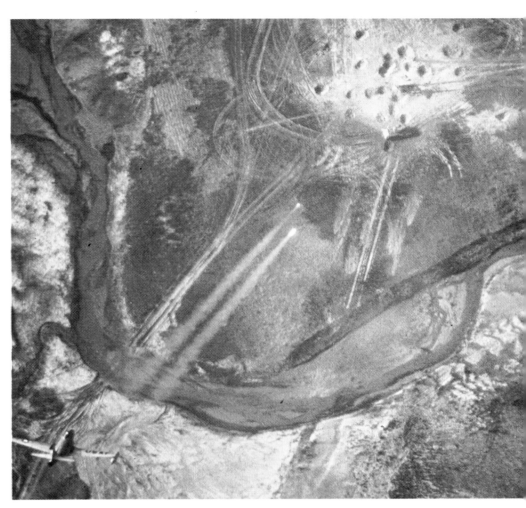

Right: Korea caught Western allies off-balance. Even shiny new jets, such as this F-80C Shooting Star rocketing North Korean tanks, were ill-adapted to harsh and distant land campaigns.

Below: September 1951 and men of the 1st Marine Division advance warily on the suspected hideout of a sniper who had been holding up the US advance. Advanced technology was often little help, to the slogging foot-soldier.

Above: Trying to climb up Mutters Ridge near the DMZ (Demilitarized Zone) north of Dong Ha, Vietnam, in 1968, Marines of the 2nd Battalion, 3rd Division throw grenades.

Below: Early in the American involvement, on 8 January 1966, M48A3 battle tanks of the 1st Infantry Division trundle slowly behind a rice-laden bullock cart heading for Trung Lap northwest of Saigon.

with all the international military menaces of a perilous world while also fending off constant suspicion at home.

The problems arising out of the history of the American armed forces ought to be pondered and have been emphasized here, because so much depends on American strength. Rising above their problems, however, the American armed forces have served their country and the the rest of the world's democracies far from badly since 1941, and it would be a distortion to paint a historical survey in wholly gloomy colors. Because offsetting the Soviet war machine does so much depend on the United States, the large size and the cost of American military power are obviously not merely a problem. The very fact that Americans can still contemplate warfare in terms of complete victories bespeaks, beyond a disconcerting immoderation, the deep reservoirs of economic strength, skilled manpower, and technological leadership they can mobilize for military purposes.

In past wars, furthermore, Americans have overcome their enemies with more than sheer material power; they have not simply transformed their gross national product into munitions and thrown it at their enemies. The Americans may have been historically an unmilitary people, but American fighting men have consistently displayed a considerable aptitude for battle. It was that aptitude, and much more than simply the material resources of the United States, that led Winston Churchill to remark of his hearing the news of Pearl Harbor and the American entry into World War II: "I had studied the American Civil War, fought out to the last desperate inch. . . . I went to bed and slept the sleep of the saved and the thankful."

Beyond the aptitude for battle, there has also been the heartening American aptitude for military leadership—which brings us back to West Point, where we began. The antique military ritual of the Point symbolizes a tradition that, though a thin current usually well separated from the mainstream of American life, and though only recently brought to the attention of the world at large, has maintained a remarkable continuity in an often inhospitable environment: the tradition of military professionalism, and of professional excellence, in the American officer corps.

Founded under President Thomas Jefferson in 1802, vitalized by Superintendent Sylvanus Thayer in 1817–1833, the United States Military Academy early began to transform military officership in America from a gentlemen's avocation to a profession. Though of course West Point is an undergraduate school, and graduate-level professional education for American officers mainly had to wait until after the Civil War, the Military Academy even before the Civil War nourished professional military attainments and study all out of proportion to the tiny size of the American army, in the teaching and writing of its Professor Dennis Hart Mahan—father of the naval strategist Alfred Thayer Mahan—and in the writing of such pupils as Henry Wager Halleck and George B. McClellan. Professional studies nourished in turn professional standards of military skill and performance. In these areas, the American officer corps of the nineteenth century was scarcely the Prussian officer corps; but because it was unhampered by the class barriers that plagued British officership, or by the political feuds of the French, the American officer corps often surpassed any Europeans except the Prussians in the early development of professional standards of military administration and command. Contrast, for example, the staff and logistical performance that sustained the Union armies over distances of thousands of miles in the Civil War with the staff and logistical work that failed to sustain a small British army in the Crimea.

Furthermore, while the actual duties of the nineteenth-century American army were largely those of policing the Indian tribes, the United

Active Duty Military Personnel, Selected Periods 1918 to 1982

Year	Army	Air Force	Navy	Marine Corps	Totals
30 June 1918	2,395,742	—	448,606	52,819	2,897,167
30 June 1939	189,839	—	125,202	19,432	334,473
31 May 1945[2]	5,983,330	2,310,436	3,359,283[1]	471,369	12,124,418
30 April 1952[3]	1,658,084	971,017	813,936[1]	242,017	3,685,054
30 June 1968[4]	1,570,343	904,850	765,457[1]	307,252	3,547,902
31 March 1982	791,762	579,503	543,703	191,957	2,106,925

1. Excluding Coast Guard.   3. Korean War peak.
2. World War II peak.   4. Vietnam Conflict peak.

All information from US Department of Defense publication, "Selected Manpower Statistics" May 1977, except 1982 statistics, from "Defense Almanac", Defense/82 Magazine.

States Army always directed its education and preparation toward eventual participation in the European military arena. When America made its debut as a world military power in the world wars, the rank and file may have performed at first with a lack of battlefield skill and wariness that produced high casualties and had to be compensated for in courage and élan. The American officer corps, in contrast, performed almost immediately at a European level of professional skill: witness as early as September 1918 the Americans' secret, concealed movement of about a million men in a three-week period, at night and over inadequate roads and railways, from the area of their St. Mihiel offensive to the concentration area for their coming Meuse-Argonne offensive, while the St. Mihiel battle was in progress. This feat was mainly the work of the young operations officer of 4th American First Army, Colonel George C. Marshall, Jr.

After a twenty-year interval spent in the scarcely larger than the old Indian wars constabulary—plus, importantly, more study and teaching in the army's schools—this same Marshall with apparently equal ease assumed the principal strategic and administrative leadership of the Anglo-American coalition's far-flung military forces in World War II, and carried them through to almost universal admiration. General Marshall was perhaps the best product of the American officer corps' tradition of professional excellence in the twentieth century, but he was also representative of the remarkably widespread ability of that officer corps to readjust almost overnight to command responsibilities over hundreds of thousands of their own and Allied forces in global war. Dwight D. Eisenhower, Douglas MacArthur, Omar N. Bradley, Carl A. Spaatz, and in the navy Ernest J. King and Chester A. Nimitz, all showed similar capacities.

Perhaps the mushroom expansion of the American armed forces has diluted the standards that in the past permitted the officers of small forces to take on large tasks so well; it is surely an understatement to say that American military leadership in the Vietnam War did not produce a George C. Marshall. Nevertheless, the quality of the American professional officer corps has remained so high through so many generations that there is good reason to hope that the tradition of excellence still persists. The democracies owe much to the American professional soldiers who led in the world wars. On their professional heirs rest many hopes for the future.

Below: Though hated by the Viet Cong, the B-52 was designed for work utterly unlike the Vietnam war. This Loran-guided B-52F is sending down 750lb bombs on what may well be empty forest.

US National Security Policy

Stephen P. Gibert, Professor of Government, Director of the National Security Studies Program and a member of the International Research Council of the Center for Strategic and International Studies, Georgetown University.

It is not often that American presidential elections can be said to turn principally on the conduct of foreign policy and national security. It is generally agreed, however, that 1980 was such a case: foreign policy and national security issues dominated the politics of 1980, not only in the race for the presidency but in Congressional races as well. Ronald Reagan not only won a decisive victory for the presidency, but Republicans also secured a 54–46 majority in the US Senate.

The Republican victory in the Senate was the more remarkable of the two events. Since 1930, the Republicans have captured the Senate only in the 1946 and 1952 elections prior to 1980; Democrats have enjoyed a Senate majority in 46 of those 50 years. Beyond this, a number of Senate Democratic stalwarts, closely identified with President Carter's foreign policy, such as Frank Church, the Chairman of the Senate Foreign Relations Committee, also went down to defeat. Clearly, the nation wanted new directions in national security policy.

What were the issues? Perhaps the most dramatic and emotional was the long-drawn-out hostage crisis; Americans felt humiliated that the Iranians had kept over 50 Americans captive so long. The incredibly bungled rescue attempt added to this sense of shame.

Perhaps the second most telling foreign policy defeat for President Carter was the failure of the US Senate to consent to ratification of the SALT II arms control treaty. Powerful and influential citizens, such as those who made up the membership of the Committee on the Present Danger, pounded home the undeniable fact that the Soviet Union had drawn ahead of the United States in strategic as well as conventional military power. Other Americans believed their nation was bearing an unfair share of the defense of the non-communist world. Still others were angry over the Panama Canal treaty. Unemployment in the automobile industry fueled a rising tide of resentment toward Japan. Illegal immigrants from Latin America took away jobs from Americans at the lower end of the economic spectrum.

Many of these things were beyond the control of President Carter or any other political leader. Nevertheless, the American people wanted change in 1980. It is now President Reagan and the Republican Party which must solve or at least ameliorate these foreign policy problems. Foremost among them is the Soviet Union and it is, therefore, appropriate to begin with a review of American-Soviet relations.

American-Soviet Relations

The Soviet "threat" and what to do about it have preoccupied American policymakers from the enunciation of the Truman Doctrine in March, 1947, until the present day. This is not surprising; since the early postwar years American leaders have been convinced that the Soviet Union is bent upon expansion, certainly in Europe, probably in the Middle East, and perhaps in Asia as well. This perception has been the dominant one, leading to the establishment of NATO and a more or less permanent American military presence in Western Europe, despite the fact that the USSR until recently

was significantly weaker than the United States in strategic power and, in fact, had behaved with prudence and restraint when confrontations, such as those in Berlin in 1948 and 1961 and Cuba in 1962, occurred between the two superpowers.

The containment school of thought dominated American discussions of superpower and East-West relationships for most of the period between 1947 and 1972. However, as early as the 1948 presidential election, a new interpretation of the Cold War – later referred to as "revisionism" – arose on the left of the American political spectrum. Bolting the Democratic Party, Roosevelt's former Vice President, Henry Wallace, campaigned in 1948 on the basis that the United States was overreacting to what were essentially Soviet defensive moves in world politics. This position did not command much support at the time and Wallace did not carry a single state in the election.

However, revisionism was later to gain more adherents, especially in academic circles. These university-based revisionists returned in their studies to the events of 1944–47, examined the origins of the Cold War, and found America, not Russia, wanting. According to revisionists, United States leader such as President Truman, Secretaries Byrnes and Acheson, Senators Vandenburg and Taft, perceived aggressive designs in what were really defensive moves on Moscow's part. While it was true that the USSR wanted "friendly" nations in Eastern Europe, revisionists claimed this did not indicate a general expansionist drive. Refusing to adjust to the realities of sphere-of-influence politics, Washington adopted a moralistic pose to hide its real intentions, which were motivated by economic necessity. American policies such as the Truman Doctrine and the Marshall Plan, and the establishment of NATO were intended to facilitate economic domination of Europe to protect American export markets. Concealing this behind the rhetoric of containment, President Truman "bombarded the American people with a 'hate the enemy' campaign", blaming it all on Soviet "aggression". This "campaign" also, according to the revisionists, contributed to the "militarization" of American foreign policy.

Revisionists, of course, represent a distinctly minority point of view, even in the universities. For, although they labored most diligently to blame the Cold War on the West, certain facts would not go away. Among the most difficult of these was the Soviet annexation, between 1939 and 1945, of some 180,000 square miles of territory, including in Europe all of Estonia, Latvia, and Lithuania and parts of Finland, Poland, and Rumania. The USSR also annexed southern Sakhalin and the Kurile Islands in the Far East and acquired a satellite in North Korea. In contrast, only China among the other major victorious powers acquired new territory. First Britain and later France divested themselves of large colonial empires and the United States granted independence to the Philippines.

As the Soviet Union approached strategic nuclear parity with the United States a new school of thought emerged—the detentists. Basically, this group came to believe that the

The US maintains a network of alliances and friendships around the world. The most important is NATO but even here there are problems. One was an attempt on the life of the US Army commander: (far left) US General Kroesen and State Minister-President Spaeth assure each other that such incidents cannot harm the "warm and deep friendship" between their countries. Deeper strains occur regularly between the US and Israel and ex-Defense Minister Sharon is shown (left) on one of his many fence-mending visits to the US. In contrast, the relationship with Egypt has been relatively stable of late, and regular exercises take place, leading to such odd companions as an A-10, MiG-15UTI, F-16 and a MiG-21 (below).

shared superpower position which arrived with parity—the total vulnerability of the United States and the Soviet Union vis-a-vis each other, and virtual invulnerability of the two countries to all other actors in the system—could become the basis for an understanding which would usher in an era of peace. At the minimum, strategic parity coupled with the doctrine and policy of assured destruction, would provide sufficient stability so that nuclear war could be prevented and a less antagonistic superpower relationship could be established.

Although detente concepts were articulated as early as the Kennedy-Johnson era, it was not until Nixon and Kissinger assumed power that detente became official American policy. Superpower strategic parity, it was argued, had produced a situation in which neither the United States nor the Soviet Union could expect to win a war with each other in any meaningful sense. Thus the basis for a new and more stable relationship existed which would eliminate superpower strategic conflict so long as each possessed invulnerable second-strike forces.

At the same time, the danger of escalation of a local conflict existed, so that it had become imperative to improve Soviet-American relations. Specifically, detente would permit agreements to be made to limit the strategic arms race and allow other actions intended to "replace confrontation with negotiation". This less dangerous situation, according to President Nixon and Secretary Kissinger, had been

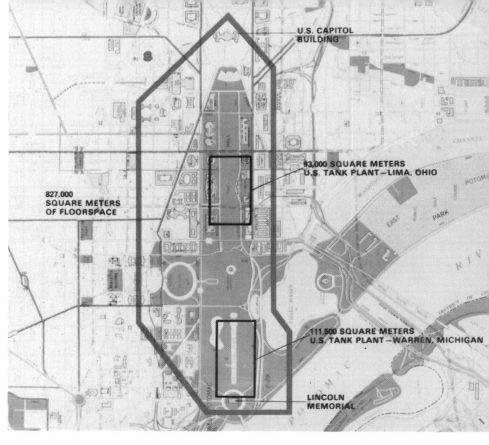

827,000 SQUARE METERS OF FLOORSPACE

93,000 SQUARE METERS U.S. TANK PLANT—LIMA, OHIO

111,500 SQUARE METERS U.S. TANK PLANT—WARREN, MICHIGAN

Below: A superconducting magnet is unloaded at a Moscow airport in the 1970s. Such gestures of friendship have ended and the US now actively opposes any transfer which might benefit Soviet defense.

Above: During the 1982 US/USSR propaganda war this DoD picture of a Soviet tank plant superimposed on a Washington map drew a Soviet response "proving" US plants to be bigger still.

realized in the SALT agreements of May 1972 and June 1973, ushering in a new era in American/Soviet relations.

Even in the halcyon days of detente in 1973, however, the Soviets were supplying sophisticated weapons to a large number of Third World countries. In October of that year, Egypt and Syria used advanced Russian Sagger and SAM missiles in their attack on Israel. In 1978, for the first time, the Soviet share of world arms exports exceeded that of the United States. Conventional arms transfer negotiations (CAT talks) were held between the two superpowers, but no agreement was reached. Could detente be divided with superpower competition continuing through client states, while tension in direct relations eased? The October War alert of Soviet airborne divisions and American strategic forces indicated that, indeed, detente was not divisible.

Moreover, direct relations between the United States and the USSR were also strained by the Soviet deployment of its fourth generation of ICBMs starting soon after the SALT I agreement. Highly accurate and powerful weapons such as the SS-18 rocket were clearly destabilizing the strategic balance. The US Department of Defense warned that in the 1980s the Soviet Union would have the ability to knock out 80 to 90 per cent of the US Minuteman force, while using only a fraction of the Soviet warheads. Such a disarming first strike would drastically alter the strategic balance, casting doubt on American retaliation and leaving Washington with the choice of city-busting attacks with the sea-based strategic forces, or negotiation under highly unfavorable conditions.

By the late 1970s the policy of detente was clearly on the wane. President Ford forbade the use of the word "detente" within his administration. Following the Soviet invasion of Afghanistan in late 1979, the long-negotiated and controversial SALT II Treaty was withdrawn from Senate consideration. In 1980 Ronald Reagan was elected President on a platform which included, *inter alia*, a commitment to pursue a more forceful foreign policy and to upgrade US military forces. Although arms control negotiations continued with the Soviet government and both superpowers pledged they would abide by the limits in the non-ratified SALT II accord, the two sides are far apart. In essence, the Soviet Union's negotiating position in the Strategic Arms

Reduction Talks (START) is "equal reductions" from current arms levels. Since the USSR currently has more launchers, missiles, and throw-weight (payload), this would leave the Soviet Union numerically superior in all critical categories of strategic weapons except warheads. The American position, in contrast, calls for "equal aggregates" at the end of the negotiations. To achieve equality, the USSR therefore would be required to make greater reductions.

In late 1982 Soviet leader Leonid Brezhnev died and was replaced by KGB Chief Yuri Andropov. The new Soviet leader immediately called for a summit meeting with President Reagan to improve the overall climate of Soviet-American relations and to further the START and intermediate nuclear forces (INF) arms reduction talks. Washington's position, however, is that the United States is no longer interested in "climate" talks. Rather, President Reagan's announced view is that the USSR must demonstrate by specific policy measures that it desires a genuine detente with the West. These concrete steps include "improvement in Soviet international behavior", especially in Afghanistan and Poland; a more "forthcoming" attitude toward arms reduction negotiations and the arresting of the Soviet military build-up; and a greater willingness on the part of Moscow to carry out in good faith the human rights provisions of the Helsinki Accords. Since there are no indications that the new Soviet leadership is any more willing than was the Brezhnev team to make concessions on those points, Soviet-American relations are likely to remain quite frigid, tempered only by the mutual desire of the superpowers to avoid an open military clash. Soviet-American detente, to the extent that it ever existed other than in terms of unrealized hopes fed by an unwarranted optimism, cannot be resurrected short of drastic changes within the Soviet Union itself.

US Security Concerns in Western Europe

It is generally agreed that, with a rough parity or a Soviet advantage in strategic forces, the conventional military balance in Europe is becoming increasingly important. The Warsaw Pact Organization is generally held to have a 2.5:1 advantage over NATO in ground combat troops. NATO depends on rapid reinforcement and prepositioned heavy equipment (POMCUS – prepositioning of materiel configured to unit sets) to prevail in any future ground conflict. In addition, NATO counts on precision guided munitions to overcome the Pact's superiority in tanks (approximately 40,000 to 12,000). In the future, NATO intends to deploy "high tech" systems to compensate for Warsaw Pact numerical superiorities. The US also is attempting to persuade, so far unsuccessfully, the European members of NATO to devote more resources to their conventional forces.

At the theater nuclear level, however, the balance of forces must also be strengthened. The Soviet Union is replacing its SS-4 and SS-5 missiles aimed at Europe with modern, three-warhead mobile SS-20 rockets. To counterbalance this, NATO in 1979 adopted the "two-track" decision. One track is not only to continue START negotiations with the Soviet Union, but also to arrange the removal of all the theater missiles, both American and Soviet, from Europe. This is the Reagan "zero option". The second track is meanwhile to deploy ground-launched cruise missiles (GLCMs) and new generation Pershing II rockets in Western Europe. The Soviets are particularly concerned about this deployment since their homeland could be struck by Pershing II warheads less than ten minutes after launch.

Soviet Defense Minister Ustinov and Foreign Minister Gromyko (the latter in Bonn, January 1983) have warned that if NATO proceeds with the deployment of the 108 Pershings and the 464 GLCMs and the United States deploys its new American-based heavy missile, the MX, the Soviet Union would have to "answer" these additions with new Soviet deployments. President Reagan's view is that the new theater and strategic deployments are necessary to convince the Soviet Union to accept strategic and theater nuclear parity through arms control negotiations. The NATO governments have pointed out that the estimated 333 Soviet SS-20 missiles, each carrying three warheads, could devastate all of Europe. In addition, it is claimed that the Soviet rocket forces have at least one "extra" missile for each SS-20 launcher. If so, the SS-20s might be able to deliver approximately 2,000 warheads on their targets.

To date, the British, German and Italian governments, and also most other NATO governments, remain committed to the deployment of the 572 US theater nuclear weapons in

Above: A test-firing of the controversial Ground-Launched Cruise Missile (GLCM). Plans to deploy GLCMs and Pershing II in Western Europe have provoked a major, widespread, and very emotional debate.

Europe, beginning in late 1983 or early 1984. The Europeans remain worried, however, that the superpowers might fight a "sanctuary war" limited to Europe, with both the Soviet Union and the United States homelands spared from attack. However unrealistic this may be, American attempts to improve NATO's theater, tactical nuclear and conventional forces fuel such doubts in European capitals. The European declaratory doctrine has been since the 1950s one of rapid escalation so that, in Henry Kissinger's phrase, any new war would take place "over their heads", with a central exchange of missiles directed at superpower homelands. The Europeans provide just enough conventional forces to keep the American government barely satisfied, but count on the

Right: A NATO E-3A Sentry AWACS aircraft. US defense contractors benefit greatly from huge NATO arms purchases and, whatever the US may say, it appears to Europeans to be very much a "one-way" street, with few reciprocal sales.

threat of rapid escalation to strategic nuclear warfare to deter any future conflict with the Soviet Union.

Another issue driving a wedge between the US and its NATO allies concerns their respective responses to events in Poland. In Poland, the first legitimate workers' union in the Communist bloc was struck down by the imposition of martial law in December 1981. Political responses to this action split the West. Sanctions aimed at the Soviet Union or the Polish government would also target European industry. Declaring Poland in default would rebound against European and American banks. A wheat embargo would hurt American farmers, while limiting other exports would injure American and especially European manufacturers.

President Reagan continued wheat exports to the USSR but banned technology exports to the Soviet Union in an effort to prevent the completion of their natural gas pipeline to Western Europe. Washington argued that Moscow could influence European political decisions by threatening to turn off the pipeline once it was in place. Further, the US government claimed that the pipeline would be the single largest generator of hard currency for the Soviet Union in the immediate future. The Europeans countered that the gas pipeline will provide only 5 per cent of their energy needs and that much of the Soviet hard currency reserves go for wheat from the United States. It was all very well for Washington to maintain ehat the wheat export and the pipeline issues were very different and warranted separate approaches. Europeans, however, regarded this as sophistry—a weak attempt by the United States to make its European allies bear the brunt of the burden in imposing sanctions on the USSR.

The differences in interest outlined above— the relative importance of trade with the East, differing perceptions of the Soviet threat, different approaches to deterrence—threaten seriously to disrupt the Atlantic Alliance. Periodically, similar fissures have been repaired in the past. There can be little doubt, however,

Above: US President Reagan, British Prime Minister Thatcher, NATO Secretary-General Luns and former German Chancellor Schmidt outside NATO HQ in Brussels. Jointly their countries face heavy responsibilities in the East-West confrontation, but NATO is the cornerstone of their response.

that relations between Western Europe and the United States are under considerable strain. Nevertheless, Western Europe and America remain linked by economic, cultural and social ties. Europe's large population, wealth, technological resources, and industrial base make it indispensable to American security. In return, without the United States, Western Europe could not, at least in the near future, successfully resist Soviet pressures. Both Europe and the United States, therefore, will find it imperative to resolve their major differences or at least to prevent such differences as may arise from obscuring the very real benefits of cooperation.

Defense Alliances and Treaties With US

● Rio Treaty
Argentina
Bolivia
Brazil
Chile
Colombia
Costa Rica
Dominican Republic
Ecuador
El Salvador
Guatemala
Haiti
Honduras
Mexico
Nicaragua
Panama
Paraguay
Peru
Trinidad/Tobago
USA
Uruguay
Venezuela

● NATO
Belgium
Canada
Denmark
France
Fed. Rep. of Germany
Greece
Italy
Luxembourg
Netherlands
Norway
Portugal
Turkey
United Kingdom
Iceland
USA

▲ Manila Pact
Australia
France
New Zealand
Philippines
Thailand
United Kingdom
USA

⋈ US · Japan
Japan
USA

✳ US · Rep. of Korea
Rep. of Korea
USA

◪ Former treaty with "Rep. of China" (Taiwan)

○ US · Philippine
Philippine
USA

▲ ANZUS
Australia
New Zealand
USA

US Security Policy in Asia

While NATO-Europe has been and remains the principal focus of United States security concerns, Washington also maintains a substantial presence in Asia. In fact, when the Nixon administration took office in 1969, the United States had much larger military forces in Asia than in Europe. Of course, the Vietnam forces, which at their largest totalled some 550,000 troops, were the major reason for this situation. Additionally, it was US policy at that time to maintain military forces sufficient to fight "two-and-a-half wars". This was defined as including a possible conflict between NATO and Warsaw Pact forces, a war between the United States and the People's Republic of China, and a "half-war" contingency elsewhere.

When US troop commitments were revised downward from a "two-and-a-half" stance, it might have been supposed that force reductions would have occurred around the world. Instead, between 1969 and 1975 the United States withdrew from Asia some 702,000 military personnel. By contrast, not a single soldier was withdrawn from Europe. Empirically, if not in theory, the Nixon administration not only terminated the Vietnam conflict but reverted to a "European-first" military posture. Elsewhere, military aid was to take the place of American soldiers. Europe was to get US troops; Asians were to get US dollars.

Such a policy was both required and justified by the downgrading of the "Chinese threat" to non-communist Asian nations and to US national security. This was accomplished through the secret Kissinger mission to Peking in 1971, followed by the Nixon trip in 1972, although full diplomatic relations with the PRC were not established. By the end of the Ford administration, Nixon's statement that "Asian hands must shape the Asian future" had been given concrete reality.

Despite the drawdown of American military strength in Asia, a broad consensus had developed by the time President Carter took office that Korea and Japan remained important to US global strategy. There was also general agreement that the continuing hostility between Moscow and Peking might be turned to American advantage. Stated differently, while the United States no longer intended to play a leading role in Southeast Asia, America would continue to regard Northeast Asia as a region

vital to US national security. Nevertheless, Washington found it very difficult to translate this consensus into concrete policy decisions.

Korean-American Relations

As regards Korean-American relations, these have been subjected to increasing stresses and strains. Although the two events may not be related, when President Nixon withdrew the Seventh Division from Korea in 1971–72, President Park declared (in December 1971) a state of emergency; martial law followed some months later (in October 1972) and in December a new constitution—referred to as the Yushin constitution—conferred new powers on the Korean chief executive. Subsequently, four emergency decrees were issued and a number of prominent opposition leaders were arrested, including a former ROK president, Yun Po-son. Supporters of President Park cited the new security situation in Asia and Korea in justifying more stringent political controls; critics claimed that these were only excuses to maintain a dictator whose support in the populace had waned.

These charges were echoed in the United States. Sentiment for removing the remaining US ground forces, which had surfaced periodically in the past, began building again in Washington. "Trial balloons" were floated,

Top: The limitations of super-power status were demonstrated clearly when two US Army officers were murdered by North Korean border guards. One of the few visible acts was to send a unit of F-111 aircraft to South Korea; that apart not very much seems to have happened, and all seems forgotten.

Above: The seemingly endless ritual of the Mixed Armistice Commission in Panmunjon drags on. Here a PRC general has joined the North Koreans, while a British brigadier sits with the US delegation. At least such talks seem to have limited the fighting.

suggesting various "options" to the retention of American forces in South Korea, especially involving the Second Division which was positioned along the demilitarized zone (DMZ) guarding the approaches to Seoul. Whether or not there was serious sentiment in the executive branch for removing or repositioning the Second Division, the collapse of South Vietnam in April 1975 effectively eliminated the possibility of such a move by the Ford Administration. In May, President Ford reaffirmed US treaty commitments to the Republic of Korea and in August Secretary of Defense Schlesinger journeyed to Seoul to emphasize the President's statement by pledging that American troops would remain in Korea and that the United States would continue to assist South Korea in its armed forces improvement program.

Reviving the arguments of the 1972–74 period, presidential candidate Jimmy Carter in May 1976 called for the withdrawal from Korea of the remaining American ground forces and the tactical nuclear weapons available to these forces. Subsequently, the new president had been in office only about a week when his Vice President, Walter Mondale, announced in Tokyo that US force withdrawals would begin but would be accompanied by "consultations" between Washington and Tokyo and Seoul. It was not mentioned precisely what these "consultations" would include since indeed the decision had not only been made prior to talks with the Koreans and the Japanese, but even before the new Secretary of State and National Security Advisor had had an opportunity to assess the situation. Undaunted by these rather peculiar circumstances, President Carter reaffirmed in March 1977 his intention to withdraw American ground forces, but in phases, and accompanied by "consultations", from the Republic of Korea.

President Carter's decision quite naturally raised the question as to whether adequate consideration had been given to the reasons for retaining the status quo. Possibly the most important of these is the belief that the presence of US forces in Korea is a highly significant symbol of American determination to play an important (although clearly not a dominant) role in shaping the course of change in Asia. It can be argued that the Second Division, placed as it is on the DMZ in "harm's way", is a symbol of US will and resolve to uphold its treaty obligations and its commitments in an era when there is, regrettably, substantial reason to doubt that it intends to do so. President Carter in his press conference of May 26, 1977, replying to criticisms of his withdrawal policy, stated that the American "commitment to South Korea is undeviating and is staunch". But would the Koreans and Japanese believe that this is true if the troops departed? Or would this action be perceived as yet another step in the waning of American power in Asia?

Eventually responding to these fears and to pleas by the South Korean government, President Carter in 1979 temporarily halted further US troop drawdowns. It was announced that three brigades of the Second Division would remain in South Korea until 1982, the final year of the phased withdrawal. The US also announced that South Korea would be given additional military aid in "compensation" for the withdrawal of troops.

Upon assuming office in 1981, Ronald Reagan made it known that his administration would not implement the Carter decision to withdraw the remaining American troops from Korea. To emphasize the new policy, South Korean President Chun Doo Hwan became the first foreign leader to visit Washington after Reagan assumed the US presidency. The 11-day visit in late January and February 1981 was intended to symbolize that the new American government was committed to maintaining the defensive alliance with the Republic of Korea. Perhaps more importantly, it signalled to the rest of Asia (and to the Soviet Union) that the United States intended to remain an Asian (as distinct from just a Pacific) power; South Korea was to be the one place in continental Asia where the United States would maintain a substantial military presence, including at least some units armed with tactical nuclear weapons.

At the summit meeting, the two leaders announced that they would resume the ROK-US security consultative meetings and pledged their cooperation to further the modernization of ROK armed forces. President Reagan reaffirmed that South Korea must be a full participant in any American negotiations with North Korea (a policy which has consistently been opposed by North Korea). Furthermore, the

US government stated that any unilateral American or allied steps toward North Korea which are not reciprocated by North Korea's allies with regard to South Korea would be unacceptable. This latter is an important policy stand; in practical effect, it means that Washington will not recognize and will oppose allied recognition of North Korea unless the Soviet Union and the People's Republic of China reciprocate by recognizing South Korea.

Cognizant of the fact that the US Second Division in Korea is the only US Army division located west of Hawaii, the current administration in Washington obviously has no plans at present to remove American military forces from Korea. This is sensible; under the present circumstances, the United States should attempt to create a more favorable political and military situation in Northeast Asia prior to troop withdrawal. This includes completing the Korean Force Improvement Plan so that the military imbalance between North and South Korea is rectified. Politically, it might include such measures as cross-recognition of the two Koreas by the United States and the Soviet Union; mutual reciprocal recognition by the North and South of each other; admission of both to the United Nations; and a North Korean-South Korean non-aggression pact.

Finally, discussions concerning unification could be encouraged between North and South Korea. The United States should play a helpful but secondary role in these negotiations which should be conducted primarily between the two Koreas themselves. While unification certainly is a long-term prospect (if ever), such talks might, as they did between West and East Germany, contribute to a less explosive confrontation between the two rivals.

Relations with Japan

While American relations with Korea have improved since President Carter postponed further US troop withdrawals in 1979, tensions between Washington and Tokyo have steadily increased over the past decade. Two critically important issues are now sharply dividing Japan and the United States.

The first issue is trade. Between 1977 and 1980 America's trade deficit with Japan was running at about a billion dollars a month. In 1981, however, this very large deficit ballooned to a yearly total of $18 billion, an increase of approximately 50 per cent, and 1982 estimates show an increase to about $20 billion. The American television industry disappeared to Japan some years ago and now the United States is concerned that the automobile industry—which recently gave up first place to Japan in total vehicle production and had the lowest sales for 20 years in 1982—will also be vanquished. Such a development carries very severe implications that go far beyond economic stresses, severe as they are, to the core of American security—the industrial base which is required to maintain the United States as an economic and military superpower. Nevertheless, it is widely accepted that the

Above: President Reagan and former Japanese Premier Suzuki seem the best of friends. The US spends more money on the defense of Japan than do the Japanese.

Below: Japan depends totally upon the US commitment to help in her defense and repays her allies by commercial warfare and industrial espionage, but for how long?

principal reasons for the decline of the American automobile industry must be attributed to shortsighted practices on the part of American automobile management executives and to slipshod work for very high wages on the part of American automobile workers. It is also the case that very high US interest rates have overvalued the dollar relative to the yen, making Japanese cars more price-competitive on the American market.

It is equally believed in the United States, however, that the Japanese are "unfair traders". As US Representative John Dingell, a prime supporter in December 1982 of a "domestic content" bill in the House of Representatives, put it: "The Japanese do not trade fairly and do not practise free trade with the US or any other of their trading partners. . . . They are going to destroy our jobs . . . and leave us and our economy colonies of Japan." As to Japanese retaliation if the US passed such legislation, Representative Richard Ottinger spoke for many when he said Japan was too vulnerable: "The Japanese dare not do that." With more than half of the total US representatives cosponsoring the law—aimed directly at Japan—only the shortness of time in the "lame duck" pre-Christmas Congressional session, coupled with President Reagan's opposition, prevented this clearly most protectionist measure in decades from becoming the law of the land.

Because the Reagan administration, many

members of the Senate, some in the House, and the prestige media are all supporters of liberal trade, it is possible—although perhaps not likely—that Japan can continue to impose substantial non-tariff barriers to American exports and fail to take other steps to ameliorate the situation without American trade retaliation. But there are virtually no influential defenders of Japan concerning the American-Japanese security relationship. With regard to security burden-sharing, the Japanese are much more vulnerable to the American charge of unreasonable and unfair behavior. Stated bluntly, Japan is a military protectorate of the United States, not an ally.

At the center of the controversy is Japan's unwillingness to allocate the resources necessary to contribute in a meaningful way to mutual security in Northeast Asia and the Western Pacific. In July 1982 the Tokyo government once more failed to live up to its previously made commitments to upgrade its defenses. While there was much discussion in Japan of the need to shoulder a greater share of the mutual security burden, the Japanese Finance Ministry set the increase in Japan's spending for 1983 at only 7.3 per cent, less than the increase in 1982 over 1981 and less than that requested by the Japanese Defense Agency. While 7 per cent does not seem an unreasonable increase, the total defense budget is so low that the increase amounts only to $760 million.

Subsequently, in December 1982, the Finance Ministry said that the defense spending increase should be limited to 5.1 per cent but this was later revised to 6.5 per cent. Total spending for 1983 is projected at $11.7 billion, representing, once again, less than 1 per cent of Japan's GNP. The Reagan administration, in contrast, plans to increase the projected FY 1983 spending of $209 billion to $247 billion in FY 1984.

The contrast between the projected Japanese increase of less than $750 *million* and the US projected increase of $38 *billion* should stagger even those few remaining American apologists for Japan. If these projected figures remain even approximately accurate, then US spending for defense will grow from about 19 times to about 21 times that of Japan. Since Japan enjoys approximately 50 per cent of the US GNP, Japan's defense expenditure is equivalent to the US spending a mere $23 billion on defense.

In March 1982 the US Department of Defense published a detailed analysis of allied (NATO plus Japan) contributions to defense as compared to indicators of ability to contribute, such as gross domestic product and a "prosperity index". Comparing the 15 nations, Japan ranked at the bottom (15th) in terms of defense spending compared to gross domestic product and 14th (above only Luxembourg) in terms of defense spending compared to the "prosperity index". Japan ranked last of the

15 nations in the ratio of active defense manpower compared to population share. On the remaining three comparisons, Japan ranked 15th, 12th, and 14th respectively. Taken as a whole, only tiny Luxembourg has as poor a record in support of defense as does Japan. The United States provides 53 per cent of the total defense spending of the 15 NATO-plus-Japan countries; Japan provides just under 4 per cent.

In November, 1982, Yasuhiro Nakasone succeeded Zenko Suzuki as Prime Minister of Japan. In his opening statements Nakasone called the United States Japan's most important trading partner and ally, and pledged his efforts to improve substantially Japanese-American trade relations. He also cited the necessity for Japan to increase significantly Japan's contributions to mutual security. While these kinds of statements have emanated previously from Tokyo, Nakasone is considered to be by far the most pro-defense leader Japan has had in decades. His cabinet choices and his advisers also reflect an unusually strong (for Japan) defense orientation.

Nakasone is clearly and obviously very concerned about the deterioration in relations with the United States. In January, 1983, the Prime Minister visited Washington for talks with President Reagan. In the course of his stay, the Japanese leader expressed his firm intention of further easing Japanese import restrictions, especially with regard to American agricultural exports. Nakasone also was quite forthright in acknowledging the need for ameliorating to the extent feasible the severe trade imbalance between the two countries. Japanese officials did point out, however, as have other foreign leaders, that high US interests are an important element in the trade problem. The Japanese also reminded the Americans that Japan, like the United States, currently confronts unprecedentedly large budget deficits. Nevertheless, Nakasone reiterated his previous statements in Tokyo that Japan would significantly strengthen its defense posture.

It is to be sincerely hoped that the Prime Minister can deliver on these promises, despite powerful political opposition certain to arise in Tokyo. If he cannot, it is not unduly alarmist to say that the end of the American-Japanese alliance is in sight.

The People's Republic of China
On December 19, 1978, President Carter ended the long diplomatic hiatus between the United States and the People's Republic of China when he "derecognized" the Republic of China on Taiwan, switching diplomatic recognition from Taipei to Peking. While the establishment of diplomatic ties with the PRC met with general approval in the United States, many in

the Congress were disturbed over the failure of the Carter administration to secure concessions from the PRC on the Taiwan issue. Congress was concerned that the United States was not making adequate provisions for Taiwan's security or for the continuation of American military aid and other measures to assist Taiwan in maintaining its independence and territorial integrity. Also, many Congressmen were offended, as were Taiwan's leaders, over the Carter administration's refusal to refer to the "Government of Taiwan" or to the "Republic of China on Taiwan". Instead, the phrase that was used to refer to America's repudiated ally was the "People on Taiwan". This was viewed as provocative and demeaning; after all, there surely existed a government on Taiwan, regardless of what it called itself.

These and other sentiments led to a heated and somewhat emotional response to the Carter initiative, even though probably a Congressional majority desired diplomatic relations with Peking. In late March, 1979, the House of Representatives by a 345 to 55 vote passed the Taiwan Relations Act. While it seems likely that President Carter secretly disapproved of the TRA, the overwhelming Congressional vote led him to praise publicly and to sign the new act into law. The TRA pledged the United States to continue less than full diplomatic relations with Taiwan, establishing new institutions in Taipei and Washington. The Coordinating Council for North American Affairs and the American Institute in Taiwan are not dejure embassies but they continue most of the form and substance of full diplomatic relations between the United States and the Republic of China on Taiwan.

The Republican Party presidential platform in 1980 and candidate Reagan's subsequent campaign deplored the "Carter Administration's mistreatment of Taiwan, our long-time ally and friend". This led many to believe that President Reagan would reverse the Carter decision and restore diplomatic ties with Taiwan. Once in office, however, it became clear that the Reagan government would pursue a policy toward the two Chinas not sharply different from that of the previous government in Washington. In June 1981, then-Secretary of State Alexander Haig paid a visit to Peking in order to reassure the Chinese leadership that, irrespective of contrary sentiments expressed during the presidential campaign, the new administration was committed to an expansion

Below: The redoubtable Dheng Zhiao-Peng during his tour of the USA. Despite surface differences, the USA and PRC have become very close friends, especially in defense, much to the chagrin of the Soviet Union.

of already developing relations between both countries. To underscore this pledge, Haig used the occasion of his trip to proclaim official US willingness to sell lethal weapons to China.

The timing and location of this announcement were deliberate because the new administration, with its strong anti-detente and anti-Soviet posture, wanted to send an unequivocal message to Moscow. Previous indications of an emerging "proto-alliance" had already given Moscow jitters, had confirmed its worst fears, and had drawn the usual stern warnings and fierce denunciations. Although the Carter administration had abandoned the policy of "evenhandedness" toward Moscow and Peking in the wake of the Soviet invasion of Afghanistan and had ceased to deny allegations of "playing the China card", Haig's trip raised Soviet anxieties about the new American administration. It appeared to signal an additional step toward a Sino-American alliance directed against Moscow, linking Russia's global antagonist to its most ardent and, although presently militarily weak, potentially powerful adversary in Asia.

By late 1982, however, it had become clear that substantial obstacles still existed to close Sino-American relations. The Taiwan issue remained a bone of contention. China's military weakness led many to believe that it was not wise for the United States to ally itself with the PRC. Beijing seemed more interested in economic modernization than in building its military forces. Signs of a possible Sino-Soviet rapprochement began to appear.

In retrospect it seems that the anti-Soviet thrust of the Reagan administration is stronger than its anti-Communist attitude. Believing in "power politics" in the classical sense and viewing the Soviet Union as the only genuine danger to the United States, Secretary Haig wanted close relations with the PRC to offset Soviet strength. This attitude also seems to be shared by Vice President Bush and other high officials in the Reagan government. Accordingly, American relations with Taiwan have not improved and perhaps have even deteriorated. But compensatory ties between Peking and Washington have not occurred. At present America's China policy is uncertain and hesitating, primarily reacting to Sino-Soviet developments rather than charting a firm direction. Both Washington and Peking seem to be having second thoughts about how close they wish to cooperate with each other and whether a genuine reconciliation is possible between societies with such antithetical views of the world.

American Security Concerns in the Middle East

The Middle East may not be as critical to America's global posture as Western Europe or Northeast Asia, but there is no question that the Middle East is of great concern to the United States. In contrast to the sharp disagreements that exist over American policy to the USSR and the concomitant preservation of European security, and over Northeast Asian policy, there seems to be a broad consensus concerning US interests in the Middle East even if there are questions as to how best to secure those interests. American policy goals are: to assist Israel in maintaining its independence and security and to settle the Arab-Israel conflict on equitable terms; to secure access to Persian Gulf oil at "reasonable" prices, both for the United States and other oil-dependent nations, especially Western Europe and Japan; and, finally, to deny "undue" influence over the Middle East to the Soviet Union.

Arab-Israel Policies

Policy choices with regard to the Arab-Israeli conflict must begin with the fundamental premise that the United States of necessity will have important relationships with both Israelis and Arabs for the foreseeable future. Polarization of the political forces in the Middle East, which would be a likely consequence of a US decision to abandon all attempts at "even-handedness" and strongly favor one or the other side, would jeopardize important American interests. Accordingly, courses of action such as reversing alliances and "abandoning" Israel on the one hand or deliberately seeking confrontation with the Arab world through total and unquestioning support of Jerusalem on the other, are not feasible.

While there are certain aspects of the Arab-Israeli dispute which lend themselves to the formulation of alternative options, there are other aspects which have come to be imperatives in US policy. These are:

The existence of Israel is not negotiable. Most Arabs have now come to accept this and the United States must not adopt a policy position which leaves any room for doubt on this question. To do otherwise, aside from the moral implications, would do irretrievable damage to US credibility and lead an isolated

Israel to adopt a declaratory nuclear retaliation policy with obvious dangerous consequences.

2. While the United States is committed to defend Israel's right to exist, it is not committed to particular boundaries. The United States supports UN Resolution 242 which calls for Israeli withdrawal from territories occupied in the 1967 war. That resolution envisions such withdrawal in the context of Arab recognition of Israel's rights to live in peace within secure and recognized borders, not mere armistice lines.

3. The United States supports "normalization" of the conflict. This means direct negotiations of issues by the immediate participants, with external powers assisting but not dictating outcomes. It also means the acceptance of negotiations as a bargaining process in which each side makes certain concessions in order to arrive at a solution not wholly satisfactory but at least minimally acceptable to all concerned.

4. Pending resolution of the dispute, the United

States must attempt to maintain a balance of military power between the two parties. It is not sufficient to maintain a military balance between Israel and the Arab opponents. While it is possible that a no-war, no-peace situation could persist a long time, the inherent instabilities make it essential to move beyond this condition to some form of settlement and US policy should be geared to this goal.

Based upon these principles, after Egyptian Prime Minister Anwar Sadat had made his dramatic peace visit to Israel, President Carter achieved the greatest foreign policy success of his term in office: the Camp David Agreement between Egypt and Israel. The Egyptian-Israeli peace treaty shattered the Arab coalition against Israel and seemingly opened the way for a genuine reconciliation between Israel and the Arab countries. Unfortunately, however, the issue of an independent Palestinian state has prevented further progress. Israel under

Prime Minister Menachem Begin has adopted an increasingly tougher line toward the now-weakened Arab front. President Reagan has been unable to persuade Israel to "freeze" new Jewish settlements on the West Bank. In contrast to previous policy, the government in Israel now shows no inclination to pursue the old formula of trading territory for formal peace agreements as was done with Egypt. Rather, Israel appears to have chosen territory over peace and by promoting Jewish settlements in the West Bank region, is laying the basis for annexing the ancient lands of Judea and Samaria.

Consistent with this more aggressive policy, the Israeli government in 1982 began seeking a pretext to move into Lebanon and destroy the Palestinian Liberation Organization as a military force. The long-sought opportunity was provided by the Arab assassination of the Israeli ambassador in London. Israel's retaliation for the death of the ambassador was deliberately disproportionate in its severity, thus provoking the anticipated Arab response. This Arab attack then provided Israel with the necessary political justification to launch the desired full-scale invasion of Lebanon. In a textbook military operation, obviously planned in advance, Israeli forces quickly advanced to Beirut. After some weeks of negotiations, led by American envoy Philip Habib, PLO forces were evacuated from Beirut and dispersed throughout the Middle East. The Israeli triumph, however, was marred by the Lebanese militia massacre of Moslem civilians in Palestinian refugee camps, ostensibly under the protection of the Israeli occupying authorities.

While it can be argued that Israel is not justified in furthering Jewish settlements in the West Bank area, and that such a policy is counterproductive, certainly Israel had the

right to attack and destroy the PLO forces. Palestinians cannot expect to regard themselves as at war with Israel and not be prepared to suffer the consequences of belligerency. The military defeat and dispersal of the PLO has opened up an opportunity for a genuine Arab-Israeli settlement. Israel is now the unquestioned militarily dominant power in the region. The Arabs, in contrast, are divided among themselves. Egypt and Jordan desire peace and Syria has been cowed into passivity. The Soviet Union, once the strongest external supporter of the Arab states, has seen its influence considerably diminished. Preoccupied with Poland and Afghanistan and concerned about the situation on its Iranian border, Moscow shows little inclination to become an active proponent of Israel's Arab neighbors. Falling oil prices, reflecting a world oil glut, has sheathed, at least for the time being, the vaunted

oil weapon. Never before has Israel been more secure.

In such circumstances, Washington has hoped that the Begin government would be conciliatory and magnanimous, thus opening up the possibility for a genuine Arab-Israeli peace settlement. Instead, the Israeli government has been quite unyielding, even at the risk of jeopardizing its close relations with the United States. To date Washington has tolerated Israeli intransigence, but it cannot be doubted that continuation of the present policy by Israel will diminish the unqualified support Israel has enjoyed in Washington in the past. More importantly, the present bright prospects for peace may dim and be irrevocably lost. Sooner or later the Arabs will regain their strength and restore some semblance of unity. Sooner or later Moscow will return to its accustomed trouble-making role in the Middle East.

The Persian Gulf

While the risk of superpower confrontation has diminished on the Mediterranean side of the Middle East, the Persian Gulf area has become more volatile and dangerous. The Middle East region provided President Carter with the single greatest foreign policy success of his presidency in the Camp David Accords, but the Middle East also handed Carter his most telling defeat in the Iranian revolution and the hostage crisis. Although he inherited and did not initiate a situation where Iran had become an "American surrogate" to maintain order in the Gulf, Carter accepted this state of affairs quite uncritically.

After the Shah went into exile, the American government engaged in an embarrassing and public display of anxiety over the Shah's medical visit to the United States, breathing a sigh of relief audible all the way to Teheran when he departed from the United States. This conduct was all the more unbecoming when it is recalled that only a short time earlier the American president had lavished praise on the Shah as a great world leader.

Perhaps this episode would have been quickly forgotten, however, had it not been for the seizure of the American Embassy in Teheran. It is difficult to attribute any single factor to President Carter's defeat in the 1980 election.

Left: A signing ceremony between Secretary of Defense Weinberger and former Israeli Defense Minister Sharon. Israel has often broken its agreements with the US although the quarrels never last.

Above: The start of another commitment as US Marines come ashore at Beirut on November 18, 1982, to begin duties with the Peacekeeping Force. Such short-term expedients may lead to long-term problems.

Below: These F-16s had their delivery to Israel delayed to show US displeasure, but the US Government always seems to relent in the end. Israel's hold over the US seems strong, but may not last for ever.

Surely, however, the ineffectual attempts to obtain the release of the American hostages and the completely inept rescue operation must be considered principal causes for the rout of the Democrats in which the Republicans not only won the White House but captured control of the Senate for the first time since 1954.

Two other events have imperiled the stability of the Gulf. The first is the Iraqi-Iranian war. The United States has attempted to remain neutral, recognizing that a decisive victory for either side could threaten other Gulf states such as Saudi Arabia and endanger the vital Persian Gulf oil supply.

More serious was the Soviet invasion of Afghanistan and the ongoing Soviet attempts to destroy Afghan resistance. Irrespective of Soviet motivations, the geopolitical reality cannot be denied: control of Afghanistan will enable the USSR to dominate militarily the Persian Gulf region. Neither the so-called Carter Doctrine nor the (untested and suspect) Rapid Deployment Force can alter the basic and fundamental fact that a Soviet-dominated Afghanistan will enable Soviet air power to reign supreme over the Persian Gulf and the surrounding seas. Thus still another area of the world, if Moscow succeeds in Afghanistan, will live under the shadow of Russian military power.

Earlier it was stated that the United States has three more or less permanent goals in the Middle East: a just and pacific settlement of the Arab-Israeli conflict; to guarantee access for the Western nations and Japan to Persian Gulf oil; and the denial of "undue" Soviet influence in the Middle East. At present the first goal is in sight, provided the United States and Israel can agree on a peace policy toward the Arab states. Israel is now in such a strong position that it may be able finally to secure a just and secure place for itself in the Middle East, if it can restrain its territorial ambitions.

As regards Persian Gulf oil, it remains a vital commodity, despite the present world oil surplus. The United States, by far the largest oil consumer in the world, can claim a major share of the credit for this more favorable situation. In 1972 the United States was consuming about 17 million barrels of oil per day and consump-

tion was rising at an annual increase of about 6 per cent. This increase was halted: in 1982, a decade later, United States consumption was about 16 million barrels per day. Although the list price of Persian Gulf light crude remained at $34 a barrel (as compared with less than $3 in 1972), the selling price in January 1983 hovered at around $28. There will be further price reductions, barring some unexpected crisis in the Gulf. Gradually but surely the world is reducing its dependence on the Persian Gulf. This is certainly fortunate, given the present very unstable political situation in the Gulf area.

As to the third US goal—preventing excessive Soviet influence in the Middle East—at the moment Soviet fortunes in the area are at their lowest ebb. But this situation can drastically change if the USSR succeeds in turning Afghanistan into a pacified vassal state. Even

Above: Preparations on board USS *Nimitz* in April 1980 for the attempt to rescue the hostages from Iran. The raid ended in fiasco at "Desert One" in an episode the US armed forces would rather forget.

if this does not happen, it is to be anticipated that Moscow will once more, at some time in the not too distant future, seek to regain an influential role in Middle Eastern affairs. Thus, preventing "undue" Soviet influence in the Middle East is a permanent task for American diplomacy.

Below: Almost home, the former hostages emerge onto the tarmac at a US airbase in West Germany. One of the lessons of this episode is that nations can deal with each other if they act rationally and follow roughly similar rules.

This felicitous state of affairs—from Washington's point of view—has been gradually undergoing change. The geopolitics of the Cold War still dictate that the areas of Soviet-American confrontation will be around the Eurasian rimland; nevertheless, the last two decades have been ones of transition in US relations with Latin America. The old hegemonic role of the past is being replaced with, if not a relationship of equals, at least one in which Washington must demonstrate a greater regard for Latin American concerns and interests. As for the Latin Americans themselves, they have in recent years rejected their dependent status and increasingly found ways to demonstrate their unwillingness to remain subject to United States political domination.

The central issue for some 20 years in US relations with Latin America has been Cuba—what to do about Castro's decision in the early 1960s to align himself closely with the Soviet Union. President Eisenhower first tried to "deal with" Castro and then largely ignored Cuba. President Kennedy inherited a plan to overthrow the Castro regime but failed, although he did succeed in the crisis of 1962 in disrupting Soviet plans to use Cuba as an intermediate range missile base. Presidents Johnson and Nixon tried economic and political sanctions; President Ford and especially President Carter attempted to entice Cuba into a more satisfactory relationship through promising various economic benefits of cooperation. Nothing worked; whatever the reasons—ideological, idiosyncratic, economic, megalomaniacal—all failed with Fidel.

Washington's troubles with Havana began in 1959 when Cuba's agrarian reform policy included the nationalization of the agricultural holdings of American citizens. To this injury Cuba added insult when it opened diplomatic

Above: The emotional involvement of the US people in the hostage drama is obvious from this banner. The US voters reacted against the Carter administration's leadership over this issue.

Latin America

One of the more pleasant myths enjoyed by North Americans is that Latin America and the United States are "good neighbors", linked in a "special relationship" dictated by geography and history.

The facts are otherwise. Latin America has never been of much consequence to the United States politically, culturally or economically. One does not have to agree with the unkind remark, attributed to a former high official in Washington, that "Latin America is a dagger pointed at the south pole" to accept the reality that only Africa has been accorded a lesser

role in American national security policy. When one reviews the landmark crises of the period since World War II the names that come to mind are Turkey and Greece, Berlin, China and Korea, Czechoslovakia, Vietnam, Israel, Taiwan, Iran, Afghanistan, Poland. Only Cuba injects a Latin American name. Thus it should have come as no surprise, after the failure of Secretary Haig's "shuttle diplomacy" between Buenos Aires and London, that, forced to choose, Washington backed Britain in the 1982 Falkland Islands crisis. To have done otherwise would have been quite astonishing.

The reality is that the United States government has viewed its role as exercising a benevolent hegemony over hemispheric affairs, primarily concerned with making certain that Latin America followed wherever the US chose to lead in world affairs and regarded US investment in Latin America with gratitude.

Below: USS *Tarawa* passing through the Panama Canal. This great seaway has never closed, but the US has shown great perception in agreeing to hand over control by the year 2000. Washington must, however, view unrest in Central America with concern because of its possible implications for the canal.

and trade relations with the Soviet Union and began to provide assistance to other Marxist-oriented Latin American revolutionary movements. Washington responded first with the abortive CIA-sponsored raid on the Bay of Pigs, then compelled the Soviet Union to withdraw its missiles in 1962, and in 1964 led the movement by the Organization of American States (OAS) to impose sanctions on Cuba. Cuba became increasingly dependent for its economic survival on its distant patron, the Soviet Union. For the first time in its history, Moscow had established a genuine alliance in the Western Hemisphere.

The United States reassessed its Cuban policy after President Ford assumed office and made several overtures to Castro: Washington dropped its insistence that Havana break off relations with Moscow as a precondition for restoring diplomatic ties with the United States; restrictions on American-owned firms abroad doing business with Cuba were modified; the US agreed in the OAS to ease OAS sanctions against Cuba; and wide-ranging discussions between the United States and Cuba began. This rapprochement ended, however, when Castro dispatched some 36,000 Cuban troops to Angola to assist the Marxist-oriented Popular Movement for the Liberation of Angola. Cuban troops also were sent to Mozambique, ostensibly to prevent an invasion by South Africa.

Subsequently, President Carter attempted to improve relations with Castro after Cuba allegedly withdrew much of its armed force from Angola. As Ford's initiative had foundered on Castro's Angolan intervention, so Carter's collapsed when in 1978 Cuba dispatched some 20,000 Cuban soldiers to Ethiopia to assist that Marxist regime in its struggle with Somalia. By the end of President Carter's term, even those persons in the United States most willing to have a reconciliation with Cuba had to admit that Cuba and the Soviet Union were coordinating military efforts to assist Marxist movements both in Africa and Central America. Under such circumstances, it is not surprising that the Reagan government, upon assuming office in 1981, made it known that no further overtures would be made to Cuba unless Havana ceased to act as a proxy warrior for the Soviet Union.

The Reagan administration in its first months in office not only toughened the US stand against Cuba but also toward the Marxist

revolutionaries in Central America, especially in El Salvador and Nicaragua. Congressional opposition, however, and the (spurious) cry of "no more Vietnams" have prevented stronger US efforts in the Central American area.

Despite Washington's preoccupation with Cuba, American-Mexican relations are of far greater importance. One reason, of course, is that Mexico is on the US border; countries are naturally concerned with adjacent nations. In the case of the United States, with its strong governing tradition of states rights, despite the fact that American states have no constitutional role in foreign policy, relations with the border nations of Mexico and Canada are exceedingly complex.

Yet Washington has ignored Mexico nearly as much as it has the rest of Latin America. Recently, however, the United States seems to have "discovered" Mexico. A major reason for this is the porous 3,000 mile border between the two countries. Especially since the insurgencies in Central America in the 1960s and 1970s, many Latin Americans have fled their homelands, crossed Mexico and entered the United States illegally. Others have left both Central

Above: A line-up of Cuban MiG-23 Flogger-E and -F aircraft provided by the Soviet Union. Former President Carter was greatly embarrassed by the revelation that there is a Soviet Army brigade on the island as well as other "advisers".

Right: An excellent quality air photograph of Sandino airfield in Nicaragua taken by a USAF U-2 reconnaissance aircraft on January 1, 1982. The picture had to be released by the US Government to prove the growing Communist infiltration of Latin America. The US position was not helped by being forced to take sides with the UK during the short-lived Argentinian occupation of the Falkland Islands in Spring 1982.

Below: US Army Special Forces instructors briefing trainees from El Salvador during an exercise at Fort Bragg. The US is in an unenviable position in Latin America, and frequently gives the impression of trying to back all sides in a desperate effort to avoid another Vietnam on its doorstep.

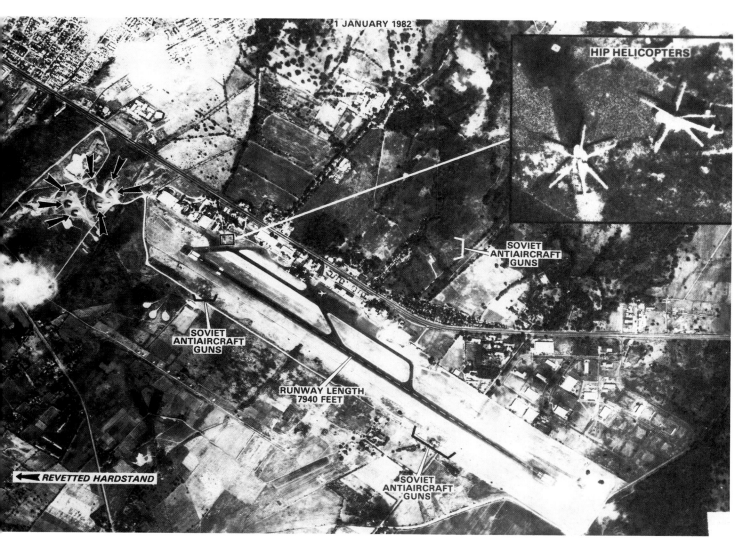

HIP HELICOPTERS

SOVIET
ANTIAIRCRAFT
GUNS

SOVIET
ANTIAIRCRAFT
GUNS

RUNWAY LENGTH
7940 FEET

← REVETTED HARDSTAND

SOVIET
ANTIAIRCRAFT
GUNS

America and Mexico itself for reasons people have always left their homelands: to seek a better life elsewhere.

Whatever the reasons, the flow of illegal migrants from Mexico to the United States is now estimated at between 500,000 and one-and-a-half million people annually. Some are un-documented workers who return to Mexico; others merge into the US population permanently. While Washington has attempted to secure Mexico's cooperation in stemming this tide, Mexico sees the illegal migration out of Mexico as a US problem but a Mexican solution. Mexico has a population of which half or more are under 15 years of age. The population growth rate is about 2.7 percent annually. Some 800,000 young people enter the job market each year but only about 350,000 jobs become available.

A second reason why Mexico has become important to the United States and to the rest of the world is the dramatic rise of Mexico as a major oil producing country. Mexico has not joined OPEC and in August 1981 made a long-term commitment to sell petroleum to the United States to fill its strategic petroleum reserve.

For a time it appeared that Mexico's oil exports would provide it with the necessary capital to continue its rapid pace of industrialization. This would not only enhance American-Mexican trade relations but also would help to stem the flow of Mexicans to the United States as job opportunities improved in Mexico.

President Reagan, with his southern California background and a greater realization than most US presidents of the importance of Mexico to the United States, came to office intent on improving Mexican-American relations. This determination was shared by President Lopez Portillo. Mexico is now the third most important US trading partner (after Canada and Japan). Mexico's anti-American rhetoric of the past has now been softened.

Unfortunately, however, the oil glut and the concomitant reduction in oil prices have caused severe economic setbacks in Mexico to what was an overly ambitious drive for industrialization. Currently Mexico is in the throes of a genuine economic crisis; relative to the dollar the peso has virtually collapsed. President Portillo's six year term in office ended in December 1982. It remains to be seen whether the recent progress in Mexican-American relations will continue.

The Future of American National Security Policy

Many of the problems noted in this essay are not the result of errors in resolve or judgement, although of course some are. Rather, the era of American dominance of world politics—roughly between the end of World War II in 1945 and the signing of the SALT I treaty (signifying Soviet-American strategic parity and equality) in 1972—has come to an end.

This was inevitable; as Europe and Japan recovered from the great world conflict it was to be expected that America's economic dominance of the world would diminish. Certainly not desirable but perhaps inevitable was the rise of the Soviet Union as a military super-power. Decolonialization and the growth of nationalism and anti-westernism in the Third World impeded the tidy solutions of the past. The extraordinary rise in oil prices and the related capability of a few relatively backward Middle Eastern countries to disrupt the global economy brought about further political and economic change.

Americans must adjust to their diminished status in world affairs. They must adjust to the fact that they may no longer be dictating solutions but arriving at them through the arduous process of negotiations, and this may be painful, but this is the situation at present and the one which lies ahead. However, the United States will remain for some time to come the world's largest economy. And if the United States, Western Europe and Japan collectively can contain the despotic and militaristic Soviet state, then a world in which the United States is an important but no longer the dominant nation ought to be one which Americans should willingly accept.

The US Defense Organization

Dr. Lawrence J. Korb, Assistant Secretary of Defense (Manpower, Reserve Affairs, and Logistics).

The heart of the US war machine is the Department of Defense (DoD), which is the largest bureaucracy within the American political system. It was created three decades ago by the National Security Act (NSA) of 1947. Prior to that time, the American military establishment was divided into two separate cabinet level departments: War and Navy. Over the past 30 years, the structure of DoD has been modified several times by legislation, executive order, and administrative fiat. The structure of the department as it now exists is outlined in Table 1.

The current organizational structure of DoD can be best understood if it is broken down into its five major levels. These are: the Office of the Secretary of Defense (OSD), the Joint Chiefs of Staff (JCS), the military departments, the defense agencies, and the field or operational commands.[1]

The Office of the Secretary of Defense (OSD)

The Department of Defense is under the control of the Secretary of Defense. He is the individual responsible for exercising the President's authority over DoD. The Secretary performs three main functions for the Chief Executive. First, he is the manager of DoD. In this capacity, the Secretary controls the Department's resources and directs all activities of the subunits of the Department. Second, he is the deputy commander-in-chief with authority and responsibility for controlling the actions of US military forces. Third, the Secretary is a principal advisor to the President on national security policy.

To assist him in carrying out his multiple responsibilities, the Secretary has a Deputy Secretary, two Under Secretaries, eight Assistant Secretaries of Defense, and a General Counsel. Collectively, this group and their staffs are referred to as the Office of the Secretary of Defense (OSD). OSD is composed of about 1,700 people, 1,250 of whom are civilians and 450 of whom are military.

When the Department was first created, the Secretary of Defense was limited to three special assistants and his total staff was only 50 people. As his responsibilities grew, so too did the size of OSD. It reached its apex in 1969, at the height of the war in Vietnam, when it climbed to 3,500 people. The 40 per cent reduction in OSD over the last decade has paraleled the cut in the size of the entire defense establishment.

A 1949 amendment to the NSA authorized the creation of a Deputy Secretary of Defense, and a 1972 amendment authorized the creation of a second Deputy. However, except for a brief period in 1976, the post of the second Deputy has not been filled. The intent of Congress in establishing the second Deputy was to allow the incumbent to focus on operational matters,[2] but the other Deputy and the Chairman of the Joint Chiefs of Staff both argued that this would encroach upon their areas of responsibility. When Robert Ellsworth served briefly as the second Deputy Secretary of Defense, he was given responsibility for intelligence activities instead of operational matters. In 1977, the position was abolished when the two Under Secretaries (one for Policy, another for Research and Engineering) were created.

The Deputy Secretary of Defense is the alter ego of the Secretary. He is responsible for coordination and supervision of the Department as directed by the Secretary. Normally the Secretary delegates a great deal of his authority to the Deputy. The number two man can issue directives to all the subunits of governmental agencies, and to international bodies, in the name of the Secretary. In recent years, the Deputy has also been given complete authority to deal with specific problem areas. David Packard, Deputy 1969–72, reformed DoD's weapons acquisition process, while William Clements, 1972–77, revised the Department's educational system, and Frank Carlucci, 1981–83, managed the budget process.

The Director, Program Analysis and Evaluation, and his personnel serve as the Secretary's analytical staff. It is their job to evaluate all of the proposals submitted to the Secretary to ensure that they are in accord with the established objectives and are cost effective. As will be noted later, their main function is to analyze the programs submitted by the military departments and agencies during the budgetary process.

This group was established in 1961 as the Systems Analysis Division in the Comptroller's office. In 1965, Systems Analysis was raised to the Assistant Secretary level, in 1976 was placed in a staff capacity to the Secretary, in 1977 was restored to the Assistant Secretary level, and in 1981, redesignated Director of Program Analysis and Evaluation. Despite the changes in its status, the functions of systems analysis have remained the same.

Current legislation allows the Secretary of Defense to have two Under Secretaries, eight Assistant Secretaries, and a General Counsel. The law does not specify the functional responsibilities or titles of the Under and Assistant Secretaries, but permits the Secretary to alter them as he demes fit. The current designations of each of these 11 individuals are self explanatory; descriptions of their responsibilities are listed in Table 1.

The Joint Chiefs of Staff (JCS)

According to law, the Joint Chiefs of Staff are composed of five military officers: The Chief of Staff of the Army, the Chief of Naval Operations (CNO), the Chief of Staff of the Air Force, and a Chairman.[3] The latter is a member of one of the armed services but during his tenure on the JCS has no service responsibilities.

All of the Joint Chiefs are appointed by the President subject to Senate confirmation. The service chiefs are appointed for a fixed non-renewable term of four years. The Chairman is appointed for a two-year term, and, except in wartime, can only be reappointed once. His term is not fixed and he serves at the pleasure of the President. Because of their tenure in office, the terms of the Chiefs carry over from one administration to the next.

By law the JCS are charged with performing eight specific functions within the DoD. They can be grouped into four broad categories.

Most aspects of the US defense establishment are on a mammoth scale. From the White House the President of the United States (left) endeavours to control the world's largest single employer and spender of the second largest military budget (after the USSR). On the President's left is Secretary of Defense Weinberger who has direct responsibility for the department which is symbolized by the mighty Pentagon building (below) which has five 921 ft (280m) sides and employs about 23,000 military and civilian personnel. The powers of both President and Pentagon are, however, circumscribed by a third element—the US Congress—which protects its prerogative with great care since the hiatus of the Vietnam War.

First, they serve as the principal military advisors to the President and the Secretary of Defense. Their input to these two individuals is made primarily through the NSC system. Second, they prepare seven short, medium, and long range strategic and logistic plans, which provide guidance for the development of the defense budgets, military aid programs, industrial mobilization plans, research and development programs, and the contingency plans of operational commanders. Third, they review and comment upon the plans, programs, and requirements of the separate services and the field commands. Fourth, the Chiefs assist the President and the Secretary of Defense in carrying out their command responsibilities; that is, the JCS provide strategic direction over the operational commands for the Commander-in-Chief.

The JCS are assisted in the exercise of their functions by a group known as the Organization of the Joint Chiefs of Staff (OJCS). OJCS is composed of approximately 1,270 people. Of these, about 650 are officers; the others are enlisted personnel and civilians. It has two major components: the Joint Staff and the other groups that support the JCS but are not part of the Joint Staff.

The Joint Staff cannot by law exceed 400 military officers, and is composed of equal numbers of officers from the three military departments, with the Marine Corps being allotted 20 per cent of the Navy complement.

The Joint Staff includes the Office of the Director, Joint Staff; the Manpower and Personnel Directorate (J-1); the Operations Directorate (J-3); the Logistics Directorate (J-4); the Plans and Policy Directorate (J-5); and the Command, Control and Communications Systems Directorate (C³S).

Above: The Joint Chiefs of Staff. Seated, left to right: Adm. James D. Watkins, USN; Gen. Edward C. Meyer, USA; Gen. John W. Vessey, Jr., USA (Chairman); Gen. Robert H. Barrow, USMC; and Gen. Charles A. Gabriel, USAF. They are responsible for the mightiest forces in the world.

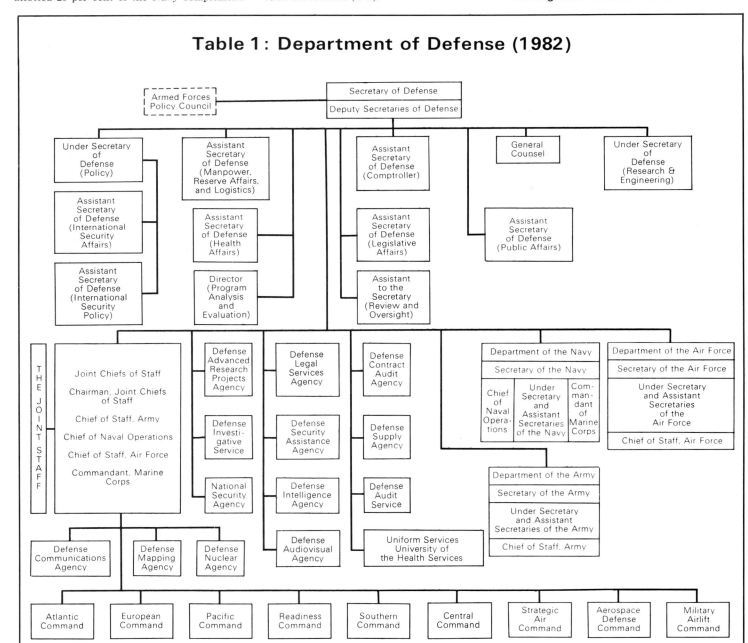

Table 1: Department of Defense (1982)

The Military Departments

Within the Department of Defense there are three military departments separately organized and administered: Army, Navy, and Air Force. However, these organizations are departments in name only. The secretaries of these departments do not have cabinet level status nor are they responsible directly to the President or Congress. For all practical purposes, the Army, Navy, and Air Force are agencies or bureaux within the Department of Defense. They carry the designation of Department because until the formation of DoD they had cabinet level status and were masters of their own affairs. Three decades after unification, the military departments are left with but few vestiges of their former prerogatives.

The primary function of the Departments of the Army, Navy, and Air Force is to recruit, train, and equip forces for the unified and specified commands. These departments have no control over military operations. The chain of command goes from the President to the Secretary of Defense and the JCS to the unified or specified commands. Moreover, in the areas "reserved" for the military departments—that is, recruiting, training, equipping—OSD can and does intervene to establish guidelines and procedures; for example, the length of recruit training, development of weapon systems. Whenever there is a conflict between a departmental position and an OSD position, the Army, Navy, and Air Force must give way.

Each military department is headed by a secretary who is in effect president of a DoD subsidiary. These individuals are usually referred to as service secretaries. The departments are organized essentially along hierarchical staff lines, which are a rough microcosm of the organization of the entire Department of Defense. Each service secretary has an under secretary, a service secretariat and a military staff.

The secretariat is composed of approximately 10 civilian officials whose responsibilities roughly parallel those of the assistant secretaries of Defense; e.g., research and development, manpower and reserve affairs, general counsel. Each of these 10 officials presides over a mixed staff of civilians and military personnel, the total size of which is now about 100.

The Military staff of each department is headed by the uniformed Chief of Service. Each service chief has a vice chief who is in charge of conducting the day-to-day operations of the service staff so that the service chief has time to

Above: Overall chief of the armed forces, of course, is the President, who surrounds himself with wise counsellors. One of them (standing) is William Clark, National Security Adviser.

devote to his corporate duties as a member of the JCS. The military staffs are normally divided into approximately 15 sections, which represent the different line and staff functions performed by the services; for example, personnel and medicine. Just as the responsibilities of the secretariat overlap with those of OSD, many of the functions of the military staff overlap with those of the defense agencies; for example, intelligence. Finally, there are the non-headquarters organizations or commands of each military department, which actually carry out the work of recruiting, training, and equipping the force. When these forces become operational, i.e., are assigned to a unified or specified command, the departments maintain only administrative control over them. The field commanders—for example, Commanding General, US Seventh Army or Commander-in-Chief US Pacific Fleet—become component commanders in the unified or specified commands.

There are certain differences in the organizational arrangements of the military departments. Generally speaking the Departments of the Army and Air Force are much more hierarchical in nature than the Navy Department, in which certain bilineal elements of pre-World War II organizational arrangements have persisted. In the Army and Air Force, the military staffs support and report to the service secretary through both the appropriate assistant secretary, and the under secretary. In the Navy, the CNO and the Commandant of the Marine Corps report directly to the Secretary of the Navy through a chain entirely separate from the civilian secretariat. Moreover, in the Navy department there are two distinct military staffs, one led by the CNO and the other managed by the Commandant of the Marine Corps.[4]

Defense Agencies

At present there are 14 organizations or groups within DoD which have the status of defense agencies. These organizations perform functions which are common to or cut across departmental lines. There are no specific restrictions on the number or functions of these organizations. The McCormack-Curtis amendment to the 1958 Defense Reorganization Act empowers the Secretary to create such agencies whenever he determines that it would be advantageous in terms of effectiveness, economy, or efficiency to provide for the performance of a common function by a single organization. Implicit in the amendment is the Secretary of Defense's power to disestablish or disband such agencies.

Secretaries of Defense Gates, McNamara, Laird, Rumsfeld, Brown, and Weinberger have used the provisions of the McCormack-Curtis amendment to create 12 defense agencies. The 13th agency, the Defense Nuclear Agency, started with the Manhattan Project in 1942, then was reformed as the Armed Forces Special Weapons Project by the Atomic Energy Act of 1946. The 14th—the National Security Agency

Below: Powerful though JCS Chairman Gen. Vessey may be, he and his JCS colleagues do not exercise operational control over the field commands. Without Secretary of Defense authority, they cannot move a ship or a squadron.

—was established in November 1952 by Presidential directive and placed under the control of the Secretary of Defense.

Ten of the agencies are under the direct management control of the Secretary of Defense; that is, their tasks are given by and they report directly to the Secretary. Three other agencies, Defense Communications, Defense Mapping, and Defense Nuclear, report directly to the JCS. The status of the Defense Intelligence Agency (DIA) is somewhat ambivalent. From its creation in 1961 through 1976, it was under the control of the JCS. In fact, as noted above, the Director of DIA serves as the J-2 for the Joint Staff. However, in 1976 control over DIA was transferred to OSD, with the provision that the JCS could still assign tasks to it directly. Table 2 contains a list of the 14 agencies along with their dates of inception, controlling agent and personnel assigned.

Seven of the agencies are headed by two- or three-star generals or admirals, while the other seven organizations are headed by senior civilians. All of the agencies are staffed by a mixed civilian military complement. The civilians are generally in a permanent career status while the military personnel are assigned for a three-year tour.

The 14 defense agencies employ over 70,000 people. About 90 per cent are civilians while the remaining 10 per cent are military on temporary assignment. The agencies range from the mammoth Defense Logistics Agency, which employs nearly 48,000 people, to the miniscule Defense Legal Services Agency, which has only 56 people on its payroll. Only the Defense Logistics Agency and Defense Mapping Agency have more than 5,000 people in their group. The median size is about 5,000 and six agencies actually have less than 1,000 people in their employ.

Although the defense agencies are the largest single organizational unit within DoD, their total budget is comparatively small. The total budget of these 14 agencies (as well as OSD and JCS) for FY 1983 was over $9 billion or nearly

Above: The White House is the place where the highest defense decisions are made. Despite Congressional powers, in emergency all real power lies with the President.

4 per cent of the total Defense budget.[5] There is one organizational reason for the fact that these groups consume such a relatively small amount of resources; that is, each of the military departments has groups within its military staff with responsibilities similar to that of the defense agencies. These service groups perform much of the basic work in the area, while the defense agencies function more or less as integrators.

The roles of the agencies
The responsibilities of the agencies vary widely. The National Security Agency (NSA) is officially designated the National Security Agency/Central Security Service. It has a two-fold responsibility. NSA safeguards the communications of the armed forces and monitors the communications of other nations for the purpose of gathering intelligence. The NSA was established in 1952 by President Truman as a replacement for the Armed Forces Security Agency. The Central Security Service was added to NSA in 1972 to emphasize the fact that NSA was being given responsibility for developing a unified cryptologic program within DoD. The three-star director of NSA also heads the Central

US Mainland Military Districts

First US Army includes:
District of Columbia,
Commonwealth of Puerto Rico,
Virgin Islands of the
United States.

Naval Districts (HQ in blue)
Army Areas
Air Force Reserve Regions
(HQ in black)

Table 2: Defense Agencies

Agency	Founded	Reports to	Personnel Military	Personnel Civilian	Personnel Total
National Security Agency	1952	OSD	Classified	Classified	Classified
Defense Advanced Research Projects Agency	1958	OSD	26	153	179
Defense Nuclear Agency	1942	JCS	483	633	1,116
Defense Communications Agency	1960	JCS	1,463	1,667	3,130
Defense Intelligence Agency	1961	JCS/OSD	1,805	2,607	4,412
Defense Logistics Agency	1961	OSD	965	46,757	47,722
Defense Contract Audit Agency	1965	OSD	—	3,536	3,536
Defense Audit Agency	1976	OSD	—	393	393
Defense Security Assistance Agency	1971	OSD	24	83	107
Defense Mapping Agency	1972	JCS	436	8,375	8,811
Defense Investigative Service	1972	OSD	142	2,446	2,588
Defense Audiovisual Agency	1979	OSD	128	472	600
Defense Legal Services Agency	1981	OSD	2	54	56
Uniformed Services University of the Health Services	1972	OSD	96	606	702
Total			5,570	67,782	73,352

ecurity Service. Because of the classified ature of its operation, there are no figures vailable on the number of NSA employees.

The purpose of the Defense Advanced Re-earch Projects Agency (DARPA) is to maintain echnological superiority for the US in the field f military hardware. DARPA undertakes and arries through to feasibility demonstration hose projects which meet one of the following riteria: those with high potential payoffs but ith too high a risk for the individual services obtain budget approval; projects which may nvolve major technological advances or break-hroughs; and projects which could have broad tilization within the entire department. After ARPA has explored a concept and determined it to be feasible, control of the project is turned over to the department or agency most directly concerned.

The Defense Nuclear Agency (DNA) is the present name of the "Manhattan Project" group, the Armed Forces Special Weapons Project, and later the Defense Atomic Support Agency. DNA manages the nuclear weapons stockpile, develops and monitors a National Nuclear Test Readiness Program, and maintains liaison for DoD with other governmental bodies concerned with nuclear matters.

The primary function of the Defense Communications Agency (DCA) is to provide support for the World-Wide Military Command and Control System, the National Military Communications System, and the Defense Communications System. The operations of these systems will be discussed more fully in the section on command and control.

The Defense Intelligence Agency (DIA) manages all of the defense intelligence programs and provides intelligence support to the Secretary of Defense and the JCS. DIA relies upon the resources of the armed services for intelligence collection and supervises the development of intelligence by the services to meet their own particular needs.

The Defense Logistics Agency supports the military services, other DoD components, federal civil agencies, foreign governments, and others (as authorized), by buying, storing, and distributing assigned materiel commodities and items of supply, including weapon systems, and providing logistics services directly associated with the supply management function, contract administration services, and other support services as directed by the Secretary of Defense. DLA presently handles two-thirds of all requisitions processed by DoD and administers military contracts with a value of more than $128 billion.

The role of the Defense Contract Audit Agency (DCAA) is to perform all the required contract auditing for DoD and to provide accounting and financial advisory services regarding defense contracts to DoD components which have responsibility for procurement and contract administration. The functions of DCAA include evaluating the acceptability of costs claimed as proposed by contractors and reviewing the efficiency and economy of contractor operations. Many other agencies of the federal government also make use of DCAA services.

Below: A contract is signed for military equipment. Such ceremonies are often the result of intense and bitter infighting, both political and financial, and there is little doubt that sometimes military factors take second, possibly even third place.

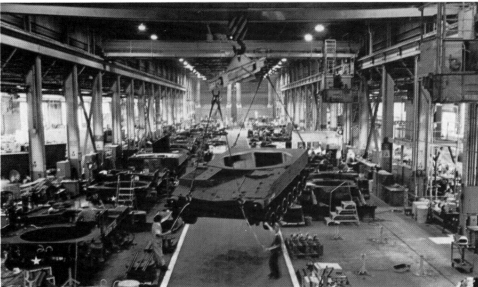

Top: The Rapid Deployment Joint Task Force was born from a perceived need to be able to project effective power to virtually any spot on Earth, though it has yet to be proven in actual combat operations.

Above: The USA possesses the most capable defense industry in the world which is able to satisfy virtually every need of its armed forces, and still have a vast excess capacity to meet export orders.

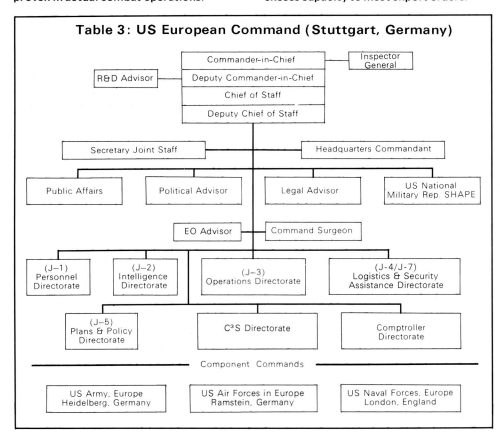

Table 3: US European Command (Stuttgart, Germany)

The Defense Security Assistance Agency (DSAA) was established to provide greater emphasis to the management control of such aid programs as military assistance and foreign military sales. Besides controlling these programs, the Director of DSAA also functions as a deputy assistant secretary of defense under the Assistant Secretary of Defense for International Security Affairs.

The Defense Mapping Agency (DMA) was established to consolidate and improve the efficiency of defense mapping, charting, and geodetic operations. DMA relies almost completely on the individual services for research and development and data collection.

The primary function of the Defense Investigative Service (DIS) is to conduct personnel security investigations on DoD civilians, military personnel, and industrial and contractor personnel involved in defense business. DIS also conducts some criminal investigations and crime prevention surveys for DoD.

The Defense Audit Service plans and performs internal audits of OSD, JCS, the Unified, Specified Commands, and all defense agencies; interservice audits in all DoD components; quick response on matters of special interest to the Secretary of Defense; and audits of the Security Assistance Program.

The Defense Audiovisual Agency (DAVA) produces, acquires, and reproduces motion picture films, video and audio tapes and discs, still photographs, and multimedia and other audiovisual media products for all DoD components. DAVA manages and operates the distribution system for its audiovisual products, provides depositories for the archival storage of DoD audiovisual products, and develops and maintains a data base for managing the DoD Audiovisual Program.

The Defense Legal Services Agency was established to provide legal advice and services for OSD and its field activities and the defense agencies; it provides technical support and assistance in developing the DoD legislative program; it provides a centralized legislative and congressional document reference and distribution point of the department; and it maintains the department's historical legislative files. The General Counsel serves as the Director of DLS.

The Uniformed Services University of the Health Sciences was established in 1974 to educate career-oriented health professionals for the military services. The graduating medical student is required to serve a period of obligation of not less than seven years. The University provides the opportunity for the military services to recruit, educate, and retain health professionals with a career commitment to the Services.

Field Commands

The operational forces of DoD are placed under the control of either a unified or specified commander. A unified command is one which has a broad continuing mission and is composed of forces of two or more services. A specified command also has a broad continuing mission but is normally composed of forces from only one service.

The operating forces of the Department of Defense are presently broken down into six unified and three specified commands. Five of the six unified are theater or area commands: Atlantic, Pacific, European, Central and Southern. The sixth unified command, the Readiness Command, is composed of forces from the Army and Air Force based in the continental United States. The Readiness Command is in effect our ready reserve or contingency command. Its primary mission is to make its forces available to reinforce the other unified or area commands.

The three specified commands are the Strategic Air Command, Aerospace Defense Command, the Military Airlift Command. Each of these commands is composed primarily of Air Force components.

The present command structure had its

rigins in World War II when the creation of heater joint and combined commands demonrated the value of unified commands for broad ilitary missions. The National Security Act of 947 authorized the President to establish combatant commands for the performance of asgned military missions. However, it was not ntil the 1958 Reorganization Act became law nat the unified and specified commands were laced directly under the control of the Secreiry of Defense. Prior to that time, the unified ommands were subject to the authority of the ilitary departments and service chiefs.

Each unified command is headed by a three- r four-star general officer. The Atlantic and acific Commands have always been headed by avy admirals, while the European, Southern, entral and Readiness Commands are normally nder the control of an Army officer. The three ecified commands are headed by Air Force enerals. The commanders of the unified and ecified commands are responsible to the resident and the Secretary of Defense for e accomplishment of their military missions. hey have full operational control over the rces assigned to them and these forces cannot e reassigned or transferred except by the ecretary of Defense. The JCS provide strategic uidance and direction to these commands rough the various joint planning and intelli- nce documents, but do not exercise opera- onal control over them. The JCS may issue ders to the unified commands only on the ithority and direction of the Secretary of efense. On their own, the Chiefs cannot move ship or squadron.

The unified and specified commands are assisted by a joint staff and the commanders of the service forces or components assigned to them. In some of the commands, the unified commander also functions as a component commander. For example, the Commander-in-Chief of the Atlantic also serves as the Commander of the Atlantic fleet. Some of the unified commanders also are allied commanders. For example, the Commander-in-Chief of Europe is also the Supreme Allied Commander Europe.

As noted above, logistics and administrative support of the nine combat commands is the responsibility of the military departments. This permits the operational commander to focus on strategic and tactical matters and to take advantage of pre-existing channels for logistics and administrative support.

Table 3 contains the organizational arrangements of the European Command. These arrangements are similar to those in each of the eight operational commands.

The Budgetary Process; Executive Phase

Since 1961 DoD has formulated its budget through the use of the Planning, Programming, and Budgeting System (PPBS). This system divides the executive phase of the budgetary process into three clearly defined cycles: planning, programming, and budgeting, and has as its foundation the Five Year Defense Plan (FYDP). The FYDP is the master plan for the entire budget process. At any given moment, it contains the approved programs with their estimated costs projected out over a five-year period. Three times each year the FYDP is

Above: A comprehensive defense capability requires a plethora of back-up facilities whose manpower far exceeds that in combat units. One such facility is the Defense Mapping Agency which is concerned with mapping, charting and geodetic activities, but with all data inputs being supplied from single-service sources.

updated to reflect decisions made in the budgetary process.

The planning cycle is the first and longest of the cycles. It begins in May and goes on for 10 months—that is, until the following February. The first step in the planning cycle involves production of the Joint Strategic Planning Document (JSPD) by the JCS for the Secretary of Defense. Based on assessment of national commitments projected over the next five years, this document contains the comprehensive military appraisal of the threat to US interests worldwide, a statement of recommended military objectives derived from national objectives, and the recommended military strategy to attain national objectives. In formulating JSPD, the JCS are guided by decisions made by the National Security Council in this area.

The JSPD includes a summary of the planning force levels, which the JCS believes could successfully execute the approved national strategy and presents views on the attainability of these forces in consideration of fiscal responsibility, manpower resources, material availability, technology and industrial capacity.

During the fall, the Secretary of Defense and his staff review JSPD and prepare the Defense

Guidance (DG), which gives a threat assessment, defense policy and strategy as well as force planning and resource allocation guidance for the defense community. The Secretary's guidance is based upon inputs of the JCS, the unified and specified commanders, the Services, the NSC, and his own conception of what the national security policy should be. The DG is reviewed and discussed in some detail by the Defense Resources Board (DRB) made up of the Secretary, Deputy Secretary, Chairman of the JCS, Service chiefs, and Secretaries, and selected members of the OSD staff.

The Secretary completes the planning cycle in February by issuing the Defense Guidance. This document presents definitive fiscal constraints and policy assumptions under which the upcoming budget will be produced. It is the primary document used by the Services and DoD components in preparing their five-year program.

The fiscal constraints set forth a total for the entire Department as well as targets for each of the subunits of the organization. The DoD target comes from the Office of Management and Budget and is arrived at through a complex series of negotiations and bargaining between the President's advisors for national security and economic affairs. The ultimate decision on the defense total is highly susceptible to such influences as the state of the US economy, the chief executive's own monetary philosophy, and the demands of other agencies as well as the international situation.

Rather than funding a particular policy, the process is generally reversed. The administration decides on the size of the entire federal budget, adds up the essentially uncontrollable or previously committed items in the budget, and then allocates some portion of the remainder to defense.

The shares of the defense total which are allocated to the individual components are based upon the missions or programs supported by each of these agencies. For example, the Navy supplies the submarine launched ballistic missile portion of the Triad in DoD's strategic program, surface combatants and tactical air for the general purpose forces program, and transport ships for the sealift mission.

The planning assumptions in the DG are influenced to some degree by guidance received from the National Security Council and to a lesser extent by inputs from the JCS. These assumptions are primarily a product of the Secretary of Defense's own interpretation of NSC and JCS inputs and his views on the likely scenarios which may lead to armed involvement by US military forces.

The programming cycle commences upon receipt of the DG by the departments and agencies and lasts through the summer. First, the military departments and agencies complete their Program Objective Memoranda (POMs). The POMs are submitted to OSD in May and express total program requirements in terms of forces, manpower and costs for each mission area of the defense budget in which the organization plays a part. The POMs must provide a rationale for any deviations from the FYDP or DG.

The POMs are scrutinized during June by the systems analysts in OSD for conformity with the fiscal and policy guidance of the DG. On the basis of this analysis, issue papers are prepared for the Secretary of Defense. These issues are the major questions that the analysts feel the Secretary and the DRB should address in their review of the POMs. They normally reflect those areas where OSD feels that the departments or agencies could meet their assigned objectives in a more cost effective manner or where a change in priorities or reallocation of funds is appropriate. Services may raise issues, but they rarely do. The analysts normally prepare a series of options for the Secretary on each issue.

During July and August the Secretary of Defense, Deputy Secretary, Chairman JCS, and OSD staff meet with the service chiefs and

Top: Explaining the national defense budget to the Press. Every year the US administration produces a vast amount of documentation for Press consumption. There can be little doubt that the US Press is able to exert a lot of influence on military programs by mobilizing opinion, especially in national and state legislatures.

Above: The author of this chapter, Lawrence J. Korb, one of the DoD's more senior civil servants who provide continuity and a great deal of expertise. Right: Congress has much power, especially over the defense budget which must be progressed through both the House of Representatives and the Senate.

department secretaries to discuss and debate these issues. These "issue paper" meetings of the DRB are considered the second "step" in the programming cycle. On the basis of these meetings, the Secretary makes a decision on each issue which he promulgates in the form of a Program Decision Memorandum (PDM). The PDMs are circulated throughout the Department for review and comment by the Director, Program Analysis and Evaluation, who is executive agent for the program review. The JCS or the individual services may disagree with any of the Secretary's judgments, and ask for a reconsideration or rehearing on the issue.

The budgetary cycle commences on October 1 when the departments and agencies submit their budget estimates for the fiscal year beginning 12 months hence. These estimates are

reviewed jointly by personnel assigned to th Assistant Secretary of Defense (Comptrolle and the National Security Analysis Branch the Office of Management and Budget (OMB Theoretically this joint examination is tec nical in nature; that is, the reviewers are su posed to determine such things as whether particular weapons system is costed out co rectly. In practice, the comptroller and OM often raise many issues with policy implica tions: for example, how many weapons ar needed.

On the basis of this review, the Secretary Defense makes certain changes in the budge of his subunits which he issues in the form Program Budget Decisions (PBDs) durir November and early December. These ar circulated throughout the Department, and th

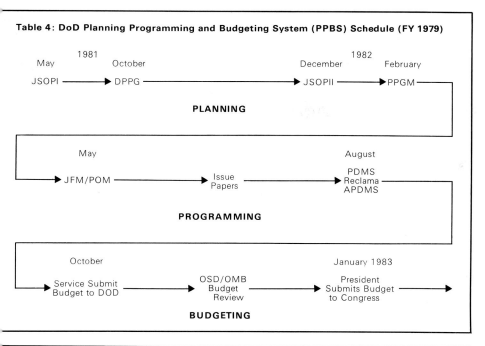

Table 4: DoD Planning Programming and Budgeting System (PPBS) Schedule (FY 1979)

1981
May — October — 1982 December — February

JSOPI → DPPG → JSOPII → PPGM

PLANNING

May — August

JFM/POM → Issue Papers → PDMS Reclama APDMS

PROGRAMMING

October — January 1983

Service Submit Budget to DOD → OSD/OMB Budget Review → President Submits Budget to Congress →

BUDGETING

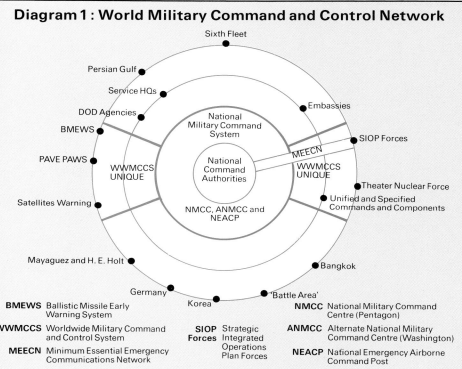

Diagram 1 : World Military Command and Control Network

Sixth Fleet
Persian Gulf
Service HQs
DOD Agencies
BMEWS
PAVE PAWS
Satellites Warning
Mayaguez and H. E. Holt
Germany
Korea
'Battle Area'
Bangkok
Unified and Specified Commands and Components
Theater Nuclear Force
SIOP Forces
Embassies

National Military Command System
National Command Authorities
NMCC, ANMCC and NEACP

MEECN

WWMCCS UNIQUE
WWMCCS UNIQUE

BMEWS Ballistic Missile Early Warning System
WWMCCS Worldwide Military Command and Control System
MEECN Minimum Essential Emergency Communications Network
SIOP Forces Strategic Integrated Operations Plan Forces
NMCC National Military Command Centre (Pentagon)
ANMCC Alternate National Military Command Centre (Washington)
NEACP National Emergency Airborne Command Post

military departments and agencies are given the opportunity to reclama those with which they disagree.

The PBD reclama process is finished in late December and the budget is then sent to the President. If the OMB examiners disagree with certain decisions of the Secretary, the Director of OMB brings these to the attention of the Chief Executive. The President normally reviews the defense budget in early January and submits it to the Congress by the middle of the month. In his review, the President usually meets with the JCS as a group to ascertain their views on the final product. The Chief Executive generally makes only marginal changes to the proposed budget. However, there are some occasions when the President will make substantial modifications. These occasions arise if the Chief Executive needs to achieve specific monetary goals which necessitate a change in the size of the total federal budget. Since the defense budget represents two-thirds of all of the controllable expenditures in the entire federal budget, it is the easiest area to change in order to alter the size of the federal budget. Table 4 recaps the steps in the budgetary process.

Legislative Phase
The legislative phase of the defense budget process begins in mid-January upon receipt of the budget from the President and lasts until late September when the budget is sent to the White House for signature. This phase has three separate stages.

The first stage consists of setting a target for, or a ceiling on, the size of the defense budget. Under the provisions of the Congressional Budget Control and Impoundment Act of 1974, the Congress must pass a budget resolution by May 15. Among other things, this resolution must establish the overall size of the federal budget. This is made on the basis of recommendations of the House and Senate Budget Committees which conduct hearings on the subject. The budget resolution deals only with the size and not the distribution of the defense budget.

The second stage in the legislative phase of the budget process consists of authorizing or approving the major weapon systems and manpower levels of DoD. Before funds can be appropriated to DoD for men and materiel, the substance of the program must be approved. The authorization hearings are conducted by the Armed Services Committees of each chamber. These committees take about one thousand hours of testimony from the Secretary of Defense, the assistant secretaries, service secretaries, and the JCS before making their recommendations. Many times issues which were decided upon within the executive branch are reopened again, and the services make their case once more to the Armed Services Committees which, for the most part, are composed of defense partisans. On many occasions these committees will authorize a program which the Secretary of Defense or the President does not want; e.g., a nuclear powered strike cruiser. The Congress normally completes action on the authorization by the end of June.

The final stage of the legislative phase is the appropriations process. The Congress may appropriate funds for any authorized program but does not have to appropriate funds for all authorized programs. The appropriations process is conducted by a subcommittee of the House and Senate Appropriations Committees. These groups take another six hundred hours of testimony on the defense budget from most of the same witnesses who appeared before the Armed Services Committees. In effect, each program in the DoD budget is subject to double jeopardy. It must be approved in both the authorization and appropriations process. Work on the defense appropriation bill is normally completed in late September.

While the defense appropriations bill is making its way through each chamber, the Congress adopts a second and binding resolution on the size of the defense budget. This figure, which must be established by September 15, is nearly identical to the May 15 target. If the defense appropriations bill falls within the binding target, the legislative phase is concluded. If not, the bill is sent back to the Appropriations Committee or the guideline is changed. Thus far, the size the defense appropriations bill has not exceeded the binding target.

Command, Control, and Communications

The command, control, and communications (C³) systems of DoD are the means through which the National Command Authorities (the President and the Secretary of Defense) and, under their direction, the military commanders control and employ the military strength of the United States. These C³ systems are composed of satellites for warning, surveillance, meteorology, and communications; ground and undersea systems; ground, shipborne, and airborne command facilities, worldwide voice, telephone, teletype, and automatic data networks; and information processing systems. A secure, well designed, and efficient C³ system is vital to the success of DoD in fulfilling its primary mission of employing military force in support of national policy. A poor C³ system can undo the best efforts of even an administratively sound organizational structure and a cost effective military force.

An overview of the present C³ structure is portrayed in Diagram 1. At the center are the National Command Authorities (NCA)—the President and the Secretary of Defense. The NCA exercise command and control over deployed forces through the Joint Chiefs of Staff. The JCS are supported directly by the National Military Command System (NMCS), which consists of the National Military Command Center (NMCC) in the Pentagon, the Alternate National Military Command Center (ANMCC), based near Washington, and the National Emergency Airborne Command Post (NEACP), along with their interconnecting telecommunications and Automated Data Processing (ADP) support. These facilities provide the personnel and equipment which can receive, evaluate and display information as well as execute national decisions for direction and control of the forces. Alerting procedures and the redundancy of the facilities, coupled with the NEACP's airborne capability, provide for an important degree of survivability if the system should come under attack.

The NMCS is under the control of the JCS. The chairman of the JCS is responsible for the operation of the three elements in this system. He is assisted in this job by the Director and Deputy Director of Operations (J-3). The Director of the Defense Communications Agency is the NMCS systems engineer and technical supervisor for the entire NMCS.

The second diagrammatic ring around the NCA represents the Defense Communications System (DCS). The DCS is the "in-place" worldwide system which serves as the foundation for wartime communication needs. It provides for common-user communication requirements and extends high volume command and control capability throughout the United States, Europe and the Pacific. Included are subsystems for voice communications by the Automatic Voice Network (AUTOVON), secure voice communications by the Automatic Secure Voice Network (AUTOSEVOCOM), and secure message and data transmission by the Automatic Digital Network (AUTODIN). For the most part, these systems consist of fixed equipment and facilities and interconnect with the primary and alternate fixed or mobile command posts of the key decision makers.

Above: Inside a Boeing E-4B Advanced Airborne Command Post (AABNCP) with the staff officers at their desks ready to deal with any national emergency.

Overseas, the DCS is mostly government owned; in the US, it is leased from commercial carriers. It serves the entire Defense community with over 1,100 AUTODIN terminals and 17,000 direct AUTOVON subscriber access lines. The systems which comprise the DCS have a preempt capability so that essential command and control messages can be accorded precedence over routine traffic. The DCS system is operated and maintained by the Defense Communications Agency.

The last ring in the diagram represents the mobile and transportable facilities and tactical networks organic to the military field force. Also included here are the post, camp, static and base fixed, internal communications systems. The communications networks of the operating forces are the means by which the highly mobile forces are maneuvered by the commanders. DoD has the capability to link the various tactical systems through the DCS to the NMCS to allow the National Command Auth-

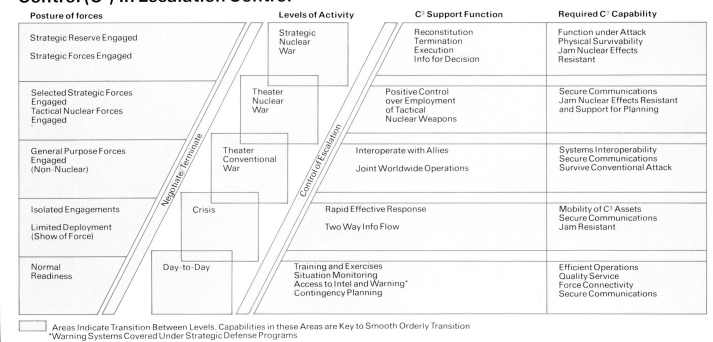

Diagram 2: The Changing Role of Communications, Command and Control (C³) in Escalation Control

Posture of forces	Levels of Activity	C³ Support Function	Required C³ Capability
Strategic Reserve Engaged / Strategic Forces Engaged	Strategic Nuclear War	Reconstitution / Termination / Execution / Info for Decision	Function under Attack / Physical Survivability / Jam Nuclear Effects Resistant
Selected Strategic Forces Engaged / Tactical Nuclear Forces Engaged	Theater Nuclear War	Positive Control over Employment of Tactical Nuclear Weapons	Secure Communications / Jam Nuclear Effects Resistant and Support for Planning
General Purpose Forces Engaged (Non-Nuclear)	Theater Conventional War	Interoperate with Allies / Joint Worldwide Operations	Systems Interoperability / Secure Communications / Survive Conventional Attack
Isolated Engagements / Limited Deployment (Show of Force)	Crisis	Rapid Effective Response / Two Way Info Flow	Mobility of C³ Assets / Secure Communications / Jam Resistant
Normal Readiness	Day-to-Day	Training and Exercises / Situation Monitoring / Access to Intel and Warning* / Contingency Planning	Efficient Operations / Quality Service / Force Connectivity / Secure Communications

Diagonal labels: Negotiate/Terminate, Control of Escalation

☐ Areas Indicate Transition Between Levels. Capabilities in these Areas are Key to Smooth Orderly Transition
*Warning Systems Covered Under Strategic Defense Programs

rities to communicate with unified and specified commanders in crisis spots and then with the on-scene commanders represented on the outer ring.

Funding and Control

The pie-shaped segments in the diagram represent the Worldwide Military Command and Control System (WWMCCS). This system includes the communication systems of the unified and specified commands, and the special systems used for control of nuclear forces. This portion of the communications network has survivability characteristics which are too expensive for incorporation in all systems but which are necessary for execution of essential functions in the event of stress, degradation, or deliberate attack. Some of the survivability characteristics are physical hardening, mobility, redundancy, antijam protection and electromagnetic pulse protection. That portion of WWMCCS designated the Minimum Essential Emergency Communications Network (MEECN) encompasses the maximum survivability and reliability features needed for essential network performance in a stressed environment. The MEECN is dedicated to providing the highest possible assurance of command and control of US strategic nuclear forces during and after any nuclear attack on the United States, which includes an attack on the communications systems.

The perimeter of the second ring contains examples of the intermediaries through which directives would flow on their way to and from the field forces. For example, communications with most operating or deployed forces would be channeled through the unified and specified commands, while communications with a military advisory group in a particular country would be handled by the embassy.

The perimeter of the outer ring contains selected examples of different areas and types of forces. The strategic nuclear forces or SIOP (Strategic Integrated Operations Plan) forces use the MEECN while theater or tactical nuclear forces communicate through WWMCCS. Communications between the NCA and the Sixth Fleet in the Mediterranean or the

Below: A Boeing E-4B AABNCP taking off on patrol. These aircraft can remain in the air for up to 72 hours with air-to-air refueling, the limits being set by crew endurance and the amount of engine oil.

US Seventh Army in Germany would use the Defense Communications System and would go via the European Command. Communications among units of the Sixth Fleet and the Seventh Army would take place via the tactical communications net.

The C^3 systems and procedures must be adaptable to rapidly changing situations ranging from day-to-day activities through crisis to conventional and nuclear war—including surprise attack on the United States—and programs have been structured to address this need. The interrelationship of force postures, levels of conflict and the command and control function required at each level is illustrated by Diagram 2.

Defense Organizational Issues

If any organizational theorist were designing an organization from scratch, it is not likely that he would design an organization in the form of the Department of Defense in 1983. However, it is important to keep in mind that DoD was not created from a tabula rasa. The three military departments, the four services, and the JCS all antedated the establishment of DoD, and their continued existence has never been seriously challenged.

Moreover, the efficiency of defense organization has always had to take a secondary role to the desire of Congress to maintain its ability to influence defense policy. The legislative branch operates on the premise that a truly centralized military establishment would decrease the impact of the Congress in the policy process. For example, the legislature has not allowed an increase in the number of assistant secretaries since 1953, nor in the size of the joint staff since 1958. Moreover, each branch has a legislative veto on the power of the Secretary to transfer roles and missions among the services.

Nonetheless, in spite of these limitations, there are still some things that can and should be changed to improve the effectiveness of defense organization. These changes can be grouped into three categories.

First, the operational command situation needs to be clarified. At present there is a great deal of potential confusion between the area or unified and the functional or specified commands. For example, it is not clear who would have control over strategic forces in the Pacific—CINCPAC or CINCSAC. The problem could be solved by dividing and placing the

operational forces into strategic, tactical, and logistics commands.

In addition, there are also some changes that could be made in the budgetary process. As it presently exists, the PPBS leaves room for some improvements. We need to expand on the macro level the idea of mission area analysis the Air Force developed to encompass all of the Defense Department's major missions. Also, DoD cannot assess the affordability of policy options in other than the grossest terms; therefore, we need an information system that portrays all defense resources in two dimensions (one that shows outputs, one that establishes categories of resource inputs and support functions)—this system should identify the distribution of those resource inputs among mission, unit types, and selected weapon systems. Finally, we should combine the Program and Budget reviews to make more time for the program review and allow major program decisions to be made closer to the end of the cycle.

The command and control and communications system has the opposite problem. It is simply too efficient. As it exists, the C^3 system can easily lead to overcontrol of field operations by Washington. During the Mayaguez incident the Pentagon and the White House were actually issuing orders to individual aircraft. Moreover, information was being made available to Washington before the on-the-scene units. No structural changes can solve the problem. The National Command Authorities must have the capability to exert whatever degree of control they feel is appropriate. The ability to resist the tendency toward overcontrol requires the development of the proper respect for military professionalism.

Footnotes

1. Data on the present organizational structure of DoD can be gathered from *United States Government Manual*, 1982/83, pp. 211–232. See also Eston T. White, *Defense Organization and Management*, Industrial College of the Armed Forces, 1980, and my *Thirty Years of Service Unification*, Naval Institute Proceedings, June 1978.
2. The post was established as a result of the unauthorized bombing of North Vietnam by the Seventh Air Force.
3. For an analysis of the organization and function of the JCS see my *The Joint Chiefs of Staff: The First Twenty-Five Years*, Bloomington: Indiana University Press, 1976.
4. Until World War II, the Department of the Navy was composed of separate bureaus, each of which was subject to the control of the Secretary of the Navy.
5. Caspar W. Weinberger, *Annual Report to Congress*, FY 1983, p. A-2.

The US Intelligence Machine

Dr. Ray S. Cline, Senior Associate, Georgetown University Center for Strategic and International Studies; former Deputy Director for Intelligence, Central Intelligence Agency.

Throughout the sweep of history military commanders have emphasized the difficulty of penetrating the "fog of war" that obscures the movement of forces as well as the intentions of opposing military leaders on the battlefield. Intelligence is the sum of reliable information available at a military headquarters; it is also the apparatus by which the commander extends the capacity of his own eyes and ears to collect the information he needs. Intelligence should encompass as much as possible of the pattern of maneuver and concentration of forces in the theater of combat. It has always been eagerly sought by great military leaders, and superior intelligence often provides the margin which wins the battle. The extraordinary achievements of British troops in North Africa and US naval forces in the Pacific in the early days of World War II, for example, were due less to superior generalship or brilliant seamanship than to the precision of data on enemy forces provided by code and cipher breaksthrough. When intelligence is good enough to give advance warning to the military high command of what the enemy is going to do as well as what he is now doing, the fortunes of war will nearly always swing to the side with the better information.

In the early days of the history of the United States, the importance of intelligence was fully appreciated by the founding fathers of the Republic. In what, after all, was a quasi-guerilla war against the generally superior British forces in North America, the supreme commander George Washington depended enormously on the superiority of the information which he could gather because of the sympathy of most of the citizens of the countryside. In this way time and again he was able to offset what was usually comparative weakness in the numbers, training, supply, and equipment of his troops.

Washington's first large expenditures, after he took command of the Continental armed forces, were made for the purpose of sending secret agents into the town of Boston, and he encouraged the procurement of spies as a central part of his plans for coping with the better organized and trained British forces in Boston. He also gave orders for the stationing of lookouts at all commanding heights. Washington urged that prisoners be captured in all skirmishes so that they could be interrogated. His view, he said, was: "do not stick at any expense" in organizing an espionage net to penetrate the enemy-controlled area.

Intelligence Requirements Today

The technology of war and the destructiveness of weapons have changed enormously in the past two centuries, but the imperative of basing military decisions on sound information about the capabilities of enemy forces and their potential movements is just as great as ever. In fact, the commanders of the armed forces of the United States today have an even more difficult job than George Washington did. He at least knew the terrain of the battles of the Revolutionary War, and he had friendly populations everywhere in British-occupied areas. Today's US armed forces have virtually a global battlefield to be concerned with in preparing for defense of their country, their

soldiers, sailors, and airmen on duty overseas, their military bases, and the territory of their allies.

Moreover, in the broadest context, armies today are intended primarily to deter potential enemies from resorting to military force as an instrument of their international policy. Hence the battlefield not only has expanded, in a sense, to cover the whole world but also the requirements for knowledge of the strength and the intentions of every potential combatant has become overwhelming. In many ways it is more important than ever before to be prepared to respond instantly and appropriately to opening phases of hostilities since the name of the game is to avoid escalation. In order to deter an enemy from attacking in some locale where the interests of the United States may force it to become involved, or to counter a local attack in such a way as to prevent further escalation, it is absolutely essential for the US to be prepared in all respects with knowledge of the ground, air, and naval capabilities of potential enemies as well as the geographical, military, and economic conditions in adversary, friendly, and neutral territory. It is also imperative to be aware of the psychology and the political factors which go into military decision-making by all parties to the potential conflict. The peacetime requirements for intelligence are staggeringly voluminous and complex.

It is necessary, therefore, for modern military intelligence officers to think not merely of the circumstances on the battlefield where armies fire on one another, although in the last analysis that is where both capabilities and the intentions of planners are tested out; it is essential in addition to make the more subtle distinctions to enable not only military commanders but all of the government officials responsible for national security affairs to understand fully the dangers around them, the risks they should or should not take, and the probable outcome of interdependent political, military, and economic factors that condition the outcome of military conflicts in which the United States may become involved.

Today the American unit commander has at his fingertips details about the locale of his operations and the character of potential enemy forces which exceed anything ever available before. The danger today is less with the paucity of information than it is with the difficulty of comprehending all of the information. Here the automation of knowledge has helped in some ways but created additional difficulties in other ways. The armed forces of the United States have in the tactical military field achieved extraordinary breakthroughs in creating display systems which provide the commander with the routine elements of information about the forces which he might meet in battle, and which give him instant retrieval of data which in the past would have had to be processed through the minds of men in his intelligence section. However, the data on the automated display system can only be as good as the input into the computers which supply that data. The computer experts are absolutely right in enunciating the idea they abbreviate as "GIGO"—which means, "garbage in, garbage out".

48

Below: This vertical photograph of Washington D.C. was taken on 2402-type film from 50,500ft. Different kinds of film defeat most attempts at camouflage, and detail is much finer than anything reproducible on this page. The SR-71 (far left) is the chief American strategic reconnaissance aircraft, and like most modern reconnaissance platforms uses radar and infra-red as well as optical photography. Just as important as information-gathering is data processing and transmission. The DSCS II (Defense Satellite Communications System II, near left) will be a key network of 18 space platforms girdling the Earth and enabling all kinds of information to be relayed in split-seconds.

In a sense, the automation of information processing is only a special modern circumstance for intelligence operations, a tool of the trade, rather than a fundamental change in the character of intelligence operations. It is still crucial to get the information to go into the automated memory bank and appear on the display panels, whatever they may be, on board ship or in command posts in battle areas.

There are two types of intelligence needed by military commanders, tactical and strategic. There is no clean dividing line between the two but units in the field have a primary concern for tactical detail about immediately opposing forces. At higher headquarters the broader sweep of information about nations and potential conflicts of all kinds is what is needed. The key point for the tactical commander is to know how to sift out of the vast data banks at national levels of intelligence analysis exactly what is relevant to his problems. Thus the fighting soldier at any level of command will have a greater chance of getting what he needs for military success if he understand the structure and functioning of the great central intelligence system that is a component part of the American military machine.

Tactical military intelligence continues to be of prime importance to the combat forces, and in time of war the intelligence (G-2) sections of every command echelon extract all the information possible from reconnaissance sweeps, prisoner interrogations, and local espionage sources. Tactical intelligence in combat situations, just as in the time of George Washington, will depend to a remarkable extent on contact with the enemy, ability to capture prisoners and interrogate them efficiently, conduct aerial and patrol reconnaissance, communicate with agents behind the enemy lines, and intercept documentary evidence about opposing forces.

The Vietnam war, in this respect, was not very different from earlier wars. It was marked primarily by the sophistication of the gadgetry, not the difference in the essential elements of information which commanders needed to know. In fact, advanced technology in gadgetry imposed an additional burden of deploying manpower and a tremendous complication in the processing of information. Interrogation centers for the interviewing of military and civilian prisoners turned out reams of information which had to be evaluated, assimilated and related to secret agent reporting, search patrols, intercepted messages (a prime source of data particularly valuable because in some cases it revealed forward plans of the enemy), and the voluminous files of film from overflying airplanes—especially the old reliable workhorse, the U-2.

These elements of tactical military intelligence, however, are not the main resource of the American military machine. In peacetime, in view of the complexity of possible future conflicts and, in fact, uncertainties as to where the battlefields may be, the main data base for United States military forces comes from the national intelligence community, which deals primarily with strategic intelligence. It is the provision of this strategic intelligence to the armed forces in the field, along with nuggets and titbits of information that are of tactical import to individual units in the field (although part of the strategic intake), that gives the American military machine its margin of superiority in being alert and ready for hostilities, able to comprehend enemy force maneuvers and deceptions, and prepared to go into combat effectively in fighting any first-phase battles.

The main element of the intelligence component of the American military machine is not the standard G-2 unit which appears under one name or another in almost all military organizations, but the national intelligence system. Encompassing all of the elements of government agencies that collect or evaluate and analyze intelligence information, this central intelligence community provides most of the basic data on which they will operate in peacetime, and on the basis of which they will go into

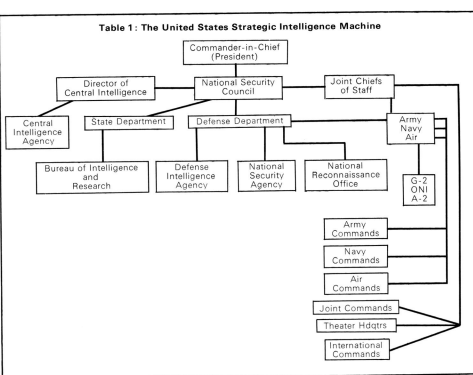

Table 1: The United States Strategic Intelligence Machine

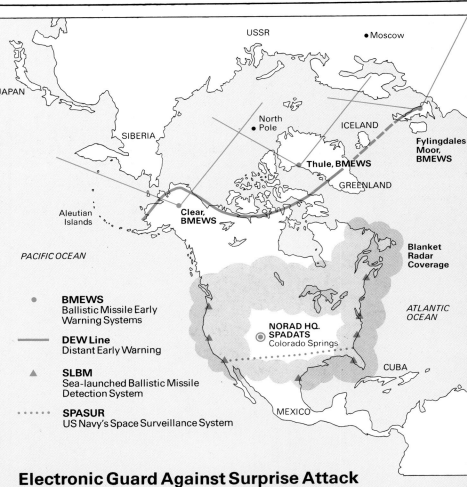

- ● **BMEWS** Ballistic Missile Early Warning Systems
- ── **DEW Line** Distant Early Warning
- ▲ **SLBM** Sea-launched Ballistic Missile Detection System
- ⋯⋯ **SPASUR** US Navy's Space Surveillance System

Electronic Guard Against Surprise Attack

These are the lacings of the electronic network covering air approaches to North America. All are tied to the North American Air Defense Command's underground Combat Operations Center within Cheyenne Mountain near Colorado Springs, Colo. At three sites near the top of the world, high-powered radar antennas of the Ballistic Missile Early Warning System (BMEWS) reach out 3,000 miles to give the alert of an intercontinental ballistic missile attack from the north. Eight radar sites of the Sea-Launched Ballistic Missile Detection and Warning System (SLBM) along the sea approaches to the US would detect a missile attack launched from submarines. Space satellites would also flash an alarm to NORAD's Combat Operations Center of a missile attack against North America. Against the manned bomber threat, NORAD employs the Distant Early Warning (DEW) Line, extending across the top of the continent, and a system of radars guarding all approaches to the US and the populated areas of Canada. Stretched across the southern US is the US Naval Space Surveillance System (SPASUR), one of the satellite detection and tracking nets reporting data on earth-orbiting space objects to NORAD's Space Defense Center inside Cheyenne Mountain.

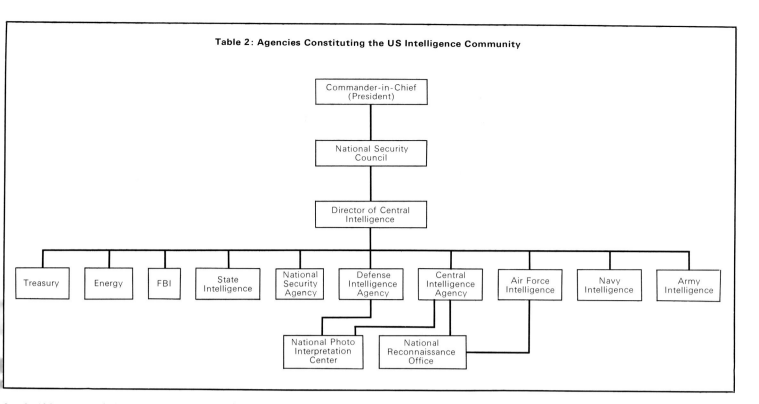

Table 2: Agencies Constituting the US Intelligence Community

- Commander-in-Chief (President)
  - National Security Council
    - Director of Central Intelligence
      - Treasury
      - Energy
      - FBI
      - State Intelligence
      - National Security Agency
      - Defense Intelligence Agency
      - Central Intelligence Agency
      - Air Force Intelligence
      - Navy Intelligence
      - Army Intelligence
        - National Photo Interpretation Center
        - National Reconnaissance Office

battle, if deterrence fails and war comes. Viewed in this sense, the American military machine is almost entirely dependent on the cogs and wheels of the intelligence community in Washington.

At present the structure of the US intelligence community is being reviewed and reorganized by the Executive Branch of the government and by the Congress. Nevertheless, the essential elements are long established and clearly identified. The military agencies provide to their own forces in the field the informational output not only of the intelligence agencies under the command of the Secretary of Defense and the Joint Chiefs of Staff, but those that are directly or indirectly tasked by civilian agencies of

Right: Routes that space satellites take as they circle the earth can be displayed on screens in NORAD's Command Post. By relaying a command to a computer, battle staff members can look at the paths a satellite will follow for as many as 12 global revolutions and know what part of the earth it will soon be crossing.

Below: High technology bases, of top strategic importance, are dotted over many remote regions, giving the USAF Satellite Control Facility global coverage.

Air Force Satellite Communications System (AFSATCOM)

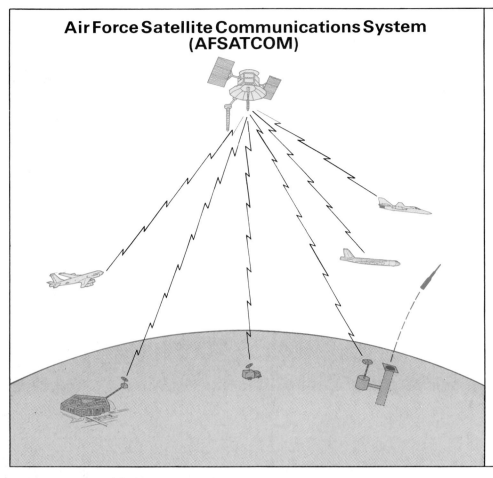

AFSATCOM (Air Force Satellite Communications System) is one of the major American systems providing "C³": command, control and communications. Providing ground and air teletype terminals and the satellites is only a minor part of the task. Every user has to have secure access to the system, to be alerted instantly of any change in the status of any satellite (caused by malfunction or possibly enemy action) and be able to "talk" to any other part of the Air Force. A fundamental part of the requirement is that it must "withstand massive physical as well as jamming attacks in the execution of its mission". Though reliability and resistance to nuclear explosions and other attacks must be high, the whole system incorporates a degree of redundancy so that loss of one or more satellites, or many ground terminals, does not degrade system capability. The links illustrated are two-way, most of them uhf (ultra high frequency), with instant-response transponders in the satellites to re-broadcast amplified and possibly clarified messages to the allotted destination(s). Of course, any major nuclear attack decision could be taken only by the President of the United States and Commander of SAC, and in any time of crisis both would be airborne in an E-4 AABNCP aircraft, as explained in the aircraft technical section. Other allied military satellite networks include the US Navy FLTSATCOM, Army SATCOM and the NATO series shown below. All are vulnerable to anti-satellite systems, an area in which the Soviets have become increasingly active.

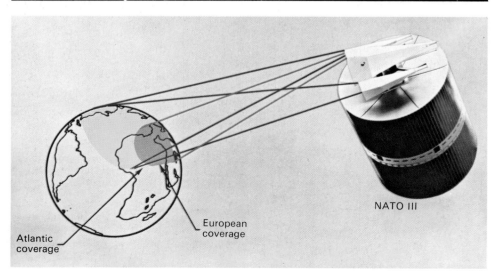

Atlantic coverage

European coverage

NATO III

government like the State Department and the Central Intelligence Agency (CIA). The superiority of strategic intelligence holdings in Washington is mainly due to the 30-year effort to coordinate and share intelligence among all agencies at the national level as prescribed in the National Security Act of 1947, which set up the Central Intelligence Agency. To know what the danger of the outbreak of hostilities is and what the character of potential attacks might be, requires more than the individual unit commander can possibly have resources to discover. Hence, from the front line back through the echelons of command of each theater, the military intelligence units are holding data which come from the massive machine managed from Washington. It is the structure and functioning of this central intelligence machine which a US military commander must appreciate if he is to use it well and to get the best information out of the sources available to him.

The first thing to realize is that a great deal of information comes from what we think of as open sources. Newspaper accounts of foreign events, periodical literature on economic, political and scientific trends, foreign broadcasts of speeches and news, the proceedings of scholarly conferences in American or foreign "think tanks": all these must be mined and the valuable nuggets distributed to the right staffs. Beyond this, US Embassy diplomatic reporting brings in data openly procured from foreign sources but passed back to Washington in confidential channels of official communications. Military intelligence and related background information of military value derive in good part from these open sources.

Among them, reporting from military

Left: Though quite different in appearance, the American DSCS III (upper) and NATO III (left) both fulfil similar functions. Each satellite holds its station over the same point whilst processing and re-transmitting many voice, teletype, facsimile (picture) and data channels. There will be 18 DSCS III satellites but only one NATO III plus a single "back-up".

attachés stationed in embassies abroad—what could be called semi-open intelligence—is extremely useful in focusing on the weapons characteristics and the force levels of nations all over the world, including the forces of allies and friends of the US, as well as these allies' views of potential enemies' forces. The attachés, of course, mainly concentrate on the information more difficult to procure, information about the forces of the Soviet Union, the greatest military power opposing the United States, and other nations which are, by political and strategic force of circumstance, adversaries if not actual enemies of the United States; for example, the People's Republic of China (Peking) and the Warsaw Pact countries of East Europe. These attaché reports are often procured through the services of friendly military agencies abroad and their detailed accounts of the structure and training levels, the readiness for combat of all kinds of forces, and the technical specifications of weapons provide the US with the basic data on which the worldwide order of battle is built. A surprising amount of useful knowledge is available from close scanning of the open broadcasts of the governments and the governmental units in the totalitarian states. Because information is so tightly controlled, things that are said about the armed forces and their plans are sometimes very revealing. CIA is the principal agency responsible for procuring foreign broadcasts and documents, though all the other intelligence components assist.

For the major adversary nations, however, like the Soviet Union and China, which try to conceal from the United States the military data which the US military machine needs to know in order to do its job of deterrence and preparedness, the open sources and semi-open official reports are not full enough to permit full reliance on them. These countries can only be brought under surveillance by the sophisticated instrumentalities of the secret and clandestine agencies of the national intelligence community.

Another reason why central intelligence at the Washington level is crucial to all military units is the fluid and problematic nature of modern conflicts. If the crucial value of intelligence is one main characteristic of military affairs today, others are the mobility of military forces, the fuzziness of battle lines, and the melding or merging of tactical and strategic considerations as military dispositions in one region or another reveal clues to the intentions of military planners in Moscow or Peking and vice versa. The whereabouts of Soviet strategic air forces and, in particular, of missile-launching submarines, becomes a prime element in calculating the probabilities of conflict throughout the regions of the world where US forces are deployed. In a total war, strategic warning would be as likely to come from the first indicators of movement to sea of Soviet submarines in unusual force in the Atlantic and the Pacific as from troop mobilization or concentrations on any front.

An American combat unit in Korea, say, might get no inkling of attack until the actual jumping off of forces near the Demilitarized Zone and yet be enormously aided in being ready for an attack by a report from the Iceland area confirming the movement to sea of unprecedented numbers of submarines from Murmansk.

All of this is to say that the subject matter of military intelligence is basically what it has

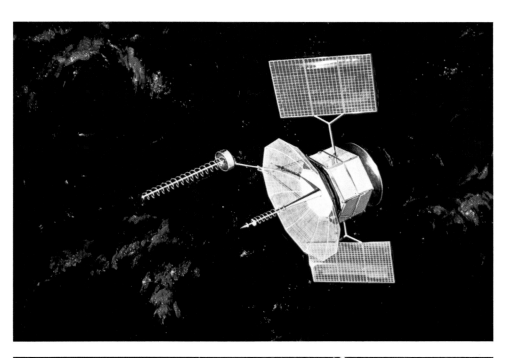

Top: FLTSATCOM (Fleet Satellite Communications) satellites began operating in 1977. Four, plus a spare, will link US Navy aircraft, ships, submarines, SAC and the Presidential command network.

Right: Second of the NATO III series, IIIB was placed in orbit hovering over a point on the Equator on January 27, 1977. It can simultaneously handle hundreds of different communications.

always been, but that the elaborate structure of the modern US intelligence community extends the range of observation—the eyes and ears of each unit commander—to a virtually unlimited global surveillance. At tactical unit or strategic force levels the intelligence sections of all commands try to keep up-to-date, reliable order of battle (strength and deployment of potential enemy forces), technical intelligence about weapons characteristics and the capabilities and vulnerabilities of all support facilities—especially transportation and communications equipment, and the main features of the terrain of potential battlefields.

All of this kind of data, when and if collected in the field, goes up the chain of command as well as directly back to Washington. In Washington all sources and all service interests are melded into one big evaluation process, from which emerges the general picture confronting the American military machine as a whole. From this national picture of the world around the US, the military agencies of the Defense Department, the Joint Chiefs of Staff, the Army, the Navy, the Air Force, the Marines, and the Coast Guard abstract the data relevant to their respective missions and construct an intelligence data base for their own reference in operational planning and also to send out to the joint theater commands and service headquarters all over the world. The theater command staffs sort out the intelligence applicable to the units under them and pass it along. Thus there is a flow of intelligence to the field for combat unit readiness purposes that is the finished product from all of the various kinds of intelligence that flows into Washington from the many agencies collecting military information and related strategic data for the entire intelligence community.

The President of the United States is under the Constitution the Commander-in-Chief of the US armed forces. Hence, at a high level of interdependence, he is nominally the recipient of all military intelligence that affects his extremely broad strategic responsibilities. A schematic rendition of the military command system in which the main cogs in the strategic intelligence machine operates is shown in Table 1.

At every command level there is an intense demand for reliable intelligence on the basis of which to prepare strategic plans, train and deploy forces, and maintain combat readiness. While reporting goes up in the various chains of command, strategic intelligence mainly goes down after it has been coordinated, evaluated, and amalgamated at the top level of each intelligence element in Washington. These tasks in peacetime simply must be done in an active interrelationship with all the other elements of the intelligence community, civilian as well as military.

After all, the best indication that hostilities may break out in some specific region where US armed forces are exposed may not be any kind of military action, but, for example, a piece of political intelligence to the effect that Soviet advisors are being withdrawn (as they were from Syria and Egypt a few days before the Yom Kippur war in October 1973), or a piece of economic intelligence (the importation or domestic production of commercial items—such as medicines—in such quantity as to exceed normal civilian requirements and reveal an urgent need for military end-use matériel).

Thus the American military machine runs primarily on the output of the strategic intelligence machine in Washington, that is, the agencies and elements of agencies operating under the interagency coordinating mechanisms headed by the Director of Intelligence. These agencies constituting the intelligence community shown in Table 2.

The ten agencies are very uneven in the contributions they make to the American military machine, but among them the work is done which creates the national intelligence data base on which all force planning, deployment, and combat readiness depend.

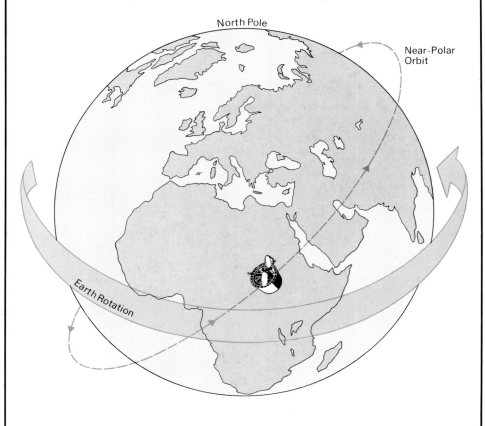

Principle of the Earth Orbiting Satellite

North Pole

Near-Polar Orbit

Earth Rotation

Above: A satellite travelling at about 17,500mph about 100 miles above the Earth's surface makes one orbit every 90 minutes. In a near-Polar orbit the Earth turns about 1,500 miles (at the Equator) between orbits, so the whole globe is eventually covered. Below 100 miles, atmospheric drag slows the satellite down quickly and it burns up. At a height of about 22,300 miles a satellite in eastwards equatorial orbit (wide band) appears to hover over one spot.

The Treasury Department's input is in the form of economic statistics and financial information derived from its intricate involvement with foreign and international financial organizations. It is represented by a Special Assistant to the Secretary of the Treasury and works very closely with the Economic Research Office of CIA.

The new Energy Department has a most specialized function to perform, mainly to contribute its specialized knowledge of energy in all its forms, but especially nuclear energy, to estimates made by the CIA and the military intelligence analysis staffs of foreign nuclear weapons inventories and characteristics. While it will also contribute to economic estimates on other forms of energy, the technical detail based on weapons development programs in the US is the best guide, or the only guide, to

Below: This black Lockheed U-2 ultra-high-flying aircraft is carrying special equipment behind the cockpit for use in upper-air and electronic surveillance experiments. They are the main intelligence research platforms.

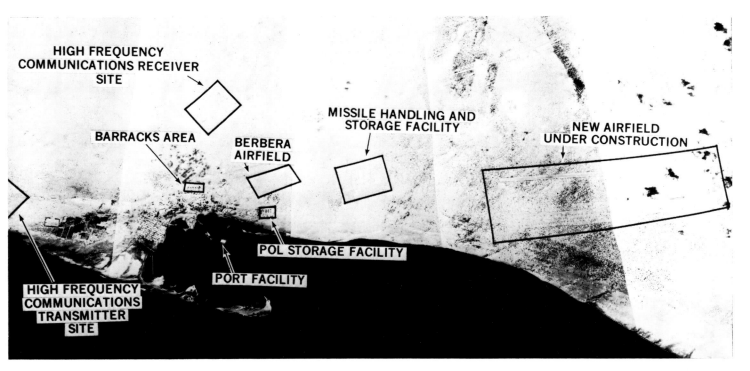

HIGH FREQUENCY
COMMUNICATIONS RECEIVER
SITE

BARRACKS AREA

BERBERA
AIRFIELD

MISSILE HANDLING AND
STORAGE FACILITY

NEW AIRFIELD
UNDER CONSTRUCTION

POL STORAGE FACILITY

PORT FACILITY

HIGH FREQUENCY
COMMUNICATIONS
TRANSMITTER
SITE

Above: An ''orientation view'' of the Somali port of Berbera, assembled from five USAF reconnaissance photographs taken during the Soviet arms build-up in 1975. Three enlargements (right) show Soviet ships unloading, a missile storage facility and the vast military airbase under construction. With modern methods of multi-spectral (many wavelengths) photography virtually no significant event can take place on the Earth's surface undetected, even by aircraft flying at great height. But with Britain's global presence gone, only the United States has the capability of watching the Soviet Union's widespread military operations.

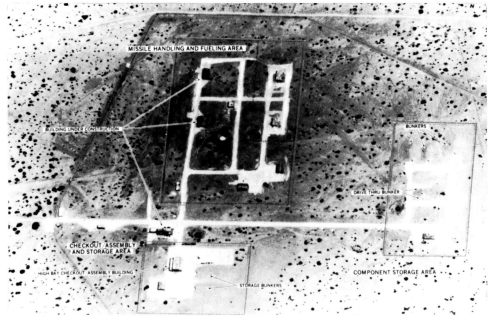

VYN CLASS
(BARRACKS SHIP)

AMUR AS
Submarine Tender

CARGO FREIGHTER

MISSILE HANDLING AND FUELING AREA

BUILDING UNDER CONSTRUCTION

BUNKERS

DRIVE THRU BUNKER

CHECKOUT/ASSEMBLY
AND STORAGE AREA

HIGH BAY CHECKOUT ASSEMBLY BUILDING

STORAGE BUNKERS

COMPONENT STORAGE AREA

PROBABLE RUNWAY UNDER CONSTRUCTION
17,500' X 300'

PARKING APRON
600' X 500'

RUNWAY UNDER CONSTRUCTION

BUILDINGS UNDER
CONSTRUCTION

14,600' X 150'

1,650'

the meaning of evidence about Soviet or Chinese nuclear weapons production. Similar technical know-how for calculations of nuclear energy use for generation of power in civilian economies—a matter of prime importance for economic research by CIA—will become increasingly important in calculating the resources of nations; but the crucial military contribution will for a long time be in the nuclear weapons field.

The FBI has a limited but important function in the intelligence community—counterespionage in the United States. It is the agency responsible for discovering and countering hostile penetrations of US government organizations and facilities by foreign governments and intelligence agencies. In this capacity the FBI works closely with CIA, which is responsible for counterespionage abroad, and with the counterintelligence staffs of the armed services. FBI information on penetration efforts could be extremely valuable tip-off evidence in the event of planned attack or sabotage of military installations. It was a crucial failure when the combined efforts of the fragmentary US intelligence services at the time of the Pearl Harbor attack of 1941 did not put together the FBI reports of Japanese data collection efforts in Hawaii with intercepted communications indicating a breakdown of diplomatic talks and an impending attack somewhere.

The US State Department is one of the most important cogs in the intelligence community machine. In the first place, it operates the embassy installations in foreign countries where US military attaches and the CIA clandestine station officers do their work. Thus, open reporting on military subjects garnered from foreign sources and the secret data passed to attaches and CIA agent-handlers are dependent upon the official hospitality and

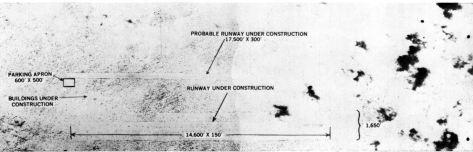

Intelligence Asset Availability

This chart depicts the various intelligence assets and organizations which work to satisfy the operational requirements of US Army generals, colonels, and captains, and the echelons at which these assets are normally assigned, attached, or in direct support.

Information demands which cannot be fulfilled with organic resources must be satisfied by those of a higher commander. For example, national level collection supports corps requirements far beyond the scope of organic capabilities, and feeds both combat information and intelligence into the corps fusion center. Division and brigade centers similarly support their commanders' needs as well as those of subordinate commanders which exceed their organic capabilities.

	GENERALS		COLONELS		CAPTAINS
	CORPS	DIVISION	BRIGADE	BATTALION	COMPANIES
National Strategic System	●				
USAF/USN Systems	●	●			
Tactical Systems					
Electromagnetic					
SIGINT					
☐COMINT	●	●	●		
☐ELINT	●	●	●		
REMS		●	●	●	●
GSR		●	●	●	●
Weapon Locating Radar		●	●		
Imagery					
Photo	●	●			
IR	●	●			
SLAR	●	●			
Human Observation					
Reconnaissance Units	●	●		●	
Troops				●	●
IPW	●	●	●		

SIGINT	Signal intelligence	**GSR**	Ground surveillance radar
COMINT	Communications intelligence	**IR**	Infra-red
ELINT	Electronic intelligence	**SLAR**	Side-looking aircraft (or airborne) radar
REMS	Remote sensors	**IPW**	Interrogation of prisoners of war

Relative Intelligence/Combat Information to Various Echelons, US Army, Europe

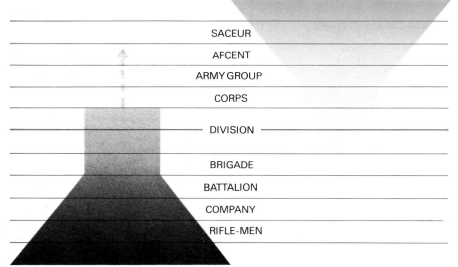

SACEUR Supreme Allied Commander Europe
AFCENT Allied Forces Central Europe

Intelligence of varying detail is required by generals, colonels, and captains. The typical requirements at corps and division are normally general in nature. Commanders at this echelon need intelligence products which provide the basis for timely decisions—they need the answers to what, where, when and in what strength. Their intelligence must be primarily decision-oriented and directed toward telling them where to concentrate their forces.

Brigade commanders move forces and assign delivery of fires; hence, they need approximately equal ratios of intelligence and combat information. Battalion commanders need some intelligence and a great deal of combat information—*they need information on enemy movements, as they take place.* Commanders of companies are almost exclusively concerned with combat information—targets.

Combat information is used for rapid tactical execution of maneuvers and fire support which respond to the fast moving enemy situation in the battle area.

Just as the lower echelons need less intelligence and more combat information, so do they perform more reporting and less analysis. The higher echelons, primarily corps and to a lesser extent division, analyze and fuse. Normally, brigades and battalions and companies report combat information up and receive combat intelligence down.

---

administrative housekeeping of the embassies. In particular, the worldwide diplomatic communications net runs through embassy facilities where secure ciphers can be used to funnel intelligence data back to the intelligence agencies in the United States. The worldwide CRITICOM (Critical Communications) Net includes State Department and CIA communications facilities as well as US overseas military headquarters channels. Through CRITICOM, intelligence reports with evidence indicating the possibility of imminence of hostilities reach the desks of senior officials in Washington promptly, often in ten minutes, nearly always in less than an hour.

Embassy reporting is supplemented in ways often invaluable for assessing military information on foreign armed forces by political and economic officers who file official dispatches on the structure, evolutionary trend, and strengths or weaknesses of the political system and the economy of the host countries. If an army, navy, or air force is caught up in domestic political strife or if an economy is riddled with corruption of sheer inefficiency in its heavy industry and weapons production facilities, such facts may tell more about military capabilities than order of battle analyses or technical training levels of armed forces. Official reporting of this kind makes up, along with open information filed from foreign press, radio, TV, and periodical literature, about half of the information circulating at top levels of government in Washington. It provides the framework which secret military information fits into or modifies.

The National Security Agency (NSA) is the central code and cipher facility of the US Government, and its cryptanalytic reports have often supplied the small but indispensable bits of information which enable analysts to fit together a jigsaw puzzle of other fragmentary intelligence. While modern high-level ciphers are extremely hard to break into, mechanical and human errors sometimes reveal significant messages meant to be hidden from outsiders. More important, traffic analysis of the senders and receivers of enciphered messages, derived from sophisticated direction-finding equipment, reveals a great deal about the structure and activity of the armed forces units to which the signals organizations being overheard are attached. Even without reading the messages, skilled NSA analysts can reconstruct radio networks that parallel armed forces organization and deployment.

During peacetime industrial production and weapons testing data from signals intelligence is vital in providing clues to armaments levels, weapons characteristics, and readiness patterns of all combat forces. Mobilization and maneuver exercises reveal strategic warning indicators and alert military commands to the possibilities of hostilities. In actual military conflict situations, such as the recent Vietnam, Korean, and Arab-Israeli wars, forces in combat of necessity resort to lower security level codes and ciphers to meet the urgencies of field situations, and in these circumstances signals intercepts become one of the richest sources of detailed knowledge about the size and deployment of armies. The Army, Navy, and Air Force provide cryptanalytic field units for operation under central NSA task guidance. A commander without signals intelligence in a local war is like a man without hearing; he is handicapped in his movements and in his awareness of dangers. Some of this intelligence is produced and used directly in the field, but most of it to be fully productive is guided from Washington and is funneled back to Washington for correlation with other data and distribution to all elements of government and the armed forces.

In view of the electronic nature of command, guidance and radar-interrogation devices in almost all military units and weapons systems, the recorded blips and beeps of electronic gadgetry are crucial pieces of knowledge for opposing combat forces. This ELINT (electronic intelligence) is a vast field of technical informa-

ion about the ever-changing technical specifications of each weapons system and the overall pattern of electronic order of battle—the deployment of radars, electronic countermeasures (jamming) equipment and defensive electronic devices (counter-countermeasures). This is the true wizard war, with the most advanced gadgetry giving a sharp edge in battle provided it does not become known sufficiently to enemy electronic intelligence collectors to be offset, evaded, or countered by devices tailored for the purpose. While much of this kind of intelligence is tactical military intelligence, it requires constant sorting out and updating at NSA Headquarters to avoid obsolescence, and possible surprise.

Since the range of interception is vastly increased by putting receivers on satellites orbiting the earth, the wizard war in the strategic field has gone into space. The electronic gear essential for recording earth-generated signals from space and sifting out the meaningful military evidence from the noise is the most difficult—and costly—of modern intelligence collection techniques. In the field of strategic warning stationary satellites positioned in orbit at the right height and speed to stay in place where certain important signals can be sensed provide the best guarantee of noting missile firings, particularly in test modes.

The electronic monitoring and reporting equipment attached to missiles by their own test headquarters so that they can observe how the weapons are performing can be overheard by others if the listening devices are correctly positioned and tuned. This particular kind of data is called telemetry and is followed closely by NSA and CIA so as to get early warning about research and development breakthrough as well as warning of readiness for hostilities. Modern military intelligence holdings are saturated with information derived from signals and telemetry.

The CIA led the way to another development of an intelligence technique that changed the nature of modern warfare. Satellites orbiting the earth can be used for sensing light and heat

Above: Right down to the level of individual ships, squadrons and army brigades advanced electronic systems are necessary to display tactical information for quick and correct decisions.

waves as well as electronic pulses. About 1960 the CIA, working closely with the US Air Force, developed satellite vehicles with extraordinarily sensitive cameras and other sensing devices that enable US intelligence analysts to survey large portions of the earth's surface in relatively short periods of time so as to detect objects of a very small size (generally of about one foot in length in any dimensions). The photographic imagery, developed for the old U-2 high-flying aircraft, has become so complex and effective that it provides a truly indispensable first-phase data base for any research or reporting that depends on counting and measuring visible objects on the earth's surface.

Right and below: Two Soviet-made T-55 tanks knocked out in south Laos, and SA-2 SAMs travelling out of Haiphong in 1972. These are examples of low-level photographs, taken by manned aircraft or RPVs, needed for pre- and post-strike intelligence. With modern ground forces such pictures are required instantly.

It is not possible to collect imagery at night or under heavy cloud cover or inside buildings and shelters. It is also impossible to photograph ideas inside men's heads. But everything else is fair game for the photo interpreter's file. There are few analytical problems, especially in military intelligence, that do not start with the skilled interpreters and analysts using the facilities of the National Photographic Interpretation Center (NPIC), a joint facility administered by CIA but used extensively by the armed services. If CIA had accomplished nothing in its 30 years but to bring the United States into the world of modern overhead reconnaissance imagery—at least five years ahead, technically, of the Soviet Union, its only rival in this exotic field of intelligence—CIA would have well repaid the country for supporting its entire effort. The costs are so great that only the richest nations can support a modern overhead reconnaissance program.

The principle of the earth-orbiting satellite is simple. A certain velocity attained by a satellite projected into space by a missile will cause it to go into orbit around the earth—its outward thrust being equalized by the pull of the earth's gravity, like a man-made moon, at heights from around 100 to a few hundreds of miles above the surface of the globe. The speed of the camera carrying satellites is so great that they circle the earth approximately every 90 minutes. If the satellite is in a near-Polar orbit, the earth turns under it about 1,500 miles at each orbit so that the camera can cover successive broad swaths of the Eurasian Continent, for example, moving across the land surface at each orbit and filling in the interstices between swaths on successive days as the earth keeps turning. This particular mode of surveillance is especially good for covering the Soviet Union which, at 8.6 million square miles, is by far the largest territory under one government, and to a lesser extent China, which is, after Canada, the next largest, that is the third largest, at 3.7 million square miles. The United States itself is the fourth largest nation with 3.6 million square miles.

Mapping large parts of the territory of the Soviet Union in very short order (a number of days) is quite feasible when weather permits. The imagery thus captured can either be catapulted out of the satellite in a film capsule, with a parachute, to be hooked by a waiting aircraft, or transmitted to ground stations in coded signals when the satellite is orbiting the right part of the earth. It is all an expensive, technically complex process taking much time, manpower, skill, and money; nevertheless, it gives US intelligence agencies a capability without which its intelligence estimates would be much spongier and its own population and the populations of US allies would be infinitely less secure.

A final important point to remember is that it is the surveillance of potential enemy territory by photographic sensors, aided by electronic intercepts of all kinds, lumped together under the term "national technical means" of verification of levels of strategic arms that makes arms limitation agreements between the USSR and the United States feasible. The precision with which the United States is able to count missile launchers in the Soviet Union, and vice versa, reassured Soviet and US national leaders sufficiently to permit the signing of the ABM limitation treaty and the SALT I missile limitation agreement. In many ways the future of arms control and limitation depends on the virtuosity of the US intelligence services. Only with adequate verification of numbers of weapons and compliance with all limitation provisions can the United States afford to limit the numbers and capabilities of its own strategic weapons. Military commanders and military intelligence agencies therefore have a tremendous vested interest in the effectiveness of these verification techniques which include the use of all kinds of analytical skills and confirming types of evidence as well as the "technical" photographic and signals intelligence itself.

One of the vital "technical means" is the array of sound-sensing devices which can be planted on ocean floors or carried in ships and submarines to detect the movement of submarines under water in the same way that other sensors detect missile and aircraft movements. This "sound ranging"—i.e. SONAR—evidence supplements photography of the construction of missile-launching submarines, filling in what would otherwise be a missing gap in US knowledge of Soviet strategic weapons and US capability to verify compliance with SALT agreements limiting submarines as well as missiles and aircraft.

CIA and the US Air Force jointly manage the operational program which develops the specific missiles and sensors and fires the payloads of imagery collecting devices into orbit. The Navy has some satellite capabilities of its own aimed at peculiarly naval targets, and, of course, it is first and foremost in the field of underwater sensors of all kinds. The whole program of national reconnaissance and imagery interpretation is the embodiment of the intelligence community at work, sharing resources, skills and intelligence products. While the State Department does not get involved in the collection program as such, it has a lively interest in tasking or targetting the sensors, and it becomes immediately and directly involved when international crises occur involving disputes over the location and activity of military forces. For instance, the State Department took the intelligence lead during the Suez Canal Zone missile controversy of 1970, when the USSR built the anti-aircraft missile defenses in depth near the Canal that eventually provided one of the key ingredients of the Egyptian initial victory in the Yom Kippur cross-Canal attack in October 1973. Consequently no intelligence agency can afford to be ignorant of the findings of the national reconnaissance and imagery interpretation

Above: How can one detect intruders and avoid false alarms (caused, for example, by animals)? This US Army device is a seismic detector for the lightest human footfall; another detector is magnetic.

machinery. No military commander could do his job properly today without having his own planners, intelligence section, and targetting staffs fully informed of the national holdings of photography and other imagery covering his area of responsibility.

The CIA itself, much maligned as it has been for the fairly limited domestic security operations and covert political interventions abroad which it got into in the Nixon-Watergate era, is fundamentally and primarily an intelligence collection and analysis agency. Clandestine services operations are aimed at using secret agents to try to elicit, buy or steal useful information that other nations are trying to hide. While the military intelligence agencies collect some clandestine information, mainly in their own areas of expertise, CIA tries to collect all of the information of strategic value — political, economic, scientific, or military—that is needed by decision-makers and policy planners at the national level of government. It operates in almost every country of the world and in countries friendly to the United States; the clandestine information taken from its own agents is supplemented by secret intelligence given in exchanges with friendly intelligence services of the host governments. CIA information reports go directly to all agencies concerned with the subject matter, although the need to protect sources often limits distribution to higher levels of officialdom.

The CIA also provides secret information reports to other agencies based on its open collection of confidential data from willing American sources who travel and work abroad. This procedure is open, not clandestine, but the

ta collected must be protected in order to protect the sources who give it to the US Government as a patriotic duty but naturally do not want their foreign interlocutors to think of em as intelligence agents—which they are ot. Surprisingly often some tidbit of technical ternational trade data that has come to light this way provides the central clue to inter-etation of a military program that cannot be operly understood on the basis of other formation available.

CIA sources, clandestine and open-confiden-al, are targetted to get at the kind of hidden formation that cannot be overheard elec-onically or detected by imagery sensors. It als mainly with people, their thoughts and ans, and the future direction of government licies of all kinds. Naturally some of the most luable material is in the military intelligence ld. For example, the penetration of the viet Union by the CIA agent, Colonel Oleg nkovsky in the early 1960s, gave the American ilitary agencies bales of secret documents on viet weapons, forces, and military thought; ir basic understanding of the Soviet military reat would be greatly impoverished if this aterial had not become available. With less ppy results, CIA distributed some sensitive andestine reports on Syrian and Egyptian ans to attack Israel in 1973 that proved to be markably accurate. Unfortunately they were smissed by most military intelligence analysts contrary to their estimates of Arab inten-ns based on other factors, until after hostili-s began.

This brings us then to the most difficult and ost crucial task of the intelligence com-unity—research, analysis, and estimating. ard factual evidence must be weighed in the ht of "softer" but crucial evidence of human rposes and perceptions to make an overall sessment of capabilities, intentions, and ssible courses of action. Here CIA has the richest and largest talent pool, ranging over the spectrum of research in economic, scientific, political, and strategic-military intelligence. Its staffs do depth research and reporting; they provide the tidbits of new data that make up the staple of current intelligence reporting to the top-levels of government, and they work with State and Defense intelligence research analysts to arrive at coordinated views on the truly difficult estimative problems where evidence is insufficient to illuminate with certainty what is going or is likely to develop.

If the policymakers and strategic planners of the national security complex of agencies require answers on the probability of various situations existing or likely to develop in some foreseen set of circumstances, the CIA-State-Defense analytical teams must give the best answers possible on the basis of the evidence held by the whole intelligence community. Often these problems are military: Will Syria attack Israel? Will North Korea attack South Korea? How many large modern missiles does the USSR have? How large a stockpile of weapons-grade nuclear energy material does Communist China have? Will there be a Thai-Cambodian war? What African countries will Cuban troops be used in? What will be the shape of the Soviet Navy in 1985? How much superior in combat capability are Warsaw Pact troops in Central Europe compared with the capability of opposing NATO forces?

These are bread-and-butter intelligence analysis tasks. CIA analysts, the analysts of the Defense Intelligence Agency (DIA), and the analysts of the State Department's Intelligence Bureau (INR) must pull together the best guesses possible on these hard questions—not necessarily (because it would not be possible) always exactly right, but as objective and accurate a setting out of real probabilities as evidence allows. On good estimates good policy can be made, as well as good military force

Above: In South-East Asia the techniques of air-dropping acoustic, seismic and combined sensors for trucks and humans reached a high pitch in the Igloo White programme. These photographs show an even more sensitive sensor, which can be dropped with a braking parachute (by F-111, above) or with its own petal-type airbrakes (inset), normally into areas where they are concealed.

projections, theater deployment plans, weapons procurement, and troop training programs. Just as the local military field commander strains to hear and see everything in his sector of command that pierces the fog of war and lets him see into the minds of potential armed enemies so as either to deter them or to counter them in battle, the whole central strategic intelligence system strains to provide the eyes and ears of national strategic high command.

As weapons become lighter, more mobile, more accurate, and more destructive, the more imperative it is for military commanders to know their terrain (whether local, regional, or global), the strength and disposition of opposing forces, and, above all, the degree of probability of various military moves of a threatening or damaging character. While every military unit struggles to increase its own alertness to local intelligence on these matters, every unit and every echelon of command must also be familiar with and extract every possible element of essential information from the vast array of experts and data that constitute a vital part of the American military machine, that is, the central intelligence collection and analysis apparatus of the United States intelligence community. It is this advanced national intelligence machine that gives US forces a potential edge in every area of the world in deterring war or winning conflicts when they occur.

The US Strategic Triad

Dr. William R. Van Cleave, Professor of International Relations, and Director of the Defense and Strategic Studies Program, University of Southern California.

The term "strategic forces" is an ambiguous one and trying to define it precisely can be a fruitless task. In any traditional strategic sense, confining the term to those intercontinental nuclear forces directed essentially toward the USSR, as is the tendency in the US, is an impoverishment of the term. This is not the place, however, to seek a more proper application, and since other sections of this book cover other forces, this section will deal with forces implied by the narrow sense of the term "strategic nuclear forces"—those intercontinental offensive and defensive systems designed principally to cope with similar Soviet forces. Following the categorization of the Annual Defense Department Report (see footnotes), strategic nuclear forces encompass intercontinental ballistic missiles (ICBMs), modern submarine launched ballistic missiles (SLBMs) on nuclear powered launcher submarines (SSBNs), intercontinental-range bombers, some cruise missiles (those on intercontinental bombers, and longer-range, nuclear land-attack missiles at sea), and the defences against such forces. In addition, one should include the intelligence, warning, command, and communications systems associated with these strategic forces, as well as systems designed to attack or to defend such systems. Due to the paucity of American bomber defences, the absence of a ballistic missile defence, the general-purpose force nature of antisubmarine defence, and the very small and unorganized civil defence effort in the US, this section must of necessity focus on strategic offensive forces.

The existing mix of strategic offensive forces —the Minuteman and Titan II ICBMs, the Polaris and Poseidon SLBMs, and the B-52 heavy bomber—has become known as the Triad, a descriptive term that has come to connote prescriptively the complementarity or synergism of the three forces. The term and its rationale have become so entrenched that it is difficult to remember that the particular Triad forces were developed and their deployment begun before their complementarity was well appreciated. Nevertheless, the rationale for a force mix that presents an enemy with very different offensive and defensive problems and that dovetails individual strengths and weaknesses into a more capable whole is eminently persuasive. That does not imply necessarily that *three* is the correct number. There are proponents of a Diad, or two-force mix, and a Diad could result willy-nilly from a failure to preserve the viability of one of the forces. Current US policy, however, does not contemplate a Diad, but officially remains committed to maintaining the Triad—a Triad improved by the addition in 1983 of long range cruise missiles to the bomber force, and in the near future by submarine-launched cruise missiles.

Before moving to present and future US strategic forces and policies, it will be helpful to outline the development of American strategic nuclear forces and the changes in American thinking about those forces.

Prologue to a Strategic Force

US demobilization after World War II was so thorough that, in 1946, Army Air Force testimony before Congress indicated that not one fully operational air wing existed. While the United States had pioneered the development of atomic weapons and held the sole capability to produce and stockpile these weapons, it did not in fact start to produce such a stockpile until the late 1940s. "Atomic diplomacy" certainly did not exist without the atomic military means. A foreign policy of containment, formulated by 1947–1948, lacked the military support and military strategy necessary to such a policy. A growing recognition within the United States Government that American military strength was seriously lacking was nurtured by the developing Cold War and Russia's acquisition of atomic weapons technology in 1949. Early in 1950, a National Security Council Report (NSC-68) summed up the situation, warned of broad-gauged Soviet military superiority and increasing threats to the West unless appropriate countermeasures were immediately taken, and recommended a crash programme to build up America's nuclear and general-purpose forces. The attack on the Republic of Korea then served as the catalyst for a rearmament that, in all probability, would not otherwise have taken place at that time or with the rapidity with which it occurred.

In 1953, the new Eisenhower Administration inaugurated a broad economically oriented strategic programme, the "New Look", which imposed severe budget constraints on the military, but at the same time selectively emphasized strategic air power, the development of a family of nuclear weapons and North American air defence.

At the start of the Korean War, American strategic forces were centred on a small number of World War II B-29 or modified B-29 (B-50) bombers. The huge six-engine (propeller) B-36, a bomber initially contracted at the start of World War II, and the six-jet B-47 medium bomber, however, began service in 1951, and also began the rejuvenation of the Strategic Air Command. Due to the range-limitations of the B-47, bases for it were established overseas and an air refuelling technique was developed. By the time production of the B-47 ended, some 2,000 of these aircraft, in different versions, had been produced.

The Korean War also gave impetus to the development and production of the B-52, an eight-jet-engine heavy bomber, which continues to be the bomber mainstay of the Triad today. The B-52 was first flown in 1952 and was first delivered to SAC in 1955. Between 1955 and 1962, when the last B-52 was delivered, a total of more than 700 B-52s of various classifications and capabilities were produced.

The speed and range, or radius (normally one-half the range), of a bomber are variable measurements. Not only does each influence the other, but each is also influenced by altitude of flight, flight profile, payload and refueling. With optimum payload and cruising speed, and high altitude flight, the B-52 could hit a target in the USSR and return to the US without refueling, a total trip of 9,000 to 10,000 miles. At higher speeds (maximum speeds range from about 550 to 650mph, depending upon the model of B-52), more payload and low-level penetra-

United States strategic doctrine is based upon a triad, a three-fold order of weapon systems, each with its own unique characteristics. Providing great range but, above all, great accuracy is the ICBM force, predominantly composed of Minuteman missiles (far left). These would be used in a counter-force role against hostile strategic forces. Lurking deep in the ocean is the SSBN fleet armed with SLBMs; some with Poseidon, but an increasing number with Trident (left). These provide the secure and survivable counter-value system. Third is the ''air-breathing leg'', the manned bombers which will soon include the first B-1s (below). These have the unparalleled advantage of crew control up to weapon launch.

Left: Soldiers of the US Army turn away to shield their eyes from the bright light flash of an atomic device, during an exercise on August 7, 1957. Troop familiarization tests such as this were not uncommon in the 1950s and early 1960s, but would be unthinkable now, and several court cases are pending from some of those who blame such tests for subsequent illness.
Right: In an earlier exercise, in November 1951, troops of a battalion combat team of 11th Airborne Division watch a plume of radioactive smoke and debris rise after an atomic explosion.
Lower left: One of the most remarkable aircraft of all time was the XB-70A "Valkyrie", the prototype of a strategic nuclear bomber intended to replace the B-52. Designed for high-level penetration, it would never have survived at the low altitude now necessary as a result of the sophisticated Soviet air defenses.

surprise attack.

The shock produced in America by the full range flight test of a Soviet ICBM in August 1957, well before any US ICBM was ready followed by the launches of the world's first man-made satellites, Sputnik in October and Sputnik II in November, caused further acceleration of the American missile program A full range ICBM flight test was accomplished with Atlas in November 1958. Despite progress being made in solid-fuel ballistic missiles, the decision was made to proceed with interim deployment of the liquid-fueled Atlas and Titan ICBMs, and the Thor and Jupiter IRBMs. The latter, having ranges of only 1,500nm, were deployed in the United Kingdom, Turkey and Italy between 1959 and 1962, when they were phased out. Approximately 200 Atlas and Titan ICBMs and 100 IRBMs were deployed by 196 when the Minuteman I ICBM became operational, at which time they were phased out.

Minuteman I, with a 5,500nm range and somewhat less than 2,000 pounds throw-weight or payload, was flight tested in February 196 and first became operational in December 1962. The first fully operational Minuteman squadron was assigned to SAC in February 1963. Titan II (a liquid-fueled ICBM, four to five times the size of the Minuteman) was developed along with Minuteman, and also first became operational in 1963, but a total of only 54 of these missiles was deployed. By the mid-1960s, Minuteman II, a follow-on missile of somewhat longer range and slightly more payload, but with more accuracy, became operational.

The first SLBM nuclear-powered submarine the USS *George Washington*, successfully launched a Polaris from underwater in July 1960, and became fully operational in 196 (The table shows the schedule of Polaris submarines.) Early boats were equipped with an interim 1,200nm missile (the A-1), until the 1,500nm A-2 and later the 2,500nm A-3, equipped with three warheads (not independently targetable), became standard.

Transition to a Modern Force and New Doctrine

The Eisenhower strategic doctrine, initially based upon maintaining superiority in strategic nuclear forces, was changed to one of "sufficiency" by 1956–1957. As Secretary of the Air Force Quarles expressed it, sufficiency depended, not necessarily upon being superior in forces or capabilities, but upon having the "forces required to accomplish the mission assigned". By the end of the 1950s a dual debate developed, centred, first, upon the nature of the mission and, second, upon whether US programs were "sufficient" to provide the forces necessary to mission success. The Eisenhower Administration left office with neither part of the debate being resolved.

In 1961, a new Administration and a new civilian team in the Department of Defense assumed office, persuaded that a change was in order away from Eisenhower's Sufficiency doc-

tion, the range would be reduced substantially, and refueling would be required for mission performance.

The 1950s also saw the development of a supersonic medium bomber, the B-58, which was first flown in 1956, but of which less than one hundred ever entered the force. A B-70 bomber, with a speed near Mach 3, designed during the mid/late 1950s as successor to the B-52, was cancelled in 1961.

The story of American strategic ballistic missiles is an interesting one, and clearly one where technology did not lead automatically to decisions on strategic forces; rather, technology encountered much resistance and was successfully turned into modern weapons systems only after the efforts of a few dedicated and determined people. One recent study of the American ICBM program summarizes it as "a long pattern of disbelief, neglect, and delay".[1]

Despite the technological headstart provided after World War II by the acquisition of German rocket experience and expertise, long-range missile weapons were subordinated in research and development priority to manned aircraft and air-breathing (cruise) missiles. In 1947, US Air Force research on long-range ballistic missiles was cancelled altogether and

not resumed until after the start of the Korean War. By 1953, less than $2 million was spent on such research. During 1953–1955, however, technological developments, evidence of a concerted Soviet rocket program, and—most particularly—the efforts of a few civilians changed neglect into a high priority development program, prudently placed outside of normal Air Force channels (but under the direction and management of an Air Force General, Bernard Schriever).[2] With strong Congressional backing, General Schriever took his case for the ICBM to President Eisenhower and the National Security Council in the middle of 1955. The result was a Presidential directive assigning the highest national priority to the ICBM. Funding for strategic ballistic missile development (ICBM and IRBM) rose to $159 million in 1955, $1.4 billion in 1957, and $2 billion in 1958.

The initial US ICBM programs, the Atlas and Titan, involved large liquid-fueled missiles. In 1955, however, a breakthrough in solid fuel technology led to the Air Force Minuteman ICBM and the Navy Polaris SLBM programs—more compact, solid-fuel missiles for deployment, respectively, in underground silos and submarines, which resulted in a missile force with much greater survivability against a

"Assured Destruction" (AD) and the later concept of "Mutual Assured Destruction" (MAD). Originally only one of several analytical tests to aid judgement on the adequacy of forces, AD became the principal criterion, then the dominant strategic concept of the American defense community, and finally a philosophical base for theories of mutual deterrence strategic stability, and strategic arms limitation. It became the necessary "conceptual framework for measuring the need and adequacy of our strategic forces".

While these concepts were evolving, force level decisions had to be made. The Eisenhower Administration left office planning some 1,100 Minuteman, Titan and Polaris missiles under the concept of Sufficiency. The new Administration, having been critical of the "assiveness" of the Eisenhower Administration and, having campaigned on a warning of "missile gap" and a cry for US strategic superiority, moved initially to redeem campaign pledges. Superiority was reinstituted as American policy for strategic force relations with the USSR (in testimony before Congress in 1963, Administration spokesmen termed US strategic superiority the "sine qua non" of Western security), and planned levels of Minuteman and Polaris were increased: Polaris to 44 boats (with 16 missiles each) and Minuteman, by some accounts, to as many as 1,600–2,000.

As strategic ballistic missiles were becoming operational, decisions were made to reduce the bomber force of SAC. In 1961, that force consisted of over 2,000 B-47s and B-52s. Secretary of Defense McNamara accelerated the phase-out of B-47s and cancelled developmental work on the advanced B-70 strategic bomber. The last B-52s and B-58s were delivered to SAC in 1962, and by then no new strategic bomber was either in production or under development. By the time that Minuteman and Polaris were fully operational, US bomber strength had been reduced to less than 700 B-52s and B-58s. (The latter were phased out in 1969, and the former suffered attrition through fatigue and Vietnam, to reduce the force further.)

Cost-effectiveness considerations along with the progressive development of American Assured Destruction thinking led to reductions in planned levels of Minuteman and Polaris early in the 1960s. ICBM levels were lowered to 1,200 Minuteman and 120 Titan II, and then to 1,000 Minuteman and 54 Titan II. Polaris levels were set at 41 boats with 656 missiles. By the mid-1960s the decision had been made to level off American strategic offensive forces at the levels then existing.

Left: An Atlas 8-E is launched from Cape Canaveral on January 24, 1961. Atlas was the USA's first true ICBM and entered service in November 1959, serving until the force was de-activated in 1965–67.

trine and the strategy of "Massive Retaliation". "Flexible Response", a phrase gleaned by President Kennedy from the writings of Army General Maxwell Taylor, and supported by RAND Corporation studies, whereby the flexibility of both general-purpose and strategic nuclear forces was to be increased, was adopted as policy. At the same time, however, the "systems analysts" who came to dominate the Pentagon sought a more systematic and measurable approach to planning strategic forces, an analytical and quantifiable theory to determine as precisely as possible "How Much is Enough?".[3] The evolution of American strategic thinking during the 1960s was the story of a contest between true Flexible Response, which tended to drive strategic force requirements upwards, and the analytical techniques and arms control corollaries of calculable force limitations, which depressed requirements.

From this contest, the term "Flexible Response" was supplanted by the doctrine of

Evolution of American Doctrine; The 1960s, Superiority to Parity

In his famous Ann Arbor, Michigan, address in 1962, Secretary McNamara set forth the tenets of a Flexible Response Doctrine based upon counterforce and damage limiting. Military strategy, he said, "should be approached in much the same way that more conventional military operations have been regarded in the past. That is to say, principal military objectives . . . should be the destruction of the enemy's military forces, not of its civilian population."[4] Deterrence of nuclear war would be based upon the ability to limit damage in the event of war, which would be accomplished by US possession of the means to destroy an enemy's military capability and by targeting restraint (*vis-à-vis* cities) on our own part, backed by the ability to escalate should the enemy do so. In 1963, McNamara said:

> "We should not think of ourselves as forced by limitations of resources to rely upon strategies of desperation and threats of vast mutual destruction. . . . The damage-limiting capability of our numerically superior force is, I believe, well worth its incremental cost."

Clearly, cost-effectiveness arguments against damage limiting had not yet impressed the Secretary, nor had the notion that MAD parity was synonymous with strategic stability.

Although biographers of McNamara generally agree that his thinking was moving away from this strategy by 1964–1965, the Defense Reports of those years repeated the same theme: In addition to an Assured Destruction capability, American forces "should have the power to limit the destruction of our own cities and population to the maximum extent practicable . . . a damage-limiting strategy appears to be the most practical and effective course for us to follow." Moreover, contradicting later assertions that Pentagon studies did not support damage-limiting strategies, one Report stated directly: "In every pertinent case we found that forces in excess of those needed simply to destroy Soviet cities would significantly reduce damage to the US and Western Europe." Assured Destruction and Damage Limiting were thus at this time the dual pillars of American strategic policy.

Change, however, came rapidly. More emphasis in public statements (and in target and force planning) came to be placed on Assured Destruction, now based upon the judgemental criterion of "unacceptable damage" measured in presumed population fatalities and gross industrial destruction. Concurrently, Secretary McNamara began to disparage both damage limiting and countermilitary targeting. Flexible Response options gave way in emphasis to countercity AD. In 1966 and 1967, he said: "Our forces must be sufficiently large to possess an 'Assured Destruction' capability." It is this capability "and not the ability partially to limit damage to ourselves" that must command our attention.

From Assured Destruction grew the mutual deterrence concept of Mutual Assured Destruction (MAD). *Both* sides were to have an AD capability against the other, and—ideally—essentially no other strategic force capabilities. Neither should develop capabilities that would appear to call into question the other's AD capability; hence, offensive and defensive capabilities that might do so were to be avoided to the extent feasible.[5] It was not merely that such capabilities were not achievable at prices the decision makers were willing to pay; they were to be avoided as incompatible with stability based upon MAD. MAD was as much an arms limitation concept as a strategic one. Thus, it was not so much that forces to counter the enemy's AD capability would upset mutual deterrence as that they would "fuel an arms race". As McNamara's Assistant Secretary of Defense expressed it, "any attempt on our part to reduce damage to our society would put pressure on the Soviets to strive for an off-

setting improvement in their assured-destruction forces, and vice versa. . . . This 'action-reaction' phenomenon is central to all strategic force planning as well as to any theory of an arms race." The corollary to this presumed "action-reaction" determinism was inaction-inaction. If the US were to refrain from challenging a Soviet AD capability, the Soviets would be satisfied and would have no need to build up their forces further. Stability would result, and strategic arms limitation agreements codifying that stability could be reached. Hence, a policy of self-restraint was adopted, and strategic force parity (later termed Sufficiency by the Nixon Administration) was substituted for the goal of Superiority. American strategic nuclear force expenditure declined, from over $18 billion (in fiscal year 1974 dollars) at the start of the 1960s to less than one-half that by 1967–68.

Soviet strategic forces were growing during this period of time, but it seems clear that this growth was not the reason for the changes in American policy. The US intelligence community chronically underestimated the growth of that force and placed very modest AD objectives on the growth. In 1965, Secretary McNamara asserted that the "Soviets have decided that they have lost the quantitative race and they are not seeking to engage us in that contest . . . there is no indication that the Soviets are seeking to develop a strategic nuclear force as large as our own."

The changes came, instead, from the progressive development of the concepts and beliefs noted above, a presumed disutility of strategic forces for anything save AD, and the goal of strategic stability (MAD) through arms limitations agreements that would be possible only when the Soviets were satisfied with their own AD capability. The "slow pace" of Soviet strategic programs perceived by US officials was to be encouraged by US restraint. As an American arms control enthusiast later acknowledged, "the strategic parity which was a prerequisite for strategic arms limitation could not have come about except for conscious restraint on the part of the US government."[6]

Technological Developments

Technological progress and force modernization may be constrained by neglect, or by policy when it seems to clash with doctrinal preferences and arms control aspirations, but technology generally advances. The problem is to adapt policy and technology to one another. While these policies were evolving, technological progress was occurring in three notable areas that seemed incompatible with those policies: ballistic missile guidance, which promised very good accuracies for ICBMs; multiple warheads, or reentry vehicles, for single missiles, each of which could be independently targeted (MIRV); and antiballistic missile (ABM) systems.

The MIRV (Multiple Independently Re-Targeted Vehicle) was originally a cost-effectiveness concept whereby expanded target coverage could be provided without increasing the size of the missile force. As evidence began to accumulate in the middle 1960s of a Soviet ABM program and air defense expansion, and in the

Right: Two Minuteman II ICBMs being launched from Vandenburg Air Force Base in December 1969. Missiles must be ready for launch at all times to prevent their destruction by a surprise pre-emptive strike.
Far right: A Minuteman II ICBM in its protective silo at Ellsworth Air Force Base. Ten such silos are grouped together to make a "flight" which has one control centre, also located underground.

Right: Six unarmed Mark 2 Multiple Independently Targetted Re-Entry Vehicles (MIRVs) approaching their targets on the American missile range near Kwajalein Atoll in the Pacific Ocean.

later 1960s of a Soviet counterforce capability against American ICBM silos, two supplementary reasons for MIRV were added: to counter a Soviet ABM and to reduce the ABM capability of Sam (Surface-to-Air Missile) air defenses; and to increase the capability of deterrent forces surviving any possible first strike. The quandary of MIRV and MAD was eased by deliberately avoiding effective hard target MIRVs (high yield, high accuracy), and designing them mostly to offset ABM and to increase soft target coverage.[7] (Hence, many reasoned, should ABM be banned in SALT, neither side should have any reason for MIRV, and MIRV could also be banned or stringently limited.) While the concept of MIRV was first proposed under an Air Force contract, the Navy Special Office, studying options to improve Polaris, adopted MIRV for future SLBMs. In 1965, development of Poseidon—a new SLBM eventually to be equipped with some ten small, .04 MT warheads—was approved. The system seemed ideal for countering an ABM and targeting soft urban-industrial targets; it did not pose a threat to ICBM silos.

MIRV was also adapted to an Air Force follow-on to Minuteman. Minuteman III (with about 2,200 pounds of throw-weight or payload capability) was designed to be equipped with three MIRV warheads, each of .17 MT. This system, with MIRV, was first tested in 1968, but neither it nor Poseidon would be deployed prior to the beginning of SALT in 1969. Deployment of the first Minuteman III was scheduled for summer, 1970, and the first Poseidon-equipped SSBN was to be delivered in 1971. Hence, MIRV became a major SALT issue in the US. Major segments of the US Government wished to reach an agreement with the USSR banning MIRV before deployment began. In the second session of SALT, in the spring of 1970, the US proposed an agreement banning MIRV, which was rejected by the USSR, even though it would have also banned ABM. The Soviet Union did not link the two systems in the US arms control sense.

ABM, even more than MIRV, was widely deemed inconsistent with MAD concepts and US SALT aspirations. American policy through the 1960s had been to continue ABM development but to forgo deployment. Steady advances in the technology, however, combined with the same Soviet development that urged MIRV and other considerations, such as expected People's Republic of China (PRC) ICBM development, strained that policy. A reluctant decision to proceed with deployment was made in 1967, but the deployment was designed and rationalized to be consistent with a MAD relationship with the USSR. Initially, that meant casting the program in terms of a light area defense against such threats as the PRC might pose in the future, but not heavy enough to cause Soviet concern about its AD capability.

Early in 1969, the new Nixon Administration modified that plan. The new deployment plan, named Safeguard, was to emphasize first the defence of Minuteman ICBM silos, whose future vulnerability was projected by continuing Soviet ICBM developments. Eventual expansion of the deployment to twelve ABM sites would be decided on an annual basis, depending upon progress in SALT and developments in Soviet counterforce capabilities. SALT agreements could still be reached to limit, or possibly ban, ABM deployment. (It might be noted that ABM defense of retaliatory forces would be logically consistent with MAD. Such a defense would not reduce an enemy's AD capability, but would only preserve one's own. In SALT, that defense might be reduced or obviated altogether if agreements reduced the projected threats to US ICBM forces. In this vein, it is noteworthy that the major Soviet initiative to stop US ABM deployment in SALT came *after* the area defense component of Safeguard was abandoned by the US in 1970, and ABM plans became restricted to defense of Minuteman. Coupled with Soviet disinterest in banning MIRV, this should have clearly re-

vealed the Soviet strategic emphasis on counterforce rather than MAD.)

By the end of the 1960s, the focus of US strategic force attention was on SALT. The Soviet Union had roughly drawn equal with the US, at least in the central strategic forces to be the subject of SALT, and "parity" was established. United States SALT expectations were high. While there were major studies of future US strategic force requirements and force modifications, they were SALT dominated and their recommendations were largely held in abeyance pending the outcome of SALT.

Early American expectations were not met. United States ABM deployment was limited by SALT to one ICBM site (since dismantled), but neither MIRV nor the continued growth and improvement of Soviet forces was constrained. The earlier US decisions to freeze numerical levels of the TRIAD and to improve the capabilities of the force qualitatively at only a modest, SALT-related pace failed to induce the Soviets to freeze their own strategic force levels or to show any similar restraint. In retrospect it must be concluded that US restraint and the concept of MAD merely contributed to the

opportunity for the Soviet Union first to achieve parity, then to gain superiority in major quantitative comparisons of strategic forces and finally to convert the latter to a counterforce and war-fighting advantage.

A "New" American Strategic Doctrine

The Nixon Administration had formalized a set of criteria that defined "Sufficiency" for American strategic forces. In addition to the Assured Destruction criterion, Crisis Stability (i.e., avoiding major force vulnerabilities), equivalent destructive capability with the USSR, and defence against light attacks were to comprise Sufficiency. In concept, there began to be a move away from the previous emphasis and reliance on Assured Destruction. Presidential statements and Department of Defense Reports began to suggest new interest in more selective targeting and in escalation control, both to enhance deterrence and to hedge against its failure. In the early 1970s, after SALT had failed to dampen the Soviet build-up, a Government study spearheaded by the Office of Secretary of Defense produced what might be regarded as a new doctrine of Sufficiency.

improve in our strategic posture" the following:

"... a capability sufficiently large, diversified, and survivable so that it will provide us at all times with high confidence of riding out even a massive surprise attack and of penetrating enemy defenses, and with the ability to withhold an assured destruction reserve for an extended period of time.

"... employment of the strategic forces in a controlled, selective, and restrained fashion.

"... the forces to execute a wide range of options in response to potential actions by an enemy, including a capability for precise attacks on both soft and hard targets, while at the same time minimizing collateral damage.

"... an offensive capability of such size and composition that all will perceive it as in overall balance with the strategic forces of any potential opponent".[8]

To a large extent, American official strategic thinking seemed to have gone full circle back to the 1962 Ann Arbor statement of McNamara. Assured Destruction was not replaced; it was essential, but inadequate; furthermore, it was again to be perceived as a last ditch coercive reserve with the objective of dampening escalation even after deterrence initially failed and strategic weapons were used. As made clear later, AD was not to be measured arbitrarily in terms of population fatalities, but rather in terms of objectives of greater political-military relevance to a war and its aftermath (hence, linking deterrence to political postwar objectives and relationships); principally, reduction of the enemy's post-attack political-economic recovery capability and postwar political-military power.

Short of such major exchanges, however, the US goal was again to limit damage to the extent feasible, through targeting restraint and discriminate targeting, multiple options to fit the situation, and targeting of military forces, soft and hard.

It was ironic that counterforce and damage limiting were eschewed as major US objectives and strategic force planning criteria in order to exercise a self-restraint that was to induce Soviet reciprocity, but again had to be seriously reconsidered precisely because the lack of any reciprocity produced a Soviet strategic force capability rendering Assured Destruction thoroughly inadequate and highly questionable as a planned response to *any* threat save a massive Soviet attack on American cities, as well as on US strategic forces. The steady growth of Soviet capabilities and steadfast rejection of MAD forced American rethinking of strategic doctrine.

Above: Three MIRV warheads on their 'bus' with the protective nose-cone beside them. These reentry vehicles can be targetted to hit points hundreds of miles apart, although in order to ensure a high probability of damage two MIRVs would be aimed at each target. One of the consequences of "MIRVing" is that the critical count in weapon comparisons is now independently targettable warheads and not just the number of missiles in the strategic inventory.

Left: Minuteman III ICBM is launched from an underground silo; note the characteristic "smoke-ring" above the missile. The USA has 550 Minuteman IIIs in service with eleven operational squadrons: some 300 of these are to be fitted with the new 330 KT Mk 12A reentry vehicle, whose increased weight results in a slight reduction in range.

Right: An ICBM sitting in its silo. The efficacy of a silo is measured in the overpressure necessary to ensure its destruction. Once 300 pounds per square inch (psi) was thought adequate, but now 3,000 psi or more is necessary.

On the basis of this study, Secretary of Defense James R. Schlesinger first announced in a press conference on January 10, 1974, that there had taken place a "a change in the strategies of the United States with regard to the hypothetical employment of central strategic forces. A change in targeting strategy as it were." He went on: "To a large extent the American doctrinal position has been wrapped around something called 'assured destruction', which implies a tendency to target Soviet cities initially and massively and that this is the principal option that the President would have. It is our intention that this not be the only option and possibly not the principal option."

Because of the enormous growth of Soviet strategic force capabilities, he said, "the range of circumstances in which an all-out strike against an opponent's cities can be contemplated has narrowed considerably and one wishes to have alternatives for the employment of strategic forces."

The FY 1975 Department of Defense Report set forth what might be regarded as a new set of "sufficiency criteria", describing as the "principal features that we propose to maintain and

American strategic forces, however, were only partly affected by this explicit change in planning. On the one hand, steps were taken to improve the targeting and ability to retarget the Minuteman force and plans were made to improve Minuteman accuracy and to install a more powerful warhead on Minuteman III (the Mark 12-A). In addition, the development of the Trident I (C-4), which would have more flexibility than the basically soft-point target Poseidon, was carried forth. On the other hand, force planning remained constrained both by the existing SALT-I agreements and by the then anticipated SALT-II limitations. The SALT ABM Treaty prohibited damage-limiting defences against ballistic missiles and also dam-

pened other means of defense. As Secretary of Defense Schlesinger put it in the FY 1976 Defense Report, "if we cannot defend ourselves against strategic missiles, there is little to gain from trying to defend ourselves against strategic bombers", to which Secretary of Defense Rumsfeld later added: "With the emphasis on active defenses substantially reduced, it was considered almost pointless to advocate a major program of passive defenses."

At the same time, however, a new attitude toward SALT was reluctantly developing, which, along with the unprecedented and still increasing pace of Soviet strategic programs, precipitated new interest in strategic force programs. The United States had continued to

exercise restraint, even in the face of a rapidly developing Soviet threat, in the hope that SALT agreements would ease strategic pressures and contribute to strategic stability. SALT II, however, was making essentially no progress toward such limitations. Instead, it became increasingly clear that an acutely dangerous strategic imbalance would occur unless the US took major steps to prevent it. SALT agreements, clearly, could not themselves do that. Consequently, the American approach to SALT changed somewhat. SALT-II agreements would be pursued, but without the previous expectations or enthusiasm. They would be acceptable to the extent that they did not impede programs necessary to prevent that imbalance. Indeed, they would be acceptable only assuming that the US was proceeding with those programs in a timely fashion.

Funds were provided for force programs scheduled to ease the problems that the United States would otherwise face by the early to middle 1980s: new, more capable ICBM (MX), redeployed to reduce its vulnerability; Trident submarines and missiles to augment the FBM force; the B-1 bomber to replace or supplement the ageing B-52 forces; and a family of cruise missiles suitable for deployment on a variety of carriers. It was possible that the Soviets would make some SALT concessions in order to stop B-1, Trident, and the MX, but by this time the Administration had decided that such programs were essential and should not be used as "bargaining chips" for SALT agreements.

In 1977, however, a new Administration more sanguine about SALT and skeptical about SNF programs, decided upon a different approach. It immediately cut nearly $3 billion from the proposed FY 1978 Defense budget, and

Far left: Trident I (C-4) Submarine-Launched Ballistic Missile (SLBM) roars off into space following an underwater launch. This missile can carry up to 14 MIRVs, although about 8 to 10 is a more likely operational figure.

Left: A missile container is loaded into its silo in an SSBN. All US SSBNs have carried 16 missiles in the past, but the latest Ohio class carries 24 Trident missiles—a truly awesome second-strike capability.

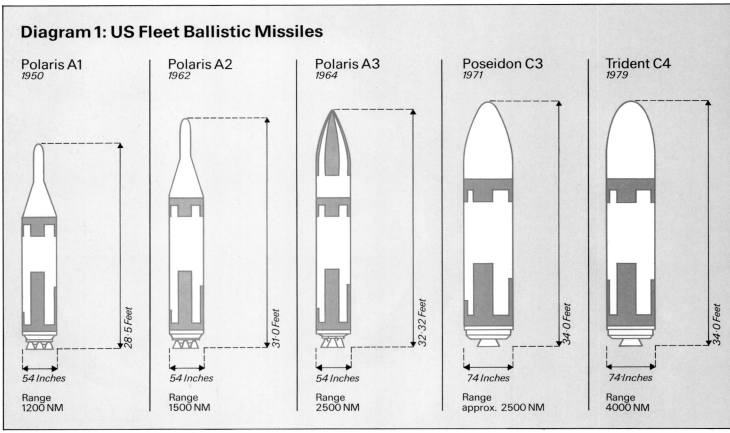

Diagram 1: US Fleet Ballistic Missiles

Polaris A1 *1950*	Polaris A2 *1962*	Polaris A3 *1964*	Poseidon C3 *1971*	Trident C4 *1979*
28·5 Feet	31·0 Feet	32·32 Feet	34·0 Feet	34·0 Feet
54 Inches	54 Inches	54 Inches	74 Inches	74 Inches
Range 1200 NM	Range 1500 NM	Range 2500 NM	Range approx. 2500 NM	Range 4000 NM

Above: ALCMs being loaded onto a B-52 long-range bomber. This missile, the AGM-86B, has had a lengthy development; just as it is due to enter service an entirely new replacement has been revealed which makes use of "stealth" technology.

reduced, delayed or—as in the notable case of the B-1 bomber—cancelled major strategic force programs. At the same time, it enthusiastically placed the highest priority on a SALT-II agreement.

Current and Future Doctrine and Forces

The rethinking of American strategic doctrine continued under the Carter Administration. Neither President Carter nor Secretary of Defense Harold Brown seemed closely in tune with the concepts and objectives enunciated in 1974. Both seemed personally closer to the philosophy of Mutual Assured Destruction, and President Carter's statements (and force decisions) emphasized restricting, not expanding, nuclear capabilities. In referring to the putative destructive power contained in one Poseidon submarine in his 1979 State of the Union message, Carter seemed to many commentators to be suggesting a minimum deterrent posture.

Nonetheless, the FY 1980 Defense Report of Secretary Brown announced a "Countervailing Strategy" policy, which seemed to be based upon most of the objectives set forth in 1974.

The FY 1980 Defense Report stated that "we must insist on essential equivalence with the Soviet Union", and to fulfil the aims of a "Countervailing Strategy", US forces must be capable of surviving even a well-executed surprise attack and then be able to "penetrate enemy defenses and destroy a comprehensive set of targets in the USSR with whatever timing, and degree of deliberation and control, proves desirable; if necessary, inflict high levels of damage on Soviet society—particularly those elements the Soviet leadership values—regardless of the measures the Soviets might take to limit the damage; and still retain a reserve capability." The capability to attack military targets selectively and to control escalation in the event that deterrence should fail was also emphasized. During 1980, this was confirmed

as official national policy with the issuance of Presidential Directive 59 (PD-59).

That major threats to American strategic forces were rapidly developing was openly acknowledged. Secretary Brown warned in the FY 1980 Report that "it would be a mistake to underestimate the problems created by the military buildup of the Soviet Union", and that "it may be too late if we wait much longer" to react. Furthermore, he reported: "Our most serious concerns—which we need to act now to meet—are about the period of the early-to-mid 1980s." By that time it was acknowledged that essentially all comparisons of strategic force capabilities would favor the Soviet Union, that American ICBMs would have questionable survivability, that the bomber force would be vulnerable to a surprise attack (only about 25 per cent were currently kept on ground alert),

Above: A B-52 in position on the biggest all-wood structure in the world. This platform is used to test aircraft for their resistance to Electromagnetic Pulse, one of the phenomena resulting from a nuclear explosion and one which can destroy electrical and electronic equipment.

and that Soviet active and passive defenses could greatly mitigate the effectiveness of surviving retaliatory forces. The Chairman of the Joint Chiefs of Staff termed this an "acutely dangerous imbalance" in his 1979 report to Congress.

It was this situation in general, and the vulnerability of land-based deterrent forces in particular, that gave rise to the term "Window of Vulnerability" during the 1980 Presidential campaign.

The Triad

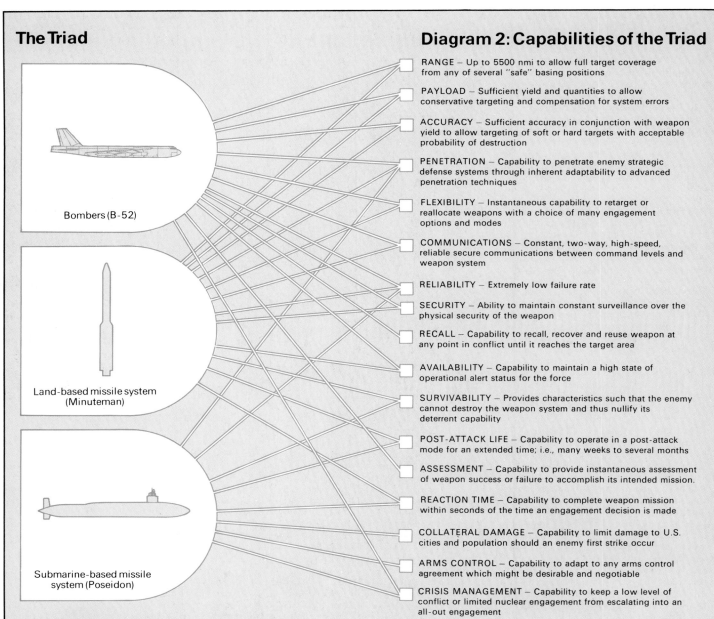

Bombers (B-52)

Land-based missile system (Minuteman)

Submarine-based missile system (Poseidon)

Diagram 2: Capabilities of the Triad

RANGE – Up to 5500 nmi to allow full target coverage from any of several "safe" basing positions

PAYLOAD – Sufficient yield and quantities to allow conservative targeting and compensation for system errors

ACCURACY – Sufficient accuracy in conjunction with weapon yield to allow targeting of soft or hard targets with acceptable probability of destruction

PENETRATION – Capability to penetrate enemy strategic defense systems through inherent adaptability to advanced penetration techniques

FLEXIBILITY – Instantaneous capability to retarget or reallocate weapons with a choice of many engagement options and modes

COMMUNICATIONS – Constant, two-way, high-speed, reliable secure communications between command levels and weapon system

RELIABILITY – Extremely low failure rate

SECURITY – Ability to maintain constant surveillance over the physical security of the weapon

RECALL – Capability to recall, recover and reuse weapon at any point in conflict until it reaches the target area

AVAILABILITY – Capability to maintain a high state of operational alert status for the force

SURVIVABILITY – Provides characteristics such that the enemy cannot destroy the weapon system and thus nullify its deterrent capability

POST-ATTACK LIFE – Capability to operate in a post-attack mode for an extended time; i.e., many weeks to several months

ASSESSMENT – Capability to provide instantaneous assessment of weapon success or failure to accomplish its intended mission.

REACTION TIME – Capability to complete weapon mission within seconds of the time an engagement decision is made

COLLATERAL DAMAGE – Capability to limit damage to U.S. cities and population should an enemy first strike occur

ARMS CONTROL – Capability to adapt to any arms control agreement which might be desirable and negotiable

CRISIS MANAGEMENT – Capability to keep a low level of conflict or limited nuclear engagement from escalating into an all-out engagement

Under President Ford it had been planned that some 500 MX ICBMs would be redeployed in a more survivable Multiple Aim Point basing mode with an IOC of 1982–83. But by 1980, the Carter Administration planned to deploy fewer than half that number, with an IOC of 1986 or later, in a multiple protective shelter (MPS), or multiple aim point (MAP) system. This would involve shuttling 200 MX missiles among 4,600 shelters in an attempt to keep their location so uncertain that any attack, for success, would have to destroy all 4,600 shelters simultaneously. While many experts agreed with the basic MPS/MAP concept, many also—including Presidential candidate Ronald Reagan—were skeptical about the particular form of the Carter plan, which was highly influenced by SALT considerations. Many still favored the system originally planned, whereby ICBMs would be hidden among a large number of vertical silo-type shelters; others advocated proceeding immediately with deployment of Minuteman in that fashion, without waiting for the development of the MX. Options were also under development by the Army for an active defence of the ICBM force—although that would require abrogation or amendment of the SALT-I ABM Treaty.

In submarine forces the larger, advanced Trident submarine was planned to replace some SSBNs as they were phased out at the end of their scheduled deployment life. Advances in Soviet anti-submarine warfare capabilities could mean that the SSBN technology of the 1950s and '60s would dangerously lag behind the ASW technology of the '70s and '80s. The Trident program involved two new missiles. The Trident I (C-4) missile, with better guidance and longer range than Poseidon, would be retrofitted into some of the present Poseidon submarines, as well as being carried by the first Trident boats. Later, in the 1990s, the Trident boats might carry the more accurate Trident II (D-5) missile. Construction of the first Trident submarine was begun in the summer of 1974; the second boat was begun a year later. Originally, three boats were to be deployed every two year, beginning in 1979. By 1979–80, however, the IOC had slipped to 1981 and the number to be produced was uncertain. A total of 13 boats was mentioned in 1979–80, but only seven boats had been authorized for the period up to 1985.

The production of 244 B-1 bombers was planned by the Ford Administration for a 1979 IOC. The B-1 was designed to relieve future problems of survivability against SLBM attack (by faster getaway time and hardening to nuclear effects) and penetration of Soviet air defenses (by very low level penetration at Mach .85, high altitude supersonic flight, and use of SRAMS, and ALCMs; the latter providing a "stand-off" attack option as well as penetration). However, the Carter Administration, incorrectly viewing the B-1 and the ALCM as alternatives, cancelled the program.

The Ford Administration also planned cruise missiles, with land and sea deployment beginning in 1980 and air deployment (ALCMs), on B-1 and on some 200 B-52s, beginning in 1981. The Carter Administration planned to equip some 120 B-52Gs with air-launched cruise missiles (ALCM), with the first squadron operational at the start of 1983. It also tentatively planned future deployment of submarine-launched cruise missiles (the Navy's Tomahawk), but programs and plans were not set.

The Carter Administration held strategic force program spending to about eight per cent of defence expenditures, but acknowledged in 1980 that this spending would have to be increased, with or without SALT-II. In fact, promises of more effort in the area of strategic

Above: Boeing B-52 launches an Air-Launched Cruise Missile (ALCM). The USAF has decided to cut back production of this AGM-86A in favor of a new missile, which will have increased survivability.

Below: B-1A seen through the operator's window of a refueling tanker. B-1 can carry carry 32 SRAM, 32 ALCM, or 75,000lb (34,020kg) free-fall bombs internally plus 40,000lb (18,144kg) externally.

forces, as well as in the overall defense budget, accompanied its SALT-II proposals. The projected increase, which in 1979–80 was debated in terms of a 3 to 5 per cent increase overall, would have applied more to General Purpose Forces than to strategic forces. Department of Defense analyses showed marked inferiority in strategic capabilities for the United States from the early 1980s, extending toward the end of the decade, but beginning to change as the MX and cruise missiles were deployed. Such analyses, however, left open more questions than they answered; for example, would the US carry through those programs assumed by the analyses? Some programs assumed for analytical purposes were far from certain: MX was one example; and, in addition, the Commander in Chief of SAC acknowledged in Senate Hearings

that bomber force improvements necessary to meet the penetration assumptions used in these analyses were not funded in the Five Year Plan.

Another question was: how could the United States expect to pass safely through the period of acknowledged Soviet superiority, even assuming that it managed eventually to turn the trends around?

Mr. Reagan, both as candidate and as President, has acknowledged the severity of these problems and has emphasized the need to move rapidly to reinvigorate US SNF. Prior to his election, Mr. Reagan declared that "our nuclear forces must be made survivable as rapidly as possible to close the window of vulnerability before it opens any wider".[9] In 1982, as President, he told the public: "The truth of the matter is that on balance the Soviet Union does have a definite margin of superiority—enough so there is risk, and there is what I have called, as you all know, several times, a window of vulnerability."[10] And the Secretary of Defense later told Congress, "unfortunately, it is true."[11]

The Administration's SNF modernization program, at the beginning of 1983, has five elements.

Perhaps the most important, and certainly the most controversial, element is ICBM modernization, or the MX program. A survivable, flexible ICBM force is essential to US strategic doctrine yet the existing vulnerability of this force is a large part of "the window of vulnerability" that Mr. Reagan pledged to close. Unfortunately, after two years of wrestling with the problem, the Reagan Administration has not yet produced an acceptable survivable basing mode for the MX missile; consequently, its future is in doubt. Congress has thus far refused to approve production funds for the missile without an acceptable way to provide for its survivability against attack.

The Reagan Administration early rejected the Carter MAP basing plan. After examining, suggesting, and discarding various alternatives, at the end of 1982 the Administration proposed Closely Spaced Basing (CSB), where super-hardened silos would be placed so closely together that, theoretically, incoming warheads would destroy their brothers ("fratricide") before they could destroy the silos. Congress has thus far rejected this questionable plan, and the Administration's failure to provide survivability has left the future of the ICBM leg of the TRIAD in doubt. Some now favor abandoning it altogether for more reliance on sea-based and air-breathing forces. Some advocate producing the MX, placing it in existing silos, and relying on launching the force upon adequate warning of a Soviet attack. Others, including the author, favor abandoning the MX missile for the rapid development of much smaller, single-warhead ICBMs, light enough (about $\frac{1}{3}$ the weight of Minuteman) to be adaptable to cost-effective multiple shelter basing, or a variety of land- and air-mobile arrangements. The size and weight of the MX (192,000lb, 87,090kg, not including its canister) explains the great difficulty in deriving a survivable basing mode for it.

Bomber force modernization includes the simultaneous production of some 100 B-1B bombers (a development of the cancelled B-1) and development of "Stealth" technology for an advanced 1990s bomber of such low radar cross section that it can penetrate Soviet air defenses. A quarter of the B-52 force (B-52D) will be retired, but the remaining 240 B-52G/H bombers will be retained as cruise missile carriers equipped with ALCM.

By 1983, the operational SSBN force had been reduced from 41 to 33, with retirement of 10 Polaris boats, and the introduction of the first two Trident submarines. Trident production, however, has been slowed to one boat per year. The Trident II (D-5) missile is under development for the 1990s, with the promise of increasing the currently limited targeting capability of the sea-based force. In addition, there are plans to deploy a few hundred Tomahawk nuclear land-attack SLCMs on 688-class attack submarines, and perhaps on selected surface ships. Unfortunately, the Tomahawk program has experienced serious technical and managerial problems, which cast doubt on at least the timing of this deployment.

Finally, important steps are being taken to improve the connectivity and survivability of strategic intelligence, warning, and communications, and modest steps are being taken to improve air defenses.

Were one to rely solely on the media, one might believe that, with these programs, the US was embarked on a major SNF buildup or "arms race". In fact, the programs are modest, and the real question is whether, in view of the enormous disparity of effort between the US and the USSR, they are adequate. According to the Department of Defense, the Soviets have

Top: A dry-launch of an MX missile prototype. This controversial project has had a long and difficult gestation period, and its problems are far from over. If the ICBM leg of the USA's strategic triad is to retain its credibility then a replacement missile is urgently needed.

Above: By May 1983 President Reagan was attempting to win Congressional support for the installation of MX missiles in existing Minuteman silos, with minimal additional equipment and new command and control systems, as shown in this artist's impression.

The original schemes for mobile basing of MX, or 'Peacekeeper', were replaced in November 1982 by the so-called 'dense pack' or Closely Spaced Basing Plan. In the face of widespread skepticism and a Congressional demand for a review of alternative proposals, and with the renewed support of the Joint Chiefs of Staff, the new plan to use Minuteman silos was revealed by Caspar Weinberger in April 1983. The diagram shows the dispersal of the two types of missile in a Minuteman field.

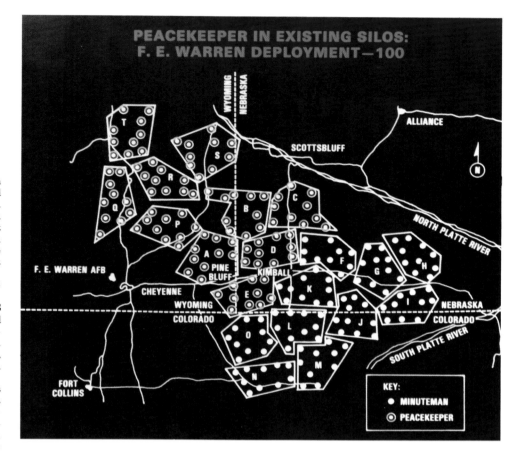

invested a minimum of $150 billion more than the US on SNF in just the last ten years (and some $700 billion in overall military spending). The SNF spending proposed by the Reagan Administration is only slightly more than that proposed in 1980 by the Carter Administration for the same period, and commands about the same share of defense expenditures ($7\frac{1}{2}$ per cent in 1982, 9 per cent in 1983).

The annual report to Congress of the US Joint Chiefs of Staff, for fiscal year 1983, contained charts and graphs that show the US inferior to the USSR in both pre-attack and post-exchange SNF as far ahead as projected—1992, or 12 years after the election of Mr. Reagan. Those projections assume successful, on-time completion of all SNF modernization programs.

Since the essence of US strategic policy is deterrence, it is essential that *surviving* forces —i.e., those that can endure enemy attacks— be capable of accomplishing the strategic missions set for them. The Reagan Administration has affirmed its commitment to the strategic doctrine and objectives that have evolved since the early 1970s, which the Carter Administration grouped under the terms "Countervailing strategy" and "Essential Equivalence". This requires a diversified strategic force capable of surviving "well-executed surprise attacks," and fulfilling a range of missions, including flexible targeting and escalation control. In addition, in both perception and reality, it would be equal to the strategic force capabilities of the USSR.

It seems clear that US SNF during the 1980s will fall short of these requirements. The prestigious US Committee on the Present Danger concluded in its 1982 assessment of the strategic balance that: "Without a major redirected effort, US strategic forces will not meet established requirements at any time in the 1980s."

The implications of this for US strategic doctrine and objectives, and for Western security, do not seem to have been thoroughly digested.

Below: Pave Paws phased array radar is part of SAC's early warning network being upgraded to detect increasingly advanced Soviet strategic missile threat.

Footnotes

The most recent DoD Report has separate sections covering Strategic Nuclear Forces, Theater Nuclear Forces, and Conventional Forces.

1. Edmund Beard, *Developing the ICBM* (New York: Columbia University Press, 1976). While the history of the development and deployment of US strategic ballistic missiles is most thoroughly contained in assorted Congressional Hearings and US Government histories, the reader is encouraged to refer to this excellent account for the ICBM story and to Harvey M. Sapolsky, *The Polaris System Development* (Cambridge, Mass: Harvard University Press, 1972) for the Polaris story.
2. The principal civilian mover was Trevor Gardner, Special Assistant for Research and Development to the Secretary of the Air Force. Under Gardner's sponsorship and guidance, a civilian Strategic Missile Evaluation Committee, chaired by John von Neumann, validated the feasibility of an ICBM and urged a greater US effort.
3. This approach is best described in Alain C. Enthoven and K. Wayle Smith, *How Much is Enough?* (New York: Harper & Row, 1971), pp. 176 and *passim*. Mr. Enthoven was Assistant Secretary of Defense for Systems Analysis during these years.
4. This address may be found in William W. Kaufmann, *The MacNamara Strategy* (New York: Harper & Row, 1964). The other quotations that follow are taken from that book, annual Department of Defense reports, or Pentagon news releases.
5. This rationale and the following quote can be found in *How Much is Enough?, op. cit.*
6. Alton Frye, "US Decision Making for SALT", in Mason Willrich and John Rhinelander, *SALT: The Moscow Agreements and Beyond* (New York: The Free Press, 1974), p. 66.
7. The throw-weight and payload limits of the light Minuteman ICBM did not allow large MIRVs anyway; a new, larger ICBM would have had to be developed and produced. One designed and proposed by the USAF was rejected by the Administration precisely to avoid the deployment of larger MIRVs and a good hard-target counterforce capability.
8. Report of Secretary of Defense Schlesinger to the Congress on the FY 1975 Defense Budget and FY 1975–1979 Defense Program, 93rd Congress, 2nd Session, March 4, 1974.
9. Speech to the American Legion National Convention, Boston, August 20, 1980.
10. News Conference of March 31, 1982. *New York Times*, April 1, 1982.
11. *Washington Post*, April 30, 1982.
12. *Has America Become Number 2? The US—Soviet Military Balance and American Defense Policies and Programs*, Washington, DC, 1982.

The United States Army

Lt. Col. Donald B. Vought, US Army (Ret.), former specialist instructor, US Army Command and General Staff College, Fort Leavenworth, Kansas, and

Lt. Col. David K. Riggs, instructor, Department of Joint and Combined Operations, US Army Command and General Staff College.

WITH SOME 790,000 personnel, the regular US Army constitutes the principal land fighting element of the US armed forces. United States military involvement in Vietnam (circa 1965–73) provided combat experience for a professional generation of officers and NCOs. This experience was, however, obtained at a price. National focus on the Vietnam struggle inhibited research and development of weapons and support systems for more conventional battle in different geographical environments. Similarly, Army organizational development suffered a "decade of neglect". Subsequent to the Vietnam War, Army modernization was low on the list of priorities, thereby slowing the transition from the Southeast Asian orientation to a force capable of employment on a global scale.

Geopolitical factors pose some considerations which affect Army structure and doctrinal development. The most prominent of these is the problem of projecting military power abroad. A question which influences Army planners is how to structure forces for possible employment anywhere in the world when the various areas and different types of employment each call for a fundamentally different force.

The need to have the capability to project military power across the world's major oceans influences US defense planners in significant ways. First is the need for air and sea forces capable of moving and sustaining Army units as well as carrying out combat functions in their own elements. This requires a distribution of resources indicated by the budgetary figures shown in the table below.

Another factor arising from the need for power projection which influences armed service planners is interservice cooperation. The necessity for unified effort involving Army, Navy and Air Force elements has prompted development of a Joint Staff system and an accompanying philosophy of cooperation. As a result, US military services have unusually close working relationships which are routinely exercised. The US Army, as the major land fighting element which is ever-sensitive to the logistics of overseas operations, plays a leading role in the joint service arena.

It is evident that US Army planners of the late 1970s faced several problems which went beyond the budget and manpower constraints inherent in democracies. We have noted power projection and the need for close inter-service cooperation. There were, in addition, problems which arose from America's worldwide defense commitments. The US Army had to be prepared to operate in widely varying geographical and climatic conditions as well as at different levels of conflict intensity. It had to be ready to fight on a relatively unsophisticated battlefield as well as against numerous, highly mechanized, technologically sophisticated forces typified by the Warsaw Pact.

Against this galaxy of needs, US assessments of possible military threats in the 1980s led the Army's leadership to two conclusions. One was that, given the numerical and technological realities, US forces could not win relying primarily on attrition and a tactical doctrine focused on defense. The second conclusion was that, while the Army would have to be organized and equipped to win on the conventional battlefield, it would also have to be prepared to respond to enemy-initiated use of chemical or nuclear weapons.

These conclusions prompted two efforts which are having profound effects on the US Army today. One is a new tactical doctrine which has been labeled the Airland Battle, and the other is an organizational change of the field forces (Corps, Divisions and divisional units) to accommodate the new doctrine and the new weapons systems scheduled for distribution over the next decade.

US Army Tactical Doctrine

The principles of US Army doctrine, and therefore the shape and form of the ground forces, are heavily influenced by economics, existing attitudes of the American people, and the perceived potential threat. US and NATO strategists envision the greatest threat, although a less probable threat, as coming from the Soviet Union or the Warsaw Pact, and being principally directed against Western Europe. Therefore, US ground forces are structured, and doctrine is developed, to address a potential war in Europe. Given an attack by the Warsaw Pact with little or no early warning, the Warsaw Pact enjoys a quantitative advantage in numbers of division, tanks, artillery and aircraft. To counter this numerical advantage, the United States has developed qualitatively superior equipment, and a tactical doctrine that is designed to defeat an attacking numerically superior enemy. A tactical concept that combines maneuver forces with artillery and close air support in addition to the other elements of the combined arms formation has been emphasized in the development of today's tactical doctrine. Tanks, infantry, attack helicopters and close air support by high performance aircraft are mutually supporting.

Budgetary Allocation by Service 1976–81
in Billion of dollars and (%)

Year	Army	Navy	Air Force	Def. Agencies
1976	21.4 (24.3)	28.5 (32.4)	26.4 (30.0)	11.6 (13.2)
1977	23.9 (25.0)	30.9 (32.3)	27.9 (29.2)	12.9 (13.5)
1978	26.0 (25.2)	33.5 (32.5)	29.2 (28.3)	14.3 (13.9)
1979	28.8 (25.0)	37.8 (32.8)	32.3 (28.1)	16.2 (14.1)
1980	34.6 (25.3)	47.1 (34.4)	41.7 (30.4)	13.6 (9.9)
1981	42.4 (25.1)	57.5 (34.2)	52.4 (31.1)	16.2 (9.6)
1982 (Projected)	53.0 (25.7)	69.7 (33.8)	65.8 (31.9)	17.8 (8.6)

The US Army's most valuable asset is its men and women, and in particular its combat troops (below). But they can do little without the backing of modern weaponry, as exemplified by the M1 Abrams main battle tank (left). The experience in Southeast Asia has now been put behind them and there is a new spirit abroad. Further, the equipment deficiencies are rapidly being made good, although many of the programs are suffering from serious cost and time overruns caused, at least in part, by a desire to be always in the forefront of technological development. Considerable thought is also being given to tactical concepts leading to the current AirLand Battle, and, in particular, to the daring and innovative AirLand Battle 2000.

Organization of the Department of the Army

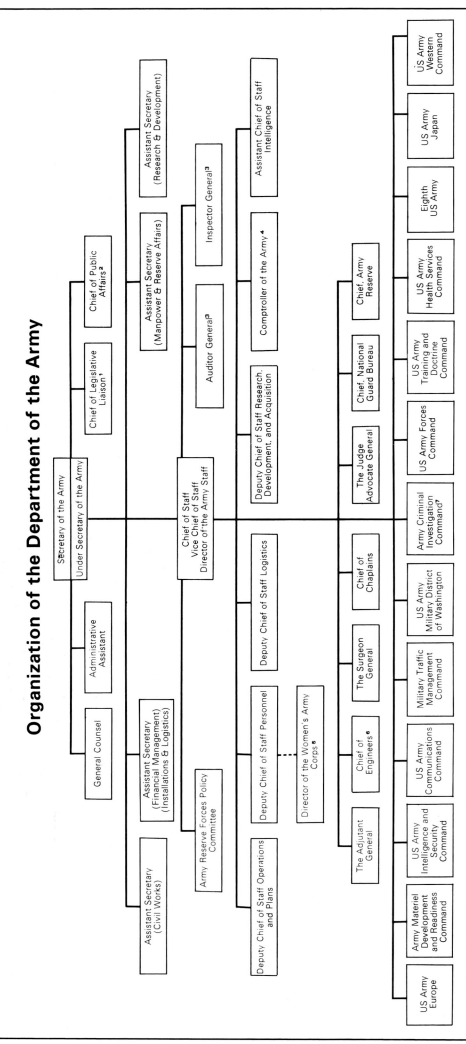

1 Chief of Legislative Liaison reports directly to the Secretary of the Army and is responsive to the Chief of Staff.
2 The Chief of Public Affairs reports directly to the Secretary of the Army and is responsive to the Chief of Staff.
3 The Inspector General and Auditor General serve as the confidential agent of and report directly to the Secretary of the Army and to the Chief of Staff upon the morale, discipline, efficiency, and economy of the Army.
4 The Comptroller of the Army is under the direction and supervision of, and is directly responsible to, the Assistant Secretary of the Army (Financial Management), with concurrent responsibility to the Chief of Staff.
5 The Director of the Women's Army Corps advises the Secretary of the Army and Chief of Staff on matters relating to Women's Army Corps and as a personal staff officer has direct access to the Chief of Staff.
6 The Chief of Engineers reports through the Assistant Secretary of the Army (Civil Works) to the Secretary of the Army on civil works matters.
7 Commander, US Army Criminal Investigation Command reports directly and concurrently to the Secretary of the Army and the Chief of Staff on criminal investigation matters.

Statutory Role of the Army, Title 10, United States Code, Section 3062

The role of the US Army is drawn from many interrelated sources—legal, philosophical, and historical. As an expression of the will and intent of the Congress, the Army's legal role—as expressed in Title 10, United States Code, Section 3062, is the principal basis of Army philosophy. Under this statute:

"(a) It is the intent of Congress to provide an Army that is capable, in conjunction with the other armed forces, of:—

"(1) preserving the peace and security, and providing for the defense, of the United States, the Territories, Commonwealths, and possessions, and any areas occupied by the United States;

"(2) supporting the national policies;

"(3) implementing the national objectives; and

"(4) overcoming any nations responsible for aggressive acts that imperil the peace and security of the United States.

"(b) In general, the Army, within the Department of the Army, includes land combat and service forces and such aviation and water transport as may be organic, therein. It shall be organized, trained, and equipped primarily for prompt and sustained combat incident to operations on land. It is responsible for the preparation of land forces necessary for the effective prosecution of war except as otherwise assigned and, in accordance with integrated joint mobilization plans, for the expansion of the peacetime components of the Army to meet the needs of war.

"(c) The Army consists of:—
"(1) the Regular Army, the Army National Guard of the United States, the Army National Guard while in the service of the United States, and the Army Reserve; and
"(2) all persons appointed or enlisted in, or conscripted into, the Army without component.

"(d) The organized peace establishment of the Army consists of all:—
"(1) military organizations of the Army with their installations and supporting and auxiliary elements, including combat, training, administrative and logistic elements; and
"(2) members of the Army, including those not assigned to units; necessary to form the basis for a complete and immediate mobilization for the national defense in the event of a national emergency."

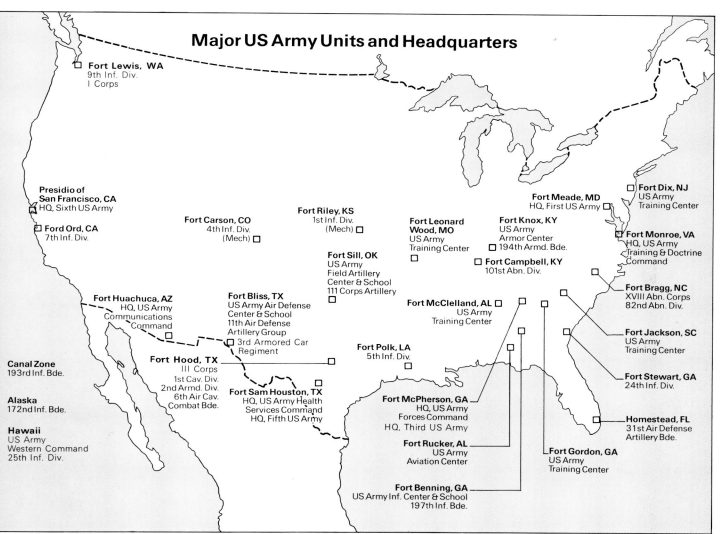

Major US Army Units and Headquarters

Fort Lewis, WA
9th Inf. Div.
I Corps

Presidio of San Francisco, CA
HQ, Sixth US Army

Ford Ord, CA
7th Inf. Div.

Fort Carson, CO
4th Inf. Div.
(Mech)

Fort Riley, KS
1st Inf. Div.
(Mech)

Fort Leonard Wood, MO
US Army
Training Center

Fort Knox, KY
US Army
Armor Center
194th Armd. Bde.

Fort Meade, MD
HQ, First US Army

Fort Dix, NJ
US Army
Training Center

Fort Monroe, VA
HQ, US Army
Training & Doctrine
Command

Fort Huachuca, AZ
HQ, US Army
Communications
Command

Fort Sill, OK
US Army
Field Artillery
Center & School
111 Corps Artillery

Fort Campbell, KY
101st Abn. Div.

Fort McClelland, AL
US Army
Training Center

Fort Bragg, NC
XVIII Abn. Corps
82nd Abn. Div.

Fort Bliss, TX
US Army Air Defense
Center & School
11th Air Defense
Artillery Group
3rd Armored Car
Regiment

Fort Jackson, SC
US Army
Training Center

Canal Zone
193rd Inf. Bde.

Fort Hood, TX
III Corps
1st Cav. Div.
2nd Armd. Div.
6th Air Cav.
Combat Bde.

Fort Polk, LA
5th Inf. Div.

Fort Stewart, GA
24th Inf. Div.

Alaska
172nd Inf. Bde.

Fort Sam Houston, TX
HQ, US Army Health
Services Command
HQ, Fifth US Army

Fort McPherson, GA
HQ, US Army
Forces Command
HQ, Third US Army

Homestead, FL
31st Air Defense
Artillery Bde.

Hawaii
US Army
Western Command
25th Inf. Div.

Fort Rucker, AL
US Army
Aviation Center

Fort Gordon, GA
US Army
Training Center

Fort Benning, GA
US Army Inf. Center & School
197th Inf. Bde.

Similarly, the Soviet force structure and doctrine are influenced by economics and the perceived threat, but additionally they are influenced by geography. The Soviet Union west of the Urals is primarily an open plain with low density population centers. Her historical enemies are the Germans in the west and the Chinese in the east, and she fears that an attack by one might stimulate an attack by the other, thus causing a two-front war. This fear and the experiences of WWII have contributed to Soviet reliance on massed forces and weapons systems to provide momentum for the attack. The Soviets hope to attain this momentum through echelonment of forces. Offensive operations in Western Europe are, however, not afforded the wide geographic expanse for maneuver these massed formations require. Instead, ground forces would be restricted by urban sprawl, numerous water obstacles, and terrain-restricted directions of attack. Blitzkrieg-type offensive operations that would be very appropriate for open country may no longer be as feasible in Western Europe as was once the case. Concentrating masses of men and materiel would provide the defender with lucrative targets, particularly if nuclear weapons were employed. The various obstacles and defenses would slow, halt, or fragment advancing forces. Even if the attacking force is able to concentrate, the attacker would still sustain staggering losses. His ability to sustain continuous operations in view of these losses and the disruption of successive echelons to the rear of the disintegrating forward elements is questionable.

Thus the Soviet war machine, offensive in nature, will be faced with critical limitations. Certainly not all Soviet forces can be or would be directed against operations in Western Europe. US strategists realize full well that, in the event of hostilities in Europe, NATO will initially be on the defensive, and the United States will be forced to fight with available

European-based forces until such time as NATO brings its full power to bear.

The US Army's tactical doctrine, as promulgated in 1976, called for countering the enemy— i.e. responding to the enemy's initiatives—an essentially defensive orientation. The new doctrine, which was officially approved in 1982, might best be summarized as follows: *to secure the initiative and exercise it aggressively to defeat the opposing forces.* This new and tactically more aggressive style is having far-reaching effects on Army training and organization. It calls, for instance, for greater use of maneuver and a greater recognition of human factors as elements of battle. As much an attitudinal change as a physical one, there are four tenets derived from the operational concept.

The first is *initiative*—to gain the ability to act and thereby cause the enemy to react to US forces rather than the reverse. Inevitably gaining and retaining the initiative will entail risks wherein the commander's judgment becomes the final determinent of where he can afford weakness in order to increase strength at the critical point(s).

Below: The M1 Abrams main battle tank is bringing a new capability to the armored units of the US Army. The 60-ton tank has a top speed on roads of 45mph (72.4km/hour) and a cruising range of 280 miles (450km). It has improved day and night fire control, better ammunition and fuel protection and superior mobility, giving a new impetus to the armored battle.

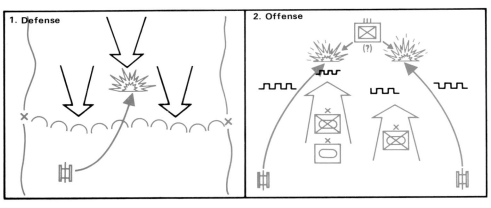

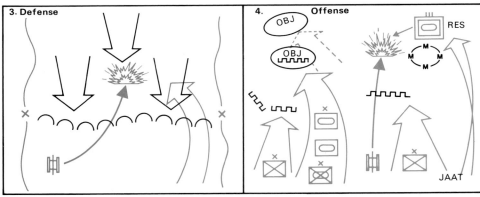

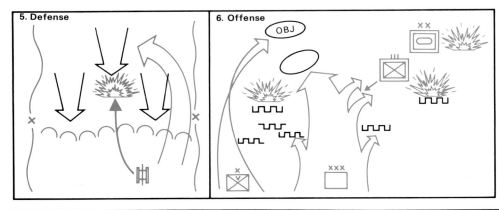

1–2: DELAY OF FORCES TO PREVENT REINFORCEMENT

The first form of depth attack is used both when in defense (1) and in attack (2). The aim is to disrupt the enemy forces in depth particularly the second echelon, to delay (or even prevent) their arrival in the battle area. This enables the enemy forces in contact to be isolated and then defeated in detail. Deception, offensive electronic warfare, artillery fire, counter-battery fire and air interdiction will all be used in this form of deep battle. The commander must decide when he needs particular enemy units isolated in this way, and this is the window of opportunity towards which all efforts are directed.

3–4: DELAY IN ENEMY FORCES TO ALLOW MANEUVER COMPLETION

The second concept also involves attacking the enemy deep forces with fire. Its aim, however, is not so much to prevent the reinforcement of committed forces, as in (1) and (2) above, but rather to prevent them from interfering with own forces' attacks or counterattacks against the flanks or rear of enemy close-battle forces. Valuable targets in the deep battle may be different from those in the close-in battle, for example, bridges may be higher value targets than tactical units when the aim is to prevent the arrival and deployment of the second echelon.

5–6: DECISIVE DEEP ATTACK

The third form of tactical operation in this concept is both more complex and more difficult to achieve. It involves the engagement of the enemy follow-on echelon with both firepower and maneuver forces at the same time as the close-in battle continues. This is designed to stop the enemy from massing, to deprive him of momentum, and, most important of all, to destroy his force in its entirety. This will require the use of every combat and support element in close harmony. It will also require very close coordination between Army air and ground maneuver forces, artillery, electronic warfare, and Air Force battlefield interdiction.

Another tenet is *depth*—a three dimensional consideration. Battlefield depth is time, resources and distance. These elements in combination provide momentum in the attack and elasticity in the defense. US commanders are expected to use their resources to gain depth for themselves while denying depth to their opponent. To do this, they will fight the "deep battle," i.e. the battle against enemy uncommitted or follow-on forces. By delaying, disrupting and/or destroying the enemy's second echelon forces, the opponent is deprived of their use, thereby isolating his committed forces which are then destroyed in close-in battle.

The third tenet is *agility*—acting faster than the enemy. This involves not only the mental flexibility to analyze, decide and plan in the face of constantly changing circumstances, but to do so more rapidly than your opponent. Equipment and information systems which allow the commander to know about critical events as they occur are needed to support Agility, as are organizational procedures which permit the rapid tailoring of forces with the proper mix of personnel and equipment to capitalize on opportunities.

Synchronization, the last tenet, is defined as an all-pervading unity of effort. Implicit in the other tenets, synchronization goes beyond the mere coordination of diverse actions. It is considered to apply in joint service and allied operations as well as at lower levels. Fundamental to synchronization is awareness of the higher commanders' intentions so that all levels and activities involved are in pursuit of the same goals.

Operationally, the new doctrine calls for a tripartite view of the contemporary battlefield. While inextricably interrelated, the three concurrent battles are labeled Deep Battle, Close-In Battle, and Rear Area Protection. Not only are the three dependent on each other and therefore coequal, but planning must also take into account conventional, nuclear, and chemical environments, should the enemy employ nuclear or chemical weapons.

Since the main or close-in battle and protection of a fighting force's rear areas are universal military considerations, the Deep Battle is the US tactical concept which raises most questions. Essentially, Deep Battle involves disrupting, delaying or destroying second and succeeding echelons of enemy forces to prevent them from influencing the close-in battle. The tactic is particularly important when the enemy has a numerical advantage since successful application prevents massing at the critical point and time.

The term "window of opportunity" has been applied to operation of Deep Battle techniques. The commander determines at what point in time he needs particular enemy units isolated or capabilities reduced to win the close-in battle. This then becomes the window of opportunity toward which Deep Battle efforts are directed. While conceptually simple, the demands on planning, target acquisition and attack resources are inordinate. Valuable targets in the Deep Battle are not always the same as those for the Close-in Battle. Bridges, defiles or bridging equipment may constitute "higher payoff" targets than maneuver units when the

purpose is to prevent the enemy's second echelon from joining the close-in battle.

Deep Battle is fought at the brigade, division and corps levels with each level operating in different context, i.e. concerned with different size enemy units and using different weapons for their attack. The corps, however, is considered the primary level for Deep Battle planning and operations. Corps is the focal point for intelligence and target acquisition information from national and allied sources as well as for joint planning with the Air Force for employment of tactical aircraft.

Offensive Operations

Fundamental to the US Army's offensive operations are five concepts—concentration, surprise, speed, flexibility and audacity. Concentration to achieve local superiority followed by rapid dispersion to disrupt the enemy defensive efforts involves logistics as well as maneuver planning and execution. The definition of surprise has been expanded somewhat to include avoiding enemy strength and attacking his weaknesses. Speed, an element implicit in all of the concepts, has been defined more broadly than mere rapidity of movement on the battlefield. Speed includes any and all actions which promote the enemy's confusion as well as contributing to friendly maneuver. Flexibility in an environment where forces may cover 30 or more miles (50 or more km) a day, calls for the ability to exploit opportunities as they arise. Audacity recognizes risk but rejects tactical gamble.

Types of offensive operations describe the

The area of influence (7) is the operational
area assigned to a commander within
which he is capable of acquiring and
fighting enemy units with assets organic to
his command, plus any assigned to him in
support of the particular operation. The
size of the area will vary according to the
prevailing conditions and the superior
officer's plans. The latter also designates
the front and flanking boundaries of
the area. The area of interest (8) extends
beyond the area of influence to include any
enemy forces capable of affecting
operations by the formation concerned.

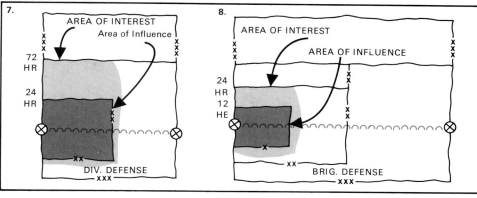

9.

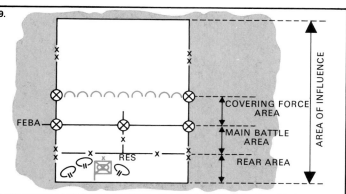

ORGANIZATION OF THE DEFENSE

The purpose of the defense is to provide an opportunity to gain the
initiative, and commanders are expected to combine elements of
static and dynamic tactical action. With this increased emphasis on
offensive action and agility, reserve forces have become
particularly important for counterattacks.

AIRLAND BATTLE 2000

The US Army's most recent battle methodology is a totally new
concept entitled AirLand Battle 2000. The central idea is a strategic
defense of NATO's central region by aggressive tactics, which
would include immediate, sustained and simultaneous attacks
both in depth and on the line of contact.

Based on a 20-year Soviet threat projection, assessments
conclude that the US Army, heavily outnumbered in both men and
equipment, would be foolish to fight a war of attrition. Rather, the
plan is for the Army to defend offensively, to strike quickly at
Soviet assault echelons, while seeing subsequent echelons, in an
attempt to finalize this stage of the battle before the enemy's
follow-up armies join the fray. The intention is to attack the enemy
throughout the depth of his formation with air, artillery and
electronic means, and by use of high maneuverability. It is planned
to confuse the enemy and cause him to fight in more than one
direction, by deploying ground maneuver forces to the rear of his
advance echelons. The Army will take advantage of the Soviet
tactics which (as they exist today) mean there is an inevitable
time-lag between follow-on echelons, such periods normally being
lulls in the intense fighting. AirLand Battle tactics will upset the
enemy's advance timetable, and force him to change his plans even
to the extent of altering routes or splitting forces, so that hopefully
subsequent defending forces will not have to face enemy forces
too strong for them to defeat.

A scenario would have a US Army brigade attack the enemy's
first echelon assault regiments while "seeing" the first echelon
assault divisions. These are attacked by a US Army division, which
at the same time "sees" the first echelon assault armies. These in
turn are attacked by the US Army corps which must also disrupt the
timetable of the second echelon divisions of the first echelon armies.

The depth attack, penetrating as much as 200 miles (321 km),
would be by fully integrated air forces (hence the air-land aspect),
indirect fire systems and by deep penetration ground units. The
concept will entail small combat units which will operate
relatively independently of each other. It also includes tactics for
fighting in 360 degrees to meet the threat posed by the Warsaw
Pact tactics; indeed, almost challenging them to attempt to
surround the Army's agile combat forces. The concept will depend
heavily on new technology, especially in communications, and in
the rapid collection and assessment of intelligence data. Brigade
commanders will have to know their superior commanders'
intent, rather than have constant dialogue with them, thus
combining the strategic and tactical levels.

---

purpose rather than a method and have not
changed from earlier listings: movement to
contact—hasty attack—deliberate attack— exploitation—pursuit.

Movement to contact is intended to develop
the situation while maintaining the commander's freedom of actions. Organization for a
movement to contact calls for a covering force
of highly mobile units to find the enemy and
provide time for the main body to deploy. An
"advance guard" is provided to prevent light
enemy resistance from delaying the main body
and to facilitate movement by obstacle removal
and bridge repair. The "main body" moves on
multiple routes in the form of combined arms
teams with their logistical support or as "pure"
units which are prepared for cross attachment
and rapid deployment. Ground units serving as
"flank" and "rear guards" are detached from
the main body to increase security during
movement.

Hasty attacks are called for as a result of a
meeting engagement or a successful defense.

Above right: Whatever the strategies and
tactics dreamt up by the generals and their
staffs, the final and decisive factor is the
human material of the army; how will
these young men fight in Europe?

Right: Airborne soldiers bringing their
105mm M102 howitzer into action after an
air-drop. The airborne units are among the
best trained and most professional in the
US Army. There are 10 airborne battalions,
9 of them in 82nd Airborne Division.

Speed in concentrating forces and surprise compensate for the lack of thorough preparation. A well-organized defense usually requires a deliberate attack involving the full range of weaponry and techniques.

Exploitation and *pursuit* follow successful attacks. Commanders exploit a successful attack by aggressively moving to disrupt enemy defenses after a penetration has been made. Pursuit of a withdrawing enemy calls for the commander to maintain pressure, thus preventing the enemy from organizing a delaying action.

Defensive Operations

As with the offense, the changes in defense called for in the 1982 Operations Manual are more spirit and operational style than mechanical or definitional. The defense is considered more a matter of purpose than form with offensive combat characterizing operations. There is no single deployment or technique prescribed for the defense. Commanders are expected to combine elements of the static and dynamic forms in light of their mission, terrain, relative strength and mobility. In this context, "static" defense implies retention of particular terrain and tends to rely on fire power to destroy the enemy. "Dynamic" defense orients more on the enemy force than on retention of terrain objectives and tends to greater use of maneuver against attacking forces.

Deep Battle techniques have affected the role and subsequently the composition of the "covering force". In order to gain maximum effects from the enemy's early deployment, which may reveal his intentions, the covering force not only establishes contact but develops the situation. Ideally, the covering force will defeat the enemy's lead elements while Deep Battle actions delay follow-on units by aerial interdiction and other means. Covering forces are organized around tank-heavy task forces with aviation, artillery, air defense artillery, engineer and intelligence support. The covering force is expected to employ a full range of tactical options in halting and forcing the enemy to deploy; delay alone will not usually suffice. Withdrawal will normally not be uniform but take place only when forced by enemy pressure. Elements of the covering force which can do so remain forward of the main battle area, hindering enemy operations, adding to the commander's surveillance capabilities, and when possible attacking enemy forces from the flank or rear.

With the increased emphasis on offensive actions and battlefield agility, reserve forces become particularly important to the commander. Formally designated reserves usually only apply at brigade and higher levels. Here, however, reserves may constitute a third of the force. Since the purpose of defense is to provide an opportunity to gain the initiative, reserves (whether fire power or maneuver units) will be employed in decisive counterattacks rather than in simply restoring the defensive position.

The heightened emphasis on rear area protection is a function of the increased demands on command and control systems as well as the high volume of fuel and ammunition consumption which the battlefield of the future will entail. Combat support and combat service support (logistics) units will be dispersed to avoid presenting lucrative targets but must be mutually supporting for possible rear area combat operations. The commander's allocation of resources and placement takes into account the probabilities of enemy air mobile, nuclear, chemical and conventional air attack along with sabotage and unconventional warfare.

Right: An 81mm mortar crew from a line infantry battalion on a training range. Airborne and special forces may have a more glamorous public image, but it is overall equality of the ordinary infantry units which is the ultimate measure of the quality and efficiency of an army.

Major US Army Units and Headquarters in Germany

NETHERLANDS

Hamburg

Bremen

Hannover

Berlin

EAST GERMANY

Dortmund

Cologne

Bonn

WEST GERMANY
(Federal Republic and West Berlin)

Frankfurt
V Corps
3rd Armored Division

Würzburg
3rd Infantry Division

Bad Kreuznach
8th Infantry Division

Heidelberg
HQ, US Army Europe and Seventh Army

Ansbach
1st Armored Division

Moerhingen
VII Corps

FRANCE

Munich

SWITZERLAND

US Armored and Mechanized Infantry Divisions in Europe		
	Armored Div.	Mechanized Inf. Div.
Tank Battalions	6	5
Mechanized Infantry Battalions	5	6
Major Weapons Systems		
M60A1 ⎫		
M60A3 ⎬ Tanks	324	316
M1 ⎭		
M113 APC	418	463
M113 TOW ⎫ Anti-	152	170
Dragon ⎬ armor Systems	244	284
M109A1 ⎫ Arty.	72	72
M110 ⎭	12	12
Chaparral ⎫ Air Defense	24	24
Vulcan ⎬ Gun/	24	24
Stinger ⎭ Missiles	72 teams	72 teams

Above: M113 armored personnel carriers are transported across a river in Germany on a Mobile Assault Bridge (MAB). In rapid advances the ability to throw bridges quickly across water obstacles is vital.

Below: American soldiers must be capable of fighting in any type of terain anywhere in the world; from Germany to Korea, from Alaska to the deserts of Africa. It is a daunting challenge, but is now accepted.

The Corps

Organizational implications of the new tactical doctrine—airland battle—are extensive. All levels of operational forces must be modified to support the new doctrine and to accommodate the rapidly changing technology. While never intended to be organizationally rigid, the type of corps which has been designed for the European Theater is shown below.

The heavy corps design envisions operating with from 3⅔ divisions to 5 divisions. A type corps will have a minimum strength of some 0,000 personnel, less assigned divisions, and be capable of expansion as needed. Design considerations include provisions for coordination with allied forces and the increased operational participation with US Tactical Air Forces.

The Division

A total of 16 divisions make up the active army ground combat force. Within these divisions are found combat support elements consisting of artillery, air defense artillery, military intelligence, signal, chemical and engineers. Combat service support elements consisting of quartermaster, transportation, military police, medical services, and those others responsible for the care and maintenance of the Army are also organic to the division.

The division is the largest force that is trained and fought as a combined arms team. It is a balanced, self-sustaining force that normally conducts operations as part of a larger force, but is capable of conducting independent operations, especially when supplemented by additional combat support and combat service support elements. Normally, the division fights as part of a corps, with three to five divisions making up the corps force. The division is designed to fight conventional operations, or a mixture of conventional and chemical-nuclear operations, in any part of the world.

While the division is the basic combined arms formation, it is the battalion (rather than the regiment, as is the case with the Soviet Ground Forces) that is the basic maneuver unit. The battalion fights as a part of a brigade, with normally three to five battalions comprising a brigade. Each division has three brigade headquarters to which battalions are assigned as the command sees fit. The HQ of the Cavalry Brigade Air Attack also has the capability of controlling ground maneuver units which, in effect, gives the division an additional brigade level headquarters.

Heavy maneuver battalions—armor and mechanized infantry—fight best in open country operations, in any part of the world. using terrain to maximum advantage. The light maneuver forces—rifle infantry, air assault infantry, airborne infantry, and ranger infantry—are ideally suited to more restricted terrain where close-in fighting becomes the norm. The maneuver elements of the division are grouped together under brigade control in accordance with the terrain, the enemy they

US Army Corps Organisation

```
                        XXX
                      [CORPS]
   I          III         X          I          X
 [HHC]      [ACR]      [AVN]    [HHB CORPS   [ARTY
                                  ARTY]      BRIG]
        X         X           III          X
      [SIG]     [MP]        [CEWI]       [ENGR]
        X         III          X          XX
      [NBC]     [ADA]       [RACO]     [COSCOM]
```

Key:
HHC = HQ HQ Co.
ACR = Armored Cav. Regt.
AVN = Aviation
HHB = HQ HQ Battery
SIG = Signals
MP = Military Police
CEWI = Combat EW Intelligence

ADA = Air Defense Artillery
RACO = Rear Area Combat Ops.
COSCOM = Corps Support Command
NBC = Nuclear/Biological/Chemical
ENGR = Engineer
ARTY = Artillery

Current Division Forces

	Active Duty Div (Bdes)	Reserve Component Div (Bdes)
AR	4 (12)	2 (6)
Mech Infantry	6 (16) +2 Reserve	1 (3)
Infantry	4 (10) +2 Reserve	5 (15)
Air Assault	1 (3)	
Airborne	1 (3)	
Total Div (Bdes)	16 (44)	8 (24)
Separate Bde (Incl 4 RO)		
AR	1	4
Mech Infantry	1	7
Infantry	0	5
CBAC	1	0
Armored Cav Rgt	3	4
Theater Force Bdes	3	4
Total Separate Bdes	9	24

face, and the mission they must accomplish.

Tank and mechanized infantry battalions rarely fight as pure organic units, but are cross-attached or task-organized by the brigade commanders to perform specific mission tasks to utilize more fully their capabilities and offset each other's vulnerabilities. After the division commander has visualized how he wishes to fight the battle, he allocates maneuver units to the brigade commanders, who in turn cross-attach these forces to optimize the weapon systems of each unit. The resultant battalion task forces are a combination of tank and mechanized infantry companies under the command of a battalion commander. A tank-heavy force would normally be structured to operate in open, rolling terrain, while the mechanized-infantry-heavy task force is better suited to operate in more restricted terrain and built-up areas. An even mix of tank and mechanized infantry results in a balanced task force that provides great flexibility to the commander. A balanced force would normally be structured when information about the enemy is vague or when the terrain is mixed and variable.

Because of global contingencies, US Army force structure must provide for several types of divisions since the division is the basic combined arms formation wherein armor, infantry, artillery and supporting functions are employed on the battlefield. Designs for light divisions (infantry, airborne, airmobile) are not firm at this time. In general terms, light divisions will have strengths of approximately 17,000. With transportability as a major factor, these divisions will rely on armor-defeating systems other than tanks, e.g. TOW missiles. Each division will have 9 or 10 infantry battalions and supporting units comparable to the heavy division but scaled to their lighter weaponry support requirements. Currently, it is anticipated that six divisions will be light (1 airborne, 1 airmobile, 4 infantry), the remaining ten heavy.

Tank Battalion

The tank battalion has 565 officers and enlisted personnel organized into four tank companies and an HQ company. Each tank company has three platoons of four tanks each. Maintenance and support functions are consolidated in the battalion HQ company, as are a scout platoon and a six-tube mortar platoon. Currently tank battalions may have M60A1, M60A3 or the M1 Abrams tank. The M60A1 has a 105mm gun which is highly effective at 2,190 yards (2000m) and a cruising range of 310 miles (50 km). The M60A3 has a similar chassis but its main gun is stabilized for firing on the move. The M1 Abrams tank is the newest system and will replace the several models of M60 over the next few years.

The new tank battalion is designed to employ 58 of the M1 tanks. With its improved day and night fire control capability, compartmentalized fuel and ammunition storage and stabilized gun, the Abrams is the primary ground combat weapons system of the US Army for the 1980s. The 60-ton Abrams has a top speed of 45mph (73 kmh) and cruising range of 280 miles (450km). While it will eventually be equipped with a 120 mm smoothbore gun of German design, the initial Abrams will have the standard U

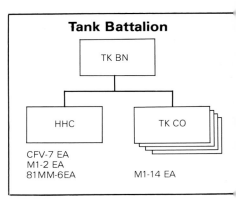

Tank Battalion

TK BN
- HHC
  - CFV-7 EA
  - M1-2 EA
  - 81MM-6EA
- TK CO
  - M1-14 EA

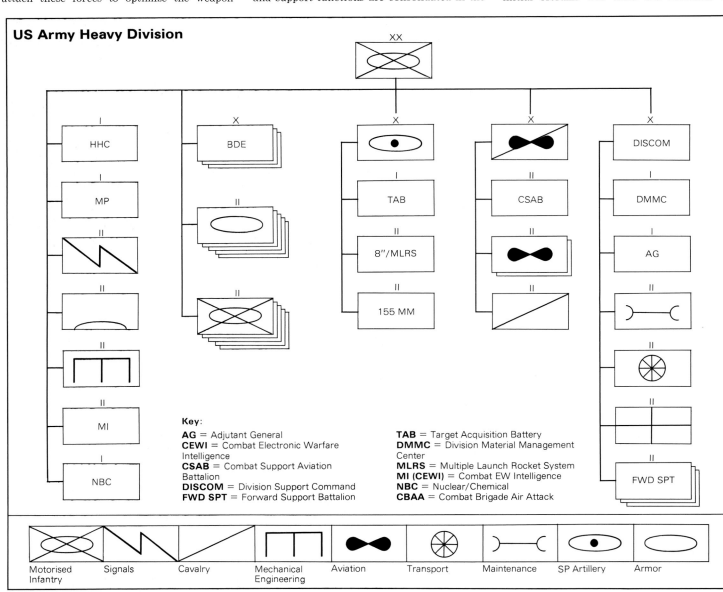

US Army Heavy Division

Key:
AG = Adjutant General
CEWI = Combat Electronic Warfare Intelligence
CSAB = Combat Support Aviation Battalion
DISCOM = Division Support Command
FWD SPT = Forward Support Battalion

TAB = Target Acquisition Battery
DMMC = Division Material Management Center
MLRS = Multiple Launch Rocket System
MI (CEWI) = Combat EW Intelligence
NBC = Nuclear/Chemical
CBAA = Combat Brigade Air Attack

Motorised Infantry · Signals · Cavalry · Mechanical Engineering · Aviation · Transport · Maintenance · SP Artillery · Armor

05mm tank gun.

Tanks use their mobility and combat power to outflank the enemy or to penetrate the enemy defenses. Once armor has broken through to the enemy rear, it destroys or disrupts the defenses in depth. Tanks are also well suited for rapid and dynamic exploitation and pursuit operations.

Mechanized Infantry Battalion

The mechanized infantry battalion has 880 officers and enlisted personnel organized into four mechanized rifle companies, an anti-armor company and an HQ company. The four-rifle-company configuration allows for cross-attachment with the similarly structured tank battalions. Each rifle company has three platoons of three squads each. Maintenance and support functions are consolidated in the battalion HQ company, along with a scout platoon and a mortar platoon. The anti-armor company has three platoons of two sections each, and contains a total of 12 Improved TOW Vehicles. (The TOW has a 3,280 yards/3,000m range.) Each rifle company has 9 Dragon (1,093 yards/1,000m range) man-portable anti-armor guided missiles.

The improved M2 Infantry Fighting Vehicle (IFV) is designed to provide infantry with cross-country mobility comparable to the Abrams tank. The 25-ton IFV has a top speed of 45mph (73kmh) a cruising range of 174 miles (280km). It carries a 25mm automatic cannon and a 62mm machinegun in a two-man turret equipped with day and night thermal sights. There are 54 IFVs in each mechanized infantry battalion.

The mechanized infantry usually operates as part of a combined arms force. The infantrymen

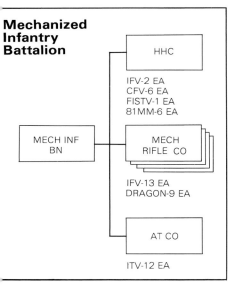

Mechanized Infantry Battalion

- MECH INF BN
  - HHC
    - IFV-2 EA
    - CFV-6 EA
    - FISTV-1 EA
    - 81MM-6 EA
  - MECH RIFLE CO
    - IFV-13 EA
    - DRAGON-9 EA
  - AT CO
    - ITV-12 EA

Top right: Although the basic **M60** tank design is now somewhat dated most are now being brought up to the M60A3 standard. This has many detailed improvements, but the main one is the fitting of a stabilizer which enables the main gun to be fired on the move. One inescapable problem is its height.

Right center: The M2 Infantry Fighting Vehicle is at last in service after a long and troubled development history. Designed to enable the infantry to have the same cross-country agility as the new M1 tanks it is extremely expensive and remains a contentious issue.

Right: DIVADS, the new divisional air defense weapon system. For years NATO pilots have warned of the effectiveness of the Soviet ZSU-23-4 air defense cannon system and it is only now that Western armies are getting something similar with which to challenge Warsaw Pact low-level air interdiction operations in forward areas.

remain mounted in their carriers until they are required to assault or forced to dismount by the enemy. The carriers displace to protected positions to provide supporting fire. The new infantry fighting vehicle (IFV) will greatly enhance the infantryman's ability to fight while mounted and protected.

Cavalry Brigade Air Attack (CBAA)

This organization of approximately 1,700 officers and enlisted personnel is designed to consolidate the aviation assets of the division as well as to provide an additional control headquarters. In addition to its headquarters troop, the CBAA has two attack helicopter battalions, a combat support aviation battalion and the division's cavalry squadron. Principal weapons of the attack helicopter battalions are their 21 AAH and 13 OH-58C (observation) aircraft. The cavalry squadron has two air cavalry troops which also have AAH and OH-58C aircraft (4 AAH, 6 OH-58C each). The two ground cavalry troops each have 19 cavalry fighting vehicles. Aerial movement of personnel and equipment, maintenance of aircraft and aerial observer support for the division artillery is provided by the combat support aviation battalion.

Below: The Hughes AH-64 is the outcome of a long development program for an armed helicopter for the US Army. The heavy armament can be seen on this aircraft as can the "black hole" engine exhaust outlets. The entire aircraft is able to withstand hits from 12.7mm rounds.

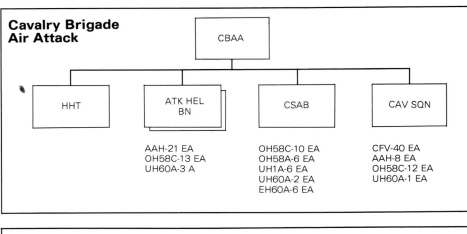

Cavalry Brigade Air Attack

CBAA

- HHT
- ATK HEL BN
  - AAH-21 EA
  - OH58C-13 EA
  - UH60A-3 A
- CSAB
  - OH58C-10 EA
  - OH58A-6 EA
  - UH1A-6 EA
  - UH60A-2 EA
  - EH60A-6 EA
- CAV SQN
  - CFV-40 EA
  - AAH-8 EA
  - OH58C-12 EA
  - UH60A-1 EA

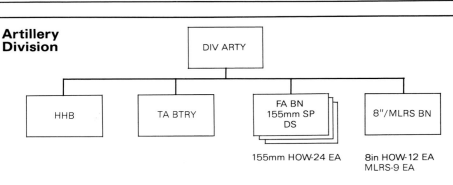

Artillery Division

DIV ARTY

- HHB
- TA BTRY
- FA BN 155mm SP DS
  - 155mm HOW-24 EA
- 8"/MLRS BN
  - 8in HOW-12 EA
  - MLRS-9 EA

Major US Army Units and Headquarters in Korea

CHINA

NORTH KOREA

SEA OF JAPAN

•Pyongyang

Camp Casey
2nd Infantry Div.
Youngsan
HQ, Eighth
US Army
Soul (Seoul)

SOUTH KOREA
28,486

•Pusan

Additionally, there are 2,364 US Army personnel serving in Japan

---

The AAH uses speed (145 knots) as well as natural and manmade cover and concealment (hills, trees, buildings, etc) to avoid enemy air defenses. Equipped with sights and night vision sensors, the two-man crew can navigate and attack in darkness or poor visibility. Upon sighting a target the AAH pops up from cover and fires one or more of its weapon systems. The weapons package for the AAH includes a 30mm chain gun, 2.75-inch rockets and the laser-homing Hellfire missile in various combinations.

The OH-58C is capable of speeds up to 120 knots and with its radar warning and heat suppression systems provides a survivable observation capability which can operate at night.

Division Artillery

With slightly over 3000 personnel, the division artillery organization follows traditional principles of direct support for the maneuver elements and a longer range capability to support the battle as a whole or general support. Each 155mm self-propelled howitzer battalion routinely supports one of the division's brigades. These battalions are fully mobile and can split their component batteries into two sections capable of independent operation. The general support battalion with its 8-inch howitzers and Multiple Launch Rocket Systems (MLRS) provides the division with an organic rocket capability as well as longer range weapons to fight the Deep Battle envisioned in the new tactical doctrine.

While the division 86 artillery has more guns than previous organizations, it is the improved responsiveness and flexibility which contributes most to its battlefield potency. Additional ammunition resupply capacity, additional fire direction capability and the integration of automated systems to speed key functions all increase artillery accuracy, lethality and responsiveness.

Left: The Sikorsky UH-60A Black Hawk is the Utility Tactical Transport System (UTTAS) for the Army and is designed to carry a squad of 11 equipped troops.

Right: The Multiple Launch Rocket System (MLRS) is organic to the division, and is an essential element of the Deep Battle concept. It has 12 rocket-tubes and the missiles have an 18-mile + (30km) range.

US Maneuver Forces mix and Locations

Armored Divisions
Ansbach, Germany
1st Armored Division
6 Armored   5 Mechanized

Fort Hood, Texas
2nd Armored Division
5 Armored   5 Mechanized
(3d Brigade in Germany)
(2 Armored   1 Mechanized)*

Frankfurt, Germany
3d Armored Division
6 Armored   5 Mechanized

Fort Hood, Texas
1st Cavalry Division
4 Armored   4 Mechanized
(2 Armored   1 Mechanized)*

Mechanized Divisions
Wurzburg, Germany
3d Infantry Division
6 Mechanized   4 Armored

Fort Carson, Colorado
4th Infantry Division
5 Mechanized   5 armored
(3d Brigade in Europe)
(1 Mechanized)

Fort Polk, Louisiana
5th Infantry Division
2 Armored   1 Mechanized (3 Infantry)*

Bad Kreuznach, Germany
8th Infantry Division
6 Mechanized   5 Armored

Fort Riley, Kansas
1st Infantry Division
5 Mechanized   5 Armored
(3d Brigade in Europe)
(1 Mechanized)*

Infantry Divisions
Korea
2nd Infantry Division
5 Infantry   2 Mechanized   1 Armored
(Still has HJ Battalion)

Fort Ord, California
7th Infantry Division
6 Infantry   (3 Infantry)*

Fort Stewart, Georgia
24th Mechanized Division
6 Infantry   (1 Armored   3 Mechanized)*

Fort Stewart, Georgia
24th Infantry Division
6 Infantry   (1 Armored   3 Mechanized)*

Hawaii
25th Infantry Division
6 Infantry

Air Assault Divisions
Fort Campbell, Kentucky
101st AASLT Division
9 Infantry (Ambl)   1 Tank Dest   1 Attack Hel

Airborne Divisions
Fort Bragg, North Carolina
82nd Airborne Division
9 Infantry (Abn)   1 Armored (Lt)

6th ACCB
Fort Hood, Texas
2 Attack Battalions   1 Air Cavalry Battalion

172d Infantry Brigade (Sep)
Fort Richardson, Alaska
3 Infantry

197th Infantry Brigade
Fort Benning, Georgia
1 Infantry   1 Mechanized   1 Armored (1 Mech)*

194th Armored Brigade
Fort Knox, Kentucky
2 Armored   1 Mechanized

Berlin Brigade
3 Infantry   1 Armored Company

193d Infantry Brigade
Panama
2 Infantry   1 Mechanized

2d Armored Cavalry Regiment
Nürnburg, Germany
3 Cavalry Squadron

3d Armored Cavalry Regiment
Fort Bliss, Texas
3 Cavalry Squadron

11th Armored Cavalry Regiment
Fulda, Germany
3 Cavalry Squadron

Ranger Battalions
Fort Stewart, Georgia
1st Battalion (Ranger)   75th Infantry

Fort Lewis, Washington
2d Battalion (Ranger)   75th Infantry

Airborne Task Force (TF)
Italy
1 Airborne (+)

Totals (Active/Roundout)

Infantry 38/9	Armored 48/6	
Airborne 10	Armored Cavalry 21	
Air Mobile 9	Air Cavalry 6	
Mechanized 47/8	Attack 3	
Ranger 2	Tank Des 1	

*Reserve Component Roundout Battalions.

Figure as of 31 Sept. 1981

U S ARMY

Deployment Considerations

While the organization, equipment and training of most ground forces is based on fighting in the European environment, with emphasis on armored and mechanized forces, recent Soviet demonstrations of the capability and willingness to project military power, directly or through proxy forces, has caused some re-evaluation of deployment considerations for US forces. The introduction during the 1980s of increasingly heavier tanks and infantry fighting vehicles and a host of mechanized supporting systems will significantly enhance the fire power and mobility of deployed forces in Europe. These same changes will significantly increase the strategic airlift and sealift required to move reinforcing units across the Atlantic.

In case of conflict between NATO and the Warsaw Pact, several factors combine to help alleviate the deployment problem. The existence of a forward base and depot structure in place in Europe, and the attendant ability to preposition both unit sets of equipment and required sustaining supplies allows rapid airlift of personnel with minimum accompanying equipment. Recent agreements between the United States and its European NATO allies will provide at least initial support by host nation support units, again reducing initial requirements to deploy logistical support forces with combat units. The commitment of European civilian cargo ships and aircraft to the deployment effort will further ease the burden on US capabilities. Finally, the advantage enjoyed by NATO forces in terms of familiarity with the terrain, established command and control systems, and exercise experience (including annual deployment exercises) combine to offer a high degree of assurance that timely reinforcement of Europe is feasible.

A similar set of circumstances, combined with a reduced requirement for armor and mechanized forces applies to deployment considerations for an outbreak of hostilities in Korea, although the distances involved are far greater.

No such advantages are currently found, however, when possible contingency requirements for Southwest Asia or other potential areas of conflict are considered. The requirement to maintain the capability to deploy forces rapidly to areas of the world where no US troops are forward deployed in peacetime, where no alliances currently exist and where equipment and supplies cannot be stockpiled in advance presents the army with critical challenges. Since such forces must not only be relatively lightly equipped for ease and rapidity of movement, yet possess sufficient firepower to combat a mechanized enemy, the Army is currently testing new organizational concepts and high-technology weapon systems to provide the required levels of both firepower and deployability. Other specially trained and equipped units (air assault, airborne and ranger) provide a current rapidly deployable force for wordwide contingencies.

The wide range of possible contingencies is reflected in the combat forces identified for employment with the Rapid Deployment Force (RDF), which include the 24th Mechanized Division, the 82nd Airborne Division, the 101st Air Assault Division, the 6th Cavalry Brigade (Air Combat), plus Ranger, Special Forces and support forces. This does not mean that all of these units would be committed to all RDF contingencies, merely that a wide mix of heavy and light forces is available for tailoring packages of Army, Air Force, Navy and Marine elements to meet specific circumstances.

Top: M60 tanks are unloaded from a ship. Despite forces being stationed overseas many men and much equipment would have to be sent by air and sea.

Right: US Army troops on exercise in the snows of northern Norway, just one of the many deployment options facing the Army and for which it must train.

Above: The Light Armored Vehicle (LAV) competition has been won by the General Motors of Canada Piranha 8 x 8, first deliveries taking place in 1983; 969 will be built. The Marine Corps will also receive many LAV-25s.

Above right: As low-level airspace becomes increasingly unfriendly for reconnaissance aircraft greater use is being made of drones and remotely piloted vehicles (RPV). Prime mission of this Lockheed RPV is to acquire targets for the MLRS system.

Below: Infantrymen deplaning from a C-141 Lockheed StarLifter of the USAF. The Army is currently testing new organizations and high technology weapons systems to give such troops the necessary levels of both airmobility and firepower.

Tactical Nuclear Weapons and US Military Capabilities*

The changing strategic balance between the US and the USSR together with growing Soviet conventional military capabilities, especially in Europe, have in recent years revived interest in the role of tactical nuclear weapons in US defense planning. Some analysts have responded to the growing Soviet challenge by advocating greater reliance on tactical nuclear weapons for both deterrence and defense; others have argued that the increased Soviet threat, including deployment by the USSR of more numerous and sophisticated theater nuclear weapons in Europe, renders ever more doubtful claims that tactical nuclear weapons add to the credibility of the Western deterrent against war in Europe and provide useful military options in the event of war.

Tactical nuclear weapons, of course, have been a source of considerable controversy since the middle 1950s. There has never been any consensus among analysts, for example, on precisely what constitutes a tactical nuclear weapon. One approach stresses the explosive power of warheads as the key indicator. The yields of US weapons deployed in Europe range from the sub-kiloton level to more than a megaton. The latter weapons have an explosive power seventy times that of the bomb which devastated Hiroshima. Emphasis on the explosive power of bombs and warheads, moreover, tends to downgrade the significance of the ranges of delivery systems and the value of targets. An attack on Moscow which employed even the smallest nuclear weapons would certainly have to be judged a strategic attack. On the other hand, even very large strategic weapons can be employed in a tactical mode, and strategic delivery systems (such as the

B-52) can be utilized tactically. For these and related reasons, most analysts now prefer to discuss tactical nuclear weapons in terms of modes of deployment and the types of targets against which they are to be utilized. Some attempt to avoid the term altogether, and talk instead about "theater nuclear weapons".

The origins of the existing United States tactical nuclear stockpile can be traced back to the late 1940s. As early as 1949 General Omar Bradley, the Chairman of the Joint Chiefs of Staff, proposed that the United States deploy tactical nuclear weapons in Europe to counter Soviet advantages in conventional military power. Testing of such weapons began in 1951, and by October 1953 the initial deployment of the 280mm "atomic cannon" in Europe was begun. "Regulus" and "Honest John" missiles followed in 1954.

The deployment of these systems, however, was not accompanied by the development of a carefully worked out doctrine for their use in war. Top Eisenhower Administration officials basically considered their deployment to represent the extension of the doctrine of massive retaliation to Europe and Northeast Asia. MC-14/2, for example, which laid down basic strategy for NATO during this period, called for a relatively light "shield" of conventional forces to serve as a tripwire to activate the US strategic "sword" in the event of a Soviet attack.

Tactical nuclear weapons, as American planners saw it, further reduced the need for large conventional forces along the Iron Curtain. Such weapons were believed to afford distinct advantages to the side seeking to defend itself against an attack, and to compensate for Soviet advantages in conventional military power especially manpower, at a bearable cost.

Insofar as attention was paid to the development of doctrine for the actual use of tactical nuclear weapons, analysts argued that allied conventional forces would "channel" first echelon elements of an invading force into massed formations which would constitute

US Ground Launched Tactical Nuclear Weapons Deployed in Europe

Name	No. of Launches	Range miles (km)	Yield of Warhead	Year first deployed
Pershing[1]	108	280 (450)	60-400 Kt	1962
Lance	36	43–68 (70–110)	1 Kt (variable)	1972
Nike-Hercules[2]	144	12 (20)	1 Kt	1958
8in howitzer M110A1	56	18 (29)	sub-to-low Kt	1962
155mm howitzer M109A1	252	8.6 (14)	sub-to-low Kt	1964

Source: The Military Balance 1981–82 (IISS).
1. Pershing II scheduled to deploy 1983 has an 1,120-mile (1800km) range.
2. Nike-Hercules is an air defensive weapon with limited surface-to-surface capability which is being phased out of the US inventory.

*Editor's note: the following analysis was contributed by Dr James E. Dornan, Jr.

convenient targets for tactical nuclear systems. It was usually assumed as well that the use of tactical nuclear weapons against appropriate communist bloc targets behind the lines would seriously disrupt second and third echelon formations and help bring the attack quickly to a halt.

Almost immediately, however, doubts arose concerning the validity of such analyses. Some commentators challenged the assertion that tactical nuclear weapons would provide a cheaper means of defense against a communist bloc attack, and denied that a nuclear equipped NATO force would require fewer troops. It was only a matter of time, they suggested, before the USSR also would deploy tactical nuclear systems; since a war in Europe in which both sides utilized nuclear weapons would result in extremely high casualty rates, they argued, NATO would require far larger forces than would be necessary to fight a conventional war. Other analysts denied that tactical nuclear weapons necessarily favored the defense. While the deployment of nuclear systems with NATO forces might act as a deterrent against the massing of troops and armor, Pact deployment of similar weapons would also force defending NATO forces to spread out, rendering NATO defense lines vulnerable to penetration by small mechanized units. Finally, grave doubts were expressed concerning the adequacy of NATO's command, control and communications systems for controlling a nuclear war in the theater. Widespread fears arose in Europe, especially after the notorious *Carte Blanche* exercise in 1955, that any use of nuclear weapons in response to a Soviet attack would result in civilian casualties on a massive scale and the consequent destruction of all of Western Europe.

Such doubts and fears led over time to new emphases in discussions by Western leaders of the role of nuclear weapons in the defense of Europe. Increasingly the role of theater nuclear

weapons in *deterring* a Soviet attack was emphasized, and the *warfighting* role of such systems played down. American articulations of the doctrine of "flexible response" as developed under the Kennedy Administration, in fact, essentially argued that the role of such systems was to deter the use of tactical nuclear weapons by the Warsaw Pact; NATO, conversely, would employ such weapons only as a last resort—in the event of an "overwhelming enemy conventional breakthrough", in the words of a recent Department of Defense posture statement. Such statements, of course, have generated fears of their own, especially in Europe. Would NATO commanders receive permission to employ tactical nuclear weapons in sufficient time to influence the outcome of the conflict? Would the use of such weapons late in the game, presumably after the Warsaw Pact had achieved substantial breakthroughs along the FEBA (Forward Edge of the Battle Area), succeed in halting the attack? Given the size of many currently deployed nuclear bombs and warheads and the ranges of existing delivery systems, the utilization of such systems after Warsaw Pact breaksthrough would mean that most of the weapons would be detonated on West German soil, with devastating impact on the industrial infrastructure and civilian population of the FRG. Reflections on these and related issues have led most European analysts to reject the American formulation of the doctrine of flexible response, and to stress instead the deterrent role of NATO-deployed nuclear systems.

By December of 1966, in any event, then-Secretary of Defense Robert S. McNamara announced that there were approximately 7,000 US nuclear warheads deployed in Western Europe. In 1968 Defense Secretary Clark Clifford stated that the total had reached 7,200. Some sources believe that by 1970 there were more than 10,000 nuclear warheads in Europe, although in that year obsolescent "Honest John" and "Sergeant" missiles began to be withdrawn and the level gradually receded once again to about 7,000. Some "Honest John" and "Sergeant" missiles remain, although these are gradually being replaced by the newer "Lance" tactical missile. The US also deploys nuclear warheads for "Pershing" missiles,

"Nike-Hercules" anti-aircraft missiles (which also could be employed in a surface-to-surface mode), nuclear projectiles for some 500 8-inch and 155mm howitzers, and a number of atomic demolition munitions. The following chart lists the ground-launched tactical nuclear systems now deployed with US NATO-based forces in Europe. It should be noted, however, that there are also 72 "Pershings" and 20 "Sergeant" missiles plus a number of nuclear-capable 8-in and 155mm howitzers in the hands of the FRG, 44 "Lance" missiles deployed by the FRG, Great Britain and Italy, and 112 "Honest Johns" in the hands of the smaller NATO countries. France has also deployed 24 "Pluton" missiles with a range of 72 nautical miles and warheads with a yield estimated at approximately 20 KT.

In addition, the United States has deployed about 550 nuclear-capable tactical aircraft in the European theater. These consists primarily of F-4s and F-111s, plus A-6 and A-7 attack aircraft deployed aboard carriers in the Mediterranean. The new F-16 will be nuclear-capable. Nuclear bombs delivered by such aircraft have yields ranging from .1 KT to 1+ MT, although most are said to be in the high KT range. Some —like the B-61 bomb—are variable-yield weapons. There are also well over 1,000 nuclear-capable aircraft in the air forces of the West European states. It is worth noting, however, that it is unlikely that more than a small fraction of these aircraft could be used to deliver nuclear ordnance in the event of war, given the demand for conventional battlefield support which would inevitably arise.

Finally, numbered among the 7,000 US nuclear warheads are a variety of sea-based ASW systems such as ASROC, SUBROC and ASTOR torpedoes and depth charges as well as "Talos" and "Terrier" surface-to-air missiles. None of these, however, would be useful against land targets, and many are being withdrawn from service due to obsolescence in any case.

Precise data concerning US nuclear systems deployed in Asia have never been made available. Published sources suggest, however, that there are approximately 300 nuclear weapons of all types deployed in Korea. These presumably include at present projectiles for 155mm and 8-in artillery pieces and a variety of air-deliverable nuclear bombs. All of the artillery projec-

Legend:
- Troops in open killed by heat/blast (red) or, several days later, radiation (blue)
- Crew killed inside
- Electronics destroyed by EMP; crew probably later succumb
- Tank knocked out but crew might survive (whereas with enhanced radiation bomb crew would die eventually)
- Radiation
- Reduced heat/blast effects
- Heat/blast effects
- Electromagnetic pulse (EMP)

tiles and perhaps the Air Force weapons as well are scheduled to be withdrawn as US ground troops are pulled out of Korea over the next four years.

During the tenure of James A. Schlesinger as Secretary of Defense, United States planners began to give serious attention to the possibility of a failure of deterrence in Europe, and to reconsider ways in which nuclear weapons might be employed in the event of a Warsaw Pact attack. Although still emphasizing the deterrent role of US strategic and theater based nuclear systems, Schlesinger sought credible options for the actual utilization of such weapons in the event that deterrence failed, and he consequently became an advocate of the modernization of the US tactical nuclear force. Recent and impending advances in military technology have made possible the development and deployment of nuclear weapons which would both improve the military effectiveness of NATO's defense forces and avoid wholesale slaughter of civilians in the process. Technology either in hand or under development, for example, will greatly improve the accuracy with which ordnance can be

delivered on targets. Electro-optical, laser-designated, infra-red seeking, beacon-guided and map-matching guidance systems are being developed and deployed both for conventional and nuclear weapons which will make possible higher "target" kill probabilities and at the same time permit the use of lower-yield nuclear weapons and the greater use of conventional ordnance against certain classes of targets. New methods are being developed for estimating desired target damage and for matching weapons and targets. Finally, so-called "tailored effects" weapons, i.e. weapons designed to achieve specific military purposes, are being developed. So-called shallow-burst nuclear munitions, for example, detonated at sufficient depths in the ground, can minimize or eliminate fireball effects on the surface, thus reducing unwanted collateral damage to civilian population, buildings, and so on.

Of the various special effects weapons now under development, the so-called neutron bomb, more properly the enhanced radiation (ER) warhead, has received the most publicity. Contrary to many press reports, the ER warhead is not entirely new, nor is it a "people killer"

weapon which is somehow less humane than existing nuclear weapons. Research and development on the ER warhead began in 1960. It is a nuclear weapon with special characteristics: it employs a relatively low-yield fission reaction to trigger a fusion reaction, and thus can release up to 80 per cent of its yield in very high-energy deadly neutrons with a longer range than neutrons generated by standard fission weapons. It thus has a larger effective radius against personnel than normal fission weapons of the same yield, which kill primarily by blast and heat. High velocity heavy neutrons easily penetrate the human body; moreover, while modern tanks are relatively impervious to blast and heat, such neutrons can easily penetrate armor and react with it to produce deadly gamma radiation.

Such characteristics mean that lower yield weapons of the ER type, with reduced blast effects and lower levels of thermal radiation and little or no fallout, can be used to perform certain military tasks. The use of such weapons would result in substantially less damage to nearby civilian and military structures. A 1-KT enhanced radiation weapon can deliver 5,00

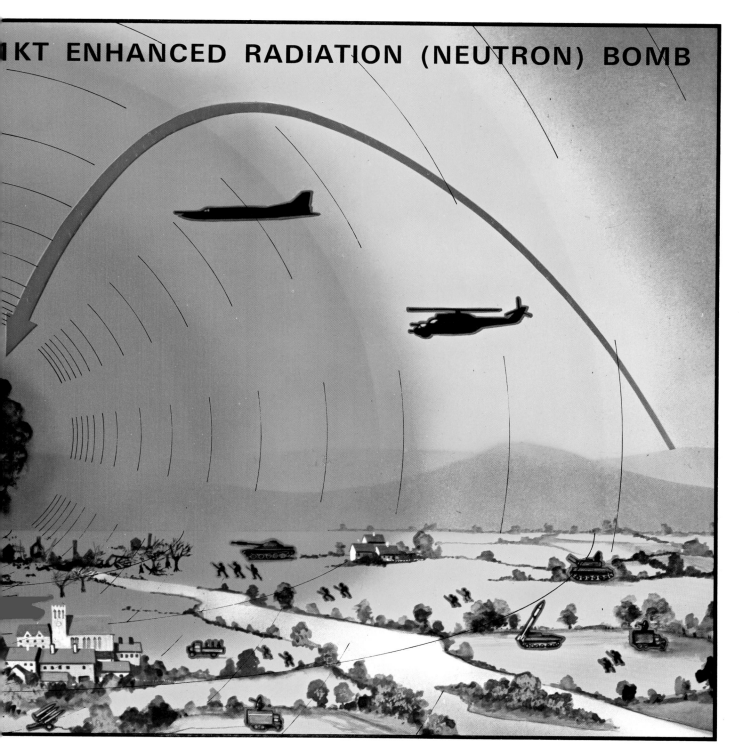

8,000 rads (the standard measure of radiation) to a distance of one-half mile, but would have little impact beyond a radius of a mile and half. It would thus be highly useful against passing enemy troop and armor formations, even on the highly populated and heavily industrialized North German plain. ER weapons would also be especially valuable to defending forces, which can dig in and shield themselves against retaliatory nuclear attacks by the attacking force—even an attacking force equipped with ER weapons. The US is presently developing the W70-3 warhead for the "Lance" missile, and the W70-9 1-KT projectile for the in howitzer; a projectile for the 155mm owitzer is also under discussion.

ER weapons have not been deployed to Europe t development is proceeding. The use of ER eapons with the new high accuracy delivery stems would undoubtedly enhance NATO's pacity to defeat Warsaw Pact mechanized rces. Added to the lesser level of destruction civilian installations, the ER weapons' mor-killing capabilities offer opportunities hich will continue to intrigue military inkers for some time to come.

This diagram attempts the difficult task of illustrating some of the effects of a conventional nuclear weapon (left half of drawing) compared with a neutron bomb (right half). The nuclear weapon is of 10 kilotons yield and the neutron bomb of 1 kiloton, and both are air-burst at a height of 330ft (100m). (The blue trajectory shows a possible rocket delivery.) A, B, C and D respectively denote radii from ground zero of 250, 880, 1,320 and 2,220 yards (229, 805, 1,207 and 2,030m). The entire area hit by the conventional weapon is desolate, affected by blast and heat (red). Yet inside the tank (foreground) the crew could survive and carry on fighting. In contrast the red area on the right is localised. EMP (electromagnetic pulse) effects are augmented, and would destroy the electronics in the radar vehicle (foreground) and in the overflying aircraft. Most important of all, the radiation (yellow) is enormously intensified on the right, killing the crews in the tanks and in the aircraft. The popular media misled the public in the West in suggesting the neutron bomb was intended to "kill humans but protect property". This misses the point, and there would be no point in protecting property about to be occupied by the enemy. The entire purpose behind the neutron bomb was to kill immediately or disable the crews of tanks, aircraft and other strongly protected manned weapons, which could not be readily knocked out in any other way except by painstakingly picking off each one with an individual counter-weapon.

US Ground Forces Weapons

Christopher F. Foss, author of *Jane's World Armoured Fighting Vehicles*; editor of *Jane's Armour and Artillery* and *Jane's Military Vehicles and Ground Support Equipment*; author of many military reference books, including Salamander's *The Illustrated Encyclopedia of Tanks and Fighting Vehicles*.

M48 Medium Tank

M48, M48C, M48A1, M48A2, M48A2C, M48A3, M48A5, M67, M67A1, M67A2, M48 AVLB

Crew: 4. **Armament:** One 90mm gun M41; one 0·3in M1919A4E1 machine-gun co-axial with the main armament (some have a 7·62mm M73 MG); one 0·5in machine-gun in commander's cupola. **Armor:** 12·7mm–120mm (0·50–4·80in). **Dimensions:** Length (including main armament) 28·3ft (8·686m); length (hull) 22ft 7 in (6·882m); width 11ft 11in (3·631m); height (including cupola) 10ft 3in (3·124m). **Weight:** Combat 104,000lb (47,173kg). **Ground pressure:** 11·80lb/in² (0·83kg/cm²). **Engine:** Continental AVDS-1790-2A 12-cylinder air-cooled diesel developing 750hp at 2,400rpm. **Performance:** Road speed 30mph (48km/h); range 288 miles (463km); vertical obstacle 3ft (0·915m); trench 8ft 6in (2·59m); gradient 60 per cent. **History:** Entered service with the United States Army in 1953. Used by Germany, Greece, Iran, Israel, Jordan, Lebanon, Morocco, Norway, Pakistan, Somalia, South Korea, Spain, Taiwan, Thailand, Tunisia, Turkey, United States and Vietnam. (*Specifications relate to M48A3.*)

Once the M47 was authorized for production, development started on a new medium tank as the M47 was only a stop-gap measure. So in October 1950 Detroit Arsenal started design work on a new medium tank armed with a 90mm gun. This design study was completed two months later and in December 1950 Chrysler was given a contract to complete the design work and build six prototypes under the designation T48. The first of these prototypes had to be completed by December 1951. Production started in 1952 and first deliveries were made to the US Army the following year. The M48, as it was now called, was followed in production by the M60, essentially an M48A3 with a 105mm gun and other detailed changes, production of this model being undertaken at the Detroit Tank Plant.

The hull of the M48 is of cast armour construction, as is the turret. The driver is seated at the front of the hull with the other three crew members located in the turret, with the commander and gunner on the right and the loader on the left. The engine and transmission are at the rear of the hull and are separated from the fighting compartment by a fireproof bulkhead. The suspension is of the torsion-bar type and consists of six road wheels, with the drive sprocket at the rear and the idler at the front. Depending on the model there are between three and five track-return rollers, and some models have a small track tensioning wheel between the sixth road wheel and the drive sprocket. The main armament consists of a 90mm gun with an elevation of +19° and a depression of −9°, traverse being 360°. A 0·3in M1919A4E1 machine-gun is mounted co-axially with the main armament, although most M48s in US (except on the M48A1 which has a simple mount). This cupola can be traversed through 360°, and the machine-gun can be elevated from −10° to +60°.

The M48 can be fitted with a dozer blade, if required, at the front of the hull. All M48s have infra-red driving lights and some an infra-red/white searchlight mounted over the main armament. The type can ford to a depth of 4ft (1·219m) without preparation or 8ft (2·438m) with the aid of a kit.

The first model to enter service was the M48, and this has a simple cupola for the commander, with the machine-gun mounted externally. The second model was the M48C, which was for training use only as it has a mild steel hull. The M48A1 was followed by the M48A2, which has many improvements including a fuel-injection system for the engine and larger capacity fuel tanks. The M48A2C was a slightly modified M48A2. The M48A3 was a significant improvement as this has a diesel engine, which increases the vehicle's operational range considerably, and a number of other modifications including a different fire-control system. Latest model is the M48A5, essentially an M48A1 or M48A2 with modifications including a new 105mm gun, new tracks, a 7·62mm M60D co-axial machine-gun and a similar weapon on the loader's hatch, plus many other detail modifications. Three flamethrower tanks were developed: the M67 (using an M48A1 chassis), the M67A1 (using an M48A2 chassis) and the M67A2 (using an M48A3 chassis). Also in service is an M48 Armored Vehicle-Launched Bridge. This has a scissors bridge which can be laid over gaps up to 60ft (18·288m) in width. The chassis of the M48A5 is used as the basis for the twin 40mm DIVAD self-propelled anti-aircraft gun (qv).

Above: The chassis of the M48A5 is used as the basis for the twin 40mm DIVAD self-propelled anti-aircraft gun.

Below: An M48A5 fitted with an M60-type turret with 105mm gun and Xenon searchlight (above the main gun).

M60 Main Battle Tank

M60, M60A1, M60A3, M60 AVLB, M728 CEV

Crew: 4. **Armament:** One 105mm gun; one 7·62mm machine-gun co-axial with main armament; one 0·5in anti-aircraft machine-gun in commander's cupola. **Armor:** 12·7mm—120mm (0·50—4·80in). **Dimensions:** Length (gun forward) 30ft 6in (9·309m); length (hull) 22ft 9½in (6·946m); width 11ft 11in (3·631m); height 10ft 8in (3·257m). **Weight:** combat 101,998lb (46,266kg). **Ground pressure:** 11·24lb/in² (0·79kg/m²). **Engine:** Continental AVDS-1790-2A 12-cylinder diesel developing 750bhp at 2,400rpm. **Performance:** Road speed 30mph (48km/h); range 310 miles (500km); vertical obstacle 3ft (0·914m); trench 8ft 6in (2·59m); gradient 60 per cent. **History:** The M60 entered service with the United States Army in 1960 and is also used by Austria, Egypt, Ethiopia, Iran, Israel, Italy, Jordan, Morocco, Saudi Arabia, Somalia, South Korea, Tunisia, Turkey, United States Marine Corps, and Yemen Arab Republic (North). (Specifications relate to M60 model.)

Above: An important improvement in the M60A3 is its shoot-on-the-move capability, brought about by gun stabilization.

In the 1950s the standard tank of the United States Army was the M48. In 1957 an M48 series tank was fitted with a new engine for trials purposes and this was followed by another three prototypes in 1958. Late in 1958 it was decided to arm the new tank with the British 105mm L7 series gun, to be built in the United States under the designation M68. In 1959 the first production order for the new tank, now called the M60, was placed with Chrysler, and the type entered production at Detroit Tank Arsenal in late 1959, with the first production tanks being completed the following year.

From late in 1962, the M60 was replaced in production by the M60A1, which has a number of improvements, the most important being the redesigned turret. The M60A1 has a turret and hull of all-cast construction. The driver is seated at the front of the hull with the other three crew members in the turret, commander and gunner on the right and the loader on the left. The engine and transmission are at the rear, the latter having one reverse and two forward ranges. The M60 has torsion-bar suspension and six road wheels, with the idler at the front and the drive sprocket at the rear; there are four track-return rollers. The 105mm gun has an elevation of +20° and a depression of −10°, and traverse is 360°. Both elevation and traverse are powered. A 7·62mm M73 machine-gun is mounted co-axially with the main armament and there is a 0·5in M85 machine-gun in the commander's cupola. The latter can be aimed and fired from within the turret, and has an elevation of +60° and a depression of −15°. Some 60 rounds of 105mm, 900 rounds of 0·5in and 5,950 rounds of 7·62mm ammunition are carried. Infra-red driving lights are fitted as standard and an infra-red/white light is mounted over the main armament. All M60s have an NBC system. The tank can also be fitted with a dozer blade on the front of the hull. The M60 can ford to a depth of 4ft (1·219m) without preparation or 8ft (2·438m) with the aid of a kit. For deep fording operations a schnorkel can be fitted, allowing the M60 to ford to a depth of 13ft 6in (4·114m).

The M60A2 was a special model armed with a 152mm gun/launcher but has now been phased out of service. Current production model is the M60A3 with numerous improvements including stabilization of main armament, top loading air cleaner fitted, passive searchlight over main armament, new tracks with removable pads, tube over bar suspension, RISE engine, thermal sleeve for main armament, laser rangefinder, passive night vision devices, new MAG 7·62mm MG, smoke dischargers each side of turret, muzzle reference system, engine smoke dischargers and improved personnel heater. Most M60A1s of the US Army are now being brought up to this new standard. By 1981 total production of the M60 series of MBTs had amounted to over 13,000 vehicles with final vehicles scheduled to be completed in 1983. Specialized versions of the M60 series include the M60 armored vehicle launched bridge and the M728 Combat Engineer Vehicle which is fitted with a bulldozer blade, 152mm demolition gun and an A-frame for lifting obstacles which is pivoted at the front of the hull. The basic vehicle can also be fitted with roller type mineclearing equipment or a dozer blade.

ER weapons have not been deployed to Europe but development is proceeding. The use of ER weapons with the new high accuracy delivery systems would undoubtedly enhance NATO's capacity to defeat Warsaw Pact mechanized forces. Added to the lesser level of destruction to civilian installations, the ER weapons' armor-killing capabilities offer opportunities which will continue to intrigue military thinkers for some time to come.

Below: Row of M60A3s with turrets reversed; the addition of a thermal imaging gunner's periscope extends day and night capability.

M1 Abrams Main Battle Tank

Crew: 4. **Armament:** One 105mm M68 gun; one 7·62mm machine-gun co-axial with main armament; one 0·5in machine-gun on commander's cupola; one 7·62mm machine-gun on loader's hatch (see text). **Armor:** Classified. **Dimensions:** Length (gun forward) 32ft 0½in (9·766m); length (hull) 25ft 11¾in (7·918m); width 11ft 11¾ (3·655m); height 7ft 9½in (2·375m). **Weight:** 120,000lb (54,432kg). **Engine:** Avco Lycoming AGT-T 1500 HP-C turbine developing 1,500hp. **Performance:** Road speed 45mph (72·4km/h); range 275 miles (475km); vertical obstacle 4ft 1in (1·244m); trench 9ft (2·743m); gradient 60 per cent. **History:** First production vehicle completed in 1980. Also being evaluated by the Swiss Army in competition with the West German Leopard 2.

In June 1973 contracts were awarded to both the Chrysler Corporation (which builds the M60 series) and the Detroit Diesel Allison Division of the General Motors Corporation (which built the MBT-70) to build prototypes of a new tank designated M1, and later named the Abrams tank. These tanks were handed over to the US Army for trials in February 1976. In November 1976 it was announced after a four-month delay that the Chrysler tank would be placed in production. Production, which commenced at the Lima Army Tank Plant in Lima, Ohio, in 1979, with the first vehicles being completed the following year, is now also under way at the Detroit Arsenal Tank plant which, like Lima, is now operated by the Land Systems Division of General Dynamics who took over Chrysler Defense Incorporated in 1982. By late 1982 over 600 M1s had been built, with the US Army having a requirement for some 7,058 by the end of fiscal year 1982. From 1985 it is expected that the 105mm M68 rifled tank gun will be replaced by the 120mm Rheinmetall smooth bore gun which is being produced under the designation XM256; this will fire both West German and American ammunition.

The M1 has a hull and turret of the new British Chobham Armour, which is claimed to make the tank immune to attack from both missiles and tank guns. Its crew consists of four, the driver at the front, the commander and gunner on the right of the turret, and the loader on the left. The main armament consists of a standard 105mm gun developed in Britain and produced under license in the United States and a 7·62mm machine-gun is mounted co-axially with the main armament. A 0·5in machine-gun is mounted at the commander's station and a 7·62mm machine-gun at the loader's station. Ammunition supply consists of 55 rounds of 105mm, 1,000 rounds of 12·7mm and 11,400 rounds of 7·62mm. Mounted each side of the turret is a bang of six British-designed smoke dischargers. The main armament can be aimed and fired on the move. The gunner first selects the target and then uses the laser rangefinder to get its range and then depresses the firing switch. The computer makes the calculations and adjustment required to ensure a hit.

The fuel tanks are separated from the crew compartment by armored bulkheads and sliding doors are provided for the ammunition stowage areas. The suspension is of the torsion-bar type with rotary shock absorbers. The tank can travel across country at a speed of 35mph (56km/h) and accelerate from 0 to 20mph (0 to 32km/h) in seven seconds, and this will make the M1 a difficult tank to engage on the battlefield. The M1 is powered by a turbine developed by Avco Lycoming, running on a variety of fuels including petrol, diesel and jet fuel. All the driver has to do is adjust a dial in his compartment. According to the manufacturers, the engine will not require an overhaul until the tank has travelled between 12,000 to 18,000 miles (19,312 to 28,968km), a great advance over existing tank engines. This engine is coupled to an Allison X-1100 transmission with four forward and two reverse gears. Great emphasis has been placed on reliability and maintenance, and it is claimed that the complete engine can be removed for replacement in under 30 minutes.

The M1 is provided with an NBC system and a full range of night-vision equipment for the commander, gunner and driver.

It is not often realized that there are hundreds of sub contractors to a major program such as a tank. On the Chrysler M1 there are eight major subcontractors: the government for the armament, Avco Lycoming for the engine, Cadillac Gage for the turret drive and the stabilization system, the Control Data Corporation for the ballistic computer, the Detroit Diesel Allison Division of General Motors for the transmission and the final drive, the Hughes Aircraft Company for the laser rangefinder, the Kollmorgen Corporation for the gunner's auxiliary sight and the Singer Kearfott Division for the line-of-sight data link.

Below: The M1's hull and turret are constructed from the British Chobham armor, said to be made up of layers of nylon micromesh bonded on both sides by sheets of titanium alloy, able to direct sideways the explosive force of enemy rounds.

Above: M1 on trials. The Army reckon the tank to be capable of operating during a 24-hour combat day without the need to refuel.

Right: The M1 has a 27 per cent lower silhouette than the M60A1 but with the same ground clearance of about 19 inches (48cm).

Below: M1 Abrams, with 1,500hp turbine engine, is fast, but operational testing has shown track and engine durability problems.

Below: The M1 made its operational debut in Autumn 1982 NATO maneuvers in Germany. Production is running at about 60 a month, to be increased to a rate of 90 a month by 1985.

Below: A prototype firing its British-designed rifled 105mm gun. Though this is well-proven and a standard NATO weapon, about half of the M1s will have German 120mm smoothbore gun.

M551 Sheridan Light Tank

Crew: 4. **Armament:** One 152mm gun/missile launcher; one 7·62mm machine-gun co-axial with main armament; one 0·5in anti-aircraft machine-gun; four smoke dischargers on each side of turret. **Armor:** Classified. **Dimensions:** Length 20ft 8in (6·299m); width 9ft 3in (2·819m); height (overall) 9ft 8in (2·946m). **Weight:** Combat 34,898lbs (15,830kg). **Ground pressure:** 6·96lb/in² (0·49kg/cm²). **Engine:** Detroit Diesel 6V53T six-cylinder diesel developing 300bhp at 2,800rpm. **Performance:** Road speed 45mph (70km/h); water speed 3·6mph (5·8km/h); range 373 miles (600km); vertical obstacle 2ft 9in (0·838m); trench 8ft 4in (2·54m); gradient 60 per cent. **History:** Entered service with United States Army in 1966 and still in service.

In August 1959 the United States Army established a requirement for a "new armored vehicle with increased capabilities over any other weapon in its own inventory and that of any adversary". The following year the Allison Division of General Motors was awarded a contract to design a vehicle called the Armored Reconnaissance Airborne Assault Vehicle (ARAAV) to meet the requirement. The first prototype, designated XM551, was completed in 1962, and this was followed by a further 11 prototypes. Late in 1965 a production contract was awarded to Allison, and the first production vehicles were completed in 1966, these being known as the M551 or Sheridan. Production was completed in 1970 after 1,700 vehicles had been built.

The hull of the Sheridan is of all-aluminium construction whilst the turret is of welded steel. The driver is seated at the front of the hull and the other three crew members are in the turret, with the loader on the left and the gunner and commander on the right. The engine and transmission are at the rear of the hull. The suspension is of the torsion-bar type and consists of five road wheels, with the drive sprocket at the rear and the idler at the front. There are no track-return rollers. The most interesting feature of the Sheridan is its armament system. This consists of a 152mm gun/launcher which has an elevation of +19° and a depression of −8°, traverse being 360°. A 7·62mm machine-gun is mounted co-axially with the main armament, and there is a 0·5in Browning machine-gun on the commander's cupola. The latter cannot be aimed and fired from within the turret, and as a result of combat experience in Vietnam many vehicles have now been fitted with a shield for this weapon. The 152mm gun/launcher, later fitted to the M60A2 and MBT-70 tanks, can fire either a Shillelagh missile or a variety of conventional ammunition including HEAT-T-MP, WP and canister, all of them having a combustible cartridge case. The Shillelagh missile was developed by the United States Army Missile Command and the Philco-Ford Corporation, and has a maximum range of about 3,281 yards (3,000m). The missile is controlled by the gunner, who simply has to keep the cross-hairs of his sight on the target to ensure a hit. This missile itself weighs 59lbs (26·7kg) and has a single-stage solid-propellant motor which has a burn time of 1·18 seconds. Once the missile leaves the gun/missile launcher, four fins at the rear of the missile unfold and it is guided to the target by a two-way infra-red command link which eliminates the need for the gunner to estimate the lead and range of the target. A Sheridan normally carries ten missiles and 20 rounds of ammunition, but this mix can be adjusted as required. In addition, 1,000 rounds of 0·5in and 3,080 rounds of 7·62mm ammunition are carried. The Sheridan is provided with a flotation screen, and when erected this enables the vehicle to propel itself across rivers and streams by its tracks. Night-vision equipment is provided as is an NBC system.

The M551 is used only by the 82nd Airborne Division (57) and the Arkansas National Guard (12), although some 330 have been assigned to the National Training Center at Fort Irwin. Many of the latter have been modified to resemble Soviet vehicles.

Above: Though effective, the M551 is regarded as a costly AFV calling for prolonged crew training. Service reliability has proven unsatisfactory. It will be replaced by the M3.

Below: The Sheridan can launch the infra-red-guided Shillelagh missile, virtually useless below 1,300 yards (1200m), but effective at longer ranges, up to 3,250 yards (3000m).

M113 Armored Personnel Carrier

M113, M113A1, M113A2, M106, M132, M163 and variants
Crew: 2 plus 11. **Armament:** One Browning 0·5in (12·7mm) machine-gun. **Armor:** 12mm–38mm (0·47–1·58in). **Dimensions:** Length 15ft 11in (4·863m); width 8ft 10in (2·686m); height 8ft 2in (2·5m). **Weight:** Combat 24,600lbs (11,156kg). **Ground pressure:** 7·82lb/in² (0·55kg/cm²). **Engine:** General Motors Model 6V53 six-cylinder water-cooled diesel developing 215bhp at 2,800rpm. **Performance:** Road speed 42mph (67·6km/h); water speed 3·6mph (5·8km/h); range 300 miles (483km); vertical obstacle 2ft (0·61m); trench 5ft 6in (1·68m); gradient 60 per cent. **History:** Entered service with the United States Army in 1960. Also used by 50 other countries.

In the early 1950s the standard United States Army APC was the M75, followed in 1954 by the M59. Neither of these was satisfactory and in 1954 foundations were laid for a new series of vehicles. In 1958 prototypes of the T113 (aluminium hull) and T117 (steel hull) armoured personnel carriers were built. A modified version of the T113, the T113E1, was cleared for production in mid-1959 and production commenced at the FMC plant at San Jose, California, in 1960. The vehicle is still in production today and so far over 70,000 have been built. It is also built in Italy by Oto Melara, which has produced a further 4,000 for the Italian Army and for export. In 1964 the M113 was replaced in production by the M113A1, identical with the earlier model but for a diesel rather than a petrol engine.

The M113A1 has a larger radius of action than the earlier vehicle. The M113 has the distinction of being the first armoured fighting vehicle of aluminium construction to enter production. The driver is seated at the front of the hull on the left, with the engine to his right. The commander's hatch is in the center of the roof and the personnel compartment is at the rear of the hull. The infantry enter and leave via a large ramp in the hull rear, although there is also a roof hatch over the troop compartment. The basic vehicle is normally armed with a pintle-mounted Browning 0·5in machine-gun, which has 2,000 rounds of ammunition. The M113 is fully amphibious and is propelled in the water by its tracks. Infra-red driving lights are fitted as standard. FMC has developed a wide variety of kits for the basic vehicle including an ambulance kit, NBC kit, heater kit, dozer-blade kit, various shield for machine-guns and so on.

The current production model is the M113A2 which is essentially an M113A1 with improved engine cooling and improved suspension. Most US Army M113 and M113A1 vehicles are now being brought up to M113A2 standard.

There are more variants of the M113 family than any other fighting vehicle in service today, and there is room here to mention only some of the more important models. The M577 is the command model, with a much higher roof and no armament. There are two mortar carriers: the M125 with an 81mm mortar, and the M106 with a 107mm mortar. The flamethrower model is known as the M132A1, and is not used outside the United States Army. The XM806 is the recovery model, and this is provided with a winch at the rear of the vehicle and spades at the rear. The anti-aircraft model is known as the Vulcan Air Defense System or M163; this is armed with a six-barrelled 20mm General Electric cannon. The M548 tracked cargo carrier is based on an M113 chassis, can carry 5 tons (5,080kg) of cargo and is fully amphibious. There are many models of the M548, including the M727, which carries three HAWK surface-to-air missiles, and the M730, which carries four Chaparral short-range surface-to-air missiles. Yet another version, the M752, carries the Lance tactical missile system, whilst the M688 carries two spare missiles.

One of the latest models is the M901 Improved TOW Vehicle (ITV) which has a retractable launcher which carries two Hughes TOW ATGWs in the ready-to-launch position. Almost 2,000 of these vehicles have been ordered for the US Army.

Below: The squat shape of the M113 is distinctive even amidst the snows of Alaska, as a squad from Company A, 1st BG, 23rd Infantry, goes through a tactical demonstration at the Fort Richardson training aids area.

Above: More M113 chassis have been built than any other since 1945. This is the M557 unarmed command post version.

Below: The Improved TOW Vehicle (ITV), whose missile components can be removed for ground-launching if necessary.

Below: M113s in convoy through a German town during "Autumn Reforger" NATO exercises in 1982. It is the standard personnel carrier in mechanized infantry units but, unable to keep pace with the M1 tank, will be replaced by the M2 IFV.

M110 Self-propelled Howitzer

M110, M0A1, M110A2

Crew: 5. **Armament:** one 8in (203mm) howitzer. **Armor:** 20mm (0·79in) maximum (estimated). **Dimensions:** Length (including gun and spade in traveling position) 35ft 2½in (10·731m); length (hull) 18ft 9in (5·72m); width 10ft 4in (3·149m); height 10ft 4in (3·143m). **Weight:** Combat 62,500lb (28,350kg). **Ground pressure:** 10·80lb/in² (0·76kg/cm²). **Engine:** Detroit Diesel Model 8V-7T eight-cylinder turbo-charged diesel developing 405bhp at 2,300rpm. **Performance:** Road speed 34mph (54.7km/h); range 325 miles (523km); vertical obstacle 3ft 4in (1·016m); trench 7ft 9in (2·362m); gradient 60 per cent. **History:** Original version M110, entered service with the United States Army in 1963. Now used by Belgium, West Germany, Greece, Iran, Israel, Italy, Japan, Jordan, Saudi Arabia, South Korea, Netherlands, Pakistan, Spain, Turkey, United Kingdom and United States.

In 1956 the United States Army issued a requirement for a range of self-propelled artillery which would be air-transportable. The Pacific Car and Foundry Company of Washington were awarded the development contract

LVTP-7 Amphibious Assault Vehicle

LVTP7, LVTC7, LVTE7, LVTH7

Crew: 3 plus 25. **Armament:** One M85 0·5in (12·7mm) machine-gun. **Armor:** 0·256–1·77in (7–45mm). **Dimensions:** Length 26ft 1in (7·943m); width, 10ft 9in (3·27m); height, 10ft 9in (3·27m). **Weight:** Combat 50,349lb (922,838kg). **Ground pressure:** 8lb/in² (0·57kg/cm²). **Engine:** Detroit Diesel Model 8V53T eight-cylinder turbocharged diesel developing 400bhp at 2,800rpm. **Performance:** Road speed 39·5mph (63·37km/h); water speed 8·5mph (13·7km/h); range (road) 300 miles (482km); vertical obstacle 3ft (0·914m); trench 8ft (2·438m); gradient, 70 per cent. **History:** Entered service with United States Marine Corps 1971. Also in service with Argentina, Italy, South Korea, Spain, Thailand and Venezuela.

The standard amphibious assault carrier in service with the United States Marines in the 1950s was the LVTP5 (Landing Vehicle Tracked Personnel 5). Although an improvement over earlier vehicles, the LVTP5 proved very difficult to maintain in service. So, in 1964, the Marines issued a requirement for a new LVTP and the FMC Corporation was selected to build 17 proto-types. The first of these was completed in 1967 under the designation of LVTPX12. Trials were carried out in Alaska, Panama and various other Marine installations, and in 1970 FMC was awarded a production contract for 942 vehicles. The first production LVTP7 was completed in August 1971 and production continued until September 1974. It has now completely replaced the older LVTP5. The role of the LVTP7 is to transport Marines from ships off shore to the beach, and, if required, to carry them inland to their objective. The hull of the LVTP7 is of all-welded aluminium construction and varies in thickness from 7 to 45mm. The engine and transmission are at the front of the hull and can be removed as a complete unit if required. The driver is seated at the front, on the left, with the commander to his rear. The LVTP7 is armed with a turret-mounted M85 0·5in machine-gun. This is mounted on the right side and has an elevation of +60° and a depression of −15°; traverse is a full 360° and a total of 2,000 rounds of ammunition is carried. The personnel compartment is at the rear of the hull, where the 25 Marines are provided with bench type seats which can be quickly stowed so that the vehicle can be used as an ambulance or cargo carrier. The usual

method of entry and exit is via a large ramp at the rear of the hull. Hatches are also provided over the troop compartment so that stores can be loaded when the vehicle is alongside a ship.

The LVTP7 is propelled in the water by two water-jets, one in each side of the hull towards the rear. These are driven by propeller shafts from the transmission. Basically pumps draw water from above the track, and this is then discharged to the rear of the vehicle. Deflectors at the rear of each unit divert the water-jet stream for steering, stopping and reversing.

There are two special versions of the LVTP7 in service. The first of these is the LVTR7. This is used to repair disabled vehicles, for which a wide

nd from 1958 built three different self-propelled weapons on the same hassis. These were the T235 (175mm gun), which became the M107, the 236 (203mm howitzer), which became the M110, and the T245 (155mm un), which was subsequently dropped from the range. These prototypes ere powered by a petrol engine, but it was soon decided to replace this by a esel engine as this could give the vehicles a much greater range of action. he M107 is no longer in service with the US Army; all have been rebuilt to 110A1 or M110A2 configuration.

The hull is of all-welded-steel construction with the driver at the front on e left with the engine to his right. The gun is mounted towards the rear of e hull. The suspension is of the torsion-bar type and consists of five road heels, with the fifth road wheel acting as the idler, the drive sprocket is at e front. Five crew are carried on the gun (driver, commander and three gun ew), the other eight crew members following in an M548 tracked vehicle his is based on the M113 APC chassis), which also carries the ammunition, s only two ready rounds are carried on the M110 itself. The 203mm owitzer has an elevation of +65° and a depression of −2°, traverse being 0° left and 30° right. Elevation and traverse are both hydraulic, although ere are manual controls for use in an emergency. The M110 fires an HE rojectile to a maximum range of 18,372 yards (16,800m) and other types f projectile that can be fired include HE carrying 104 HE grenades, HE arrying 195 grenades, Agent GB or VX and tactical nuclear. A large ydraulically-operated spade is mounted at the rear of the hull and is lowered to position before the gun opens fire, and the suspension can also be cked when the gun is fired to provide a more stable firing platform. The un can officially fire one round per minute, but a well trained crew can fire least two rounds a minute. As the projectile is very heavy, an hydraulic oist is provided to position the projectile on the ramming tray; the round is en pushed into the breech hydraulically before the charge is pushed home, e breechlock closed and the weapon is then fired. The M110 can ford reams to a maximum depth of 3ft 6in (1·066m) but has no amphibious apability. Infra-red driving lights are fitted as standard but the type does not ave an NBC system.

All M110s in US Army service, and in an increasing number of NATO ountries as well, are being brought up to M110A1 or M110A2 configura- on. The M110A1 has a new and longer barrel, while the M110A2 is entical to the M110A1 but has a double baffle muzzle brake. The M110A1 an fire up to charge eight while the M110A2 can fire up to charge nine. The 110A1/M110A2 can fire all of the rounds of the M110 but in addition nary, High Explosive Rocket Assisted and the improved conventional unition which contains 195 M42 grenades. The latter two have a maximum nge, with charge nine, of 31,824 yards (29,100m). One of the problems ith heavy artillery of this type is keeping the guns supplied with sufficient mmunition. As noted above the weapon is supported by an M548 tracked ehicle, and this in turn is kept supplied by 5- or 10-ton trucks.

eft: The M110A2, improved version of the Army's heaviest annon artillery weapon, has conventional and nuclear capability. ll of the Army's M110s (and M107s) have been converted.

nge of equipment is carried, including an hydraulic crane and winch. The econd model is the LVTC7, a special command model, with additional adios and other equipment. Two other models, the LVTE7 (Engineer) and VTH7 (Howitzer) were not placed in production.

All LVTP7s are now being rebuilt to the LVTP7A1 standard and fitted with ew Cummins VT400 8-cylinder diesel and many other improvements ncluding smoke generators, passive night vision equipment, improved fire uppression system, installation of PLARS, improved crew/troop compart- ent ventilation and improved electric weapon station. In addition, vehicles re now being produced to the LVTP7A1 standard.

elow: This rear view of an LVTP-7 shows the large full-section ailgate, which when closed is sealed against water ingress. On ach side are the large curved deflectors at the rear of the quare-section water jets for sea propulsion.

M109 Self-propelled Howitzer

Crew: 6. **Armament:** One 155mm howitzer; one ·5in (12·7mm) Browning anti-aircraft machine-gun. **Armor:** 20mm (0·79in) maximum, estimated. **Dimensions:** Length (including armament) 21ft 8in (6·612m); length (hull) 20ft 6in (6·256m); width 10ft 10in (3·295m); height (including anti-aircraft machine-gun) 10ft 10in (3·295m). **Weight:** Combat 52,438lbs (23,786kg). **Ground pressure:** 10·95lb/in² (0·77kg/cm²). **Engine:** Detroit Diesel Model 8V71T eight-cylinder turbocharged diesel developing 405bhp at 2,300rpm. **Performance:** Road speed 35mph (56km/h); range 242 miles (390km); vertical obstacle 1ft 9in (0·533m); trench 6ft (1·828m); gradient 60 per cent. **History:** Entered service with the United States Army in 1963. Also used by Austria, Belgium, Canada, Denmark, Germany, Great Britain, Ethiopia, Greece, Iran, Israel, Italy, Jordan, Kampuchea, Kuwait, Libya, Morocco, the Netherlands, Norway, Oman, Pakistan, Saudi Arabia, Spain, South Korea, Switzerland, Taiwan, Tunisia and Turkey. Still in production.

The first production models of the M109 were completed in 1962, and some 3,700 examples have now been built, making the M109 the most widely used self-propelled howitzer in the world. It has a hull of all-welded aluminum construction, providing the crew with protection from small arms fire. The driver is seated at the front of the hull on the left, with the engine to his right. The other five crew members are the commander, gunner and three ammunition members, all located in the turret at the rear of the hull. There is a large door in the rear of the hull for ammunition resupply purposes. Hatches are also provided in the sides and rear of the turret. There are two hatches in the roof of the turret, the commander's hatch being on the right. A 0·5in (12·7mm) Browning machine-gun is mounted on this for anti- aircraft defense. The suspension is of the torsion-bar type and consists of seven road wheels, with the drive sprocket at the front and the idler at the rear, and there are no track-return rollers.

The 155mm howitzer has an elevation of +75° and a depression of −3°, and the turret can be traversed through 360°. Elevation and traverse are powered, with manual controls for emergency use. The weapon can fire a variety of ammunition, including HE, tactical nuclear, illuminating, smoke and chemical rounds. A total of 28 rounds of separate-loading ammunition is carried, as well as 500 rounds of machine-gun ammunition. The latest models to enter service are the M109A1/M109A2, identical with the M109 apart from a much longer barrel, which is provided with a fume extractor as well as a muzzle-brake. The fume extractor removes propellent gases from the barrel after a round has been fired and thus prevents fumes from entering the fighting compartment. The M109 fires a round to a maximum range of 16,076 yards (14,700m), whilst the M109A1 fires to a maximum range of 19,685 yards (18,000m). The M109 can ford streams to a maximum depth of 6ft (1·828m). A special amphibious kit has been developed for the vehicle but this is not widely used. It consists of nine inflatable airbags, normally carried by a truck. Four of these are fitted to each side of the hull and the last to the front of the hull. The vehicle is then propelled in the water by its tracks at a maximum speed of 4mph (6·4km/h). The M109 is provided with infra-red driving lights and some vehicles also have an NBC system.

To keep the M109 supplied with ammunition in the field Bowen- McLaughlin-York have recently developed the M992 Field Artillery Ammunition Support Vehicle which is expected to enter production in the near future.

Below: Head-on view of an M109 of the 2nd Field Artillery in Exercise Reforger 76 in Germany.

M2 Mechanized Infantry Combat Vehicle

Crew: 3 plus 6. **Armament:** One 25mm cannon; one 7·62mm machine-gun co-axial with main armament; twin launcher for Hughes TOW ATGW. **Armor:** Classified. **Dimensions:** Length 21ft 2in (6·45m); width 10ft 6in (3.20m); height 9ft 9in (2·97m). **Weight:** 50,000lb (22,680kg). **Ground pressure:** 7·7lb/in² (0·54kg/cm²). **Engine:** Cummins VTA-903T water-cooled 4-cycle diesel developing 506bhp. **Performance:** Road speed 41mph (66km/h); water speed 4·5mph; range 300 miles (384km); vertical obstacle 3ft (0·91m); trench 8ft 4in (2·54m); gradient 60 per cent. **History:** Entered US Army service in 1983.

The United States Army has had a requirement for an MICV for well over 15 years. The first American MICV was the XM701, developed in the early 1960s on the M107/M110 self-propelled gun chassis. This proved un-satisfactory during trials. The Americans then tried to modify the current M113 to meet the MICV role: a variety of different models was built and tested, but again these vehicles failed to meet the army requirement. As a result of a competition held in 1972, the FMC Corporation, which still builds the M113A2, was awarded a contract to design an MICV designated the XM723. The XM723 did not meet the requirements of the US Army and further development, based on the same chassis, resulted in the Fighting Vehicle System (FVS) which comprised two vehicles, the XM2 Infantry Fighting Vehicle and the XM3 Cavalry Fighting Vehicle. These were eventually accepted for service as the M2 and M3 Bradley Fighting Vehicles. The US Army has a requirement for some 6,882 M2/M3 vehicles, and the first battalion of M2s was formed in 1983.

The M2 will replace some, but not all, of the current M113 APCs, as the latter are more than adequate for many roles on the battlefield. The M2 will have three major advances over the existing M113 APC. First, the IFV will have greater mobility and better cross-country speed, enabling it to keep up with the M1 MBT when acting as part of the tank/infantry team. Second, it has much greater firepower. Third, it has superior armor protection. The tank provides long-range firepower whilst the MICV provides firepower against softer, close-in targets. The M2's infantry also assist the tank by locating and destroying enemy anti-tank weapons.

The hull of the M2 is of all-welded aluminium construction with an applique layer of steel armor welded to the hull front, upper sides and rear for added protection. The hull sides also have a thin layer of steel armor, the space between the aluminium and steel being filled with foam to increase the buoyancy of the vehicle. The driver is seated at the front of the vehicle on the left, with the engine to his right. The two-man turret is in the center of the hull and the personnel compartment is at the rear. Personnel entry is

Above: The M2 Bradley Infantry Fighting vehicle showing that its overall mobility compares with that of the M1 Abrams tank.

effected through a large power-operated ramp in the hull rear. The two-man power operated turret is fully stabilized and is armed with a 25mm Hughes Helicopters Chain Gun and a co-axial 7·62mm machine gun. The weapon can be elevated to +60° and depressed to −10°, turret traverse being 360°. Mounted on the left side of the turret is a twin launcher for the Hughes TOW ATGW. A total of 900 rounds of 25mm, 2,340 rounds of 7·62mm and seven TOW missiles are carried. The troop compartment is provided with six firing ports (two in each side and two at the rear) for the 5·56mm M231 weapon. Three M72A2 light anti-tank weapons are also carried.

The M2 is fully amphibious, being propelled in the water by its tracks. An NBC system is fitted as is a full range of night vision equipment. The M3 Cavalry Fighting Vehicle is similar to the M2 but has no firing ports, a crew of two plus three, and carries more ammunition. The chassis of the M2/M3 is also used as the basis for the Vought Multiple Launch Rocket System and the Armored, Forward-Area, Rearm Vehicle (AFARV) which has been designed to supply MBTs with ammunition when they are in the battlefield area.

Below: M2 IFV with the twin launcher for the Hughes TOW ATGW in the traveling position alongside the two-man turret.

155mm M114 Howitzer

Calibre: 155mm. **Crew:** 11. **Weight:** 12,786lb (5800kg). **Length traveling:** 23·9ft (7·315m), **Width traveling:** 7·99ft (2·438m). **Height traveling:** 5·9ft (1·8m). **Elevation:** −2° to +63°. **Traverse:** 25° right and 24° left. **Range:** 15,966 yards (14,600m).

In 1939, Rock Island Arsenal started the development of a new 155mm towed howitzer to replace the 155mm M1918 howitzer which at that time was the standard 155mm howitzer of the US Army (this was basically a modified French 155mm weapon built in the United States). This new 155mm weapon was designated the M1 and first production weapons were completed in 1942. Production continued until after the end of the war by which time over 6,000 weapons had been built. After the war the M1 was redesignated the M114. The 4·5 inch gun M1 used the same carriage as the M114 but none of these remain in service today. A self-propelled model called the M41 was also built, but again, none of these remain in service with the US Army.

When the weapon is in the firing position, it is supported on its trails and firing jack which is mounted under the carriage. When in the traveling position, the trails are locked together and attached to the prime mover, which is generally a 6×6 truck. The M114 can also be carried slung under a Boeing CH-47 Chinook helicopter.

Its recoil system is of the hydropneumatic variable type and its breech-block is of the stepped thread/interrupted screw type. The M114 can fire a variety of ammunition of the separate loading (eg, the projectile and a charge) including an HE round weighing 95lb (43kg), tactical nuclear, illuminating and chemical. Sustained rate of fire is one round per minute. It cannot however fire the new Rocket Assisted Round which has a longer range than the standard 155mm round. The M114A2 is the M114A1 with a new barrel, which enables it to fire the same ammunition as the new M198 howitzer.

Armored and mechanized divisions of the US Army use the 155mm M109A1/M109A2 self-propelled howitzers, but the infantry, airborne and airmobile divisions still use the M114, although it is being rapidly replaced by the new 155mm M198 howitzer. The armored and mechanized divisions do not use the M114 as these weapons are towed by trucks and therefore have limited cross-country mobility and would be unable to keep up with mechanized forces. Each M114 battalion normally has 18 M114 s in three batteries, each with six weapons. In addition to being used by the United States the weapon is also used by some thirty other countries and is likely to remain in service for some years to come.

Above: In action the M114 is jacked up until the wheels are clear of the ground. The weapon can be towed by truck or slung-loaded beneath a helicopter.

155mm M198 Towed Howitzer

Crew: 10. **Weight:** 15,560lb (7076kg). **Length firing:** 37ft 1in (11·302m). **Length traveling:** 23ft 3in (7·086m). **Width firing:** 28ft (8·534m). **Width traveling:** 9ft 2in (2·79m). **Height firing (minimum):** ·91ft (1·803m). **Height traveling:** 9·92ft (3·023m). **Ground clearance:** 13in (0·33m). **Elevation:** −5° to +72°. **Traverse:** 22½° left and right; 360° with speed traverse. **Range:** 32,808 yards (30,000m) with RAP; 24,864 yards (24,000m) with conventional round.

In the late 1960's, Rock Island Arsenal started work on a new 155mm howitzer to replace the M114, and this was given the development designation of the XM198. The first two prototypes were followed by eight further prototypes, and during extensive trials these weapons fired over 15,000 rounds of ammunition. The M198 is now in production at Rock Island; the Army has a requirement for 435 M198s while the Marine Corps requires 282. It has also been adopted by a number of other countries including Australia, India, Greece, Pakistan, Thailand and Saudi Arabia. The M198 is used by airborne, airmobile and infantry divisions. Other divisions will continue to use self-propelled artillery. The weapon will be deployed in battalions of 18 guns, each battery having 6 weapons. The M198 is normally towed by a 6×6 5-ton truck or a tracked M548 cargo carrier, the latter being a member of the M113 family of tracked vehicles. It can also be carried under a Boeing CH-47 Chinook or a CH-54 helicopter.

When in the traveling position, the barrel is swung through 180° so that it rests over the trails. This reduces the overall length of the weapon. When in the firing position the trails are opened out and the suspension system is raised so that the weapon rests on a non-anchored firing platform. A hydraulic ram cylinder and a 24in (0·609m) diameter float mounted in the bottom carriage at the on-carriage traverse centreline, provides for rapid shift of the carriage to ensure 360° traverse. This enables the weapon to be quickly laid onto a new target.

The weapon has a recoil system of the hydropneumatic type and the barrel is provided with a double baffle muzzle brake. The M198 uses separate loading ammunition (e.g. a projectile and a separate propelling charge) and can fire an HE round to a maximum range of 24,000m, or out to 30,000m with a Rocket Assisted Projectile. The latter is basically a conventional HE shell with a small rocket motor fitted at the rear to increase the range of the shell. The weapon will also fire the new Cannon Launched Guided Projectile (or Copperhead), nuclear and Improved Conventional Munitions as well as rounds at present used with the M114. It will also be able to fire the range of ammunition developed for the FH70. The latter is a joint development between Britain, Germany and Italy and is now in production. Maximum rate of fire is four rounds per minute and a thermal warning device is provided so that the gun crew know when the barrel is becoming too hot.

Below: A prototype XM198 seen at 40° elevation during tests at Rock Island Arsenal in November 1970. Heavier than the M114, it has much greater muzzle velocity and range.

105mm M101A1 Howitzer

Calibre: 105mm. **Crew:** 8. **Weight:** 4,977lb (2258kg). **Length traveling:** 19·6ft (5·991m). **Width traveling:** 7ft (2·159m). **Height traveling:** 5·163ft (1·574m). **Ground clearance:** 14in (0·356m). **Elevation:** −4.5° to +66° **Traverse:** 23° left and right. **Range:** 12,234 yards (11,270m).

After the end of World War I, the United States Army formed a committee called the Westervelt Board to examine the performance of the field artillery in that war, and also to lay the foundations for a complete range of new artillery. One of the requirements was for a 105mm howitzer which, after many years of development owing to a shortage of funds, entered production at Rock Island Arsenal as the 105mm M2 in 1939. During World War II the M2 (later known as M101) was made by a number of companies and by the time production was completed in 1953, no less than 10,202 weapons had been built. Many self-propelled models were also developed and one of these, the M7 Priest (on a Sherman chassis), remains in service to this day, although not with the United States Army. Since the end of the war, there have been many attempts to reduce the weight and improve the mobility of the M101, but none of these have progressed past the trials stage. Today at least fifty armies around the world still use the M2 (M101). The main difference between the M101 and the M101A1 is that the M101 has the M2A1 carriage while the M101A1 has the M2A2 carriage.

The M101A1 has a carriage with split trails and is provided with a shield to protect the crew from small arms fire and shell splinters. Its breechblock is of the horizontal sliding wedge type and its recoil system is of the hydropneumatic type. The barrel, which is not provided with a muzzle brake, has a life of 20,000 rounds. The weapon can fire a wide variety of ammunition including an HE round weighing 33lb, High Explosive Anti-Tank — this round will penetrate 102mm of armor at 1,640 yards (1500m) —smoke, white phosphorous, chemical, illuminating, High Explosive Plastic — Tracer (an anti-tank round), leaflet, anti-personnel and the more recent Rocket Assisted Projectile. The latter has a range of 15,857 yards (14,500m). Its maximum rate of fire is 8 rounds per minute for 30 seconds, or 3rpm sustained. The M101 is normally towed by a 6×6 truck and can be airlifted by a Boeing Chinook helicopter.

Although obsolete by today's standards, the M101 is still in service in some numbers with the United States Army as each infantry division has three battalions each of which has 18 M101A1's (in three batteries of six guns). In Vietnam, it was found that the M101 was rather heavy in this type of terrain and as a result the 105mm M102 was developed at Rock Island Arsenal, this is however only used by Airborne and Airmobile Divisions. Both the M101 and the M102 were to have been replaced by the 105mm XM204, but development of this weapon was stopped by Congress. They are now being replaced by the 155mm M198 howitzer.

Above: The M101 is still standard light artillery of the US Army, despite obsolescence. Picture taken during annual operational readiness tests at Grafenwohr, Germany.

105mm M192 Light Howitzer

Calibre: 105mm. **Crew:** 8. **Weight:** 3,298lb (1,496kg). **Length firing:** 22ft (6·718m). **Length traveling:** 17ft (5·182m). **Height firing:** 4·29ft (1·308m). **Height traveling:** 5·22ft (1·594m). **Width:** 6·44ft (1·964m). **Ground clearance:** 1·08ft (0·33m). **Elevation:** −5° to +75°. **Traverse:** 360°. **Range:** 12,576 yards (11,500m); standard ammunition: 16,513 yards (15,100m) with RAP.

The 105mm M102 was developed at Rock Island Arsenal to replace the standard 105mm M101 howitzer in both airborne and airmobile divisions. The first prototype was completed in 1962 and the weapon entered service in 1966. It was widely used in Vietnam. Improvements over the M101 include a reduction in weight, longer range, and it can be quickly traversed through 360°. Both the M101 and M102 were to have been replaced by a new 105mm howitzer called the XM204, but this was cancelled by Congress in 1977 owing to both tactical and technical problems.

The M102 is normally deployed in battalions of 18 guns (each of these having three batteries each with 6 guns), and both the 82nd Airborne and 101st Airmobile/Air Assault Divisions each have three battalions of M102s, but these are now being replaced by the 155mm M198. It is normally towed by the M561 (6×6) Gama Goat vehicle or a 2½ ton 6×6 truck, and can be carried slung underneath a Boeing Chinook CH-47 helicopter.

When in the firing position the wheels are raised off the ground and the weapon rests on a turntable under the front of the carriage, a roller tyre is mounted at the rear of the trail and this enables the weapon to be quickly traversed through 360° to be laid onto a new target. The M102 has an unusual bow shape box type trail which is of aluminum construction to reduce weight. Its breechblock is of the vertical sliding wedge type and its recoil system is of the hydropneumatic type. The barrel is not provided with a muzzle brake, although this was fitted to the prototype weapons. A wide range of ammunition can be fitted including high explosive, high explosive anti-tank, anti-personnel, illuminating, smoke, chemical, HEP-T and leaflet. Ten rounds per minute can be fired for the first three minutes, and 3 rounds per minute in the sustained fire role.

Above right: The M102 is the only modern light artillery in US Army service. It is more stable than most.

Right: Layout of ammo at Normandy drop zone at Fort Bragg for fire mission support. The M102 is one of the lightest 105mm weapons and can be lifted by quite small helicopters.

M88 Medium Armored Recovery Vehicle

Crew: 4 (commander, driver, co-driver, mechanic). **Armament:** One 0·50 M2 HB machine gun. **Dimensions:** Length (without dozer blade): 27·15ft (8·267m); width 11·24ft (3·428m); height with anti-aircraft machine gun 10·58ft (3·225m). **Weight:** 111,993lb (50,800kg). **Ground pressure:** 10·63lb/in² (0·74kg/cm²). **Engine:** Continental AVSI-1790-6A, twelve cylinder petrol engine developing 980bhp at 2,800rpm. **Performance:** road speed 26mph (42km/hr); range 223 miles (360km); vertical obstacle 3·49ft (1·066m); trench 8·58ft (2·616m); gradient 60 percent.

The standard medium armored recovery vehicle used by the US Army in the early 1950s was the M74. This was based on a Sherman tank chassis but could not handle the heavier tanks which were then entering service. In 1954, work on a new medium armored recovery vehicle commenced and three prototypes, designated the T88, were built by Bowen-McLaughlin-York. After trials, a batch of pre-production vehicles were built and then Bowen-McLaughlin-York were awarded a production contract for the vehicle which was standardized as the M88. Just over 1,000 M88s were built between 1961 and 1964, and some were also exported abroad. The M88 uses many automotive components of the M48 tank, and can recover AFV's up to and including the M60 MBT. Its role on the battlefield is to recover damaged and disabled tanks and other AFV's, and it can, if required, remove major components from tanks such as complete turrets. When the M88 first entered service it was armed with a 0·50 calibre machine gun mounted in a turret but this was subsequently replaced by a simple pintle mounted 0·50 machine gun.

The hull of the M88 is of cast armor construction and provides the crew with protection from small arms fire and shell splinters. The crew compartment is at the front of the hull and the engine and transmission is at the rear. A hydraulically operated dozer blade is mounted at the front of the hull and this is used to stabilize the vehicle when the winch or "A" frame is being used, and can also be used for normal dozing operations. The "A" type frame is pivoted at the front of the hull, and when not required this lays in

Above: The M88A1 can recover every type of AFV in the inventory, including M1. Here the A frame used to change major components, such as turrets, is stowed to the rear.

the horizontal position on top of the hull. This frame can lift a maximum load of six tons (5443kg), or 25 tons (22,680kg) with the dozer blade in the lowered position.

The M88 is provided with two winches and both of these are mounted under the crew compartment. The main winch is provided with 200ft (61m) of 32mm cable and has a maximum pull of 40 tons, whilst the secondary winch, which is used for hoisting operations, has 200ft (61m) of 16mm cable. The vehicle is provided with a full range of tools and an auxiliary fuel pump. This enables the vehicle to transfer fuel to other armored vehicles.

All M88s of the US Army have now been brought up to M88A1 standard and are fitted with the Continental AVDS-1790-2DR diesel engine developing 750bhp at 2,400rpm. This gives the vehicle a longer operating range of 280 miles (450km) compared to the original M88. It is also fitted with an APU and can also be fitted with a NBC system. Current production model is M88A1 which has also been exported to many parts of the world.

M578 Light Armored Recovery Vehicle

Crew: 3. **Armament:** One 0·50 M2 HB machine gun. **Dimensions:** length overall 21ft (6·42m); width 10·331ft (3·149m); height with machine gun 11·20ft (3·416m). **Weight:** 53,572lb (24,300kg). **Ground pressure:** 10·56lb/in² (0·71kg/cm²). **Engine:** General Motors Model 8V71T eight cylinder liquid diesel developing 425bhp at 2,300rpm. **Performance:** road speed 34mph (54·71km/h); range 450 miles (725km); vertical obstacle 3·3ft (1·016m); trench 7·76ft (2·362m); gradient 60 percent.

In the mid-1950s, the Pacific Car and Foundry Company of Renton, Washington, were awarded a contract by the US Army to build a new range of self-propelled artillery, all of which were to use the same common chassis. These three weapons were the T235 (which eventually entered service as the 175mm M107), the T236 (which entered service as the 8inch M110) and the T245 (this was a 155mm weapon but was not developed past the prototype stage). In 1957, it was decided to build a range of light armored recovery vehicles using the same chassis as the self-propelled guns. Three different prototypes were built. Further development resulted in the T120E1 which had a diesel engine, and this entered service as the M578.

The first production M578 was completed by the FMC Corporation in 1962, and since then the vehicle has been produced by the designers,

Pacific Car and Foundry, and more recently by Bowen-McLaughlin-York. Between FY 1976 and FY 1978, the US Army requested some 64 million dollars to purchase an additional 283 M578s.

The M578 is used by all arms including self-propelled artillery battalions, mechanized infantry battalions and armored cavalry regiments. Apart from recovering such vehicles as the M110 and M109, the vehicle is also used to change major components in the field, such as engines, transmissions and tank barrels.

The hull of the M578 is identical to that of the M107 and M110 self-propelled guns, with the driver being seated at the front of the hull on the left side and the engine to his right. The crane is mounted at the rear of the hull and this can be traversed through a full 360 degrees. The commander and mechanic are seated in the turret and a standard 0·50 Browning M2 HB machine gun is mounted on the roof for anti-aircraft protection. The crane can lift a maximum of 13·38 tons (13,600kg) and the main winch is provided with 229ft (70m) of 25mm cable. This has a maximum capacity of 26·57 tons (27,000kg). A large spade is mounted at the rear of the hull to stabilize the vehicle when the winch or crane is being used, in addition, the suspension can be locked out if required. Unlike most MBTs, the M578 is not provided with a NBC system and it has no amphibious capability, infra-red driving lights are normally fitted.

Below: Standard light armored recovery vehicle is the M578. Recovery and repair of main battle tanks, and other weapons, is obviously an important role in a highly mobile army.

M79 Grenade Launcher

Calibre: 40mm. **Weight of grenade:** 0·610lb (0·277kg). **Length of launcher:** 29in (73·7cm). **Length of barrel:** 14in (35·6cm). **Weight of launcher:** (empty) 5·99lb (2·72kg); loaded, 6·5lb (2·95kg). **Muzzle velocity:** 249ft/s (76m/s). **Range:** 437·4 yards (400m) maximum; 383 yards (350m) effective, area targets; 164 yards (150m) effective, point targets. **Effective casualty radius:** 5·46 yards (5m). **Rate of fire:** 5 rounds per minute.

The 40mm M79 Grenade Launcher was developed to give the infantryman the capability to deliver accurate firepower to a greater range than could be achieved with a conventional rifle grenade. The M79 is a single shot, break-open weapon and is fired from the shoulder. It is breech loaded and fires a variety of different types of ammunition including high explosive, high explosive air burst, CS gas and smoke. Its fore sight is of the blade type and its rear sight is of the folding leaf adjustable type. The latter is graduated from 82 yards (75m) to 410 yards (375m) in about 27 yards (25m) increments. When the rear sight is in the horizontal position, the fixed sight may be used to engage targets up to 109·3 yards (100m). The M79 has been replaced in front line units by the M203 grenade launcher which is fitted to the standard M16A1 rifle.

Right: The M79 grenade launcher fires the full range of 40mm grenades. There is also a version for use by helicopters with automatic feed of grenades. The M79 is largely replaced by the M203/M16A1 rifle combination.

81mm M29 Mortar

Calibre: 81mm. **Weight of barrel:** 27·99lb (12·7kg). **Weight of base-plate:** 24·91lb (11·3kg). **Weight of bipod:** 40lb (18·15kg). **Total weight with sight:** 115lb (52·2kg). **Elevation:** +40° to +85°. **Traverse:** 4° left and 4° right. **Maximum range:** 5,025 yards (4595m) with M374A2 HE bomb. **Rate of fire:** 27rpm for 1 minute; 4rpm sustained.

In service with US Army and some Allied countries, the 81mm M29 mortar is the standard medium mortar of the US Army and is in service in two basic models, infantry and self-propelled. The standard infantry model can be disassembled into three components, each of which can be carried by one man—baseplate, barrel, mount and sight. The exterior of the barrel is helically grooved both to reduce weight and to dissipate heat when a high rate of fire is being achieved.

The mortar is also mounted in the rear of a modified member of the M113 APC family called the M125A1. In this vehicle the mortar is mounted on a turntable and this enables it to be traversed quickly through 360° to be laid onto a new target. A total of 114 81mm mortar bombs are carried in the vehicle.

The mortar can fire a variety of mortar bombs including HE (the M374 bomb has a maximum range of 5,025 yards (4595m)), white phosphorus (the M375 bomb has a maximum range of 5,180 yards (4737m)) and illuminating (the M301 bomb has a maximum range of 3,444 yards (3150m)). The 81mm M29 has been replaced in certain units by the new 60mm M224 Lightweight Company Mortar. The US Army expects to replace the 81mm M29 by the British 81mm L16 which has a range of 6,190 yards (5660m) when compared to the M29. The US Army also uses the 107mm M30 mortar in both standard and self-propelled versions.

Right: Here seen in the infantry role, the M29 is the standard US Army medium mortar. It is also used by many NATO countries, some of which claim up to 32 bombs in one minute.

60mm M224 Lightweight Company Mortar

Below: The M224 60mm Lightweight Company Mortar can be used with a circular base plate and a bipod, or hand held. Included among its mortar bombs is the new M720 HE round.

During the Vietnam campaign, it was found that the standard 81mm M29 mortar was too heavy for the infantry to transport in rough terrain, even when disassembled into its three main components. In its place the old 60mm M19 mortar was used, but this had a short range. The M224 (development designation XM224) has been developed to replace the 81mm M29 mortar in non-mechanized infantry, airmobile and airborne units at company level, and is also issued to the US Marine Corps. The weapon comprises a lightweight finned barrel, sight, baseplate and bipod, although if required it can also be used without the baseplate and bipod. The complete mortar weighs only 45lb (20·4kg) compared to the 81mm mortar which weighs 115lb (52kg). The M224 fires an HE bomb which provides a substantial portion of the lethality of the 81mm mortar with a waterproof "horseshoe" snap-off propellant increments, and a multi-option fuze. The latter allows proximity, near surface, point detonating and delay options, simply by the rotation of the fuze head.

The mortar will be used in conjunction with the AN/GVS-5 hand held laser rangefinder, this can range up to 10,936 yards (10,000m) to an accuracy of ±10·936 yards (±10m), this enables the mortar to engage a target without firing a ranging bomb first. The M224 fires a variety of mortar bombs to a maximum range of 3,828 yards (3500m) and is currently in production at Watervliet Arsenal. The army has ordered 1,590 of these mortars while the Marine Corps has ordered 698.

20mm Vulcan Air Defense System

Crew: 1 (on gun). **Weight (firing and traveling):** 3,500lb (1588kg). **Length traveling:** 16ft (4·9m). **Width traveling:** 6·49ft (1·98m). **Height traveling:** 6·68ft (2·03m). **Elevation:** −5° to +80°. **Traverse:** 360°. **Effective range:** 2,187 yards (2000m).
Note: the above data relate to the towed version.

The 20mm Vulcan is the standard light anti-aircraft gun of the US Army and has been in service since 1968, it is also used by Belgium, Israel and Jordan. There are two versions of the Vulcan system in service, one towed and the other self-propelled. The towed version is known as the M167 and this is mounted on a two wheeled carriage and is normally towed by an M715 or M37 truck. When in the firing position the weapon rests on three outriggers to provide a more stable firing platform. The self-propelled model is known as the M163 and this is mounted on a modified M113A1 APC chassis, the chassis itself being the M741. The latter will be replaced by the twin 40mm DIVAD.

The 20mm cannon used in the system is a modified version of the air-cooled six-barrel M61 Vulcan cannon developed by General Electric. It is also the standard air-to-air cannon of the US Air Force and is installed in many aircraft including the F-104, F-111, F-15 and F-16. The Vulcan cannon has two rates of fire, 1,000 or 3,000 rounds per minute, and the gunner can select either 10, 30, 60 or 100 round bursts. The M163 has 500 rounds of linked ready-use ammunition while the self-propelled model has 1,100 rounds of ready-use ammunition.

The fire control system consists of an M61 gyro lead-computing gun sight, a range-only radar mounted on the right side of the turret (developed by Lockheed Electronics), and a sight current generator. The gunner normally visually acquires and tracks the target while the radar supplies range and range rate data to the sight current generator. These imputs are converted to proper current for use in the sight. With this current the sight computes the correct lead angle and adds the required super elevation. The turret has full power traverse and elevation, slewing rate being 60°/second, and elevation rate being 45°/second. Power is provided by an auxiliary generator.

The Vulcan air defense system is normally used in conjunction with the Chaparral SAM. Each Vulcan/Chaparrel battalion has 24 Chaparral units

Above: The M167 towed version. Vulcan guns in fighter aircraft fire at rates up to 6,000 shots/minute.

and 24 self-propelled Vulcan systems. Airborne and Airmobile divisions have a total of 48 towed Vulcan systems. The Vulcan system is normally used in conjunction with the Saunders TPQ-32 or MPQ-49 Forward Area Alerting Radar, which provides the weapons with basic information such as from which direction the targets are approaching.

The 20mm cannon has a maximum effective range in the anti-aircraft role of 2,187 yards (2000m) but can also be used in the ground role, and was deployed to Vietnam for this purpose. A variety of different types of ammunition can be fired, including armor piercing, armor piercing incendiary, and high-explosive incendiary. The weapon is also produced for export without the range-only radar. All American M167 VADS now have dual road wheels for improved stability.

In addition to being used by the Army and Air Force, a modified version of the 20mm Vulcan is being used by the US Navy for its Close-In Weapon System (or Vulcan Phalanx). This has been developed to protect warships against attack from cruise missiles.

66mm M72 Light Anti-tank Weapon (LAW)

Calibre: 66mm. **Length of rocket:** 20in (50·8cm). **Weight of rocket:** 2lb (1kg). **Muzzle velocity:** 476ft/s (145m/s). **Maximum effective range:** 984ft (300m). **Length of launcher closed:** 25·7in (65·5cm). **Length of launcher extended** 35in (89·3cm). **Weight complete:** 5·22lb (2·37kg).

The M72 is the standard Light Anti-Tank Weapon (LAW) of the US Army and is also used by many armies around the world. Development of the weapon started in 1958 with the first production LAWs being completed by the Hesse Eastern Company of Brockton, Massachusetts, in 1962. It is

also manufactured under licence in Norway by Raufoss. The LAW is a lightweight, shoulder-fired rocket launcher and its rocket has a HEAT warhead which will penetrate over 11·8in (300mm) of armor. It can also be used against bunkers, pillboxes and other battlefield fortifications.

When the M72 is required for action, the infantryman removes the safety pins, which open the end covers, and the inner tube is telescoped outwards, cocking the firing mechanism. The launcher tube is then held over the shoulder, aimed and the weapon fired. The launcher is then discarded. Improved models are known as the M72A1 and the more recent M72A2. The M72 LAW is due to be replaced by the General Dynamics Viper which is covered in the "missiles" section.

Below: Effective range of the M72A2 LAW against moving targets is considered to be about half of that against stationary ones.

7.62mm M60 General Purpose Machine Gun

Calibre: 7·62mm. **Length:** 43·3in (110cm). **Length of barrel:** 22in (56cm). **Weight:** 23lb (10.48kg) with bipod; 39·6lb (18kg) with tripod. **Maximum effective range (bipod):** 984 yards (900m). **Maximum effective range (tripod):** 1,968 yards (1800m). **Rate of fire:** 550rpm (cyclic); 200rpm (automatic).

The M60 is the standard GPMG of the US Army and has now replaced the older 0·30 Browning machine gun. The weapon was developed by the Bridge Tool and Die Works and the Inland Division of General Motors Corporation, under the direction of Springfield Armory. Production of the M60 commenced in 1959 by the Maremont Corporation of Saco, Maine, and the weapon is still in production today.

The M60 is gas-operated, air-cooled and is normally used with a 100-round belt of ammunition. To avoid overheating the barrel is normally changed after 500 rounds have been fired. Its fore sight is of the fixed blade type and its rear sight is of the U-notch type and is graduated from about 656ft to 3,937ft (200 to 1200m) in about 328ft (100m) steps. The weapon is provided with a stock, carrying handle and a built in bipod. The M60 can also be used on an M122 tripod mount, M4 pedestal mount and M142 gun mount for vehicles. Other versions include the M60C remote for helicopters, M60D pintle mount for vehicles and helicopters and the M60E2 internal model for AFVs.

Above: The M60 in standard infantry form, with stock, pistol-grip trigger and bipod. The helicopter model (M60D), has twin grips at the rear and pintle mount.

12.7mm M2 HB Heavy Machine Gun

Calibre: 0·50in (12·7mm). **Length overall:** 65·07in (165·3cm). **Length of barrel:** 44·99in (114·3cm). **Weight (gun only):** 83·33lb (37·8kg); 127·8lb (57·98kg) with tripod. **Range:** 1,996 yards (1825m) effective in ground role; 7,470 yards (6830m) maximum; 820 yards (750m) anti-aircraft role. **Rate of fire:** 450/575rpm.

The 0·50 calibre M2 Heavy Barrel (HB) machine gun was developed for the US Army in the early 1930s, as the replacement for the 0·50 M1921A1 MG. The weapon was developed by John Browning (who designed many other famous weapons including the Browning Automatic Rifle and the Browning 0·30 machine gun), and the Colt Firearms company of Hartford, Connecticut.

The M2 is air-cooled and recoil operated, and is fed from a disintegrating metallic link belt. The weapon can fire either single shots or fully automatic, and various types of ammunition can be fired including ball, tracer, armor-piercing and armor-piercing incendiary. For ground targets the weapon is mounted on the M3 tripod while for the anti-aircraft role the M63 mount is used. It is also mounted on many armored fighting vehicles including the

M113A1 series of APC (and variants), the M109/M108 SPH and the M57 and M88 ARV. The M55 anti-aircraft system (no longer in service with the US Army) has four M2s, and the M2 is also mounted in helicopters and in some commanders' turrets as the M85. The M2 HB MG is still being produced in the United States by Ramo Incorporated and the Maremont Corporation.

Above: 0·50 calibre Browning M2 HB machine gun on M3 tripod, with box of ready-use ammunition.

90mm M67 Recoilless Rifle

Calibre: 90mm. **Crew:** 2. **Weight:** 34·98lb (15·876kg). **Length:** 53in (134·6cm). **Range:** 503 yards (460m) effective anti-tank; 2,296 yards (2100m) maximum.

The M67 was the standard Medium Anti-Tank Weapon (MAW) of the US Army for many years, but has now almost been replaced in units by the M47 Dragon anti-tank guided missile. The M67 consists of a front-mounting bracket group, cable assembly, face shield group, breech and hinge mechanism group, rear mounting bracket group and the rifled tube itself. The telescopic sight has a magnification of ×3 and a 10° field of view. A normal team would consist of two men, one M67 MAW and five rounds of ammunition. It can be fired from the shoulder, or from the ground using the

rear bipod mount and forward monopod for stability.

The M371 HEAT round is fin-stabilized and has a maximum effective range of 437 yards (400m), it weighs 9·2lb (4·19kg). The M590A1 anti-personnel round weighs 6·7lb (3·04kg) and has a maximum effective range of 328 yards (300m). A training round, weighing 9.23lb (4·19kg), is also available.

After firing five rounds in quick succession, a 15 minute cooling period must elapse before fire is resumed as the barrel quickly overheats. The weapon also has a danger area, due to backblast, which extends 33 yards (30m) to the rear. The M67 is still used by the US Army's Berlin Brigade and is now manufactured in South Korea.

Below: The M67 is one of very few types of recoilless rifle of around 4in (100mm) calibre usable by a single infantryman.

5.56mm M16A1 Rifle

Calibre: 5·56mm. **Length overall (with flash suppressor):** 38·9in (99cm). **Length of barrel:** 19·9in (50·8cm). **Weight (including 30 round loaded magazine):** 8·42lb (3·82kg). **Range:** 503 yards (460m) maximum effective). **Rate of fire:** 700–950rpm (cyclic); 150–200rpm automatic); 45–65rpm (semi-automatic). **Muzzle velocity:** 3,280ft/s 1000m/s).

The M16 (previously the AR-15) was designed by Eugene Stoner and was a development of the earlier 7·62mm AR-10 assault rifle. It was first adopted by the US Air Force, and at a later date the US Army adopted the weapon or use in Vietnam. When first used in combat numerous faults became apparent and most of these were traced to a lack of training and poor maintenance. Since then the M16 has replaced the 7·62mm M14 as the standard rifle of the United States forces. To date over 5,000,000 have been manufactured, most by Colt Firearms and the weapon was also made under licence in Singapore, South Korea and the Philippines. Twenty-one armies use the M16. The weapon is gas-operated and the user can select either full automatic or semi-automatic. Both 20- and 30-round magazine can be fitted, as can a bipod, bayonet, telescope and night sight. The weapon can also be fitted with the M203 40mm grenade launcher, and this fires a variety of 40mm grenades to a maximum range of 382 yards (350m). The M203 has now replaced the M79 grenade launcher on a one-for-one basis. The Colt Commando is a special version of the M16 and this has a shorter barrel, flash supressor and a telescopic sight, reducing the overall length of the weapon to 27·9in (71cm). The M231 is a special model which can be fired from within the M2 Bradley Infantry Fighting Vehicle.

Below: Training with an M16 fitted with a laser transmitter and receiver simulator system (clipped under the muzzle) with which accuracy can be checked without necessarily firing.

0.45 Caliber M1911A1 Pistol

Calibre: 0·45in (11·43mm). **Length:** 8·63in (21·93cm). **Length of barrel:** ·03in (12·78cm). **Weight loaded:** 2·99lb (1·36kg). **Weight empty:** ·49lb (1·13kg). **Effective range:** 65ft (20m). **Muzzle velocity:** 826ft/s 252m/s).

The 0·45 calibre M1911 pistol was the standard American sidearm of World War I. In 1923, work on an improved model commenced at Springfield Armory, and this was standardized as the M1911A1 in 1926, and since then the weapon has been the standard sidearm of the US Army. The Army does, however, use other pistols for special missions, as the M1911A1 is rather heavy and has quite a recoil. Between 1937 and 1945, over 19 million M1911A1 pistols were manufactured by Colt, Ithaca and Remington. The weapon is semi-automatic, and all the user has to do is to pull the trigger each time he wants to fire. The magazine, which is in the grip, holds a total of seven rounds. The fore sight is of the fixed blade type and the rear sight consists of a U notch on dovetail slide. The weapon has three safety devices: the grip safety on the handle, the safety lock, and the half cock position on the hammer.

Right: Demonstrating the position used in competition shooting with sidearms; this body and arm posture provides the shooter with maximum stability. Without doubt, the next standard US Army sidearm will have much smaller calibre.

The United States Navy

Bruce F. Powers, Senior Fellow, Strategic Concepts Development Center, National Defense University, Washington, DC.

Nations have navies to exert some control over the oceans. The United States is no exception. The far-flung successes of the US Navy as World War II ended made it dominant in many parts of the world. This dominance continued after demobilization and into the 1960s. Today's US Navy has 481 ships and 550,000 men and women on active duty. The number of ships is half as many as 20 years ago, despite some recent growth. Even so, the US Navy deploys versatile, capable fleets overseas and operates additional effective forces closer to the United States during peacetime. It is still the most capable navy in the world.

The US Navy—the ships and aircraft in it and how it is used—has been shaped by many forces. This chapter begins by identifying them. The composition of today's Navy is then described, as well as changes in its composition that can be foreseen. Finally, unanswered questions concerning the Navy's future are examined.

Forces that have shaped the Navy

The most important force shaping the Navy is the set of broad objectives the United States has for it. These are discussed first, followed by descriptions of the Navy's most likely conflicts and its peacetime posture. The likely conflicts point out the characteristics of opposing navies most needing US Navy attention. Improvements in technology create opportunities to shape a navy; limited budgets impose constraints. These, too, are discussed.

US objectives for its Navy

The United States, allied, and friendly countries dominate the World Ocean, a loosely-defined geographic area which is tied together by economic interdependence and trade. Its limits are roughly defined by Alaska, Japan/Korea, the Malay Archipelago, Australia, Cape Horn, South Africa and NATO Europe. The seas and airspace surrounding the United States serve as a convenient means for access to other members of the World Ocean as well as the final bastions for defense of the US homeland. Their control is vital to the security of the nation.

US peacetime objectives include free use of the seas by friendly merchant shipping and influencing events far from US shores. The US Congress requires that the Navy be prepared to fight quickly when called upon, and to keep fighting when necessary. In order to achieve these objectives, US Navy officers focus on more specific missions—establishing control of sea and air space and projecting air, missile, or amphibious forces ashore.

As the United States became increasingly dependent on foreign trade during the past century, its Navy grew to insure the uninterrupted flow of that trade. One reason US Navy ships are deployed far from US shores is to maintain that flow by deterring potential threats to it. These deployed forces also affect events ashore by their ability to intervene. Earlier in this century, intervention ashore meant several miles—the range of a nval gun or an independent landing party. More recently, carrier-based aircraft and helicopter-borne marines

extended intervention ranges to tens and even hundreds of miles. Cruise missiles now appearing aboard ships in numbers extend the range still farther.

Naval forces can move freely in peacetime. This flexibility becomes very important in crises, when naval forces can help signal their governments' intents by the stations they assume. Some of this stationing can be threatening but, if done outside territorial waters, the option to stop short of combat and pull away is retained. If, on the other hand, land forces are to influence crises, they must generally be so placed that the act of placement is itself hostile. Naval forces are therefore preferred for crisis management. US naval forces bring a wide range of potential capabilities to a crisis—from a few interceptor sorties that can cover the ground forces of a small ally to large air strikes or amphibious assaults. This versatility gives added flexibility to the US government in a crisis. If the crisis turns to combat, the versatility permits US participation without the full-scale commitment implied by the introduction of sizeable ground forces. If a full-scale commitment is decided upon, naval forces are often—because of their position and the range of their capabilities—the first committed. (The first American strikes against North Vietnam, for instance, were conducted by US Navy forces in 1964. The demand for air sorties to support friendly troops in South Vietnam rose quickly in 1965. Even though it may be less expensive to fly air sorties from land bases, such bases take months to build. While construction was going on in 1965, an extra carrier flew the sorties needed.)

When a crisis does turn into a conflict, one US objective is to control it. Because the United States has major interests overseas, including the well-being of many allies there, local conflicts that spill over can be very damaging. Employing needed US Navy capabilities far from American shores enhances the likelihood of keeping conflict confined, and also away from North America or other areas of vital concern.

In addition to operating at long distances, the US Navy is expected to respond promptly and to continue to fight for months or even years. To go into action quickly means that naval forces must be nearby and ready. This is achieved by keeping them manned and equipped and exercising them regularly. The exercises stress likely combat employment and tend to be more sophisticated the closer the forces are to the scene of their likely employment. In particular, the forces regularly stationed in the Mediterranean Sea, the Indian Ocean, and the western Pacific Ocean conduct multi-ship exercises that stress several types of naval warfare within the space of a few days.

The requirement to fight on also influences the design of the US Navy. Staying power is built into individual ships; it also is achieved by providing both relief warships and ships that can replenish warships engaged in combat with ammunition, fuel, spare parts, and food. The replenishment ships permit warships to keep fighting, and to do so several thousand miles from the United States rather than returning

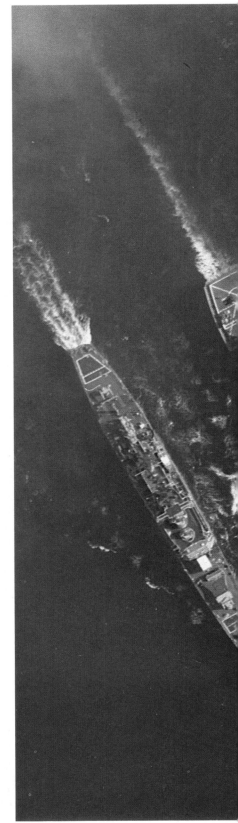

The enormous power of the United States Navy is summed up in these two pictures. On the left a Trident C-4 SLBM blasts away from an underwater launch epitomising the USN's role in providing the survivable counter-value deterrent force. The Navy has 32 SSBNs in service of which some 17 are at sea at any one time. These possess truly formidable firepower. The second element of the fleet is the conventional force represented below by ships of a Carrier Task Force undergoing Replenishment at Sea (RAS). The ships are the carrier USS *Constellation* (CV-64), the combat stores ship USS *Niagara Falls* (AFS-3) and the cruiser USS *Leahy* (CG-16). The ability to project airpower from mobile bases is a priceless asset.

home for replenishment. A network of overseas bases increases the flexibility and decreases the distances over which these replenishment ships must sail. Typically, warships retire a hundred miles or more from the combat area to replenish and then return to it. When warships need repairs or crew rest, the relief warships fill their place. Relief warships operate near the coasts of the United States in peacetime.

Specific missions

To achieve the objectives described above, US Navy officers focus on specific missions. The most important is establishing and maintaining control of sea and air space. Others are projecting military forces ashore and operating in peacetime to reassure allies and warn potential foes.

Establishing sea control is generally viewed as a prerequisite to projecting naval forces ashore. For example, moving a division or more of troops to assault a distant shore requires many transports. Such ships are lightly armed; their path must be kept safe from opposing forces. Even if the path is cleared beforehand, heavily armed escorts are needed to fend off opposing forces that may enter the cleared lane. The clearing and escort tasks amount to establishment of control over sea and air space. Similar tasks are obviously required for a massive resupply by unarmed convoys, and even for the transit of battle groups whose principal ships are aircraft carriers. Once an amphibious or carrier force has reached its operating area, control of the sea and air space there is also necessary; if control of the operating area is subject to interruption, projection of air or landing forces ashore cannot be achieved reliably.

Emphasis has been shifting among US Navy missions since World War II. Such broad objectives as insuring free use of the seas and influencing distant events ashore have remained fixed. But specific Navy missions, such as projecting forces ashore, have shifted in relative importance as technology and the capabilities of potential opponents have evolved.

After World War II, the US Navy quickly demobilized from 3.4 million men and thousands of ships to 350,000 men and a few hundred ships. It soon remobilized to more than a thousand ships. Because the fleets of the United States and its allies faced no important opponents at sea, the US Navy was still able to dominate the oceans. During the Korean War of 1950–53, for instance, ships of the US Navy and the navies of some other UN members operated several thousand miles from the United States. Unchallenged at seas, this force devoted itself entirely to air attack of targets ashore, shore bombardment with naval guns, and amphibious landings.

About that time, US Navy aircraft aboard carriers were assigned the mission of delivering nuclear weapons on targets in the Soviet Union. This mission influenced the design of carriers and their aircraft. Some aircraft became larger to carry the large nuclear devices of the time and to strike targets at ranges of a thousand or more miles. The carriers were also built larger to accommodate the larger aircraft. Except for amphibious transports, the Navy subordinated its other large surface ships to escort or replenishment of the carriers. Beginning in 1960, the carriers gradually transferred the long-range delivery of nuclear weapons to submarines.

The US Navy has operated nuclear-powered submarines since 1960. Their mission is firing ballistic missiles with nuclear warheads. These early "Polaris", and "Poseidon", and now "Trident" missiles can be launched from beneath the ocean's surface against targets in the Soviet Union or elsewhere. The submarine-launched missiles account for only some of the United States' intercontinental nuclear weapons; the entire capability is described in more detail in the chapter on "strategic" forces.

As the carriers turned over the mission of delivery of nuclear weapons against the Soviet

Above: View along the deck of USS *Ohio* with caps of the Trident launch tubes open; 24 Trident I C4 missiles are carried. Below: *Ohio* launches a Trident on February 18, 1982. The missile has a range of 3,830 miles (7,100km) and carries 8 MIRVs.

Right: Following its launch, USS *Phoenix* a Los Angeles class SSN, slides past Ohio class SSBNs under construction. The latter will be armed with a total of 72 missiles, each with 8 MIRVs, enabling 572 targets to be engaged.

tion to submarines, they resumed their
earlier attention to closer targets. This shift of
attention was accelerated in 1964–72 by the
requirements for air sorties during the Vietnam
war. Here, as in Korea, the absence of a naval
threat permitted the carriers to mount sorties
with maximum bombloads from close to shore
and free their escorts occasionally to bombard

Potential challenges at sea have also caused
shifts in emphasis among Navy missions. The
Soviet Navy began its first regular deployments
outside home waters by deploying to the
Mediterranean Sea in 1964. In 1967, such deployments became continuous. During that
year, an Egyptian ship launched a cruise missile at the Israeli destroyer *Eilat* and sank it.
Similar missiles were carried by some of the
Soviet ships that had recently arrived in the
Mediterranean. There—and, later, elsewhere
as US Navy operations in Vietnam decreased—
the Navy developed and exercised procedures
for dealing with opposing surface forces armed
with cruise missiles.

These long-term shifts in US Navy emphasis
are matched by short-term crises that call for
the application of naval power ashore. At
places where the Soviet Navy concentrates
forces, virtually all US Navy resources in the
vicinity will have to be directed to dealing with
the concentrated Soviet forces—as with classical naval operations—before USN attention
can return to events ashore. In places where the
Soviet Navy is absent or weak—such as in some
Third World settings—the threat to the US
Navy's unfettered activities is reduced, and so
some USN attention can be concentrated on
events ashore from the outset.

Submarines have been a major concern to the
Navy even longer than have cruise missiles,
particularly in the Atlantic. German submarines nearly stopped the flow of supplies to
Europe in 1918 and again in 1942. After 1945, the
Soviet Union expanded its submarine force. Beginning in the mid-1950s, some older US aircraft
carriers were assigned exclusively to anti-
submarine duty. They were therefore allotted
antisubmarine helicopters and fixed-wing anti-
submarine aircraft. Beginning in the early
'70s, for budgetary reasons, the carrier-cap-
able antisubmarine aircraft have been placed
aboard all carriers; the older carriers devoted
to antisubmarine work have been retired. At

the same time, nuclear-powered submarines
besides those fitted with ballistic missiles have
entered the US Navy in large numbers, adding
significantly to its antisubmarine strength.
However, the ongoing modernization of the
Soviet Navy's attack submarines with nuclear-
powered ones—which are harder to detect than
diesel submarines involved in frequent battery
charges—has kept US Navy attention on
Soviet submarines. So has the regular appearance in sizable numbers of Soviet submarines in the Mediterranean Sea and in the
Pacific and Indian oceans.

Although nuclear weapons for delivery by
carrier-based aircraft were at first designed for
use against the Soviet homeland, later nuclear
weapons were developed for both offensive and
defensive war at sea. Such weapons are no
longer limited to aircraft carriers.

Likely wartime employment
The Secretary of Defense has directed the Navy
to assist NATO if attacked by Warsaw Pact
forces, to conduct operations near the Persian
Gulf, for similarly-scaled contingencies elsewhere, and to manage crises. US forces are
supposed to be able to deal with the NATO war

**Above: USS *Los Angeles*, nameship of a
class of SSNs which could number some
60 units, the greatest national investment
ever in one class of submarine.**

and with combat elsewhere as well. For the
Navy, the current planning assumption could
mean simultaneous fighting in three oceans—
Atlantic/Mediterranean, Indian, and Pacific.

A NATO war would place great stress on US
naval forces. In such a war, they might be called
upon to provide NATO ground forces with air
support from carriers or to assist by landing
Marines. To do either would require control of
sea and air space in the vicinity. If the war went
on for weeks or months, extensive sea control
operations would be required of NATO navies
so that NATO armies and air forces engaged in
Europe could be supplied by merchant shipping
from North America. Any of these missions,
moreover, might involve use of tactical nuclear
weapons.

With or without nuclear weapons, the US
Navy might be expected to participate extensively in such sea control while providing NATO
land forces with more direct support. In such a
conflict, the US fleet would have to help fend

off Soviet attacks at sea and cope with Warsaw Pact air defenses ashore. NATO, with the combined capabilities of its navies including the US Navy, would find its hands full in dealing with these threats. If the US Navy were called upon to fight a lesser war elsewhere at the same time, NATO would be especially taxed.

In recent years, US defense circles have debated whether the US Navy's power should be used to open new geographic fronts in response to Soviet aggression in one theater. For example, Soviet successes in Europe might be countered by naval attacks on targets in the Soviet Far East. The debate turns on whether such attacks would be viewed as damaging enough by the Soviets for them to divert significant resources and attention to the new theater.

Lesser contingencies that might require US forces include the Middle East, Persian Gulf, and Korea. The US Navy would probably play a large role in these contingencies. Because of its access to each area from the sea, the capabilities that the Navy has developed to be ready for a NATO war make it a tool the US government is apt to use in these more geographically constrained wars. Combat there might be slower than NATO combat and the opponents might be weaker than the Soviet Union. It is because of the potential Soviet foe that the US Navy has acquired highly sophisticated weapons systems, such as the F-14 interceptor. Without the demands of a NATO war, such systems might not be needed in the US fleet. But, because they are there, the US fleet could tip the balance in lesser conflicts.

Still lesser contingencies are rising in relative likelihood of occurrence. Within the Third World, rapid political changes—caused by burgeoning populations, religious upheavals, resource discoveries, and the like—and growing military power made available by purchases of advanced-technology weaponry by newly-rich nations combine to form a dangerous mixture. The resulting explosions, when viewed against the background of increasing economic interdependence in the world, can be more disruptive than a decade or two ago. Containment and neutralization of them will sometimes fall to the US Navy. Its responses will have to be flexible and deft to avoid making the mixture even more explosive.

An important example of these lesser but likely contingencies can arise from exploitation of the oceans' resources. Despite largely successful Law-of-the-sea negotiations under UN auspices over the past decade, the various maritime boundaries—continental shelf, territorial waters, exclusive economic zones, and seabed mining areas—claimed by nations are still not free of dispute.

Peacetime deployment posture

The peacetime deployment posture of the US Navy reflects a compromise between which areas of the world are most important and where the Navy is most likely to be employed in wartime and crises. The details of the peacetime disposition of the Navy will be described later, but the general character of the Navy's peacetime posture bears description now. It, too, has shaped the Navy.

The US Navy deploys forward one-seventh to one-third of its warships—depending on class—in peacetime. Current practice has a third of the aircraft carriers thousands of miles from the United States. On a typical day, at least one US carrier is deployed to the Mediterranean Sea, at least one other to the western Pacific Ocean, and another operates in the Indian Ocean. A fourth is usually either in the Mediterranean Sea or western Pacific. (Carriers deploy overseas for approximately six months at a time.) These four carriers are backed up by ten others assigned to bases in the continental United States. Because of the great distances from home and a policy of "relief on station", one of the ten is often enroute to or from one of the forward stations. The ten carriers based in the United States are in various states of opera-

tional training and repair, including one or two in overhaul. (In addition, during the 1980s, the four carriers commissioned in the 1950s are undergoing extraordinarily extensive 28-month overhauls, one at a time. These overhauls will extend the carriers' lives to 45 years.) A fifteenth carrier—one without ammunition storage—is used for training new pilots. It does not deploy.

A carrier, its embarked aircraft, their pilots, the escorting ships, and their crews customarily train together for a deployment. This period of preparation builds working relationships and mutual confidence. Training includes advanced exercises in, for example, the North Atlantic during preparation for deployment to the Mediterranean. When a group of ships and aircraft deploys, it generally operates together as a battle group. This arrangement takes advantage of the smooth working relationship built during work-up training. Amphibious ships are similarly grouped; because the embarked Marines make up a single fighting unit once they have landed and their effectiveness ashore depends partly on how well their landing is coordinated, there are obvious advantages to grouping their transports.

Forward deployed ships can be dispatched elsewhere if the need arises. (Forward deployed

ships move regularly for exercises and po[rt] visits.) The forces deployed forward are rea[dy] for combat, some of those to the rear are rea[dy] to augment those forward, and all have th[e] ability common to all naval forces—the fre[e]dom to move in crises that was described earlie[r.] In cases of potential conflict, the carriers in tha[t] part of the world, together with escorts an[d] other ships such as transports, are usual[ly] moved closer to the trouble spot. An addition[al] carrier with supporting ships is sometim[es] dispatched from the United States. At least on[e] such carrier on each coast can be dispatche[d] immediately, arriving in the Mediterranean [in] 4 to 5 days, in the western Pacific in 8 to 10, [or] in the Arabian Sea in 12 to 25—depending [on] the risks in using the Suez Canal. Anoth[er] carrier on each coast can be dispatched 3 to [4] days later.

If a war lasted at least six months, requir[ing] it, and theaters elsewhere could spare a tem[-]porary loan of forces, as many as 12 carrie[rs] could be sent to the combat theater. A muc[h] longer war would permit construction of add[i-]tional carriers.

Naval bases

Naval bases in the United States provide t[he] full range of services needed, including: ove[r-]

US/USSR Maritime Bases and Facilities

● United States Bases and Facilities　　○ Soviet Bases and Facilities　　+ Soviet Anchorages

Above left: A Lockheed Orion P-3F of the Iranian Air Force is intercepted by a USN F-14 over the Indian Ocean. One US carrier is always on station in the area.

Above: A Kitty Hawk class carrier, her flight deck covered with aircraft, epitomises the power-projection capability of the Navy, something the Soviets are trying to emulate.

Right: USS *Nimitz* (CVN-68) is eased out of her home base by tugs. Only in CONUS do the bases provide all the services required by the Navy's massive fleet.

haul, refueling, aircraft rework, ordnance storage, sensor calibration, and recreation. Recoring of nuclear power plants is also available. US Navy bases overseas tend to provide a narrower range of services. Overhauls, including recoring, are not done overseas. Nor are repairs that can be deferred until the end of a deployment. Overseas bases exist to provide the services a deployed fleet must have to stay ready. In wartime, large-scale operations using Marines are often conducted to seize such bases overseas.

One way to ease the burden of a peacetime policy that puts so much of the fleet's warships forward is to station some of them overseas indefinitely, saving transit times. But, because all overhauls are done in the United States, indefinite overseas stationing has not been adopted. Instead, a compromise has been arranged for some submarine and destroyer tenders and the command ships that serve as flagships overseas and some combatant ships. It is known as "homeporting", and assigns some ships overseas for the full 4 to 7 years between overhauls. In the mid-1970s, a squadron of destroyers was "homeported" in Greece for three years. An aircraft carrier, a cruiser, and a squadron of destroyers are now "homeported" in Japan, and a cruiser and a pair of conventionally powered submarines are "homeported" in the Philippines.

Past technological improvements

About 125 years ago, the United States Navy converted its ships from sail to steam. Steam was faster but required coaling stations along the routes. Moreover, because steam made large-scale operations more reliable, fleets covered larger areas. Since conversion from coal to oil, which is more easily transferred at sea than coal, direct and frequent dependence on bases for refueling has decreased. (The bases

now serve more as storage points for such consumables as ammunition, jet fuel, and oil for ships, and as transit points for the spare parts on which the fleet increasingly depends.) Thirteen of the Navy's surface ships, being propelled by nuclear power plants, are virtually free of the usual refueling requirements; however, the four large aircraft carriers, *Enterprise*, *Nimitz*, *Eisenhower*, and *Vinson*, need occasional replenishment of their aviation fuel. (A conventionally propelled carrier must, every few days, take on ship fuel as well as aviation fuel.) All US Navy submarines constructed since 1960 have nuclear propulsion, making them less vulnerable to radar and visual detection than the diesel-electric submarines that regularly have to break the surface of the water.

The outcome of sea battles has always depended, in large part, on the ranges at which ships could detect each other, on weapon ranges, and on the ability of ships to absorb hits. The introduction of ironclad ships over a hundred years ago was followed by the development of armor-piercing ammunition for naval guns. The range of these guns was slowly extended to the range of the visual horizon, about 20 miles (32 km), and then slightly beyond. Accuracy also improved. Aircraft first operated from ships to extend the range at which targets could be detected and identified—beyond ship horizons—so that naval gunfire could be concentrated against them. Later, the aircraft began to carry bombs and torpedoes. World War II proved surface ships to be vulnerable to attacks by aircraft; the carrier became the preeminent ship of the line. As with naval guns earlier, the range of aircraft operating from ships was increased. Their speed was improved by the introduction of jet engines in the late 1940s. This was followed by increases in the speed and altitude of aircraft designed to fight other aircraft and in the range and bomb-

Above: Six US Navy nuclear-powered cruisers operating together during Exercise READEX 1-81. Nuclear power makes ships such as these virtually free of range constraints, vital to a navy faced with patrolling vast areas of ocean in a future war.

load of aircraft designed to strike surface targets, at sea and on land.

Detection of targets had been largely visual, but World War II brought radar and sonar to ships, and radar to aircraft. Shipborne radar permitted detection of air targets far beyond the range of naval guns; guided anti-air missiles named "Tartar", "Terrier", and "Talos" began to replace guns aboard US Navy ships in the late 1950s, to take advantage of the larger detection range made possible by the radar and the greater accuracy of the missiles. In the late 1970s, "Harpoon" surface-to-surface mis-

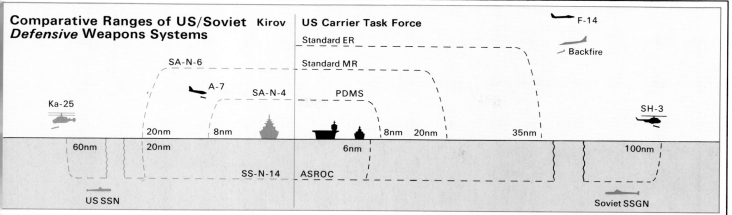

Comparative Ranges of US/Soviet *Defensive* Weapons Systems

Kirov | US Carrier Task Force

F-14

Backfire

Standard ER
Standard MR

SA-N-6
A-7
SA-N-4
PDMS

Ka-25

20nm 8nm 8nm 20nm 35nm

SH-3

60nm 20nm 6nm 100nm

SS-N-14 ASROC

US SSN

Soviet SSGN

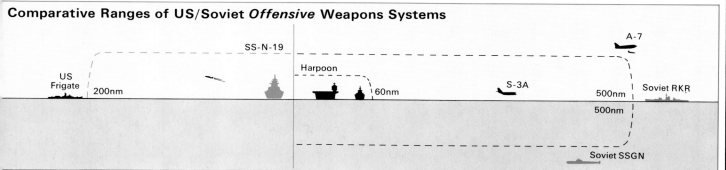

Comparative Ranges of US/Soviet *Offensive* Weapons Systems

SS-N-19

A-7

Harpoon

US Frigate

200nm 60nm S-3A 500nm Soviet RKR

500nm

Soviet SSGN

Above: Many critics of NATO ships point to the great number of weapons carried on Soviet ships and draw unfavorable comparisons with Western practice. These diagrams show that the imbalance is the other way: that NATO weapons have longer range and greater terminal effects. The balance may start to be redressed when new Soviet carriers enter service, but they will need a carrier-borne AEW aircraft if they are to avoid the problems which beset the British in the Falklands.

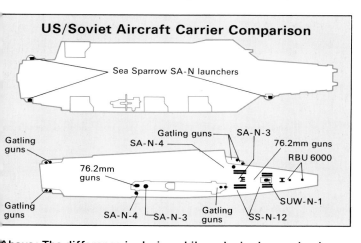

US/Soviet Aircraft Carrier Comparison

Sea Sparrow SA-N launchers

Gatling guns

Gatling guns
SA-N-3
76.2mm guns
RBU 6000

76.2mm guns
SA-N-4

Gatling guns

SUW-N-1

Gatling guns
SA-N-4 SA-N-3 Gatling guns SS-N-12

Above: The difference in design philosophy is shown clearly, with *Nimitz* having basic ship's armament (3×BPDMS) while *Kiev* is a very heavily armed warship in her own right.

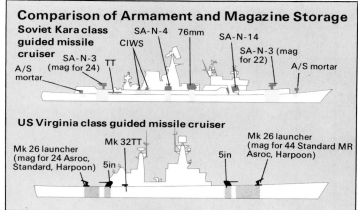

Comparison of Armament and Magazine Storage

Soviet Kara class guided missile cruiser

SA-N-4 76mm SA-N-14
CIWS
SA-N-3
A/S mortar SA-N-3 (mag for 24) TT SA-N-3 (mag for 22) A/S mortar

US Virginia class guided missile cruiser

Mk 26 launcher (mag for 24 Asroc, Standard, Harpoon) Mk 32TT 5in 5in Mk 26 launcher (mag for 44 Standard MR Asroc, Harpoon)

Above: Outwardly *Kara* is better armed than *Virginia,* but the American ship actually has much greater magazine capacity, dual-function launchers and a far more flexible electronic outfit.

---

les began to supplant still more naval guns. he introduction of "Tomahawk" surface-to-rface missiles in the early 1980s continues at trend. For several reasons—to return 16-ch guns to the fleet, to increase the size of the avy relatively inexpensively, to insure that rge numbers of cruise-missile hits can be ken by some ships—four World War II battle-ips are being reactivated in the 1980s. (The st, USS *New Jersey*, was recommissioned by esident Reagan as 1982 ended.) These 59,000-n battleships are being modernized with arpoon and Tomahawk, but nonetheless will ten operate under the cover of aircraft from rriers.

High-powered shipborne sonars, such as the QS-26, which arrived in the 1960s, extended e range at which submerged submarines uld be detected. Airborne radar, used at first r antisubmarine work and detections of

ft: Another example of American rsatility is the Tomahawk SLCM, unched from a standard submarine rpedo unit.

surface ships, was later extended to anti-air warfare. Radar allowed interceptors to detect other aircraft beyond visual range; air-to-air missiles of greater range than air-to-air guns soon followed. The heat-seeking (passive infra-red homing) "Sidewinder" of 2 to 3 miles (c. 3 to 4 km) range came first. Its early models had to attack from the rear of the target. The "Spar-row" missile, permitting attack at 10 to 15 miles (16 to 24 km) and from any heading because of its radar guidance, followed. Only one Sparrow at a time could be controlled by the F-4 inter-ceptor that had fired it. This limitation was overcome in the mid-1970s by introduction of the F-14 interceptor with 60-mile range "Phoe-nix missiles; the F-14 can control six at a time.

Force coordination

The arrival of long-range weapons and sensors in quantity in the US fleet has made coordina-tion of forces especially useful. When several ships and aircraft operate together in a battle group, as is customary, the capabilities of their sensors and weapons overlap, often beyond the range at which any one of the ships or aircraft

could, alone, destroy the target. Coordination of the sensors or weapons on several ships or aircraft is needed to take advantage of the overlap.

Coordination occurs by visual signals, as well as by radio, which was added in the past 75 years, and by high-speed computers, which arrived in the past 25. All US Navy aircraft carriers, all cruisers, and several other sur-face ships have the Navy Tactical Data System (NTDS), providing computer-assisted target tracking and quick radio exchange of tracking data among ships. The 1980s will bring the more-sophisticated AEGIS control system (de-scribed later) into the fleet.

The carrier-based E-2 aircraft, whose capa-bilities include a look-down radar for detecting and tracking targets that ships may not be able to detect, has an Air Tactical Data System comparable to the NTDS. It permits linking with the ships' NTDS, so that tracking data can be shared among all units. (Ships also have the potential to draw on the tracking data produced by the larger, land-based E-3 "AWACS" air-craft.) The most recent version of the land-

Above: A corner of the operations room on board *Nimitz* (CVN-68). Inputs come from sensors on the ship and its aircraft.

Table 1: Composition of the US Navy, 1982

Active ships

Aircraft carriers (62,000 to 93,000 tons)		3
Conventionally-powered	9	
Nuclear-powered	4	
Battleships (59,000 tons)		1
Cruisers (7,800 to 17,500 tons)		28
Conventionally-powered	19	
Nuclear-powered	9	
Destroyers (4,000 to 7,300 tons)		80
Frigates (2,600 to 3,500 tons)		84
Attack submarines		96
Diesel-electric	5	
Nuclear-powered	91	
Amphibious transports		61
Mine warfare ships		3
Patrol boats		5
Underway replenishment ships		36
Auxiliaries		41
Ballistic missile submarines		33
With Trident missiles	14	
With Poseidon missiles	19	
Total		**481**
Reserve ships		
Destroyers		7
Amphibious transports		4
Mine warfare ships		18
Auxiliaries	6	
Total		**35**
Grand total		**516**
Additional ships of interest		
Aircraft carriers		
In 28-month overhaul		1
Training		1
Battleships (to be reactivated in the 1980s		3

Table 2: Fleets of the US Navy

Fleet	Operating Area	Home Port of Flagship
Second	Atlantic Ocean	Norfolk, Virginia
Third	Eastern Pacific Ocean	Pearl Harbor, Hawaii (headquarters ashore)
Sixth	Mediterranean Sea	Gaeta, Italy
Seventh	Western Pacific Ocean and Indian Ocean	Yokosuka, Japan

Table 3: Peacetime Composition of Deployed US Fleets, 1983

Sixth Fleet

Task Force 60
2 carriers
14 surface combatants

Task Force 61
5 amphibious ships

Task Force 62
1 reinforced USMC battalion

Task Force 63
6 to 7 underway replenishment ships
4 auxiliaries

Task Force 67
1½ maritime patrol squadrons
1 reconnaissance squadron

Task Force 69
4 to 5 attack submarines

Seventh Fleet

Task Force 72
3½ maritime patrol squadrons
1 reconnaissance squadron

Task Force 73
7 to 9 underway replenishment ships
6 to 7 auxiliaries

Task Force 74
6 attack submarines

Task Force 76
8 amphibious ships

Task Force 77
2 carriers
19 surface combatants

Task Force 79
2 reinforced USMC battalions

Task Force 70
Indian Ocean of about 20 ships
seconded from the other task
forces in this table

Table 4: Fleet Organization, US Navy, 1983

Commander-in-Chief Pacific Fleet — Pearl Harbor, Hawaii	Commander-in-Chief Atlantic Fleet — Norfolk, Virginia	Commander-in-Chief Naval Forces, Europe Naples, Italy (Deputy in London, England)
Seventh Fleet / Third Fleet	Second Fleet	Sixth Fleet / MidEast Force

based P-3 antisubmarine aircraft has the computer and communications capability to participate in this linking; carrier-based interceptors do, too. Though ships without NTDS have significant radio capacity and other means of control, the margin provided by NTDS often causes an NTDS ship to be chosen by a battle group commander as his flagship.

The coordination capability of the US Navy has been displayed many times, none more impressively than in combat in 1972. Five aircraft carriers with attendant escorts, air control ships and replenishment ships, operated together in the Gulf of Tonkin. At times, this force operated more than a hundred aircraft in combat, tracking both them and potentially hostile aircraft, providing airborne refueling aircraft as needed, recovering downed pilots whose planes had been hit over North Vietnam, tracking surface targets, keeping an eye out for submarines, and refueling and rearming ships while in motion.

Increasing ship size
Because ships now carry computers, large radars, large sonars, and missile systems, they are larger than ever before. The equipment itself, the additional men that must operate it, and greater comfort for those crews all have contributed to this growth. So have greater magazine and fuel capacities, to lengthen the time between replenishments. Most classes of US Navy ships have at least doubled in size since World War II. The newest aircraft carriers displace 93,000 tons when fully loaded. However, despite added manning for sophisticated weapon systems, the ratio of manpower to ship tonnage is down sharply from World War II. Rising relative manpower costs have induced it; automation and streamlined damage-control measures have permitted it.

Constraints on the US Navy
The US Navy faces obstacles in achieving the objectives the United States has for it, and in taking advantage of the technological opportunities it creates and that are presented to it. One obstacle is limited funds. Although almost $60,000 million will be spent in 1983 on the US Navy and Marine Corps (whose avaiation and amphibious budgets are closely coordinated), many programes compete for these funds. In anti-air warfare, for example, shipborne surface-to-air missiles compete with interceptors. Should new missiles be funded or existing interceptors be provided with more spare parts? Once such issues are resolved within the Navy Department, a proposed budget is sent to the Secretary of Defense. That budget competes with others for the limited funds available to the Defense Department. Similar competition occurs as the budget moves toward Congress for final approval. The net result is that most programs do not get the funds their Navy sponsors week. The reductions take on meaning when another obstacle, the capabilities of potential opponents, is considered.

The principal potential opponent of the US

Navy is the Soviet Navy. It has more ships than the US Navy, though less tonnage. The sophistication and breadth of its operations have increased substantially in the past 20 years. The posture of the Soviet Navy had been principally defensive, emphasizing protection of the Soviet homeland by denying portions of the nearby seas to Western navies. Such denial capabilities have taken greater focus in the apparent Soviet intent to preserve their SSBNs in bastions north and east of the USSR. Moreover, in the past 15 years, deployments by the Soviet Navy far from the Soviet Union have become common. These deployments permit

localized denial or at least neutralization Western navies near trouble spots.

Today the Soviet Navy has about as ma ships in the Mediterranean as the US Nav Occasionally, they deploy a ship—such as th *Moskva*, *Leningrad* or *Kiev*—that is capable operating aircraft. More important, several the ships and submarines on the scene car antiship cruise missiles. Both the number of th missile-equipped ships and the total numbe can be doubled within a month, as was done October 1973. Although the Soviet ships ten to stay in the eastern Mediterranean and th US ships in the western Mediterranean

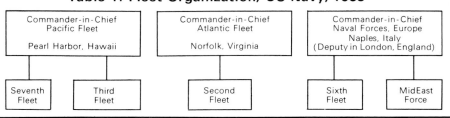

Above: Lockheed P-3B Orion, the US Navy's only land-based ASW aircraft. Many hundreds are deployed around the world constantly policing the Soviet threat.

Above: USS *New Jersey* (BB-62) is now back in commission as a result of a still-controversial decision to reactivate and update the armament of these battleships.

routine peacetime operations, ships of both nations roam throughout the sea. (In periods of force commitment ashore, as with Marine peacekeeping in Lebanon, the distribution of supporting ships is skewed appropriately.) During crises, US and Soviet ships tend to intermingle. At such close quarters, the potency of the Soviet shipboard missiles, when combined with proximity to Soviet bases for missile-equipped aircraft, as in the Mediterranean, makes a massed attack particularly threatening. If US forces were to take the initiative in such circumstances, they would pose a serious threat to the Soviet Navy. The advantage to the force that strikes first inhibits the action both governments take with their fleets.

Some obstacles to orderly development of a navy cannot be foreseen. In the case of the US Navy, the Vietnam War was such an interruption. Its emphasis on projection ashore demanded funds for carriers and their aircraft, for ships with naval guns, and for the unexpectedly large amounts of ammunition used. At the same time, the Navy's share of the Defense budget shrank because the combat loss rates of Army and Air Force equipment ashore had been unforeseen. The net result for Navy forces designed for sea control was accelerated obsolescence and relative inattention to replacement forces. That is being corrected with a plan to return to Navy of 600 ships, as will be seen later.

Today's US Navy

Having traced the forces that have shaped the navy, the discussion now turns to what today's navy is like—its composition, disposition, organization, leadership, manning, and capabilities.

Composition and organization

Table 1 shows the early 1983 composition of the US Navy (The designation of cruisers, destroyers, and frigates changed in the mid-1970s.) Groups of US Navy surface ships tend to be built around a carrier, amphibious ships or replenishment ships. Each such group will need surface combatants with it in wartime. The total number of cruisers, destroyers and frigates is about 13 times as large as the number of carriers plus the battleship. Twenty to thirty surface combatants will provide defense as the lightly armed amphibious ships transit to the landing area and shore bombardment once there. A like number would escort the 8 to 10 groups of underway replenishment ships that would be needed to keep fighting ships on

station. Yet others would be needed for convoy duty. All these wartime demands, when combined with the other demands likely in Latin American and African waters and elsewhere, would quickly tap the 189 surface combatants.

Besides the 516 ships assigned to the Navy, there are 5,559 aircraft assigned to the Navy and Marine Corps. Approximately 1,000 are aboard large aircraft carriers. Another few hundred, mostly helicopters, are aboard smaller ships, including amphibious assault ships. Land-based aircraft include 24 squadrons of nine P-3s each.

Some attack submarines would be assigned to antisubmarine work in wartime, including one to three submarines to each of the battle groups built around a carrier. These groups also would each include four to seven surface combatants and be supported by their own carrier-based aircraft and by P-3s.

Each ship and aircraft in the US Navy is assigned to one of four fleets for operational control. Table 2 shows the four fleets and their customary operating areas. The fleet to which any one ship or aircraft is assigned changes with time. Deployments overseas mean assignment to the Sixth or Seventh Fleet for several months. The approximate peacetime composition of those fleets is shown in Table 3. After a deployment is concluded, the ship or aircraft squadron returns to the Second or Third Fleet, respectively. Then the ship or squadron begins a new training cycle.

The overall management of this rotation is conducted by theater commanders-in-chief. The

organization of operational control is shown in Table 4, where the locations of the headquarters of the commanders-in-chief are also shown. The US Navy organization for management of force rotation is not symmetrical. In the Pacific Fleet, forces in the Third Fleet preparing for deployment are still controlled by the same commander-in-chief when assigned to the Seventh Fleet. When forces are moved to Sixth Fleet from Second Fleet, their operations are controlled by separate commanders-in-chief. This asymmetry stems from the unified command structure of worldwide US forces. That structure stresses three theaters, the Pacific, Atlantic, and Europe. (A "Central" command was formed in 1983 to encompass Southwest Asia and the northwest Indian Ocean. It evolves from the Rapid Deployment Force command created in 1979.) Unlike US Navy and US Marine Corps forces, which are integrated within fleets as shown in Table 3, the forces of the US Army, the US Navy, and the US Air Force report to their unified theater commanders-in-chief through component commanders-in-chief such as those shown in Table 4. (The MidEast Force is a 20-year-old three-ship entity that has operated largely within the Persian Gulf. Since late 1979, about 20 ships from the Seventh Fleet have operated in the nearby Arabian Sea.) In Europe, the unified US commander-in-chief has an Army component

Below: US and Australian Navy units on joint exercises in the Indian Ocean. The carrier *Midway* (CV-41) is surrounded by military sealift command oiler *Navasota,* frigate *Knox,* guided missile destroyer *Parsons,* Australian frigate HMAS *Torrens,* frigate *Stein* and nuclear powered guided missile cruiser *Bainbridge*

commander-in-chief, an Air Force component commander-in-chief, and a Navy component commander-in-chief (the C-in-C, US Naval Forces, Europe).

The Commanders-in-Chief of the Pacific and Atlantic Fleets each have several subordinate commanders charged with administrative control of various types of forces. Each of these subordinate commanders tends to be concerned with one type of ship only—such as submarines —and is responsible for development of tactics and doctrine and for provision of manpower, spare parts, safety standards, etc. to the ships. The ships and aircraft assigned to the Sixth Fleet are under the administrative control of the Commander-in-Chief, Atlantic Fleet.

The Navy commanders-in-chief are autonomous in some respects. Operating doctrine and procedures for their forces can vary. Because the forces and personnel under their control rotate, these variations are not great. The ultimate unifying influence in the US Navy is provided by the Chief of Naval Operations (CNO). The CNO commands no forces. He does, however, select the forces that will make up the Navy. He does so by considering the operational problems faced by fleet commanders, the postulated threat, guidance on US strategy from the Secretary of Defense, emerging technologies, available manpower, and budget constraints. In selecting the forces that will make up the Navy, most of the CNO's effect on it comes 5 to 35 years after his decisions. The CNO is also responsible for more immediate concerns—the provision of manpower and other resources to the fleet commanders-in-chief and for overall Navy policies. The current CNO, Admiral James D. Watkin's, began his four-year term in mid-1982. The CNO also serves as the Navy member of the Joint Chiefs of Staff, who advise the President and Secretary of Defense on direction of worldwide US forces commanded by the unified commanders-in-chief.

The US Navy has about 550,000 men and women on active duty; all are volunteers. About 62,000 are officers, and 4,350 are officer candidates. Before 1973, when the United States ended conscription, the Navy was composed almost entirely of volunteers. The end of conscription has been accompanied by substantial increase in pay, now almost $6,900 a year for recruits. In the post-conscription period, Navy manpower managers have stressed proper selection of recruits. Such indicators as graduation from secondary school are scrutinized to increase the chances of successful completion of enlistment and of the Navy's many schools that prepare recruits to operate and maintain increasingly sophisticated equipment.

Capabilities of forces

The operational strengths and weaknesses of the US Navy are best reviewed by recalling that it is structured to assert control over the oceans and, when necessary, over adjacent territory. Its principal potential opponent, the Soviet Navy, is, on the other hand, structured to deny that control.

In antisubmarine warfare, the US Navy enjoys significant technological advantages that are buttressed by geographical advantages. US antisubmarine sensors permit detections that allow attacks to be made at long range. Off-ship sensors and information-processing capabilities permit tracking of submarines, thus increasing the likelihood that attacks will be successful. Widespread and well-placed US air bases for operation of P-3 antisubmarine

Top: No. 3 prototype F-18 Hornet armed with AIM-9L missiles. A mix of these aircraft, A-6s, A-7s and F-14s will form the strike force on US Navy attack carriers, supported by AEW and ASW types; a potent force, indeed.

Right: Two Grumman EA-6B Prowlers in the circuit around the new USS Carl Vinson. Such ECM/ESM aircraft are important to the USN's overall air capability.

Above: An SH-2D Seasprite ASW helicopter from the frigate USS *Standley* (DLG-32) keeping a close watch on a Soviet Foxtrot class diesel submarine. It is absolutely vital to establish the normal pattern of Soviet submarine operations and deployments so that any deviation can be quickly spotted and analyzed.

planes give them an advantage. Because the large Soviet submarine force must move out of home waters in wartime if it is to help deny contested areas to Western naval forces, and since the exit from those waters to the North Atlantic, in particular, is narrow, US defenses can be concentrated. Attack submarines could be stationed in barriers to take advantage of this. Despite these US advantages, the size of the Soviet force and the slow pace of any antisubmarine campaign is apt to present vexing problems. If the Soviets deploy their submarines significantly before combat, high initial US losses are possible.

The Soviets learned well the lesson taught by Japanese kamikaze attacks on American and British surface ships toward the end of World War II. Cruise missiles (low-flying homing weapons) have been fitted on some Soviet submarines and are now widely deployed on Soviet cruisers and destroyers. These pilotless missiles are directed against surface ships; they can be redirected in flight. They have proved their potency, as in the *Eliath* sinking and, when fired by aircraft, in the 1982 sinkings of HMS *Sheffield* and the *Atlantic Conveyor* near the Falkland Islands. As described earlier, the intermingling of forces that sometimes occurs in crises tends to offer great advantage to the side that shoots first if it is willing to incur the risks of a war. The potential harm to US surface ships from Soviet cruise missiles fired from intermingled positions is made more severe by the added possibility of prompt follow-up attacks with torpedoes fired by submarines. This combination, if effectively delivered, could disable many US ships.

With reasonable prospects for eventual, if not immediate, establishment of sea control, US capabilities to project naval power ashore can be addressed. It is here that most of the combat experience gained in Vietnam resides. Each US aircraft carrier is a potent force. Its 24 A-7s or A-18s, 13 A-6s, 24 F-14s or F-18s, and 20 to 25 other aircraft can mount a devastating strike of about 40 aircraft on several hours' notice. In a strike of this kind, half the aircraft may carry bombs or air-to-surface missiles. The loads possible on today's carrier-based aircraft mean that such a strike could deliver 75 tons of bombs on targets as far as 300 to 400 miles (c. 480 to 640 km) from the carrier. When, instead of major strikes, more routine production of sorties is required, as often happened in Vietnam, a large carrier is capable of 110 to 120 sorties a day when operating aircraft for 12 hours and then resting for 12. This performance is possible at night as well as in daylight, and is readily sustained for a month or more.

Such output can be interrupted, however. The example of the North Vietnamese Air Force shows how. This force of no more than 100 fighter aircraft prevented carriers in the Gulf of Tonkin and larger numbers of US Air Force bases ashore from achieving maximum output. The usual way to measure fighter performance is the exchange ratio: in the case of the Vietnam War, MiGs lost versus US fighters lost. The MiGs initially held their own at that, but were later overwhelmed. However, detections of MiGs near strike groups over North Vietnam sometimes caused heavily-laden attack aircraft to jettison their bombloads before reaching the target so as to decrease vulnerability to the MiGs. This, too, is a useful measure of the effect of the North Vietnamese Air Force. The most subtle measure captures the most pervasive effect the MiGs had. Ten to fifteen per cent of the sorties flown from carriers in the Gulf of Tonkin were launched with air-to-air missiles instead of air-to-ground bombs in case MiGs should appear; they almost never did. Thousands of sorties that might have carried bombs did not.

Despite the possibilities for interruption of carrier strikes or diversion of some of their aircraft to other missions, a carrier near a friendly country's shoreline poses a considerable problem for a potential invader. Similarly, the amphibious assault capabilities of US Marines embarked in Navy ships permit rapid landing of an effective force. Amphibious transports can move at 20 knots and thereby create uncertainty regarding the choice of a landing site. The large replenishment force of the US Navy can keep up with the amphibious force. It can also replenish the faster carrier battle groups while they are underway, day or night.

Despite many strengths, the US Navy is noticeably weak in some areas. The problems of dealing with massed missile attacks have already been described. Battle groups without carriers are limited in their ability to detect, identify, and track ships beyond visual range. As a result, effective use of the surface-to-surface Harpoon and Tomahawk missiles that are being installed in large numbers of surface combatants will be limited to visual or radar ranges unless friendly aircraft can help. The threat of large-scale use of mines by the Soviet Navy is not matched by large-scale mine countermeasure forces or exercises in the US Navy— the present active inventory includes only three mine warfare ships. The substantial ability of the US Navy to manage massed forces at sea has depended on high-frequency (HF) radio communications. These signals, readily detectable at ranges beyond the horizon and susceptible to interference by jamming, are another weakness of the US fleet.

Tomorrow's US Navy
The composition of any navy changes only

Below: USS *Carl Vinson* (CVN-70), the latest nuclear carrier to join the fleet. These huge carriers deploy what amounts to a complete tactical air force of their own on a mobile and strongly protected base.

slowly because ships normally have useful lifetimes of 20 to 40 years. (Aircraft last about half as long.) In 1963, the US Navy was composed of 916 ships, many of which were built towards the end of World War II and retired by the mid-1970s; many others were constructed during the 1950s, as Korea and the Cold War pushed up the size of the Navy. In 1963, the US Navy had 24 aircraft carriers; nine were smaller ones configured for antisubmarine work. There were 280 surface combatants, mainly World War II destroyers. The conversion to a nuclear-powered submarine force is now just underway. There were 12 nuclear-powered ballistic missile submarines and 16 such attack submarines. There are now 33 and 91, respectively. (Eight of the 91 are former ballistic missile submarines that no longer carry missiles.) Eighty-one of the 86 diesel-powered submarines that were in the 1963 inventory have now been retired. Most of the reduction in inventory since 1963 has come in mine warfare ships (from 87 ships to 3), underway replenishment ships (from 75 to 36), and auxiliaries (from 189 to 41).

Moderate growth in the number of US Navy ships is planned for the coming decade. The Navy goal is 600 ships. (Some of the progress toward it comes from adding reserve and civilian-manned ships controlled by fleet commanders to the count of active ships.) But the full costs of modern ships are very high, and Congress is showing increasing concern for costs in the early 1980s. Since Congress authorizes shipbuilding only one year at a time, the fleet's future composition cannot be specified. The most substantial recent growth in numbers of ships has been frigates and destroyers, but two new nuclear-powered aircraft carriers were authorized by Congress in 1982. (The nuclear-powered carrier authorized by Congress in 1980 is now being built. It will be commissioned in 1987 as USS *Theodore Roosevelt* and permit the retirement of a 40-year-old carrier.)

New ships and aircraft

Four Trident ballistic-missile submarines had entered the inventory by early 1983. Ten are planned. These large (18,700-ton) submarines carry 24 ballistic missiles each. The missiles have a 4,350-mile (7,000 km) range, permitting operation of the submarines over a much wider area than the Polaris submarines with Poseidon missiles which they replace. The increase in operating area, the increased number of missiles per submarine, the quieter operation, and the expected reduction in frequency of overhauls should all make the Trident force a more invulnerable and potent ballistic missile force.

Before proceeding with a description of other weapon systems that will soon be entering the US fleet, it is worth noting that eventual performance in the fleet seldom matches the claims made for a system before it is deployed. Those claims are generally made with implicit assumptions of near-perfect maintenance, a cooperative atmosphere or ocean, and perfect information available to commanders. Though such assumptions are unjustified, they color nearly all descriptions of future weapon systems.

Antisubmarine helicopters called "LAMPS" (Light Airborne Multi-Purpose System) are already aboard approximately 75 surface combatants. They are there to permit weapon delivery more quickly after detection and at longer range than possible while waiting for the surface combatant to move toward the contact. A replacement, "LAMPS Mark III", begins entering the fleet in 1983. Its longer range, greater sonobuoy capacity, and advanced information processing capability permits it to take greater advantage of the longer-range detections expected from high-powered sonars and towed passive sonar arrays on surface combatants. These arrays consist of hydrophones embedded in a cable several hundred feet in length that is towed behind a surface combatant or submarine. Engine or other characteristic noise emitted by an opposing submarine can be heard through the hydrophones. The wide separation between hydrophones permits accurate determination of the opposing submarine's bearing, and the separation of the array from the noise made by the towing ship as it moves through the water permits clear interpretation of the submarine's emitted noise. These capabilities, combined with improved data processing aboard the ship, should make possible more effective attacks with LAMPS III or other antisubmarine weapons aboard surface combatants.

Another antisubmarine weapon, but one that does not require a ship's presence to be effective, is now entering the inventory. It is "Captor", enCAPsulated TORpedo. After drop by aircraft or ship, it moors itself to the bottom, and waits. Mine-like, it senses the passage of a submarine and then realses its torpedo at the submarine. The potential cost savings over maintaining barriers continually with ships or planes are obvious.

It has been 25 years since nuclear-powered attack submarines began joining the US fleet in quantity. These boats were of 3,000 to 4,000 tons submerged displacement. Their replacements, the SSN-688 class of 6,900 tons submerged displacement, have already joined the fleet in numbers and will continue to do so through the 1980s. The 688-class boats are much quieter than their predecessors, and are fitted with the long-range BQQ-5 hull-mounted sonar. By 1990, there will be almost 40 of them in the US fleet.

Anti-air warfare capabilities in the US Navy should also be upgraded by the arrival of new systems. Prominent among these is the "Aegis" combat system, which was introduced with the commissioning of the cruiser *Ticonderoga* early

Below: A Kaman SH-2F anti-submarine helicopter dropping a sonobuoy. These aircraft were the first in a program for a Light Airborne Multi-Purpose System (LAMPS); the latest is LAMPS III, the Sikorski SH-60B, some 200 of which have been ordered.

Table 6: Department of the Navy Shipbuilding and Conversion, Navy (SCN) Five Year Plan						
New construction	FY 1983	FY 1984	FY 1985	FY 1986	FY 1987	FY 1983–FY 1987
Aircraft carrier (CVN-72/73)	2	–	–	–	–	2
Trident submarine (SSBN)	2	1	1	1	1	6
Attack submarine (SSN-688)	2	3	4	4	4	17
AEGIS cruiser (CG-47)	3	3	3	4	4	17
Destroyer (DDG-51)	–	–	1	–	3	4
Destroyer (DD-963)	–	–	–	2	1	3
Frigate (FFG-7)	2	2	2	3	3	12
Ocean surveillance ship (AGOS)	–	1	–	2	3	6
Mine countermeasures ship (MCM)	4	4	5	–	–	13
Coastal minehunter (MSH-1)	–	1	–	5	5	11
Dock landing ship (LSD-41)	1	–	2	2	2	8
Amphibious warfare ship (LHD-1)	–	1	–	–	1	2
Fast combat support ship (AOE)	–	–	1	1	2	4
Fleet oiler (TAO)	1	3	4	4	6	18
Salvage ship (ARS)	1	1	–	–	–	2
Cable laying ship (T-ARC)	–	–	–	1	–	1
Nuclear cruiser (CGN-42)	–	–	–	–	1	1
Ammunition ship (AE)	–	–	1	2	1	4
Destroyer tender (AD)	–	–	–	1	1	2
Conversion/acquisition						
Battleship activation (BB)	1	1	1	–	–	3
FBM supply ship (TAK) (C)	–	–	1	–	–	1
CV-SLEP	1	–	1	–	1	3
Fast logistics ship (TAKRX) (C)	4	–	–	–	–	4
Survey ship (TAGS) (C)	–	–	2	–	–	2
Hospital ship (TAHX) (C)	1	1	–	–	–	2
Range ship (TAGM) (C)	–	–	–	1	–	1
Total number of ships	**25**	**23**	**29**	**33**	**39**	**149**

A total of six Trident submarines are budgeted for the five-year period. A total of 17 each SSN-688s and CG-47s are budgeted through 1987, with a fairly level stream of construction planned for both during the five-year period. Likewise, a total of 12 FFG-7s are budgeted through 1987 with either two or three scheduled in each of the five years. In the case of Mine Countermeasure Ships (MCMs), however, all of the new construction of 13 ships are budgeted for the first three years of the five-year period. Eighteen fleet oilers (TAOs) are budgeted for FY 1983 through FY 1987.

Source: US Secretary of Navy testimony before Defense Subcommittee Senate Appropriations Committee (RADM Miller statement) March 1982.

Above: USS *Ticonderoga* (CG-47) the first of the new AEGIS ships. The AEGIS system is designed to combat the Soviet saturation missile attacks which will probably form the basis of their future tactics.

Right: The 1982 naval war in the Falklands showed only too clearly the danger posed by aircraft and missiles. Therefore, even more attention is being devoted to weapons such as this Vulcan/Phalanx CIWS capable of a cyclic rate of fire of 3,000rds/min.

1983. Aegis depends on the SPY-1 phased array radar, permitting automatic detection and tracking, and on the "Standard" SM-2 surface-to-air missile. Aegis cruisers are variants of the *Spruance* (DD-963) hulls propelled by gas turbines that were introduced in the mid-1970s. (These Spruance destroyers were the first US ships constructed in large blocs by modular assembly techniques in a single shipyard.) Eventually, at least one Aegis cruiser will operate with each carrier battle group. Anti-air capabilities are also being upgraded by installation of the Phalanx gun system, a six-barreled 20mm rapid-fire system designed to shoot down cruise missiles that pass through such outer defenses as Aegis.

The sophisticated swing-wing F-14s began replacing F-4 interceptors in the mid-1970s, and that modernization is now essentially complete. The F-14s are very expensive, and a less costly complement to them was therefore sought for carrier service. The F-18 began appearing in the Navy and Marine Corps in 1982. Initially conceived as a relatively simple aircraft, the addition of many features has driven the cost for a massive planned purchase of almost 1,400 aircraft above $40,000 million. Despite a cost approaching that of an F-14, the F-18 offers an advantage by using the same airframe for an attack airplane, the A-18. It will replace the A-7s introduced aboard the carriers in the mid-1960s. Current plans call for first carrier embarkations of F-18s and A-18s on the 62,000-ton carriers of World War II design; these cannot operate F-14s. The effectiveness of all carrier-based interceptors has been increased by development of an improved version of the last air-to-air missile, Sidewinder. Because of greatly increased sensitivity to the heat emitted

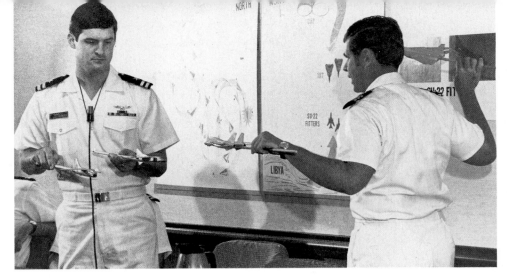

by opposing aircraft, the new Sidewinder will not be limited to attacks from the rear of its target aircraft, but can be used from any bearing.

Defense against antiship cruise missiles is being buttressed by widespread deployment of NATO Seasparrow missiles on US surface ships, including both combatants and replenishment ships. This system employs the 20-year-old Sparrow air-to-air missile in a surface-to-air mode with a range exceeding five miles. It is a high-performance version of the Sparrow, with folding fins and 8-round box launcher. It is to be aboard the battleships and 1950s carriers as they emerge from 1980s refits. Several other NATO countries and Japan are also deploying Seasparrow on their ships.

The longer range Tomahawk is augmenting the 60-mile (96km) Harpoons that are now on many ships. (These surface-to-surface missiles restore offensive punch to surface ships after a long eclipse. The eclipse began when surface combatants were subordinated to defense of aircraft carriers and some of their guns were replaced to make way for surface-to-air missile systems.) When LAMPS is aboard the firing ship, identification of targets at ranges beyond the horizon is possible. LAMPS III extends that range further. So should satellite systems for the detection and identification of surface targets. In fact, systems that stress manage-

Above: An example of how unexpectedly an incident can arise occurred on August 19, 1981 over the Gulf of Sidra. Two US Navy F-14s operating from USS _Nimitz,_ flying in international airspace, were attacked by two Libyan Su-22 fighters. Here the US pilots show how they shot the Libyans down. In February 1983 the _Nimitz_ was sent back to the area to deter fresh Libyan threats, this time to neighboring Sudan.

ment and processing of information rather than direct destruction of targets will claim an increasing share of US Navy resources as it moves into the 21st century.

Another current example is a set of communications satellites that use ultra-high-frequency (UHF) radio signals. Unlike the widely used high-frequency (HF) signals that bounce off the ionosphere, UHF radio cannot be detected beyond the 20-mile (32km) line-of-sight horizon of the transmitting ship. Since the satellite is above the ship, it can receive the signal and relay it to distant points without

Below: USS _Oliver Hazard Perry_ (FFG-7) undergoing a mine-resistance test. Much more attention is being paid to mine warfare in NATO navies as the scale of the Soviet threat in this area increases.

betraying the position of the transmitting ship.

The US Navy's amphibious force has been upgraded by delivery of five large ships called LHAs. As with the Spruance destroyers, they were constructed by modular shipbuilding techniques. They offer large flight decks for helicopter lift of troops and cargo to the beach, well decks for ship-to-shore landing craft carrying tanks and other heavy equipment, and enough internal capacity to carry a reinforced battalion of troops and equipment. Until now USMC battalions deployed at sea were generally spread among four or five ships.

Unanswered Questions

Some characteristics of the future US Navy cannot be seen clearly. The major questions include:

Which should be stressed more in structuring the Navy, NATO or the Third World?

What is the role and future distribution of aircraft at sea?

How vulnerable are surface ships?

Can distant targets be located and identified accurately enough to use Navy surface-to-surface missiles at their maximum ranges?

How many surface ships should have nuclear propulsion?

How should attacks that employ nuclear weapons be countered?

A further question that underlies much of the current debate, both inside and outside the US Defense Department, over the future of the US Navy is: Should the Navy be structured for wars against concentrated Soviet naval forces and homeland territory or for less-concentrated Soviet forces and intervention in the Third World?

The first alternative is very demanding and therefore will be costly. The choice will affect the entire Navy; its effect can be seen clearly in carrier and amphibious forces. If the US Navy and Marine Corps are to be used against concentrated Soviet forces, enough carriers must be built to make sure that—after losses—enough will be operating near Eurasia's coast when their air sorties are needed. (They are expected to be necessary in the Mediterranean and Arabian Sea, may be necessary in northern Europe and the Far East, and could even be required in central Europe.) Similarly, if USMC ground forces were employed in central Europe or against Soviet concentrations elsewhere, they might require more tanks and other heavy equipment than they now have. If such ground forces were to move to Eurasia in amphibious ships, those ships would need more capacity.

If, on the other hand, naval challenges

Above: The scene on board USS *Nimitz* in the Indian Ocean on February 5, 1980, as the crews of RH-53 helicopters began to train for the April 25 rescue attempt in Iran. US airpower has been used in such raids before, not always with success, despite bold planning and much courage.

Above right: A potential revolution in naval warfare in the unique shape of the AV-8B Harrier prototype. Protagonists of V/STOL had their theories proved again in the Falklands War, but the full promise of this aircraft has yet to be realised, despite several hundred now in service.

oviet forces close to USSR borders could be destepped, and if NATO land armies could hold he line without help from amphibious troops, arriers and Marines would be able to concenate on preparations for Third World operaons. This might mean fewer carriers would be eeded in the US inventory and that their airaft might not face opponents as sophisticated as concentrated as those in Europe. For the arines, it would probably mean lighter forces esigned to intervene quickly and withdraw uickly. In either case, significant forces to ep the supply line to Europe open would be ecessary in a long war.

Whether the Navy is oriented toward the oviet periphery or toward the Third World, e future of sea-based aircraft will be the bject of continuing debate. There is general greement that aircraft based on ships will be a ntinuing feature of the US Navy, but how any aircraft, their design, and that of the ips that will operate them is not entirely ear. As noted earlier, the number of carriers is been going down as the size of their aircraft is been going up. Meanwhile, the Soviets ve deployed cruise missiles in quantities that ight be able to put some carriers out of action rly in a war. If the Soviets could attack veral carriers successfully, a significant porn of the US Navy's offensive punch would be unted.

A possible answer lies in aircraft that can ke off and land vertically or over a runway a w hundred feet in length. This technology, own as V/STOL, may produce aircraft that n perform in flight as effectively as convenonal aircraft. If such aircraft could be deloped, smaller, more numerous ships could erate the aircraft. What size ships would be propriate to operate them? How many? How any aircraft per ship? To begin to answer ese questions, a squadron of V/STOL Harrs was deployed to the Sixth Fleet along with nventional aircraft aboard the carrier *F. D. osevelt* at the end of 1976. The Harriers proled some answers and also reemphasized me questions. How reliable must aircraft be at are dispatched to smaller ships if they are continue operating from them—rather than ling their limited deck space with aircraft

awaiting parts? How should aircraft maintenance be managed? If many ships with aircraft operate far apart, will they need additional communications to coordinate all the aircraft? Which is more easily defeated—a force of many smaller ships or a force of a few large ships? These questions were thoroughly debated in the United States in recent years. The results: keep the question of aircraft type open by continuing development of V/STOLs, but build additional large aircraft carriers.

How vulnerable are surface ships in an era of widespread cruise missiles? Proponents of submarines and of land-based aircraft say that the era of navies built around surface ships is passing, and cite British ship losses in the Falklands as examples. Surface ships, however, cannot be matched for a combination of easy communications and on-station times running to weeks or months. Because of this, efforts to fashion effective defenses against antiship cruise missiles continue. These include direct defenses, such as Aegis, Phalanx, and F-14s, and indirect ones, such as electronic deception and shifting radio communications to UHF.

Another element of the decentralization of US Navy offensive power is the widespread deployment of Harpoon and now the 300-mile antiship Tomahawk aboard surface combatants. As described earlier, taking advantage of these ranges requires a capability to detect, identify, hit and assess the damage to targets well beyond the horizon. This means integrating and passing information among ships and aircraft in such timely and reliable fashion that doing it presents major problems to the US Navy—a navy that already has made important advances in the management of information.

How many surface ships should be propelled by nuclear power? The tactical advantages of the carefully-designed US plants can be substantial—greater propulsion reliability and speed, and reduced replenishment frequencies. For an aircraft carrier, though, the investment in such propulsion costs up to twice as much as conventional propulsion. Over the carrier's lifetime, however, the costs of its aircraft are dominant and they do not depend on the means of ship propulsion. The tactical advantages have to be balanced against the cost differences.

Building programs in the remainder of the century can produce somewhat different numbers of ships, depending on which propulsion plants are selected for them. (All six aircraft carriers authorized since *J. F. Kennedy*, which was commissioned in 1968, have been authorized by Congress to have nuclear propulsion.)

Attacks conducted with nuclear weapons present acute problems in defending a fleet. Soviet naval writers tend not to distinguish between use of nuclear and conventional weapons as US writers do. Soviet writers also stress "decisive strikes" (although some recent writings claim that naval conflict will not necessarily be brief). If strikes with nuclear weapons are to be the means to achieve these goals, defeating them will require more than defeating conventional strikes. Because nuclear weapons are more powerful and therefore need not be as accurate, stopping more of them is necessary to protect a fleet. Depending on the size of the warheads on the attacking weapons, it may be necessary to stop all of them—a much more demanding task than stopping most. If systems such as Aegis and Phalanx cannot achieve it, then dispersal of defending ships may be necessary to prevent more than one from being disabled by a nuclear detonation. As the separation distance between ships increases, the communication that permits coordination of ships and aircraft becomes more difficult to maintain. If attacks with nuclear weapons are this disruptive to a fleet, then their use offers more advantage to the side whose mission is sea denial than to the side trying to control the seas.

The world's naval officers and other students of naval warfare have not yet reached agreement on which factors are most important in winning war at sea. Although it is possible to get general agreement on which factors—the ranges of weapons, quality of fighting personnel, staying power of ships, ability to mass and coordinate forces, and the many other considerations discussed in this chapter—are important, it is much more difficult to rank the factors in order of importance. It is presently impossible to relate changes in one factor to changes in another in any systematic way. Because of that, debate over how to build and operate more effective navies and how to predict which of them will prevail in combat continues. Such debate is ordinarily illuminated by combat experience, but there has been no conflict between major navies for more than 35 years. Navies are already quite different from what they were then; they will continue to change. The debate will go on.

US Warships

John Jordan, a contributor to many important defense journals, a consultant to the Soviet section of "Jane's Fighting Ships", and author of several technical books on modern warships.

The following technical descriptions cover the more important warships, auxiliary classes and torpedoes in the US Navy inventory. The warships are presented by ship type, with combat vessels arranged approximately by size.

Nimitz Class

CVN

Completed: 1975 onwards.
Names: CVN 68 *Nimitz*; CVN 69 *Dwight D. Eisenhower*; CVN 70 *Carl Vinson*, CVN 71 *Theodore Roosevelt*, (building).
Displacement: 81,600t standard; 91,400t full load.
Dimensions: Length 1,092ft oa (332.8m); Beam 251ft (76.4m); Draught 37ft (11.3m).
Propulsion: 4-shaft nuclear; 2 A4W reactors; 260,000shp = 30kts.
Armament: *AAW:* 3 BPDMS launchers Mk 25 (3x8).
Aircraft: 24 F-14A Tomcat; 24 A-7E Corsair; 10 A-6E Intruder + 4 KA-6D; 4 E-2C Hawkeye; 4 EA-6B Prowler; 10 S-3A Viking; 6 SH-3H Sea King.

The Nimitz class was originally envisaged as a replacement for the three Midway-class carriers. The completion of the first nuclear-powered carrier, *Enterprise*, had been followed by the construction of two conventionally powered ships, *America* and *John F. Kennedy*. The latter had, however, only ever been thought of as "interim" designs to plug the gap between *Enterprise* and a second generation of nuclear carriers which would employ smaller numbers of more advanced reactors to provide the necessary power, and which would, it was hoped, cost less to build. The two A4W reactors which power the Nimitz class each produce approximately 130,000shp compared with only 35,000shp for each of the eight A2W reactors aboard *Enterprise*. Moreover, the uranium cores need replacing far less frequently than those originally used in *Enterprise*, giving a full 13-year period between refuellings.

The reduction in the number of reactors from eight to two allowed for major improvements in the internal arrangements below hangar-deck level. Whereas in *Enterprise* the entire centre section of the ship is occupied by the machinery rooms, with the aviation fuel compartments and munitions

magazines pushed out towards the ends of the ship, in *Nimitz* the propulsion machinery is dvided into two separate units, with the magazines between them and forward of them. The improved arrangement has resulted in a increase of 20 per cent in aviation fuel capacity and a similar increase in th volume available for munitions and stores.

Flight deck layout, electronics and defensive weapons are on a par with *John F. Kennedy*. Three Mk 25 BPDMS launchers are fitted at present, bu these will shortly be replaced by the Mk 29 launcher for NATO Sea Sparrow (IPDMS). The class is also scheduled to receive three Phalanx CIWS guns.

Problems were experienced from the outset in the construction of thes

Above: USS *Eisenhower* (CVN-69) showing the vast size of the flight deck 1,092ft (333m), or one-fifth of a mile, long.

ships. *Nimitz* was four years late in commissioning and took seven years build (*Enterprise* took only four). Her construction was plagued by shortage of skilled labour and frequent strikes at the Newport New Shipyard. When she was finally completed in 1973, vital components for th A4W reactors had still not been delivered, and a further two years were t elapse before commissioning. This delayed the start of *Eisenhower* by further four years, and produced a knock-on effect which resulted rocketing costs. President Carter attempted, unsuccessfully, to block th authorisation of funds for the construction of a fourth carrier in favour of th smaller, less capable, but less costly CVV design. The CVV, however, wa never popular with the Navy, and the Reagan administration has no committed itself to the continuation of the CVN programme. A fourth ship a modified Nimitz type, *Theodore Roosevelt*, was laid down in late 1981, ar two further units are projected.

Above: *Nimitz* (CVN-68), with lifts lowered and F-4s, A-6s and E-2Cs included on deck.

Below: Side view of Nimitz class emphasises the enormous size o the vessel. These carriers possess more air power than many Thir World air forces. Note the three side lifts and radar.

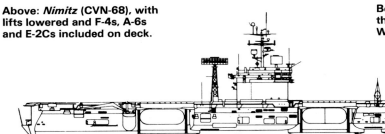

Enterprise

Completed:	1961
Name:	CVN 65 *Enterprise*
Displacement:	75,700t standard; 89,600t full load.
Dimensions:	Length 1,123ft oa (342.3m); Beam 248ft (75.7m); Draught 36ft (10.9m).
Propulsion:	4-shaft nuclear; 8 A2W reactors; 280,000shp = 30kts.
Armament:	3 NATO Sea Sparrow launchers Mk 29 (3x8); 3 Phalanx CIWS (3x6).
Aircraft:	24 F-14A Tomcat; 24 A-7E Corsair; 10 A-6E Intruder + 4 KA-6D; 4 E-2C Hawkeye; 4 EA-6B Prowler; 10 S-3A Viking; 6 SH-3H Sea King.

Laid down shortly after the US Navy's first nuclear-powered surface ship, the cruiser *Long Beach, Enterprise* was completed in the remarkably short space of 3 years 9 months. The initial development work on her propulsion plant had begun as early as 1950, and the design of the reactors had benefited from the evaluation of early models installed in submarines. Even so, the problem of producing the required 280,000shp on four shafts employing first-generation reactors resulted in a solution that was costly in terms of internal volume; two A2W reactors are coupled to each shaft and the entire centre section of the ship is taken up by machinery.

Enterprise was also costly in terms of the initial purchase price—nearly double that of her conventionally-powered contemporaries of the Kitty Hawk class—but a number of strong arguments were advanced in favour of nuclear power. Reduced life-cycle costs due to infrequent refuellings made the nuclear-powered carrier a more economic proposition in the longer term, and the CVAN would be capable of undertaking lengthy transits and operations in high-threat areas at a high sustained speed. Moreover, the elimination of ship's fuel bunkers in *Enterprise* allowed a 50 per cent increase in aviation fuel capacity, and consequently in the number of consecutive days of strike operations she could sustain.

Below: USS *Enterprise* (CVN-65) flying-off. Among the aircraft to be seen are F-4 Phantoms, A-4 Skyhawks and an RA-5 Vigilante.

Below: The *Enterprise* leaves the notorious Alcatraz prison island as she steams out of San Francisco Bay in March 1982.

Above: USS *Enterprise* (CVN-65) at sea in the late 1970s. She was the first carrier to operate the F-14, of which six can be seen.

In size and general layout *Enterprise* is similar to *Kitty Hawk*. The most significant difference as completed was in the shape of the island, which comprised a "box" structure on which were mounted SPS-32/33 "billboard" radars, surmounted by a large cone for ECM and ESM antennae. The SPS-32/33 radars proved difficult to maintain, however, and when *Enterprise* was refitted in 1979-81, the entire island was removed and replaced by a more conventional structure similar to that of the *Nimitz*. As refitted, she will carry conventional rotating radars of the latest types.

Like the carriers of the Kitty Hawk class *Enterprise* was to have received two Mk 10 launchers for Terrier missiles. She was completed with the large sponsons aft, but Terrier was not installed initially in a bid to keep down costs. When Terrier lost favour as a carrier weapon in the mid-1960s, it was decided instead to fit two BPDMS Sea Sparrow launchers on the after sponsons. After her current refit *Enterprise* will carry three Mk 29 launchers for NATO Sea Sparrow, and three Phalanx CIWS guns.

Kitty Hawk Class
CV

Completed: 1961-8.
Names: CV63 *Kitty Hawk*; CV64 *Constellation*; CV 66 *America*; CV 67 *John F. Kennedy*.
Displacement: 60,100-61,000t standard; 80,800-82,000t full load.
Dimensions: Length 1,048-1,073ft oa (319.3-326.9m); Beam 250-268ft (76.2-81.5m); Draught 36ft (11m).
Propulsion: 4-shaft geared steam turbines; 280,000shp = 30kts.
Armament: CV63: 2 NATO Sea Sparrow launchers Mk29 (2x8); CV64: 2 twin Mk 10 launchers (40 + 40) for Terrier missiles; CV66-7: 3 NATO Sea Sparrow launchers Mk29 (2x8), 3 Phalanx CIWS.
Aircraft: 24 F-14A Tomcat; 24 A-7E Corsair; 10 A-6E Intruder + 4 KA-6D; 4 E-2C Hawkeye; 4 EA-6B Prowler; 10 S-3A Viking; 6 SH-3H Sea King.

Although there are significant differences between the first pair completed and the last two vessels—*John F. Kennedy* is officially considered as a separate single-ship class—these four carriers are generally grouped together because of their common propulsion system and flight-deck layout.

Kitty Hawk and *Constellation* were ordered as improved Forrestals, incorporating a number of important modifications. The flight deck showed a slight increase in area, and the arrangement of the lifts was revised to improve aircraft-handling arrangements. The single port-side lift, which on the Forrestals was located at the forward end of the flight deck—and was therefore unusable during landing operations—was repositioned at the after end of the overhang, outside the line of the angled deck. The respective positions of the centre lift on the starboard side and the island structure were reversed, so that two lifts were available to serve the forward catapults. A further improved feature of the lifts was that they were no longer strictly rectangular, but had an additional angled section at their forward end which enabled longer aircraft to be accommodated. The new arrangement proved so successful that it was adopted by all subsequent US carriers.

Kitty Hawk and *Constellation* were designed at a time when long-range surface-to-air missiles were just entering service with the US Navy. In place of the eight 5-inch (127mm) guns of the Forrestal class these ships therefore received two Mk 10 launchers for Terrier missiles positioned on sponsons aft just below the level of the flight deck, with their 40-missile magazines

behind them. *America*, the third ship of the class, was completed after a ga‹ of four years and therefore incorporated a number of further modification‹ She has a narrower smokestack and is fitted with an SQS-23 sonar—th only US carrier so equipped.

In 1963 it was decided that the new carrier due to be laid down in FY 196 would be nuclear-powered, but Congress baulked at the cost, and the sh was finally laid down as a conventionally powered carrier of a modified Kit Hawk design. *John F. Kennedy* can be distinguished externally from h near-sisters by her canted stack—designed to keep the corrosive exhau gases clear of the flight deck—and by the shape of the forward end of th angled deck. Of even greater significance was the abandonment of th expensive long-range Terrier system, which took up valuable space an

Forrestal Class
CV

Completed: 1952-5.
Names: CV 59 *Forrestal*; CV 60 *Saratoga*; CV 61 *Ranger*; CV 62 *Independence*.
Displacement: 60,000t standard; 78,000t full load.
Dimensions: Length 1,039-1,047ft oa (316.7-319m); Beam 238ft (72.5m); Draught 37ft (11.3m)
Propulsion: 4-shaft geared steam turbines; 260-280,000shp = 33kts.
Armament: CV 59-60: 2 BPDMS launchers Mk 25 (2x8); CV 61-62: 2 NATO Sea Sparrow launchers Mk 29 (2x8).
Aircraft: 24 F-4J Phantom; 24 A-7E Corsair; 10 A-6E Intruder + 4 KA-6D; 4 E-2C Hawkeye; 4 EA-6B Prowler; 10 S-3A Viking; 6 SH-3H Sea King.

Authorisation of the Forrestal class was a direct consequence of the Korean War, which re-established the value of the carrier for projecting air power against land targets. The new class was to operate the A-3 Skywarrior strategic bomber, which weighed fully 78,000lb (35,455kg) and dimensions and hangar height were increased accordingly. The original design was for a

carrier similar in configuration to the ill-fated *United States*, which had flush deck, together with a retractable bridge, and two waist catapul‹ angled out on sponsons in addition to the standard pair of catapults forward

The advent of the angled deck, which was tested by the US Navy in 195 on the Essex-class carrier *Antietam*, led to the modification of *Forrestal* whi building to incorporate this new development. The result was the distinctiv configuration which has been adopted by all subsequent US carrie construction: a massive flight deck with considerable overhang supporte by sponsons to the sides, with a small island incorporating the smokestack starboard. The Forrestals were the first US carriers to have the flight deck ‹ the strength deck—in previous ships it was the hangar deck—and consequence side lifts were adopted in preference to centreline lifts an incorporated in the overhang. This resulted in a large uninterrupted hanga in which more than half the ship's aircraft could be struck down. The layou of the four side lifts proved less than satisfactory, however; in particular th port-side lift, which is at the forward end of the angled deck, cannot be use during landing operations, and the Kitty Hawk class which followed had modified arrangement.

All four ships of the class were completed with eight 5-inch (127mn single mountings on sponsons fore and aft. The forward sponsons create

Below: USS *Saratoga* (CV-60) steaming at speed with an attendant destroyer in her wake. This carrier is the first of the class to undergo the Service Life Extension Programme (SLEP), a major refit lasting from October 1980 to February 1983. This cost $514 million at FY1981 prices, but the remaining ships will cost more.

**ove: USS *John F Kennedy* (CV-67) is officially a separate class
t is normally grouped in the Kitty Hawk class. Note the funnel.**

rely duplicated similar area defence systems on the carrier escorts, in
our of the Basic Point Defence Missile System (BPDMS), for which three
tuple launchers were fitted.
John F. Kennedy marks the high point of US carrier construction, and the
lier three ships of the Kitty Hawk class are now being refitted to the same
ndard. In particular the Terrier launchers, together with the fire control
lars, are being removed and replaced by Mk 29 launchers for NATO Sea
arrow. It is envisaged that all four ships will eventually carry three Mk 29
nchers and three Phalanx CIWS guns.

**Above: USS *Kitty Hawk* (CV-63) underway in the Pacific Ocean.
The four E-2C AEW aircraft emphasize the huge area of the deck.**

oblems in heavy seas, however, and the three ships based in the Atlantic
d both guns and sponsons removed in the early 1960s (*Ranger* lost her
ward guns but retained the sponsons). During the 1970s all guns were
olaced by BPDMS Mk 25 or IPDMS Mk 29 launchers. Eventually all four
os will have three Mk 29 launchers and three Phalanx CIWS guns.
The electronics suite has undergone considerable change and expansion
ce the 1950s, and in 1980 *Saratoga* was taken in hand for a 3-year major

modernisation, as part of the Service Life Extension Program (SLEP).
Unlike later carriers, the Forrestal class do not operate the F-14 Tomcat,
but retain the F-4 Phantom. It is envisaged that the latter will eventually be
replaced by the F-18 Hornet.

**Below: This silhouette shows the three side lifts and the
uncluttered deck broken only by the small bridge structure.**

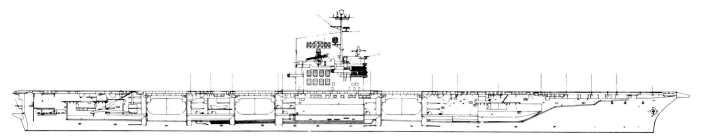

**Left: USS *Forrestal* (CV-59) underway in the Mediterranean, a sea
she knows well. She was the first of the "super-carriers" to be built
in the early 1950s and revolutionized naval thinking.**

**Below: USS *Independence* (CV-62), her flight deck covered in
aircraft. The Forrestals were the first carriers to operate the
angledeck and steam catapult, both invented in the UK.**

Midway Class

CV

Completed: 1945-7.
Names: CV 41 *Midway*; CV 43 *Coral Sea*.
Displacement: 51-52,000t standard; 64,000t full load.
Dimensions: Length 979ft oa (298.4m); Beam 236-259ft (71.9-78.8); Draught 36ft (11m).
Propulsion: 4-shaft geared steam turbines; 212,000shp = 32kts.
Armament: 2 BPDMS launchers Mk 25 (2x8—CV 41 only); 3 Phalanx CIWS.
Aircraft: 24 F-4J Phantom; 24 A-7E Corsair; 10 A-6E Intruder + 4 KA-6D; 4 E-2C Hawkeye; 4 EA-6B Prowler.

These ships were the last war-built US carriers. Three units were completed but *Franklin D. Roosevelt* was stricken in 1977. As built, the Midway class had an axial flight deck with two centre-line lifts and a side lift amidships on the port side. They were armed with a heavy battery of 14-18 5-inch (127mm) guns and numerous smaller AA weapons. The original design was quickly overtaken by developments in jet aircraft, and the class underwent a major modernisation during the 1950s in which an 8-degree angled deck was built, incorporating the side lift at its forward end; the after lift, which would have obstructed landing operations, was removed and replaced by a second side lift to starboard aft of the island. The armament was significantly reduced and the latest 3-D and air search radars fitted. C-11 steam catapults were installed to enable the ships to operate the new generation of various types of jet aircraft.

Coral Sea, which was the last of the three to be modernised, incorporated a number of further modifications as a result of experience with her two sisters and with the Forrestal class. The position of the port-side lift was found to be unsatisfactory, and it was moved aft to clear the angled deck altogether. This enabled the angled deck itself to be extended forward with a consequent increase in deck space, and a third C-11 catapult was installed. The position of the forward centre-line lift was found to be equally unsatisfactory, as it was situated between the forward catapults and was therefore unusable during take-off operations. It was therefore removed and replaced by a third side lift forward of the island. New sponsons were bu for the six remaining guns, which were now just below flight-deck level.

The conversion of *Coral Sea* was particularly successful, and s remained largely unaltered–except for the removal of the remainir guns–throughout the following two decades. Since 1978 she has been t thirteenth carrier in a 12-carrier force and has only recently been reactivat to replace *Saratoga* while the latter undergoes her SLEP.

In 1966 *Midway* was taken in hand for a major modernisation whic would enable her to operate the same aircraft as the more modern U carriers. The flight deck was completely rebuilt–its total area was increase by approximately one-third–and the lifts rearranged on the patte

Ohio Class

SSBN

Completed: 1981 onwards. No. in Class: 1 (+ 6 building).
Displacement: 16,600t surfaced; 18,700t submerged.
Dimensions: Length 560ft (170.7m); Beam 42ft (12.8m); Draught 36ft 6in (11.1m).
Propulsion: 1-shaft nuclear; 1 S8G reactor; ? shp = 20+kts
Armament: 24 tubes for Trident C-4 SLBM; 4 21-inch (533mm) torpedo tubes Mk 68.

While the programme of upgrading the later Polaris SLBM submarines to carry Poseidon was under way in the early 1970s development of an entirely new missile was started. This was to have a much longer range—4,400 miles (7,100km)—which in turn necessitated a new and much larger submarine to carry it. The missile, Trident 1, is now in service on converted Lafayette class SSBNs, while the first of the submarines purpose-built for Trident, USS *Ohio*, has just joined the fleet. Initially Congress baulked at the immense cost of the new system—but then the Soviet Navy introduced its own long-range SLBM, the 4,200-mile (6,760km) SS-N-8, in the Delta class. This was followed in 1976 by the firing of the first of the increased-range SS-N18s (4,846 miles, 7,800km). US reaction was to speed up the Trident programme, and the first of the Ohio class submarines was laid down on 10 April 1976.

The eventual number of Trident-carrying SSBNs depends on tv principal factors. The first is the outcome of the new round of Str tegic Arms Limitation Talks (or Strategic Arms Reduction Talks) b tween the Reagan administration and the USSR, which will then, course, have to be ratified by the US Congress. Any such agreeme would presumably include, as in SALT-II proposals, the maximu numbers of SLBMs and launch platforms that each super-power w prepared to permit the other to possess. The other factor is th development of new types of long-range cruise missiles, some which can be used in a strategic role even when launched from standard 21in (533mm) submerged torpedo tube. This, and simil progress in other fields, may restrict the need for large numbers SLBMs in huge and very expensive SSBNs. The great advantag however, of the current generation of very long-range SLBMs is th they can be launched from American or Soviet home waters, th making detection of the launch platform and destruction of either t submarine or the missiles launched from it extremely difficult, if n virtually impossible.

Below: USS *Ohio* (SSBN-726) alongside a missile wharf is loaded with a Trident I C-4 SLBM. She carries 24 of these missiles, which have a range of 4,400 miles (7,100km) and carry 8 100KT MIRVs.

established by *Coral Sea*. (The new lifts are much larger, however, and have
a capacity of 130,000lb (59,100kg) compared with 74,000lb (33,636kg)
for those of her sister-ship). Two C-13 catapults were installed forward,
enabling *Midway* to handle the latest aircraft. The armament was reduced to
three 5-inch (127mm) guns (these were replaced in 1979 by two BPDMS
launchers). NTDS was installed during the modernisation and the island has
recently been extended to incorporate the latest sensors. Three Phalanx
CIWS guns are to be fitted in the near future.

Midway, which is based in Japan, is due to remain in service until 1988,
when she will replace *Coral Sea* as a training ship. Her principal limitations
compared with later carriers are those inherent in the initial design; a hangar

**Above left: An overhead view of USS *Coral Sea* (CV-43). Three
Midway class carriers were built in 1943-44; only *Coral Sea* and
Midway remain; *Franklin Roosevelt* was scrapped in 1977.**

**Above: USS *Midway* (CV-41) shows off to advantage her angled
flightdeck as she steams under the Golden Gate bridge.**

height of only 17ft 6in (5.3m) and a limited aviation fuel capacity. In spite of
their CV designation neither *Midway* nor *Coral Sea* operate fixed- or rotary-
wing ASW aircraft, and both continue to operate the F-4 Phantom in place of
the F-14 Tomcat.

Lafayette Class
SSBN

Completed: 1963-67. No. in Class: 19/12.
Displacement: 7,250t surfaced; 8,250t submerged.
Dimensions: Length 425ft (129.5m); Beam 33ft (10.1m);
Draguht 31ft 6in (9.6m).
Propulsion: 1-shaft nuclear; 1 S5W reactor;
15,000shp = 25kts.
Armament: 16 tubes for Poseidon C-3 or Trident C-4 SLBM;
4 21-inch (533mm) torpedo tubes Mk 65.

The 31 Lafayette class SSBNs were the definitive US submarines of
the 1960s and 1970s. The first eight were originally fitted with Polaris
A-2 missiles, while the remaining 23 had the improved Polaris A-3
with a range of 2,855 miles (4,594km) and three 200KT MRV warheads. The first five boats launched their missiles with compressed air,
but the remainder use a rocket motor to produce a gas-steam mixture
to eject the missiles from their tubes. All Lafayettes have now been
fitted to take Poseidon C-3 SLBMs, which have a range of about
3,230 miles (5,200km) with ten 50KT MIRVs.

The Lafayettes are slightly enlarged and improved versions of the
Ethan Allen design, and are almost indistinguishable from that class.
The last 12 Lafayettes differ considerably from the earlier boats and
are sometimes referred to as the Benjamin Franklin class. They have
improved, quieter machinery and 28 more crewmen. Twelve of these
are being refitted to take the larger three-stage Trident 1 C-4 SLBM,
which has a range of about 4,400 miles (7,100km) and carries eight
100KT MIRVs. Although these SSBNs do not have the underwater
performance of the SSNs, they have a respectable capability against
surface ships or other submarines and are armed with conventional
wire-guided torpedoes and Subroc. Normally, however, they would
attempt to evade detection or contact.

Daniel Webster (SSBN-626) of this class has been fitted with diving
planes on a raised bow sonar instead of on the fin; although this has
been successful, it has not been copied on other SSBNs.

**Above: USS *Lafayette* (SSBN-616) underway on the surface in
Hampton Roads, Virginia in December 1968. She was laid down in
January 1961, launched in May and commissioned April 1963.**

**Below: An SSBN of the Lafayette class travelling on the surface.
These submarines were first fitted with Polaris and then with
Poseidon; now 12 are being converted to take Trident I C-4.**

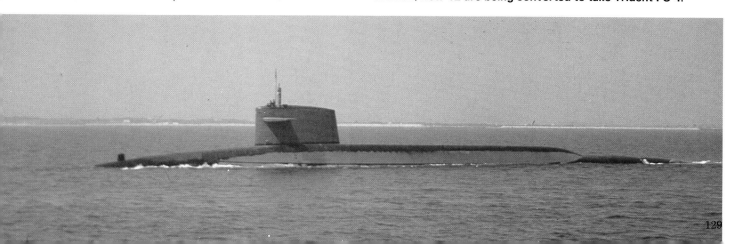

Skipjack Class

Completed: 1959-61. No. in Class: 5.
Displacement: 3,075t surfaced; 3,500t submerged.
Dimensions: Length 252ft (76.7m); Beam 32ft (9.6m);
Draught 28ft (8.5m).
Propulsion: 1-shaft nuclear; 1 S5W reactor;
15,000shp = 30+kts.
Armament: 6 21-in (533mm) torpedo tubes Mk 59.

The Skipjack class SSNs were the first nuclear submarines to incorporate the teardrop hull developed in the conventionally-powered USS *Albacore* (AGSS-569). Hence, whereas her predecessors had a submerged speed of some 20+ knots, USS *Skipjack*, with her new hull form, is capable of well over 30 knots, although her surface performance is poor in comparison. As well as the improved speed, underwater manoeuvrability is also increased, although the use of only one screw brings its own problems and means that stern torpedo tubes can no longer be fitted.

One of this class, *Scorpion* (SSN-589), was modified on the slip to become the first of the George Washington class SSBNs, and the materials for another of the Skipjack class were appropriated for USS *Patrick Henry.* Ultimately, six Skipjacks were built between 1956 and 1961, but *Scorpion* (SSN-589) was lost with all hands in the Atlantic in May 1968.

All engine fittings in the Skipjacks (except for the reactor and the propeller) are duplicated to minimise the danger of a breakdown. They have had their original sonar equipment updated, but these old boats will not be fitted with the BQQ-5 sonar because they have their torpedo tubes in the old bow position. They were the first boats to use

Above: USS *Skipjack* (SSN-585) has a surface speed of about 16 knots, which is poor in comparison with her submerged speed of 30+ knots.

the S5W nuclear reactor, but they are now reaching the terminatio of their active lives.

Sturgeon Class/Narwhal

Completed: 1967-75. No. in Class: 37/1.
Displacement: 3,640t surfaced; 4,650t submerged.
Dimensions: Length 292ft (89m); Beam 32ft (9.65m);
Draught 29ft 6in (8.9m).
Propulsion: 1-shaft nuclear; 1 S5W reactor;
15,000shp = 30kts.
Armament: Harpoon SSMs; SUBROC; 4 21-inch (533mm)
torpedo tubes Mk 63.

The 37 Sturgeon class SSNs are slightly enlarged and improved versions of the Permit (Thresher) class. Like them, the Sturgeons have an elongated teardrop hull with torpedo tubes set amidships, with the bow taken up by the various components of the BQQ-2 sonar system. The Sturgeon is distinguished visually from the Permit by its taller fin with the driving planes set farther down. Several problems arose between the USN and the builders of this class: *Pogy* (SSN-647) was re-allocated to another yard for completion, while *Guitarro* (SSN-665) was delayed for more than two years after sinking in 35ft (10.7m) of water while being fitted out, in an incident later described by a Congressional committee as 'wholly avoidable'.

In an attempt to reduce noise, the Sturgeon class is fitted with two contra-rotating propellers on the same shaft. Although American submarines are already significantly quieter than their Soviet counterparts, any developments which can reduce noise (and therefore the distance at which the submarine can be detected) are speedily introduced. The Sturgeons, like the Permits, will be fitted during the course of routine overhauls with the BQQ-5 sonar system introduced in the Los Angeles class.

Narwhal (SSN-671), an experimental SSN based on the Permit/

Above: Sturgeon class submarines like USS *Sea Devil* (SSN-664), here seen surfacing, have a diving depth in excess of 1,320ft (400m

Sturgeon design, was built in 1967-69 to test the S5G free-circulatic reactor, which has no pumps and is therefore quieter than previou US reactors. Although *Narwhal* retains this system and is still in servic no further submarines have been built with such a system.

Tullibee/Permit (Thresher) Class

Completed: 1960-68. No. in Class: 1/13.
Displacement: 3,750t surfaced; 4,300-4,600t submerged.
Dimensions: Length 279-297ft (84.9-89.5m);
Beam 32ft (9.6m); Draught 29ft (8.8m).
Propulsion: 1-shaft nuclear; 1 S5W reactor;
15,000shp = 30kts.
Armament: Harpoon SSMs; SUBROC; 4 21-inch (533mm)
torpedo tubes Mk 63.

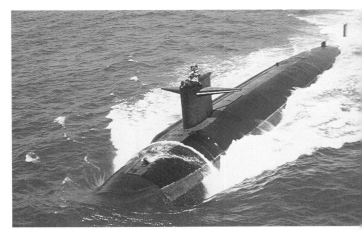

Tullibee is one of the smallest SSNs to be built, displacing only 2,640 tons submerged, and was an early attempt at the ideal hunter-killer submarine. The small size meant that she was very manoeuvrable and thus more likely to detect a hostile submarine before herself being detected. The torpedo tubes were fitted amidships for the first time in order to free the bows for the then new BQQ-2 conformal sonar array. She was also fitted with turbo-electric drive to eliminate the noise made by the reduction gears in earlier boats. However, small size also led to a low submerged speed, and *Tullibee* lacked space to carry the more sophisticated (and inevitably larger) equipment and electronics. No more SSNs of this size have been built for the US Navy. *Tullibee* remains in service but is no longer considered a first-line unit.

Above: An unmarked SSN of the Permit class cruising on the surface. Class name was changed after *Thresher* was lost in 1963

Right: The experimental hunter/killer USS *Tullibee* (SSN-597); small, manoeuvrable but lacking in equipment space and speed.

ipscomb/
os Angeles Class

Completed:	1974 onwards. No. in Class: 1/19 (+14 building).
Displacement:	6,000t surfaced; 6,900t submerged.
Dimensions:	Length 360ft (109.7m); Beam 33ft (10.1m); Draught 32ft 4in (9.85m).
Propulsion:	1-shaft nuclear; 1 S6G reactor; 30,000shp = 30+kts.
Armament:	Harpoon SSMs; SUBROC; 4 21-inch (533mm) torpedo tubes Mk 67.

USS *Glenard P. Lipscomb* was launched in 1973, the outcome of a evelopment programme for a 'quiet' submarine stretching back to USS *Tullibee* of the early 1960s. *Lipscomb* has many interesting features to achieve silent running, many of them subsequently incorporated into the Los Angeles class. Like *Tullibee*, *Lipscomb* is powered y a pressurised-water cooled reactor driving a turbo-electric plant. This removes the requirement for gearing, which is one of the prime ources of noise in submarines. Although *Lipscomb* remains in frontine service, this particular drive system was not repeated in the submarines of the Los Angeles class.

The first Los Angeles SSN entered service in 1976; nineteen are now n commission and fourteen are under construction. They are much arger than any previous SSN and have a higher submerged speed. They have the BQQ-5 sonar system and can operate Subroc, Sub-Harpoon nd Tomahawk as well as conventional and wire-guided torpedoes. Thus, like all later US SSNs, although they are intended to hunt other ubmarines and to protect SSBNs they can also be used without modifiation to sink surface ships at long range with Sub-Harpoon. Further,

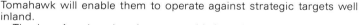

Right: A splendid picture of USS *Philadelphia* (SSN-690) running on the surface during her immediate pre-commissioning trials in 1977. With a displacement of 6,900 tons, the Los Angeles class SSNs are the largest and most powerful hunter/killers in any navy.

Below: USS *Atlanta* (SSN-712) on sea trials in the Atlantic Ocean. The cost of each boat was $221.25 million in 1976, but this has risen rapidly to $991.7 million each for the two boats built in FY1981. Even the USA cannot spend money at this rate for ever.

Tomahawk will enable them to operate against strategic targets well inland.

The Los Angeles class is very sophisticated and each boat is an extremely potent fighting machine. With a production run of at least 37, it must be considered a very successful design. However, these boats are becoming very expensive: in 1976 the cost of each one was estimated at $221.25 million; the boat bought in 1979 cost $325.6 million; the two in 1981 will cost $495.8 million each. Not even the USA can continue to spend money at that rate.

Nevertheless, the Reagan Administration has ordered a speeding up of the Los Angeles building programme, calling for two in 1982 and three per year thereafter. The Tomahawk missile programme is also being accelerated: Tomahawk will be fitted from SSN-719 (the twenty-second boat to be launched, in 1983) onward.

A design for a smaller and cheaper SSN, under consideration in 1980 as a result of Congressional pressure, has now been shelved. There are now plans to improve the Los Angeles boats—especially their sensors, weapon systems and control equipment—and consideration is also being given to a vertically-launched cruise missile system which would comprise 12 vertical tubes, possibly mounted in the forward main ballast tank area.

All the better features of *Tullibee* were incorporated into the Thresher class, which, after the loss of the name ship in the Atlantic in April 1963, was redesignated the Permit class. Built between 1960 and 1966, four of these boats were originally designed to take the Regulus II cruise missile: they were re-ordered as SSNs when the Regulus II was cancelled in favour of the Polaris SLBM in 1958. The last three of the class (SSN-614, -615 and -621) have a larger hull than the earlier boats; *Jack* (SSN-605) has a modified hull to accommodate contra-rotating propellers, as one of the US Navy's many attempts to find a really quiet propulsion system. The principal anti-submarine weapon is Subroc, controlled by the BQQ-2 sonar sytem; the Permits can also fire the anti-ship Harpoon missile. They will in time be fitted to take the Tomahawk SLCM and will also be retrofitted with the BQQ-5 sonar.

Below: USS *Barb* (SSN-976). The Permit class was the first to carry Subroc missiles guided by the BQQ-2 sonar system; they can also fire the anti-ship Harpoon missile and, in future, Tomahawk.

George Washington Class/ SSN
Ethan Allen Class

Completed: 1959-63. No. in Class: 3/5.
Displacement*: 6,955t surfaced; 7,900t submerged.
Dimensions*: Length 411ft (125.1m); Beam 33ft (10.1m);
Draught 30ft (9.1m).
Propulsion: 1-shaft nuclear; 1 S5W reactor;
15,000shp = 25kts.
Armament: 4 21-inch (533mm) torpedo tubes Mk 65.
*Details for Ethan Allen

The George Washington class were the US Navy's first ballistic missile submarines. In order to get Polaris to sea as quickly as possible the design was based on that of the Skipjack class SSN. In fact, *George Washington* (SSBN-598) herself was laid down as *Scorpion* (SSN-589), and was lengthened by the addition of a 130ft (40m) insert while on the stocks. The original powerplant and much of the SSN-type equipment was retained in the SSBN. The five George Washington SSBNs were in service for seven years before the first of the Soviet equivalents, the Yankee class, became operational. By the mid-1960s the relatively short range of the Polaris A-1 missiles was making the George Washingtons vulnerable to Soviet countermeasures, so during their first re-coring they were fitted with the 2,855-mile (4,595km) Polaris A-3. Their electronics were also upgraded.

Two of this class (*Theodore Roosevelt* and *Abraham Lincoln*) had their missile compartments removed in 1980 and the spent fuel disposed of. Although the bow and stern sections were then rejoined, the decommissioned hulks are now being cannibalized for spares prior to disposal. The three remaining boats are being converted to SSNs by removing all missiles and associated equipment; cement will be put into the missile tubes as ballast compensation. The cost of conversion is a mere $400,000 per boat. As SSNs, their main use will be in training and as targets on ASW exercises, thus releasing more modern SSNs for front-line duties. The three boats will only be used in this way

for two to three years, however, because of the short life remaining in their nuclear cores.

Whereas the George Washington class was built to a modified SSN design in order to get the Polaris into service as soon as possible, the five Ethan Allen SSBNs were the first to be specially designed as such. While generally similar to the George Washingtons, they are nearly 30ft (9.1m) longer and, when first commissioned, were armed with the Polaris A-2, which had a range of 1,725 miles (2,776km). They had greatly improved crew quarters, an important factor in boats which remained submerged for more than sixty days at a time. *Ethan Allen* herself became the first SSBN to fire a live SLBM, on 6 May 1962; this detonated successfully on the Christmas Island test range. These boats were fitted with Polaris A-3, but, like the George Washingtons, they will not be fitted with Poseidon or Trident. All five are now being converted to SSNs and will operate in the attack role through to the end of the 1980s at least.

Below: Seen as an SSBN this Ethan Allen boat is now being converted to give a few more years service as an SSN.

Below: An SSBN of the George Washington class. These boats were rushed into service in the 1960s and have been first class.

Ticonderoga Class CG

Completed: 1983 onwards. No. in Class: 1 (+ 2 building).
Displacement: 9,100t full load.
Dimensions: Length 563ft oa (171.7m); Beam 55ft (17m);
Draught 31ft (9.4m).
Propulsion: 2-shaft COGAG; 4 LM2500 gas turbines;
80,000bhp = 30kts.
Armament: *AAW:* 2 twin Mk 26 launchers (44 + 44) for Standard MR SM-2 missiles; 2 5-inch (127mm) Mk 45 (2x1);
2 Phalanx CIWS.
ASW: ASROC missiles from Mk 26 launcher;
2 LAMPS helicopters; 6 12.75-inch (324mm) torpedo tubes Mk 32 (2x3).
SSM: 8 Harpoon missiles (2x4).

The new missile cruiser *Ticonderoga* is the first operational vessel to be fitted with the Aegis Combat System. It was originally envisaged that this system would be installed in nuclear-powered escorts such as the Strike Cruiser (CSGN) and the CGN 42 variant of the Virginia class, but the enormous cost of Aegis combined with that of nuclear propulsion proved to be prohibitive under the restrictive budgets of the late 1970s. Moreover, two Aegis escorts were required for each of the twelve carrier battle groups, and as not all of the carriers concerned were nuclear-powered, it was decided to utilise the growth potential of the fossil-fuelled Spruance design to incorporate the necessary electronics.

The Aegis Combat System was developed to counter the saturation missile attacks which could be expected to form the basis of Soviet anti-carrier tactics during the 1980s. Conventional rotating radars are limited

both in data rate and in number of target tracks they can handle, whereas saturation missile attacks require sensors which can react immediately and have a virtually unlimited tracking capacity. The solution adopted in the Aegis system is to mount four fixed planar antennae each covering a sector of 45 degrees on the superstructure of the ship. Each SPY-1 array has more than 4000 radiating elements that shape and direct multiple beams. Targets satisfying predetermined criteria are evaluated, arranged in sequence of threat and engaged, either automatically or with manual override, by variety of defensive systems.

At longer ranges air targets will be engaged by the SM-2 missile, fired from one of two Mk 26 launchers. The SM-2 differs from previous missiles in requiring target illumination only in the terminal phase of flight. In the initial and mid-flight phase the missile flies under auto-pilot towards a predicted interception point with initial guidance data and limited mid-course guidance supplied by the Aegis system. This means that no less than 18 missiles can be kept in the air in addition to the four in the terminal phase, and the Mk 9 illuminators switch rapidly from one target to the next under computer control. At closer ranges back-up is provided by the two 5-inch guns, while "last-ditch" self-defence is provided by two Phalanx CIWS guns, assisted by ECM jammers and chaff dispensers.

Ticonderoga and her sisters are designed to serve as flagships, and will be equipped with an elaborate Combat Information Centre (CIC) possessing an integral flag function able to accept and coordinate data from other ships and aircraft. Eighteen units are currently projected, and it is envisaged that they will operate in conjunction with specialised ASW destroyers (the Spruance class) and a new type of AAW destroyer (the DDG-51).

Right: USS *Ticonderoga* (CG-47) the first of the Aegis guided missile cruisers on sea trials in the Gulf of Mexico in May 1982.

Above: USS *Thomas Jefferson* (SSN-618) will be the last of her class to operate as an SSBN; she will be converted in FY1984.

Barbel Class

Completed: 1959. No. in Class: 3.
Displacement: 2,145t surfaced; 2,895t submerged.
Dimensions: Length 220ft (66.9m); Beam 29ft (8.8m); Draught 28ft (8.5m).
Propulsion: 1-shaft; 3 FM diesels, 4,800bhp = 15kts (sur.); 2 GM electric motors, 3,150hp = 25kts (sub.).
Armament: 6 21-inch (533mm) torpedo tubes Mk 58.

The Barbel class will almost certainly go down in history as the last conventional submarines to be built for the US Navy. They have the 'tear-drop' hull tested by USS *Albacore,* which gives exceptionally high underwater speed for a non-nuclear submarine, albeit at the expense of performance on the surface. The Barbels still perform a useful function for the US Navy, acting as training boats, demonstrating the problems and abilities of conventional submarines in exercises with the rest of the fleet. The general Barbel design has been followed abroad in several classes; eg, the Japanese Uzushio and the Dutch Zwaardvis.

Above and below: USS *Barbel* (SS-580) is the nameship of what is almost certainly the final class of non-nuclear submarines in the US Navy. They have an Albacore-type hull giving an underwater speed in excess of 25 knots, but are used mainly to train ASW forces.

Virginia Class
CGN

Completed: 1976-80. No. in Class: 4.
Displacement: 11,000t full load.
Dimensions: Length 585ft oa (178m); Beam 63ft (19m);
Draught 30ft (9m).
Propulsion: 2-shaft nuclear; 2 D2G reactors; 60,000shp = 30kts.
Armament: *AAW:* 2 twin Mk 26 launchers (44 + 24) for Standard MR
missiles; 2 5-inch (127mm) Mk 45 (2x1).
ASW: 1 LAMPS helicopter (see notes); ASROC missiles
from fwd Mk 26 launcher; 6 12.75-inch (324mm)
torpedo tubes Mk 32 (2x3).
SSM: 8 Harpoon missiles (2x4) being fitted.

Following closely upon the two CGNs of the California class, the *Virginia* incorporated a number of significant modifications. While the basic layout of the class is identical to that of their predecessors, the single-arm Mk 13 launchers of the *California* were superseded by the new Mk 26 twin launcher forward, and a helicopter hangar was built into the stern.

The magazine associated with Mk 26 launcher has a continuous belt feed system with vertical stowage capable of accommodating a variety of missiles, including the standard MR surface-to-air missile, ASROC and Harpoon. The elimination of the separate ASROC launcher and its associated reloading deckhouse has saved 5m (16.4ft) in length compared with *California*.

The installation of an internal helicopter hangar in a ship other than an aircraft carrier is unique in the postwar US Navy. The hangar itself is 42ft by 14ft (12.8 x 4.3m) and is served by a stern elevator covered by a folding hatch. Although it is envisaged that SH-2F helicopters will eventually be assigned, the ships do not at present have helicopters embarked.

The electronics outfit is on a par with *California*, with two important differences. The first is the replacement of the SQS-26 sonar by the more advanced solid-state SQS-53, and the older Mk 114 ASW FC system by the digital Mk 116. The second is the retention of only the after pair of SPG-5 tracker/illuminators, reducing the number of available channels (including the SPG-60) from five to three. This modification looks forward to the conversion of the ships to fire the SM-2 missile, which requires target illumination only in the terminal phase. The ships are also scheduled to receive Harpoon, Tomahawk, and two Phalanx CIWS guns at future refits.

California Class
CGN

Completed: 1974-5. No. in Class: 2.
Displacement: 10,150t full load.
Dimensions: Length 596ft oa (182m); Beam 61ft (18.6m);
Draught 32ft (9.6m).
Propulsion: 2-shaft nuclear; 2 D2G reactors; 60,000shp = 30kts.
Armament: *AAW:* 2 single Mk 13 launchers (40 + 40) Standard
MR missiles, 2 5-inch (127mm) Mk 45 (2x1).
ASW: ASROC launcher Mk 16 (1x8, reloads);
4 12.75-inch (324mm) torpedo tubes (4x1, fixed).
SSM: 8 Harpoon missiles (2x4) being fitted.

California and her sister *South Carolina* were built in response to the need for a new class of nuclear escorts to accompany the CVNs of the *Nimitz* class. A third ship was approved in FY 1968, but this was later cancelled in favour of the improved *Virginia* design.

Compared with previous CGNs, *California* is a much larger, more sophisticated vessel. The design reverted to the "double-ended" layout of *Bainbridge*, but single Mk 13 Tartar launchers were adopted in preference to the Mk 10. This was in some ways a retrograde step in that it limited the ships to the medium-range (MR) version of the Standard missile, whereas earlier

Right: USS *California* (CGN-36); note the single Mark 13 launchers which distinguish her from later CGNs. She was the first US ship to receive the 5in (127mm) Mk 45 gun and the Mark 86 fire control.

Belknap Class
CG

Completed: 1964-7. No. In Class: 9 + 1 CGN.
Displacement: 6,570t standard; 7,930t full load.
Dimensions: Length 547ft oa (166.7m); Beam 55ft (16.7m);
Draught 29ft (8.7m).
Propulsion: 2-shaft geared steam turbines; 85,000shp = 33kts.
Armaments: *AAW:* twin Mk 10 launcher (60) for Standard ER missiles;
1 5-inch (127mm) Mk 42; 2 Phalanx CIWS being fitted.
ASW: ASROC missiles from Mk 10 launcher;
1 SH-2F helicopter; 6 12.75 (324mm) torpedo tubes
Mk 32 (2x3).
SSM: 8 Harpoon missiles (2x4).

The nine ships of the Belknap class, together with their nuclear-powered half-sister *Truxtun*, constitute the final group of AAW "frigates" completed for the US Navy during the 1960s. Outwardly they resemble their predecessors of the Leahy class, with which they share a common hull-form and superstructure layout. A closer look, however, reveals a shift in emphasis in favour of significantly increased anti-submarine capabilities.

In the Belknaps the "double-ended" missile launcher arrangement was ▶

Right: USS *Jouett* (CG-29) in the Mediterranean. The Mark 10 launcher fires both standard ER and ASROC missiles, of which 60 are carried.

Far right: USS *Truxton* (CGN-35); note the distinctive lattice masts which carry the surveillance radars. Her weapons fit is similar to the Belknap class, but the layout is reversed. Only one was built.

The original requirement was for eleven ships of this class, which would then combine with earlier CGNs to provide each of the CVANs projected at that time with four nuclear-powered escorts. After only four units of the class had been laid down, however, further orders were suspended while consideration was given first to the Strike Cruiser (CSGN) and then to a modified CGN 38 design with Aegis. Both these projects were abandoned in favour of the conventionally powered CG-47 now under construction, but the CGN 42 Aegis proposal has recently been revived.

Above left: USS *Virginia* (CGN-38) underway in the Indian Ocean. Nuclear power makes these ships ideally suited to the traditional cruiser role of long-range operations protecting the capital ships.

Above: Stern view of USS *Mississippi* (CGN-40). The twin launcher arms on the Mark 26 mounting distinguish her from the earlier California class. The 5 inch (127mm) gun seems small in its Mark 45 housing, and the missile launcher must reduce its arc of fire.

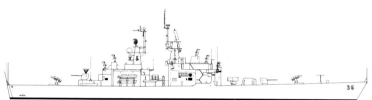

Above: USS *California* (CGN-36), showing ASROC launcher and, forward of it, its prominent deckhouse magazine behind the 5 inch (127mm) gun. Its defensive armament is to be improved by the addition of Phalanx CIWS guns.

CGs and CGNs could be retro-fitted with the extended-range (ER) version. It also necessitated the provision of a separate ASROC launcher, forward of which there is a magazine surmounted by a prominent deckhouse into which the missiles are hoisted before reloading.

California was the first ship to be fitted with the new lightweight 5-inch (127mm) gun, and the first to have the digital Mk 86 FC system installed. The anti-surface element of the latter—the SPQ-9 antenna—is housed within a radome on the after side of the mainmast, while the SPG-60 antenna, which besides tracking air targets can serve as a fifth illuminating channel for the missiles, is located directly above the bridge. Both ships will be fitted with Harpoon, Tomahawk, and two Phalanx CIWS guns at future refits.

abandoned and the 5-inch gun reinstated—a reflection, in part, of concern about the diminishing number of vessels capable of fire support operations. The Mk 10 Terrier launcher was given a third 20-round magazine ring located below and between the other two. The extra capacity was used, however, not to compensate for the reduction in Terrier rounds compared with the *Leahy*, but in order to dispense with a separate ASROC launcher. The upper two rings carry alternate Terrier/Standard and ASROC rounds, while the third, which carries only SAM rounds, serves as a feed for the two upper rings. *Truxtun* has the position of the 5-inch gun and the Mk 10 launcher reversed as compared with the conventionally-powered ships, and can otherwise be distinguished by the absence of funnel uptakes and by her two tall lattice masts.

The Belknaps were the first DLGs to incorporate a helicopter platform and hangar. It was originally envisaged that they would operate the ill-fated drone anti-submarine helicopter (DASH) but the programme was abandoned before any drones were embarked. Instead, the Belknaps became the trial class for the LAMPS helicopter programme in the early 1970s, and introduced manned ASW helicopters to the US Navy with conspicuous success.

As completed the Belknaps carried an altogether more advanced electronics outfit than the Leahy class. In particular the SQS-23 sonar was replaced by the much more powerful SQS-26, and target and fire control data were coordinated by the US Navy's first computer-based Naval Tactical Data System (NTDS). Moreover, these systems have been constantly updated in order to keep abreast of the aerial threat. Since 1977 *Wainwright* has been modified to conduct evaluation of the SM-2 missile, which will eventually be carried by all ships of the class. *Belknap*, which had her entire upper works destroyed by fire following a collision with the carrier *John F. Kennedy* in 1975, has been rebuilt with a completely updated sensor outfit. All ships have now been fitted with quadruple Harpoon launchers in place of the former 3-inch (76mm) AA guns amidships, and each will receive two Phalanx CIWS guns in the near future.

Leahy Class

CGN

Completed: 1962-4. No. in Class: 9 + 1 CGN.
Displacement: 5,670t standard; 7,800t full load.
Dimensions: Length 533ft oa (162.5m); Beam 55ft (16.8m);
Draught 25ft (7.6m).
Propulsion: 2-shaft geared steam turbines; 85,000shp = 32kts.
Armament: *AAW:* 2 twin Mk 10 launchers (40 + 40) for Standard ER missiles, 4 3-inch (76mm, 2x2) in some ships;
2 Phalanx CIWS being fitted.
ASW: ASROC launcher Mk 16 (1x8); 6 12.75-inch (324mm) torpedo tubes Mk 32 (2x3).
SSM: 8 Harpoon missiles (2x4) being fitted in place 3-inch (76mm) guns.

The nine ships of the Leahy class, together with their nuclear-powered half-sister *Bainbridge*, constitute the second group of AAW "frigates" completed for the US Navy during the 1960s. They were designed at a time when it was thought that guns would disappear altogether from the inventory of naval weapons. They were therefore the first US Navy ships to have an all-missile main armament. They also introduced the "mack" (combined mast and stack) to US Navy construction as a means of conserving valuable centre-line deck space.

A "double-ended" layout was adopted with twin Mk 10 Terrier launchers fore and aft. There are 20-round magazine rings in line with each launcher arm, and the missiles are lifted from the top of the ring and run up at an angle of 15 degrees through a wedge-shaped deckhouse onto the launcher. Target tracking and illumination are provided by paired SPG-55B FC radars mounted atop the fore and after superstructures.

As in the earlier Coontz class, there is an 8-round ASROC launcher forward of the bridge, but no reloads are carried.

From 1967 until 1972 the Leahy class underwent an extensive

Above: USS *Leahy* (CG-16). Note the large planar array for SPS-48

modernisation programme aimed at bringing their electronics up to the same standard as the Belknaps. From 1974 onwards *Bainbridge* underwent an even more comprehensive refit involving not only the installation of new surveillance radars and NTDS but also the complete remodelling of her superstructure, which now comprises two distinct blocks with much greater internal volume. The forward block is surmounted by a broad lattice mast and the after block by a heavy pole mainmast. All ships have now had their 3-inch (76mm) AA guns removed, and quadruple Harpoon launchers are being fitted in their place. They are scheduled to receive two Phalanx CIWS guns.

Below: USS *Halsey* (CG-23). The "double-ended" missile launcher layout (2 Mk 10s) distinguishes this class from the later Belknaps.

Below: USS *Bainbridge* (CGN-25) off the California coast; only three of the class serve in the Atlantic, the rest are in the Pacific.

Above: USS *Horne* (CG-30) of the Belknap class, which is the standard conventional AAW escort for carrier task groups.

Above left: USS *William H Standley* (CG-32) in the Mediterranean. The Mark 10 launcher fires both Standard ER and ASROC missiles.

Long Beach CGN

Completed: 1961. No. in Class: 1.
Displacement: 14,200t standard; 17,350t full load.
Dimensions: Length 721ft oa (219.8m); Beam 73ft (22.3m); Draught 29ft (8.8m).
Propulsion: 2-shaft nuclear; 2 C1W reactors; 80,000shp = 30kts.
Armament: AAW: 2 twin Mk 10 launchers (40 + 80) for Standard ER missiles; 2 5-inch (127mm) Mk 30 (2x1).
ASW: ASROC launcher Mk 16 (1x8); 6 12.75-inch (324mm) torpedo tubes Mk 32 (2x3).
SSM: 16 Harpoon missiles (4x4).

Long Beach was the US Navy's first all-missile warship, and the first surface ship with nuclear power. She was designed as an escort for the carrier *Enterprise*, and has performed this role throughout the past two decades.

As completed she had two Mk 10 Terrier launchers forward and a Mk 12 launcher aft for the long-range Talos. The depth of the hull enabled an extra pair of magazine rings to be worked in beneath the second Mk 10 launcher, giving *Long Beach* a total capacity of no less than 166 surface-to-air missiles. There was an ASROC box launcher amidships, and shortly after the ship entered service two 5-inch (127mm) guns of an older pattern were fitted to provide defence against small surface craft.

Electronics were on a par with *Enterprise* herself, with large fixed SPS-32/33 "billboard" radars mounted on a similar "turret" superstructure block. The latter proved to be a major maintenance problem, and the FY 1978 budget provided funds to fit *Long Beach* with the Aegis system. The proposed conversion was quickly cancelled, however, as it was feared that this expenditure might result in reductions in the new CG 47 programme.

Talos was removed in 1979 and the after launcher replaced by quadruple Harpoon launchers. The following year *Long Beach* began a major refit at which the SPS-32/33 radars will be removed and their functions taken over

Above: USS *Long Beach* (CGN-9) showing her massive SPS-32 and SPS-33 planar radar arrays. These are being removed to be replaced by more conventional SPS-48 and SPS-49 arrays.

by an SPS 48.3-D radar and an SPS-49 air search radar--the latter atop lattice mainmast. Two Phalanx CIWS guns will be installed on the after superstructure, and there will eventually be launchers for Tomahawk aft.

Below: The *Long Beach* was the world's first nuclear-powered warship and the first in the US Navy to have an all-missile armament.

Kidd Class

DDG

Completed: 1981-2. No. in Class: 4.
Displacement: 8,140t full load.
Dimensions: Length 563ft oa (171.1m); Beam 55ft (16.8m);
Draught 30ft (9m).
Propulsion: 2-shaft COGAG; 4 LM2500 gas turbines;
80,000bhp = 30kts.
Armament: *AAW:* 2 twin Mk 26 launchers (24 + 44) for Standard MR
missiles; 2 5-inch (127mm) Mk 45 (2x1).
ASW: ASROC missiles from Mk 26 launcher;
2 LAMPS helicopters; 6 12.75-inch (324mm) torpedo
tubes Mk 32 (2x3).
SSM: 8 Harpoon missiles (2x4).

Above: USS *Chandler* (DDG-996). Built for the Iranian Navy the ships were taken over by the USN after the fall of the Shah.

The four ships of the Kidd class are AAW modifications of the Spruance-class destroyer originally ordered by Iran but acquired by the US Navy in 1979 following the fall of the Shah.

The allowances made in the Spruance design for the modular installation of a number of weapon systems then in production or under development made redesign a simple matter, as the AAW modification had been one of the variations originally envisaged. In the Kidd class twin-arm Mk 26 launchers have been fitted fore and aft in place of the ASROC and Sea Sparrow launchers of the ASW version. The forward magazine is the smaller of the two, the original intention being to fit the now-defunct 8-inch (205mm) Mk 71 gun in place of the forward 5-inch (127mm) mounting. Contrary to US Navy practice, an SPS-48 3-D radar is fitted, but there is no independent air search radar. There are also only two SPG-51 tracker/illuminators—one above the bridge and the other on a raised superstructure immediately abaft the mainmast. The electronics outfit is therefore austere by US Navy standards, but this will be remedied over the next few years by the addition of systems currently being fitted to other ships of similar capabilities. Two Phalanx CIWS guns are to be fitted in the near future.

The Kidd-class destroyers can fire ASROC missiles from their forward M 26 launcher, resulting in an ASW capability not far short of that of the standard Spruance.

The provision of extra air-conditioning capacity and dust separators fo the gas-turbine air intakes makes these ships well suited to operations i tropical conditions.

Spruance Class

DD

Completed: 1975-80. No. in Class: 30 (+ 1 building).
Displacement: 7,800t full load.
Dimensions: Length 563ft oa (171.1m); Beam 55ft (16.8m);
Draught 29ft (8.8m).
Propulsion: 2-shaft COGAG; 4 LM2500 gas turbines;
80,000bhp = 30 + kts.
Armament: *ASW:* ASROC launcher Mk 16 (1x8, 24 reloads);
2 SH-2F helicopters (only one embarked); 6 12.75-inch
(324mm) torpedo tubes Mk 32 (2x3).
AAW: NATO Sea Sparrow launcher Mk 29 (1x8, 16
reloads). 2 5-inch (127mm) Mk 45 (2x1); 2 Phalanx
CIWS being fitted.
SSM: 8 Harpoon missiles (2x4).

The most controversial ships to be built for the US Navy since World War II, the Spruance class was designed to replace the war-built destroyers of the Gearing and Allen M. Sumner classes, which had undergone FRAM ASW modification programmes during the 1960s but by the early 1970s were nearing the end of their useful lives.

At 7,800t full load—more than twice the displacement of the destroyers it was to replace—the *Spruance* epitomised the US Navy's design philosophy of the 1970s. This philosophy envisaged the construction of large hulls with block superstructures which maximised internal volume, fitted out with machinery that could be easily maintained and, if necessary, replaced, and equipped with high-technology weapon systems that could be added to and updated by modular replacement at a later stage. The object was to minimise "platform" costs, which have no military pay-off, in favour of greater expenditure on weapon systems ("payload") in order to ensure that the ships would remain first-line units throughout the 30-year life-expectancy of their hulls.

In a further attempt to minimise "platform" costs the entire class was ordered from a single shipbuilder, the Litton/Ingalls Corporation, which invested heavily in a major production facility at Pascagoula, using advanced modular construction techniques.

The only "visible" weapons aboard *Spruance* when she was completed were 5-inch (127mm) Mk 45 lightweight gun mountings fore and aft and an ASROC box launcher forward of the bridge. In view of the size and cost of the ships this caused an immediate public outcry.

The advanced ASW qualities of the Spruance class are, however, largely hidden within the hull and the bulky superstructures. The ASROC launcher, for example, has a magazine beneath it containing no less than 24 reloads, and the large hangar to port of the after-funnel uptakes can accommodate two LAMPS helicopters. The bow sonar is the powerful SQS-53, which can operate in a variety of active and passive modes. The adoption of an all-gas-turbine propulsion system, which employs paired LM2500 turbines *en echelon* in a unit arrangement, and which was selected partly because of the ease with which it can be maintained and because of its low manning requirements, has resulted in a significant reduction in underwater noise emission. The Spruance is therefore capable of near-silent ASW operations.

Moreover, besides the weapon systems fitted on completion, the Spruance class was designed to accept a variety of other systems then at the development stage. Most ships have now received NATO Sea Sparrow and Harpoon, and the class is scheduled to receive the SQR-19 TACTAS towed

Above: USS *Oldendorf* (DD-972) showing off to advantage the handsome lines of the Spruance class destroyer. This class has been under criticism since its inception, but has proved its worth.

Right: USS *Leftwich* (DD-984). Large areas of empty deck led ill-informed critics to say the class lacked all necessary armament, and compared it unfavourably with Soviet practice.

array when it becomes available.

The flexibility of the Spruance design is such that it has formed the basi both for the AAW destroyers originally ordered for Iran (see Kidd class) an of the new Aegis cruiser (see Ticonderoga class).

One additional ship of the Spruance class was ordered in 1979. DD 99 was originally to have had increased hangar and flight-deck space fo helicopter and VTOL operations, but it was a modification which foun greater favour with Congress than with the US Navy, which has sinc decided to complete the ship to the standard Spruance configuration.

Decatur Class

DDG

Completed: 1956-9. No. in Class: 4.
Displacement: 4,150t full load.
Dimensions: Length 418ft oa (127.5m); Beam 45ft (13.8m);
Draught 20ft (6.1m).
Propulsion: 2-shaft geared steam turbines; 70,000shp = 32.5kts.
Armament: *AAW:* single Mk 13 launcher (40) for Standard MR
missiles; 1 5-inch (127mm) Mk 42.
ASW: ASROC launcher Mk 16 (1x8); 6 12.75-inch
(324mm) torpedo tubes Mk 32 (2x3).
SSM: Harpoon missiles will be fired from Mk 13 launcher.

These four ships were originally conventionally armed destroyers of the
Forrest Sherman class. From 1965 until 1968 they underwent a major
conversion to bring them up to a similar standard to the DDGs of the Charles
F Adams class.

The three-year refit included the removal of the after 5-inch (127mm)
guns and their replacement by the Tartar missile system. A Mk 13 single-arm
launcher together with its cylindrical magazine replaced the after gun
mounting, and immediately forward of it a large deckhouse carrying a
single SPG-51 tracker/illuminator was constructed. Two massive lattice
masts replaced the original tripods, giving the ships a distinctive profile. The
purpose of the new mainmast was to carry the large SPS-48 3-D radar,
which was just entering service. The initial conversion plan envisaged the
operation of DASH anti-submarine drones, but when the DASH programme
ran into problems, it was decided to fit an ASROC launcher instead.

It was originally intended that the entire Forrest Sherman class should
undergo a similar conversion, but the cost of the programme proved to be
prohibitive. Nor has the conversion proved to be particularly successful; the
Decatur class suffers from excessive topweight, and although costly long-
range detection and tracking facilities have been provided, the ships are
limited to a single tracker/illuminator.

**Above: USS *John Paul Jones* (DDG-32), bearer of one of the great
names of American naval history. The four ships of the Decatur
class were converted in 1965-68 from the Forrest Sherman class.**

**Above: USS *Elliott* (DD-967) showing her tight turning circle. Gas
turbines give her a rapid response and a low noise signature, both
crucial factors in the ASW operations for which she is designed.**

**Below: *Arthur W Radford* (DD-968). The large hull and block super-
structures maximise internal volume. The high technology weapons
systems are fitted in modular units for easy replacement.**

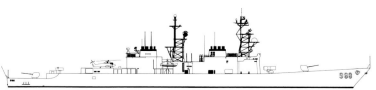

Charles F. Adams Class   DDG

Completed: 1960-4. No. in Class: 23.
Displacement: 3,370t standard; 4,500t full load.
Dimensions: Length 437ft oa (133.2m); Beam 47ft (14.3m);
Draught 22ft (6.7m).
Propulsion: 2-shaft geared steam turbines; 70,000shp = 31.5kts.
Armament: AAW: twin Mk 11 launcher (42) or single Mk 13 launcher
(40) for Standard MR missiles; 2 5-inch (127mm)
Mk 42 (2x1).
ASW: ASROC launcher Mk 16 (1x8);
6 12.75-inch (324mm) torpedo tubes MK 32 (2x3).
SSM: Harpoon missiles from Mk 13 launcher.

The Charles F. Adams class is derived from the Forrest Sherman, with a
Tartar launcher in place of the third 5-inch (127mm) gun mounting. It is still
the standard AAW destroyer in service with the US Navy, and is employed
together with the larger CGs to provide anti-air defence for the carrier battle
groups.

The first 13 ships of the class were fitted with the twin-arm Mk 11
launcher but later ships have the single-arm Mk 13. The Mk 13 is a
lightweight launcher with a high rate of fire—8 rounds per minute—which
compensates in part for the single arm. Both launchers employ a cylindrical
magazine containing two concentric rings of missiles. Overall length was
increased by about 29.5ft (9m) to accommodate a Mk 16 ASROC launcher
between the funnels. The installation of Tartar and ASROC made the *Charles
F. Adams* one of the most formidably armed destroyers of its period, and the
design was adopted by the Federal German and the Australian Navies.

In spite of their age these ships are still highly regarded in the US Navy.
They have proved to be extremely useful, well balanced ships, whose only
major defect has been their temperamental high-pressure boilers. In the late
1970s it was therefore proposed that they should undergo a major
modernisation programme which would extend their service life beyond the
nominal 30-year mark. Funding was to have been authorised in FY 1980-3
but it was feared that expenditure of this magnitude would adversely affect
the programme of new construction, and six of the later ships will now
receive a less fundamental modernisation involving a complete overhaul and
updating of their electronics.

It is envisaged that the class will eventually be replaced by the DDG-51
destroyers now projected.

**Above: A bow view of a DDG of the Charles F. Adams class, one of
the most successful destroyer designs of recent years. The USN
received 23 and 3 each were built for West Germany and Australia**

**Left: A DDG of the Charles F. Adams class in heavy weather in the
North Atlantic. This unit has the older twin-arm Tartar launcher aft**

Forrest Sherman Class   DD

Completed: 1955-9. No. in Class: 14.
Displacement: 2,800t standard, 4,050t full load.
Dimensions: Length 418ft oa (127.5m); Beam 45 (13.7m);
Draught 22ft (6.7m).
Propulsion: 2-shaft geared steam turbines; 70,00shp = 32.5kts.
Armament: (Unmodified units) ASW: 6 12.75-inch (324mm) torpedo
tubes Mk 32 (2x3).
AAW: 3 5-inch (127mm) Mk 42 (3x1).
(ASW Conversions). ASW: ASROC launcher Mk 16 (1x8);
6 12.75-inch (324mm) torpedo tubes Mk 32 (2x3).
AAW: 2 5-inch (127mm) Mk 42.

The Forrest Sherman class were the first postwar US destroyers. Although
conventionally armed, they followed current tactical thinking in abandoning
anti-ship torpedoes, which were replaced by four fixed 21-inch (533mm)
"long" ASW torpedoes, and in mounting a lesser number of guns with higher

**Right: Aerial view of a converted Forrest Sherman class destroyer,
showing clearly the ASROC launcher aft. Eight ships of the class
were converted from 1967-71 to improve their anti-submarine
warfare capabilities. Navy plans are for all ships of the class to be
replaced by new-build Spruance-class destroyers, starting at the
end of this decade.**

Coontz Class

DDG

Completed:	1959-61. No. in Class: 10.
Displacement:	4,700t standard; 5,800t full load.
Dimensions:	Length 513ft oa (156.2m); Beam 53ft (15.9m); Draught 25ft (7.6m).
Propulsion:	2-shaft geared steam turbines; 85,000shp = 33kts.
Armament:	*AAW:* twin Mk 10 launcher (40) for Standard ER missiles; 1 5-inch (127mm) Mk 42.
	ASW: ASROC launcher Mk 16 (1x8); 6 12.75-inch (324mm) torpedo tubes Mk 32 (2x3).
	SSM: 8 Harpoon missiles (2x4).

Above: USS *Luce* (DDG-38) in the Mediterranean. The Coontz class have an aluminium superstructure to lessen topweight.

The ten ships of the Coontz class constitute the first group of AAW "frigates" completed for the US Navy during the 1960s. Unlike the later ships of the Leahy and Belknap classes they have a flush-decked hull, and this feature, together with their twin lattice mast/funnel arrangement, reveals their derivation from the all-gun DLs of the early 1950s. They also have much lower endurance than later ships, and this factor appears to have been largely responsible for their redesignation as DDGs in 1975 (the Leahy and Belknap classes became CGs). They nevertheless carry a similar armament to the later ships, have been brought up to the same standard as regards electronics, and perform an identical mission in defence of the carrier battle groups.

The *Coontz* has a twin Mk 10 launcher aft, a single 5-inch (127mm) gun forward, an ASROC box launcher above it in "B" position, and triple anti-submarine tubes amidships. From 1968 until 1976 the class underwent a major modernisation similar to that of the *Leahy*. The electronics were updated and NTDS was installed. *Farragut* had her ASW capability enhanced by the provision of a reloading magazine for ASROC at the forward end of the superstructure, but she remained the only ship thus fitted. All ships had the original 3-inch (76mm) AA guns removed, and these were lated replaced by Harpoon. In 1979 *Mahan* received the SM-2 missile, and this will eventually be fitted to the rest of the class. They are also scheduled to receive the SQQ-23 PAIR sonar, but will not be fitted with Phalanx.

Below: USS *Macdonough* (DDG-39). This picture shows very clearly the great number of radio and radar antennas required on a modern warship giving the electronic engineer a major problem.

performance than those of their war-built predecessors.

The conventional armament was quickly overtaken by new technological developments—in particular the advent of the nuclear submarine and the surface-to-air missile—and an extensive conversion programme was drawn up. Four ships were given the Tartar missile system (see Decatur class) but the cost of the conversion precluded its extension to the rest of the class. Eight ships were therefore given a limited ASW conversion between 1967 and 1971. The second gun mounting was replaced by an ASROC launcher and the fixed A/S tubes by triple Mk 32 trainable tubes; surveillance radars were updated and an independent variable depth sonar fitted above the stern.

Even this limited conversion programme ran into cost problems, and the remaining six ships of the class received only those modifications which entailed a minimum of structural alterations. They retained all three 5-inch (127mm) guns and were not fitted with ASROC or VDS.

From 1975 onwards *Hull* served as trial ship for the 8-inch (205mm) Mk 71 Major Calibre Light Weight Gun (MCLWG). The mounting replaced the forward gun until 1979, when it was removed. *Edson* is now in reserve, but it is anticipated that the other units will remain active for some years yet.

Left: USS *Forrest Sherman* (DD-931) underway, retaining her original configuration with three 5-inch (127mm) guns. She was one of six of this class (others being *Bigelow, Mullinix, Hull, Edson* and *Turner Joy*) which were not modernized, because of cost considerations.

Oliver Hazard Perry Class   FFG

Completed: 1977 onwards. No. in Class: 23 (+ 17 building).
Displacement: 3,710t full load.
Dimensions: Length 445ft oa (135.6m); Beam 45ft (13.7m);
Draught 25ft (7.5m).
Propulsion: 1-shaft COGAG; 2 LM2500 gas turbines;
40,000bhp = 28kts.
Armament: *AAW:* single Mk 13 launcher (40) for standard MR
missiles; 1 3-inch (76mm) Mk 75; 1 Phalanx CIWS being
fitted.
ASW: 2 LAMPS helicopters; 6 12.75-inch (324mm)
torpedo tubes Mk 32 (2x3).
SSM: Harpoon missiles from Mk 13 launcher.

The FFG 7 design has its origins in the Patrol Frigate first proposed in
September 1970. The latter was to constitute the "low" end of the so-called
"high/low" mix, providing large numbers of cheap second-rate escorts with
reduced capabilities to counterbalance the sophisticated but costly specialist
ASW and AAW vessels whose primary mission was to protect the carriers.
Strict limitations were therefore imposed on cost, displacement and
manpower requirements.

Like the frigates which preceded her, the *Oliver Hazard Perry* has a
"second-class" propulsion plant on one screw. The layout is, however, much
more compact than that of the *Knox* as a result of the adoption of gas
turbines. Two LM2500s – the same model as that installed in the *Spruance* – are
located side-by-side in a single engine room. Two small retractable
propulsion pods fitted just aft of the sonar dome provide back-up during
docking procedures, and these can drive the ship at 6 knots in an
emergency.

The balance of the armament is more closely oriented to AAW than that of
the *Knox*, which was a specialist ASW design. The FFG 7 has a Mk 13
launcher forward for Standard MR surface-to-air missiles and Harpoon anti-
ship missiles, and an OTO-Melara 3-inch (76mm) quick-firing gun atop the
bulky superstructure block. ASROC has been abandoned altogether, but
there is a broad hangar aft for two LAMPS helicopters. The sonar, which is
hull-mounted inside a rubber dome, is a new austere type which has neither
the long range nor the multi-mode capability of the SQS-26 fitted to previous
frigates. It is, however, envisaged that the FFG 7 would operate in
conjunction with other frigates equipped with the SQS-26 and would receive
target information from their sonars via data links.

Whereas the *Spruance* was designed to incorporate a large amount of
space for future growth, the FFG 7 has been strictly tailored to accommodate
only those systems envisaged in the near future. These include the SH-60
Seahawk LAMPS III (together with its RAST recovery system), the SQR-19
tactical towed array, fin stabilisers, a Link 11 data transfer system, and a
single Phalanx CIWS gun. These items alone represent a log of growth. Once

Above: ***Oliver Hazard Perry*** **(FFG-7) name ship of a class of at leas**
40 Patrol Frigates. Everything about her design is "austere"; simpl
construction techniques have been used to save money.

these modifications have been made, however, there remains only a 50-to
margin for further growth, and if any additional items of equipment are to b
fitted, others will have to be removed.

Knox Class   FF

Completed: 1969-74. No. in Class: 46.
Displacement: 3,011t standard; 4,100t full load.
Dimensions: Length 438ft oa (133.5m); Beam 47ft (14.3m);
Draught 25ft (7.6m).
Propulsion: 1-shaft geared steam turbine; 35,000shp = 27kts.
Armament: *ASW:* ASROC launcher Mk 16 (1x8, reloadable);
1 SH-2F helicopter; 4 12.75-inch (324mm) torpedo
tubes Mk 32 (4x1).
AAW: BPDMS launcher Mk 25 (1x8) in 31 ships;
1 5-inch (127mm) Mk 42.
SSM: Harpoon missiles from ASROC Launcher.

The Knox class began as a Design Work Study of the Brooke-class missile
escort. Congressional opposition to the mounting costs of fitting escorts
with the Tartar system resulted, however, in the abandonment of the latter
class after only six units had been laid down, The *Knox* was therefore
redesigned as an ASW Escort.

Although the *Knox* retained the one-shaft propulsion system of the
Garcia/Brooke design, the complex pressure-fired boilers of the latter were
abandoned in favour of a "safer", more conventional steam plant. This
necessitated an increase in size without creating any extra space for
weapons.

Originally the two 5-inch (127mm) Mk 38 guns of the *Garcia* were to have

Above: An aerial view of USS Stein (FF-1065) of the Knox class.
Note the enlarged helicopter platform and the telescopic hangar.

been replaced by a combination of a single 5-inch Mk 42 and the ill-fated Se
Mauler point-defence missile. The Sea Mauler was eventually replaced by th
Sea Sparrow BPDMS—a system not contemplated when the *Knox* wa
designed. The *Knox* was also to have operated the DASH anti-submarin
drone, but when the latter programme was abandoned it was decided t
extend the flight deck and to fit the hangar with a telescopic extension t
enable the ships to operate a LAMPS 1 manned helicopter. Taken togethe
with the reloadable ASROC launcher and the SQS-26 sonar, this gave th
Knox a first-class anti-submarine outfit, which rescued the design from a
unpromising beginning.

Besides the Sea Sparrow BPDMS, many ships have received the SQS-3
independent variable depth sonar since completion. All will receive the SQ
18 towed array in the near future. Most ships have now had their ASRO
launchers modified to fire Harpoon, and it is planned to replace Sea Sparro
with a single Phalanx CIWS mounting.

Left: USS ***Joseph L Hawes*** **(FF-1078) with the 5in (127mm) Mk 42**
gun and the BPDMS gun clearly visible on the foredeck. After som
early problems the Knox class has proved versatile and useful.

Bronstein Class/ Garcia Class/ Brooke Class

FF/FFG

Completed:	1963-68. No. in Class: 2/10/6.
Displacement:	2,360t standard; 2,650t full load, (Bronstein).
	2,620t standard; 3,400t full load. (Garcia).
	2,640t standard; 3,245t full load. (Brooke).
Dimensions:	(Bronstein) Length 372ft oa (113.2m); beam 41ft (12.3m); draught 23ft (7m). (Garcia, Brooke) Length 415ft oa (126.3m); beam 44ft (13.5m); draught 24ft (7.3m).
Propulsion:	(Bronstein) 1-shaft geared steam turbine; 20,000shp = 24kts.
	(Garcia, Brooke) 1-shaft geared steam turbine; 35,000shp = 27kts.
Armament:	(Bronstein) *ASW:* ASROC launcher Mk 16 (1x8); 6 12.75-inch (324mm) torpedo tubes Mk 32 (2x3). *AAW:* 2 3-inch (76mm) Mk 33 (1x2).
	(Garcia) *ASW:* ASROC launcher Mk 16 (1x8, reloadable in FF 1047-5.1). 1 SH-2F helicopter (except FF 1048, 1050) 6 12.75-inch (324mm) torpedo tubes Mk 32 (2x3). *AAW:* 2 5-inch (127mm) Mk 30 (2x1).
	(Brooke) *AAW:* single Mk 22 launcher (16) for Standard MR missiles; 1 5-inch (127mm) Mk 30.

Below: USS *Julius A Furer* (FFG-6). The sloping bridge-face conceals an ASROC reload magazine fitted to the last three ships.

The two ships of the Bronstein class were the first of a new type of ocean escort designed in the late 1950s. The design stressed anti-submarine qualities at the expense of all others. The ASW outfit was based on a combination of the ASROC missile and the powerful SQS-26 bow sonar. Air defence qualities, on the other hand, were minimal and a relatively modest speed on a single shaft was accepted. The propulsion plant was particularly compact and employed pressure-fired boilers.

The ten ships of the Garcia class, which became in effect the production model, were larger, had a heavier gun armament and were provided with a hangar and flight deck aft for DASH anti-submarine drones.

The Brooke class is a Tartar modification of the Garcia class, with a single Mk 22 Tartar launcher in place of the second 5-inch (127mm) gun of the latter. The Mk 22 launcher has a single-ring magazine with a much-reduced capacity of 16 rounds compared with the 40-round installation which is standard to larger vessels. The above-water sensor outfit is also comparatively austere; there is an SPS-52 3-D radar but no independent air search antenna, and only a single SPG-51 tracker/illuminator. In spite of this Congress baulked at the $11m increase in cost compared with the gun-armed *Garcia*, and only six units were completed.

Modifications have been made to all three classes since their completion. In the mid-1970s the Bronsteins had the original quarterdeck 3-inch (76mm) gun removed to make room for a large towed array. The Garcia and Brooke classes have had the two Mk 25 torpedo tubes initially incorporated in the stern removed and, following the abandonment of the DASH programme, have had their hangar enlarged and fitted with a telescopic extension to accommodate a LAMPS helicopter.

Above: USS *Bronstein* (FF-1037) name ship of a class of two, the precursors of the mass-produced Garcia, Brooke and Knox classes.

Above: USS *Bradley* (FF-1041) with her telescopic hangar partially extended. The after 5in (127mm) gun is visible forward of hangar.

Pegasus Class

PHM

Completed: 1977-82. No. in Class: 3 (+3 building).
Displacement: 231t full load.
Dimensions: Length 132ft oa (40m); Beam 28ft (8.6m);
Draught 6ft (1.9m).
Propulsion: (hullborne) 2 Mercedes-Benz diesels; 1600bhp = 12 kts.
(foilborne) 1 General Electric gas-turbine;
18,000bhp = 40kts.
Armament: 8 Harpoon (2x4); 1 3-inch (76mm) Mk 75.

The PHM was one of the four new designs in the "low" programme advocated in Zumalt's Project 60. It was envisaged that squadrons of these fast patrol craft would be deployed at the various choke-points—in particular those in the Mediterranean and the NW Pacific—through which the surface units of the Soviet Navy needed to pass in order to reach open waters. High speed and a heavy armament of anti-ship missiles would enable the PHM to make rapid interceptions, and the relatively low unit cost meant that large numbers could be bought.

The Italian and Federal German Navies, with similar requirements in the Mediterranean and the Baltic respectively, participated in the development of the design. The Germans planned to build 12 units of their own in addition to the 30 originally projected for the US Navy.

Technical problems with the hydrofoil system resulted in cost increases, and opponents of the PHM programme, pointing to the limited capabilities of the design, tried to obtain cancellation of all except the lead vessel. Congress insisted, however, on the construction of the six units for which funds had already been authorised.

The propulsion system of the PHM comprises separate diesels driving two waterjets for hullborne operation and a single gas turbine for high-speed foilborne operation.

Above: *Pegasus* **(PHM-1) makes 40 knots foilborne and is well-armed with eight Harpoon missiles and a 76mm (3in) gun forward**

In order to fit in with the requirements of the NATO navies the OTO-Melar 76mm gun and a Dutch fire control system were adopted. The original ant ship missile armament has been doubled, with two quadruple mount replacing the four singles first envisaged.

Avenger Class

MCM

Completed: 1984-onwards. No. in Class: (1 ordered).
Displacement: 1,032t full load.
Dimensions: Length 213ft (64.9m); Beam 38ft (11.7m);
Draught: 10ft (3.1m).
Propulsion: 2 shafts; 4 x Waukesha L-1616 diesels; 2,400bhp =
14kts.
Armament: None.

Ordered in June 1982, *Avenger* is the first mine countermeasures vessel to be built for the US Navy since the 1950s. Although large by contemporary European standards, the design is conservative; the traditional wooden hull

has been retained, the superstructure being of fibreglass and the diesels (non-magnetic alloy. *Avenger* will be able to sweep deep-moored mines dow to 60ft (180m) as well as magnetic and acoustic mines. The mines will b located by the new SQQ-30 minehunting sonar (an improved version of th SQQ-14), which is lowered from the hull of the ship. A mine countermeasure information centre will be installed to coordinate data from the sonar, an plotting and relocating minefields will be assisted by the installation of th SSN-2 precise integrated navigation system. Mine destruction manoeuvre will be aided by the provision of bow thrusters.

It is envisaged that fourteen units of this class will be built. They will b complemented by a smaller coastal MCM type designated the MSH; the fir of these is to be requested in FY 1984. Considering recent Soviet advance in mine technology, there is an obvious need for these vessels.

Blue Ridge Class

LCC

Completed: 1970-71. No. in Class: 2.
Displacement: 19,290t full load.
Dimensions: Length 620ft oa (188.5m); Beam 108ft (33m);
Draught 27ft (8.2m).
Propulsion: 1-shaft steam turbine; 22,000shp = 20kts.
Armament: 2 BPDMS launchers Mk 25
4 3-inch (76mm) Mk 33 (2x2).

These two vessels were built to provide specialised command facilities for the amphibious fleets in the Pacific and Atlantic respectively. They replaced the more numerous war-built AGFs, which had inadequate speed for the new 20-knot amphibious squadrons. The basic design is that of the Iwo Jima-class LPH, with the former hangar occupied by command spaces, offices and accommodation. Prominent sponsons for LCPLs and ships' boats project from the sides, and the broad flat upper deck is lined with a variety of surveillance, ECM/ESM and communications aerials. The LCCs are fitted with the Naval Tactical Data System (NTDS), the Amphibious Command Information System (ACIS) and the Naval Intelligence Processing

Above: The very specialized command ships *Blue Ridge* **and** *Moun Whitney* **are now the flagships of the US 7th and 2nd fleets.**

System (NIPS). As completed, they had only two twin 3-inch (76mn mountings for defence against aircraft, but two BPDMS launchers we added in 1974. Two utility helicopters are generally operated from the fligl pad aft but there are no hangar or maintenance facilities.

The command facilities originally provided for a naval Command Amphibious Task Group (CATG), a Marine Landing Force Command (LFC), Air Control Group Commander, and their respective staffs, wi accommodation for up to 200 officers and 500 enlisted men in addition the 780-man crew.

There were plans for a third ship (AGC 21), which would have provide both fleet command and amphibious command facilities, but inadequa speed for fleet work was an important factor in her cancellation. With th demise of the Cleveland-class CGs fleet flagships in the late 1970s, howeve *Blue Ridge* and *Mount Whitney* became flagships of the Seventh (W. Pacifi and the Second (Atlantic) Fleets respectively.

Below: USS *Blue Ridge* **(LCC-19) showing the numerous antennas necessary for her role as a fleet command and control ship.**

Tarawa Class

Completed: 1976-80. No. in Class: 5.
Displacement: 39,300t full load.
Dimensions: Length 820ft oa (249.9m); Beam 126ft (38.4m);
Draught 26ft (7.9m).
Propulsion: 2-shaft geared steam turbines; 70,000shp = 24kts.
Armament: 2 BPDMS launchers Mk 25 (2x8); 3 5-inch (127mm)
Mk 45 (3x1); 6 20mm (6x1).
Aircraft: 30 helicopters (CH-46D, CH-53D/E, AH-1T, UH-1N).
Troops: 2,000.
Landing-craft: 4 LCU, 2 LCM.

The last in a series of ocean-going amphibious vessels ordered during the
1960s, the Tarawa-class LHAs were to combine in a single hull capabilities
which had previously required a number of separate specialist types—the
LPH, the LSD, the LPD, the LCC and the LKA (see following entries). The
result is a truly massive ship with more than twice the displacement of any
previous amphibious unit and with dimensions approaching those of
a conventional aircraft carrier. Nine ships were originally projected, to be
constructed by means of advanced modular techniques at the same
Litton/Ingalls yard that built the Spruance-class destroyers. In 1971,
however, with the Vietnam War drawing to a close, the order was reduced
to five, resulting in some financial penalties.

The increase in size of these ships is a direct consequence of the need to
provide a helicopter hangar *and* a docking-well. The hangar is located
directly above the docking-well; both are 268ft in length and 78ft wide (81.6
x 23.7m), and the hangar has a 20ft (6m) overhead to enable the latest
heavy-lift helicopters to be accommodated. The flight deck is served by a side
lift to port and a larger centre-line lift set into the stern. AV-8 Harrier STOVL
aircraft can be operated in addition to the customary assault helicopters.

The docking-well can accommodate four LCUs. Two LCM-6 landing-craft,
which can each carry 80 troops or 34 tons of cargo, are stowed immediately
aft of the island and are handled by a large crane. The docking-well is divided
into two by a central support structure incorporating a conveyor belt, which
runs forward onto the vehicle decks. The conveyor belt is served by a group
of three cargo elevators at its forward end, and by a further two elevators in
the docking-well area. The elevators bring supplies for the landing force,
stored in pallets each weighing approximately one ton, up from the cargo
holds deep in the ship. The pallets are transferred to the landing-craft by one
of 11 monorail cars which work overhead in the welldeck area. The after pair
of elevators can also lift pallets directly to the hangar deck, where they are
loaded onto transporters. An angled ramp leads from the hangar deck to the
forward end of the island, enabling the transfer of pallets to the flight deck
for loading onto the helicopters.

Forward of the docking-well are the vehicle decks, interconnected by a
series of ramps and able to accommodate some 200 vehicles, including up
to 40 LVTP-7 amphibious personnel carriers. Above the vehicle decks is the
accommodation deck, which incorporates an acclimatisation room at its
forward end and a well-equipped hospital at its after end.

**Above: The massive stern door of a Tarawa class LHA which gives
access to the capacious 268 x 78ft (81.6 x 23.7m) docking-well.**

The large block superstructure houses extensive command facilities, with
accommodation for both the Commander Amphibious Task Group (CATG)
and the Landing Force Commander (LFC) and their respective staffs. To
enable these officers to exercise full tactical control over amphibious
operations the LHAs are provided with a computer-based Integrated Tactical
Amphibious Warfare Data System (ITAWDS), which keeps track of the
position of troops, helicopters, vehicles, landing-craft and cargo after they
leave the ship. The system also tracks the position of designated targets
ashore, and aims and fires the ship's armament, which is orientated towards
fire support and short-range anti-aircraft defence.

The versatility of the LHAs enables them to combine with any of the other
amphibious types in the US Navy inventory. A typical PhibRon deployment
would combine an LHA with an LPD and one/two LSTs. The only major
limitation of the design appears to be the inability to accommodate more
than one of the new air-cushion landing-craft (AALC) because of the layout
of the docking-well.

**Below: *Tarawa* (LHA-1) showing her massive flight deck, the
forward pair of 3in guns, and a BPDMS launcher.**

Iwo Jima Class

LPH

Completed:	1961-70. No. in Class: 7.
Displacement:	17,000t light; 18,300t full load.
Dimensions:	Length 592ft oa (180m); Beam 112ft (34.1m); Draught 26ft (7.9m).
Propulsion:	1-shaft geared steam turbine; 22,000shp = 20kts.
Armament:	2 BPDMS launchers Mk 25 (2x8); 4 3-inch (76mm) Mk 33 (2x2).
Aircraft:	25 helicopters (CH-46D, CH-53D, AH-1T, UH-1N).

The Iwo Jima class were the world's first purpose-built helicopter assault ships. As they were amphibious—not fleet—units, many of the refinements associated with first-line vessels were dispensed with in the interests of economy. The design was based on a mercantile hull with a one-shaft propulsion system capable of a sustained 20 knots. A large central box hangar was adopted with 20ft (6.5m) clearance, a capacity of about 20 helicopters, and with side lifts disposed *en echelon* at either end. The side lifts fold upwards to close the hangar openings. Fore and aft of the hangar there is accommodation for a Marine battalion, and the ships have a well equipped hospital with 300 beds.

The flight deck is marked out with five helo spots along the port side and two to starboard. No catapults or arresting wires are fitted. Helicopter assault operations are directed from a specialised Command Centre housed in the island. The radar outfit is austere: air search and aircraft control antennae are fitted but these ships do not have the large 3-D antennae of the first-line carriers.

As completed, the *Iwo Jima* class had two twin 3-inch (76mm) mountings at the forward end of the island and two further mountings just below the after end of the flight deck. Between 1970 and 1974 the after port mounting and the first of the two forward mountings were replaced by BPDMS launchers.

From 1972 until 1974 *Guam* was test ship for the Sea Control Ship concept. In this role she operated ASW helicopters and a squadron of marine

Right: USS *Tripoli* (LPH-10) entering Subic Bay in the Philippines following mine-clearing operations off the North Vietnamese coast.

Below: A US Marine Corps AV-8A Harrier on the after elevator of the USS *Guam* during trials of the Sea Control Ship (SCS) concept.

AV-8 Harrier aircraft. Although operations with the Harrier were particular successful and have been continued on a routine basis in the larger Tarawa class LHAs, the Sea Control Ship did not find favour with the US Navy, an *Guam* has since reverted to her assault ship role.

The Iwo Jima class generally operates in conjunction with ships of th LPD, LSD and LST types. Although *Inchon*, the last ship built, carries tw LCVPs, the LPHs have no significant ability to land troops, equipment an supplies by any means other than by helicopter. The troops are therefor lightly equipped and would be employed as an advance echelon, landin behind the enemy's shore defences and relying on a follow-up frontal assau staged by more heavily equipped units brought ashore by landing-craft fro the other vessels in the squadron.

Whidbey Island Class

LSD

Completed:	1984 onwards. No. in Class: (1 building).
Displacement:	11,140t light; 15,745t full load.
Dimensions:	Length 609ft oa (185.6m); Beam 84ft (25.6m); Draught 20ft (5.9m).
Propulsion:	2-shaft diesels; 4 SEMT-Pielstick 16-cyl.; 34,000shp = 20kts.
Armament:	2 Phalanx CIWS.
Troops:	340.
Landing-craft:	4 LCAC.

The LSD 41 design was prepared in the mid-1970s as a replacement for the eight Thomaston-class ships. The project was subjected to delaying tactics by the Carter Administration pending a reassessment of the Navy's requirement for amphibious lift. In 1981, however, pressure from Congress compelled the Administration to order the prototype for the class, and nine follow-on ships are included in the first 5-year programme of the Reagan Administration.

Although not a particularly innovative design, the LSD 41 shows a number of improvements over its immediate predecessor, the Anchorage class. The large flight deck aft extends right to the stern, and is strong enough to accept the powerful CH-53E Super Stallion cargo-carrying helicopter now entering service with the Marines. The docking-well is identical in width to that of earlier LSDs but is 10ft (3m) longer than that of *Anchorage*. It is designed to accommodate four of the new air-cushion landing-craft (LCAC), with which it is intended to replace all conventional LCU-type landing-craft in the late 1980s. The LCAC has bow and stern ramps and can carry an M-60 tank or 120,000lb (54,545kg) of cargo. This is a lower lift capacity than the

Above: An artist's concept of the LSD 41 design, the prototype of which is now being built, following pressure from Congress.

conventional LCU, but the LCAC will compensate for this by carrying its loa to the beach at a speed of 50 knots.

The LSD 41 will be built by modular construction techniques, and diffe from previous amphibious vessels in adopting diesel propulsion in place steam turbines. Four SEMT-Pielstick diesels, manufactured under licenc will be installed in two independent paired units. An annual fuel saving of million gallons over a steam plant of similar power is anticipated.

Raleigh Class/Austin Class LPD

Completed:	1962-71. No. in Class: 3/12.
Displacement:	10,000t light; 16,900t full load.
Dimensions*:	Length 570ft oa (173.3m); Beam 84ft (25.6m); Draught 23ft (7m).
Propulsion:	2-shaft geared steam turbines; 24,000shp = 20kts.
Armament:	4 3-inch (76mm) Mk 33 (2x2).
Aircraft:	up to 6 CH-46D (see notes).
Troops:	840-930.
Landing-craft:	1 LCU, 3 LCM-6.

*Details for Austin class

The three ships of the Raleigh class were the prototypes of a new amphibious class employing the "balanced load" concept. Previous amphibious task forces carried troops in Attack Transports (APA), cargo in Attack Cargo Ships (AKA), and landing-craft and tanks in Dock Landing Ships (LSD). The basic principle of the "balanced force" concept is that these three capabilities are combined in a single hull. The docking-well in the Raleigh class therefore occupies only the after part of the ship, while forward of the well there are vehicle decks, cargo holds and substantial troop accommodation decks. The well itself measures 168ft x 50ft (51.2x15.2m)—less than half the length of the docking-well in the most modern LSDs—and is served overhead by six monorail cars, which load cargo into the awaiting landing-craft. The docking-well can accommodate one LCU and three LCM-6s, or four LCM-8s. Two further LCM-6s and four LCPLs are carried at the after end of the superstructure, and are handled by a large crane. The docking-well is covered by a helicopter landing platform, which can receive any of the major types of helicopter in service with the Marines.

The major modification in the succeeding Austin type was the insertion of a 50ft (15.2m) hull section forward of the docking-well. This resulted in a significant increase in vehicle space and cargo capacity (3,900 tons compared to only 2,000 tons for the Raleigh class). The additional length available for flying operations enabled a large telescopic hangar to be worked in immediately aft of the superstructure, giving these ships the maintenance facilities which were lacking in the Raleigh class. Seven of the 12 ships are configured as amphibious squadron (PhibRon) flagships and can accommodate only 840 troops. They can be outwardly distinguished by their extra bridge level.

La Salle, of the Raleigh class, serves as a Command Ship for the US Middle East Force. She was specially converted in 1980 for this role and is now numbered AGF 3.

Above: USS *Coronada* (LPD-11) in company with an Iwo Jima class LPH. The 64ft (19.5m) long telescopic hangar can be seen.

Below: USS *Vancouver* (LPD-2) with a Marines battalion on flight-deck, without hangar or maintenance facilities for helicopters.

Anchorage Class LSD

Completed:	1969-72. No. in Class: 5.
Displacement:	8,600t light; 13,700t full load.
Dimensions:	Length 553ft oa (168.6m); Beam 84ft (25.6m); Draught 19ft (5.6m).
Propulsion:	2-shaft geared steam turbines; 24,000shp = 20kts.
Armament:	6 3-inch (76mm) Mk 33 (3x2).
Troops:	375
Landing-craft:	3 LCU, 1 LCM-6.

The five dock landing ships of the Anchorage class were among the last units to be completed in the large amphibious ship programme of the 1960s. In spite of the advent of the LPD with its "balanced load" concept, there was still a requirement for LSDs to carry additional landing-craft to the assault area. The Anchorage class was therefore built to replace the ageing war-built vessels, which had inadequate speed for the new PhibRons. It is a development of the Thomaston class, from which its ships can be distinguished by their tripod mast and their longer hull.

The docking-well measures 430ft by 50ft (131 x 15.2m)—an increase of 30ft (9m) in length over the Thomastons—and can accommodate three of the big LCUs or nine LCM-8s, with an alternative loading of 50 LVTP-7s. There is space on deck for a single LCM-6, and an LCPL and an LCVP are carried on davits. As in the Thomaston class, there are vehicle decks above the docking-well amidships, served by two 50-ton cranes. The Anchorage class was designed to transport up to 30 helicopters, and there is a removable flight deck aft for heavy-lift cargo helicopters.

The sensor outfit and armament are on a par with the contemporary LPDs of the Austin class.

Below: USS *Pensacola* (LSD-38) with an LCU 1610 entering the large docking well. The flight deck can be removed.

147

Thomaston Class

LSD

Completed: 1954-7. No. in Class: 8.
Displacement: 6,880t light; 11,270-12,150t full load.
Dimensions: Length 510ft oa (155.5m); Beam 84ft (25.6m);
Draught 19ft (5.8m).
Propulsion: 2-shaft geared steam turbines; 24,000shp = 22.5kts.
Armament: 6 3-inch (76mm) Mk 33 (3x2).
Troops: 340.
Landing-craft 3 LCU.

The Thomaston class was the first postwar LSD design and was a result of the renewed interest in amphibious operations during the Korean War. The basic conception of the wartime LSD was retained but the Thomaston class incorporated a number of improvements. The ships have a large, more seaworthy hull, with greater sheer and flare in the bows, and can steam at a sustained speed of over 20 knots compared to only 15 knots for their war-built counterparts. The docking-well, which measures 391ft by 48ft (119.1 x 14.6m), is wider and more than half as long again, and can accommodate three LCUs or nine LCM-8s. There is a vehicle deck amidships but no access to the docking-well. Cargo and vehicles are therefore preloaded in the landing-craft or handled by the two 50-ton cranes. The after part of the docking-well is covered by a short removable platform for cargo-carrying helicopters, but there are no hangar or maintenance facilities.

As completed, the Thomaston class were armed with eight twin 3-inch (76mm) mountings but five of these, together with all fire-control radars, have since been removed.

In 1980 *Spiegel Grove* conducted evaluation trials for the Jeff-B

Above: USS *Hermitage* (LSD-34). The Thomaston class will be replaced by the Whidbey Island class in the mid-80s.

aircushion landing-craft (AALC). Three such craft could be accommodated in the docking-well of the Thomaston class, but it is possible that some of these ships will be retired before the production LCAC enters service.

Newport Class

LST

Completed: 1969-72. No. in Class: 20.
Displacement: 8,342t full load.
Dimensions: Length 562ft oa (171.3m); Beam 70ft (21.2m);
Draught 18ft (5.3m).
Propulsion: 2-shaft diesels; 6 GM (1179-81)/Alco (others);
16,500bhp = 20kts.
Armament: 4 3-inch (76mm) Mk 33 (2x2).

The twenty LSTs of the Newport class are larger and faster than the war-built vessels they replaced. In order to match the 20-knot speed of the other amphibious units built during the 1960s the traditional bow doors were suppressed in favour of a 112ft (34m) ramp which is lowered over the bows of the ship between twin fixed derrick arms. This arrangement also allowed for an increase in draught in line with the increase in displacement.

There is a large integral flight deck aft for utility helicopters. Pontoons can be slung on either side of the flight deck for use in landing operations. Each can carry an MBT and they can be mated with the stern gate. They are handled by twin derricks located immediately aft of the staggered funnel uptakes.

Below decks there is a total parking area of 19,000sq ft (5,300m²) for a cargo capacity of 500 tons of vehicles. The forecastle is connected to the vehicle deck by a ramp and to the flight deck by a passageway through the superstructure. A through-hull bow thruster is provided to maintain the ship's position while unloading offshore.

The twin 3-inch (76mm) gun mounts, located at the after end of the superstructure will be replaced by Phalanx CIWS guns when these become

Above: A tank-landing ship of the Newport class positioning her bow ramp prior to offloading vehicles on an amphibious exercise.

available. Several ships of the Newport class have recently been assigned to the Naval Reserve Force (NRF).

Yellowstone Class/ Samuel Gompers Class

AD

Completed: 1967 onwards. No. in Class: 2/4.
Displacement: (AD 37,38) 22,260t full load.
(AD 41-44) 22,800t full load.
Dimensions: Length 643ft oa (196m); Beam 85ft (25.9m);
Draught 23ft (6.9m).
Propulsion: 1-shaft geared steam turbine; 20,000shp = 18kts.
Armament: 4 20mm (4x1) in AD 37,8; 2 40mm (2x1), 2 20mm (2x1) in AD 41-4.

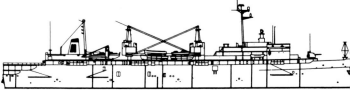

Samuel Gompers and *Puget Sound* were the Navy's first destroyer tenders built to a postwar design. They are similar in size and general configuration to the contemporary SSBN tenders of the Simon Lake class, but were specifically fitted out to support surface combatants on forward deployment. They can furnish in-port service to six cruiser/destroyer types alongside simultaneously. The high-sided hull and the superstructures contain approximately 60 workshops to enable these ships to maintain and repair the latest equipment, including missile systems, ASW weapons, advanced communications and electronics and nuclear propulsion plants.

The Yellowstone class is a follow-on design incorporating improvements in stowage and layout. They carry spare gas-turbines for the latest surface ships.

Right: The photo and side-view drawing show the lines of USS *Samuel Gompers* (AD-37), a destroyer tender capable of supporting up to six cruiser/destroyers alongside. The kingpost cranes handle heavy items while the small travelling cranes handle lighter stores.

L.Y. Spear Class/ Emory S. Land Class

AS

Completed: 1970-81. No. in Class: 2/3.
Displacement: (AS 36, 37) 12,700t light; 22,628t full load.
(AS 39-41) 13,842t light; 23,000t full load.
Dimensions: Length 646ft oa (196.8m); Beam 85ft (25.9m);
Draught 25ft (7.5m).
Propulsion: 1-shaft geared steam turbine; 20,000shp = 18kts.
Armament: 4 20mm (4x1)in AS 36.7, 240mm (2x1), 420mm
(4x1) in AS 39-41.

Derived from the SSBN tenders of the Simon Lake class, *L. Y. Spear* and *Dixon* were the first submarine tenders to be designed to support SSNs, for which they provide repairs, spare parts, provisions, ordnance and medical facilities. There are three Ship Alongside Service (SAS) stations supplied through four switchboards. Services supplied include compressed air, oxygen, nitrogen, 150-lb (68kg) steam, oil, water and electrical power.

The Emory S. Land class is a follow-on design fitted specifically for the support of SSNs of the Los Angeles class.

Below: USS *Dixon* (AS-37) a submarine tender of the L.Y. Spear class, designed to support nuclear-propelled attack boats. The three ships of the Emory S. Land class support Los Angeles SSNs.

Simon Lake Class

AS

Completed: 1964-5. No. in Class: 2.
Displacement: 21,500t full load.
Dimensions: Length 644ft oa (196.2m); Beam 85ft (25.9m);
Draught 25ft (7.5m).
Propulsion: 1-shaft geared steam turbine; 20,000shp = 18kts.
Armament: 4 3-inch (76mm) Mk 33 (2x2).

The two SSBN tenders of the Simon Lake class are larger than their immediate predecessors of the Hunley class and have a much improved layout. The funnel and machinery are well aft, leaving the midships section clear for cranage and services to support up to three submarines lying alongside. There is a full reactor support capability and facilities are provided for the handling, replacement and limited servicing of SLBMs. Both ships were modified 1969-71 to enable them to handle Poseidon, and Simon Lake has recently been fitted for Trident.

Right: The two tenders of the Lake class serve with the Atlantic Fleet supporting Lafayette class SSBNs. A third ship was cancelled.

Hunley Class

AS

Completed: 1961-3. No. in Class: 2.
Displacement: 10,500t standard; 18,300t full load.
Dimensions: Length 599ft oa (182.6m); Beam 83ft (25.3m);
Draught 24ft (7.3m).
Propulsion: 1-shaft diesel-electric; 6 Fairbanks-Morse diesels;
15,000bhp = 19kts.
Armament: 4 20mm (2x2).

These were the first purpose-built SSBN tenders. They can supply services to three submarines alongside simultaneously and support a squadron of nine. There are 52 workshops and extensive stowage facilities, including vertical stowage for SLBMs. Both ships were modified 1973-5 to enable them to handle Poseidon missiles. Machinery and funnel were located amidships, which proved unsatisfactory and was avoided in the later tenders of the Emory S. Land class and its successors.

Right: *Hunley* (AS-31) the first purpose-built tender for Polaris submarines and later converted to support Poseidon boats. The stowage silos for the missiles can be seen between the jibs of the large kingpost cranes. The helipad is for VERTREP operations.

Kilauea Class

AE

Completed: 1968-72. No. in Class: 7.
Displacement: 20,500t full load.
Dimensions: Length 564ft oa (171.9m); Beam 81ft (24.7m);
Draught 26ft (7.8m).
Propulsion: 1-shaft geared steam turbine; 22,000shp = 20kts.
Armament: 4 3-inch (76mm) Mk 33 (2x2)—not in T-AE 26.
Helicopters: 2 UH-46 Sea Knight.

The eight ammunition ships of the Kilauea class belong to the generation of under way replenishment vessels constructed during the 1960s. They are similar in size to the combat stores ships of the Mars class, but specialise in the transfer of missiles and other munitions. Cargo capacity is approximately 6,500 tons. Four transfer stations are provided on either side forward of the bridge, two abreast of the funnel and another two at the after end of the hangar. Fin stabilisers are fitted to ensure a steady platform for the transfer of delicate stores. Twin hangars 50ft x 18ft (15.2 x 5.3m) can accommodate two UH-46 VERTREP helicopters. Two twin 3in (76mm) gun mounts are fitted and these will be supplemented by two Phalanx CIWS systems.

Right: The ammunition ship *Kilauea* (AE-26) underway. The transfer stations can be seen clearly on this picture, as can the twin 3in gun mounts above the bows. *Kilauea* herself has been transferred to the civilian-manned Military Sealift Command to save manpower.

Mars Class

AFS

Completed: 1963-70. No. in Class: 7.
Displacement: 16,500t full load.
Dimensions: Length 581ft oa (177.1m); Beam 79ft (24.1m);
Draught 24ft (7.3m).
Propulsion: 1-shaft geared steam turbine; 22,000shp = 20kts.
Armament: 4 3-inch (76mm) Mk 33 (2x2).
Helicopters: 2 UH-46 Sea Knight.

The seven combat stores ships of the Mars class were the first of a new generation of under-way replenishment vessels completed during the 1960s to support carrier task force deployments. They combine the functions of store ships (AF), stores-issue ships (AKS), and aviation store ships (AVS). They were the first ships to incorporate the Fast Automatic Shuttle Transfer system (FAST), which revolutionised the handling of stores and munitions. Five "M" frames replace the conventional kingposts and booms of previous vessels and these have automatic tensioning devices to keep the transfer lines taut while replenishing. Cargo capacity is 7,000 tons in five cargo holds. Computers provide up-to-the-minute data on stock status with the data displayed on closed-circuit-television.

Right: The combat stores ship *Mars* (AFS-1) underway off Hawaii. The *Mars* class was the first to be fitted with the FAST transfer system which revolutionised stores and munitions handling at sea.

Cimarron Class

AO

Completed: 1980 onwards. No. in Class: 4 (+ 1 building).
Displacement: 27,500t full load.
Dimensions: Length 592ft oa (178m); Beam 88ft (26.8m);
Draught 34ft (10.2m).
Propulsion: 1-shaft geared steam turbine; 24,000shp = 20kts.
Armament: 2 Phalanx CIWS (not in T-AO 186).

The new fleet oilers of the Cimarron class are the first ships in that category to be completed since the mid-1950s. They are significantly smaller than previous vessels; they have been deliberately "sized" to provide two complete refuellings of a fossil-fuelled carrier and six to eight escorts, and have a total capacity of 120,000 barrels of fuel oil. There are four replenishment stations to port and three to starboard, and there is a large platform aft for VERTREP helicopters, but no hangar or support facilities are provided.

Right: USS *Cimarron* (AO-177) under full power during her sea trials in November 1980. Capacity is 120,000 barrels of fuel oil.

Below: *Cimmaron* is smaller than previous USN oilers. Note bridge structure aft, together with a flight deck for VERTREP helicopters.

Neosho Class

AO

Completed: 1954-56. No. in Class: 6.
Displacement: 11,600t light; 38-40,000t full load.
Dimensions: Length 655ft oa (199.6m); Beam 86ft (26.2m);
Draught 35ft (10.7m).
Propulsion: 2-shaft geared steam turbines; 28,000shp = 20kts.
Armament: Removed.

These were the first major under-way replenishment vessels to be built postwar, and they are the largest fleet oilers in the US Navy. They have a capacity of approximately 180,000 barrels of fuel oil, and have been fitted since the 1960s with a modern rig for abeam replenishment. They were designed to serve as flagships of the service forces, and were given accommodation for the Service Force Commander and his staff. All ships are part of Military Sealift Command and are civilian manned.

Right: The oiler *Neosho* (AO-143) underway. The six ships of this class were the first major replenishment at sea (RAS) vessels to be built for the US Navy after World War II in the years 1955-57.

Sacramento Class

AOE

Completed: 1964-70. No. in Class: 4.
Displacement: 19,200t light; 53,600t full load.
Dimensions: Length 793ft oa (241.7m); Beam 107ft (32.6m);
Draught 39ft (12m).
Propulsion: 2-shaft geared steam turbines; 100,000shp = 26kts.
Armament: 1 NATO Sea Sparrow launcher Mk 29 (1x8);
4 3-inch (76mm). Mk 33 (2x2).
Helicopters: 2 UH-46 Sea Knight.

The world's largest under-way replenishment vessels, the fast combat support ships of the Sacramento class are designed to supply a carrier battle group with all its basic needs. They combine the functions of fleet oilers (AO), ammunition ships (AE), stores ships (AF) and cargo ships (AK). They have exceptionally high speed for their type to enable them to keep pace with fleet units.

Cargo capacity is 177,000 barrels of fuel oil, 2,150 tons of munitions, 250 tons of dry stores and 250 tons of refrigerated stores. The Sacramento class was one of the first two designs to employ the FAST automatic transfer system. There is a large helicopter landing deck aft with a three-bay hangar for VERTREP helicopters.

Below: USS *Camden* (AOE-2), second of the Sacramento class cost $70 million when she was built in 1965 and a fifth ship was cancelled when it was decided that they were too expensive.

Wichita Class

AOR

Completed: 1969-75. No. in Class: 7.
Displacement: 38,100t full load.
Dimensions: Length 659ft oa (206.9m); Beam 96ft (29.3m);
Draught 33ft (10.2m).
Propulsion: 2-shaft geared steam turbines; 32,000shp = 20kts.
Armament: 1 NATO Sea Sparrow launcher Mk 29 (1x8) in AOR 3,7;
4 3-inch (76mm) Mk 33 (2x2) in AOR 1, 4, 6;
2/4 20mm (2/4x1) in AOR 2,7.
Helicopters: 2 UH-46 Sea Knights in AOR 2-3,5,7.

The Wichita-class replenishment oilers, like the fast combat support ships of the Sacramento class, are designed for the support of the carrier battle groups. They are smaller vessels with much-reduced speed but have proved to be very successful ships. They carry a similar quantity of fuel oil to the larger AOEs but have only a limited capacity for provisions and munitions. Cargo capacity is 160,000 barrels of fuel, 600 tons of munitions, 200 tons of dry stores and 100 tons of refrigerated stores.

The last ship was completed with a double helicopter hanger, and all other ships of the class are now being similarly fitted.

Right: USS *Wichita* (AOR-1) leadship of a class of seven built as a less costly (and slightly less capable) alternative to the Sacramento.

Weapons and Sensors

SPS-48
SURVEILLANCE RADAR

In service: 1965 (first operational installation).
Long-range (230nm, 426km) 3-D radar used to provide target data for Terrier/Standard ER missile in CGs and for aircraft control in CVs. Large square planar antenna.

SPS-30
SURVEILLANCE RADAR

In service: 1962.
Long-range 3-D radar used for aircraft control in older CVs. Large solid dish antenna with prominent feed-horn. Being replaced by SPS-48.

SPS-39/52
3D RADAR

In service: 1960/1966.
3-D radar used to provide target data for Tartar/Standard MR missile in DDGs and FFGs. Rectangular planar antenna.

SPS-49
AIR SEARCH RADAR

In service: 1976.
Long-range air search radar. In FFG-7 and to be retro-fitted to all major classes in place of SPS-37/37A/43/43A. Elliptical lattice antenna.

SPS-37A/43A
AIR SEARCH RADAR

In service: 1961.
Long-range (300nm, 556km) air search radar in CVs. 13-metre (42.6ft) rectangular lattice antenna.

SPS-37/43
AIR SEARCH RADAR

In service: 1960/1961.
Long-range (230nm, 426km) air search radar in CGs and some DDs and DDGs. Rectangular mattress antenna.

SPS-40
AIR SEARCH RADAR

In service: 1962.
Medium-range (150-80nm, 278-334-km)) air search radar in DDs, FFs, some DDGs, and amphibious vessels. Elliptical lattice antenna with feed-horn above.

Above: SPS-48 is the standard three-dimensional radar on cruisers. Range, depending on conditions, is some 230nm (426km).

Below: Frigates of the Brooke class (foreground) and Knox class showing typical radar arrays. The square planar array is an SPS-52 while the Knox has the SPS-40 air search radar. Both have SPS-10.

SPS-55

SURFACE SEARCH RADAR

In service: 1975.
surface search radar. Has replaced SPS-10 in new construction.

SPS-10

SURFACE SEARCH RADAR

In service: 1953.
urface search radar. Standard on all but most recent units. To be upgraded
 SPS-67.

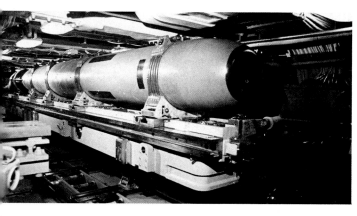

bove: The torpedo room on board USS *Ohio* (SSBN-726). Four
 in (533mm) tubes are fitted. The torpedo is a Mark 68.

Mk 46 Torpedo

ASW

service: 1967.
ength: 8.5ft (2.6m)
iameter: 12.75in (324mm).
uidance: active/passive acoustic homing.
red from triple trainable or single fixed Mk 32 tubes on all surface
arships. Normal payload of ASROC missile. NEARTIP update.

SQS-26/53

LF SONAR

service: 1962/1975.
rge LF bow sonar. Simultaneous active/passive operation in a variety of
odes (incl. bottom bounce, convergence zone). Detection ranges out to
st convergence zone (25-35nm, 46.3-65km). Fitted in most FFs and all
ajor surface units since mid-1960s. SQS-53 has solid-state electronics and
gital interface with Mk 116 UFCS.

SQS-23

LF SONAR

In service: 1958.
Predecessor of above. LF sonar with detection ranges of 6nm (11.1km)
approx. In all major surface warships built late 1950s/early 1960s. To be
upgraded to SQQ-23 status with active/passive operation.

SQS-56

MF SONAR

In service: 1977.
Austere MF hull sonar designed for FFG 7. Latest technology but modest
range.

SQS-35

MF SONAR

In service: 1968.
Independent MF variable depth sonar fitted in stern counter of Knox-class
FFs. SQR-18 passive array (in service 1978) can be streamed from towed
body.

5-inch/54 cal. Mk 45

TWIN GUN

In service: 1974.
Fire Control: SPG-60, SPQ-9 with Mk 86 GFCS.
Lightweight D-P gun with modest performance but good reliability and low
manning requirements.

5-inch/54 cal. Mk 42

SINGLE GUN

In service: 1953.
Fire Control: SPG-53 with Mk 68 GFCS.
High-performance D-P gun. Complex and not always reliable.

76mm/62 cal. Mk 75

SINGLE GUN

In service: 1977.
Fire Control: Mk 92 GFCS.
Lightweight high-performance gun manufactured under licence from
OTO-Melara for FFG-7 and PHM.

20mm/76 cal. Mk 15

CIWS

In service: 1980.
Fire Control: Local radar.
Phalanx Close-In Weapon System (CIWS). 3,000rpm. To be fitted as
standard "last-ditch" anti-missile weapon in 250 warships. Three to be fitted
in CVs, two in all other major surface units, including amphibious vessels.

Below: 20mm CIWS disposes of an incoming missile.

The United States Air Force

Doug Richardson, Editor of *Defence Materiel*, former Defence Editor, *Flight International*
and
Bill Gunston, Assistant Compiler of *Jane's All The World's Aircraft*; author of many technical books and papers on military affairs

The United States Air Force is undoubtedly a most formidable military machine. Equipped with the most advanced fighters currently available, advanced early-warning aircraft equipped with "look-down" surveillance radar, a fleet of intercontinental-range jet transports capable of projecting military power across the globe, more than 200 long-range heavy bombers capable of attacking targets with free-falling bombs or the latest cruise missiles, and a land-based deterrent in the shape of more than 1,000 intercontinental missiles, it represents a military capability which no other nation can match. Whereas USAF's F-15 Eagle fighter entered service in the mid 1970s, the nearest Soviet equivalent—the MiG-29 Fulcrum—is probably only just becoming operational, and the F-16 Fighting Falcon provides the yardstick against which the performance of future Soviet air-combat fighters must be judged.

The air arm of the United States did not achieve its status as an independent service until 1947, having been a branch of the US Army until then. It started life in 1907 as the Aeronautical Division of the Signal Corps, later being renamed the Aviation Section of the Signal Corps. In 1918 it became the Army Air Service, but was elevated to the status of the Army Air Corps in 1926. The latter title was retained until 1941, when a further "promotion" introduced the title Army Air Forces. Final independence came on September 18, 1947, and the service has been known as the United States Air Force since that date.

It may be that this late transition to the status of a separate service had a detrimental influence on the procurement and operating policies in the decades which followed. Certainly, the USAF has twice adopted US Navy front-line aircraft—the F-4 Phantom and the A-7 Corsair II—while the service's "kill ratio" against North Vietnamese fighters for a long time lagged behind that of the US Navy.

Organization

Main components of the USAF are Strategic Air Command (SAC), Tactical Air Command (TAC), Military Airlift Command (MAC), Air Training Command (ATC), United States Air Forces in Europe (USAFE), Pacific Air Force (PAF), and Alaskan Air Command (AAC).

These are supported by four further Commands—Air Force Communications Command (AFCC), Air Force Logistics Command (AFLC), Air Force Systems Command (AFSC), and Electronic Security Command (ESC). Further support is given by 13 Separate Operating Agencies (SOAs), covering fields from commissary and safety to legal and counter-intelligence services, plus a number of Direct Reporting Units (DRUs) such as the Air Force Academy, Air Reserve Personnel Center and the Simpson Historical Research Center.

Like most air arms, the USAF front-line aircraft strength can vary from year to year. During the early 1980s the number showed a slight annual increase. In Fiscal Year 1983, a total of 7,305 aircraft were deployed. A further 485 were available from the Air Force Reserve, and 458 from the Air National Guard.

Most fighter or attack squadrons have either 18 or 24 aircraft. Bomber squadrons can have anything from 12 to 19 aircraft, 12 or 13 in the case of FB-111 units. Typical transport squadrons have 16 C-130 Hercules, 17 to 18 C-5A Galaxies or 18 C-141 StarLifters. Units operating specialized aircraft tend to vary in strength. An E-3A Sentry squadron for example could have between 2 and 17 aircraft.

The USAF has 94 bases in the USA, plus 43 main bases in overseas nations. The Air National Guard and Air Force Reserve operate from a total of 85 bases in the USA. Some are shared with the USAF.

Just over 80 percent of the USAF personnel ing specialized aircraft tend to vary in strength. account for 17 percent, the remainder being cadets. More than 85,000 black personnel serve with the USAF, making up some 15 percent of the enlisted manpower, and five percent of the officers. Black personnel form an above-average share of enlisted ranks such as staff sergeant, sergeant and senior airman, but are less well represented at the higher levels of command. Women play an ever-growing role in USAF strength, making up about 10 percent of the total.

Service personnel are well educated. More than 1,000 officers plus a handful of enlisted personnel have Doctoral or professional degrees, while virtually all officers have a Batchelor's or Master's degree. The later qualifications are also held by around two percent of enlisted personnel, while around 20 percent have some level of college education. Seventy-five percent of all enlisted personnel have a High School education, with only a few percent falling below this category.

Strategic Air Command

Strategic Air Command is responsible for the ground and airborne portions of the "triad" of US strategic forces. When Boeing engineers designed the B-52 bomber in the early 1950s, they could have had no idea that the aircraft would serve into the 1980s. The search for an eventual replacement has run for two decades, the Mach-3 B-70 having been cancelled in the 1960s, with the later B-1 being delayed by President Carter's decision to cancel the original program.

By the mid-1980s, the average age of USAF's B-52s will be a quarter of a century. The original projected airframe life was only 5,000 hours, a figure which even the youngest passed more than a decade ago, but a massive structural rebuild program has prolonged service life and enabled the aircraft to cope with the stresses involved in low-level flight.

The main bomber force consists of 269 B-52G and B-52H bombers (plus some sharply differing B-52Ds now being withdrawn from the active inventory). In order to improve avionics performance and to eliminate the problems associated with the maintenance of elderly vacuum-tube (thermionic valve) avionics, these aircraft are being re-equipped with modern solid-state electronics hardened to resist the effects of electro-magnetic pulses from nuclear explosions. The new avionics include a modernized radar, and new inertial navigation and bombing systems.

The USAF retains its unique position as the world's most technically advanced air arm. Its roles are wide-ranging, spreading across the whole spectrum of land-based astronautics —from air defense, through low-level strategic strike and satellite reconnaissance, to the quick-fire response of the Rapid Deployment Force (see unusually camouflaged KC-135 of RDJTF, left). But there is a growing feeling among defense experts that this huge fighting arm, in developing high technology combat aircraft heavily reliant on fixed bases such as that below, is digging its own grave. A Soviet first strike on such bases could cripple the Air Force to such an extent that its retaliatory capability would be nil.

Under another program, the B-52G is being converted to carry AGM-86 ALCM cruise missiles. The first squadron of ALCM-armed B-52Gs became operational at Griffiss AFB, NY, late in 1982, and a total of 104 will receive this armament. From 1986 onwards a total of 96 turbofan-engined B-52H bombers will also be converted into cruise-missile carriers.

Using the current AGM-86B missile, the B-52 force will be able to reach 85 percent of all strategic targets from launch positions outside of Soviet airspace, and beyond the range of many defensive systems. The newer AGM-86C will have greater range, allowing all targets to

be attacked from offshore launch areas and giving USAF planners greater flexibility to deceive the Soviet defences by routing the incoming cruise missiles on deceptive flight paths incorporating major changes of course.

The need to cope with cruise missiles seems to have forced many engineering changes to the new Soviet SA-10 surface-to-air missile system, delaying the latter's entry into service by several years. The development of a Soviet long-range air-to-air missile—perhaps an air-breathing weapon in the class of the now-abandoned Martin Marietta ASALM—seems likely, since the Soviet Union is now thought to

Above: Aerial refueling is a vital part of SAC's operations and confers a global capability on the bomber force. The B-1B (similar to the B-1A seen here) will join SAC in 1985 to replace the B-52s, which are already nearly 25 years old.

be focussing its anti-cruise missile defens efforts on engaging the carrier aircraft befor ACLMs have been released.

The B-52G and H models are currently suppl mented by 80 B-52Ds. The latter were refu bished between 1975 and 1977, being fitted wit improved avionics and radar. During the Vie nam War, the high-explosive payload of thes aircraft was increased by modifications to th bomb bay and the provision of external or nance racks. These aircraft are expected t remain in service until the mid-1980s.

In addition to its nuclear role, SAC als deploys its bombers in conventional roles. B-5: provide maritime-reconnaissance facilities ov the Indian Ocean, using Australia for trans facilities. Six B-52s flew nonstop from the US to Egypt and back in 1981 in support of Exerci Bright Star 82. Each dropped 27 500lb hig explosive bombs during low-level flight over a Egyptian weapons range.

Like most USAF aircraft, the B-52 is equippe for airborne refuelling and supported by a fle of KC-135 tankers. Up to half of these vetera are being re-engined and fitted with improve refuelling equipment and avionics. These wi be supplemented by up to 60 KC-10A wid bodied cargo-tanker aircraft.

The latter will have a dramatic effect on th ability of the United States to reinforce i allies during a crisis. A fleet of 17 KC-10A cou refuel an F-4 squadron flying from the USA Europe, and carry the associated personnel an ground equipment. To achieve the same resu using the KC-135 would involve 40 tankers an a similar number acting simply as transports

The ability of the B-52 to penetrate the late Soviet defenses must be limited, despite th

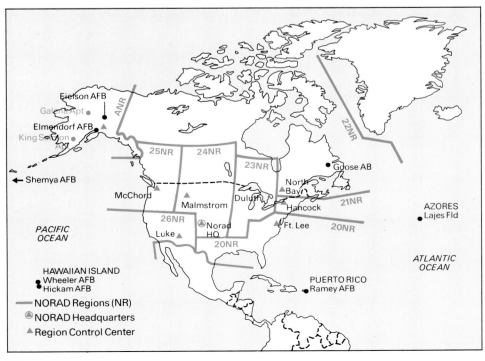

addition of a massive array of internal electronic countermeasures. The CIA has estimated that the aircraft will remain effective until 1990, but more pessimistic studies suggest a date in the mid-1980s. Long-term penetration capability will require the deployment of the "Stealth" bomber currently being developed by Northrop in conjunction with Lockheed and probably becoming operational late in 1990.

In the interim, the USAF intends to deploy 100 B-1B bombers in the mid-1980s. The radar cross-section of this aircraft is only a tenth that of the original B-1 design, and a hundredth that of a B-52, but it seems safe to predict that the aircraft will spend most of its service career as a cruise missile carrier, avoiding the Soviet defences of the 1990s.

A second "stealth" program is known to exist. Prototype hardware has been flown by Lockheed since 1977, and a tactical reconnaissance aircraft similar in size to the F-18 may already be in service. Like the current SR-71 and U-2 aircraft, this may well be operated by SAC.

Faced with the growing threat posed by high-accuracy Soviet ICBMs, the US has upgraded its Minuteman ICBM force to improve survivability. The 450 Minuteman IIIs originally deployed are being supplemented by the modernization of 50 Minuteman II installations to the Minuteman III standard. Missile silos are being modified by the addition of improved suspension for the round, anti-shock mountings for the checkout equipment, additional concrete on the silo lids and the installation of bins to catch debris thrown up by nearby nuclear explosions.

The liquid-propellant Titan II missile is now to be phased out of the SAC inventory. A series of accidents in recent years focussed attention on the weapons' safety and reliability, the force being reduced from 53 rounds to 52 after a silo was destroyed by an accidental explosion.

The failure to establish an acceptable basing mode for the new Peacekeeper missile (formerly

MX) emphasises the problems associated with maintaining a future land-based deterrent. None of the schemes suggested to date combines long-term survivability with acceptable financial or environmental costs.

Command and control facilities for the US strategic forces are partly maintained by a fleet of airborne command posts. The earlier examples are based on the KC-135, but the newer E-4 uses the airframe of the Boeing 747 wide-bodied airliner. When the refurbishment of the first three E-4A Airborne Command Posts to the E-4B standard is completed, these will serve alongside the three examples of the latter standard being built as new aircraft. The B version carries improved command, control and

Below: An ageing B-52D makes a low-level run on an American bombing range. Given the losses over Vietnam, will these old aircraft be capable of penetrating the sophisticated defenses of the Soviet Union?

communications equipment better equipped to survive the effects of electro-magnetic pulse radiation. Airborne refuelling equipment will stretch the maximum mission duration to the 72 hours dictated by the capacity of the engine oil tanks and the endurance of the crew.

Space Command

The USAF set up a Space Defense Operations Center (SPADOC) at the Cheyenne Mountain Complex in Fiscal Year 1980. This was intended to control US space surveillance systems and the two planned anti-satellite (ASAT) squadrons. Formation of USAF Space Command was announced on June 21, 1982 and took place on September 1 of the same year. This is based alongside the existing Aerospace Defense Command facilities at Colorado Springs, Colorado. Several new facilities are planned or under construction.

Main operational unit will be the planned Consolidated Space Operations Center at Peterson AFB, Colorado. This will supervise USAF shuttle missions in the late 1980s and beyond and will back up existing facilities at the Johnson Space Center.

One of the control rooms at Johnson center is being electromagnetically screened to prevent inadvertent "leakage" of classified data due to stray electromagnetic radiation from computers or other digital data-processing equipment.

Peterson AFB is also the headquarters of 1st Space Wing. Set up in January 1, 1983, this is responsible for the world-wide network of space surveillance and missile early-warning stations originally established by SAC.

Latest of these systems to enter service is the Ground-based Electro-Optical Deep-Space Surveillance System (GEODSS). Tracking stations for this sytem have been built at the White Sands Missile Range, New Mexico, cn the island of Maui in Hawaii, at Diego Garcia in the Indian Ocean and near Taegu in South Korea. Construction of a fifth and final station is due to begin in 1985.

All are equipped with two Contraves Goertz 40 inch (　　) telescopes of 86 inch (　　) focal length. These gather light from the object under

Right: Powerful telescopes probe deep into space from a GEODSS test site at White Sands N.M. America's newest ground-based surveillance system, GEODSS will be fully operational at five sites by 1987.

Major Active Air Force Installations in the US

McChord AFB (MAC)
Fairchild AFB (SAC)
Malmstrom AFB (SAC)
Minot AFB (SAC)
Grand Forks AFB (SAC)
Duluth IAP
K. I. Sawyer AFB (SAC)
Wurtsm AFB (SA
Kingsley Field (ADC)
Mountain Home AFB (TAC)
Ellsworth AFB (SAC)
Se
Beale AFB (SAC)
McClellan AFB (AFLC)
Mather AFB (ATC)
Hill AFB (AFLC)
Francis E. Warren AFB (SAC)
Offutt AFB (SAC)
O'Hare IAP
Gr
AF
Travis AFB (MAC)
Lowry AFB (ATC)
Chanute AFB (ATC)
W
Patt
AFB
Castle AFB (SAC)
United States Air Force Academy
Peterson Field (ADC)
Richards-Gebaur AFB (AFCS)
Whiteman AFB (SAC)
Scott AFB (MAC)
Indian Springs AF Auxiliary Fields
McConnell AFB (SAC)
Edwards AFB (AFSC)
Nellis AFB (TAC)
Vance AFB (ATC)
Arnold AFS (AFSC)
Vandenberg AFB (SAC)
George AFB (TAC)
Blytheville AFB (SAC)
Los Angeles AFS (AFSC)
Norton AFB (MAC)
Kirtland AFB (AFSC)
Tinker AFB (AFLC)
Little Rock AFB (MAC)
Dobb
(A
March AFB (SAC)
Luke AFB (TAC)
Cannon AFB (TAC)
Altus AFB (MAC)
Columbus AFB (ATC)
Gur
AFS (A
Williams AFB (ATC)
Holloman AFB (TAC)
Sheppard AFB (ATC)
Carswell AFB (SAC)
Craig AFB (ATC)
Davis-Monthan AFB (TAC)
Reese AFB (ATC)
Dyess AFB (SAC)
Barksdale AFB (SAC)
Maxwe
Keesler AFB (Al
Goodfellow AFB (USAFSS)
Bergstrom AFB (TAC)
England AFB (TAC)
Lackland AFB (ATC)
Randolph AFB (ATC)
Kelly AFB (AFLC)
Brooks AFB (AFSC)
Laughlin AFB (ATC)

Hurlburt Field (AFSC)
Eglin AFB (AFSC)
Tyndall AFB (ADC

An Air Force Magazine Map

AB	Air Base
ADC	Aerospace Defense Command
AFB	Air Force Base
AFCS	Air Force Communications Servi
AFLC	Air Force Logistics Command
AFRES	Air Force Reserve
AFS	Air Force Station
AFSC	Air Force Systems Command
ALCOM	Alaskan Command

surveillance and feed it to video sensors for conversion into digital data for signal processing and enhancement.

System software is able to differentiate between the light from stars and from man-made objects; the former is automatically filtered out, and the "signature" and position of the spacecraft under surveillance can be checked against a catalog of more than 800 objects which is maintained by NORAD. Some 8,000 to 10,000 observations are made each month, and the results passed to NORAD. In an emergency, data on any suspect object located by the sensors can be passed within minutes to Cheyenne Mountain.

The degree to which GEODSS sensors may examine the physical shape and appearance remains classified, but the fact that such a capability exists was highlighted in 1981 during the first orbital flight of the Space Shuttle. Ground-based cameras were used to examine the lower surface of the orbiting spacecraft to check whether some of the heat-insulating tiles have come loose.

Existing projects involving space weapons and rocket propulsion are now being handled by the Space Technology Center which has been set up at Kirtland AFB, New Mexico.

Tactical Air Command

Tactical Air Command is the arm of USAF which would provide quick-reaction air reinforcements for use overseas. It is currently involved in a major re-equipment program, with the F-15 Eagle and F-16 Fighting Falcon entering service in increasing numbers. Deployment of the A-10 Thunderbolt II ground-attack aircraft has virtually been completed. The ability of the force to survive the Soviet defenses of the mid-1980s and beyond is being enhanced by the massive ECM capabilities of the EF-111A Electric Fox, two squadrons of which are earmarked for deployment in the UK from 1984 onwards.

Most immediate future fighter project is the planned F-4 replacement for the ground-attack role. The service would like to procure both the F-15E version of the Eagle and the delta-winged F-16E, but Congress is likely to insist that a single type be selected.

In the longer term, the USAF wants a Stol Advanced Tactical Fighter capable of operating out of airstrips only 1,000 to 2,000ft (approx. 300 to 600m) long. This demanding specification calls for an aircraft able to cruise at Mach 2 at 50,000ft (15,240m) or Mach 1.6 at low level, have a 700nm (1,290km) tactical radius, and weigh no more than 50,000lb (22,680kg) when

Above: Part of SAC's responsibility is the military side of the Space Shuttle system. From the Orbiter's cargo bay, "spy" satellites will be deployed and retrieved at will.

carrying a 10,000lb (4,536kg) ordnance load.

In the mid-1970s, TAC were able to rely on a large pool of combat-experienced aircrew from the Vietnam War, but had the good sense to ensure that this experience was not lost as these men moved to desk jobs or retired from the service. The massive Red Flag exercises held at Nellis AFB, Nevada, are unique in the West, if not in the world. Flying against typical European targets defended by F-5E "MiG simulators" (Aggressors) and simulated Soviet ground radars, SAMs and anti-aircraft artillery, crews can develop the skills normally won in the crucial first combat sorties which inflict such massive losses on inexperienced aircrew.

Less well known are the Chequered Flag exercises under which TAC squadrons prepare for their wartime deployment to other bases in

Below: A KC-10 Extender refuels a Holloman-based F-15 Eagle. Compared with the more widely used flexible hose system, flying boom tanking is only operational on a large scale with the USAF.

the USA or overseas, Green Flag which focusses on ECM training and tactics, and to other "Flag" exercise programs intended to improve the performance of ground crews and facilities.

With the disbanding of Aerospace Defense Command, TAC is now responsible for the defense of US airspace. SAC still provides long-range warning facilities to guard against missile attack, but TAC mans the small force of air-defense radars, control centers and interceptors which now guards the continental USA. The contrast between this tiny force and the massive defenses which guard Soviet airspace is dramatic: the Soviet Air Force allocates 2,500 interceptors, 1,000 SAM sites with 10,000 missiles and a total of 7,000 radars to air defense; the best that TAC can offer is several hundred interceptors backed up by 120 radar sites. No SAMs are deployed as part of the US air defenses.

Above: Even after 20 years service, the Phantom is still an important type in the TAC inventory. Aerodynamic improvements enable it to continue to match its Soviet rivals. Shrike and Standard ARM hang beneath this F-4G Wild Weasel.

The current USAF interceptor force consists of a single squadron of F-15 Eagles, five F-106 squadrons, plus an F-4 squadron based in Iceland. The Air National Guard provides a further five F-106 squadrons, four units equipped with F-4s, plus one armed with the obsolescent F-101 Voodoo. The F-106s will

Below: This EF-111 Electric Fox electronic warfare aircraft was originally a standard USAF-operated F-111A. Converted by Grumman along with 41 other F-111s, it now performs the vital task of reducing the enemy's radar capability.

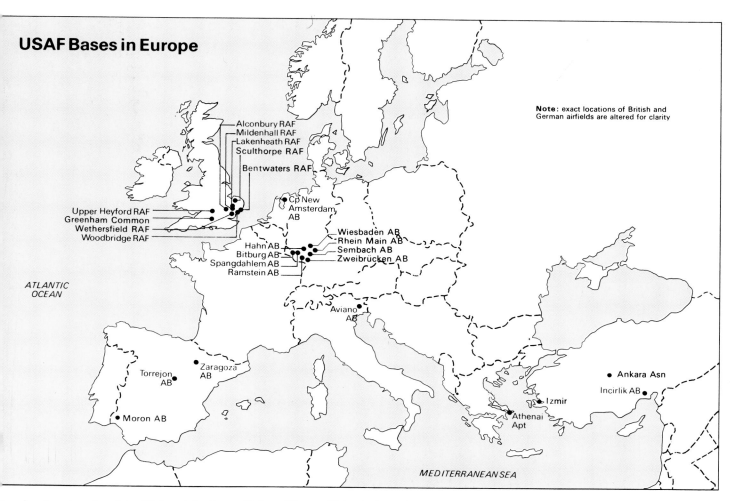

USAF Bases in Europe

Note: exact locations of British and German airfields are altered for clarity

Alconbury RAF
Mildenhall RAF
Lakenheath RAF
Sculthorpe RAF
Bentwaters RAF
Upper Heyford RAF
Greenham Common
Wethersfield RAF
Woodbridge RAF
Cp New Amsterdam AB
Wiesbaden AB
Rhein Main AB
Hahn AB
Sembach AB
Bitburg AB
Zweibrücken AB
Spangdahlem AB
Ramstein AB
Aviano AB
ATLANTIC OCEAN
Torrejon AB
Zaragoza AB
Moron AB
Ankara Asn
Incirlik AB
Izmir
Athenai Apt
MEDITERRANEAN SEA

...ased out and replaced by F-15s, while the ...101 will be replaced by the F-4. The ANG also ...ans an EB-57 equipped "friendly enemy" unit ...sed to exercise the defenses.

552nd Airborne Warning and Control Wing ...erates the E-3A Sentry, with squadrons ...ployed at three bases in the USA and at ...eflavik in Iceland, and Kadena in Okinawa. ...veral E-3s have also been deployed in Saudi ...rabia since 1980.

S Air Forces Europe

...ore than 30 USAF squqdrons serve in the 3rd, ...th and 17th Air Forces which make up the ...nited States Air Forces in Europe (USAFE). ...ke TAC, these are being re-equipped to meet ...e threat posed by next-generation Soviet ...uipment. The F-15C and D replace the earlier ...15A/B standard, while the F-16 is slowly ...placing the veteran F-4. First USAFE unit to ...nvert to the F-16 was the 50th Tactical

Fighter Wing at Hahn in West Germany. F-4s made available by this upgrading may now be issued to other USAFE units or US Allies.

The sparsely-equipped A-10 is more suited to US conditions than to the bad weather prevalent in Western Europe, but both this aircraft and the F-16 are due to be equipped with the LANTIRN FLIR system and associated wide-angle holographic HUD.

"Heavy punch" of USAFE remains seven squadrons of F-111E and F-111F strike aircraft based in the UK. Earlier F-111A models of this variable-geometry fighter-bomber have been rebuilt to create the EF-111 Electric Fox ECM aircraft. While the latter jams hostile radars, USAFE's F-4G Wild Weasel aircraft will use APG-38 homing systems to locate and attack radar installations by means of Shrike, Standard ARM or Maverick missiles, plus unguided ordnance such as the Rockeye cluster munition. From 1986 onwards, these will be supplemented

by the new HARM anti-radar missile.

In the long term, USAFE will receive the AIM-120 Advanced Medium-Range Air-to-Air Missile for use against multiple targets at long range, but for the moment will receive interim high-performance weapons such as the AIM-9M version of Sidewinder which offers better acquisition and tracking and improved resistance to countermeasures, plus the AIM-7M "look-down/shoot-down" version of Sparrow. The monopulse radar seeker fitted to the latter is less vulnerable to deceptive jamming than the earlier versions of the missile.

SAC SR-71 Blackbird and RC-135 reconnaissance aircraft are frequent "guests" of USAFE, operating from RAF Mildenhall in the UK. Additional reconnaissance capability is now available in Europe thanks to the deployment in the UK of the TR-1. This will not attempt to overfly hostile territory, but will fly along the border, using sideways-looking radar to gather information. The Precision Location Strike System planned for this aircraft will be able to locate radar systems and direct anti-radar attacks.

Alaskan Air Command
Alaskan Air Command is equipped with the F-15-equipped 43rd Tactical Fighter Squadron and 21st tactical Fighter Wing, plus the close support facilities afforded by the A-10 Thunderbolts of the 18th Tactical Fighter Squadron and O-2 support from the 25th Tactical Air Support Squadron. A total of 13 Aircraft Control and Warning squadrons operate radar sites scattered throughout Alaska's 586,000 square miles (1,500,000km²) of territory.

Pacific Air Forces
New equipment has transformed the front line of Pacific Air Command's 5th Air Force. The Tactical Fighter Wing at Kadena in Okinawa is fully equipped with three squadrons of F-15C/D Eagles plus E-3A Sentries, while the 8th Tactical Fighter Wing at Kusan in South Korea has been equipped with F-16 Fighting Falcons. Osan AB in Korea also operates the new OA-37B FAC aircraft, a rebuilt version of

---

United States Air Forces in Europe (USAFE) Major Units

Headquarters: Ramstein AB, W. Germany

3rd Air Force (Headquarters: RAF Mildenhall, UK)
16th Air Force (Headquarters: Torrejon, Spain)
17th Air Force (Headquarters: Sembach, W. Germany)

Main Units

Greece
7206th and 7276th Air Base Group (support & communications)

Italy
40th Tactical Group (various USAFE aircraft on rotation)
7275th Air Base Group (support & communications)

Netherlands
32nd Tactical Fighter Squadron (F-15)

Spain
401st Tactical Fighter Wing (F-4)

406th Tactical Fighter Training Wing (KC-135/range support & weapons training)

United Kingdom
20th and 48th Tactical Fighter Wing (F-111)
81st Tactical Fighter Wing (A-10)
10th Tactical Reconnaissance wing (RF-4/F-5)
513th Tactical Airlift Wing (C-130/KC-135)
7020th Air Base Group (KC-135)
7273rd Air Base Group (GLCM cruise missiles)
7274th Air Base Group (support & communications)

W. Germany
36th Tactical Fighter Wing (F-15)
50th Tactical Fighter Wing (F-16)
52nd and 86th Tactical Fighter Wings (F-4)
26th Tactical Reconnaissance Wing (RF-4)
435th Tactical Airlift Wing (C-9/C-130)
600th Tactical Control Wing (command, control & communications)
601st Tactical Control Wing (OV-10/CH-53)
7100th Air Base Group (command, control & communications)
7350th Air Base Group (support & communications)

the A-37 Dragonfly formerly operated by the
US Air Force Reserve.

Military Airlift Command

Even by airline standards, Military Airlift
Command is a formidable organization, operating a fleet which includes 77 wide-bodied aircraft, 275 four-engined jet transports and more
than 250 four-turboprop freighters. The entire
fleet, including the smaller helicopters and
transports, numbers almost 1,000 aircraft.

Long-range mainstay of the Command is the
C-5 Galaxy fleet. Seventy are being rebuilt with
new wings in a program due for completion in
1987, and are expected to serve into the 21st
century. USAF would like to acquire 50 new
strategic transports, and is likely to receive the
C-5B version of the Galaxy. This will incorporate the new wing and improved TF39
turbofans.

In another massive rebuilding program, Lockheed stretched 271 C-141A StarLifters to create
the present C-141B fleet. These incorporate a
refuelling receptacle located in a fairing mounted on top of the forward fuselage, making the
aircraft less dependent on landing rights during
wartime resupply missions.

Main tactical transport is the seemingly
irreplaceable C-130 Hercules. The mid-1970s
YC-14 and YC-15 jet transports were planned as
Hercules replacements, but Congress decided
that the best C-130 replacement was a new C-130
and the program was allowed to die. Latest
projected replacement is the McDonnell
C-17 four-jet transport. Although delayed by
Congress, this could enter service later this
decade.

Aerospace Rescue and Recovery Service
(ARRS) at Scott AFB, Illinois, is probably the
most exotic MAC unit. Its most publicized
activity is combat search and rescue using
specially equipped HC-130 Hercules plus
Sikorsky HH-3 and HH-53 rescue helicopters.
Most complex of the latter is probably the HH-
53H Pave Low 3, which carries a comprehensive
avionics suite for all-weather rescue missions,
including a terrain-following radar, stabilized
FLIR plus Doppler and inertial navigation
units. These rotary-wing types are due to be
joined by the new HH-60D Nighthawk version
of the Black Hawk helicopter.

ARRS also flies various models of C-130 and
C-135 for weather reconnaissance, air sampling
(a means of detecting clandestine nuclear
testing), and to support Space Shuttle and
Stratetic Air Command operations.

Air Training Command

Approximately a fifth of all USAF sorties are
flown by Air Training Command using a fleet of
T-37, T-38 Talon, T-41A, T-43A and UV-18B
aircraft. The new Fairchild T-46 trainer is due
to enter service in 1987 as a replacement for the
veteran T-37. A total of 650 are to be built.

ATC handles initial flying training, plus basic
military and technical training, but can also
handle undergraduate, postgraduate and professional training tasks. Basic flying is handled
by 14th, 47th, 64th, 71st, 80th and 82nd Flying
Training Wings, while the 323rd Flying Training Wing handles navigator training. All are
located in the Central or Southern USA where
the favorable climate creates training conditions greatly superior to those found in most
European nations. As a result, some non-US
NATO air arms send pilots and navigators to
the USA for ATC training, such candidates
making up about a tenth of the total.

At Sheppard AFB, in Texas, home of the 80th
Flying Training Wing, the US and its NATO
Allies have set up a Euro-NATO Joint Jet Pilot
Training program under which USAF and
NATO pilots will train together.

USAF Reserves

The United States is the only nation able to
afford large-scale reserve air arms and to equip
these with modern aircraft. Like the units of the
regular Air Force, Air Force Reserve squadrons
have in many cases been upgraded with better

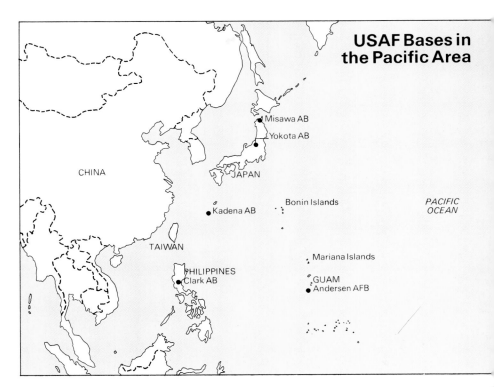

USAF Bases in the Pacific Area

Above: Worldwide political commitments
emphasize the need for a large, efficient
airlift force and the MAC has almost 1,000
transport aircraft and helicopters. The
Hercules forms the tactical element.

Below: Tomorrow's front-line pilots are
today's trainees flying such types as the
T-38s seen here. A replacement for the
T-37 basic trainer has been selected, but
what will replace the T-38?

Military Airlift Command fleet (major aircraft)

Lockheed C-5 Galaxy	77
Lockheed C-141 Starlifter	270
Lockheed C-130 Hercules	259
McDonnell Douglas C-9 (militarized DC-9)	23
Boeing C-137 (militarized 707)	5
Sikorsky CH-3/HH-3	46
Sikorsky CH-53/HH-53	21

USAF strength (Fiscal Year 1983)

Strategic Bombers	363
ICBMs	1,052
Fighter/attack aircraft	3,026
Reconnaissance & electronic warfare	392
Flight-refueling tankers	544
Transports	828
Helicopters	238
Utility, observation, SAR	250
Trainers	1,664
Personnel (military)	599,000
Personnel (civilian)	243,000

quipment such as the A-10, and are due to eceive the F-16. Air Force Reserve is organized nto three air forces—4th, 10th and 14th. Main teeth" flying units are four F-4 squadrons, ve A-10 squadrons, two A-7 squadrons, one Wild Weasel unit equipped with the F105D/F, hree KC-135 tanker squadrons, and 12 squadrons with the C-130.

The Air National Guard is equipping with x-TAC F-4s and A-7s and is also receiving some ew-production A-7s. The ANG boasts a total of 1 squadrons which make up 17 percent of USAF strength. Main combat types are the -4C/D, RF-4C, F-105G, F-106, A-7D, A-10, A-37, C-130 and KC-135.

nadequacies and Continuing Problems

The contribution of the various US Air Force upporting elements to the combat capabilities f the tactical air forces is significant but ifficult to quantify. Easily discernible, however, is the 25 percent Soviet numerical superiity over the US in operational tactical ircraft. Equally visible is the Warsaw Pact's to-1 superiority in ground forces and 5-to-1 uperiority over the armored forces of NATO.

To cope with the Soviets' quantitative advanges US tactical air forces are relying on a umber of qualitative factors:

elow: Such is the efficiency of the huge -5A—it can carry almost every type of S military vehicle—the USAF has decided o order a modernized version known as the -5B with a new wing and engines.

Above: The Hercules replacement? A McDonnell Douglas project, known as the C-17, proposed as a follow-on transport from 1990 for the C-130 and C-141.

Below: Stringent budgetary cuts forced the USAF into "stretching" each of its fleet of 270 C-141 StarLifters. The result was the equivalent of 90 new aircraft.

a continuing, though diminishing lead in technology;

modernization of tactical forces after a long relative lull in production;

superior aircraft such as the F-15 and F-16 which are expected to outperform any opposition throughout the 1980s;

superior capabilities for surveillance, command, control, and communication;

improved defense suppression techniques, especially in the currently marginal electronics countermeasures capability;

balancing costs, quantity and quality through the concept of the high-low mix;

superior capabilities of American precision guided munitions;

more highly trained and combat-experienced personnel;

superior strategic and tactical air mobility to help compensate for potential Soviet geographical advantages;

superior logistics support of combat forces;

superior tactical nuclear capability;

potential reinforcement of tactical forces, under some scenarios, by the conventional or nuclear capability of strategic forces.

Undoubtedly, these factors are impressive to the Soviets. Many analysts believe that they would be sufficient to cope with numerically superior Soviet tactical air forces in the event of war. Less certain is their ability to compensate for Warsaw Pact superiority on the ground. Hopefully, USAF's tactical air forces, under the strategic nuclear umbrella, will not have to prove the point in combat.

Though the American aerospace industry can in general produce better aircraft and supporting hardware than any other country, and certainly can do it quicker, the price is a severe deterrent to any US administration. Even that of President Reagan, which has been trying to rectify the deferred and negative decisions of the 1970s, has had to look for ways to cut $13

Below: The A-10 Thunderbolt might be one of the most heavily armored ground-attack aircraft ever built, but will it survive in a Central Front war in Europe? The pilots say it would; and that it would give a good account of itself.

billion from the defense budget between now and FY84 (Fiscal Year 1984, which ends on June 30 of that year). Several commentators have said that this means actual cuts in "total obligational authority" of roughly twice this amount, and it means that some major programs will have to go.

In the quality of its hardware, and the skill, dedication and professionalism of its people, the USAF has never been as good as today, but in its strength to preserve world peace the picture is rather bleak. Abandonment of the nuclear tripwire policy of the 1955–65 era meant that there had to be immensely powerful forces ready to deter aggression anywhere. As these forces have shrunk, so has the President tried to muster a Rapid Deployment Force intended to make a small but effective sharp cutting edge available within 24 hours almost anywhere. Such a force is ill-adapted to counter either the colossal manpower and firepower of the Soviet Union or the religious fanatics and urban terrorists who have chosen to prey upon American lives and property in recent years. Moreover, for any really large force the USAF would be hard-pressed to provide sufficient airlift. Even if the C-5A did not have to be re-winged, the need for global airlift over intercontinental distances, possibly terminating at austere airstrips, cannot at present be met, and newer types (KC-10s and C-17s) cannot be procured in anything approaching the necessary numbers.

As detailed above, apart from a very small force of some 50 FB-111A bombers, the entire winged strength of Strategic Air Command continues to reside in the remaining ageing B-52G and H bombers, although the need for a modern long-range deterrent aircraft has been self-evident for 20 years, and the only encouragement that can be drawn from the fact that none has been provided is that today the B-70 (RS-70) would not be the optimum aircraft, just as the B-1 will not be the optimum in 1990. So much time has gone by that any B-1 is better than nothing, and the B-1B, if put into the inventory as at present planned from 1986, will restore credibility to the deterrent that has kept the peace for so long.

For the more distant future a "stealth" bomber which has been under study for many

years could be very important indeed, if the U[S] has the will to produce it. The word "stealth" has come to mean an aircraft offering minima[l] signatures to defensive detection system[s] Stealth characteristics can be achieved by [a] combination of aircraft shape, exterior surfac[e] quality, materials and several other factor[s] most importantly the EW (electronic warfar[e] subsystems carried on board the aircraf[t] Surviving in hostile airspace by high fligh[t] speed or altitude is no longer viable but, afte[r] prolonged effort, stealth technology ha[s]

Distribution of Personnel
(Typical pattern in early 1980s)

US Territory	456,100
West Germany	36,600
United Kingdom	22,400
Japan & Okinawa	14,200
South Korea	9,300
Philippines	8,500
Spain	4,800
Italy	4,200
Turkey	3,800
Panama	1,800
Canada	250
Saudi Arabia	310
Egypt	80
Other European locations	7,200
Other E. Asian/Pacific locations	300
Other Locations in Western Hemisphere	60
Other locations in Middle East, Africa & Asia	90

Above: The best defensive equipment US technology can devise is packed into these SAC B-52s, but massive Soviet defenses would prevent these big aircraft from even getting to their targets.

Below: Phantoms still equip a number of squadrons in USAF Europe, but this large and not-so-young two-seater is now well supported by F-15 fighters and increasing numbers of the smaller F-16.

Main Overseas Air Bases

Azores: Lajes
Greece: Hellenikon, Iraklion
Greenland: Sondestrom, Thule
Iceland: Keflavik
Italy: Aviano, Cosimo, San Vito
Japan: Kadena, Misawa, Yokota
Netherlands: Camp New Amsterdam
Panama: Howard
Philippines: Clark
S. Korea: Kunsan, Kwang Ju, Osan, Suwon, Taegu
Spain: Torrejon, Zaragoza
Turkey: Ankara, Incirlik, Izmir
United Kingdom: Alconbury, Bentwaters, Chicksands, Fairford, Greenham Common, Lakenheath, Mildenhall, Upper Heyford, Woodbridge
W. Germany: Bitburg, Hahn, Hessish-Oldendorf, Linsey, Ramstein, Rhein-Main, Sembach, Spangdahlem, Tempelhof, Zweibrucken

reached the point at which it dominates the design of offensive aircraft, not excepting cruise missiles. The USAF is now funding at an increasing rate an ATB (Advanced Technology Bomber) which it is hoped will supplement the B-1B in the SAC inventory from about 1992. Northrop's appointment as prime contractor generated slightly misleading speculation that the ATB would be a YB-49 type of flying wing. The California company is teamed with Boeing and Vought, with GE providing the vitally important "zero signature" propulsion.

In the much shorter term Lockheed, which is supplying the TR-1 reconnaissance aircraft designed to non-stealth technology, has for some time been using stealth technology in a relatively small tactical platform called CSIRS (Covert Survivable Inweather Recon/Strike), intended to enter USAF service as early as 1983-4. Using some of the advanced aerodynamics of the SR-71 and GTD-21 RPV, the CSIRS tries to avoid being shot down on multi-sensor reconnaissance and precision attack missions by a combination of high performance and as much stealth technology as could be incorporated in the timescale, for the available budget. It is planned to deploy 20 CSIRS aircraft, with possibly more to follow of a more advanced derived type, but the work is largely classified and cannot be referred to as a regular USAF type in the inventory that follows.

At a totally different level, another machine not included in the following inventory is the Piper Enforcer. Unbelievably, this is derived from the P-51 Mustang, first flown to British order in 1940 and subsequently one of the best fighter/bomber aircraft of World War II and the Korean war. During the Vietnam war it often came into discussion, and Cavalier Aircraft sold almost new-build P-51s to the Air Force and Army, though only in small numbers for training and evaluation. Piper, a leading general aviation builder, was asked to produce a largely redesigned Mustang with a turboprop engine to meet a possible need for a light close-support attack aircraft. Piper announced the start of flight testing of the first Enforcer on 29 April 1971, the chosen engine being the Lycoming T55. Subsequently, Piper made no further announcement, and many observers were surprised when in 1981 the company was awarded a three-year contract, for some $2 million, to fly two further Enforcers with many new features. That there must be a place for a very small, agile, propeller- or fan-engined tactical aircraft, pulling 7g turns at about 300 knots and able to kill tanks and other battlefield targets, appears indisputable. The wisdom of basing it on even a redesigned Mustang is highly questionable.

Today's "Mustang", of course, is the F-16, and this is perhaps the brightest star in the entire Air Force inventory. Out of a very

Above: No base commander would wish to be confronted by this scene in wartime, yet the US fixed basing policy remains one dangerous shortcoming in American defense planning.

limited Light Weight Fighter program, whose main objective was to see if a useful fighter could be made smaller and cheaper than the F-15, has come a tactical aircraft whose limitations are already hard to probe and are being pushed wider all the time. Perhaps the single event that did most to convert the doubters—whose opinion of the F-16 rested on supposed

Below: One of the very few all-weather, low-level strike aircraft available in the West is the F-111. In wartime F-111s are tasked with deep penetration missions into Warsaw Pact territory aimed at hitting airfields and back-area targets.

inadequate avionics, so that it could not do a real job in the bad weather of northern Europe—was the RAF's annual tac-bombing contest held in mid-1981. A team of seven F-16s from the 388th TFW not only won the contest, beating such specialized attack systems as the Jaguar Buccaneer and F-111F, but set a remarkable new record in scoring 7,831 of the possible 8,000 points. This aircraft will continue to develop for at least the next 20 years, and will probably be the most numerous aircraft in the inventory for most of that time.

Dangerous Basing Policy
Almost the only shortcoming of the F-16, and it is a shortcoming of every other aeroplane in the USAF, is that it is tied to airfields whose precise position is known to potential enemies. Those potential enemies having the capability to do so, such as the Soviet Union, could wipe out those bases in minutes. It is simply a matter of everyday fact that, should it choose to do so, the Soviet Union could suddenly and totally destroy every airfield used by all the air forces of NATO, including every operating base of the USAF. It would then be too late to rectify the folly of not deploying strong forces of V/STOL aircraft dispersed so completely through the countryside—if possible at locations offering natural ski jumps—that no amount of satellite reconnaissance could find them, and the task of destroying them by missiles would be uneconomic.

Since 1960 the USAF's position on V/STOL has been variously negative, non-existent and ridiculous. The fact that the only V/STOL aircraft actually deployed (in the West) has been of British origin has served to warp and diminish USAF interest in the only survivable form of modern airpower.

Billions spent on B-1B, stealth aircraft and even the agile F-16 will be wasted if at 11 tomorrow morning someone presses a button and sends the whole lot up in fireballs as they stand on their airfield ramps. There would then no longer be any USAF, except perhaps for the planning staffs in the Pentagon and at Air Force Systems Command, who would be left to ponder on where they went wrong. . . .

Above: Small, cheap and available—the lightweight F-16 could be termed the USAF's savior. Over the next 20 years, this combat-proven aircraft will be developed far beyond its present performance envelope. Hill-based F-16s are seen here.

Below: The Eagle is considered to be the match of any Soviet fighter, current or presently projected. However, given Russian numerical superiority of 3–1, these USAFE Bitburg-based aircraft would find the going pretty rough.

US Combat Aircraft

Bill Gunston, **Assistant Compiler of Jane's** *All the World's Aircraft*; **author of many technical books and papers on military affairs.**

This catalogue includes the major combat aircraft in service with the US armed forces, and important projects under development. They are arranged in alphabetical order of manufacturers' names.

Bell 209 HueyCobra

AH-1G to -1T HueyCobra (data for -1S)

Origin: Bell Helicopter Textron, Fort Worth.
Type: Two-seat combat helicopter.
Engine: 1,800shp Lycoming T53-L-703 turboshaft.
Dimensions: Main-rotor diameter 44ft (13.4m); overall length (rotors turning) 52ft 11½in (16.14m); length of fuselage 44ft 5in (13.54m); height 13ft 5½in (4.1m).
Weights: Empty 6,598lb (2,993kg); maximum 10,000lb (4,536kg).
Performance: Maximum speed (TOW configuration) 141mph (227km/h); max rate of climb (SL, rated power) 1,620ft (494m)/min; service ceiling (rated power) 12,200 ft (3,719m); hovering ceiling in ground effect, same: range (max fuel, SL, 8% reserve) 315 miles (507km).
Armament: M65 system with nose telescope sight and crew helmet sights for cueing and guiding eight TOW missiles on outboard underwing pylons; chin turret (to 100th AH-1S) M28 with 7.62mm Minigun and 40mm M129 grenade launcher with 300 bombs, (from No 101) GE Universal turret with 20mm M197 three-barrel gun (or alternative 30mm); also wide range of cluster/fuel-air explosive and other weapons or five types of rocket fired from 7 or 19-tube launchers.
History: First flight 7 September 1965; combat service June 1967 (TOW-Cobra January 1973, AH-1S March 1977).

Below: *Canned Heat* was a standard early AH-1G, with M28 system and lateral rocket launchers. It served in the Vietnam war with the USA's "Blue Max" 20th Aerial Rocket Artillery.

Development: First flown in 1965 after only six months of development the HueyCobra is a combat development of the UH-1 Iroquois family. It combines the dynamic parts—engine, transmission and rotor system—of the original Huey with a new streamlined fuselage providing for a gunner in the front and pilot above and behind him and for a wide range of fixed and power-aimed armament systems. The first version was the US Army AH-1G, with 1,100hp T53 engine, of which 1,124 were delivered, including eight to the Spanish Navy for anti-ship strike and 38 as trainers to the US Marine Corps. The AH-1Q is an anti-armor version often called TOWCobra because it carries eight TOW missile pods as well as the appropriate sighting system. The AH-1J SeaCobra of the Marine Corps and Iranian Army has twin engines, the 1,800hp UAC Twin Pac having two T400 power sections driving one shaft. Latest versions are the -1Q, -1R, -1S and -1T, with more power and new equipment. All Cobras can have a great variety of armament.

Above: One of the very latest AH-S TowCobras firing a Tow missile; note flat-plate canopy.

Below: One of the first Tow firings from the first missile-armed version, the interim AH-1Q, probably pictured in mid-1973. Note the revised nose outline caused by the large Hughes TSU (telescopic sight unit) into which the gunner is looking.

Bell "Huey" family

XH-40, UH-1 Iroquois series
(Models 204, 205 and 212)

Origin: Bell Helicopter Textron, Fort Worth.

Type: Multi-role utility and transport helicopter.

Engine: Originally, one Lycoming T53 free-turbine turboshaft rated at 700-640shp, later rising in stages to 825, 930, 1,100 and 1,400shp; (212) 1,800 shp P&WC PT6T-3 (T400) coupled turboshafts, flat-rated at 1,250shp and with 900shp immediately available from either following failure of the other.

Dimensions: Diameter of twin-blade main rotor (204, UH-1B, C) 44ft 0in (13.41m), (205, 212) 48ft 0in (14.63m) (tracking tips, 48ft 2¼in, 14.69m); (214) 50ft 0in (15.24m); overall length (rotors turning) (early) 53ft 0in (16.15m) (virtually all modern versions) 57ft 3¼in (17.46m); height overall modern, typical) 14ft 4¾in (4.39m).

Weights: Empty (XH-40) about 4,000lb (1,814kg), (typical 205) 4,667lb (2,11kg), (typical 212) 5,549lb (2,517kg); maximum loaded (XH-40) 5,800lb (2,631kg), (typical 205) 9,500lb (4,309kg), 212/UH-1N 10,500lb (4,762kg).

Performance: Maximum speed (all) typically 127mph (204km/h); econ cruise speed, usually same; max range with useful payload, typically 248 miles (400km).

Armament: See text.

History: First flight (XH-40) 22 October 1956, (production UH-1) 1958, (205) August 1961, (212) 1969.

Development: Used by more air forces, and built in greater numbers, than any other military aircraft since World War II, the "Huey" family of helicopters grew from a single prototype, the XH-40, for the US Army. Over years the gross weight has been almost multiplied by three, though the size has changed only slightly. Early versions seat eight to ten, carried the occasional machine-gun, and included the TH-1L Seawolf trainer for the US Navy. Prior to 1962 the Army/Navy designation was basically HU-1, which gave rise to the name Huey, though the (rarely used) official name Iroquois. Since 1962 the basic designation has been UH-1 (utility helicopter type 1). In August 1961 Bell flew the first Model 205 with many changes of which the greatest was a longer fuselage giving room for up to 14 passengers of troops, or six litters (stretchers) and an attendant, or up 3,880lb (1,759kg) of cargo. All versions have blind-flying instruments, night lighting, FM/VHF/UHF radios, IFF transponder, DF/VOR, powered controls and searchlight. Options include a hook for a slung load, rescue hoist and various fits of simple weapons or armor. Newest and most important of the Model 205 helicopters in US military service is the UH-1H, which remained in production until 1980. Ten have been converted to UH-1H Quick Fix EW (electronic-warfare) machines, but this role has been taken over by the more powerful EH-60A. Two were given augmented avionics and special equipment as UH-1V medevac transports. The US Army plans to retain at least 2,700 improved UH-1Hs beyond the year 2000 for a wide range of duties, and apart from fitting glassfibre composite blades they will be completely upgraded with over 220 new items or improvements including a radar-warning receiver, chaff/flare dispenser, IR jammer, exhaust IR suppressor, radar altimeter, DME and secure communications even in NOE (nap of the Earth) flying. The Model 212 twin-engine helicopter is used by the US Navy, Marines and Air Force (total of 300) with designation UH-1N.

Above: Standard utility model of the Huey in US service (all branches of the armed forces) is the T53-powered UH-1H, two of which are seen on armed assault with M60 guns in the doorway.

Above: Troops of the USA 1st Cavalry (Airmobile) jump from a UH-1D during Operation Oregon in Vietnam in August 1967.

Bell Kiowa and JetRanger

OH-58A to D and TH-57

Origin: Bell Helicopter Textron, Fort Worth.

Type: Light multi-role helicopter.

Engine: (OH-58A, TH-57A) one 317shp Allison T63-700 turboshaft, (OH-58C) 420shp T63-720, (OH-58D) 650shp Allison 250-C30R.

Dimensions: Diameter of two-blade main rotor 35ft 4in (10.77m); length overall (rotors turning) 40ft 11¾in (12.49m); height 9ft 6½in (2.91m).

Weights: Empty (C) 1,585lb (719kg), (D) 2,825lb (1,281kg); maximum (C) 3,200lb (1,451kg), (D) 4,500lb (2,041kg).

Performance: Maximum speed (C) 139mph (224km/h), (D) 147mph (237km/h); service ceiling (C) 19,000ft (5,791m), (D) over 12,000ft (3,658m); range (SL, no weapons, 10% reserve) 299 miles (481km), (D) no reserve) 345 miles (556km).

Armament: Usually none (see text).

History: First flight (OH-4A) 8 December 1962, (206A) 10 January 1966, production OH-58C) 1978, (D) 1983.

Development: First flown as the OH-4A, loser in the US Army Light Observation Helicopter contest of 1962, the 206 was marketed as the civil JetRanger, this family growing to encompass the more powerful 206B and more capacious 206L LongRanger. In 1968 the US Army re-opened the LOH competition, naming Bell now winner and buying 2,200 OH-58A was similar to the 206A but with larger main rotor. US Navy trainers are the TH-57A SeaRangers, the 36 survivors of this model being supplemented in 1982 by seven more. Since 1976 Bell has been rebuilding 275 OH-58A Kiowas to OH-58C standard with uprated engine, flat-plate canopy to reduce glint, new instrument panel, improved avionics and many minor improvements. Standard armament kit, not always fitted, is the M27 with a 7.62mm Minigun firing ahead. In 1981 Bell was named winner of the AHIP (Army Helicopter Improvement Program) for a 'near-term scout'. The first of five prototype Model 406 AHIP machines should fly before this book appears and a total of 578 existing OH-58As could be rebuilt to AHIP standard with designation OH-58D, at an estimated cost in 1981 dollars of $2 billion. Features include a new rotor with four composite blades driven by a much more powerful T63-type (Model 250) engine, very comprehensive protection systems and a mast-mounted ball with TV and FLIR (forward-looking infra-red), laser ranger/designator, inertial navigation and one or two pairs of MLMS missiles.

Below: Flat glass cockpit panels and IR-suppressed exhaust stacks identify this Kiowa as uprated to OH-58C standard.

Boeing B-52 Stratofortress

B-52D, G and H

Origin: Boeing Airplane Company (from May 1961 The Boeing Company), Seattle, Washington.

Type: Heavy bomber and missile platform.

Engines: (D) eight 12,1001lb (5,489kg) thrust P&WA J57-19W or 29W turbojets, (G) eight 13,750lb (6,237kg) thrust P&WA J57-43W or -43WB turbojets, (H) eight 17,000lb (7,711kg) thrust P&WA TF33-1 or -3 turbofans.

Dimensions: Span 185ft 0in (56.39m); length (D, and G/H as built) 157ft 7in (48.0m), (G/H modified) 160ft 11in (49.05m); height (D) 48ft 4½in (14.7m), (G/H) 40ft 8in (12.4m); wing area 4,000sq ft (371.6m²).

Weights: Empty (D) about 175,000lb (79,380kg), (G/H) about 195,000lb (88,450kg); loaded (D) about 470,000lb (213,200kg), (G) 505,000lb (229,000kg), (H) 505,000 at takeoff, inflight refuel to 566,000lb (256,738kg).

Performance: Maximum speed (true airspeed, clean), (D) 575mph (925km/h), (G/H) 595mph (957km/h); penetration speed at low altitude (all) about 405mph (652km/h, Mach 0.53); service ceiling (D) 45,000ft (13.7km), (G) 46,000ft (14.0km), (H) 47,000ft (14.3km); range (max fuel, no external bombs/missiles, optimum hi-alt cruise) (D) 7.370 miles (11,861km), (G) 8,406 miles (13,528km), (H) 10,130 miles (16,303km); takeoff run, (D) 11,100ft (3,383m), (G) 10,000ft (3,050m), (H) 9,500ft (2895m).

Armament: (D) four 0.5in (12.7mm) guns in occupied tail turret, MD-9 system, plus 84 bombs of nominal 500lb (227kg) in bomb bay plus 24 of nominal 750lb (340kg) on wing pylons, total 60,000lb (27,215kg); (G) four 0.5in (12.7mm) guns in remote-control tail turret, ASG-15 system, plus 8 nuclear bombs or up to 20 SRAM, ALCM or mix (eight on internal dispenser plus 12 on wing pylons); (H) single 20mm six-barrel gun in remote-control tail turret, ASG-21 system, plus bombload as G.

History: First flight 15 April 1952; later, see text.

Development: Destined to be the longest-lived aircraft in all aviation history, the B-52 was designed to the very limits of the state of the art in 1948-49 to meet the demands of SAC for a long-range bomber and yet achieve the high performance possible with jet propulsion. The two prototypes had tandem pilot positions and were notable for their great size and fuel capacity, four double engine pods and four twin-wheel landing trucks which could be slewed to crab the aircraft on to the runway in a crosswind landing. The B-52A changed to a side-by-side pilot cockpit in the

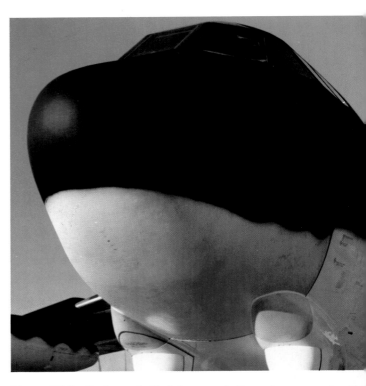

Above: While the lower half of the nose is the radome covering the scanner of the main radar, the twin ventral blisters cover the sensor heads of the EVS (electro-optical viewing system), with a steerable low-light TV and a forward-looking infra-red.

Right: In a cost-conscious SAC the expense of deploying the 32ft (9.75m) braking parachute is seldom justfied—though brakes are expensive as well and one thing the B-52 has never had is thrust reversers. This B-52H was pictured in 1981 complete with all the avionic updates including ALQ-153 pulse-doppler blisters on the fin to warn of approaching missiles.

Boeing C-135 family

C-135 Stratolifter and KC-135 Stratotanker family (data KC-135A)

Origin: Boeing Airplane Company (from May 1961 The Boeing Company), Seattle, Washington.

Type: Tankers, transports, EW, Elint, command-post and research aircraft.

Engines: (A and derivatives) four 13,750lb (6,237kg) thrust P&WA J57-59W or -43WB turbojets, (B and derivatives) four 18,000lb (8,165kg) thrust P&WA TF33-3 turbofans, (RE) four 22,000lb (9,979kg) thrust CFM56-1B11 turbofans.

Dimensions: Span (basic) 130ft 10in (39.88m); length (basic) 134ft 6in (40.99m); height (basic) 38ft 4in (11,68m) (tall fin) 41ft 8in (12.69m; wing area 2,433sq ft (226m²).

Weights: Empty (KC-135A basic) 98,466lb (44,664kg), (KC, operating weight) 106,306lb (48,220kg), (C-135B) 102,300lb (46,403kg); loaded (KC, original) 297,000lb (134,719kg), (KC, later max) 316,000lb (143,338kg), (C-135B) 275,000lb (124,740kg) (typical of special variants).

Performance: Maximum speed (all) about 580mph (933km/h); typical high-speed cruise, 532mph (856km/h) at 35,000ft (10.7km); initial climb (J57, typical) 1,290ft (393m)/min, (TF33) 4,900ft (1,494m)/min; service ceiling (KC, full load) 36,000ft (10.9km), (C-135B) 44,000ft (13.4km); mission radius (KC) 3,450 miles (5,552km) to offload 24,000lb (10,886kg) transfer fuel, 1,150 miles (1,950km) to offload 120,000lb (54,432kg); field length (KC, ISA+17°C) 13,700ft (4,176m).

Armament: None.

History: First flight 31 August 1956, variants see text.

Development: Boeing risked more than the company's net worth to build a prototype jetliner, first flown in July 1954. An important factor behind the gamble was the belief the USAF would buy a jet tanker/transport to replace the Boeing KC-97 family, and this belief was justified by the announcement of an initial order for 29 only three weeks after the company prototype flew, and long before it had done any inflight refuelling tests. The KC-135A Stratotanker differed only in minor respects from the original prototype, whereas the civil 707 developed in a parallel programme was a totally fresh design with a wider fuselage, airframe of 2024 alloy designed on fail-safe principles and totally revised systems. The KC-135A was thus a rapid programme and deliveries began on 30 April 1957, building up to a frantic 20 per month and eventually reaching 732 aircraft.

The basic KC-135A has a windowless main fuselage with 80 tip-up troop or ground-crew seats and a cargo floor with tiedown fittings. Fuel is carried in 12 wing tanks and nine in the fuselage, only one of the latter being above the main floor (at the extreme tail). All but 1,000 US gal (3,785 lit) may be

used as transfer fuel, pumped out via a Boeing high-speed extensible boom steered by a boom operator lying prone in the bottom of the rear fuselage. Only one receiver aircraft can be refuelled at a time, keeping station by watching rows of lights along the underside of the forward fuselage. The original short fin was later superseded by a tall fin and powered rudder, and many tankers were given an ARR (air refuelling receiver) boom receptacle. The KC force numbers 615 active aircraft in 35 squadrons, including 8 aircraft in Reserve units. The 100th ARW (Air Refueling Wing) at Beale AFB exclusively uses the KC-135Q with special avionics and JP-7 fuel for the SR-71 aircraft.

NASA tested a modified KC-135 with large winglets, but though these reduced drag by some eight per cent, calculated to save about 23 million gallons (105 million litres) of fuel per year for the USAF tanker force, they have not been fitted to squadron aircraft. Since 1975 lower wing skins have been replaced, extending life by 27,000h per airframe, and in 1983-8 some 300 tankers are being converted to KC-135R standard with CFM56

ose and entered service in August 1954, becoming operational in June 955. Subsequently 744 aircraft were built in eight major types, all of which ave been withdrawn except the B-52D, G and H.

The B-52D fleet numbered 170 (55-068/-117, 56-580/-630 built at eattle and 55-049/-067, 55-673/-680 and 56-657/-698 built at Wichita) elivered at 20 per month alongside the same rate for KC-135 tankers in upport. The B-52G was the most numerous variant, 193 being delivered om early 1959 (57-6468/-6520, 58-158/-258 and 59-2564/-2602, all om Wichita), introducing a wet (integral-tank) wing which increased ternal fuel from 35,550 to 46,575 US gal and also featured shaft-driven enerators, roll control by spoilers only, powered tail controls, injection ater in the leading edge, a short vertical tail, rear gunner moved to the main ressurized crew compartment and an inner wing stressed for a large pylon n each side. The final model, the B-52H, numbered 102 (60-001/-062 and 1-001/-040), and was essentially a G with the new TF33 fan engine and a ew tail gun.

During the Vietnam war the B-52D was structurally rebuilt for HDB (high-ensity bombing) with conventional bombs, never considered in the original esign. The wings were given inboard pylons of great length for four tandem iplets of bombs on each side, and as noted in the data 108 bombs could be rried in all with a true weight not the 'book value' given but closer to 9,100lb (40,400kg). Another far-reaching and costly series of structural odifications was needed on all models to permit sustained operations at low level, to keep as far as possible under hostile radars, again not previously considered. The newest models, the G and H were given a stability augmentation system from 1969 to improve comfort and airframe life in turbulent dense air. From 1972 these aircraft were outfitted to carry the SRAM (Short-Range Attack Missile), some 1,300 of which are still with the SAC Bomb Wings. Next came the EVS (Electro-optical Viewing System) which added twin chin bulges. The Phase VI ECM (electronic counter-measures) cost $362.5 million from 1973. Quick Start added cartridge engine starters to the G and H for a quick getaway to escape missile attack. Next came a new threat-warning system, a satellite link and 'smart noise' jammers to thwart enemy radars. From 1980 the venerable D-force was updated by a $126.3 million digital nav/bombing system. Further major changes to the G and H include the OAS (offensive avionics system) which is now in progress costing $1,662 million. The equally big CMI (cruise-missile interface) will eventually fit the G-force for 12 AGM-86B missiles on the pylons; 173 aircraft are being converted and the first 12 became operational at Griffiss AFB in December 1982. Later, probably about 1986, the bomb bays may be rebuilt to carry an ALCM dispenser, and the USAF has an option to have 96 B-52H bombers to carry ALCM from 1984.

Altogether about 340 B-52s remain in SAC's active inventory, 70 being conventional-bomb D-models and 270 the very different and more sophisticated G and H. These equip 17 Bomb Wings all with home bases in the Continental US. A further 187 aircraft are in storage.

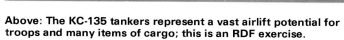

Above: The KC-135 tankers represent a vast airlift potential for troops and many items of cargo; this is an RDF exercise.

Left: SAC uses 14 EC-135C airborne command posts, which retain the boom but have TF33 engines and a mass of extra aerials.

135A, radio link (SAC post-attack command control system); EC-135B, AF Systems Command, ex-RIA (Range Instrumented Aircraft) mainly twice-rebuilt; EC-135C, SAC command posts; EC-135G, ICBM launch and radio link (with boom); EC-135H, airborne command posts; EC-135J, airborne command posts (Pacaf); EC-135K, airborne command posts (TAC); EC-135L, special SAC relay platforms; EC-135N, now C-135N, Apollo range, four with A-LOTS pod tracker; EC-135P, communications/command posts; KC-135A, original designation retained for SAC relay links; RC-135R, special recon/EW rebuilds; NC135A, USAF, NASA and AEC above-ground nuclear-test and other radiation studies; NKC-135A, Systems Command fleet for ECM/ECCM, laser, ionosphere, missile vulnerability, icing, comsat, weightless, boom and other research; RC135B and C, recon aircraft with SLAR cheeks and other sensors; RC135D, different SLARs and thimble noses; RC-135E, glassfibre forward fuselage and inboard wing pods; RC-135M, numerous electronic installations, fan engines; RC-135S, most M installations plus many others; RC-135T, single special SAC aircraft; RC-135U, special sensors and aerials cover almost entire airframe, including SLAR cheeks, extended tailcone and various chin, dorsal, ventral and fin aerials; RC-135V, rebuild of seven Cs and one U with nose thimble, wire aerials and ventral blades; RC-135W, latest recon model mostly rebuilt from M with SLAR cheeks added; WC-135B, standard MAC weather platforms.

gines giving 95 per cent smaller noise footprint, better takeoff and climb d 150 per cent more transfer fuel at long range. Another 18 were re-gined in 1982 with TF33 (JT3D-3B) engines taken from retired American lines 707s, becoming KC-135Es.

MATS, now MAC, bought 15 C-135A and 30 C-135B Stratolifter nsports, the Bs with fan engines with reversers and much sprightlier rformance with less noise and smoke. These remained windowless but d the refuelling boom removed (though retaining the operator's blister) d were equipped for 126 troops or 89,000lb (40,370kg) cargo loaded ough a large door forward on the left side. In MATS these aircraft were on replaced by the C-141. The final new-build versions were the four RC-5A survey/mapping aircraft for MATS and ten RC-135B for strategic connaissance. Thus, total C-135 production for the USAF numbered 808, mpleted in February 1965.

Since then the family has swelled by modification to become perhaps the st diverse in aviation history, the following all being USAF variants: EC-

Boeing E-3 Sentry

E-3A

Origin: Boeing Aerospace Company, Kent, Washington.
Type: Airborne Warning and Control System (AWACS) platform.
Engines: Four 21,000lb (952kg) thrust P&WA TF33-100/100A turbofans.
Dimensions: Span 145ft 9in (44,42m); length 152ft 11in (46.61m); height 41ft 4in (12.6m) (over fin); wing area 3,050sq ft (283.4m²).
Weights: Empty, not disclosed but about 162,000lb (73,480kg), loaded 325,000lb (147,400kg).
Performance: Maximum speed 530mph (853km/h); normal operating speed, about 350mph (563km/h); service ceiling, over 29,000ft (8.85km); endurance on station 1,000 miles (1,609km) from base, 6h.
Armament: None.
History: First flight (EC-137D) 5 February 1972, (E-3A) 31 October 1975; service delivery (E-3A) 24 March 1977.

Development: The USAF had been one of the pioneers of overland surveillance platforms, mainly using EC-121 Warning Stars (based on the Super Constellation, and continuing in unpublicized service until almost 1980). During the 1960s radar technology had reached the point at which, with greater power and rapid digital processing, an OTH (over the horizon) capability could be achieved, plus clear vision looking almost straight down to detect and follow high-speed aircraft flying only just above the Earth's surface. One vital ingredient was the pulse-doppler kind of radar, in which the 'doppler shift' in received frequency caused by relative motion between the target and the radar can be used to separate out all reflections except those from genuine moving targets. Very clever signal processing is needed to eliminate returns from such false 'moving targets' as leaves violently disturbed by wind, and the most difficult of all is the motion of the sea surface and blown spray in an ocean gale. For this reason even more clever radars are needed for the overwater mission, and the USAF did not attempt to accomplish it until quite recently.

While Hughes and Westinghouse fought to develop the new ODR

Boeing E-4 AABNCP

E-4B

Origin: Boeing Aerospace Company, Kent, Washington.
Type: Advanced airborne command post.
Engines: Four 52,500lb (23,814kg) thrust General Electric F103-100 turbofans.
Dimensions: Span 195ft 8in (59.64m); leight 231ft 4in (70.5m); height 63ft 5in (19.33m); wing area 5,500sq ft (511m²).
Weights: Empty, not disclosed but about 410,000lb (186 tonnes); loaded 820,000lb (371,945kg).
Performance: Maximum speed, 700,000lb (317,515kg) at 30,000ft (9,144m), 602mph (969km/h); typical cruising speed, 583mph (939km/h) at 35,000ft (10,670m); maximum range with full tanks, 7,100 miles (11,426km); takeoff field length, ISA, 10,400ft (317m); cruise ceiling, 45,000ft (13,715m).
Armament: None.
History: First flight (747 prototype) 9 February 1969, (E-4A) 13 June 1973.

Development: This unique variant of the commercial 747 transport is being procured in small numbers to replace the various EC-135 airborne command posts of the US National Military Command System and SAC. Under the 481B AABNCP (Advanced Airborne National Command Post) programme the Air Force Electronic Systems Division awarded Boeing a contract in February 1973 for the first two unequipped aircraft, designated E-4A and powered by JT9D engines, to which a third aircraft was added in July 1973. E-Systems won the contract to instal interim equipment in these three E-4A aircraft, the first of which was delivered to Andrews AFB in December 1974. The next two were delivered in 1975.

The third E-4A differed in being powered by the GE F103 engine, and this

was made standard and subsequently retrofitted to the first two aircraft. December 1973 a fourth aircraft was contracted for, and this was fitted wit more advanced equipment resulting in the designation E-4B. All AABNC aircraft have been brought up to the same standard and are designated E 4B. The first E-4B ('75-0125), the fourth in the E-4 series, was delivered c 21 December 1979. The E-4B has accommodation for a larger battle sta on its 4,620 sq ft (429.2m²) main deck, which is divided into six operatin areas: the National Comand Authorities area, conference room, briefin room, battle staff, communications control centre and rest area. The flig deck includes a special navigation station (not in 747s) and crew rest are essential for air-refuelled missions lasting up to 72 hours. Lobe areas und the main deck house technical controls and stores for on-board maintenanc

One of the world's most costly military aircraft types, the E-4B is designe for unique capabilities. Its extraordinary avionics, mainly communications b including many other types of system, were created by a team includin Electrospace Systems, Collins, Rockwell, RCA and Burroughes, co-ordinate by E-Systems and Boeing. Each engine drives two 150kVA alternators, an a large air-conditioning system (separate from that for the main cabin) provided to cool the avionics compartments. Nuclear thermal shielding extensive, and among the communications are an LF/VLF using a wire aer trailed several miles behind the aircraft, and an SHF (super high frequenc system whose aerials are housed in the dorsal blister that was absent fro the E-4A. Since November 1975 the sole operational management for th AABNCP force has been vested in SAC, and the main base is Offutt AF Nebraska. This is home to the 55th Strategic Recon Wing, user of the E 135 command posts, but it has not been announced whether the E-4Bs a also assigned to this wing. Planned force is six aircraft, five of which were use in 1982.

Below: A production E-4A (aircraft 80-1676) seen operating in 1980 on Pratt & Whitney engines before conversion to E-4B standard with F103 engines and the "doghouse" satellite link.

(overland downlook radar), Boeing was awarded a prime contract on 8 July 1970 for the AWACS (Airborne Warning And Control System). Their proposal was based on the commercial 707-320; to give enhanced on-station endurance it was to be powered by eight TF34 engines, but to cut costs this was abandoned and the original engines retained though driving high-power electric generators. The aerial for the main radar, back-to-back with an IFF (identification friend or foe) aerial and communications aerials, is mounted on a pylon above the rear fuselage and streamlined by adding two D-shaped radomes of glassfibre sandwich which turn the girder-like aerial array into a deep circular rotodome of 30ft (9.14m) diameter. This turns very slowly to keep the bearings lubricated; when on-station it rotates at 6rpm (once every ten seconds) and the searchlight-like beam is electronically scanned under computer control to sweep from the ground up to the sky and space, picking out every kind of moving target and processing the resulting signals at the rate of 710,000 complete 'words' per second. The rival radars were flown in two EC-137D aircraft rebuilt from existing 707s, and the winning Westinghouse APY-1 radar was built into the first E-3A in 1975. The first E-3A force was built up in TAC, to support quick-reaction deployment and tactical operation by all TAC units. The 552nd AWAC Wing received its first E-3A at Tinker AFB, Oklahoma, on 24 March 1977, and went on operational duty a year later. Subsequently the 552nd have operated in many parts of the world. It was augmented from 1979 by NORAD (North American Air Defense) personnel whose mission is the surveillance of all North American airspace and the control of NORAD forces over the Continental USA.

From the 22nd aircraft in 1981 an overwater capability has been incorporated, and from No 24 the systems are to an upgraded standard linked into the JTIDS (Joint Tactical Information Distribution System) shared by all US services as well as NATO forces which use 18 similar aircraft. The planned USAF force is 34 aircraft, funded at two per year and due to be complete in 1985.

Left: Costing well over $100,000,000, this E-3A Sentry was delivered to the 963rd AWAC Squadron at Tinker AFB, part of the 552nd AWAC Wing. It has seen service in Saudi Arabia.

Boeing T-43

T-43A

Origin: The Boeing Company, Seattle, Washington.
Type: Navigator trainer.
Engines: Two 14,500lb (6,577kg) thrust P&WA JT8D-9 turbofans.
Dimensions: Span 93ft 0in (28.35m); length 100ft 0in (30.48m); wing area 980 sq ft (91.05m²).
Weights: Empty 64,090lb (29,071kg); loaded 115,500lb (52,391kg).
Performance: Maximum cruising speed 562mph (904km/h); normal cruising speed, about 464mph (747km/h) at 35,000ft (10.67km); range with MIL-C-5011A reserves, 2,995 miles (4,820km).
Armament: None.
History: First flight (737-100) 9 April 1967, (T-43A) 10 April 1973.

Development: Vietnam experience revealed a serious deficiency of facilities for training modern navigators, the only aircraft for this purpose being 77 T-29 piston-engined machines based on the immediate post-war Convair-Liner. In May 1971 the Air Force announced an $87.1 million order for 19 off-the-shelf Boeing 737-200s, with an option (not taken up) for a further ten. The 19 aircraft were delivered in the 12 months from June 1973, and all have since operated with the 323rd Flying Training Wing at Mather AFB, California. Numerous change orders were issued to the basic

Above: Standard navigation trainer, the T-42A has never been named, nor have its engines received a military designation.

737-200, though engines and equipment items are treated as commercial (there is no military designation for the JT8D). There is only a single door and nine windows along each side of the cabin, the floor is strengthened to carry heavy avionics consoles and operating desks, there are additional avionics aerials, and an 800 US-gal (3027 lit) auxiliary fuel tank is installed in the aft cargo compartment. In addition to the two pilots and supernumerary there are stations for 12 pupil navigators, four advanced trainees and three instructors. Training is given under all weather conditions and at all heights, with equipment which is often modified to reflect that in operational types.

Boeing VC-137

VC-137B, C

Origin: The Boeing Company, Seattle, Washington.
Type: Special missions transport.
Engines: Four 18,000lb (8,165kg) thrust P&WA JT3D-3 turbofans.
Dimensions: Span (B) 130ft 10in (39.87m), (C) 145ft 9in (44.42m); length (B) 144ft 6in (44.04m), (C) 152ft 11in (46.61m); wing area (B) 2,433sq ft (226m²), (C) 3,010sq ft (279.64m²).
Weights: Empty (B) about 124,000lb (56,250kg), (C) about 140,500lb (63,730kg); loaded (B) 258,000lb (117,025kg), (C) 322,000lb (146,059kg).
Performance: Maximum speed (B) 623mph (1002km/h), (C) 627mph (1010km/h); maximum cruise, (B) 618mph (995km/h) (C) 600mph (966km/h); initial climb (B) 5,050ft (1539m)/min, (C) 3,550ft (1,082m)/min; service ceiling (B) 42,000ft (12.8km), (C) 38,500ft (11.73km); range, maximum payload, (B) 4,235 miles (6,820km), (C), 6,160 miles (9915km).
Armament: None.
History: First flight (civil -120B) 22 June 1960, (-320B) 31 January 1962.

Development: These aircraft bear no direct relationship to the prolific C135 family but were commercial airliners (hence the civil engine designation) bought off-the-shelf but specially furnished for the MAC 89th Military Airlift Group, based at Andrews AFB, Maryland, to fly the President and other senior executive officials. All have rear cabins with regular airline seating but a special midships HQ/conference section and a forward communications centre with special avionics in contact with stations on land, sea, in the air

Above: Most polished aircraft in the world, USAF 72-7000, serves with 89th MAG; when the President boards, it is Air Force One.

and in space. There are special security provisions. The two VC-137Bs were bought as early 707-153s with JT3C-6 engines and were redesignated on fitting turbofan engines. The first VC-137CC (62-6000), a much larger aircraft equivalent to a 707-320B, was the original Presidential Air Force One. It is now back-up to today's Air Force One, 72-7000.

Boeing-Vertol CH-47 Chinook

CH-47A, B, C and D Chinook (data for D)

Origin: Boeing-Vertol Company, Philadelphia.
Type: Medium transport helicopter with normal crew of two/three.
Engines: Two Avco Lycoming T55-L-712 turboshafts rated at 3,750shp (emergency rating 4,500shp).
Dimensions: Diameter of main rotors 60ft (18.29m); length, rotors turning, 99ft (30.2m); length of fuselage 51ft (15.54m); height 18ft 7in (5.67m).
Weights: Empty 23,093lb (10,475kg); loaded (max SL) 53,000lb (24,267kg).
Performance: Maximum speed (33,000lb/14,968kg) 185mph (298km/h); average cruise (50,000lb/22,679kg) 159mph (256km/h); max rate of climb (SL) 1,485ft (455m)/min; range (22,686lb/10,290kg external load) 34.5 miles (55.5km).
Armament: Normally, none.
History: First flight (YCH-47A) 21 September 1961; (CH-47C) 14 October 1967.

Development: Development of the Vertol 114 began in 1956 to meet the need of the US Army for a turbine-engined all-weather cargo helicopter able to operate effectively in the most adverse conditions of altitude and temperature. Retaining the tandem-rotor configuration, the first YCH-47A flew on the power of two 2,200shp Lycoming T55 turboshaft engines an led directly to the production CH-47A. With an unobstructed cabin 7½ (2.29m) wide, 6½ft (1.98m) high and over 30ft (9.2m) long, the Chinoo proved a valuable vehicle, soon standardized as US Army medium helicopte and deployed all over the world. By 1972 more than 550 had served i Vietnam, mainly in the battlefield airlift of troops and weapons but als rescuing civilians (on one occasion 147 refugees and their belongings wer carried to safety in one Chinook) and lifting back for salvage or repa 11,500 disabled aircraft valued at more than $3,000 million. The A mode gave way to the CH-47B, with 2,850hp engines and numerous improve ments, and then to the much more powerful (3,750shp T55s) CH-47 which in 1983 was the standard model, 213 being retrofitted wit glassfibre composite blades. In 1976 Boeing Vertol modified three earlie Chinooks to CH-47D standard, and the first production go-ahead followe in 1980. Among 13 major improvements are a new transmission to take th emergency (single-engine) power of the new engines, a new flight deck new flight-control/hydraulic/electrical systems, a gas-turbine APU (auxiliar power unit), upgraded avionics, single-point pressure fuelling and trip cargo hooks. Normal load limits are 44 equipped troops, 28,000 (12,700kg) cargo or 24 litters (stretchers) plus two attendants. The US hopes to rebuild 436 earlier Chinooks to CH-47D standard in 1983-199

Below: In theory the CH-47C could bring in several of these M102 light howitzers at a time, because each weighs a mere 3,196lb. (1,450kg). The Army has no alternatives to the gun or the CH-47.

Boeing-Vertol H-46 family

CH-46 and UH-46 Sea Knight

Origin: Boeing-Vertol, Philadelphia.
Type: Transport, search/rescue, minesweeping.
Engines: Two 1,400 or 1,870shp General Electric T58 turboshafts.
Dimensions: Diameter of each three-blade main rotor 50ft 0in (15.24m); fuselage length 44ft 10in (13.66m); height 16ft 8½in (5.09m).
Weights: Empty (KV-107/II-2) 10,732lb (4,868kg), (CH-46E) 11585lb (5,240kg); maximum loaded (KV) 19,000lb (8,618kg), (E) 21,400lb (9,706kg).
Performance: Typical cruise 120mph (193km/h); range with 30min reserve (6,600lb, 3,000kg payload) 109 miles (175km), (2,400lb, 1,088kg payload) 633 miles (1,020km).
History: First flight (107) April 1958, (prototype CH-46A) 27 August 1959, (E) 1977.

Development: The CH-46A Sea Knight was an assault transport carrying up to 25 equipped troops or 4,000lb (1,814kg) cargo. Boeing-Vertol delivered 624 basically similar Marine CH-46 and Navy UH-46 Sea Knights for assault transport, vertical replenishment of ships and utility transport, and (HH-46) sea/air rescue, these entering service in 1964-71. Since 1977 the survivors have been progressively re-equipped with glassfibre composite rotor blades, and the Marines at MCAS Cherry Point are updating their machines to CH-46E standard with the 1,870shp T58-16 engine, 'crashworthy' seats and fuel system and improved rescue system. Boeing-Vertol is expected to deliver 368 kits in 1985-88 to upgrade all surviving machines for reduced-cost service to at least 1999.

Above: An amphibious warfare team marches out to a CH-46D of Marine Corps squadron HMM-164 "Flying Clamors" whose home base is Futenma, Okinawa. All Marine Sea Knights are being total rebuilt and updated to CH-46E standard by the end of the decade

British Aerospace AV-8 Harrier I

AV-8A, TAV-8A and AV-8C

Origin: British Aerospace, UK.

Type: Single-seat attack and close-support, (TAV) dual combat-capable trainer.

Engine: One 21,500lb (9,752kg) Rolls-Royce Pegasus 103 vectored-thrust turbofan.

Dimensions: Span 25ft 3in (7.7m); length 45ft 7in (13.89m); height 11ft 4in (3.45m); wing area 201.1sq ft (18.68m²).

Weights: Empty (AV) 12,020lb (5,452kg); maximum (not VTOL) 25,000lb (11,340kg).

Performance: Maximum speed (SL, clean) over 737mph (1,186km/h); dive Mach limit, 1.3; time from vertical lift-off to 40,000ft (12.2km) 2min 23s; range with one inflight refuelling, over 3,455 miles (5,560km).

Armament: Two 30mm Aden gun each with 130 rounds; external weapon load of up to total of 5,000lb (2,270kg) including bombs, Paveway smart bombs, Mavericks, cluster dispensers, rocket launchers and Sidewinder AAMs.

History: First flight (AV-8A) August 1970, (AV-8C) May 1979.

Development: Adopted in 1969 by the US Marine Corps as a close-support multirole aircraft for use in amphibious assaults, the AV-8A is a slightly Americanized and simplified version of the RAF Harrier GR.3, lacking the latter's inertial navigation and laser nose but with certain US equipment specified by the customer. A total of 102 were supplied, together with eight TAV-8A dual trainers, deliveries beginning in January 1971. Units equipped have always been the training squadron, VMA(T)-203 at MCAS Cherry Point and three combat squadrons, VMA-231, 513 and 542. Attrition has at times been severe, mainly through reasons other than failures of the aircraft, and prolonged and generally very successful operations have been mounted from every kind of ship and shore airfield. In 1979-84 a total of 47 AV-8As have been upgraded to AV-8C standard with life-improving strakes and retractable flap under the fuselage, a liquid-oxygen system, secure voice radio and improved UHF, passive radar receivers facing to front and rear and a flare/chaff dispenser. The C-model is the standard USMC Harrier until the arrival in October 1983 of the Harrier II.

Above: AV-8As in the powered-lift hovering mode prior to being converted to AV-8C standard. It is in this mode that today's AV-8B Harrier II shows to the greatest advantage, the new wing, flaps, inlets and nozzles giving several tons extra lift.

Cessna T-37

Model 318, T-37B, A-37B Dragonfly

Origin: Cessna Aircraft Company, Wichita, Kansas.

Type: T-37, primary trainer; A-37, light attack.

Engines: (T) two 1,025lb (465kg) thrust Teledyne CAE J69-25 turbojets, (A) two 2,850lb (1293kg) thrust General Electric J85-17A turbojets.

Dimensions: Span (T) 33ft 9.3in (10.3m), (A, over tanks) 35ft 10.5in (10.93m); length (T) 29ft 3in (8.92m), (A, excl refuelling probe) 28ft 3.25in (8.62m); wing area 183.9 sq ft (17.09m²).

Weights: Empty (T) 3,870lb (1,755kg), (A) 6,211lb (2,817kg); loaded (T) 6,600lb (2,993kg), (A) 14,000lb (6,350kg).

Performance: Maximum speed (T) 426mph (685km/h), (A) 507mph (816km/h); normal cruising speed (T) 380mph (612km/h), (A, clean) 489mph (787km/h); initial climb (T) 3,020ft (920m)/min, (A) 6,990ft (2,130m)/min; service ceiling (T) 35,100ft (10,700m), (A) 41,765ft (12,730m); range (T, 5% reserves, 25,000ft/7,620m cruise) 604 miles (972km), (A, max fuel, four drop tanks) 1,012 miles (1628km), (A, max payload including 4100lb/1860kg ordnance) 460 miles (740km).

Armament: (T) None, (A) GAU-2B/A 7.62mm Minigun in fuselage, eight underwing pylons (four inners 870lb/394kg each, next 600lb/272kg and outers 500lb/227kg) for large number of weapons, pods, dispensers, clusters, launchers or recon/EW equipment.

History: First flight (T) 12 October 1954, (A) 22 October 1963.

Development: After prolonged study the Air Force decided in 1952 to adopt a jet primary pilot trainer, and after a design competition the Cessna Model 318 was selected. Features included all-metal stressed-skin construction, side-by-side seating in a cockpit with ejection seats and a single broad clamshell canopy, two small engines in the wing roots with nozzles at the trailing edge, fixed tailplane half-way up the fin, manual controls with electric trim, hydraulic slotted flaps and hydraulic tricycle landing gear of exceptional track but short length, placing the parked aircraft low on the ground. The introduction was delayed by numerous trivial modifications and even when service use began in 1957 pupils were first trained on the T-34. Altogether 534 T-37As were built, but all were brought up to the standard of the T-37B, of 1959, which had more powerful J69 engines, improved radio, navaids and revised instrument panel. After 41 had been converted to A-37As further T-37As were bought in 1967 to bring the total of this model to 447. They serve in roughly equal numbers with the advanced T-38A at all the USAF's pilot schools: 12th Flying Training Wing at Randolph; 14th at Columbus (Miss); 47th at Laughlin; 64th at Reese; 71st at Vance; 80th at Sheppard and 82nd at Williams.

The A-37 was derived to meet a need in the early 1960s for a light attack aircraft to fly Co-In (counter-insurgent) missions. Cessna had previously produced two T-37C armed trainers (many of this model were later supplied to Foreign Aid recipients, including South Vietnam in the 1960s and later these aircraft were then rebuilt as AT-37 prototypes (designation YAT-37D) with much more powerful engines and airframes restressed for increased weights which, in stages, were raised to 14,000lb

(6,350kg). No fewer than eight underwing pylons plus wingtip tanks were added, giving a great weapon-carrying capability whilst offering performance significantly higher than that of the trainer. Redesignated A-37A, a squadron converted from T-37Bs on the production line was evaluated in Vietnam in 1967. Altogether 39 A-37As were built by converting T-37Bs on the line, followed by 511 of the regular USAF production model with full-rated J85 engines, 6g structure, flight-refuelling probe, greater internal tankage and other changes. The A-37 Dragonfly proved valuable in south-east Asia, where many were left in South Vietnamese hands after the US withdrawal. After the end of the US involvement the A-37B was withdrawn from regular USAF service but it continues to equip a Reserve wing and two Air National Guard groups. The AFR's 434th TFW flies the A-37B at Grissom AFB, Bunker Hill, Indiana, and the ANG units are the 174th TFG (Syracuse, NY) and the 175th (Baltimore, Md).

Below: While the A-37B Dragonfly has proved a popular and low-cost light attack platform (camouflaged aircraft) it has never been able to rival its progenitor, the T-37B (unpainted) as a major USAF type. Many are becoming OA-37B FAC platforms.

Fairchild A-10 Thunderbolt II

A-10A, A-10/T, A-10/NAW

Origin: Fairchild Republic Company, Farmingdale, NY.
Type: Close-support attack aircraft.
Engines: Two 9,065lb (4,112kg) thrust General Electric TF34-100 turbofans.
Dimensions: Span 57ft 6in (17.53m); length 53ft 4in (16.26m); height (regular) 14ft 8in (4.47m), (NAW) 15ft 4in (4.67m); wing area 506sq ft (47m²).
Weights: Empty 21,519lb (9761kg); forward airstrip weight (no fuel but four Mk 82 bombs and 750 rounds) 32,730lb (14,846kg); maximum 50,000lb (22,680kg). Operating weight empty, 24,918lb (11,302kg), (NAW) 28,630lb (12,986kg).
Performance: Maximum speed, (max weight, A-10A) 423mph (681km/h), (NAW) 420mph (676km/h); cruising speed at sea level (both) 345mph (555km/h); stabilized speed below 8,000ft (2,440m) in 45° dive at weight 35,125lb (15,932kg), 299mph (481km/h); maximum climb at basic design weight of 31,790lb (14,420kg), 6,000ft (1,828m)/min; service ceiling not stated; takeoff run to 50ft (15m) at maximum weight, 4,000ft (1,220m); operating radius in CAS mission with 1.8 hour loiter and reserves, 288 miles (463km); radius for single deep strike penetration, 620 miles (1,000km); ferry range with allowances, 2,542 miles (4091km).
Armament: One GAU-8/A Avenger 30mm seven-barrel gun with 1,174 rounds, total external ordnance load of 16,000lb (7,257kg) hung on 11 pylons, three side-by-side on body and four under each wing; several hundred combinations of stores up to individual weight of 5,000lb (2,268kg) with maximum total weight 14,638lb (6,640kg) with full internal fuel.
History: First flight (YA-10A) 10 May 1972; (production A-10A) 21 October 1975, (NAW) 4 May 1979.

Development: After prolonged study of lightweight Co-In and light armed reconnaissance aircraft the Air Force in 1967 initiated the A-X programme

for a new-generation CAS (close air support) aircraft. It had never had suc an aircraft, this mission being previously flown by fighters, bombers, attac and even FAC platforms, including such diverse types as the F-105 and A-1 Emphasis in A-X was not on speed but on lethality against surface target (especially armour), survivability against ground fire (not including SAMs heavy ordnance load and long mission endurance. Low priority was paid t advanced nav/attack avionics, the fit being officially described as 'austere After a major competition the Northrop A-9A and Fairchild A-10A wer pitted against each other in a flyoff contest throughout 1972, after whic the A-10A was announced the Air Force's choice on 18 January 1973 Including six DT&E (development, test and evaluation) aircraft the planne force was to number 733, to be deployed in TAC wings in the USA an Europe, and also to a growing number of AFR and ANG squadrons.

The original A-10A was a basically simple single-seater, larger than mos tactical attack aircraft and carefully designed as a compromise betwee capability, survivability and low cost. As an example of the latter many of th major parts, including flaps, main landing gears and movable tail surface are interchangeable left/right, and systems and engineering features wer designed with duplication and redundancy to survive parts being shot awa The unusual engine location minimizes infra-red signature and makes almost simple to fly with one engine inoperative or even shot off. Weapo pylons were added from tip to tip, but the chief tank-killing ordnance is th gun, the most powerful (in terms of muzzle horsepower) ever mounted in a aircraft, firing milk-bottle-size rounds at rates hydraulically controlled a

Right: Two pairs of AGM-65A Maverick precision missiles are hung on this aircraft of the 354th TFW from Myrtle Beach. It does not have the Pave Penny laser receiver installed on the pylo under the right side of the nose. The 11 pylons are clearly seen.

Below: Funded by Fairchild Republic, this N/AW (night/adverse weather) two-seater never went into production but outwardly resembles the A-10A combat-ready trainer version now forming a small part of the force. N/AW capability is being enhanced.

General Dynamics F-106 Delta Dart

F-106A, B

Origin: General Dynamics Convair Division, San Diego, California.
Type: All-weather interceptor, (B) operational trainer.
Engine: One 24,500lb (11,130kg) thrust Pratt & Whitney J75-17 afterburning turbojet.
Dimensions: Span 38ft 3in (11.67m); length (both) 70ft 8¾in (21.55m); wing area 661.5 sq ft (61.52m²).
Weights: Empty (A) about 24,420lb (11,077kg); loaded (normal) 34,510lb (15,668kg).
Performance: Maximum speed (both) 1,525mph (2,455km/h) or Mach 2.3 at 36,000ft (11km); initial climb, about 29,000ft (8,839m)/min; service ceiling 57,000ft (17,374m); range with drop tanks 1,800 miles (2,897km).
Armament: One 20mm M61A-1 gun, two AIM-4F plus two AIM-4G Falcons, plus one AIR-2A or -2G Genie nuclear rocket.
History: First flight (aerodynamic prototype) 26 December 1956, (B) 9 April 1958; squadron delivery June 1959.

Development: Derived from the earlier F-102 Delta Dagger, the F-106 had a maximum speed approximately twice as high and completely met the

requirements of Aerospace Defense Command (Adcom) for a manne interceptor to defend the continental United States. Linked via its comple and bulky MA-1 electronic fire-control system through a digital data link in the nationwide SAGE (semi-automatic ground environment), the 10 served much longer than intended and in fact never did see a successo despite the continued threat of the manned bomber, though there wer numerous engineering improvements and some substantial updates includir the addition of the gun (in a neat installation in the missile bay, causing slight ventral bulge) as well as improved avionics, an infra-red sensor of gre sensitivity facing ahead for detecting heat from hostile aircraft and assistir the lock-on of AAMs, and a flight-refuelling boom receptacle. Conva completed many other studies including improved electric power syster solid-state computer, the AIMS (aircraft identification monitoring syster and an enhanced-capability variant for Awacs control. The last of 277 106As and 63 tandem-seat F-106B armed trainers were delivered in 196 Adcom was disbanded in 1980 and the F-106 is now flown only by fight interceptor units in TAC and in the ANG, assigned to TAC.

Right: F-106As gathered at Tyndall AFB during one of the annual TAC "William Tell" air-to-air combat proficiency meetings. Over 70 per cent of the dwindling interceptor force is now provided by units of the US Air National Guard, based in Massachusetts, New Jersey, Montana, California and Florida.

100 or 4,200 shots/min. The gun is mounted 2° nose-down and offset to ▐e left so that the firing barrel is always on the centreline (the nose landing ▐ar being offset to the right).

The basic aircraft has a HUD (head-up display), good communications fit ▐d both Tacan and an inertial system, as well as ECM and radar homing and ▐arning. Deliveries to the 354th TFW at Myrtle Beach, South Carolina, ▐gan in 1977, and over 500 have since been received by units in TAC, ▐SAFE (including the 81st TFW in England and 601 TCW at Sembach) and ▐rious other commands including the Reserve and ANG. Though relatively ▐w and ungainly the 'Thud-II' has won over any pilot who might have ▐ked askance at it, and has demonstrated in its first 100,000 hours the ▐lity to do a major job under increasingly hazardous conditions and at the ▐west height normally practised by any jet aircraft. Nevertheless attrition at ▐aircraft per 100,000 hours in 1981 was double expectation, resulting in an

increase in the overall programme to 825 to sustain the desired force to the mid-1990s. Significantly, half the 60 aircraft in the FY81 budget were two-seaters, which though priced $600,000 higher are expected to effect savings by reducing the demand for chase aircraft.

In 1979 Fairchild flew a company-funded NAW (night/adverse weather) demonstrator with augmented avionics and a rear cockpit for a WSO seated at a higher level and with good forward view. Both the regular and NAW aircraft can carry a Pave Penny laser seeker pod under the nose, vital for laser-guided munitions, and the NAW also has a Ferranti laser ranger, FLIR (forward-looking infra-red), GE low-light TV and many other items including a Westinghouse multimode radar with WSO display. It is probable that during the rest of the decade A-10As will be brought at least close to the NAW standard, while the two-seat NAW might be procured alongside or in place of future buys of the basic A-10A.

General Dynamics F-16 Fighting Falcon

F-16A, B

Origin: General Dynamics Corporation, Fort Worth.
Type: Multi-role fighter (B) operational fighter/trainer.
Engine: One 23,840lb (10,814kg) thrust Pratt & Whitney F100-200 afterburning turbofan.
Dimensions: Span 31ft 0in (9.449m) (32ft 10in/1.01m over missile fins); length (both versions, excl probe) 47ft 7.7in (14.52m); wing area 300.0 sq ft (27.87m²).
Weights: Empty (A) 15,137lb (6,866kg), (B) 15,778lb (7,157kg); loaded (AAMs only) (A) 23,357lb (10,594kg), (B) 22,814lb (10,348kg), (max external load) (both) 35,400lb (16,057kg). (Block 25 on) 37,500lb (17,010kg).
Performance: Maximum speed (both, AAMs only) 1,350mph (2,173km/h, Mach 2.05) at 40,000ft (12.19km); maximum at SL, 915mph (1,472km/h, Mach 1.2); initial climb (AAMs only) 50,000ft (15.24km)/min; service ceiling, over 50,000ft (15.24km); tactical radius (A, six Mk 82, internal fuel, HI-LO-HI) 340 miles (547km); ferry range, 2,415 miles (3,890km).
Armament: One M61A-1 20mm gun with 500/515 rounds, centreline pylon for 300 US gal (1,136 lit) drop tank or 2,200lb (998kg) bomb, inboard wing pylons for 3,500lb (1,587kg) each, middle wing pylons for 2,500lb (1,134kg) each (being uprated under MSIP-1 to 3,500lb), outer wing pylons for 250lb (113.4kg), all ratings being at 9 g.
History: First flight (YF) 20 January 1974, (production F-16A) 7 August 1978; service delivery (A) 17 August 1978.

Development: The Fighting Falcon originated through a belief by the Air Force that there might be a more cost/effective fighter than the outstanding but necessarily expensive F-15. In a Lightweight Fighter (LWF) programme of 1972 it sought bids from many design teams, picked GD's Model 401 and Northrop's simplified P.530 and evaluated two prototypes of each as the YF-16 and YF-17. GD's engineering team created a totally new aircraft with such advanced features as relaxed static stability (a basic distribution of shapes and masses to attain greater combat agility, overcoming a marginal longitudinal stability by the digital flight-control system), large wing/body flare to enhance lift at high angles of attack and house a gun and extra fuel, a straight wing with hinged leading and trailing flaps used to increase manoeuvrability in combat (the trailing surfaces being rapid-action flaperons), fly-by-wire electrically signalled flight controls, a futuristic cockpit with reclining zero/zero seat for best resistance to g, with a sidestick controller instead of a control column and one-piece canopy/windscreen of blown polycarbonate, and a miniature multi-mode pulse-doppler radar. On 13 January 1975 the Air Force announced full development of the F-16 not just as a simple day air-combat fighter but also to meet a greatly expanded requirement calling for comprehensive all-weather navigation and weapon delivery in the air/surface role.

This vitally important programme growth was triggered largely by the recognition that there existed a near-term European market, and in June 1975 orders were announced by four European NATO countries (Belgium, Denmark, Netherlands and Norway). These organized with GD and P&WA a large multinational manufacturing programme which in the longer term has greatly expanded the production base. In July 1975 the Air Force ordered six pre-production F-16As and two F-16Bs with tandem dual controls and internal fuel reduced from 1,072.5 US gal (4,060lit) to 889.8 (3,368). Both introduced a flight-refuelling boom receptacle (into which a probe can be inserted) and provision for a 300 US gal (1,136lit) centreline drop tank and two 370gal (1,400lit) wing tanks. All eight aircraft were delivered by June 1978, by which time the Air Force had announced a programme for 1,184 F-16As and 204 F-16Bs, with the name Fighting Falcon.

Few aircraft have been as excitedly received as the F-16, which by sheer engineering excellence and painstaking development is as close to the optimum combat aircraft as it is possible to get in its timescale. Even so, it was naturally prey to occasional troubles, notably the prolonged stall stagnation engine difficulty that had earlier hit the F-15 with an almost identical engine. Following intensive test programmes at Edwards, Nellis and by an MOT&E (multi-national operational test and evaluation) team the 388th TFW at Hill AFB, Utah, began to convert on 6 January 1979 and has subsequently not only achieved a string of 'firsts' with the F-16 but has set impressive records in the process. Next came the 56th TFW at MacDill, Florida, followed by the 474th at Nellis, Nevada, the 8th TFW at Kunsan, S Korea, the 50th TFW at Hahn, W. Germany (in USAFE) and the 363rd at Shaw, S. Carolina. Thanks to the large production base and wide international deployment (extending to Israel, S Korea, Egypt, Pakistan and other countries beyond those previously listed) global deployment of Air Force F-16 units is proving exceptionally simple, the aircraft having swiftly attained an exceptional level of reliabilty which is enhanced by outstanding maintenance and self-test features.

Enthusiasm by pilots and ground crew has been exceptional, but an event which dramatically highlighted how far the F-16 had come since 1974 was its first participation in a numerically scored inter-service competition. In the searching USAF/RAF contest held at RAF Lossiemouth on 16-19 June 1981 teams of F-16s (388th TFW), F-111s, Jaguars and Buccaneers were required under realistic wartime scenarios to penetrate defended airspace, engage hostile fighters and bomb airfields and road convoys. The F-16s were the only aircraft to hit all assigned surface targets, while in air combat their score was 86 kills against no losses; rival teams suffered 42 losses and collectively scored but a single kill. The F-16 also scored very much better against Rapier SAM threats, while in the ground-crew part of the contest the 388th achieved an average turnround time between sorties of 10½ minutes including refuelling, loading six Mk 82 bombs and 515 rounds of ammunition. Since its introduction to TAC the F-16 has had the highest Mission Capable Rate in the command, and has been the only multirole aircraft to achieve the command goal of 70%.

In 1982 production had passed 600 aircraft, with plenty of spare capacity at Fort Worth for up to 45 per month if necessary. Though this excellent output was attained by sticking to an agreed standard of build, improvements have been continual, and many more are in prospect. During production the inlet was strengthened to carry EO/FLIR and laser pods, a graphite/epoxy tailplane of larger size was introduced to match increased gross weight (see data), and the central computer and avionics were changed for a much 'expanded package'. Later the 30mm GEpod gun, Maverick missile, Lantirn and AMRAAM advanced missile will be introduced, the new AAM being linked with the programmable APG-66 radar for stand-off interception capability. Later still the striking bat-like SCAMP (supersonic-cruise aircraft modification program) may result in still higher performance with doubled bombloads.

Opposite top: One of the first block F-16A Fighting Falcons was used in 1981 for the initial evaluation trials of the Hughes Amraam (Advanced medium-range AAM) which was later chosen over a rival from Raytheon. Later F-16s will fire Amraam, which was well into firing trials with fully guided rounds late in 1982.

Right: First of two F-16XL development prototypes (FSD F-16A No 75-0749) in the startlingly successful Scamp programme, which will double range or bombload while reducing field length and improving agility. It could lead to a production F-16E with new airframe and the General Electric F110 (F101DFE) engine.

Below: Two of the 1980 production Fighting Falcons serving with the 8th TFW (Wolf Pack) at Kunsan AB, South Korea. These early aircraft have the original (small size) horizontal tailplanes.

Below: The F-16B dual-pilot trainer has full weapons capability but about 17 per cent less internal fuel. The cockpits are stepped just enough for good instructor view without a periscope, though the half-inch polycarbonate canopy has a metal frame at roughly mid-length, and a metal rear section. The USAF brought 204 in the initial 1,388 F-16s and expects to add another 100.

Below: Visually less striking than the F-16XL above, the AFTI (Advanced Fighter Technology Integration) testbed is at least as significant. A new flight-control system, with ventral canards, enables manoeuvres to be made in any direction without the prior need to point the aircraft in that direction—potentially a great boon for the fighter pilot.

General Dynamics F-111

F-111A, D, E and F, FB-111A and EF-111A

Origin: (except EF) General Dynamics Corporation, Fort Worth.
(EF) Grumman Aerospace Corporation, Bethpage, NY.
Type: A,D,E,F, all-weather attack; FB, strategic attack; EF, tactical ECM jammer.
Powerplant: Two Pratt & Whitney TF30 afterburning turbofans, as follow, (A, C, EF) 18,500lb (8,390kg) TF30-3, (D,E) 19,600lb (8,891kg) TF30-9, (FB) 20,350lb (9,231kg) TF30-7, (F) 25,100lb (11,385kg) TF30-100.
Dimensions: Span (fully spread) (A,D,E,F,EF) 63ft 0in (19.2m), (FB) 70ft 0in (21.34m), (fully swept) (A,D,E,F,EF) 31ft 11½in (9.74m), (FB) 33ft 11in (10.34m); length (except EF) (A,D,E,F,EF) 73ft 6in (22.4m), (EF) 77ft 1.6in (23.51m); wing area (A,D,E,F,EF, gross, 16°) 525 sq ft (48.77m²).
Weights: Empty (A) 46,172lb (20,943kg), (D) 49,090lb (22,267kg), (E) about 47,000lb (21,319kg), (EF) 55,275lb (25,072kg), (F) 47,481lb (21,537kg), (FB) close to 50,000lb (22,680kg); loaded (A) 91,500lb (41,500kg), (D,E) 92,500lb (41,954kg), (F) 100,000lb (45,360kg), (FB) 114,300lb (51,846kg), (EF) 89,000lb (40,370kg).
Performance: Maximum speed at 36,000ft (11km), clean and with max afterburner, (A,D,E) Mach 2.2, 1,450mph (2,335km/h), (FB) Mach 2, 1,320mph (2,124km/h), (F) Mach 2.5, 1,653mph (2,660km/h), (EF) Mach 1.75, 1,160mph (1,865km/h); cruising speed, penetration, 571mph (919km/h); initial climb (EF) 3,592ft (1,095m)/min; service ceiling at combat weight, max afterburner, (A) 51,000ft (15,500m), (F) 60,000ft (18,290m), (EF) 54,700ft (16,670m); range with max internal fuel (A,D) 3,165 miles (5,093km), (F) 2,925 miles (4,707km), (EF) 2,484 miles (3,998km); takeoff run (A) 4,000ft (1,219m), (F) under 3,000ft (914m), (FB) 4,700ft (1,433m), (EF) 3,250ft (991m).
Armament: Internal weapon bay for two B43 bombs or (D,F) one B43 and one M61 gun; three pylons under each wing (four inboard swivelling with wing, outers being fixed and usable only at 16°, otherwise being jettisoned) for max external load 31,500lb (14,288kg); (FB only) provision for up to six SRAM, two internal; (EF) no armament.
History: First flight 21 December 1964, service delivery (A) June 1967, (EF) July 1981.

Development: In 1960 the Department of Defense masterminded the TFX (tactical fighter experimental) as a gigantic programme to meet all the fighter and attack needs of the Air Force, Navy and Marine Corps, despite the disparate requirements of these services, and expected the resultant aircraft to be bought throughout the non-Communist world. In fact, so severe were the demands for weapon load and, in particular, mission range that on the low power available the aircraft had inadequate air-combat capability and in fact it was destined never to serve in this role, though it is still loosely described as a 'tactical fighter'. After prolonged technical problems involving escalation in weight, severe aerodynamic drag, engine/inlet mismatch and, extending into the early 1970s, structural failures, the F-111 eventually matured as the world's best long-range interdiction attack aircraft which in the hands of dedicated and courageous Air Force crews pioneered the new art of 'skiing'—riding the ski-toe locus of a TFR (terrain-following radar) over hills, mountains and steep-sided valleys in blind conditions, in blizzards or by night, holding a steady 200ft (91m) distance from the ground at high-subsonic speed, finally to plant a bomb automatically within a few metres of a previously computed target.

Basic features of the F-111 include a variable-sweep 'swing wing' (the first in production in the world) with limits of 16° and 72.5°, with exceptional high-lift devices, side-by-side seating for the pilot and right-seat navigator (usually also a pilot) or (EF) electronic-warfare officer, large main gears with low-pressure tyres for no-flare landings on soft strips (these prevent the carriage of ordnance on fuselage pylons), a small internal weapon bay, great internal fuel capacity (typically 5,022 US gal, 19,010 litres), and emergency escape by jettisoning the entire crew compartment, which has its own parachutes and can serve as a survival shelter or boat.

General Dynamics cleared the original aircraft for service in 2½ years, and built 141 of this F-111A version, which equips 366TFW at Mountain Home AFB, Idaho (others have been reserved for conversion into the EF-111A). It is planned to update the A by fitting a digital computer to the original analog type AJQ-20A nav/bomb system, together with the Air Force standard INS and a new control/display set. The F-111E was similar but had larger inlet ducts and engines of slightly greater power; 94 were delivered and survivors equip the 20th TFW at Upper Heyford, England. These are to receive the same updates as the A. Next came the F-111D, which at great cost was fitted with an almost completely different avionic system of a basically digital nature including the APQ-30 attack radar, APN-189 doppler and HUDs for both crew-members. This aircraft had great potential but caused severe

Above: KC-135 boom operator's view of an FB-111A of SAC as it comes in for refuelling. It is carrying four SRAM missiles.

technical and manpower problems in service and never fully realized its capabilities, though it remains a major advance on the A and E. The 96 built have always equipped the 27th TFW at Cannon AFB, New Mexico. The F-111F is by far the best of all tactical F-111 versions, almost entirely because Pratt & Whitney at last produced a really powerful TF30 which incorporated many other advanced features giving enhanced life with fewer problems. With much greater performance than any other model the F could if necessary double in an air-combat role though it has no weapons for this role except the gun and if necessary AIM-9. The 106 of this model served at Mountain Home until transfer to the 48th TFW in England, at Lakenheath. The most important of all F-111 post-delivery modifications has been the conversion of the F force to use the Pave Tack pod, normally stowed in the weapon bay but rotated out on a cradle for use. This complex package provides a day/night all-weather capability to acquire, track, designate and

Grumman A-6 Intruder and Prowler

Grumman A-6A, B, C, E, EA-6A and B and KA-6D

Origin: Grumman Aerospace.
Type: (A-6A, B, C, E) two-seat carrier-based all-weather attack; (EA-6A) two-seat ECM/attack; (EA-6B) four-seat ECM; (KA-6D) two-seat air-refuelling tanker.
Engines: (Except EA-6B) two 9,300lb (4,218kg) thrust Pratt & Whitney J52-8B two-shaft turbojets; (EA-6B) two 11,200lb (5,080kg) J52-408.
Dimensions: Span 53ft (16.15m); length (except EA-6B) 54ft 7in (16.64m); (EA-6B) 59ft 10in (18.24m); height (A-6A, A-6C, KA-6D) 15ft 7in (4.75m); (A-6E, EA-6A and B) 16ft 3in (4.95m).
Weights: Empty (A-6A) 25,684lb (11,650kg); (EA-6A) 27,769lb (12,596kg); (EA-6B) 34,581lb (15,686kg); (A-6E) 25,630lb (11,625kg); maximum loaded (A-6A and E) 60,626lb (27,500kg); (EA-6A) 56,500lb (25,628kg); (EA-6B) 65,000lb (29,484kg).
Performance: Maximum speed (clean A-6A) 685mph (1,102km/h) at sea level or 625 mph (1,006km/h, Mach 0.94) at height; (EA-6A) over 630mph; (EA-6B) 651mph (1,042km/h) at sea level; (A-6E) 648mph (1,037km/h) at sea level; initial climb (A-6E, clean) 8,600ft (2,621m)/min; service ceiling (A-6A) 41,660ft (12,700m); (A-6E) 44,600ft (13,595m); (EA-6B) 39,000ft. (11,582m); range with full combat load (A-6E) 1,077 miles (1,733km); ferry range with external fuel (all) about 3,100 miles (4,890km).
Armament: All attack versions, including EA-6A, five stores locations each rated at 3,600lb (1,633kg) with maximum total load of 15,000lb (6,840kg); typical load thirty 500lb (227kg) bombs; (EA-6B) none.
History: First flight (YA2F-1) 19 April 1960; service acceptance of A-6A 1 February 1963; first flight (EA-6A) 1963; (KA-6D) 23 May 1966; (EA-6B) 25 May 1968; (A-6E) 27 February 1970; final delivery 1975.

Development: Selected from 11 competing designs in December 1957, the Intruder was specifically planned for first-pass blind attack on point surface targets at night or in any weather. Though area ruled, the aircraft (originally designated A2F) was designed to be subsonic and is powered by two straight turbojets which in the original design were arranged with tilting jetpipes to help give lift for STOL (short takeoff and landing). Despite its considerable gross weight—much more than twice the empty weight and heavier than most of the heavy World War II four-engine bombers—the Intruder has excellent slow-flying qualities with full span slats and flaps. The crew sit side-by-side under a broad sliding canopy giving a marvellous view in all directions, the navigator having control of the extremely comprehensive navigation, radar and attack systems which are integrated into DIANE (Digital Integrated Attack Navigation Equipment). In Vietnam the A-6A worked round the clock making pinpoint attacks on targets which could not be accurately bombed by any other aircraft until the arrival of the F-111. The A-6E introduced a new multi-mode radar and computer and supplanted earlier versions in Navy and Marine Corps squadrons. The EA-6A introduced a valuable group of ECM (electronic countermeasures) while retaining partial attack capability; 27 were built and remain in use. The KA-6D is a conversion of the A-6A for inflight-refuelling tanker missions with a single hosereel and drogue in the rear fuselage; the 62 in service retain attack capability. By far the most costly model, the EA-6B is a complete redesign as the standard Navy and Marine Corps EW (electronic warfare) platform, with a crew of four to manage several major systems of which by far the largest is the ALQ-99 system which groups receiver aerials in the fin pod and high-power jammers in up to five pylon-hung pods each powered by a nose windmill and each tailored to a particular three waveband. Grumman is expected to build the 102nd and last Prowler in 1986. Current A-6Es, which remain in production with 318 delivered, have the Tram (Target Recognition and attack multisensor) chin turret, and 50 are being equipped to fire Harpoon missiles (six per aircraft).

Right: The small pimple under the nose is the Tram (Target-recognition and attack multisensor) with infra-red and laser equipment, now fitted to most Navy and Marines A-6E Intruders. This one belongs to VA-65 "Tigers", USS _Dwight D. Eisenhower_.

hit surface targets using EO, IR or laser guided weapons. The first squadron to convert was the 48th TFW's 494th TFS, in September 1981. Their operations officer, Maj Bob Rudiger, has said: 'Important targets that once required several aircraft can now be disabled with a single Pave Tack aircraft; the radar tells the pod where to look, and the laser allows us to put the weapon precisely on target.'

The long-span FB-111A was bought to replace the B-58 and early models of B-52 in SAC, though the rising price resulted in a cut in procurement from 210 to 76, entering service in October 1969. It has so-called Mk IIB avionics, derived from those of the D but configured for SAC missions using nuclear bombs or SRAMs. With strengthened structure and landing gear the FB has a capability of carrying 41,250lb (18,711kg) of bombs, made up of 50 bombs of 825lb (nominal 750lb size) each. This is not normally used, and the outer pylons associated with this load are not normally installed. The FB

equips SAC's 380th BW at Plattsburgh AFB, NY, and the 509th at Pease, New Hampshire. No go-ahead has been received for numerous extremely capable stretched FB versions.

Last of the F-111 variants, the EF-111A is the USAF's dedicated EW platform, managed by Grumman (partner on the original Navy F-111B version) and produced by rebuilding F-111As. The USA acknowledges the Soviet Union to have a lead in both ground and air EW, and thousands of radars and other defence emitters in Eastern Europe would make penetration by NATO aircraft extremely dangerous. The vast masking power of the EF-111A, which equals that of the Navy EA-6B and in fact uses almost the same ALQ-99E tac-jam system (but with a crew of only two instead of four), is expected to be able to suppress these 'eyes' and enable NATO aircraft to survive. An aerodynamic prototype flew in March 1977, the ALQ-99 was flying in an F-111 in May 1977, and production deliveries began in mid-1981 to the 366th TFW. The Air Force plans to have 42 aircraft rebuilt as EFs, for service with all USAFE penetrating attack units and others in TAC and possibly other commands.

Grumman F-14 Tomcat

F-14A and C

Origin: Grumman Aerospace.
Type: Two-seat carrier-based multi-role fighter.
Engines: (F-14A) two 20,900lb (9,480kg) thrust Pratt & Whitney TF30-412A two-shaft afterburning turbofans; (C) TF30-414A, same rating.
Dimensions: Span (68° sweep) 38ft 2in (11.63m), (20° sweep) 64ft 1½in (19.54m); length 62ft 8in (19.1m); height 16ft (4.88m).
Weights: Empty 39,762lb (18,036kg); loaded (normal) 58,539lb (26,553kg), (max) 74,348lb (33,724kg).
Performance: Maximum speed, 1,564mph (2,517km/h, Mach 2.34) at height, 910mph (1,470km/h, Mach 1.2) at sea level; inital climb at normal gross weight, over 30,000ft (9,144m)/min; service ceiling over 56,000ft (17,070m); range (fighter with external fuel) about 2,000 miles (3,200km).
Armament: One 20mm M61-A1 multi-barrel cannon in fuselage; four AIM-7 Sparrow and four or eight AIM-9 Sidewinder air-to-air missiles, or up to six AIM-54 Phoenix and two AIM-9; maximum external weapon load in surface attack role 14,500lb (6,577kg).
History: First flight 21 December 1970; initial deployment with US Navy carriers October 1972; first flight of F-14B 12 September 1973.

Development: When Congress finally halted development of the compromised F-111B version of the TFX in mid-1968 Grumman was already well advanced with the project design of a replacement. After a competition for the VFX requirement Grumman was awarded a contract for the F-14 in January 1969. The company had to produce a detailed mock-up by May and build 12 development aircraft. Despite sudden loss of the first aircraft on its second flight, due to total hydraulic failure, the programme has been a complete technical success and produced one of the world's outstanding combat aircraft. Basic features include use of a variable-sweep wing, to match the aircraft to the conflicting needs of carrier compatability, dogfighting and attack on surface targets at low level; pilot and naval flight officer (observer) in tandem; an extremely advanced airframe, with tailplane skins of boron-epoxy composite and similar novel construction methods, and one canted vertical tail above each engine; and the extremely powerful

Hughes AWG-9 radar which, used in conjunction with the Phoenix missile (carried by no other combat aircraft), can pick out and destroy a chosen aircraft from a formation over 100 miles (160km/h) away. For close-in fighting the gun is used in conjunction with snap-shoot missiles, with the tremendous advantage that, as a launch platform, the Tomcat is unsurpassed (Grumman claim it to be unrivalled, and to be able—by automatic variation of wing sweep—to out-manoeuvre all previous combat aircraft). Introduction to the US Navy has been smooth and enthusiastic, with VF-1 and -2 serving aboard *Enterprise* in 1974. The export appeal of the F-14 is obvious and Iran is introducing 80 from 1976. But costs have run well beyond prediction, Grumman refusing at one time to continue the programme and claiming its existing contracts would result in a loss of $105 million. For the same reason the re-engined F-14B, with the later-technology and much more powerful F401 engine, was held to a single prototype. In 1975 ongoing production agreements were concluded and by 1983 total deliveries amounted to a useful 468 aircraft, excluding 80 supplied to Iran. The basic aircraft has remained virtually unchanged, though prolonged trouble with the engines has led to the P-414A version of the TF30 which is hoped to improve safety and reliability. This engine comes with the F-14C in late 1983 together with a new radar, programmable signal processor, a new target identification system embodying Northrop's TCS (TV camera set) which has been slowly retrofitted to existing Tomcats since 1981, a laser gyro inertial system, completely new cockpit displays and completely new threat-warning and internal self-protection jammer system. In 1980-81 as a replacement for the RA-5C and RF-8G, 49 F-14As were fitted with Tarps (tac air recon pod system), containing optical cameras and an infra-red sensor. Because of severe cost-escalation of the 'cheap' F/A-18A the latter is now more expensive than the Tomcat, which is accordingly expected to be expanded from a 497-aircraft programme to a total of 845, delivered at about 24 per year into the 1990s.

Right: This fine picture was taken during the firing trials with 94 of the new Amraam missiles from the Pacific Missile Test Center at Pt Mugu; aircraft 158625 has one Amraam installed.

Below: Formerly the most flamboyantly painted fighters, F-1A Tomcats are being progressively finished in low-contrast grey.

Grumman E-2 Hawkeye

E-2A, B and C Hawkeye, TE-2C and C-2A Greyhound

Origin: Grumman Aerospace.
Type: E-2 series, AEW aircraft; C-2, COD transport.
Engines: Two 4,910ehp Allison T56-425 single-shaft turboprops.
Dimensions: Span 80ft 7in (24.56m); length 57ft 7in (17.55m); (C-2A) 56ft 8in; height (E-2) 18ft 4in (5.59m); (C-2) 16ft 11in (5.16m).
Weights: Empty (E-2C) 37,616lb (17,062kg), (C-2A) 31,154lb (14,131 kg); loaded (E-2C) 51,817lb (23,503kg), (C-2A) 54,354lb (24,654kg).
Performance: Maximum speed (E-2C) 374mph (602km/h); (C-2A) 352mph (567km/h); inital climb (C-2A) 2,330ft (710m)/min; service ceiling (both) about 31,000ft (9,450,m); range (both) about 1,700 miles (2,736km).
Armament: None.
History: First flight (W2F-1) 21 October 1960; (production E-2A) 19 April 1961; (E-2B) 20 February 1969; (E-2C) 20 January 1971; (C-2A) 18 November 1964; growth E-2C, possibly late 1977.

Development: Originally designated W2F-1, the E-2A Hawkeye was the first aircraft designed from scratch as an airborne early-warning surveillance platform (all previous AEW machines being modifications of existing types). Equipped with an APS-96 long-range radar with scanner rotating six times per minute inside a 24ft diameter radome, the E-2A has a flight crew of two and three controllers seated aft in the Airborne Tactical Data

System (ATDS) compartment, which is constantly linked with the Naval Tactical Data System (NTDS) in Fleet HQ or the appropriate land base. The E-2A can handle an entire air situation and direct all friendly air operations in attacking or defensive missions. From the E-2A were derived the E-2B, with microelectric computer, and the C-2A Greyhound COD (carrier on-board delivery) transport, able to make catapult takeoffs and arrested landings with 39 passengers or bulky freight. The final version was the dramatically new E-2C, with APS-120 radar and APA-171 aerial system, with OL-93 radar data processor serving a Combat Information Center (CIC) staff with complete knowledge of all airborne targets even in a land-clutter environment. Though it has an advanced and costly airframe, more than three-quarters of the price of an E-2C is accounted for by electronics. This version entered service with squadron VAW-123 at NAS Norfolk, Virginia, in November 1973. Production was expected to end in 1977, but since then orders have increased the total to 95, delivered at five per year until completion in 1987. In addition two TE-2C trainers are in Navy service. With the original radar aircraft could be detected within radius of some 300 miles (480km) but the improved APS-125 now fitted can detect cruise missiles at over 115 miles (185km), track more than 250 targets simultaneously, control more than 30 air interceptions (normally by F-14) and give a clear display to the three controllers. An ALR-59 passive detection system detects hostile radio or radar signals at over-the-horizon distances up to more than 500 miles (800km).

Right: One of the key men aboard a carrier is the Landing Signals Officer, here seen on recovery of a Hawkeye from a shore-based training unit practising actual carrier landings.

Above: Seen here taxiing on land with everything folded, the E-2C is one of the most compact aircraft ever built. All E-2Cs in operational US Navy service are embarked in carriers.

Grumman OV-1 Mohawk

OV-1A to -1D, EV-1, JOV, RV

Origin: Grumman Aerospace.
Type: (OV) multi-sensor tactical observation and reconnaissance; (EV) electronic warfare; (JOV) armed reconnaissance; (RV) electronic reconnaissance.
Engines: Two 1,005shp Lycoming T53-7 or -15 free-turbine turboprops; (OV-1D) two 1,160shp T53-701.
Dimensions: Span (-1A, -C) 42ft (12.8m); (-1, -D) 48ft (14.63m); length 41ft (12.5m); (-1D with SLAR, 44ft 11in); height 12ft 8in (3.86m).
Weights: Empty (-1A) 9,937lb (4,507kg); (-1B) 11,067lb (5,020kg); (-1C) 10,400lb (4,717kg); (-1D) 12,054lb (5,467kg); maximum loaded (-1A) 15,031lb (6,818kg); (11B, C) 19,230lb (8,722kg); (-1D) 18,109lb (8,214kg).
Performance: Maximum speed (all) 297-310mph (480-500km/h); initial climb (-1A) 2,950ft (900m)/min; (-1B) 2,250ft (716m)/min; (-1C) 2,670ft (814m)/min; (-1D) 3,618ft (1,103m)/min; service ceiling (all) 28,800-31,000ft (8,534-9,449m); range with external fuel (-1A) 1,410 miles (2,270km); (-1B) 1,230 miles (1,980km); (-1C) 1,330 miles (2,140km): (-1D) 1,011 miles (1,627km).
Armament: Not normally fitted, but can include a wide variety of air-to-ground weapons including grenade launchers, Minigun pods and small guided missiles.
History: First flight (YOV-1A) 14 April 1959; service delivery, February 1961; final delivery (new aircraft) December 1970.

Above: USA OV-1D Mohawks are being reworked and modernized, and also repainted in overall low-contrast grey (see facing page).

Development: Representing a unique class of military aircraft, the OV-1 Mohawk is a specially designed battlefield surveillance machine with characteristics roughly midway between lightplanes and jet fighters. One of its requirements was to operate from rough forward airstrips and it has exceptional STOL (short takeoff and landing) qualities and good low-speed

Hughes AH-64 Apache

Model 77, AH-64

Origin: Hughes Helicopters, Culver City.
Type: Armed helicopter.
Engines: Two 1,536shp General Electric T700-700 free-turbine turboshafts.
Dimensions: Diameter of four-blade main rotor 48ft 0in (14.63m); length overall (rotors turning) 57ft ½in (17.39m); length of fuselage 49ft 1½in (14.97m); height to top of hub 13ft 10in (4.22m).
Weights: Empty 10,268lb (4,657kg); maximum loaded 17,650lb (8,006kg).
Performance: Maximum speed (13,925lb/6,316kg) 192mph (309km/h); maximum cruising speed 182mph (293km/h); max vertical climb 2,880ft (878m)/min; max range on internal fuel 380 miles (611km); ferry range 1,121 miles (1,804km).
Armament: Four wing hardpoints can carry 16 Hellfire missiles or 76 rockets (or mix of these weapons); turret under fuselage (designed to collapse harmlessly upwards in crash landing) houses 30mm Chain Gun with 1,200 rounds of varied types of ammunition.
History: First flight (YAH-64) 30 September 1975; entry into service scheduled 1984.

Development: A generation later than the cancelled Lockheed AH-56A Cheyenne (the world's first dedicated armed escort and attack helicopter), the AH-64 was selected as the US Army's standard future attack helicopter

in December 1976. This followed competitive evaluation with the rival Bell YAH-63, which had tricycle landing gear and the pilot seated in front of the co-pilot/gunner. The basic development contract also included the Chain Gun, a lightweight gun (in 30mm calibre in this application) with a rotating lockless bolt. In 1977 development began of the advanced avionics, electro-optics and weapon-control systems, progressively fitted to three more prototypes, followed by a further three—designated Total Systems Aircraft—flown by early 1980. The 56-month development ended in mid 1981, and a production decision was due before the end of that year. Hughes is responsible for the rotors and dynamic components, while Teledyne Ryan produces the bulk of the rest of the airframe (fuselage, wings, engine nacelles, avionic bays, canopy and tail unit). The entire structure is designed to withstand hits with any type of ammunition up to 23mm calibre. The main blades, for example, each have five stainless-steel spars, with structural glassfibre tube linings, a laminated stainless-steel skin and composite rear section, all bonded together. The main sensors are PNVS (pilot's night vision system) and TADS (target acquisition and designation sight) jointly developed by Martin Marietta and Northrop.

Both crew members are equipped with the Honeywell IHADSS (integrated helmet and display sight system) and each can in emergency fly the helicopter and control its weapons. The helicopter's nose sight incorporates day/night FLIR (forward-looking infra-red, laser ranger/designator and laser tracker.

Below: Three of the AH-64 development machines pictured during advanced weapons trials. Speeds up to 237mph (382km/h) have been reached during manoeuvres of these nine-ton battlewagons.

control with full-span slats and triple fans and rudders. Pilot and observer sit in side-by-side Martin Baker J5 seats and all versions have extremely good all-round view and very comprehensive navigation and communications equipment. All versions carry cameras and upward-firing flares for night photography. Most variants carry UAS-4 infra-red surveillance equipment and the -1B carries APS-94 SLAR (side-looking airborne radar) in a long pod under the right side of the fuselage, with automatic film processing giving, within seconds of exposure, a permanent film record of radar image on either side of the flight path. The -1D combined the functions of the two previous versions in being quickly convertible to either IR or SLAR missions. Underwing pylons can carry 150 US gal drop tanks, ECM (electronic countermeasures) pods, flare/chaff dispensers, or, in the OV-1A such weapons as FFAR pods, 0.50in gun pods or 500lb (227kg) bombs—though a 1965 Department of Defense rule forbids the US Army to arm its fixed-wing aircraft! The EV-1 is the OV-1B converted to electronic surveillance with an ALQ-133 target locator system in centerline and tip pods. The RV-1C and -1D are conversions of the OV-1C and -1D for permanent use in the electronic reconnaissance role. Total production of all versions was 375, and since the mid-1970s the USA has maintained a continuing modernization programme involving (by 1983) 91 earlier models to OV-1D standard, and four to RV-1D, to maintain a force of 110 OV-1Ds and 36 RV-1Ds into the 1990s.

Right: Though this USA OV-1D is painted in the original olive drab it actually looks more like today's medium grey (photo opposite looks falsely white). This particular Mohawk was using SLAR and IR to monitor the Mount St Helens volcanic eruption.

Hughes OH-6 Cayuse and 500M

OH-6 Cayuse, 500M and Defender

Origin: Hughes Helicopters, Culver City.
Type: Light multi-role helicopter.
Engine: One Allison turboshaft, (OH-6A) T63-5A flat-rated at 252.5shp, (500M) 250-C18A flat-rated at 278shp.
Dimensions: Diameter of four-blade main rotor 26ft 4in (8.03m); length overall (rotors turning) 30ft 3¾in (9.24m); height overall.8ft 1½in (2.48m).
Weights: Empty (OH) 1,229lb (557kg), (500M) 1,130lb (512kg); maximum loaded (OH) 2,700lb (1,225kg), (500M) 3,000lb (1,361kg).
Performance: Max cruise at S/L 150mph (241km/h); typical range on normal fuel 380 miles (611km).
Armament: See text.
History: First flight (OH-6A) 27 February 1963, (500M) early 1968.

Development: Orignal winner of the controversial LOH (Light Observation helicopter) competition of the US Army in 1961, the OH-6A Cayuse is one of the most compact flying machines in history, relative to its capability. The standard machine carries two crew and four equipped troops, or up to 1,000lb (454kg) of electronics and weapons including the XM-27 gun or XM-75 grenade launcher plus a wide range of other infantry weapons. The US Army bought 1,434, and several hundred other military or para-military examples have been built by Hughes or its licensees. In 1982 Hughes was in production with, or offering, nine military helicopters all significantly

Above: Despite losing to Bell in the AHIP (see Bell Kiowa) the OH-6D as an OH-6A Cayuse rebuild remains an attractive possibility.

uprated compared with the Cayuse, and bristling with advanced avionics, sensors, weapons and protective features, but the only sale to the US military has been USA funding of a single research Notar (NO TAil Rotor) helicopter modified from an OH-6A.

Below: Widely used elsewhere, the Model 500MD with Tow missiles and nose-mounted sight is another OH-6A modification.

Kaman SH-2 Seasprite

UH-2, HH-2 and SH-2 in many versions (data for SH-2D)

Origin: Kaman Aerospace Corp.
Type: Ship-based multi-role helicopter (ASW, anti-missile defence, observation, search/rescue and utility).
Engine(s): Original versions, one 1,050 or 1,250hp General Electric T58 free-turbine turboshaft, all current versions, two 1,350hp T58-8F.
Dimensions: Main rotor diameter 44ft (13.41m); overall length (blades turning) 52ft 7in (16m); fuselage length 40ft 6in (12.3m); height 13ft 7in (4.14m).
Weights: Empty 6,953lb (3,153kg); maximum loaded 13,300lb (6,033kg).
Performance: Maximum speed 168mph (270km/h); maximum rate of climb (not vertical) 2,440ft (744m)/min; service ceiling 22,500ft (6,858m); range 422 miles (679km).
Armament: See text.
History: First flight (XHU2K-1) 2 July 1959; service delivery (HU2K-1, later called UH-2A) 18 December 1962; final delivery (new) 1972, (conversion) 1975, (rebuild) 1982.

Above: An SH-2F Seasprite from HSL-31 (Light helicopter anti-submarine squadron 31) which operates in the training role from NAS North Island (San Diego), California. Note Mk 46 torpedo.

Right: Refuelling at sea in the hover is one of the routines practised by Atlantic Fleet training squadron HSL-32 from Norfolk this machine is assigned to Knox class frigate *W.S.Sims*.

Development: Originally designated HU2K-1 and named Seasprite, this exceptionally neat helicopter was at first powered by a single turbine engine mounted close under the rotor hub and was able to carry a wide range of loads, including nine passengers, in its unobstructed central cabin, with two crew in the nose. The main units of the tailwheel-type landing gear retracted fully. About 190 were delivered and all were later converted to have two T58 engines in nacelles on each side. Some are HH-2C rescue/utility with armour and various armament including chin Minigun turret and waist-mounted machine guns or cannon; others are unarmed HH-2D. One has been used in missile-firing (Sparrow III and Sidewinder) trials in the missile-defence role. All Seasprites have since 1970 been drastically converted to serve in the LAMPS (light airborne multi-purpose system) for anti-submarine and anti-missile defence. The SH-2D has more than two tons of special equipment including powerful chin radar, sonobuoys, MAD gear, ECM, new navigation and communications systems and Mk 44 and/or Mk 46 torpedoes. All will eventually be brought up to SH-2F standard with improved rotor, higher gross weight and improved sensors and weapons. Though

only the interim LAMPS platform the SH-2 is a substantial programme. Th first of 88 new SH-2F Seasprites became operational with squadron HSL-3 in mid-1973, and 88 were delivered by the end of the decade. Kaman ha since been rebuilding the earlier SH- and HH-2D helicopters in the sam configuration, this being completed in March 1982. By this time 220 SH-2 or -2F detachments had served on long ocean cruises aboard eight classe of surface warship, the DD-963 and FFG-7 class vessels having two LAMP helicopters each. Though LAMPS III (SH-60B) is now entering service th SH-2F will remain operational throughout the 1990s.

Lockheed C-5A Galaxy

C-5A

Origin: Lockheed-Georgia Company, Marietta, Ga.
Type: Heavy strategic airlift transport.
Powerplant: Four 41,000lb (18,597kg) thrust General Electric TF39-1 turbofans.
Dimensions: Span 222ft 8½in (67.88m); length 247ft 10in (75.54m); height 65ft 1½in (19.85m); wing area 6,200sq ft (576.0m²).
Weights: Empty (basic operating) 337,937lb (153,285kg), loaded (2,25g) 769,000lb (348,810kg).
Performance: Maximum speed (max weight, 25,000ft/7,620m) 571mph (760km/h); normal long-range cruising speed, 518mph (834km/h); initial climb at max wt., rated thrust, 1,800ft (549m)/min; service ceiling, (615,000lb/278,950kg) 34,000ft (10.36km); range with design payload of 220, 967lb (100,228kg), 3,749 miles (6,033km); range with 112,600lb (51,074kg) payload 6,529 miles (10,507km); ferry range 7,991 miles (12,860km); takeoff distance at max wt. over 50ft (15m), 8,400ft (2,560m); landing from 50ft (15m), 3,600ft (1,097m).
Armament: None.
History: First flight 30 June 1968; service delivery, 17 December 1969; final delivery from new, May 1973.

Above: Looking like a stranded whale, this C-5A is just opening its nose to disgorge heavy cargo. The leading edges are drooped in this photograph taken at a MAC base.

Right: The C-5A is one of very few aircraft in the USAF which dwarfs the KC-10A Extender, seen here during the latter's first air-refuelling hook-up with a Galaxy. C-5A is aircraft 69-0013.

Development: Growing appreciation of the need for an extremely large logistics transport to permit deployment of the heaviest hardware items on a global basis led in 1963 to the CX-HLS (Heavy Logistics System) specification calling for a payload of 250,000lb (113,400kg) over a coast-to-coast range and half this load over the extremely challenging unrefuelled range of 8,000 miles (12,875km); it also demanded the abililty to fly such loads into a 4,000ft (1,220m) rough forward airstrip. Such performance was theoretically possible using a new species of turbofan, of high bypass ratio, much more powerful than existing engines. In August 1965 GE won the engine contract, and two months later Lockheed won the C-5A aircraft. Design was undertaken under extreme pressure, the wing being assigned to CDI, a group of British engineers from the cancelled HS.115 and TSR.2 programmes. About half the value of each airframe was subcontracted to suppliers in the US and Canada, and construction of the first aircraft (66-8303) began as early as August 1966.

Meeting the requirements proved impossible, and cost-inflation reduced the total buy from 115 (six squadrons) to 81 (four squadrons), of which 30 were delivered by the end of 1970. As a cargo airlifter the C-5A proved in a class of its own, with main-deck width of 19ft (5.79m) and full-section access at front and rear. The upper deck houses the flight crew of five, a rest area for a further 15 and a rear (aft of the wing) area with 75 seats. Features include high-lift slats and flaps, an air-refuelling receptacle, advanced forward-looking radars and a unique landing gear with 28 wheels offering the required 'high flotation' for unpaved surfaces, as well as free castoring to facilitate ground manoeuvring, an offset (20° to left or right) swivelling

capability for use in crosswinds, fully modulating anti-skid brakes and th ability to kneel to bring the main deck close to the ground. Despite high publicized faults, most of which were quickly rectified, the C-5A was soo giving invaluable service; but a deep-rooted difficulty was that the win accrued fatigue damage much more rapidly than had been predicte Several costly modification programmes proved incomplete solutions, ar in 1978 Lockheed's proposal for the introduction of a new wing wa accepted. This wing uses a totally different detailed design in differer materials, and though the moving surfaces are largely unchanged even thes are to be manufactured again, the slats, ailerons and flap tracks for th second time being assigned to Canadair. Between 1982-87 all 77 survivir aircraft are to be re-winged. This is being done with minimal reduction airlift capability by MAC's 60th MAW at Travis, 436th at Dover, Delawar and 443rd at Altus AFB, Oklahoma.

In 1982 the Reagan administration recommended purchase of a additional 50 aircraft costing $8 billion, instead of C-17s. These C-5Ns wi have long crack-free airframe life, improved avionics and easier serviceabilit but will have performance essentially identical to the existing aircraf Engines will be TF39-1Cs with modifications purely to increase life an reduce cost. In USAF service the designation of the C-5N will be C-5B, and deliveries are expected at a modest rate from 1988.

Lockheed C-130 Hercules

C-130A to C-130R (sub-variants, see text)

Origin: Lockheed-Georgia Company, Marietta, Ga.
Type: Originally, multirole airlift transport; special variants, see text.
Powerplant: Four Allison T56 turboprops, (B and E families) 4,050ehp T56-7, (H family) 4,910ehp T56-15 flat-rated at 4,508ehp.
Dimensions: Span 132ft 7in (40.41m); length (basic) 97ft 9in (29.79m), (HC-130H, arms spread) 106ft 4in (32.41m); wing area 1,745sq ft (162.12m²).
Weights: Empty (basic E, H) 72,892lb (33,063kg); operating weight (H) 75,832lb (34,397kg); loaded (E,H) 155,000lb (70,310kg), max overload 175,000lb (79,380kg).
Performance: Maximum speed at 175,000lb (E, H), also max cruising speed, 386mph (621km/h); economical cruise, 345mph (556km/h); initial SL climb (E) 1,830ft (558m)/min, (H) 1,900ft (579m)/min; service ceiling at 155,000lb, (E) 23,000ft (7,010m), (H) 26,500ft (8,075m); range (H with max payload of 43,399lb (19,685kg) 2,487 miles (4,002km); 4,606 miles (7,412km); takeoff to 50ft (15m) (H at 175,000lb), 5,160ft (1,573m); landing from 50ft (15m) (H at 100,000lb/45,360kg), 2,700ft (823m).
Armament: Normally none.
History: First flight (YC-130A) 23 August 1954, (production C-130A) 7 April 1955; service delivery December 1956.

Development: When the Berlin Airlift and Korean war highlighted the need for more capable military transport aircraft, several obvious features were waiting to be combined in one design. Among these were a high wing and unobstructed cargo compartment, a flat level floor at truck-bed height above the ground, pressurization and air-conditioning, full-section rear door and vehicle ramp, turboprop propulsion for high performance, a modern flight deck with all-round vision, and retractable landing gear with 'high flotation' tyres for use from unprepared airstrips. All were incorporated in the Lockheed Model 82 which in June 1951 won an Air Force requirement for a new and versatile transport for TAC. By sheer good fortune the Allison single-shaft T56 turboprop matured at precisely the right time, along with a new species of advanced Aeroproducts or HamStan propeller and several other new-technology items including high-strength 2024 aluminium alloy, machined skin planks for the wings and cargo floor, metal/metal bonding and titanium alloys for the nacelles and flap skins. Another new feature was a miniature APU (auxiliary power unit) in one of the landing-gear blisters to provide ground power for air-conditioning and main-engine pneumatic starting.

Two YC-130 prototypes were built at Burbank, with 3,250hp T56-1 engines, but long before these were completed the programme was moved to the vast Government Plant 6 in Georgia which had been built to produce the B-29 under Bell management and restored to active use by Lockheed in January 1951. The new transport was ordered as the C-130A in September 1952 and the work phased in well with the tapering off of the B-47. When the 130, soon dubbed the Herky-bird, joined the 463rd Troop Carrier Wing at Ardmore in 1956 it caused a stir of a kind never before associated with a mere cargo transport. Pilots began to fly their big airlifters like fighters, and to explore the limits of what appeared to be an aircraft so willing it would do impossible demands. This was despite increases in permitted gross weight

Above: Delivery of an M551 Sheridan light Shillelagh-firing tank by the ground-proximity (no parachute) extraction method.

Below: The remaining first-line user of the AC-130H is the 1st Special Ops Wing (TAC 9th AF) at Hurlburt Field, Florida.

Lockheed C-141 StarLifter

C-141A and B

Origin: Lockheed-Georgia Company, Marietta, Ga.
Type: Strategic airlift and aeromedical transport.
Powerplant: Four 21,000lb (9,525kg) thrust Pratt & Whitney TF33-7 turbofans.
Dimensions: Span 159ft 11in (48.74m); length (A) 145ft. 0in (44.2m), (B) 168ft 3½in (51.29m); wing area 3,228sq. ft (299.9m²).
Weights: Empty (A) 133,733lb (60,678kg), (B) 148,120lb (67,186kg); loaded (A) 316,600lb (143,600kg), (B) 343,000lb (155,585kg).
Performance: Maximum speed (A) 571mph (919km/h), (B, also max cruising speed) 566mph (910km/h); long-range cruising speed (both) 495mph (796km/h), initial climb (A) 3,100ft (945m)/min, (B) 2,920ft (890m)/min; service ceiling, 41,600ft (12,68km), range with maximum payload of (A, 70,847lb/32,136kg) 4,080 miles (6,565km), (B, 90,880lb/41,222kg) 2,935 miles (4,725km); takeoff to 50ft (15m) (B) 5,800ft (1,768m).
Armament: None.
History: First flight 17 December 1963; service delivery 19 October 1964; first flight of C-141B, 24 March 1977.

Development: In the late 1950s MATS (now MAC) anticipated a severe future shortage of long-range airlift capacity, the C-133 being an interim propeller aircraft and the much larger C-132 being cancelled. As interim solutions orders were placed for the C-135 jet and for a long-range version of the C-130, but on 4 May 1960 a requirement was issued for a purpose-designed transport which was won by Lockheed's Model 300 submission in March 1961. Ordered at once as the C-141, it followed the lines of the C-130, and even had the same 10ft x 9ft (3.1 x 2.77m) body cross-section (a choice which perhaps proved erroneous, as from the start the internal cube volume was totally inadequate for the available weightlifting ability). The

Above: A pre-modification StarLifter, a C-141A of 438th MAW, McGuire AFB, NJ; compare it with the stretched version, C-141B shown far right.

C-141 was, in other respects, much larger, with a wing of almost twice the area, swept at only 23° (¼-chord) for good field length but resulting in lower speeds than equivalent civil transports. Features included a full-section

om 102,000lb to 116,000 and then to 124,200lb (56,335kg). At an early
age the nose grew a characteristic pimple from switching to the APN-59
radar, and provision was made for eight 1,000lb (454kg) Aerojet assisted
takeoff rockets to be clipped to the sides of the fuselage, to augment the
thrust of full-rated 3,750hp engines.

In December 1958 Lockheed flew the first extended-range C-130B with
more powerful engines driving four-blade propellers. The Air Force bought
132 to supplement the 204 A-models, the latter progressively being rebuilt
as AC-130 gunships, DC-130 drone (RPV) controllers, JC-130 spacecraft
tracking and retrieval aircraft and C-130D wheel/ski aircraft with
Arctic/Antarctic equipment. The next basic model, and bought in largest
numbers (389), was the E, first flown on 25 August 1961. With this a minor
structural rework enabled wing pylons to carry large drop tanks of 1,360 US
gal (5,145lit), meeting the strategic range requirements of MATS (now
MAC) and thus opening up a new market for the 130 beyond the tactical
sphere. MATS (MAC) received 130 of the E model, and TAC re-equipped
with 245 and transferred the A and B models to the ANG and Reserve,
giving these reserve forces undreamed-of airlift capability. Some B-models
were converted for other roles, new duties including weather reconnaissance
(WC-130) and a single STOL aircraft with extra pod-mounted T56 engines
supplying a boundary-layer control system, designated NC-130. Among
currently serving rebuilds of the E are the EC-130E tactical command and
control platform, with several unique avionic systems, and the MC-130E
used with special avionics and low-level flight techniques for clandestine
exfiltration and airdrop missions.

Latest basic type is the C-130H, first delivered in April 1975, with more

**Left: Landing lights aglow, an HC-130H of the USAF Aerospace
Rescue and Recovery Service is marshalled during a winter
exercise. Some versions have heated ski/wheel landing gears.**

**Above: The 7th Airborne Command and Control Sqn at Keesler
AFB, Mississippi, is an operator of the EC-130E battlefield
command/control platform with 20 communications systems.**

powerful engines flat-rated at the previous level to give improved takeoff
from hot/high airstrips. Variations include the HC-130H extended-range
model for the Aerospace Rescue and Recovery Service with a fold-out nose
installation for the snatching of people or payloads from the ground. The
JHC-130H model has further gear for aerial recovery of space capsules. A
more advanced model, with special direction-finding receivers but without
long-range tanks, is the HC-130N. The HC-130P model combines the mid-
air retrieval capability with a tanking and air-refuelling function for
helicopters.

This evergreen aircraft is by far the most important Air Force tactical
airlifter and fulfils a host of secondary functions. Though civil and RAF
versions have been stretched to match capacity to payload, this has not been
done by the USAF. Production continues, and six H models were ordered for
the AFRes and ANG in July 1981. New roles being studied by the Air Force
include the C-130H-MP maritime patroller with offshore surveillance
equipment, and the CAML (cargo aircraft minelayer) system using
hydraulically powered pallets for rapid-sequence deployment of large sea
mines. Should CAML be adopted, Air Force C-130s could fly minelaying
missions for the Navy.

The Navy itself uses many C-130s, but was pipped to the post by the
Marines who began in August 1957 with C-130As used in the tanker role.
Subsequently the Marines bought 46 KC-130F and (so far) 14 KC-130R
tankers with twin hosereels in wingtip pods. Among Navy versions are the
EC-130G and EC-130Q Tacamo (special communications, especially for
ballistic-missile submarines), DC-130 drone directors and LC-130F and R
wheel/ski aircraft used mainly in Antarctica.

---

ramp/door, side paratroop doors, upper-surface roll/airbrake spoilers, four
reversers, tape instruments, an all-weather landing system and advanced
loading and positioning systems for pallets and other loads.

The first five C-141As were ordered in August 1961, at which time the
requirement was for 132 aircraft, but following extremely rapid development
and service introduction further orders were placed for a total of 285.
Several of the first block were structurally modified to improve the ability of
the floor to support the skids of a containerized Minuteman ICBM, a weight
of 86,207lb (39,103kg). One of these aircraft set a world record in
parachuting a single mass of 70,195lb (31,840kg). Standard loads included
10 regular 463L cargo pallets, 154 troops, 123 paratroops or 80 litter
(stretcher) patients plus 16 medical attendants. Usable volume was 5,290
cu ft (150m³), not including the ramp. Service experience proved exemplary
and in the Vietnam war C-141s, many of them specially equipped for medical
missions and flown with extraordinary skill to ensure a smooth ride even
through severe weather, maintained essentially a daily schedule on a
10,000-mile (16,000km) trip with full loads both ways.

It was this full-load experience which finally drove home the lesson that the
C-141 could use more cubic capacity. Lockheed devised a cost/effective
stretch which adds 'plugs' ahead of and behind the wing which extend the
usable length by 23ft 4in (7.11m), increasing the usable volume (including
the ramp) to 11,399cu ft (322.71m³). The extended aircraft, designated
C-141B, carries 13 pallets or much larger numbers of personnel. It also
incorporates an improved wing/body fairing which reduces drag and fuel
burn per unit distance flown, while among other modifications the most
prominent is a dorsal bulge aft of the flight deck housing a universal (boom or
drogue) flight-refuelling receptacle. The first conversion, the YC-141B, was
so successful that the Air Force decided to have Lockheed rework all the
surviving aircraft (277), to give in effect the airlift ability of 90 additional
aircraft with no extra fuel consumption.

In fact only 270 C-141B StarLifters were produced, the last being
delivered from Marietta on 29 June 1982. The entire rebuild programme
was completed ahead of schedule and below cost. They are assigned to the

**Above: This four-colour camouflage is one of several colour
schemes which were investigated on large aircraft in 1980. There
is no intention to depart at present from the standard all-grey
colour of the MAC C-141Bs though some have white tops.**

following MAWs: 60th at Travis, California; 63rd at Norton, California;
437th at Charleston, S Carolina; 438th at McGuire, NJ; 443rd at Altus,
Oklahoma; and to part of the 314th TAW at Little Rock, Arkansas.

Lockheed P-3 Orion

P-3A, -3B and -3C with derivatives

Origin: Lockheed-California Co.

Type: Marine reconnaissance and anti-submarine, normally with flight crew of five and tactical crew of five; variants, see text.

Engines: Four Allison T56 single-shaft turboprops; (P-3A) T56-10W, 4,500ehp with water injection; (remainder) T56-14, 4,910ehp.

Dimensions: Span 99ft 8in (30.37m); length 116ft 10in (35.61m); height 33ft 8½in (10.29m); wing area 1,300sq ft (120.77m²).

Weights: Empty (typical B, C) 61,491lb (27,890kg); maximum loaded 142,000lb (64,410kg).

Performance: Maximum speed 473mph (761km/h); initial climb 1,950ft (594m)/min; service ceiling 28,300ft (8,625m); range 4,800 miles (7,725km).

Armament: Very varied load in bulged unpressurized weapon bay ahead of wing and on ten wing pylons; maximum internal load 7,252lb (3,290kg) can include two depth bombs, four Mk 44 torpedoes, 87 sonobuoys and many other sensing and marking devices; underwing load can include six 2,000lb (907kg) mines or various mixes of torpedoes, bombs, rockets or missiles. Maximum expendable load 20,000lb (9,071kg).

History: First flight (aerodynamic prototype) 19 August 1958; (YP-3A) 25 November 1959; (production P-3A) 15 April 1961; (P-3C) 18 September 1968.

Development: In August 1957 the US Navy issued a requirement for a "off the shelf" anti-submarine patrol aircraft derived from an established type, and this was met in April 1958 by Lockheed's proposal for a conversion of the Electra turboprop airliner. The third Electra was quickly modified as an aerodynamic prototype and deliveries of production P-3As began in August 1962. From the 110th aircraft the Deltic system was fitted with improved sensors, and after delivering 157 P-3As production switched to the P-3B with the more powerful Dash-14 engine which does not need water/alcohol injection system. Lockheed supplied the US Navy with 124 of the B-model, surviving examples of which have been improved in various ways. By far the most important version is the P-3C, flown in 1968, which has largely new sensors and displays all linked by a digital computer. This soon became the definitive variant but has itself been the subject of successive Update programmes. From 1975 the P-3C Update introduced better navigation, sensor and data-processing capability. In 1976 Update II introduced an infra-red detection system in a chin turret, sonobuoy reference system and the capability to fire Harpoon missiles from wing pylons. A much more extensive revision was started in 1978 as Update III with completely altered ASW avionics, deliveries of this sub-type being due to start in April 1984. Deliveries of all P-3C versions reached 211 by 1983, with five per year expected through 1988. Rebuilds include WP-3A weather aircraft and various EP-3 Elint (electronic intelligence) aircraft serving with VQ-1 and -2.

Below: Pictured before delivery, this is a P-3C Update II of the 1977 period, which from 1984 will give way to the Update III.

Lockheed S-3 Viking

S-3A Viking, US-3A and S-3B

Origin: Lockheed-California Co.

Type: (S-3A, S-3B) four-seat carrier-based anti-submarine aircraft; (US-3A) carrier on-board delivery transport.

Engines: Two 9,275lb (4,207kg) General Electric TF34-400A two-shaft turbofans.

Dimensions: Span 68ft 8in (20.93m); length 53ft 4in (16.26m); height **22ft 9in (6.93m); wing area 598sq ft (55.55m²).**

Weights: Empty 26,600lb (12,065kg); normal loaded for carrier operation 42,500lb (19,277kg); maximum loaded 52,539lb (23,831kg).

Performance: Maximum speed 506mph (814km/h); initial climb, over 4,200ft (1,280m)/min; service ceiling, above 35,000ft (10,670m); combat range, more than 2,303 miles (3,705km); ferry range, more than 3,454 miles (5,558km).

Armament: Split internal weapon bays can house four Mk 46 torpedoes, four Mk 82 bombs, four various depth bombs or four mines; two wing pylons can carry single or triple ejectors for bombs, rocket pods, missiles, tanks or other stores.

History: First flight 21 January 1972; service delivery October 1973; operational use (VS-41) 20 February 1974; final delivery after 1980.

Development: Designed to replace the evergreen Grumman S-2, the S-3 is perhaps the most remarkable exercise in packaging in the history of aviation. It is also an example of an aircraft in which the operational equipment costs considerably more than the aircraft itself. Lockheed-California won the Navy competition in partnership with LTV (Vought) which makes the wing, engine pods, tail and F-8 type landing gear. To increase transit speed the refuelling probe, MAD tail boom, FLIR (forward-looking infra-red) and certain other sensors all retract, while the extremely modern specially designed APS-116 radar is within the nose. Equipment includes CAINS (carrier aircraft inertial navigation system), comprehensive sonobuoy dispensing and control systems, doppler, very extensive radio navaid and altitude systems, radar

warning and ECM systems, extensive communications, and a Univac digital processor to manage all tactical and navigation information. By the middle of 1978 production of the 187 S-3As for the US Navy had been completed the bulk of these aircraft being deployed in the 13 carrier air groups embarked in large attack carriers as the standard ASW type. Three early Vikings have been modified to the US-3A COD (Carrier On-board Delivery) transport configuration with accommodation for 4,000lb (1,814kg) of cargo in two large underwing containers and six passengers and a little additional cargo in the fuselage. A redesigned large-body COD version has not been procured neither has the impressive KS-3A tanker which, like the demonstrator US-3A, was evaluated in 1980. Nevertheless tooling exists for possible future procurement. Meanwhile in 1982-88 Lockheed is converting planned 160 S-3As to S-3B standard with greatly augmented acoustic and radar processing capacity, expanded ESM (electronic support measures), a new APU (auxiliary power unit), new sonobuoy receiver and capability to fire the Harpoon anti-ship missile.

Below: Indistinguishable externally (from a distance) from the S-3B, these S-3As were photographed serving with VS-22 "Checkmates" from Cecil Field or embarked aboard USS Saratoga

Lockheed SR-71

SR-71 A, B and C

Origin: Lockheed-California Co.

Type: A, strategic reconnaissance; B, C, trainer.

Powerplant: Two 32,500lb (14,742kg) thrust Pratt & Whitney J58-1 (JT11D-20B) continuous-bleed afterburning turbojets.

Dimensions: Span 55ft 7in (16.94m); length 107ft 5in (32.74m); wing area 1,800sq ft (167.2m²); height 18ft 6in (5.64m).

Weights: Empty, not disclosed, but about 65,000lb (29.5t); loaded 170,000lb (77,112kg).

Performance: Maximum speed (also maximum cruising speed), about 2,100mph (3,380km/h) at over 60,000ft (18.29km), world record speed over 15/25km course, 2,193mph (3,530km/h, Mach 3.31); maximum sustained height (also world record), 85,069ft (25,929m); range at 78,740ft (24km) at 1,983mph (3191km/h, Mach 3) on internal fuel, 2,982 miles (4,800km); corresponding endurance, 1h 30min; endurance at loiter speed, up to 7h.

Armament: None.

History: First flight (A-11) 26 April 1962; (SR-71A) 22 December 1964; service delivery, January 1966.

Development: Unbelievably, Lockheed and the Air Force succeeded in designing, building and completing the flight-test programme of these extremely large and noisy aircraft in total secrecy. President Johnson disclosed the existence of the basic A-11 design in February 1964. It was created by Lockheed's Advanced Development Projects team-- the so-called Skunk Works--under vice-president C.L. 'Kelly' Johnson in 1959-61. The requirement was for a platform able to succeed the U-2 for clandestine reconnaissance, and as height was no longer sufficient protection, speed had to be added (which in turn translated into still greater height). Unprecedented engineering problems were encountered with the airframe made principally from titanium and its alloys, never before used for primary structure, the propulsion system (which at cruising speed glows orange-white at the nozzles yet gets most of its thrust from the inlets) and even the hydraulic system (which uses completely new materials and techniques). Basic features included a modified delta wing with pronounced camber on the outer leading edges, extremely large lifting strakes extended forwards along the body and nacelles, twin inwards-canted pivoted fins above the nacelles, outboard ailerons, inboard elevators and main gears with three wheels side-by-side. The original A-11 shape also featured fixed ventral fins under the rear of the nacelles and a larger hinged central ventral fin.

The first three aircraft (60-6934/6) were built as YF-12A interceptors, with a pressurized cockpit for a pilot and air interception officer, Hughes ASG-18 pulse-doppler radar, side chines cut back to avoid the radome and provide lateral locations for two IR seekers, and tandem

Above: No American aircraft fly stranger nor less publicized missions than the SR-71s of 9th SRW; this one is being parked.

Below: Ship 61-7955 bears the snake emblem on its fins which shows it flew combat missions over Southeast Asia in 1967-73.

missile bays for (usually) eight AIM-47 AAMs. In 1969-72 two participated in a joint programme with NASA to investigate many aspects of flight at around Mach 3. These aircraft investigated surface finishes other than the normal bluish-black which resulted in the popular name of 'Blackbird' for all aircraft of this family.

It is believed that about 15 aircraft were delivered to the Air Force with a generally similar standard of build, though configured for the reconnaissance/strike role. Designated A-11, they could carry a centreline pod which could be a 1-megaton bomb but was usually a GTD-21 reconnaissance drone looking like a scaled-down single-engined A-11 and with cameras, IR and (variously, according to mission) other sensors in a bay behind the multi-shock centrebody nose inlet. Some dozens of these RPVs were delivered, painted the same heat-reflective black and with similar flight performance (engine has not been disclosed) but with rather shorter endurance. Those not consumed in missions (about 17) were stored at Davis-Monthan.

The A-11/GTD-21 held the fort until, in 1964, the definitive long-range

Above: Touchdown by an SR-71B trainer, with full left rudder (the entire tails move) and 40ft chute deployed.

recon/strike RS-71A came into service. (It was announced by President Johnson as the SR-71A and as he was never corrected the 'SR' designation became accepted.) This also can carry a 1-MT bomb pod or GTD-21 or derived RPV, but details of missions and payloads have not been disclosed. With an airframe and increased-capacity fuel system first flown on the fourth A-11 (designated YF-12C) it is longer, has no rear ventrals, optimized forward chines extending to the tip of the nose, and no missile bay but extremely comprehensive and in some cases unique reconnaissance systems for the surveillance of from 60,000 to 80,000 square miles (155,000 to 207,000km²) per hour. The backseater, with a separate clamshell canopy with inserted panes of heat-resistant glass, is the RSO, reconnaissance systems officer. Both crew wear Astronaut suits and follow pre-flight procedures based on those of space missions. The first SR-71A was assigned to a new unit, the 4,200th SRW, at Beale AFB, California, in 1966, which worked up the optimum operating procedures and techniques for best coverage, optimum fuel consumption, minimal signatures and precision navigation, burning special JP-7 fuel topped up in flight by KC-135Q tankers also based at Beale. To facilitate the demanding process of crew conversion to this extremely costly aircraft an operational trainer, the SR-71B, was purchased, at least two being slotted into the main batch of 29 (or more) which began at 61-7950. This has a raised instructor cockpit and dual pilot controls, and also includes the reconnaissance systems for RSO training.

After the first crews had qualified as fully operational, in 1971, the parent wing was restyled the 9th SRW, with two squadrons. This has ever since operated in a clandestine manner, rarely more than two aircraft being despatched to any overseas theatre and missions normally being flown by single aircraft. It is not known to what extent subsonic cruise is used; in the normal high-speed regime the skin temperature rises from -49°C to 550/595°C, and the fuel serves as the heat sink and rises to a temperature of about 320°C before reaching the engines. At least one SR-71C was produced as an SR-71A rebuild, following loss of an SR-71B. It has been estimated that the SR-71As seldom fly more than 200 hours per year, mainly on training exercises. No recent estimate has been published of their vulnerability.

Lockheed TR-1

U-2A, B, C, CT, D, R, WU-2 family and TR-1A & B.

Origin: Lockheed-California Co.

Engine: One Pratt & Whitney unaugmented turbojet, (A and some derivatives) 11,200lb (5,080kg) thrust J57-13A or -37A, (most other U-2) versions, one 17,000lb (7,711kg) thrust J75-13, (TR-1) 17,000lb (7,711kg) J75-13B.

Dimensions: Span (A,B,C,D,CT) 80ft 0in (24,38m), (R, WU-2C, TR-1), 103ft 0in (31.39m)ength (typical of early versions) 49ft 7in (15.1m), (R,TR) 63ft 0in (19.2m); wing area (early) 565sq ft (52.49m²), (R, TR) 1,000sq ft (92.9m²).

Weights: Empty (A) 9,920lb (4,500kg), (B,C,CT,D) typically 11,700lb (5,305kg), (R) 14,990lb (6,800kg), (TR) about 16,000lb (7,258kg); loaded (A) 14,800lb (6,713kg), (B,C,CT,D, clean) typically 16,000lb (7,258kg), (with 89 US gal wing tanks) 17,270lb (7,833kg), (R) 29,000lb (13,154kg), (TR) 40,000lb (18,144kg).

Performance: Maximum speed (A) 494mph (795km/h), (B,C,CT,D) 528mph (850km/h), (R) about 510mph (821km/h), (TR) probably about 495mph (797km/h); maximum cruising speed (most) 460mph (740km/h), (TR) 430mph (692km/h); operational ceiling (A) 70,000ft (21.34km), (B,C, CT, D) 85,000ft (25.9km), (R,TR) about 90,000ft (27.43km); maximum range (A) 2,200 miles (3,540km), (B,C,CT,D) 3,000 miles (4,830km), (R) about 3,500 miles (5,833km), (TR) about 4,000 miles (6,437km); endurance on internal fuel (A) 5½ h, (B,C,CT,D) 6½ h, (R) 7½ h, (TR) 12 h.

Armament: None.

History: First flight (A) 1 August 1955; service delivery February 1956; operational service, June 1957; (TR) September 1981.

Development: First of the two families of clandestine surveillance aircraft produced by Lockheed's 'Skunk Works' under the brilliant engineering leadership of C.L. 'Kelly' Johnson, the U-2 was conceived in spring 1954 to meet an unannounced joint USAF/CIA requirement for a reconnaissance and research aircraft to cruise at the highest attainable altitudes. The entire programme was cloaked in secrecy, test flying (under Tony LeVier) took place at remote Watertown Strip, Nevada, and no announcement was made of delivery to the Air Force of 56-675 and -676, the two prototypes. The original order comprised 48 single-seaters and five tandem-seat aircraft, initially the back-seater being an observer or systems operator. The operating unit was styled Weather Reconnaissance Squadron, Provisional (1st) and soon moved to Atsugi AB, Japan, while the WRS,P (2nd) moved to Wiesbaden, Germany, with basing also at Lakenheath, England. The WRS,P(3rd) remained at Edwards to develop techniques and handle research.

Intense interest in the aircraft, grey and without markings, prompted an announcement that they were NASA research aircraft, with Utility designation

Below: Because of its much greater weight the TR-1 is slightly less difficult to land than early U-2s but it still needs great skill and concentration. It comes to rest on a wingtip.

U-2, but after numerous unmolested missions over the Soviet Union, China and other territories, one of the CIA aircraft was shot down near Sverdlovsk on 1 May 1960. Future missions were flown by USAF pilots in uniform, with USAF markings on the aircraft. Several more J75-powered aircraft were shot down over China and Cuba, and attrition was also fairly high from accidents, because the U-2 is possibly the most difficult of all modern aircraft to fly. Features include an all-metal airframe of sailplane-like qualities, with lightly loaded and extremely flexible wing, tandem bicycle landing gears, outrigger twin-wheel units jettisoned on takeoff (the landing tipping on to downturned wingtip), an unpressurized cockpit with UV-protected sliding canopy of F-104 type, special low-volatility fuel, and large flaps, airbrake and braking parachute.

McDonnell Douglas A-4 Skyhawk

A-4A to A-4S and TA-4 series

Origin: Douglas Aircraft Co, El Segundo (now division of McDonnell Douglas, Long Beach).

Type: Single-seat attack bomber; TA, dual-control trainer.

Engine: (B, C, L, P, Q, S) one 7,700lb (3,493kg) thrust Wright J65-16A single-shaft turbojet (US Sapphire); (E, J) 8,500lb (3,856kg) Pratt & Whitney J52-6 two-shaft turbojet; (F, G, H, K) 9,300lb (4,218kg) J52-8A; (M, N) 11,200lb (5,080kg) J52-408A.

Dimensions: Span 27ft 6in (8.38m); length (A)39ft 1in; (B) 39ft 6in (42ft 10¾in over FR probe); (E, F, G, H, K, L, P, Q, S) 40ft 1½in (12.22m); (M, N) 40ft 3¼in (12.27m); (TA series, excluding probe) 42ft 7¼in (12.98m); height 15ft (4.57m); (early single-seaters 15ft 2in, TA series 15ft 3in).

Weights: Empty (A) 7,700lb; (E) 9,284lb; (typical modern single-seat, eg M) 10,465lb (4,747kg); (TA-4F) 10,602lb (4,809kg); maximum loaded (A) 17,000lb; (B) 22,000lb; (all others, shipboard) 24,500lb (11,113kg); (land-based) 27,420lb (12,437kg).

Performance: Maximum speed (clean) (B) 676mph; (E) 685mph; (M) 670mph (1,078km/h) (TA-4F) 675mph; maximum speed (4,000lb 1,814kg bomb load) (F) 593mph; (M) 645mph; initial climb (F) 5,620ft (1,713m)/ min; (M) 8,440ft (2,572m)/min; service ceiling (all, clean) about 49,000ft (14,935m); range (clean, or with 4,000lb weapons and max fuel, all late versions) about 920 miles (1,480km); maximum range (M) 2,055 miles (3,307km).

Armament: Standard on most versions, two 20mm Mk 12 cannon, each with 200 rounds; (H, N, and optional on other export versions) two 30mm DEFA 553, each with 150 rounds. Pylons under fuselage and wings for total ordnance load of (A, B, C) 5,000lb (2,268kg); (E, F, G, H, K, L, P, Q, S) 8,200lb (3,720kg); (M, N) 9,155lb (4,153kg).

History: First flight (XA4D-1) 22 June 1954; (A-4A) 14 August 1954; squadron delivery October 1956; (A-4C) August 1959; (A-4E) July 1961; (A-4F) August 1966; (A-4M) April 1970; (A-4N) June 1972; first of TA series (TA-4E) June 1965.

Development: Most expert opinion in the US Navy refused to believe the claim of Ed Heinemann, chief engineer of what was then Douglas El Segundo, that he could build a jet attack bomber weighing half the 30,000lb specified by the Navy. The first Skyhawk, nicknamed "Heinemann's Hot

Rod", not only flew but gained a world record by flying a 500km circuit at over 695mph. Today some 30 years later, greatly developed versions are still in use. These late versions do weigh close to 30,000lb, but only because the basic design has been improved with more powerful engines, increased fuel capacity and much heavier weapon load. The wing was made in a single unit, forming an integral fuel tank and so small it did not need to fold. Hundreds of Skyhawks have served aboard carriers, but in the US involvement in SE Asia "The Scooter" (as it was affectionately known) flew many kinds of mission from land bases. In early versions the emphasis was on improving range and load and the addition of all-weather avionics. The model introduced the dorsal hump containing additional avionics, and the M, the so-called Skyhawk II, marked a major increase in mission effectiveness. Most of the TA-4 trainers closely resembled the corresponding single-seater but the TA-4J and certain other models have simplified avionics and are used not only for advanced pilot training but also by the "Top Gun" and similar fighter-pilot training units for dissimilar aircraft combat training. Though production was completed in 1979 after 26 unbroken years, with deliveries amounting to 2,405 attack models and 555 two-seaters; updating programmes continue to improve survivors in Navy and Marine Corps service. There is also a major rebuild programme which since 1980 has given the Marines 23 two-seat TA-4F trainers rebuilt as OA-4M FAC (Forward Air Control) platforms with avionics basically as in the A-4M and the rear canopy section faired into the "camel hump".

From 1959 the J75 engine was installed, and with the U-2C the inlets were splayed out at the front, the U-2D being the original two-seat version and the U-2CT (conversion trainer) being one of at least six rebuilds, in this example as a dual-control pilot trainer with the instructor seated at an upper level. Most CTs have been stationed at the Air Force Flight Test Center and Test Pilot School, both at Edwards. The AFFTC also uses several other versions, including D variants with special instrumentation, dorsal or ventral inlets for sampling, and various external payloads, with a variety of black, white and other paint schemes. Both C and D models have large dorsal 'doghouse' fairings for sampling, sensing or avionic equipment.

Because of high attrition the line was reopened in 1968 with 12 considerably larger aircraft styled U-2R (68-10329 to 10340). While most earlier models could carry 80 US gal (336lit) tanks on the leading edge, the R was supplied with large wing pods permanently installed and accommodating various payloads as well as 105 US gal (398lit) fuel. Wet wings increased internal capacity, and the R also introduced a stretched airframe able to accommodate all necessary fuel and equipment internally. Front and rear main gears were moved closer together and the rear fuselage was formed into a bulged upper platform carrying the tailplane. All known U-2R aircraft have been matt black, serving with various overseas commands.

The latest variant, the TR-1, is basically a further updated U-2R with ASARS (Advanced Synthetic-Aperture Radar System), in the form of the UPD-X side-looking airborne radar, and with dramatically increased integral-tank fuel capacity, which results in very much higher gross weight. A single-seater, like the R, the TR-1A carries extensive new avionics in its pods, as well as much more comprehensive ECM. Mission equipment is also carried in the nose, in the Q-bay behind the cockpit and between the inlet ducts. Because of the long endurance the Astronaut-suited pilot has special facilities for his personal comfort and for taking warm food. The first batch comprised two TR-1As (80-1061 and 1062) and a third aircraft (1063) which was actually first to be delivered, on 10 June 1981, via the Air Force to NASA with designation ER-2 for earth-resource missions. Next followed three more TR-1As and a two-seat TR-1B, the eventual fleet expected to number 33 As and two Bs. Ten of the single-seaters are to be allocated to the PLSS (Precision Location Strike System) mission for pinpointing and destroying electronic emitters far into hostile territory. Of the remaining 25 aircraft 18 are to be based at RAF Alconbury, England, where operations began under SAC control in early 1983. Forward operating locations in Germany and elsewhere will extend mission endurance over Warsaw Pact frontiers.

Below: Externally almost identical to a TR-1A, this is actually a U-2R (No 68-10329) which has totally different mission equipment.

Below: Much smaller, and half the weight of a TR-1, this U-2L was one of several converted from U-2B configuration to carry out upper-atmosphere radiation measurements (mainly following foreign nuclear-weapon testing). Several are still in use.

Left: An A-4M Skyhawk II of Marine Corps attack squadron VMA-214 seen on deployment from its base at El Toro to weapons practice at Yuma, Arizona. Loads comprised tank, rocket pods and ECM pods. Marine A-4s are shortly to be replaced by Harrier IIs.

Above: One of the standard A-4 weapons continues to be the AGM-45 Shrike anti-radar missile, though of course VA-55 of the Navy no longer flies the A-4. Considerable numbers of seven major versions are now stored and unlikely to be needed.

McDonnell Douglas/ BAe AV-8B Harrier II

AV-8B

Origin: McDonnell Douglas (St Louis), USA, and BAe, UK.
Type: Single-seat attack and close support aircraft.
Engine: One 22,000lb (9,979kg) Pratt & Whitney F402-RR-406 (Pegasus 11-21) vectored-thrust turbofan.
Dimensions: Span 30ft 4in (9.25m); length 46ft 4in (14.12m); height 11ft 7¾in (3.55m); wing area 230sq ft (21.37m²).
Weights: Empty 12,750lb (5,783kg); loaded (VTO) 19,550lb (8,867kg); maximum 29,750lb (13,494kg).
Performance: Maximum speed (clean, SL) 673mph (1,083km/h); takeoff run at max weight 1,200ft (366m); combat radius (seven Mk 82 Snakeye bombs and tanks) 748 miles (1,204km); ferry range 3,310 miles (5,328km).
Armament: One 25mm GAU-12/U gun with 300 rounds; seven external pylons for maximum load of 7,000lb (3,175kg) for VTO or 17,000lb (7,711kg) for rolling takeoff, including 16 GP bombs, 10 Paveway weapons, 2/4 AIM-9L Sidewinders or AGM-65A or E Mavericks and very wide range of other stores including ALQ-164 ECM pod on centreline.
History: First flight (YAV-8B) 9 November 1978, (AV-8B) 5 November 1981; service delivery October 1983.

Development: The British government's shortsighted withdrawal from a common programme of development of an Advanced Harrier in 1973 resulted in 1981 in the RAF having to accept the McDonnell Douglas-developed AV-8B, which accordingly was then permitted to go ahead into FSD (full-scale development) after having for three years lain in the doldrums while US money was poured into the same company's F/A-18A. Though Rolls-Royce could have done many things to increase power of the engine there was no money for this purpose, so the F402 (US designation) will have features aimed at increasing life and reducing costs. It does, however, have long zero-scarf (cut square) front nozzles which increase lift in the VTO mode, and the inlets are redesigned for higher thrust and efficiency. The main airframe change is a totally new long-span wing, with deep super critical section and less sweep, which with other changes increases internal fuel by more than 50 per cent. Very large flaps are lowered in the VTO mode and combined with lift-improvement devices under the fuselage and the new nozzles result in more than 7,500lb (3,402kg) more VTO lift and even greater gains in rolling takeoffs. Extra pylons handle the greater weapon loads possible, and combined with the increased fuel capacity result in payload/range figures improved by roughly 100 per cent over the earlier AV-8A or C. Further changes include a raised cockpit and canopy (not the same as in the British Sea Harrier), retractable inflight-refuelling probe, Stencel seat, LERXs (leading-edge root extensions to enhance inflight agility) and greatly updated avionics including the Angle Rate Bombing System, advanced HUD and cockpit displays, inertial system and IBM digital computer. British Aerospace has 40 per cent of the main programme of 336 aircraft for the US Marine Corps inventory, which by 1989 are expected to replace the AV-8C in VMA(T)-203, VMA-231 and 542. The Marines are also expected to buy 18 dual TAV-8B trainers, and further sales are likely for other missions and possibly for the Navy or other US services.

Right: Now in full production, the AV-8B Harrier II, seen here fitted with the definitive wing with LERX, is to be supplemented by the TAV-8B dual conversion trainer.

McDonnell Douglas F-4 Phantom II

F-4A to F-4S, RF-4 and QF-4

Origin: McDonnell Aircraft, division of McDonnell Douglas Corp, St Louis.
Type: Originally carrier-based all-weather interceptor, now all-weather multi-role fighter for ship or land operation; (RF) all-weather multisensor reconnaissance; (QF) RPV; (F-4G) defence-suppression aircraft.
Engines: (B) two 17,000lb (7,711kg) thrust General Electric J79-8 single-shaft turbojets with afterburner; (C, D) 17,000lb J79-15; (E, F, G) 17,900lb (8,120kg) J79-17; (J, N, S) 17,900lb J79-10.
Dimensions: Span 38ft 5in (11.7m); length (B, C, D, J, N, S) 58ft 3in (17.76m); (E, F and all RF versions) 62ft 11in or 63ft (19.2m); (K, M) 57ft 7in (17.55m); height (all) 16ft 3in (4.96m).
Weights: Empty (B) 28,000lb (12,700kg), (C, D, J) 28,200lb (12,792kg), (RF) 29,300lb (13,290kg), (E) 30,328lb (13,757kg), (G) 30,900lb (14,016kg); maximum (B) 54,600lb (24,767kg); (C, D, J, RF) 58,000lb (26,309kg), (E, G) 60,360lb (27,379kg).
Performance: Maximum speed with Sparrow missiles only (low) 910mph (1,464km/h, Mach 1.19), (high) 1,500mph (2,414km/h, Mach 2.27); initial climb, typically 28,000ft (8,534m)/min; service ceiling, over 60,000ft (19,685m) with J79 engines, 60,000ft with Spey; range on internal fuel (no weapons) about 1,750 miles (2,817km); ferry range with external fuel, typically 2,300 miles (3,700km) (E and variants, 2,600 miles (4,184km).
Armament: (All versions except RF, QF which have no armament) four AIM-7 Sparrow air-to-air missiles recessed under fuselage; inner wing pylons can carry two more AIM-7 or four AIM-9 Sidewinder missiles; in addition all E versions except RF have internal 20mm M-61 multi-barrel gun, and virtually all versions can carry the same gun in external centreline pod; all except RF, QF have centreline and four wing pylons for tanks, bombs or other stores to total weight of 16,000lb (7,257kg).
History: First flight (XF4H-1) 27 May 1958; service delivery (F-4A) February 1960 (carrier trials), February 1961 (inventory); first flight (Air Force F-4C) 27 May 1963; (F-4E) 30 June 1967; (EF-4E) 1976; final delivery March 1979.

Development: McDonnell designed the greatest fighter of the postwar era as a company venture to meet anticipated future needs. Planned as an attack aircraft with four 20mm guns, it was changed into a very advanced gunless all-weather interceptor with advanced radar and missile armament. In this form it entered service as the F-4A, soon followed by the F-4B used in large numbers (635) by the US Navy and Marine Corps, with Westinghouse APQ-72 radar, IR detector in a small fairing under the nose, and many weapon options. Pilot and radar intercept officer sit in tandem and the aircraft has blown flaps and extremely comprehensive combat equipment. A level Mach number of 2.6 was achieved and many world records were set for speed, altitude and rate of climb. Not replaced by the abandoned F-111B, the carrier-based Phantom continued in production for 19 years through the F-4G with digital communications, F-4J with AWG-10 pulse-doppler radar, drooping ailerons, slatted tail and increased power, and the N (rebuilt B). In 1973-5 Navy facilities delivered 178 F-4Ns with completely revised avionics and strengthened airframe, as well as conversions of the original F-4A to TF-4A trainers and F-4Bs to QF-4B remotely piloted drones, since used in substantial numbers as missile targets and for other purposes. The F-4Gs were returned to normal (N) standard and the designation was later used for a totally different USAF model. The final Navy/Marines variant is the F-4S, 265 of which were produced in-house by rebuilding F-4Js with

improved avionics, strengthened structure (including completely new outer wings with slats) and a total electrical rewiring.

These outstanding aircraft outperformed and outnumbered all other US combat aircraft of the 1960s. Vastly increased production, rising to a remarkable 75 per month in 1967, stemmed not only from the Vietnam war but also because the Air Force recognized that the F-4 beat even the specialist land-based types at their own missions, and after prolonged study decided to buy the basic F-4B version with minimal changes. The original Air Force designation of F-110 Spectre was changed to F-4C Phantom under the unified 1962 system, the F-4C being a minimum-change version of the Navy B and preceded (from 24 January 1962) by the loan to TAC of 30 B models ex-Navy.

After buying 583 F-4Cs with dual controls, a boom receptacle, Dash-15 engines with cartridge starters, larger tyres and increased-capacity brakes, inertial navigation and improved weapon aiming, the Air Force procured 793 of the F-4D model which was tailored to its own land-based missions, with APQ-109 radar, ASG-22 servoed sight, ASQ-91 weapon-release computer for nuclear LABS manoeuvres, improved inertial system and 30 kVA alternators. Visually, many Ds could be distinguished by removal of the AAA-4 IR detector in a pod under the radar, always present on the C. Next came the extremely sophisticated RF-4C multi-sensor reconnaissance aircraft, a major rebuild in a programme which preceded the D by two years and was the first Air Force variant to be authorized. Designed to supplement and then replace the RF-101 family the RF-4C was unarmed but was modified to carry a battery of forward-looking and oblique cameras, IR linescan, SLAR (side-looking airborne radar) and a small forward oblique mapping radar, as well as more than 20 auxiliary fits including photo flash/flare cartridges in the top of the rear fuselage, special ECM and HF shunt aerials built into the fin behind the leading edge on each side. TAC purchased 505 of this model in 1964-73.

All these variants were very heavily engaged in the war in SE Asia 1966-73, where political rules combined with other problems to reduce their air-combat performance. Prolonged call for an internal gun resulted in the F-4E, which had the most powerful J79 engine to permit the flight performance to be maintained despite adding weight at both ends. In the nose was the new solid-state APQ-120 radar and the M61 gun, slanting down on

the ventral centreline with the 6 o'clock firing barrel near-horizontal, and at the rear was a new (No 7) fuel cell giving enhanced range. The first E was delivered to TAC on 3 October 1967, about three months after first flight, and a total of 949 in all were supplied to maintain the F-4 as leading TAC aircraft with an average of 16 wings equipped throughout the period 1967/77. From 1972 all Es were rebuilt with a slatted leading edge, replacing the previous blown droop which permitted much tighter accelerative manoeuvres to be made, especially at high weights, without stall/spin accidents of the kind which had caused many losses in Vietnam.

The final Air Force variant is the F-4G, the standard Advanced Wild Weasel platform replacing the F-105F and G which pioneered Wild Weasel missions in the late 1960s. The name covers all dedicated EW and anti-SAM missions in which specially equipped electronic aircraft hunt down hostile SAM installations (using radar for lock-on, tracking or missile guidance) and destroy them before or during an attack by other friendly aircraft on nearby targets. The F-4G (the same designation was used previously for modified F-4Bs of the Navy) is a rebuild of late-model F-4E (F-4E-42 through -45) fighters, and has almost the same airframe. It is the successor to the EF-4C, two squadrons of which were fielded by TAC from 1968 and which demonstrated excellent performance with a simpler system. In the F-4G the main EW system is the AN/APR-38, which provides very comprehensive radar homing and warning and uses no fewer than 52 special aerials, of which the most obvious are pods facing forward under the nose (replacing the gun) and facing to the rear at the top of the vertical tail. The system is governed by a Texas Instruments reprogrammable software routine which thus keeps up to date on all known hostile emitters. Offensive weapons normally comprise triple AGM-65 EO-guided Mavericks on each inboard pylon plus a Shrike on each outer pylon; alternatively weapons can include the big Standard ARM (Anti-Radiation Missile), AGM-88 HARM (High-speed ARM) or various other precision air/ground weapons. A Westinghouse ALQ-119 jammer pod is fitted in the left front missile recess, the other three recesses carrying Sparrow AAMs for self-protection. Another change is to fit the F-15 type centreline tank which can take 5g when full with 600 US gal (2,271lit). The G total is 116 aircraft.

Above: One of the famed USAF units still flying the F-4E is the 4th Tactical Fighter Wing based at Seymour Johnson AFB, North Carolina, whose badge appears on the inlet (with TAC badge on fin). The 4th has dual-base commitments to NATO in Europe.

Left: A Maverick missile can be seen on this F-4G Advanced Wild Weasel of the 35th Tac Fighter Wing based at George AFB, Ca. Camouflage is the standard tan/dark green/medium green.

Below: ALQ-119(V)8 ECM pods nestle under the fuselages of these F-4Es departing on a mission in Exercise Team Spirit '82.

McDonnell Douglas F-15 Eagle

F-15A,B,C,D and E

Origin: McDonnell Aircraft Company, St Louis, Missouri.
Type: Air-superiority fighter with secondary attack role.
Powerplant: Two 23,930lb (10,855kg) thrust Pratt & Whitney F100-100 afterburning turbofans.
Dimensions: Span 42ft 9¾in (13.05m); length (all) 63ft 9in (19.43m); wing area 608sq ft (56.5m²); height 18ft 5½in (5.63m).
Weights: Empty (basic equipped) 28,000lb (12.7t); loaded (interception mission, max internal fuel plus four AIM-7, F-15A) 41,500lb (18,824kg), (C) 44,500lb (20,185kg); maximum with max external load (A) 56,500lb (25,628kg), (C) 68,000lb (30,845kg).
Performance: Maximum speed (over 36,000ft/10 973m with no external load except four AIM-7), 1,653mph (2,660km/h, Mach 2.5); with max external load or at low level, not published; initial climb (clean) over 50,000ft (15.24km)/min, (max wt) 29,000ft (8.8km)/min; service ceiling 65,000ft (19.8km); takeoff run (clean) 900ft (274m); landing run (clean, without brake chute) 2,500ft (762m); ferry range with three external tanks, over 2,878 miles (4,631km), (with Fast packs also) over 3,450 miles (5,560km).
Armament: One 20mm M61A-1 gun with 940 rounds, four AIM-7F (later AMRAAM) fitting against fuselage, four AIM-9L (later Asraam) on flanks of wing pylons, total additional ordnance load 16,000lb (7,257kg) on five stations (two each wing, one centreline).
History: First flight (A) 27 July 1972, (B) 7 July 1973; service delivery (Cat II test) March 1974, (inventory) November 1974.
Development: Recognizing its urgent need for a superior long-range air-combat fighter the Air Force requested development funds in 1965 and issued an RFP in September 1968 for the FX, the McDonnell proposal being selected in late 1969, with the F100 engine and Hughes APG-63 radar following in 1970. Inevitably the demand for long range resulted in a large aircraft, the wing having to be so large to meet the manoeuvre requirement that it has a fixed leading edge and plain unblown trailing-edge flaps. Two of the extremely powerful engines were needed to achieve the desired ratio of thrust/weight, which near sea level in the clean condition exceeds unity. The inlet ducts form the walls of the broad fuselage, with plain vertical rectangular inlets giving external compression from the forward-raked upper lip and with the entire inlet pivoted at the top and positioned at the optimum angle for each flight regime. The upper wall of the inlet forms a variable ramp, and the lower edge of the fuselage is tailored to snug fitting of the four medium-range AAMs. The gun is in the bulged strake at the root of the right wing, drawing ammunition from a tank inboard of the duct. There is

no fuel between the engines but abundant room in the integral-tank inner wing and between the ducts for 11,600lb (5,260kg, 1,739 US gal 6,592lit), and three 600 US gal (2,270lit) drop tanks can be carried each stressed to 5g manoeuvres when full. Roll is by ailerons only at low speeds the dogtoothed slab tailplanes taking over entirely at over Mach 1, together with the twin rudders, which are vertical.

Avionics and flight/weapon control systems are typical of the 1970 period, with a flat-plate scanner pulse-doppler radar, vertical situation display presenting ADI (attitude/director indicator), radar and EO information on one picture, a HUD, INS and central digital computer. In its integral ECM/IFF subsystems the F-15 was far better than most Western fighters, with Loral radar warning (with front/rear aerials on the left fin tip), Northrop ALQ-135 internal counter measures system, Magnavox EW warning set and Hazeltine APX-76 IFF with Litton reply-evaluator. High-power jammers, however, must still be hung externally, any of various Westinghouse

Above: Dive bombing F-15B which has been used for many trials and has served as the prototype Enhanced Tactical Fighter.

Left: Inspection of the Hughes multimode pulse-doppler radar type APG-63, in one of the first block of F-15A aircraft. For dogfighting the radar acquires target on the Head-up Display.

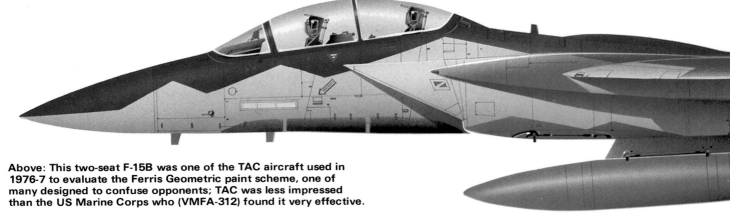

Above: This two-seat F-15B was one of the TAC aircraft used in 1976-7 to evaluate the Ferris Geometric paint scheme, one of many designed to confuse opponents; TAC was less impressed than the US Marine Corps who (VMFA-312) found it very effective.

pods normally occupying an outer wing pylon. The APG-63 offered a fantastic increase in ability to detect and track low-flying targets, and to display only features of interest to the pilot. Another advance was Hotas (Hands On Throttle and Stick) technology in the cockpit which dramatically improved dogfight performance. Though it was, and remains, concerned at the price, the Air Force got in the F-15A everything it was looking for and in 1973 announced a force of 729 aircraft including a proportion of tandem dual-control F-15B operational trainers.

Production at St Louis has been running at 90 to 144 aircraft per year, with 815 delivered by the time this book appears. Recipient units began with TAC's 57th TTW at Nellis, 58th TTW at Luke, 1st TFW at Langley, 36th TFW at Bitburg (Germany), 49th TFW at Holloman, 33rd TFW at Eglin, 32nd TFS at Camp New Amsterdam (Netherlands) and 18th TFW at Kadena (Okinawa). Some of these units have received the current production variants, the F-15C and two-seat F-15D. These have a vital electronic modification in a reprogrammable signal processor, giving instant ability to switch from one locked-on target to another, to keep looking whilst already locked to one target, to switch between air and ground targets and, by virtue of an increase in memory from 24K to 96K (96,000 'words'), to go into a high-resolution mode giving the ability to pick one target from a tight formation even at near the limit of radar range. To some extent the latter capability will remain not fully realized until a later medium-range AAM is used (the Air Force has studied the Navy AIM-54 Phoenix but not adopted it). The British Sky Flash would give a major improvement now, especially in severe jamming, but again has not been adopted. The C and D also have 2,000lb (907kg) of additional internal fuel and can carry the Fast (Fuel and sensor, tactical) packs cunningly devised by McDonnell to fit flush along the sides of the fuselage. These actually reduce subsonic drag and offer far less

Above: Start of peel-off manoeuvre by fully armed F-15As of the 32nd Tactical Fighter Wing from Camp New Amsterdam, Netherlands. The 32nd has won several proficiency awards.

Below: There are actually three F-15As in this photograph, which was taken from the back seat of an F-15B. Their unit is the 405th Tactical Training Wing at Luke AFB, near Phoenix, Arizona.

supersonic drag than the drop tanks whilst adding a further 9,750lb (4,422kg) fuel, or an assortment of sensors (cameras, FLIR, EO, LLTV or laser designator) or a mix of fuel and sensors.

In the second half of 1981 the F-15C re-equipped the 48th FIS at Langley, previously an F-106A unit in now-defunct Adcom, and the Air Force is now procuring aircraft beyond the original 729 force level, partly in order to replace the aged F-106 in CONUS defence. For the future, while one variant of F-15 has been subjected to prolonged study as the USAF's Asat (Anti-satellite) aircraft, firing a large air/space missile based on a SRAM motor followed by an Altair II carrying a nuclear warhead, prolonged testing and demonstration of a company-funded Strike Eagle has now led to the F-15E which may be on order by the time this book appears. This could serve as the Enhanced Tactical Fighter to replace the F-111 (the alternative being the Panavia Tornado) and also as the Advanced Wild Weasel (with far greater capability than the F-4G). The key is the SAR (synthetic-aperture radar) built into the APG-63, which very greatly improves resolution of fine detail against even distant ground targets. With a Pave Tack (FLIR/laser) pod the backseater in the two-seat F-15E can handle what are considered to be the best tactical navigation/target/weapon avionics in the world (apart from the strictly comparable Tornado). External weapon carriage is increased to 24,000lb (10,885kg), including laser-guided and anti-radiation weapons, Harpoon anti-ship missiles, dispensers and other stores. Whether the large existing F-15 force can eventually be brought up to this impressive standard is doubtful. In 1982 the 21st TFW in Alaska converted to the F-15C/D, and in 1983 the 1st TFW (Rapid Deployment Force) had converted to the C/D and was receiving the first Fast packs. The F-15E was engaged in a flyoff against the F-16XL; discounting the possible 400 of this version the USAF is expected to receive 1,395 Eagles by 1995, excluding the 20 development aircraft.

McDonnell Douglas F/A-18 Hornet

F/A-18A, TF/A-18A and RF-18

Origin: McDonnell Douglas (St Louis); Northrop is principal subcontractor.
Type: Single-seat carrier-based strike fighter, (TF) combat-capable dual trainer, (RF) unarmed recon.
Engines: Two GE F404-400 augmented low-ratio turbofans (bypass turbojets) each "in 16,000lb (7,257kg) class".
Dimensions: Span (basic) 37ft 6in (11.43m), (over AAMs) 40ft 4¾in (12.31m); length 56ft 0in (17.07m); height 15ft 3½in (4.66m); wing area 400sq ft (37.16m²).
Weights: Empty 22,460lb (10,188kg); loaded (fighter) 33,585lb (15,234kg), (attack) 48,253lb (21,887kg).
Performance: Maximum speed (hi, clean) 1,200mph (1,931km/h, Mach 1.82); combat ceiling about 50,000ft (15km); combat radius (fighter, hi) 460 miles (740km), (attack, three tanks) 633 miles (1,019km).
Armament: M61A-1 20mm gun with 570 rounds; nine external pylons for total load of up to 17,000lb (7,711kg) including all normal Navy/Marines bombs, rockets, ASMs, 300US gal (1,136lit) tanks, AIM-9 and AIM-7 (later Amraam) AAMs, laser spot tracker, forward-looking infra-red and ECM pods.
History: First flight (YF-17) 9 June 1974, (first of 11 prototype F-18s) 18 November 1978; production delivery (for evaluation) May 1980.

Development: In 1974 the Navy was instructed by Congress to discontinue its new-design VFAX project for a low-cost lightweight fighter and instead study derivatives of the USAF YF-16 or YF-17. Called NACF (Navy Air Combat Fighter), the best submission turned out to be the Hornet proposed by McDonnell Douglas on the basis of the Northrop YF-17. Compared with the latter it has a larger wing, wider fuselage with much greater fuel capacity, bypass engines of increased thrust, heavier and more diverse weapon loads, and carrier features including folding wings and landing gear stressed for 24ft (7.32m)/s rate of descent and nose-tow catapult launch. The nose is enlarged to house the Hughes APG-65 liquid-cooled multimode digital radar able to track ten targets and display eight, and with illumination features for Sparrow or Amraam missiles. The gun is mounted in the upper part of the nose immediately behind the radar. The single-seat cockpit is more conventional than that of the F-16 but has extremely advanced displays. From the start severe numerical requirements for ease of maintenance had to be met, despite the dense packaging of the entire aircraft.

Originally it was planned to develop an F-18A fighter and an A-18 attack aircraft for the Marines, but eventually the differences were whittled away until a single standard was reached with the unique dual-role designation F/A-18A. This has been developed to replace the F-4 in the interceptor role and the A-4 and A-7 in the attack mission. The TF/A-18A has a rear instructor cockpit, and retains weapon capability but with about 6 per cent less internal

Above: Four F-18A Hornets of the US Navy's Air Test and Development Squadron VX-4 at Point Mugu.

Right: Fourth prototype of the F/A-18A, shown on level bombing trials with Mk 83 bombs carried in pairs.

fuel. The RF-18 reconnaissance version, first tested in late 1982, has a large camera/IR sensor package installed in the nose, the gun being removed; it can be identified by a ventral bulge. This model had not been ordered when this book went to press, but could be produced by field conversion if the standard aircraft were suitably modified for this additional role.

Development was swift but marked by several major problems which combined with inevitable inflation, caused very severe escalation in price. The 11 development aircraft were all flying by March 1980. Eventually the more difficult problems, such as inadequate rate of roll, were overcome (the wing finally emerged with ailerons extending to the tips and with a full-span hinged leading edge without the dogtooth discontinuities of the early aircraft). The first nine production Hornets were funded in fiscal year 1979, 25 in 1980, 60 in 1981, 63 in 1982 and 84 in 1983. It was the original intention to buy 1,366 aircraft for the Navy/Marines inventory, to be delivered until 1992 (probably later, as the funding rates have fallen short of the original 1978 plan). VFA-125 was formed as the Navy development squadron at NAS Lemoore in November 1980 and by 1983 some 105 Hornets had been delivered to Navy and Marines units. Despite foreign sales to Canada, Australia and Spain the rise in price has been so large that an F/A-18A is now more expensive than the larger and generally more capable F-14C (the price of which was the reason for developing the Hornet in the first place). In 1982 the Navy Secretary drew attention to this and threatened to delete all F-18 procurement after Fiscal 1983, buying instead further F-14 and A-6 aircraft (which were to be kept in production anyway). It is unlikely that the F-18 programme will be terminated at this early date, but its cost troubles are symptomatic of those afflicting most modern weapon systems.

McDonnell Douglas KC-10 Extender

KC-10A

Origin: Douglas Aircraft Company, Long Beach, California.
Type: Air-refuelling tanker and heavy cargo transport.
Powerplant: Three 52,500lb (23,814kg) thrust General Electric F103 (CF6-50C2) turbofans.
Dimensions: Span 165ft 4.4in (50.41m); length 181ft 7in (55.35m); height 58ft 1in (17.7m); wing area 3,958sq ft (367.7m²).
Weights: Empty (tanker role) 240,026lb (108,874kg); maximum loaded 590,000lb (267,620kg).
Performance: Maximum speed (max weight, tanker) about 600mph (966km/h) at 25,000ft (7,620m), maximum cruising speed, 555mph (893km/h) at 30,000ft (9,144m); takeoff field length, 10,400ft (3,170m); maximum range with maximum cargo load, 4,370 miles (7,032km); maximum range with max internal fuel, 11,500 miles (18,507km); landing speed at max landing weight, 171mph (275km/h).
Armament: None.
History: First flight (DC-10) 29 August 1970, (KC-10A) 12 July 1980.

Development: During the early 1970s the Air Force studied available commercial wide-body transports as a possible ATCA (Advanced Tanker/Cargo Aircraft), and on 19 December 1977 announced the choice of a special version of the DC-10-30CF. The need had been highlighted by the difficulty of airlifting and air-fuelling USAF air units to the Middle East during the 1973 war, when some countries refused the USAF refuelling rights and the KC-135 and supporting cargo force found mission planning extremely difficult. The ATCA was bought to fly global missions not only with several times the overall payload of the KC-135, to a maximum of 169,409lb (76,842kg), but with the ability to provide tanker support to combat units whilst simultaneously carrying spares and support personnel. Compared with the DC-10-30 the KC-10A has a windowless main cabin, with large freight door and five passenger doors, a McDD high-speed boom with fly-by-wire control and able to transfer fuel at 1,500 US gal (5,678lit)/min, and a completely redesigned lower lobe to the fuselage housing seven Goodyear rubberized fabric fuel cells with capacity of about 18,125 US gal (68,610lit). Together with its own fuel the KC-10A has the ability to transfer 200,000lb

Above: Refuelling an F-15 Eagle from the 49th TFW affords a startling indication of the size of the KC-10A; another F-15 waits much nearer the camera. The Extender not only has a new design of boom but also a hose-drum unit and drogue alongside.

(90,718kg) to receiver aircraft at a distance of 2,200 miles (3,540km) from home base, and accompany the refuelled aircraft to destination. The cargo floor has improved power rollers and portable winch handling systems, and can accommodate 27 standard USAF Type 463L pallets.

The Air Force hopes eventually to be able to fund 36 KC-10A Extenders, though only at a low rate. In FY79 two aircraft were bought ($148 million, including some engineering costs), in FY80 a total of four, and in FY81 six. The second aircraft (79-0434) was the first to be delivered, to SAC at Braksdale AFB, Louisiana, on 17 March 1981. By July 1983 a total of 16 Extenders had been delivered, and, while commercial DC-10 production has been completed, the KC-10A line is likely to be kept open throughout the decade to a planned total force of 60 aircraft.

McDonnell Douglas/BAe T-45 Hawk

T-45A and B

Origin: McDonnell Douglas, Long Beach, USA; British Aerospace is principal subcontractor.

Type: Advanced pilot trainer.

Engine: One 5,340lb (2,422kg) Rolls-Royce/Turboméca Adour 851 turbofan.

Dimensions: Span 30ft 9¾in (9.39m); length 36ft 7¾in (11.17m); height 13ft 3in (4.04m); wing area 179.6sq ft (16.69m²).

Weights: Empty (A) approx 8,756lb (3,972kg); loaded (clean) 12,440lb (5,642kg).

Performance: Maximum speed 645mph (1,038km/h); dive Mach limit 1.2; max rate of climb (gross wt) 9,300ft (2,835m)/min; service ceiling 50,000ft (15.24km); sortie endurance 4h.

Armament: Has full Hawk capability but no requirement for weapons at present.

History: First flight (Hawk) 21 August 1974, (T-45B) 1987, (A) 1988.

Development: Having had perhaps the quickest and most troublefree development of any modern military aircraft, the basic Hawk T.1 for the RAF entered service as a replacement for the Hunter and Gnat in 1976 and has subsequently set the world's best-ever record for any jet combat aircraft for low maintenance burden and low attrition (in the first 130,000 hours one aircraft was lost, through collision with a ship). In November 1981 a proposal by McDonnell Douglas, British Aerospace and Sperry Flight Systems was outright winner of the US Navy VT/XTS contest for a future undergraduate pilot trainer to replace the T-2C Buckeye and TA-4J Skyhawk. The three companies proposed a total system, of which aircraft and direct support represented some 85 per cent by value. Despite Congressional opposition the win was so clear-cut that it has been allowed to go ahead, and the first FSD (full-scale development) contact was signed in September 1982. The first stage involves delivery of 54 T-45B Hawk trainers from 1987 for land-based training. These are basically similar to the Hawk T.1 but have a strengthened landing gear with long-stroke main legs and twin-wheel nose gear, a modified rear fuselage with twin lateral airbrakes and revised cockpit instrumentation and avionics. From 1988 these would be

Above: ZA101 was the British Aerospace Hawk demonstrator which confirmed the selection of the type as the basis for the T-45.

Below: On the ground the VT/XTS demonstrator shows several differences from the T-45, including nose gear and airbrakes.

supplemented by the T-45A, of which 253 are to be delivered, which in addition will have a nose-tow catapult facility and arrester hook. Though the fuel savings over today's aircraft are calculated at 35 to 55 per cent, the T-45A is not scheduled to enter service until 1991.

Northrop F-5

F-5A Freedom Fighter, F-5B, F-5E Tiger II, F-5F

Origin: Northrop Corporation, Hawthorne, California.
Type: Light tactical fighter.
Powerplant: Two General Electric J85 afterburning turbojets, (A/B) 4,080lb (1,850kg) thrust J85-13 or -13A, (E/F) 5,000lb (2,270kg) thrust -21A.
Dimensions: Span (A/B) 25ft 3in (7.7m) (A/B over tip tanks) 25ft 10in (7.87m), (E/F) 26ft 8in (8.13m), (E/F over AAMs) 27ft 11in (8.53m); length (A) 47ft 2in (14.38m), (B) 46ft 4in (14.12m), (E) 48ft 2in (14.68m), (F) 51ft 7in (15.72m); wing area (A/B) 170sq ft (15.79m²), (E/F) 186sq ft (17.3m²).
Weights: Empty (A) 8,085lb (3,667kg), (B) 8,36lb (3,792kg), (E) 9,683lb (4,392kg), (F) 10,567lb (4,793kg); max loaded (A) 20,576lb (9,333kg), (B) 20,116lb (9,124kg), (E) 24,676lb (11,193kg), (F) 25,225lb (11,442kg).
Performance: Maximum speed at 36,000ft (11km), (A) 925mph (1,489km/h, Mach 1.4), (B) 886mph (1,425km/h, Mach 1.34), (E) 1,077mph (1,734km/h, Mach 1.63), (F) 1,011mph (1,628km/h, Mach 1.53); typical cruising speed 562mph (904km/h, Mach 0.85); initial climb (A/B) 28,700ft (8,750m)/min, (E) 34,500ft (10,516m)/min, (F) 32,890ft (1,025m)/min; service ceiling (all) about 51,000ft (15.54km); combat radius with max weapon load and allowances, (A, hi-lo-hi) 215 miles (346km), (E, lo-lo-lo) 138 miles (222km); range with max fuel (all hi, tanks dropped, with reserves) (A) 1,565 miles (2,518km), (E) 1,779 miles (2,863km).
Armament: (A/B) total military load 6,200lb (2,812kg) including two 20mm M-39 guns and wide variety of underwing stores, plus AIM-9 AAMs

Above: An F-5E of the USAF Fighter Weapons School (part of the 57th Fighter Weapons Wing) at Nellis, in an Aggressors scheme.

for air combat; (E/F) Very wide range of ordnance to total of 7,000lb (3,175kg) not including two (F-5F, one) M-39A2 guns each with 280 rounds and two AIM-9 missiles on tip rails.
History: First flight (XT-38) 10 April 1959, (N-156F) 30 July 1959, (F-5A) 19 May 1964, (F-5E) 11 August 1972, (F-5F) 25 September 1974.

Development: The Air Force showed almost no interest in Northrop's N-156C Freedom Fighter, which was built with company funds and rolled out in

Northrop T-38 Talon

T-38A

Origin: Northrop Corporation, Hawthorne, California.
Type: Advanced trainer.
Powerplant: Two 3,850lb (1,746kg) thrust Genral Electric J85-5A afterburning turbojets.
Dimensions: Span 25ft 3in (7.7m); length 46ft 4½in (14.1m); wing area 170sq ft (15.79m²).
Weights: Empty 7,200lb (3,266kg); loaded 11,820lb (5,361kg).
Performance: Maximum speed, 858mph (1,381km/h, Mach 1.3) at 36,000 (11km); maximum cruising speed, 627mph (1,009km/h) at same height; initial climb 33,600ft (10.24km)/min; service ceiling 53,600ft (16.34km); range (max fuel, 20min loiter at 10,000ft/3km), 1,140 miles (1,835km).
Armament: None.
History: First flight (YT-38) 10 April 1959, (T-38A) May 1960; service delivery 17 March 1961.

Development: Throughout the second half of the 1950s Northrop's project team under Welko Gasich studied advanced lightweight fighters of novel design for land and carrier operation, but the first genuine service interest was in the N-156T trainer, a contract for Air Force prototypes being signed in December 1956. Unique in the world, except for the Japanese FST-2, in being designed from the outset as a jet basic trainer with supersonic speed on the level, the T-38 was an attractive lightweight version

Above: Popularly known as the White Rocket, the T-38A has been the standard graduation pilot trainer of the USAF since 1961. The type was replaced in the Thunderbirds team by the F-16A.

Rockwell OV-10 Bronco

OV-10A

Origin: Rockwell International, designed and built at Columbus, Ohio, Division of North American Aircraft Operations (now Columbus plant of NAA Division).
Type: Forward air control.
Powerplant: Two 715ehp Garrett T76-416/417 turboprops.
Dimensions: Span 40ft 0in (12.19m); length 41ft 7in (12.67m); wing area 291sq ft (27.03m²).
Weights: Empty 6,893lb (3,127kg); loaded 9,908lb (4,494kg), overload 14,444lb (6,552kg).
Performance: Maximum speed (sea level, clean) 281mph (452km/h); initial climb (normal weight), 2,600ft (790m)/min; service ceiling, 24,000ft (7,315m); takeoff run (normal weight), 740ft (226m); landing run, same; combat radius (max weapon load, low level, no loiter), 228 miles (367km); ferry range, 1,382 miles (2,224km).
Armament: Carried on five external attachments, one on centreline rated at 1,200lb (544kg) and four rated at 600lb (272kg) on short body sponsons which also house four 7.62mm M60 machine guns with 500 rounds each.
History: First flight 16 July 1965, (production OV-10A) 6 August 1967; USAF combat duty, June 1968.

Development: This unique warplane was the chief tangible outcome of prolonged DoD studies in 1959-65 of Co-In (Counter-Insurgency) aircraft tailored to the unanticipated needs of so-called brushfire wars using limited weapons in rough terrain. The Marines issued a LARA (Light Armed Recon Aircraft) specification, which was won by NAA's NA-300 in August 1964.

959 without US markings. Eventually Northrop secured orders for over ,000 F-5A and B fighters for foreign customers, and 12 of the MAP (Mutual Assistance Program) F-5As were evaluated by the Air Force in Vietnam in a project called Skoshi Tiger, which demonstrated the rather limited capability of this light tactical machine, as well as its economy and strong pilot appeal. When the USAF withdrew from SE Asia it left behind many F-5As and Bs, most having been formally transferred to South Vietnam, and few of these remain in the inventory. In contrast the slightly more powerful and generally updated F-5E Tiger II succeeded in winning Air Force support from the start, and the training of foreign recipients was handled mainly by TAC, with ATC assistance. The first service delivery of this version was to TAC's 425th TFS in April 1973. This unit at Williams AFB, Arizona (a detached part of the 58th TTW at Luke), proved the training and combat procedures and also later introduced the longer F which retains both the fire-control system and most fuselage fuel despite the second seat. Ultimately the Air Force bought 112 F-5Es, both as tactical fighters and over half the total) as Aggressor aircraft simulating potential enemy aircraft in DACT (Dissimilar Air Combat Training). About 60 F-5Es and a small number of Fs continue in Air Force service in the development of air-combat techniques, in Aggressor roles, in the monitoring of fighter weapons meets and various hack duties. The F-5Es are painted in at least eight different color schemes, three of which reproduce Warsaw Pact camouflage schemes while others are low-visibility schemes. The F-5Fs at Williams are silver, with broad yellow bands and vertical tails. User units include the 58th TW (425th TFS, as described), 57th TTW at Nellis (a major tactical and air combat centre for the entire Air Force), 3rd TFW, Clark AFB, Philippines (Pacaf), 527th Aggressor TFS, attached to the 10th TRW at RAF Alconbury, England, and various Systems Command establishments. In addition eight F-5Es are used by the Navy for Top Gun fighter-pilot training at the Naval Fighter Weapons School at NAS Miramar, California.

Above: Loaded only with data-link instrumentation probes, these four "Aggressors" F-5Es from the 527th Tactical Fighter Squadron at RAF Alconbury show all four current colour schemes.

of contemporary fighters, with twin afterburning engines, extremely small sharp-edged wings, area fuling for reduced transonic drag, inboard powered ailerons and slab tailplanes with slight anhedral. The instructor is seated behind and 10in (0.25m) higher than his pupil, both having rocket-assisted seats. To assist the pilot, yaw and pitch flight-control channels incorporate stability augmenters, and great care was taken in 1959-61 to produce an aircraft that pupils could handle. Strictly classed as a basic pilot trainer, the T-38A nevertheless is an advanced machine to which undergraduate pilots come only after completing their weed-out on the T-41A and their complete piloting course on the T-37A jet. The Air Force procured about 1,114 Talons, of which some 800 remain in inventory service with ATC. Their accident rate of some 0.9/11,2 per 1000,000 flight hours is half that for the USAF as a whole. An Advanced Squadron of T-38As is based at each ATC school (see Cessna T-37 for list). Many Talons are used as hacks by senior officers, for command liaison and for research, while others are assigned to TAC's 479th TTW at Holloman.

Below: This T-38A serves with TAC's 479th Tactical Training Wing at Holloman AFB (note WarPac number on nose), which also uses the AT-38B attack trainer.

Features included superb all-round view for the pilot and observer seated in tandem ejection seats, STOL rough-strip performance and a rear cargo compartment usable by five paratroops or two casualties plus attendant. Of the initial batch of 271 the Air Force took 157 for use in the FAC role, deploying them immediately in Vietnam. Their ability to respond immediately with light fire against surface targets proved very valuable, and the OV-10 was always popular and a delight to fly. In 1970 LTV Electrosystems modified 11 for night-FAC duty with sensors for detecting surface targets and directing accompanying attack aircraft, but most OV-10s now in use are of the original model. Units include TAC's 1st SOW at Hurlburt Field, Florida; the 602nd TACW, Bergstrom AFB, Texas; the 601st TCW, Sembach AB, Germany; Pacaf's 51st CW, Osan, Korea; and certain specialized schools. The Marine Corps received 114 OV-10As to a standard differing only in detail (such as radio equipment) from the USAF model. They have served with various VMO (observation) squadrons, duties including helicopter escort, FAC and armed recon. Since 1978 Rockwell has converted 17 to OV-10D standard for the NOS (night observation surveillance) role with a FLIR (forward-looking infra-red) and laser designator in a nose ball turret and an M97 three-barrel 20mm gun in a chin turret which can be slaved to the ball sensors.

Left: Carrying a 150-US gallon (568-liter) drop tank, this OV-10A was photographed on a training mission with the 51st Composite Wing from Osan AB in South Korea. In mid-1983 these aircraft were expected to be transferred to replace the light Cessna O-2A aircraft at Wheeler AFB, Hawaii. In turn they were to be replaced at Osan by the Cessna OA-37B, the A-37B reconfigured for FAC and observation duties on withdrawal from AFRES service. There is no move to fit the NOS systems to USAF OV-10s.

Rockwell B-1

B-1A, B

Origin: Rockwell International, North American Aircraft Operations, El Segundo, California.
Type: Strategic bomber and missile platform.
Powerplant: Four General Electric F101-GE-102 augmented turbofans each rated at 29,900lb (13,563kg) with full afterburner.
to 67° 30mins) 78ft 2½in (23.84m); length (including probe) 150ft 2½in
Dimensions: (B-1A) Span (fully spread) 136ft 8½in (41.67m), (fully swept, (45.78m); wing area (spread, gross) 1,950sq ft (181.2m²).
Weights: Empty (B-1A) about 145,000lb (65,772kg), (B) over 160,000lb (72,576kg); maximum loaded (A) 395,000lb (179,172kg), (B) 477,000lb (216,367kg).
Performance: Maximum speed (B, over 36,000ft/11km, clean), 825mph (1,328km/h, Mach 1.25); low penetration (B, clean) over 600mph (966km/h); high-alt cruising speed 620mph (1,000km/h); range (hi, unrefuelled) 7,455 miles (12,000km); field length, approx 4,500ft (1,372m).
Armament: Eight ALCM internal plus 14 external; 24 SRAM internal plus 14 external; 12 B28 or B43 internal plus 8/14 external; 24 B61 or B83 internal plus 14 external; 84 Mk 82 internal plus 44 (80,000lb, 36,288kg).
History: Original (AMSA) study 1962; contracts for engine and airframe 5 June 1970; first flight 23 December 1974; decision against production June 1977; termination of flight-test programme 30 April 1981; announcement of intention to produce for inventory, September 1981; planned IOC, 1 July 1987.

Above: The fourth B-1 prototype escorted in April 1981 by a chase F-111A. The B-1B will lack the long dorsal spine.

Development: Subject of a programme whose length in years far outstrips the genesis of any other aircraft, the B-1 was the final outcome of more than ten years of study to find a successor to the cancelled B-70 and RS-70 and subsonic in-service B-52. Originally planned as an extremely capable swing wing aircraft with dash performance over Mach 2, the four prototypes had variable engine inlets and ejectable crew capsules of extremely advanced design. The latter feature was abandoned to save costs, and though the second aircraft reached Mach 2.22 in October 1978 this end of the speed spectrum steadily became of small importance. By 1978 the emphasis was totally on low-level penetration at subsonic speeds with protection deriving entirely from defensive electronics and so-called 'stealth' characteristics. Not very much could be done to reduce radar cross-section, but actual radar signature could be substantially modified, and the effort applied to research and development of bomber defensive electronic systems did not diminish.

The original B-1A featured a blended wing/body shape with the four engines in paired nacelles under the fixed inboard wing immediately outboard of the bogie main gears. Though designed more than ten years ago, the aerodynamics and structure of the B-1 remain highly competitive and the extremely large and comprehensive defensive electronics system (managed by AIL Division of Cutler-Hammer under the overall avionic integration of Boeing Aerospace) far surpassed those designed into any other known aircraft, and could not reasonably have been added as post-flight modifications. During prototype construction it was decided to save further costs by dropping the variable engine inlets, which were redesigned to be optimized at the high-subsonic cruise regime. Another problem, as with the B-52, was the increased length of the chosen ALCM, which meant that the original SRAM-size rotary launcher was no longer compatible. The original B-1 was designed with three tandem weapon bays, each able to house many free-fall bombs or one eight-round launcher. Provision was also made for external loads (see data). A particular feature was the LARC (Low Altitude Ride Control), an active-control modification which by sensing vertical accelerations due to atmospheric gusts at low level and countering these by deflecting small foreplanes and the bottom rudder section greatly reduced fatigue of crew and airframe during low-level penetration. All four prototypes flew initially from Palmdale and exceeded planned qualities. The

Left: Close-up of the tail of the No 4 aircraft showing the lack of projections (except vortex generators) despite the avionics.

Sikorsky S-61 Family

SH-3A and -3D Sea King, HH-3A, RH-3A and many other variants

Origin: Sikorsky Aircraft, Division of United Technologies.
Type: See text.
Engines: Two General Electric T58 free-turbine turboshaft; (SH-3A and derivatives) 1,250shp T58-8B; (SH-3D and derivatives) 1,400shp T58-10; (S-61R versions) 1,500hp T58-5.
Dimensions: Diameter of main rotor 62ft (18.9m); length overall 72ft 8in (22.15m); (61R) 73ft; height overall 16ft 10in (5.13m).
Weights: Empty (simple transport versions, typical) 9,763lb (4,428kg); (ASW, typical) 11,865lb (5,382kg); (armed CH-3E) 13,255lb (6,010kg); maximum loaded (ASW) about 18,626lb (8,449kg); (transport) usually 21,500lb (9,750kg); (CH-3E) 22,050lb (10,000kg).
Performance: Maximum speed (typical, maximum weight) 166mph (267km/h); initial climb (not vertical but maximum) varies from 2,200 to 1,310ft (670-400m)/min, depending on weight; service ceiling, typically 14,700ft (4,480m); range with maximum fuel, typically 625 miles (1,005km).
Armament: Very variable.
History: First flight 11 March 1959.

Development: Representing a quantum jump in helicopter capability, the S-61 family soon became a staple product of Sikorsky Aircraft, founded in March 1923 by Igor Sikorsky who left Russia after the Revolution and settled in the United States. He flew the first wholly practical helicopter in 1940, and his R-4 was the first helicopter in the world put into mass production (in 1942). A development, the S-51, was in 1947 licensed to the British firm Westland Aircraft, starting collaboration reviewed on later pages. The S-55 and S-58 were made in great numbers in the 1950s for many civil and military purposes, both now flying with various turbine engines. The S-61 featured an amphibious hull, twin turbine engines located above the hull close to the drive gearbox and an advanced flight-control system.

Above: A standard SH-3D anti-submarine helicopter from USS *Kitty Hawk* with ASW Sqn HS-4 within Carrier Air Wing CVW-2.

First versions carried anti-submarine warfare (ASW) sensors and weapons, and were developed for the US Navy as the HSS-2, entering service in 1961-62 as the SH-3 series, with the name Sea King. By the early 1960s later variants were equipped for various transport duties, minesweeping, drone or spacecraft recovery (eg lifting astronauts from the sea), electronic surveillance and (S-61R series) transport/gunship and other combat duties. The S-61R family has a tricycle landing gear, the main wheels retracting forwards into sponsons and the cabin having a full-section rear loading ramp/door and a 2,000lb (907kg) roof-rail winch. The USAF model in this family was the CH-3E, 50 of which were rebuilt for combat operations with armour, self-sealing tanks, various weapons, rescue hoist and retractable flight-refuelling probe, and designated HH-3E Jolly Green Giant. The Coast Guard name for the HH-3F sea search version is Pelican. Total production of military models exceeded 770 by Sikorsky.

Above: The third prototype, with black radome, generally resembles the B-1B except for the spine, engine inlets and wing/engine fairings.

ird was fitted with the ECM system and DBS (doppler beam-sharpening) the main radar, while the fourth had complete offensive and defensive ectronics and was almost a production B-1A. The Carter administration ecided not to build the B-1 for the inventory, and the four aircraft were ored in flyable condition after completing 1,985.2h in 347 missions.

After further prolonged evaluation against stretched FB-111 proposals e Reagan administration decided in favour of a derived B-1B, and nounced in September 1981 the intention to put 100 into the SAC ventory from 1986, with IOC the following year. The B-1B dispenses with rther high-altitude dash features, the wing sweep being reduced to about

59° 30mins. As well as refined engines the B-1B can carry much more fuel; a detailed weight-reduction programme reduces empty weight, while gross weight is raised by over 37 tonnes. Main gears are stronger, wing gloves and engine inlets totally redesigned, many parts (ride-control fins, flaps and bomb doors, for example) made of composite material, pneumatic starters with cross-bleed fitted, offensive avionics completely updated (main radar is Westinghouse's APG-66), the ALQ-161 defensive avionics subsystem fitted, RAM (radar-absorbent material) fitted at some 85 loctions throughout the airframe, and the whole aircraft nuclear-hardened and given Multiplex wiring. Radar cross-section will be less than one-hundredth that of a B-52. Deploying this LRCA (Long-Range Combat Aircraft) is intended to bridge the gap until a next-generation 'stealth' aircraft can be fielded towards the end of the century.

Sikorsky S-64

-64, CH-54A and B Tarhe

rigin: Sikorsky Aircraft Division of United Technologies, Stratford.
pe: Crane helicopter.
gines: (CH-54A) two 4,500shp Pratt & Whitney T73-1 turboshafts, H-54B) two 4,800shp T73-700.
imensions: Diameter of six-blade main rotor 72ft 0in (21.95m); length erall (rotors turning) 88ft 6in (26.97m); height overall 18ft 7in (5.67m).
eights: Empty (A) 19,234lb (8,724kg); maximum loaded (A) 42,000lb 9,050kg), (B) 47,000lb (21,318kg).
rformance: Maximum cruise 105mph (169km/h); hovering ceiling out ground effect 6,900ft (2,100m); range with max fuel and 10 per cent serve (typical) 230 miles (370km).
rmament: Normally none.
story: First flight (S-64) 9 May 1962; service delivery (CH-54A) late 064, (B) late 1969.

evelopment: Developed from the first large US Army helicopter, the 56, via the piston-engined S-60, the S-64 is an efficient weight-lifter hich in Vietnam carried loads weighing up to 20,000lb (9,072kg). The 1-54A Tarhes used in that campaign retrieved more than 380 shot-down rcraft, saving an estimated $210 million, and carried special vans housing to 87 combat-equipped troops. The improved CH-54B, distinguished ternally by twin main wheels, has lifted loads up to 40,780lb (18,497kg) d reached a height of 36,122ft (11,010m). There is no fuselage, just a ructural beam joining the tail rotor to the cockpit in which seats are ovided for three pilots, one facing to the rear for manoeuvring with loads. e dynamic components (rotor, gearboxes, shafting) were used as the sis for those of the S-65. With cancellation of the HLH (Heavy-Lift elicopter) the S-64 remains the only large crane helicopter in the West. total of just over 100 were built, all the last batches being very small imbers for a late emerging civil market. By 1981 the CH-54 could be tperformed by the latest Chinook and Super Stallion, but its withdrawal om the USA is not scheduled until late in the decade.

Above: The CH-54A Tarhe has single mainwheels and one is seen here prior to installation of large inlet particle separators.

Sikorsky S-65

CH-53, HH-53 and RH-53 Sea Stallion, HH-53 Super Jolly (Green), CH-53E Super Stallion and export models

Origin: Sikorsky Aircraft, Division of United Technologies.
Type: See text.
Engines: (Early versions) two 2,850shp General Electric T64-6 free-turbine shaft; (CH-53D and G) 3,925shp T64 versions; (RH-53D) 4,380shp T64 versions; (CH-53E) three 4,380shp T64-415.
Dimensions: Diameter of main rotor (most, six blades) 72ft 3in (22.02m), (CH-53E, seven blades) 79ft 0in (24.08m); length overall (rotors turning) 88ft 3in (26.9m), (CH-53E, 99ft 1in, 30.2m); length of fuselage 67ft 2in (20.47m), (E, 73ft 4in, 22.35m); height overall 24ft 11in (7.6m), (E, 28ft 5in, 8.66m).
Weights: Empty (CH-53D) 23,485lb (10,653kg), (E) 32,878lb (14,913kg); maximum loaded (most) 42,000lb (19,050kg), (RH-53D) 50,000lb (22,680kg), (E) 73,500lb (33,339kg).
Performance: Maximum speed 196mph (315km/h); typical cruising speed 173mphj (278km/h); initial climb (most) 2,180ft (664m)/min, (E) 2,750ft (838m)/min; range (with payload, optimum cruise) (most) 540 miles (869km), (E) 1,290 miles (2,075km).
Armament: See text.
History: First flight 14 October 1964, (E) 1 March 1974; service delivery (CH-53A) May 1966, (E) March 1981.

Development: Obviously developed from the S-61, the S-65 family includes the largest and most powerful helicopters in production outside the Soviet Union. The dynamic parts (rotors, gearboxes and control system) were originally similar to those of the S-64 Skycrane family, but using titanium and with folding main-rotor blades. Most versions served in Vietnam from January 1967, performing countless tasks including recovery of downed aircraft. In 1968 a standard CH-53A completed a prolonged series of loops and rolls, while others set records for speed and payload. Most of the initial run of 139 CH-53As were for the Marine Corps, whose need for a heavy assault helicopter launched the programme in August 1962. A total of 15 were transferred to the Navy as RH-53A mine countermeasures (mine-sweeping) helicopters, and five to the USAF. Normal load is 38 troops, 24 stretchers and four attendants or 8,000lb (3,629kg) of cargo loaded through full section rear ramp/doors. To meet Vietnam needs the HH-53B Super Jolly was flown in March 1967, with a six-man crew, three Miniguns or cannon, armour, flight refuelling, extra fuel and rescue hoist. The CH-53C was a related transport version. The CH-53D had more power and auto-folding blades, with accommodation for 55 troops; 126 were built for the Marines in 1969-72 and most export versions are similar. The Navy took

Above: One of the original 5,700shp CH-53A assault transports of the US Marine Corps, which is now re-equipping with the 13,140shp CH-53E from which stems the Navy's MH-53E.

20 RH-53D, with long-range sponson/drop tanks and refuelling probe, an small numbers are being supplied toJapan. The HH-53H Super Jolly is USAF rebuild of HH-53Cs with Pave Low night/all-weather search/rescu equipment including B-52 type inertial navigation, doppler, projected ma display, AAQ-10 infra-red and APQ-158 terrain-following radar. The much needed but costly CH-53E Super Stallion is virtually a different helicopte selected in 1973 and finally ordered into production after costly delay (of political origin) in 1978. The rotor has seven blades, of greater lengt and titanium/glassfibre construction, the transmission rating is more tha doubled in capacity to 13,140hp, the fuselage is longer and many othe changes include a redesigned tail which, with the enlarged rotor, lean 20° to the left. The tailplanes were mounted low, but the productio CH-53E has a kinked gull tailplane on the right. The first production machin flew on 13 December 1980 and funding began with six in 1978, 14 in 1979 15 in 1980, 14 in 1981, 12 in 1982 and 11 in 1983, a total of 72. Deliverie by 1983 totalled 34. Total Navy requirement is put at 200, of which abou two-thirds are for the Marines and 57 will comprise the MH-53E MCN (mine countermeasures) version. This has giant sponsons adding 1,000 U gal (3,785 litres) extra fuel and extremely complete minesweeping equip ment; the first (the 35th aircraft modified) was to fly in September 1983

Vought A-7 Corsair II

Vought A-7A to E, A-7K and TA-7C

Origin: Vought Systems Division of LTV, Dallas.
Type: Single-seat attack bomber (carrier- or land-based); (K, TA) dual trainer.
Engine: (A) one 11,350lb (5,150kg) thrust Pratt & Whitney TF30-6 two-shaft turbofan; (B, C) 12,200lb (5,534kg) TF30-8; (D) 14,250lb (6,465kg) Allison TF41-1 (Rolls-Royce Spey derivative) of same layout; (E) 15,000lb (6,804kg) TF41-2.
Dimensions: Span 38ft 9in (11.80m); length 46ft 1½in (14.06m); (TA) 48ft 2in (14.68m); height 16ft 0¾in (4.90m); (TA) 16ft 5in.
Weights: Empty (A) 15,904lb (7,214kg); (D) 19,781lb (8,972kg); maximum loaded (A) 32,500lb (14,750kg); (D) 42,000lb (19,050kg).
Performance: Maximum speed (all single-seat versions, clean) 698mph (1,123km/h) at low level; climb and ceiling, not reported (seldom relevant); tactical radius with weapon load, typically 71 miles (1,150km); ferry range with four external tanks, typically 4,100 miles (6,600km).
Armament: (A, B) two 20mm Colt Mk 12 in nose; six wing and two fuselage pylons for weapon load of 15,000lb (6,804kg). (D, E) one 20mm M61 Vulcan cannon on left side of fuselage with 1,000-round drum; external load up to theoretical 20,000lb (9,072kg).
History: First flight 27 September 1965; service delivery October 1966; first flight of D, 26 September 1968.

Development: Though derived from the Crusader, the Corsair II is a totally different aircraft. By restricting performance to high subsonic speed, structure weight was reduced, range dramatically increased and weapon load multiplied by about 4. Development was outstandingly quick, as was production. Vought built 199 7-A, used in action in the Gulf of Tonkin on 3 December 1967, followed by 196 B models. The C designation was used for the first 67 E models which retained the TF30 engine. In 1966 the Corsair II was adopted by the US Air Force. Compared with the Navy aircraft the A-7D introduced a more powerful engine (derived from the Rolls-Royce Spey) with gas-turbine self-starting, a multi-barrel gun, and above all a totally revised avionic system for continuous solution of navigation problems and precision placement of free-fall weapons in all weather. The folding wings and arrester hook were retained, and other features include a strike camera, boom receptacle instead of a probe, boron carbide armour over cockpit and engine, and a McDonnell Douglas Escapac seat. Avionics have been further improved over the years, but the

Sikorsky S-70

S-70, UH-60A Black Hawk, EH-60 (SOTAS), SH-60B Seahawk and UH-60D Night Hawk

Origin: Sikorsky Aircraft, Division of United Technologies Corporation.
Type: (UH) combat assault transport, (EH) electronic warfare and target acquisition, (SH) ASW and anti-ship helicopter.
Engines: (UH, EH) two 1,560shp General Electric T700-700 free-turbine turboshafts, (SH) two 1,690shp T700-401 turboshafts.
Dimensions: Diameter of four-blade rotor 53ft 8in (16.36m); length overall (rotors turning) 64ft 10in (19.76m); length (rotors/tail folded) (UH) 41ft 4in (12.6m), (SH) 41ft 0½in (12.5m); height overall (UH) 16ft 10in (5.13m); (SH) 17ft 2in (5.23m).
Weights: Empty (UH) 10,624lb (4,819kg), (SH) 13,648lb (6,191kg); maximum loaded (UH) 20,250lb (9,185kg) (normal mission weight 16,260lb, 7,375kg), (SH) 21,488lb (9,926kg).
Performance: Maximum speed, 184mph (296km/h); cruising speed (UH) 167mph (269km/h), (SH) 155mph (249km/h); range at max wt, 30 min reserves, (UH) 373 miles (600km), (SH) about 500 miles (805km).
Armament: (UH) provision for two M60 LMGs firing from side of cabin, plus chaff/flare dispensers; (EH) electronic only; (SH) two Mk 46 torpedoes and alternative dropped stores, plus offensive avionics.
History: First flight (YUH) 17 October 1974, (production UH) October 1978, (SH) 12 December 1979; serivce delivery (UH) June 1979.

Development: The UH-60 was picked in December 1976 after four years of competition with Boeing Vertol for a UTTAS (utility tactical transport aircraft system) for the US Army. Designed to carry a squad of 11 equipped troops and a crew of three, the Black Hawk can have eight troop seats replaced by four litters (stretchers), and an 8,000lb (3,628kg) cargo load can be slung externally. The titanium/glassfibre/Nomex honeycomb rotor is electrically de-iced, as are the pilot windscreens, and equipment includes comprehensive navaids, communications and radar warning. Deliveries to the 101st Airborne Division took place in 1979-81, followed by a further block of 100 to the 82nd Division in 1981. The EH-60A is an ECM (electronic countermeasures) version with Quick Fix II (as used in the Bell EH-1H) radar warning augmentation, chaff/flare dispenser and infra-red jammer. The EH-60B SOTAS (stand-off target acquisition system) is a dedicated platform for detecting and classifying moving battlefield targets under all weather conditions, with a data terminal in the cabin fed from a large rotating surveillance radar aerial under the fuselage (the main wheels retracting to avoid it). The Navy SH-60B is the air-vehicle portion of the LAMPS III (light airborne multi-purpose system), for which IBM is prime contractor. Though using the S-70 airframe, it is a totally different helicopter with equipment for ASW (anti-submarine warfare), ASST (anti-ship

Above: Sikorsky SH-60B Seahawk.

Below: Sikorsky UH-60A Black Hawk.

surveillance and targeting), search/rescue, casevac and vertical replenishment at sea. An APS-124 radar is mounted in the forward fuselage, 25 pneumatic launch tubes for sonobuoys in the left fuselage side and an ASQ-81 towed MAD (magnetic anomaly detector) bird on the right side at the rear. The Navy has indicated a requirement for 204 of these large and costly machines for service aboard the latest destroyers and frigates. Orders totalled 18 by mid-1982, additional to prototypes, and deliveries were to begin in 1983. By 1983 S-70 type helicopters may also be on order for the USAF. From December 1982 this service was to receive an initial 11 Black Hawks designated UH-60D with winterization gear and rescue hoist. They were expected to be followed by 90 HH-60D Night Hawk combat SAR machines with terrain-following radar, forward-looking infra-red, extra fuel, rescue hoist, comprehensive protection features and armament of Miniguns and Stinger (MLMS) missiles.

APQ-126 radar has been retained, programmable to ten operating models, together with British HUD, inertial system, doppler radar, direct-view storage tube for radar or Walleye guidance, and central ASN-91 digital computer. For laser-guided weapons the Pave Penny installation is hung externally in a pod, but the ALR-46(V) digital radar warning system is hung internal. There is no internal jamming capability, however, and the usual ECM payload is an ALQ-101 or -119 hung in place of part of the bombload.

Production of the A-7D has long been completed, but Vought has recently also delivered 30 of a planned 42 tandem dual-control A-7K Corsairs with full weapons capability. It is planned that 16 will be assigned to the ANG's 162nd TFTG at Tucson, and a pair to each of the 11 ANG's 13 operational units equipped with the A-7D. These units are the 112th TFG, Pittsburgh, Pennsylvania; 114th TFG, Sioux Falls, Iowa; 121st TFW, Rickenbacker AFB, Ohio; 127th TFW, Selfridge AFB, Michigan; 132nd TFW, Des Moines, Iowa; 138th TFG, Tulsa, Oklahoma; 140th TFW, Buckley, Colorado; 150th TFG, Kirtland AFB, New Mexico; 156th TFG, San Juan, Puerto Rico; 162nd TFG (TFG), Tucson; 169th TFG, McEntire Field, S. Carolina; 178th TFG, Springfield, Ohio; and the 185th TFG, Sioux City, Iowa. In the 1981 Gunsmoke tactical gunnery meet at Nellis the 140th, from Colorado, shot their way to the top team title with an exceptional 8,800 out of 10,000 points (the team chief, Lt-Col Wayne Schultz, winning the Top Gun individual award). The meet involves not only gunnery but bombing and maintenance/loaded contests. The chief of the judges said: 'Some of the scores are phenomenal—pilots are so accurate they don't need high explosive to destroy a target, they are hitting within 1½ to 2 metres, with ordinary free-fall bombs.' Few tactical aircraft are as good at attack on surface targets.

Apart from the A-7K the last model remaining in production for US service use was the ultimate Navy model, the A-7E. First flown as early as November 1968, this has an even more powerful TF41 than the USAF versions, but were otherwise very similar, with almost the same nav/attack systems, the only other major difference being replacement of the dorsal boom receptacle by a retractable probe. The E has been intensively used from the start, and the last of 596 was delivered in March 1981. From 1978 equipment included a FLIR (forward-looking infra-red) pod under the right wing and Marconi raster-HUD display for improved night and bad weather capability. It is not expected that the whole force will be thus equipped though 231 installations have been produced.

Left: Snakeye retarded bombs drop and fall smartly astern of an A-7D Corsair II of the USAF 23rd Tactical Fighter Wing at England AFB, Louisiana. This wing is one of those which has been re-equipped with the A-10A Thunderbolt II.

The United States Marine Corps

Dr. Alan Ned Sabrosky, Senior Fellow in Political Military Studies at The Center for Strategic and International Studies, Washington, D.C.; Professorial Lecturer in Government and Adjunct Professor of National Security Studies, Georgetown University; Lecturer in Political Science, University of Pennsylvania.

Every nation has a *corps d'elite* whose military reputation stands above that of its other armed forces as a whole. Great Britain has its Brigade of Guards: France has its Foreign Legion, and then its paratroopers; and the United States has its Marine Corps. For over two hundred years, Marines have participated in every major war fought by the United States, as well as in innumerable police actions and armed interventions in virtually every part of the world. The list of battle honors earned by the Marine Corps from its inceptions in 1775 through the final days of the recent war in Indo-China bears testimony to its impressive record. Certainly, the performances of the Marine Corps at places such as Belleau Wood, Guadalcanal, Iwo Jima, the Chosin Reservoir, and Khe Sanh have earned it a prominent place in the lexicon of military history.

As with any military establishment, the US Marine Corps has its own set of traditions, reflecting an institutional interpretation of the Corps' past performance. In part, of course, such traditions are self-serving, highlighting only that which is worthy of emulation and ignoring or discarding anything that is not. Yet traditions cannot be dismissed lightly, especially in the case of a military institution. For such traditions not only influence the way in which the Corps sees itself, and how others view the Corps. They also shape the missions assigned to the Corps, and the way in which it organizes itself for battle.

Over the years, the Marine Corps has traditionally viewed itself as an elite force of infantry, highly disciplined and reliable (its motto is *Semper Fidelis,* or "Always Faithful"), which consititued the "cutting edge" of American diplomacy and power. The dictum that "every Marine was first and foremost a rifleman", while often only nominally accurate, reflected this perception. Even today, the fact that Marine ground combat formations are relatively large units with a high proportion of infantry is evidence of its continued significance.

Further, the fact that Marines were stationed aboard major naval vessels, and traditionally operated in conjunction with the fleet, made them the logical choice for expeditionary forces abroad (sometimes in conjunction with members of the Army and Navy as well). This was particularly true in the years before strategic airlift capabilities became part of the American arsenal. But even then, Marines were still used as the initial ground combat forces in a variety of recent interventions (such as Lebanon in 1958, the Dominican Republic and South Vietnam in 1965), and as a "fire brigade" to relieve pressure on beleaguered American forces (for instance, in Korea in 1950), evacuate American citizens in the face of enemy attack (Phnom Penh and Saigon in 1975), recover lost American property (the Mayagüez incident in 1975), and join in a multinational peacekeeping force to help re-establish order in war-torn localities (Beirut in 1982-1983). For the Marine Corps, in other words, being "first to fight" has had more than lyrical significance.

More recently, however, a new set of institutional traditions has been superimposed on those that originally existed. Since World War I, the Marine Corps has come to see itself as an elite assault force, in addition to whatever other qualifications it may have. The skill and ferocity of the Fourth Marine Brigade at Belleau Wood (subsequently renamed the "Wood of the Marine Brigade") earned them the accolade of Georges Clemenceau for "saving Paris", and the name of *Teufelhunde* ("devil dogs") from the Germans whom they defeated. Yet in that battle, and others like it, Marines had fought as line infantry. A unique mission was missing. That mission began to take shape in the years between the two world wars, at the same time as the Marine Corps was receiving a foretaste of Vietnam in the counterguerrilla operations in several Central American republics. During those interwar years, the Marines began experimenting with amphibious operations.

When World War II began, and the Marines began to direct their activity to the problems confronting them in the Pacific Basin, these traditions merged to produce an amphibious assault force whose maintenance has since been the principal *raison d'être* for the US Marine Corps. Finally, the evolution of Marine aviation units provided the Corps with its own "air force", something which has been a bone of contention within the American armed services for years. After the reorganization of the US defense establishment in 1947, this capability allowed the Marine Corps to lay claim to being a unique, combined-arms, ground-air team with a special competence in amphibious warfare. This was the basic configuration of the Corps when it fought in the Korean and Vietnam wars, and which it retains today. The "Modern Marine Corps" had arrived.

The Modern Marine Corps

The position of the US Marine Corps in the American defense establishment today reflects a legislative legitimization of the status of the Corps at the end of World War II. That position was delineated by the National Security Act of 1947, as amended in 1952 and afterwards. It entailed a specification of: (1) the relationship of the Marine Corps to the other services in general, and to the Navy in particular; (2) the missions to be performed by the Corps; and (3) the basic force structure of the Corps.

The anomalous position of the Marine Corps within the US defense establishment is highlighted by its relationship to the other services. It is the only branch of the armed services not to be in a separate department. Instead, it has co-equal status with the Navy within the Department of the Navy, the Commandant Marine Corps (CMC) and the Chief of Naval Operations both reporting to the Secretary of the Navy.

The Commandant of the Marine Corps (CMC), like the other three service chiefs, acts as a military adviser to the President in his capacity as Commander in Chief of the armed forces. Until 1978, however, this "four

Below: "When you hit the beach, keep moving and give 'em hell." Amphibious landings are one of the most hazardous types of assault. All the cards are generally with the defenders—dug-in emplacements, mines and beach obstacles, heavy fire to cut down the invader—all designed to inflict enormous casualties on even the most determined fighting force. Yet this type of battle has become synonymous with the US Marines. Guadalcanal, Iwo Jima, Tarawa . . . all form some of the bloody battle honours of this élite American force. Today, helicopter-borne assaults mean the USMC is closely allied with aviation in its fighting role, as shown in this parachute training from the rear ramp of a Sea Knight helicopter.

services in three departments" organization precluded the Commandant from having a regular seat on the Joint Chiefs of Staff (JCS), although he was permitted to participate in discussions with the other chiefs on a co-equal basis when matters pertaining directly to the Marine Corps were under discussion. From 1978 onwards, Congress has authorized the Commandant to sit on the JCS as a permanent member equal in status with his Army, Air Force, and Navy counterparts.

The missions assigned to the Marine Corps fall into three broad categories. The principal mission of the Corps is to maintain an amphibious capability to be used in conjunction with fleet operations, including the seizure and defense of advanced naval bases and the conduct of land operations essential to the successful execution of a maritime campaign. In addition, the Corps is required to provide security detachments for naval bases and facilities, as well as for the Navy's principal warships. Finally, the Corps carries out additional duties at the discretion of the President, so long as they do not detract from the Corps' ability to conduct effective amphibious operations and to augment its operations forces upon wartime mobilization.

The third feature of the Marine Corps' position within the Department of Defense is also unique: the Corps is the only service to have its basic force structure defined by statutory law. According to the amended National Security Act of 1947, the Marine Corps will maintain a regular Fleet Marine Force of no less than three divisions and three aircraft wings, with the additional combat, combat support, and service units (force troops) necessary to maintain those divisions and air wings. Active-duty Marine Corps force levels cannot exceed 400,000 personnel, although no minimum force levels are specified. Provision is also made for reserve components to permit the expansion of the regular Marine Corps whenever mobilization occurs.

Current Strength and Organization
The current active-duty strength of the Marine Corps is approximately 194,000 personnel, including 4,000 women. This represents a slight decline from the originally specified manpower levels, but an improvement over that during the 1970s, when recruiting problems associated with the introduction of the all-volunteer force (AVF) concept in the US defense establishment as a whole produced more significant shortfalls. Recent

developments, such as better pay and benefits coupled with extraordinarily high unemployment rates in the United States, have made it easier for all of the American armed services to obtain and retain better personnel. The uniformed active-duty force is complemented by a civilian workforce of approximately 20,000 personnel. Organized Marine Corps Reserves consist of approximately 38,000 personnel as of FY 1983. The Marine Corps intends to try to bring all of its Reserve units up to full wartime strength by FY 1986.

For nominal operational purposes, regular and reserve Marine Corps personnel are organized in four divisions (three regular and one reserve), four aircraft wings (three regular and one reserve), and supporting units upon which these formations draw when operational (e.g., force service support groups, radio battalions, force reconnaissance companies, communications battalions). Perhaps the most significant characteristic of both the divisional and aircraft wing

Above: Holding their M16 automatic rifles well clear of the water, Marines clear the deck of an LCM in classic assault style to establish a beach head during an amphibious exercise.

organization is their size. Each is larger than its counterparts in the other branches of the armed forces, and reflects the Marine emphasis on multi-purpose assault forces.

This is particularly apparent in the case of the Marine divisional structure. Even more than its advocacy of the combined-arms ground-air team organizing concept, the Marine Corps retains its basic faith in the central role of infantry in combat. Thus, the 18,000-man Marine Division (counting attached Navy personnel but excluding supporting personnel who would normally deploy with divisional units) includes a high proportion of infantry. The Marine divisions are the largest in the US defense establishment, exceeding by 20 per cent the size of their closest

Chart 1: Structure of the Marine Division

Note: The artillery regiments of the 1st and 2nd Marine Divisions include five batteries of self-propelled artillery (155mm and 8in howitzers, 175mm guns), organized into general support artillery battalions, in addition to their three direct support battalions with 105mm and 155mm towed howitzers. The 3rd Marine Division (including the 1st Marine Brigade based in Hawaii) has only direct support artillery battalions.

- Division (XX)
  - Infantry Regiments (III)
    - Infantry Battalions (II)
  - Artillery Regiment (III)
  - Tank Battalion (II)
  - Reconnaissance Battalion (II)
  - Engineer Battalion (II)
  - Light Armored Assault Battalion (II)
  - Headquarters Battalion (II)
  - Service Battalion (II)
  - Shore Party Battalion (II)
  - Medical Battalion (II)
  - Motor Transport Battalion (II)

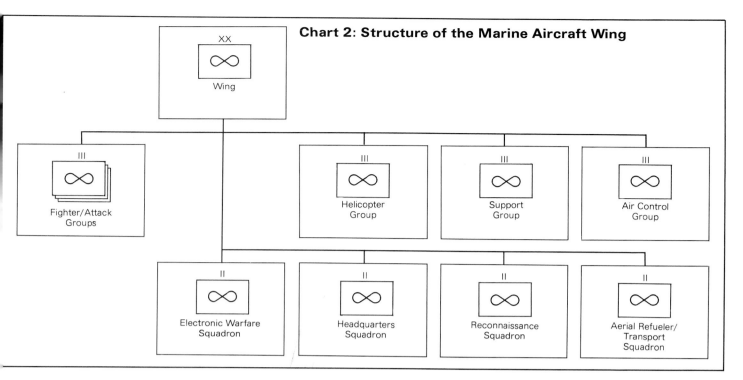

Chart 2: Structure of the Marine Aircraft Wing

- Wing (XX)
  - Fighter/Attack Groups (III)
  - Helicopter Group (III)
  - Support Group (III)
  - Air Control Group (III)
  - Electronic Warfare Squadron (II)
  - Headquarters Squadron (II)
  - Reconnaissance Squadron (II)
  - Aerial Refueler/ Transport Squadron (II)

analogue in the US Army. Yet this advantage in size does not result in greater firepower or mobility for the Marine Division. In fact, with few exceptions, Marine ground combat formations are larger, less mobile and possess less organic firepower than their principal Army counterparts, although a number of programs (to be discussed later in this chapter) are underway to give Marine ground formations more mobility and firepower than is currently at their disposal.

The basic structure of the Marine Division, as it is presented in Chart I, is essentially the old "triangular" model of World War II vintage, albeit that some changes have recently occurred or are programed for the next five years. The Division is organized around three infantry regiments, each of which has three infantry battalions and a headquarters element. The structure of the infantry battalion, which until recently consisted of a headquarters company and four large rifle companies, has undergone a major change which is still in the process of being implemented. When completed, the new Marine infantry battalion will have a headquarters company, a weapons company (with assault/anti-tank/mortar capability) and three rifle companies, with each of the latter being approximately 80 per cent as large as their predecessors. A fourth rifle company had been programmed for the new battalion, but manpower and budgetary constraints are not likely to permit it to be organized.

In addition to the infantry regiments, each Marine division has an artillery regiment with three direct support artillery battalions (equipped with 105mm and 155mm towed howitzers); batteries of self-propelled artillery (155m and 8in howitzers and 175mm guns) are also available, and currently assigned to the artillery regiments of two divisions. Other divisional units include a tank battalion, an armored amphibian battalion, a reconnaissance battalion, a combat engineer battalion, and a headquarters battalion; and each division will soon add a new formation—a "light armored assault battalion" (LAAB) equipped with a new family of armored vehicles currently being developed by the Corps.

For their part, the Marine aircraft wings, whose basic structure is presented in Chart II, are both large and multipurpose. They are larger than both their Air Force and Navy counterparts, and considerably more diverse in composition than an Air Force wing, which conventionally contains aircraft of only one type. An Air Force wing, for example, will usually have three squadrons with 18 to 24 aircraft per squadron, for a total of 54 to 72 aircraft per wing (except for the Strategic Air Command bomber squadrons, which are smaller), of the same type. A Navy aircraft wing will have nine squadrons of varying size (reflecting the varying missions they are to perform), with a total of approximately 86 aircraft. But the standard Marine aircraft wing will have from 18 to 21 squadrons with a total of 286 to 315 aircraft, running the gamut from fighter-attack squadrons (with F-4s and F/A-18s, light and medium attack squadrons with A-4s, A-6s and the once-controversial but now accepted AV-8A/B Harriers), and a tanker/transport squadron

Below: British-designed AV-8A Harriers give the Marines air power when they want it, where they want it, without the need of vulnerable fixed airbases. These two are from VMA-231 operating from Cherry Point NAS.

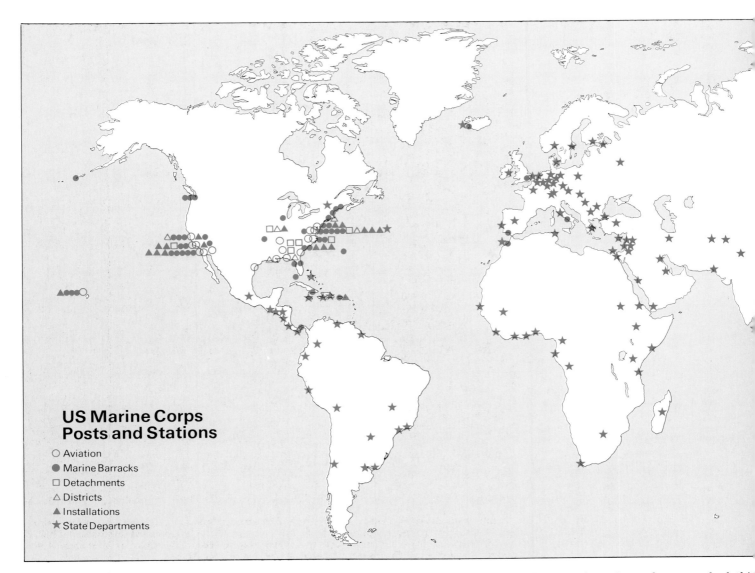

US Marine Corps Posts and Stations

○ Aviation
● Marine Barracks
□ Detachments
△ Districts
▲ Installations
★ State Departments

(with KC-130s), to transport and attack helicopter squadrons (with AH-1s, CH-53s, CH-46s, and UH-1s), plus a trio of electronic warfare, observation, and reconnaissance squadrons. These squadrons are organized into three fighter/attack groups, a helicopter group, and separate special-purpose squadrons, in addition to a wing headquarters squadron, support group, and air control group.

Task Organization and Deployment

For both administrative and operational purposes at the most general level, the Corps has traditionally paired a Marine division and a Marine aircraft wing (plus logistical support units), and divides the three active (or "regular") division-wing teams between its two principal Fleet Marine Forces (FMF). Currently, two division-wing teams are assigned to the Fleet Marine Force Pacific (FMF PAC), with responsibility for Marine Corps operations in the Pacific Ocean and Indian Ocean regions. One of these division-wing teams, composed of the Third Marine Division (reinforced) and the First Marine Aircraft Wing, is based in the Western Pacific and Hawaii. Two-thirds of this division-wing team, comprising under normal circumstances approximately 23,000 Marines, are conventionally deployed in the Western Pacific, principally on Okinawa. The remaining one-third of this division-wing team, organized into the First Marine Brigade (reinforced), is based in Hawaii. The other division-wing team with the Fleet Marine Force-Pacific is based on the West Coast of the United States. This team, which is structured around the First Marine Division (reinforced) at Camp Pendleton, California, and the Third Marine Aircraft Wing at El Toro, California, is principally oriented toward operations in the Pacific Basin. However, it also provides

back-up forces for operations elsewhere, as in the Cuban Missile Crisis of 1962 and the US intervention in the Dominican Republic in 1965. The remaining division-wing team is assigned to the Fleet Marine Force Atlantic (FMF LANT), which has responsibility for operations in the Atlantic Ocean, Caribbean Sea, and Mediterranean Sea regions. This team consists of the Second Marine Division, headquartered at Camp Lejeune, North Carolina, and the second Marine Aircraft Wing, headquartered at Cherry Point, North Carolina.

All major formations based within the US proper provide both individual replacements and, on a unit deployment basis, maneuver units (infantry battalions and aviation squadrons) on a rotational basis for Marine formations headquartered in the Western Pacific for six-month tours of overseas duty. (Longer tours of duty are permitted for some individuals assigned to regimental or higher headquarters, or to certain base support units. Reinforced infantry battalions (called "battalion landing teams," or BLTs) also form the core of Marine formations regularly assigned to the 6th Fleet in the Mediterranean and the 7th Fleet (in the Western Pacific), and are occasionally deployed elsewhere as contingencies arise, to provide American commanders with an amphibious assault force capable of being put ashore and committed to action at short notice. Smaller detachments of regular Marines are assigned to Marine Barracks ships, and security detachments across the world.

Finally, the reserve division-wing team, made up of the Fourth Marine Division with supporting units and the Fourth Marine Aircraft Wing, with supporting units, is located entirely within the US itself. Divided among localities within the six Marine Corps

Districts, the units and personnel of this division-wing team are intended to augment and to reinforce the regular division-wing teams.

The extent of Marine assignments, both within the US and elsewhere, is apparent from the portrayal of US Marine Corps Posts and Stations in the map; the current deployment status of Marine maneuver formations (infantry battalions, helicopter squadrons and fixed-wing aviation squadrons) with their parent headquarters, is presented in Table 1.

The size of both the Marine division and the Marine aircraft wing, the built-in reliance of the division on reinforcing elements from the FMF, and the diversity and multi-purpose flexibility of the aircraft wing reflect a basic element in Marine Corps organization, planning, and doctrine. This is the importance of "tailoring" combined-arms forces with a mix of ground and air components to perform a specific mission. This is known as the "Marine Air-Ground Task Force" (MAGTF) concept, and assumes that the relative composition of each MAGTF (and especially both the size and the mix of its ground and aviation combat components) would vary according to the mission it was expected to perform. The basic "building block" in this approach is the infantry battalion, aviation squadron, and service/support unit which may be combined into a Marine Amphibious Unit (MAU), which is intended to be a quick reaction force. Larger formations are the Marine Amphibious Brigade, or MAB (with from two to five MAUs), and the Marine Amphibious Force, or MAF (which can comprise up to two full division-wing teams). A present the MAB is considered in many circles to be the formation most capable of being deployed in likely combat operations that ar

Top: Standard USMC assault helicopter is the Sea Knight seen here operating off the USS *Peleleu* during exercise Kernel Egress. They carry 25 troops.

Above: Standard heavy machine gun used by the American ground forces is the M2. Here a Marine blasts a target at some 450 rounds a minute.

Table 1: Unit Deployment Status (December 1982)—Maneuver Formations Only

INFANTRY BATTALIONS

Hawaii	Camp Pendleton			29 Palms	Camp Lejeune			Med	WestPac	Okinawa	
3rd Mar	*1stMar*	*5thMar*	*7thMar*		*2ndMar*	*6thMar*	*8thMar*	*24th MAU*	*31ST MAU*	*4thMar*	*9thMar*
1/3	1/9	1/5	1/7	1/4	1/2	1/6	1/8	BLT 3/8	BLT 2/3	2/2	2/1
3/3	1/1	2/5	2/7		3/2	2/6	2/8			3/4	2/9
	3/1	3/5	3/7		2/4	3/6					3/9

FIXED-WING SQUADRONS

Hawaii	El Toro	Yuma	Cherry Pt	Beaufort	Iwakuni
MAG-24	*MAG-11*		*MAG-14*	*MAG-31*	*MAG-12*
VMFA-232	VMFA-314	VMFAT-101	VMA(AW)-224	HAMS-31	VMA(AW)-121
VMFA-235	VMFA-323	VMA-513	VMA(AW)-332	VMFA-115	VMA-331
	VMFA-531		VMA(AW)-533	VMFA-122	
	VMFP-3(-)		VMGR-252	VMFA-251	
			VMAQ-2(-)	VMFA-333	
	MAG-13			VMFA-451	*MAG-15*
	VMA-211		*MAG-32*		
	VMA-214		HAMS-32		VMFA-212
	VMA-311		VMA-223		VMFA-312
	VMA(AW)-242		VMA-231		Det VMFP-3 (WestPac)
	VMGR-352		VMA-542		VMGR-152(Oki)
	HAMS-13				Det VMO-1
					Det VMO-2

HELICOPTER SQUADRONS

Hawaii	Camp Pendleton	Tustin	New River	Med	WestPac	Okinawa
MAG-24	*MAG-39*	*MAG-16*	*MAG-26*	*24th MAU*	*31st MAU*	*MAG-36*
HMM-165	HMA-169	HMM-163	HMM-162	HMM-263(-)Rein	HMM-262(-)Rein	HMM-161
HMM-265	HMA-369(-)	HMM-164	HMM-261			HMH-361
HMH-463	HML-267(-)	HMM-268	HMM-264			HAMS-36
Det A HML-367	HML-367(-)	HMM-363	HMM-365			Det B HML-267
	VMO-2(-)	HMH-462	HMH-362			Det B HMA-369
		HMH-465	HMH-461(-)			
			HMH-464			
			MAG-29			
			HML-167			
			HMA-269			
			VMO-1(-)			

Abbreviations

Med=Mediterranean (6th Fleet) **WestPac**=Western Pacific (7th Fleet) **Mar**=Marines, short for "Marine Regiment" (e.g., "3rd Mar" is 3rd Marine Regiment) **1/3**=denotes battalion/regiment (here, 1st battalion/3rd Marine Regiment) **MAU**=Marine Amphibious Unit (reinforced battalion landing team plus composite helicopter squadron) **MAG**=Marine Aircraft Group (aviation equivalent of Marine Regiment) **VMFA**=fighter/attack squadron **VMA**=attack squadron (VMA/AW=all-weather attack squadron) **HMH**=heavy helicopter squadron **HMM**=medium helicopter squadron **HML**=light helicopter squadron **HMA**=attack helicopter squadron **VMO**=observation squadron

Note: Rotation of infantry battalions and aviation squadrons between US and Western Pacific occasionally produces organizational "marriages" in which a regimental HQ may control battalions, from another regiment, as when the 1st Marines (above) included a battalion from the 9th Marines (1/9) in addition to two battalions from the 1st Marines.

not amenable to being handled by a simple quick-reaction MAU.

A number of programs or plans are in various stages of development, all of them intended to enhance the ability of the Marine Corps to deploy combined-arms task forces more rapidly, more efficiently, and more extensively than in the past. One involves the prepositioning of equipment in certain key areas to reduce the transportation requirements for the insertion and employment of at least the initial Marine contingents. It is, for example, planned to preposition in Norway equipment and supplies adequate for a full Marine Amphibious Brigade. The Near-Term Prepositioning Force (NTPF) program, employing ships based out of Diego Garcia in the India Ocean, is likewise intended to provide equipment and stocks for an initial Marine component of any intervention force in that region.

Second, to enhance the ability of the Marine Corps to operate more effectively in armor-heavy environments (something that the Marine Corps has traditionally not been prepared to deal with), work is being done on the concept of the Mechanized Combined Arms Task Force (MCATF). Such a task force would be an *ad hoc* organization with a mix of armored units taken from divisional and Force Troops assets, plus three support components for logistical backup. Movement in this direction reflects an acknowledgement that some contingencies (e.g., the Middle East) will require the Marine Corps to have a more sophisticated armored option at its disposal than is now the case. Supporters of this concept argue that it will provide the Marine Corps with a highly maneuverable combined-arms team capable of dealing with a wide array of threat environments. Critics assert that the concept implies a greater change in Marine Corps task organization and doctrine than is actually taking place, or likely to occur, and that the MCATF concept is at best a limited response to a changing threat environment. The debate, it should be noted, is by no means closed here.

Finally, plans are being developed to make better use of existing organizational assets

Above: A Marine detachment using an 81mm mortar. An improved version lighter in weight and with more range will enter service in 1984. With a skilled crew, the present weapon can deliver up to 30 rounds per minute.

Below left: With origins going back to the Amtracs of World War Two, the LVTP-7 is currently the amphibious workhorse of the Marines. It was surplus vehicles of this type that spearheaded the Argentinian invasion of the Falklands in April 1982.

within the MAF/MAB/MAU framework. This is implicitly based upon the recognition of the fact that the reduced manning levels of most Marine units means that only part of a division (with its reinforcing and aviation components) could actually be deployed, or be considered deployable, at any one time. In theory, that is, the 27 Marine infantry battalions (three in each of the three regiments in each of the three divisions in the active Marine Corps) should provide the basis for the same number of Marine Amphibious Units (MAUs). In fact, nothing

approaching that number could be readied for use. Thus, what might be called a "field force" approach to task force organization is being considered, which would give the Marine Corps a rapidly employable force of three Marine Amphibious Forces (MAF), each of two Marine Amphibious Brigades (MAB) each MAB, in turn, would have two MAUs. The proposed structure is outlined in Table 2 it should be noted that MAF/MAB/MAU designations would not automatically correspond to existing division/regiment battalion designations.

Doctrine and Weapons

Perhaps the single dominant characteristic of Marine tactical doctrine is the emphasis on the principle of the offensive. This applies not only to combined-arms amphibious operations with their projected mix of seaborne and helicopter-borne assault groups attacking with naval gunfire and tactical air support, but to all other operations as well. In theory, the tactical repertoire of the Marine Corps is as varied as that of any other modern military organization. Certainly, it includes major emphasis on the closely coordinated employment of close air support and (where available and feasible) naval gunfire support as well. Yet, in practice, it often seems that the institutional precedence given to the ability to provide assault forces, coupled with the relatively limited tactical flexibility permitted to amphibious assault forces in the initial stage of an operation, has continued to predominate the actual or proposed changes noted above in organization (and, to a certain degree, in doctrine as well) notwithstanding. And in point of fact, it ought not to be surprising that

Table 2: Standing Task Force Structure Using Existing Unit Designators

Marine Amphibious Force (MAF)	Marine Amphibious Brigade (MAB)	Marine Amphibious Unit (MAU)
I	5th	15, 17
	7th	11, 13
II	4th	26, 28
	6th	22, 24
III	1st	31, 33
	9th	35, 37

Above: The likelihood that in future conflicts the Marines will have to operate in armor-heavy situations, has prompted the concept that the force should have a more extensive armored option at its disposal than is now the case.

Right: Marine artillery is also due for modernisation. The ageing 105mm M101 howitzer seen here and the larger 155mm gun will be replaced by a new Mk 198 weapon of 155mm calibre. Unusually it will be towed and not self mobile.

an institution such as the Marine Corps, which has built its *persona* around the image of an assault force, should prefer to operate in such a manner whenever possible.

That preference notwithstanding, and despite an institutional ethos that endorses the principle of the offensive to an extraordinary degree, the Marine Corps is taking a number of steps to increase both its firepower and its mobility in the 1980s. First, the reorganization of the basic infantry battalion noted earlier will have the effect of reducing the number of personnel in each battalion by approximately 10 per cent, while giving the new battalion considerably more firepower and mobility than its predecessor possessed. Improved M16 rifles will be issued as the basic infantry weapon. Each squad, which has been reduced in size from 13 men to 11 men, organized into two fire teams in place of three in the larger squad, will have a new 5.56mm M249 FN Belgian-made Squad Automatic Weapon (SAW) in each fire team. This will give each squad a capability it has not had since the Browning Automatic Rifle (BAR) was phased out nearly two decades ago, in addition to the 7.62mm M60 machine guns and 60mm mortars within the company weapons platoon. The battalion weapons company will also acquire a new heavy machinegun platoon with eight firing teams, each of which will man a vehicle with a .50 caliber heavy machine gun and the new Mk19 40mm "machinegun"—a *de facto* automatic grenade launcher; the battalion weapons company's mortar platoon will also receive an improved version of the 81mm mortar, with more range and lighter weight than the current weapon, beginning in FY 1984. What

the Commandant Marine Corps referred to in 1983 as the "basic tactical unit of ground combat power and a balanced force of combined arms"—the Marine infantry battalion—stands a good chance of becoming just that in short order, and a formidable contender on any battlefield.

Second, changes are underway in the artillery, aviation, and armor capabilities of the Corps. To enhance counterbattery capability, the Marines will acquire three target acquisition batteries over the next five years. The towed 105mm and 155mm howitzers currently in the Marine Corps divisional artillery regiments will be replaced by a new Mk198, 155mm howitzer. Oddly enough, however, this will also be a towed weapon—something of an anomaly, given the prevailing trend in most armed forces toward self-propelled artillery. Some of the 105mm howitzers, however, will be

retained in a "contingency reserve" during the transition, perhaps as a hedge against the fact that the new 155mm howitzers will be heavier than the older 105mm weapons, and thus less mobile. There will also be an increase in the number of 155mm SP (self-propelled) weapons in the inventory, with a total of five new batteries being acquired over the next six years.

Modernization of Marine aviation is likewise proceeding, with an eye to enhancing both close air support (CAS) and tactical airlift capabilities in support of the divisional formations. Two squadrons of CH-53Es, with a 16-ton lift capacity (adequate for more than 90 per cent of the Corps' equipment), will become operational in 1983. Acquisition proceeds with the F/A-18 dual-purpose air-superiority/ground attack aircraft, equipped with both Sparrow and Sidewinder missiles in addition to its other ordanance. Further, the Falklands war of 1982 reaffirmed the Marine Corps' faith in the value of the Harrier V/STOL aircraft; beginning in 1985, it will take delivery of the improved AV-8B version.

Finally, although far less important in the Marine Corps than in other major ground combat forces of the world, armor is continuing to receive attention. The M60A1 tanks, the mainstay of Marine Corps armor for years, are being upgraded to extend their service life into the late 1980s. The Marine Corps is working with the US Army on a Mobile Protected Gun System (MPGS), an air-mobile dual-purpose weapon with a clear antitank capability in addition to a direct-fire capability against open targets. Of greatest importance, however, is the programed acquisition of the Light Armored Vehicle (LAV), principally but not exclusively for the Light Armored Assault Battalions (LAAB) being added to each Marine division between 1983 and 1986. Each LAAB will consist of 1,038 men with 145 LAVs. A total of 744 LAVs is to be acquired by the Corps, at a cost of approximately $400,000 each (in current dollars), in eight variants: light assault, assault gun, antitank, air defense, command, mortar, logistics, and recovery. When available in strength, the LAV will add considerably to the Marine Corps' combat power in fluid combat environments.

If having better air and armor capabilities adds to the ability of the Corps to wage modern war, the ability to counter an opponent's aircraft and armor is at least as important. Control of the air has always been an important element in planning amphibious operations. It is equally essential for amphibious forces ashore to have an independent capability to defend themselves against attacking aircraft. Similarly, the relative dearth of armored fighting vehicles available to the MAU and its larger multiples argues for enhancing their anti-armor capabilities as well. Both anti-aircraft and anti-armor capabilities become of even greater importance to

the Corps if one contemplates employing Marine units in either European or Middle Eastern theaters of operations. Even the projected augmentation of Marine aviation and armored forces will not appreciably alter this consideration.

Two basic weapons systems are available to the Marine Corps for anti-aircraft defense. First, each of the Fleet Marine Forces has a light anti-aircraft missile (LAAM) battalion equipped with Hawk surface-to-air missiles. Second, for close-in defense, the Marine Air Control Group (MACG) of each Marine aircraft wing has a Forward Area Air Defense (FAAD) battery equipped with 75 launchers

Above: Redeye close air-defence missiles being aimed at a target. Being a first generation infantry SAM it has a number of shortcomings and a replacement was inevitable. This will take the form of the enhanced capability Stinger being developed by General Dynamics.

Below: Almost prehistoric in appearance when crawling from the water, the LVTP-7 will be with the Marine Corps for some years yet. Existing vehicles will undergo a phased modernisation program and the Service plans to buy more than 300 improved versions.

for Redeye shoulder-fired surface-to-air missiles. One section of this battery, with five Redeye launchers, would normally be deployed with each MAU. In addition, each Hawk LAAM battalion has four Redeye teams for close-in defense. In the coming years, the Hawk missiles are to be upgraded. The Redeye missiles are being replaced by an enhanced-capability infrared missile called the Stinger for short-range defense against low-altitude attacks. The number of such missiles will also be increased, with each Marine Aircraft Wing (MAW) eventually having four firing platoons for FAAD.

Although once limited to the 106mm recoilless rifle and the 3.5in rocket launcher, Marine Corps anti-armor capabilities have grown considerably in recent years, with further growth projected in the future. The M60A1 tanks now in service, and the Light Armored Vehicles (LAV) coming on line in 1983, are certain to be the mobile "core" of this capability, reinforced by the Mobile Protected Gun System (MPGS) discussed above when it comes on line later in this decade. A new High Mobility Multi-Purpose Wheeled Vehicle (HMMWV), although not primarily designed for anti-armor roles, will nonetheless have the capability to carry antitank missiles and the Mk19 40mm machine guns; 14,000 of these vehicles are to be procured, and will replace 26,000 wheeled vehicles now used in a variety of roles by the Corps.

In addition, the family of anti-tank missiles being deployed by the Marine Corps is growing in number and diversity. Three principal variants exist: the heavy/long-range TOW, the medium-range Dragon, and the short-range LAW (light assault weapon). Each of the LAAB battalions will include a platoon of 15 LAVs equipped with TOWs; a TOW platoon with 24 launchers will be added to each infantry regiment between 1985 and 1987, increasing the total of divisional TOW platoons to 18 (six per division); the divisional tank battalion will include an antitank company with 72 TOW launchers; and the TOW system itself will be enhanced by the acquisition of the TOW-2 system with improved guidance systems and warheads (this will be retrofitted on existing TOW launchers). The number of Dragons available will also be increased in the near future from 24 launchers to 32 launchers per infantry battalion, giving each division when this process is completed a total of 288 Dragons. The LAW, while providing some protection against enemy armor, has not been entirely satisfactory, and an improved version is scheduled to come on line.

Last, but certainly not least for an institution such as the Marine Corps, is the question of amphibious capability. Although not entirely a Marine Corps issue, given the role of the Navy in such operations, it is nonetheless a matter that weighs heavily in Marine Corps planning and procurement. The mainstay of the amphibious assault force is the classic "Amtrac", the LVTP-7 and its variants, a total of 47 of all types (including 43 LVTP-7s) being in each LVT (Landing Vehicle Tracked) unit. The service life of these vehicles is to be extended by a phased modernization program. In addition, the Marine Corps is to procure between 329 and 382 improved versions of the basic LVT system in order to meet the pre-positioning requirements of three Marine Amphibious Brigades in coming years.

A new type of assault craft, the Landing Craft Air Cushion (LCAC), with a 60-ton payload and a speed of 40-50 knots (plus across-the-beach and inland capability), will become operational in 1986, when Amphibious Craft Unit-5 is activated with six LCACs, followed the next year by a similar detachment. In addition to the amphibious ships (e.g., LHAs) currently available, the Navy's plans to proceed with the development and deployment of the Landing Ship Dock (LSD)-41 class, of which eight are to be built;

the LHD-1 (General Purpose Assault Ship) of 40,000 tons displacement, scheduled to replace the existing LPHs; and the recommissioning of the battleship *New Jersey*, with its 16in guns and array of missiles and secondary batteries, plus the requested recommissioning of its sister ships, all point in favor of greater amphibious assault capability for the Marine Corps.

The Modern Marine Corps: A Net Assessment
On balance, it is clear that the Marine Corps, as it is presently configured, has a number of distinct assets. *First,* it is clearly a highly cost-effective force, providing a considerable degree of combat power at relatively low cost. In FY 1982, for example, only 4 per cent of the entire defense budget was allocated to the Marine Corps. For that expenditure, the Corps provided 9 per cent of the military personnel, 12 per cent of the general-purpose forces, 12 per cent of the tactical air forces, and 15 per cent of the ground combat forces in the entire US defense establishment.

Second, within its basic ground combat formations, the Marine Corps maintains a very high "teeth-to-tail" (combat : support) ratio of 60:40. This is the highest in the American defense establishment, and comes the closest of any American formation to the combat : support ratio of the very "toothy" Soviet formations. Combined with its previously mentioned cost-effectiveness, the ability of the Corps to provide "the most [combat power] for the least [outlay of personnel and resources]" seems demonstrated.

Third, the combined-arms ground-air team concept which is at the foundation of Marine Corps operational doctrine provides a framework for the integrated use of all combat arms to a degree greater than that which exists elsewhere in the US defense establishment. In this highly flexible and well-coordinated framework, the Marines employ a very high ratio of tactical air:infantry capabilities as a surrogate for the armor and artillery in which the Corps is lacking (at least by Army standards). This enhances the combat power of Marine formations beyond what might be expected from an inspection of the tables of organization and equipment of the ground combat elements.

Fourth, while there is some doubt about the utility of a large amphibious capability, there is little doubt about the need to have *some* ability to project combat power ashore via an amphibious assault, as that is currently

conceived in US doctrine. Here, the Corps' forte stands out. It has the greatest experience with amphibious operations, and possesses the greatest number of personnel trained to manage such operations, of any force in the world. Airborne formations certainly can deploy more rapidly than seaborne Marines. But in some instances (e.g., Lebanon, 1958, Dominican Republic, 1965, and the Mayagüez incident, 1975) an amphibious force on station in a trouble spot may still be preferable to a more mobile force which would have to be deployed overseas from the US itself. Certainly, the amphibious assault ships (LHAs), which can carry 2,000 Marines with their artillery and armor, plus helicopters, are clear assets in this regard, as are the previously mentioned amphibious assault ships now in production or development.

On the other hand, the Corps retains a number of liabilities as well. *First* is the fact that the Marine Corps is still a very "light" organization, despite current and projected changes in its mobility and firepower. "Lightness" is, of course, a relative term. Against most Asian, African, or Latin American units, a Marine battalion (reinforced) would be considered a very *heavy* unit. Yet unless Marine operations in the future can be limited to the Third World, the ability of the Corps to operate effectively against much heavier Soviet formations must be considered questionable.

Second, it is very clear that the close-air support (CAS) on which the Corps has placed great reliance in the past may no longer retain the same usefulness. The families of Soviet-designed surface-to-air missiles and radar-directed multiple automatic AA cannon have, as the 1973 Arab-Israeli war demonstrated, made reliance on close-air support a very chancy thing. More recent conflicts in both Lebanon and the South Atlantic have clouded that picture somewhat, to be sure, but in all cases the combination of training plus technology produces a very complex equation. The sale of increasingly sophisticated weapons to an ever-larger number of countries means that the technological barriers between first-line military establishments and those of smaller countries may not be quite so

Below: The Landing Craft Air Cushion (LCAC) project by Bell Aerosystems is very much alive and should enter service in 1986. Up to 60 tons of tanks, trucks and stores can be carried in the centre deck.

Above: The F-18 Hornet entered service in 1982 under fire from critics of its offensive capability, and threats to McDonnell Douglas that production would be cut if the price per aircraft wasn't reduced. Sidewinder missiles arm the eighth prototype seen here during test flying.

Below: A Thomaston class Landing Ships dock (LSD) disgorging a fully loaded LCU landing craft. Like all assault ships, these custom-built vessels are highly vulnerable to attack when conducting amphibious operations, emphasizing the need for protective air cover.

pronounced in the future as they were in the past, for example.

Overall, however, there is a more fundamental question here that goes beyond single wars; that is, undermining the reliability of CAS also calls into question the utility of the air-ground team concept basic to USMC force structure and doctrine. Questions of inter-service competition aside, it may become increasingly difficult to justify the "heavy" Marine aircraft wings in a combat environment ever more hostile to CAS. If those wings are attenuated, then the Corps would either have to acquire more armor and firepower to allow it to act without CAS, or forgo such augmentations and preclude engaging in operations outside of the Third World. Neither option would justify a continuation of the Corps, as it is now constituted, at its present force levels.

Third, the Corps' ability to conduct amphibious operations with the support necessary for good prospects of success is decreasing, although not because of deficiencies on its part. The current fleet of amphibious warfare ships is relatively new, and newer ships yet are coming on line to replace older vessels. But trends in amphibious shipping over nearly two decades demonstrate clearly that there now exist fewer ships with less lift and less naval gunfire (NGF) support than was the case at the beginning of the Vietnam War. The simple fact that the United States now has the ability to provide adequate amphibious lift for only the assault echelon of one Marine Amphibious Force—barely one-half of what US planners have considered essential—cannot be considered desirable. Moreover, although the recommissioning of the battleship *New Jersey* is a step in the right direction insofar as NGF is concerned, the sharp decline in on-line NGF capability over the years has reached the point where the ability of a Marine assault force to make a forcible entry against a determined defense in the absence of clear tactical air superiority is doubtful. Unless these deficiencies are remedied, the ability of the Marine Corps to maintain a viable amphibious assault capability against established opposition will become increasingly open to question.

Basic Questions About the Marine Corps
From the end of the Vietnam War to the present, a general reassessment of American defense policy raised questions about the place of the Marine Corps in the defense establishment. As the Vietnam War receded in public memory somewhat, and as concern about the growth in Soviet military power partially replaced apprehension about American military misadventures overseas, only vestiges of the earlier questions remained. Some still questioned whether the US needed a Marine Corps; others wondered precisely what mission the Corps should have; and some—perhaps the most persistent of those who expressed concern—cast a wary eye at the Corps' manpower policies, in the light of the problems it had encountered during the transition to an all-volunteer force by the entire US defense establishment. All agreed that the foundation of the Marine Corps, whatever its role, was and remains well-trained and well-disciplined personnel. If that failed, then the entire edifice could become an institutional house of cards—something that many who remain concerned about the modifications that have taken place in the traditionally intense basic training fear may come back to haunt the Corps in the future.

It is readily apparent that the Marine Corps' history and record are sufficiently meritorious to commend it as a model for other military institutions to emulate. Recent criticism directed at the Corps as an institution is far from unusual. After World War II and the Korean War, the need for a Marine Corps was called into question, and the post-Vietnam experience simply fits the pattern.

Yet it was, and is, clearly in the national interest of the US to have at its disposal an elite combat force, even—and, perhaps, especially—in an era of technologically sophisticated weaponry.

On the other hand, it must be recognized that the Corps' response to the most recent round of criticism has been less than persuasive. It can certainly be argued that there remains a need to retain an amphibious assault capability in the modern world. But it is a very different matter to argue that there is a need for a major, multi-division amphibious capability, and that the Marine Corps should be able to participate in operations in Europe, if the need arises.

Memories of the past notwithstanding, it is all too likely that any adversary large enough to merit, for example, a MAF-level amphibious assault would also have the capability to concentrate massive firepower on a most inviting target: an amphibious force, lying (even at some distance) off a shoreline, preparing to send in the landing force via helicopter and assault landing craft or armored amphibians. What may have been perfectly feasible in the years before the advent of nuclear weapons and precision-guided munitions, or even in the era of US nuclear superiority, does not necessarily apply today.

Furthermore, it should be clear that the only way the Marine Corps could realistically hope to be able to conduct operations in a European war is for it to acquire a substantial mechanized capability. Yet this would make it functionally equivalent to the Army,

thereby undermining the presumption of uniqueness on which its existence as a separate entity was, and remains, based. Indeed, the decision of the Corps to incorporate a family of light armored vehicles (LAVs) into its divisional structure, while talking of the Mechanized Combined Arms Task Force (MCATF) concept, is all too obviously an attempt to find an institutionally tolerable way out of this dilemma.

One thing must be admitted fairly. The Marine Corps, despite extensive rationales to the contrary, has evolved to the point where its size and force structure bear only a tangential relationship to the purpose, scope, and realistic missions of an elite *force d'interventions*. Nor would augmenting the mechanized warfare capability of the Corps ease the problem. In fact, the Corps is caught on the horns of a dilemma, and one which is of its own making. If it remains as it is presently configured, the Corps risks becoming a functional anachronism, as outmoded as horse cavalry in an era of machine guns, organizing itself around the doctrine of major amphibious operations in a world where the feasibility of such operations has become doubtful. Yet if it moves closer to the Army in terms of its organization, equipment, weapons, and tactical doctrine (for example, regarding the conduct of mechanized operations), it risks losing both its institutional uniqueness *and* the mobility necessary for it to be able to carry out the rapid deployments essential for an intervention force, amphibious or not.

What, then, should the Marine Corps do? It is clear that there is no rational basis for

Above: Sea Stallion heavy transport, the most powerful helicopter in Marine service until the arrival of the Super Sea Stallion.

the Corps to become a second Army, replete with mechanized formations; nor to compete with the other services for the possession of a major tactical air capability; nor even to remain a "light" force in a world of "heavy" conflicts. On the other hand, it is equally clear that what really gave the Marine Corps its presumptions of uniqueness and elite status in the past reflected its institutional values more than its operational characteristics. What made the Marine Corps different was not the missions it was intended to perform. It was the overall caliber of the forces available for *whatever* missions they were called upon to carry out. And it is there that the Corps should base its future position, and not simply retreat to periodic restatements of missions that hark back to the days of Tarawa and Iwo Jima.

The Future of the Marine Corps: America's Rapid Deployment Force

Beginning on the last year of the Carter Administration, the USA began talking about the need to have a force capable of intervening rapidly abroad, especially in Southwest Asia in the aftermath of the Soviet invasion of Afghanistan and the collapse of a pro-American government in Iran. This force, originally called the "Rapid Deployment Force" and subsequently re-christened the "Rapid Deployment Joint Task Force", became a separate task force

217

reporting to the National Command Authority (NCA) via the Joint Chiefs of Staff in October 1981. As of January 1, 1983, it became the "US Central Command", reflecting the broader mandate for operations it was gradually assuming. The missions assigned to the RDJTF were ambitious, and remain so more than three years after its inception. Certainly, questions of time and distance (i.e., could the USA move sufficient forces with proper equipment into place in time to counter a threat, especially one including or supported actively by the Soviet Union?) were, and are, of considerable importance.

What is important here, however, is not an appraisal of the missions the RDJTF is intended to perform. It is an assessment of the selection of the forces assigned to the RDJTF. To many, the RDJTF concept seemed to be an idea whose time had come. Thus, each of the services wanted a role—especially the Army, which saw in the advent of the RDJTF a chance to rectify the damage done to its institutional reputation by the Vietnam War, and thereby remain ahead of the bureaucratic "power curve" in the game of Washington interservice politics.

Therefore, elements of all four services were designated for the RDJTF: from the Army, the 82nd and 101st Airborne divisions, the 24th Mechanized Infantry Division, the 6th Air Combat Cavalry Brigade, and head-quarters, Ranger, and Special Forces units; from the Air Force, two bomber squadrons, twelve fighter squadrons, two tactical recon-naissance squadrons, and nine tactical airlift squadrons; from the Navy, three carrier battle groups, one surface action force, and five maritime patrol squadrons; and from the Marine Corps, one Marine amphibious force and the 7th Marine amphibious brigade.

Somewhat lost in this nominally impressive array of forces was one problem: despite the existence of a separate command for the RDJTF, and the designation of the above units for RDJTF missions, none was ever transferred for administrative and operational purposes from its existing command. Thus, in

the event of a crisis, the commander of the RDJTF would necessarily have to assemble an *ad hoc* task force composed of units from all of the services with their inherent differences in training, doctrine, and tactics. Few, if any, of those units (except for their headquarters and communications echelons) could reasonably have been expected to have operated together in the recent past, given the experience to date. And the force, assembled under a strange commander, beset with near-certain questions of inter-service rivalry and competing administrative and

Above: Peace keeping plays large part in the role of a present-day Marine. He is more than ever a political instrument of government, often being called in to provide a presence in a divided country. Here in the Lebanon troops have just disembarked from the USS *Saginaw.*

Below: Marine Air Wings like their Navy counterparts use dedicated electronic warfare aircraft to confuse enemy communications. Principal types are the EA-6B Prowler (below) and EA-6A Intruder.

operational command structures, would then have to deploy quickly into a hostile environment in the face of probable shortages of shipping and supplies, given current and projected air- and sea-lift capabilities. Like the multiservice task force assembled for Operation Eagle Claw in 1980 (the abortive rescue attempt of American hostages held in the US Embassy in Tehran, which ended in flaming ruin)—a task force that was simply an RDJTF in miniature—the potential for disaster is all too great.

Correcting this situation is obviously a matter of great urgency, given the instability in the Third World likely to prevail during the 1980s and thereafter. The United States needs a force capable of carrying out interventions in parts of the world that do not carry with them the spectre of nuclear war or an armored battle on the plains of Europe (or at least what remains of them!). It does *not* need a hybrid force such as the RDJTF in its current configuration, devoid of forces per-

manently assigned to it, and of little practical (as opposed to symbolic) comfort to those who might depend upon such a collage of forces to come to their assistance.

It is here that the Marine Corps, obviously acting in conjunction with the Navy, could assume the role most appropriate for it in the modern world. The assets required for the "rapid deployment force" concept to be realized exist in their entirety within the Department of the Navy; the ground force assets necessary to effect a forcible entry in a variety of hostile conflict environments either exist within the Marine Corps, or could be incorporated into it with little difficulty after a relatively brief transition period. (For example, parachute drops by large formations, while impressive in peacetime maneuvers, are rare in modern combat operations. Some airborne capability, however, should be maintained, and the Corps—which had parachute battalions in World War II—would have to re-acquire such a capability.)

Too often overlooked is the historical fact that, until World War II, the Navy and the Marine Corps together *were* the US "rapid deployment force", participating in literally scores of operations around the world that would today fall under the rubric of "rapid deployment force contingencies". Indeed, the operational heart and soul of the "rapid deployment force" concept are that of the Marine Corps: the ability to act quickly and decisively in low-intensity combat environments

under circumstances requiring the use of minimum force to achieve politically acceptable outcomes.

It is clear that the Navy and the Marine Corps, acting in concert, should be America's Rapid Deployment Force, with the Marine Corps assuming all of the ground force missions now divided between the Marine Corps and the Army. It is all too obvious in Washington (and, I suspect, to most outside analysts) that only bureaucratic infighting among the US armed services, magnified by the desire on the part of the Air Force and the Army to remain competitive with the Navy and the Marine Corps in the annual Pentagon budget sweepstakes, precluded that from being done in the past. Such luxuries are something the United States simply cannot afford any longer in the name of "Defense Department 'politics as usual' ", if only because neither America nor its allies can afford to risk having to deal with the spectacle of the failure of an intervention by the RDJTF in its current convoluted incarnation.

To effect this transformation would require a number of changes within the American defense establishment, not least of which would be in the way in which defense politics prevail over strategic necessity in far too many instances. At a minimum, this would entail an increase in the strategic airlift capability of the Navy, plus an increase in both tactical airlift capability (fixed-wing and helicopter alike) and assault aviation assets for the Marine Corps. This redefinition of the Marine Corps' requirements for tactical aviation, given the budgetary and manpower constraints with which the US is virtually certain to have to live for the foreseeable future, will necessarily entail the elimination of its fixed-wing "heavy" fighter/air-superiority aviation components—a step that ought to be taken in any event to reduce the duplication of effort that now exists among the armed services. It would require the Marine Corps to acquire an airborne/airmobile capability in addition to its amphibious assault capability, making it America's sole intervention force, with the Army divesting itself of its airborne/ airmobile forces and concentrating its full resources on general war requirements. It might well be advisable for the Marine Corps to separate itself from the Navy, forming a new Service Department, as the Air Force did when it separated itself from the Army after World War II, if only to underscore the new mission of the Corps and its new standing in the interplay of Pentagon politics. Finally, it would be desirable to station a full Marine Amphibious Brigade in Southern Europe, less to participate in some European war than to provide a forward-based intervention capability in Africa and the Middle East analogous to that which the Corps currently maintains in the Western Pacific.

The political obstacles to implementing the proposals outlined above are doubtless formidable, especially within the Pentagon. The Corps itself would probably resist any attenuation in its fixed-wing aviation capability, even if that was offset in the aggregate by the acquisition of other aviation assets. The Army would resist losing the airborne/airmobile capability whose forces (or at least the parachute and air assault badges its members wear) have become marks of status with that service. The Department of the Navy would object to losing control of the Marine Corps, just as the Army resisted losing control of the Air Force.

Yet if these steps, and others needed to transform a general design into operational reality, could be put into effect, they could well produce a Rapid Deployment Force worthy of the name and a Marine Corps capable of serving both its country and itself to the fullest measure possible in the years ahead. Perhaps that would be a good lesson in the true meaning of "Semper Fidelis".

US Reserves and National Guard

Roy A. Werner, Corporate Director, Policy Research, Northrop Corporation: formerly Principal Deputy Assistant Secretary of the Army.

The question of readiness and value of reserve forces is again a major question in US strategic doctrine, which currently calls for reservists "to be the initial and primary source for augmentation of the active forces". But with a small volunteer military, reserve forces are the only means of quickly expanding manpower in an emergency. Thus, to be useful, the 820,000 personnel in selected US reserve units must be ready. If reserve personnel cannot readily deploy, the doctrine is faulty and changes are necessary.

The necessity for rapidly deployable reserve units is clear given the dismantling of the Selective Service System and the possibility of brief, high-intensity wars. Four months, however, would be necessary to select and train draftee replacements. Moreover, even immediate enlistments would require two to three months of training. Hence, reservists are the sole source of additional manpower for the first ninety days of any future conflict.

But is this concept viable? Unless reserve units are combat ready and capable of meeting exacting deployment schedules, the strategic doctrine fails. Evidence suggests that currently many US reserve units cannot meet the probable schedules. According to Brig. General Randall D. Peat, USAF, Plans and Policy Directorate, JCS, "It is the current Joint Chiefs of Staff (JCS) assessment that a large proportion of Reserve Forces, especially ground combat units and surface ships, are less than combat ready."[1] However, the force posture in the 1980s still represents a substantial improvement over the preceding decade. As the Chairman of the Senate Armed Services Subcommittee on Preparedness noted, "A poor state of readiness within the Reserve components . . . calls into question the sustainability and—ultimately—the survivability of US Forces in combat."[2] Thus, restructuring is necessary to develop capable reserve forces. If such revamping is opposed, the reserves at their present levels are not a "national security bargain" and should not be perpetuated.

The Planning Process

Logically the planning process for arriving at an optimum defense force structure begins with an appreciation of the threat, then proceeds to structure forces and missions to counter the perceived threat. However, gaps inevitably arise between the "ideal force" and budgetary constraints. This fiscal reality and the desire to maintain an "insurance" factor, leads to reliance upon reserve forces. Although optimizing for a specific conflict is recommended, forces are not always substitutable between potential scenarios. It is easier, of course, to adjust reserve forces to wage a sustained war of attrition than to cope effectively with a *blitzkrieg*. Yet, because the likely adversary of the United States has a maneuver doctrine, the reserve structure and doctrine may be inadequate.

Despite noticeable alterations in foreign policy, defense strategies, weapons technology, and active force levels, the structure and missions of US reserve forces have remained nearly constant. A re-evaluation is long overdue.

Missions which can be performed only by active forces and those for which an active-reserve mix is both prudent and economical must be distinguished. Obviously the level, duration, and intensity of possible conflicts are crucial factors. For example, prospects of a prolonged low-intensity conflict seem remote. Moreover, because of political consequences and lethal new weapons, the probability of a lengthy high-intensity war seem equally remote. Therefore, the most probable conflict is a short, intense war—possibly designed for only limited goals. In such a case what then are reserve force missions? If deterrence fails, reserves must defeat aggression by means sufficient to serve political objectives. Thus, reserve combat elements should be deployable between within 1 to 30 days, and a training and logistical base sufficient to expand the military services should a prolonged conflict develop. Clearly then, higher priorities must be assigned to deploying units early with a low priority being given to sustaining support personnel and units. The many men on active duty in the USSR help to maintain a vast reserve pool of nearly nine million personnel over current five year intervals and in association with Warsaw Pact allies outproduce NATO in most categories of equipment for conventional warfare.

Force Structure

Force structures and strategy reflect past political and military decisions (or non-decisions). Presently, US reserves are ill-prepared to fight and win a high-intensity, short duration, war in Europe. Yet, many authorities anticipate precisely such a "short intense war."[3] Current strategy which assumes a three week warning of Soviet attack and up to sixty days for reinforcements to arrive[4] is dubious. If we remember Czechoslovakia in 1968 and consider the deployment pattern of Soviet forces, these assumptions become debatable propositions.

Obviously, the partial shifting of initial defensive burdens to the reserves because NATO members are unwilling to sustain sufficient active forces has important consequences. First, reserve reinforcements must be deployable immediately given the Soviet doctrinal emphasis on shock and speed and armor assets. But reserve units require more time to prepare for overseas deployment and US stockpiles still need rebuilding. Moreover, if these resupply and staging areas were overrun early in a conflict, equipment would be lost. Second, nine of the Army's eleven active divisions based in the United States rely upon reservists to fill their wartime manning levels, hence these divisions will be less effective if deployed within the initial weeks of combat. Third, while ignoring categories of reserve effectiveness, it is obvious that the Warsaw Pact alliance can field more reservists and enjoys much shorter logistical lines. Thus, the need for NATO superiority in weapons technology and planning is crucial. A Soviet attack launched in bad weather, utilizing smoke, electronic warfare and chemicals, might well achieve a breakthrough given comparative strengths and still mal-deployed NATO forces. When the weather clears, air power can be fully utilized but it may be too late. NATO must then

Although the reserves, with over 800,000 personnel, form a substantial proportion of the US armed forces' total strength, the equipment depicted here would be of little use in modern warfare, even if it could be activated readily. Moreover, it has been estimated that several months' post-mobilization training might be required before Army reserves could be deployed overseas in brigade or divisional formations, and deficiencies in sea-lift capability would prevent the immediate deployment of armored and mechanized divisions. Far left: Army reservist laying a mine during training. Left: Part of the US Navy's "mothball fleet" at San Diego. Below: Some of the obsolete aircraft preserved at Davis Monathan AFB, Arizona.

declare either to gain territory through conventional warfare or to threaten escalation to nuclear warfare. If a conventional role is decided upon, NATO is dependent upon reserves. Is such reliance justified?

If reserve units are incapable of both rapid deployment and mission success, NATO must either accept a *fait accompli* or escalate. Thus, adequate reserves can support deterrence. However, reserve force structure may not be sending out such a positive signal. Only the Air Force has basically altered its force structure since pre-Vietnam days. A decreased emphasis upon air defense interceptor roles and a sharper focus on tactical fighters, air refueling and airlift capabilities by the Air Force reflect both missions and reserve training capabilities. Table 3 reveals the scope of these changes. An even better indication of the Air Force modernization of its force structure is provided by examining the inter-meshing of regular and reserve units (Table 4). More significantly, Air Force reserve units probably receive the best training of any reserve component.

Modern equipment, however, is not present in the Naval reserve inventory. The Navy has passed on to the reserves modernized World War II destroyers (Gearing class) that lack fully modern sensors and helicopters for ASW purposes. Such ships obviously have little capability against Soviet nuclear submarines. Nor are these destroyers very effective against modern diesel powered submarines which, when submerged and running on batteries, are more difficult to detect than nuclear boats. These vessels are also vulnerable to Soviet surface combatants that can kill US ships with anti-ship missiles at a distance beyond the destroyer gun ranges. Adequate shipboard training for inland naval reservists remains a problem despite occasional "fly-ins" for sea duty. More fundamentally, sea control will be difficult in the early stages of NATO conflict given the vulnerability of surface vessels to anti-ship missiles, submarines and Soviet naval aircraft. These factors thus combine to assert a need for structural reform. A Korean War type reactivation would be of limited use, even if 549 mothballed

Below: Ex-USAF A-7D Corsairs in service with the 140th Tac Ftr Wing, Air National Guard, at Buckley Field, Colorado. With modern equipment, and a higher proportion of full-time personnel, the Air Force reserves are reasonably combat-ready, and are allocated definite missions alongside or in support of active units.

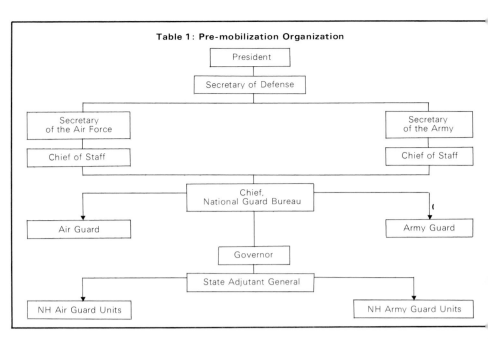

Table 1: Pre-mobilization Organization

- President
  - Secretary of Defense
    - Secretary of the Air Force
      - Chief of Staff
    - Secretary of the Army
      - Chief of Staff
    - Chief, National Guard Bureau
      - Air Guard
      - Army Guard
      - Governor
        - State Adjutant General
          - NH Air Guard Units
          - NH Army Guard Units

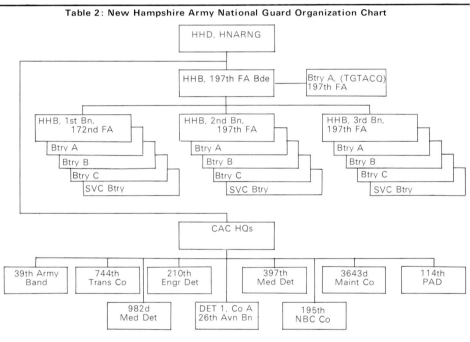

Table 2: New Hampshire Army National Guard Organization Chart

- HHD, HNARNG
  - HHB, 197th FA Bde — Btry A, (TGTACQ) 197th FA
    - HHB, 1st Bn, 172nd FA
      - Btry A
      - Btry B
      - Btry C
      - SVC Btry
    - HHB, 2nd Bn, 197th FA
      - Btry A
      - Btry B
      - Btry C
      - SVC Btry
    - HHB, 3rd Bn, 197th FA
      - Btry A
      - Btry B
      - Btry C
      - SVC Btry
  - CAC HQs
    - 39th Army Band
    - 744th Trans Co
    - 210th Engr Det
    - 397th Med Det
    - 3643d Maint Co
    - 114th PAD
    - 982d Med Det
    - DET 1, Co A 26th Avn Bn
    - 195th NBC Co

hips were available again. The latest weapons, vessel speeds, and surveillance capabilities make the reserve fleet obsolete. Because any future naval conflict is likely to be a war of platform attrition, surface effect ships, V/STOL carriers and hydrofoils — in large numbers — are the most useful ships. It is time to realize that merely continuing the past force structure will not suffice. The US surface naval reserve, if it is to contribute, must find new approaches to force composition simultaneously with new technology and vessels.

The composition of the Navy's active-reserve mix is found in Table 5 and clearly reveals the limited reserve capabilities. Meanwhile the Army, like the Navy, has been slow to modernize its reserve elements. Although excessive divisions headquarters with understrength units have been reduced, the Army's mission capabilities are much the same. A high intensity war generally demands armor and mechanized units. Yet, the present structure of 19 active Army and Marine divisions has nine light infantry divisions. Thus, almost half of the US ground combat strength is primarily designed for low-intensity operations — not the primary threat identified earlier. While it is true that some general capabilities must be maintained and that no scenario can hope to respond to all possible threats, the imbalance seems striking if rapid NATO reinforcements are needed. Of course, to a degree, it is more sensible to retain light infantry in the reserves to respond to the need for manpower above the active duty numbers. Further, with additional training and equipment, light infantry can assume other roles. But such shifts require time which only lower priority reserve units can spare. It would therefore seem reasonable to make some of these units anti-tank formations. Such an assignment would more clearly relate to potential conflicts in Europe, in Korea, or in the Middle East.

Another difficulty with the ground combat elements is that the US is deficient in lift capacities for high and mid-intensity wars. Capacity and time frame are the critical elements in such conflicts, wherever they may occur. Yet, there is insufficient sealift to move immediately the armor and mechanized divisions and US airmobile forces appear not to be suitably equipped. Moreover, light infantry delivered via air transport could find stockpiles captured and some airfields closed. When readiness is also evaluated, it is not surprising that one analyst concluded that it may take the six National Guard divisions designated as NATO combat replacements eight or more weeks after M-day (Mobilization Day) to arrive in Europe.[5]

Without revisions of reserve force structure, it may well be that neither the Army or Navy reserves will make significant contributions to a brief, high-intensity war. Another methodology for examining force structure as related to military doctrine is to analyse mission percentages between reserve and active forces. Table 6 presents such a comparison.

Whether one anticipates a brief or prolonged war, logic demands that planners maximize funding and training for early deploying units. The first step in that process is to identify priority and non-priority units. The elimination of some units may also be desirable. Such units include Navy Seabees, Army military police hospital guard units, and a host of other personnel, maintenance, engineer support, legal, public information and historical units. All these are job specialities for which civilian skills are easily transferable. In the event of mobilization for a longer conflict, these slots will be readily filled. The savings from these unnecessary units could then be directed to modernize equipment, improve training and tailor reserve units to specific missions. If such deletions are not made,

Right: Rows of B-52s at Davis-Monthan look like impressive air power, but each lacks engines, weapons, radar and other vital parts, and to refurbish one for combat duty would cost millions.

Table 3: Air Force Reserve and Air National Guard Flying Squadrons

	1960	1967	1974	1976
Wing Headquarters:	39	36	36	36
Fighter Interceptor Squadrons	42	22	21	11
Tactical Fighter Squadrons	24	23	33	38
Tactical Reconnaissance Squadrons	16	12	7	8
Air Commando/SOF	0	4	3	0
Tactical Airlift Squadrons	46	22	36	37
Military Airlift Squadrons	6	44	20	17
Aeromedical Airlift Squadrons	5	0	1	1
Air Refueling Squadrons	0	5	9	12
Tactical Air Support Squadrons	0	0	5	7
Tactical Electronic Warfare Squadrons	0	0	2	4
Special Operations Squadrons	0	0	6	2
Air Rescue and Recovery Squadrons	5	5	4	6
Weather	0	0	0	1

Sources: Congressional Testimony, *Air Force Magazine* and Dept. of the Air Force data.

Table 4: Air Force Flying Squadrons Functional Mix

	Active	Reserve
Wing Headquarters:	68	36
Fighter Interceptor Squadrons	6	11
Tactical Fighter Squadrons	74	38
Tactical Reconnaissance Squadrons	9	8
Tactical Airlift Squadrons	15	37
Military Airlift Squadrons	17	17
Aeromedical Airlift Squadrons	3	1
Air Refueling Squadrons	35	12
Tactical Air Support Squadrons	9	7
Tactical Electronic Warfare Squadrons	1	4
Special Operation Squadrons	5	2
Air Rescue and Recovery Squadrons	6	6
Weather Squadrons	2	1
Bomber Squadrons	25	0
Strategic Reconnaissance Squadrons	2	0

Sources: Adapted from Air Force Reserve, Air National Guard data and *Air Force Magazine*.

existing reserve force levels will require even more money to become combat ready. But, given fiscal realities, more money is unlikely and there is no alternative to pruning.

Readiness

Even if the reserve force structure had the ideal combination of units to respond to both short and prolonged war, the crucial issue is readiness. In October, 1961, three "high priority" Army divisions (2 infantry and 1 training) were mobilized for the Berlin crisis. But, the two priority combat divisions required nine months to achieve combat readiness.[6] In comparison it took only three more months to start from the beginning—form a cadre, basic training, individual proficiency and unit training—and to deploy the Ninth Infantry Division in 1965. Thus, even if we accept as valid the "insurance requirement" for both training and logistical support units for a prolonged war, it may be asked whether hundreds of thousands of reservists are necessary if they are not deployable much faster than volunteers and draftees. Are possible months of delay, perhaps even defeat, acceptable given the billions spent annually on reserves?

Clearly a huge reservoir of partially trained manpower, not readily deployable, is wasteful. The case for reserve organizations must rest upon these forces being deployable to combat theaters within the first month for high priority units and within two to three months for the lower priority sustaining units. Yet, in an exchange between Senator John Culver and then Secretary of Defense, James Schlesinger, the Senator stated, "What you are saying . . . is that it is hard to envision any real combat role within a ninety-day period?" Schlesinger responded, "I would not want to exclude it, but I think it is lower down on a probability scale."[7]

Another major disadvantage for the US, unlike European nations which can emphasize a territorial home defense role, is that US reserves must be capable of complex mobile warfare. Therefore, the training of maneuver battalions and elements to interact in battle is crucial, yet few and often inadequate field exercises at such levels are a common feature of US reserve forces.

This persistent doubt about the early deployment of reserve forces was also evident at a recent Army Operations Research symposium. An analysis of post-mobilization training at the battalion level only led Major Thomas A. Wilson, II (Hq. Force Command) and Dr. John R. Chiarini (Litton Systems) to estimate that two weeks would be required between the altering and the onset of active training and another seven weeks for post-mobilization training.[8] Even more time would be necessary if the units were to deploy as brigades or divisions—some four to six months. These discouraging estimates confirm earlier studies completed by the Army War College Strategic Studies Institute.

It may therefore be unrealistic to expect a reserve component maneuver unit, except for aviation elements, to deploy within thirty days. Armor units, for example, fire only once a year and cannot complete two of the eight gunnery tables without additional post-mobilization training. Thus, reserve units possessing generally only 39 training days a year (15 days active duty and 48 drill periods of four hours each), are hard pressed to meet their readiness criteria. As former Defense Secretary Schlesinger said, "We should stop pretending that we can use all of them as full substitutes for active duty ground forces."[9]

Other reserve elements experience poor training. Air defense units seldom train in, or experience, electronic warfare environments. Engineer, artillery, signal units, and naval surface crews all require extensive teamwork. Such units seldom receive the necessary collective training. A naval reservist recently noted that except for the Naval Reserve Force destroyers and other small reserve ships . . . "the surface reserve sailor gets little practical shipboard-type training."[10]

The single service reasonably ready is the US

Table 5: Naval Ships, Functional Mix[1]			
	Active	**Reserve**	**Custody**[2]
Sea Control (Surface Warfare, ASW, etc)			
Destroyers	84	5	8
Cruisers	27	0	7
Frigates	79	4	0
Minesweepers	3	22	0
Submarines, Attack[3]	90	0	3
Projection			
Amphibious[4]	65	4	17
Battleships	10	0	4
Carriers	14	0	6
Submarines, SSBN	32	0	0
Other			
Patrol	26	0	0
Command	0	0	2
Auxiliary	111	2 (LST)	34

Source: IISS Military Balance, 1982–83.
1. This table excludes the seventh reserve component, the Coast Guard and the forty-two vessels assigned to the Military Sealift Command.
2. This category includes mothball ships held by the Navy, and the Maritime Administration vessels already identified for Navy utilization. Data is from 1976.
3. Eighty-five are nuclear powered.
4. Assumes a primary role of naval gunfire support for land combat operations (as in Vietnam). Obviously, in an era of ship-to-ship missiles, these vessels are unlikely to engage other ships. Excludes 90 LCU ships and smaller vessels.

Air Force. Its reserve elements have visible missions, participate alongside active forces, have generally the same equipment as active components, and possess significantly higher percentages of full-time personnel. Both Air National Guard and Air Force Reserve airlift squadrons directly support the Rapid Deployment Force. Missions include KC-135 tanker aircraft and the P-3 airplane for maritime patrol. The USAF tactical fighter reserve squadrons deployed in the January and May, 1968, mobilizations attained the highest performance ratings in their respective four wings. The results show. Naval aviators learned the importance of training on the same aircraft they will fly when mobilized in 1968. Six squadrons were delayed in that mobilization because of re-equipping and re-training requirements necessary to convert the crews to new aircraft.

After the aviation elements in readiness comes the Fourth Marine Division. The Marines possess many of the same advantages as the Air Force reserves, especially active duty involvement and guidance. Probably only in such a fashion can reservists assume the awesome burden of national defense while providing significant cost savings.

Another problem is the growing technological disparity between the regular and the reservist. Equipment is becoming increasingly complex and a reservist who does not train regularly on laser guided weapons, for example, is going to be less proficient. Obviously this disparity will be greater for radar and sonar operators as compared to infantrymen. Moreover, even effective training on outdated equipment, regardless of enthusiasm, is of little value if that equipment cannot be deployable or if stockpiles contain different gear.

The problems are thus centered in the Army's reserve components and naval crews. The Office of the Secretary of Defense conducted a Reserve Component Test Program between 1972 and 1974 of Army divisions and separate brigades. The majority of these units did not attain company level (basic combat unit) proficiency. Recent reforms stressing "hands-on" mission-essential training have somewhat improved the situation. In essence, although defense policy prescribes missions for reserve units, there is scepticism that these units could successfully accomplish their missions without extensive post-mobilization training.

Personnel

The ever-present problem of reserve personnel strength is illustrated by the fact that the then Major Dwight D. Eisenhower wrote his 192? Army War College research topic on "An Enlisted Reserve for the Regular Army". Personnel problems continue to plague selected reserve forces.

Below: AFRES (Air Force Reserve) pilot on pre-flight check of an A-37A Dragonfly of 434th Tac Ftr Wing.

Official estimates[11] are that the Army needs 125,000 individual ready reservists (IRR) to meet emergency demands in the first 90 to 120 days of war. But, in August 1982, the IRR total was only 234,000. More troubling is the imbalance between support and combat arms personnel. Hence, the extreme shortage is of junior enlisted personnel with combat arms experience. Moreover, since analysts expect up to a 25 per cent "no-show" rate because of physical disabilities, hardships, and administrative problems, another 130,000 troops are necessary. Thus, the Army IRR total is 555,000 – a shortfall of 321,000 in August 1982. Possible recall of retirees will be of marginal help, but of little assistance in combat-oriented enlisted slots. The decline from over 1,000,000 in 1972 is obvious. Recommendations have been made to return to an eight year military service obligation, including reserve time (as it was prior to 1956) and to pay bonuses for extending IRR obligations. However, any "solution" before 1990 is unlikely.

Personnel problems, however, may doom any reform of the reserve forces that does not shrink force levels. The Reserve Forces Policy Board, a mixture of civilian and military advisors, in a November 1976 statement warned that an economic recovery "will intensify the recruiting and retention problem." Recent statistics show the combined reserve shortfall to be about 90,000 personnel. Even more disturbing is the failure of Army reserve components to retain more than half of their enlisted personnel. Moreover, it is not certain that enacting a variety of financial benefits will solve the recruitment and retention problems. If the root of the problem is attitudinal in nature, such incentives will have little effect. The adequacy of individual ready reservists (IRR) is also dubious. This massive manpower pool formerly had no realistic training requirements. More importantly, volunteer military forces are constantly shrinking these numbers. In addition, without proper training the value of this manpower is questionable. Thus, the reserve personnel system neither

delivers a continuing flow of manpower nor adequately trains and retains what manpower it does recruit.

Yet another difficulty in personnel is the buddy-system of officer appointments made possible by geographical dispersion. An innovative approach to opening these closed shops has been made by the 97th US Army Reserve Command (ARCOM). Utilizing senior officers from subordinate commands, the officer career management board publicizes widely all 0–5 and 0–6 positions, interviews interested parties and makes recommendations to the Commander. In the words of one general officer member, the problem is to "identify the qualified, ambitious, effective" officer as well as the "ineffective officers" and place them both "where they belong".[12] An additional aid for the Army reserve components will be the recent changes in AR 140–10 which limit key command and staff slots to three year tours.

Yet another issue is what mix of prior service (generally ex-active duty) and non-prior service personnel is desirable. Obviously, if a trained individual can be acquired, efficiency and readiness should be enhanced. Since Vietnam reserve units have relied on prior service, short-term enlistments to fill the ranks. Although veterans minimize shortfalls, they increase turbulence, grade and longevity, and result in higher personnel costs. Hence, more inexperienced personnel are desirable given cost, retention, and age efficiencies. The one advantage of "veterans" is that they are generally qualified in their respective job skills.

Another personnel problem is the mobilization process itself. After readiness, mobilization

speed is probably the most significant issue in reserve policy considerations. Israeli and South Korea forces mobilize within 72 hours (many sooner). Both these systems thus signal potential adversaries and probably aid deterrence. Yet, aside from the Berlin 1961 mobilization and the limited call-up in 1968, no full scale US mobilization exercises have been conducted. Ideally, units should be tested within a reasonable time period by alerting them and then moving the unit out for two weeks of annual training. Such an evaluation might impose some hardships, but it would present a more complete picture of the system's capabilities to include possible "no shows" due to health standards, one of today's unknowns. Another option is the unannounced Marine Corps Mobilization Operational Test. These exercises check personnel and mobilization time, equipment, and unit proficiency. Until such realistic tests are conducted, planners cannot be confident of reserve personnel capabilities.

Although MOBEX 78 and 80 exercises tested primarily higher headquarters and plans, they have revealed numerous deficiencies. Yet, mobilization capabilities have been significantly enhanced by the many corrective actions taken, and mobilization planning is now a reality.

An argument is made, however, that regardless of readiness, political and diplomatic factors will determine any future mobilization decision. Certainly, political authorities have recently been reluctant to call up more than a minimum of reserve forces in a crisis. Recent crises—Berlin, Vietnam, the Pueblo Incident of 1968—have seen small numbers of reservists called up to dramatize US resolve. However, the demise of conscription and a recent statute granting the President authority to activate 100,000 reservists without declaring a national emergency suggest reserve activation is indeed policy. More importantly, reserve forces perceived as capable of early battlefield deployment aid both deterrence and crisis management by expanding readily deployable military forces.

As the newly assigned Director of the Army

Table 6: Selected Reserve Forces as a percentage of the Department of Defense functional mix

Army	Per cent
Divisional forces	38
Medical units	46
Tactical support forces	67
Nondivisional forces	69
Navy and Marine Corps	
Carrier air wings	14
Marine division/wing strength	25
Marine anti-aircraft missile battalions	33
Maritime patrol squadrons	35
Military Sealift Command personnel	60
Minesweepers	88
Air Force	
Strategic airlift crews	48
Tactical reconnaissance	57
Tactical airlift	59
Air defense interceptors	69
Combat communications and air traffic control	70+
Aerial spraying capability	100

Source: DoD data, 1982.

Table 7: Readiness of selected reserve forces

Type	1981 Number	Combat Rated
Strategic Forces		
Air refueling squadrons	16	16
Air defense squadrons	10	8
General Purpose Forces		
Land		
Army divisions	8	8
Army brigades and regiments	28	28
Marine divisions	1	1
Naval[1]		
Destroyers	5	8
Minesweepers	22	15
Amphibious ships	6	1
Air[2]		
Air Force squadrons	44	43
Marine squadrons	15	15
Navy squadrons	62	59
Tactical airlift squadrons	36	33
Associated military airlift wings	6	6

Notes:
1. Excludes ships destined for deactivation, conversion overhaul or restricted availability.
2. includes fixed- and rotary-wing aircraft.

Source: DoD data, 1982.

Table 8: Selected equipment shortfalls

Army	
Tanks	1,949
Trucks	9,161
Personnel carriers	5,214
Aircraft	1,167
Navy and Marine Corps	
Ships	34
Communications/electronics	1,357
Motor transportation	1,392
Aircraft	300
Air Force	
Aircraft	130
Vehicles	1,918
Support equipment	4,426

Estimated funding necessary to eliminate shortfalls in 1982 $, 17.8 billion.

Source: DoD data, 1982.

National Guard, Major General Herbert R. Temple, Jr, said, "we won't have time to put units together with equipment they have never seen or used before"[13] in the next war. Readiness, nevertheless, improved over the 1970s. For example, the 2nd Battalion of the 252nd Armor of the North Carolina Guard, a "roundout" unit of the 2nd Armored Division, is due to receive M1 tanks in 1983.

Equipment
Shortages of modern equipment continue to plague reserve forces and degrade readiness.

As the Deputy Assistant Secretary of Defense for Reserve Affairs said recently, "I would suggest . . . that the equipment problem is the most critical . . .".[14] Yet, as Senator Humphrey elicited from the JCS representative at the same hearings, "you feel that the Joint Chiefs are very comfortable for the first 90 days with regard to equipment in that scenario (Warsaw Pact attack)?" Answer, "Yes."[15] Obviously, the critical shortages are smaller and more targetable for corrective action.

Corrective measures in the near term include issuing the M60 main battle tank to all early deploying roundout or affiliate units (those completing active forces wartime manning tables). The Air Force is accelerating transfer of one hundred and twenty-eight KC-135 tankers to its reserve components. Additionally the army is supplying M198 howitzers and trucks; the Naval Reserve is getting 12 modern Knox-class frigates; the Air Force Reserve and National Guard are receiving some new aircraft. Block obsolescence of aircraft is a particular problem. At the end of FY80 the average age of USAFR was 16.3 years, the Air National Guard 14.3 years, US Marine Corps Reserve attack aircraft 13 to 17 years, and fighters, 14 years. Naval reserve aircraft have similar time frames and technological backwardness, and C-118s used for airlift will be unsupportable by 1984. Indeed, engine modification is needed to reduce smoke trails left by USAFR F-4 aircraft. Less costly, unique reserve aircraft with modern avionics systems capable of using force multiplying weapons may be both desirable and more effective. Presently A-10 ground attack aircraft

go directly to reserve units, F-4C/Ds are transferred to reserve squadrons, and the first F-16A planes will go to the USAFR in 1983. Hence, at best there is only manageable vertical obsolescence, pushing a few new aircraft annually into the force structure. Yet, these positive examples nevertheless reveal a budgetary constraint. Because the cost of equipping both active and reserve forces with fully modern equipment is so high, as older major stock items are phased out of active forces, they are transferred to reserve components.

Many units are not, however, combat ready because of equipment shortfalls. Table 8 illustrates those units not at their highest stage of readiness. Further, when equipment is short, costs rise and readiness decreases. Over many years various equipment programs have been promulgated that historically do not succeed. The Army told Congress that all Army Reserve units would be at or near authorized equipment levels by FY 1977 in the FY 1973 hearings[16], yet reserve units were still quite short. These shortages degrade mission capabilities. While granting that budget dollars, production line schedules and some foreign military sales all adversely affect the reserves, corrective action is necessary. "We simply cannot afford to spend $5.5 billion annually on a force oriented solely toward a lengthy mobilization of the type envisioned in the past," the Assistant Secretary of Defense for Manpower Reserve Affairs told Congress in 1975.[17]

Emerging Issues
The Laird decision in 1970 to return to traditional policy and rely upon reservists, not conscripts, as the initial reinforcement was accompanied by increased reserve budgets and a focusing on reserve problems by senior defense officials. Obviously, however, reform of reserve units to reflect viable policy options has not been accomplished. The United States can no longer endure the luxury of ill-prepared reservists on M-day (Mobilization Day). Therefore changes are mandatory. The starting point is to ask why the aviation components excel? One of the principal reasons for their success is a full-time manning level of about 20 percent. These levels

Left: As well as veterans of earlier wars, the Army reserve includes personnel without prior service, such as this grenade thrower shown in training.

were designed to provide maintenance care and to enable the units to conduct missions alongside regular units. Obviously not all reserve units can assist active forces. But all reserve units could increase their full-time personnel.[18] The Marines also gain from such augmentation and these active duty personnel may be assigned to the unit upon mobilization. Such methods are one way of infusing recent experience into reserve units.

A crucial immediate issue is, of course, whether reserve units can overcome their manpower shortfalls. Recently some civilian political and military officials have called for a return to conscription. In December 1976, Major General Henry Mohr, Chief of the Army Reserve, for example, argued that the only way reserve manpower needs will "be solved with any degree of effectiveness is with some sort of restoration of the draft". Such a judgment, however, ignores political realities. Nor would a "reserve only" draft produce viable fighting units with conscripts manning the platoons. It was exactly such attitudinal and generational conflict that recently plagued the active military. In prosperous societies the military is seldom popular and reserve units are no exception. Finally, in view of the declining demographic rates in the 1980s for persons of entry level age into military service, it is unlikely that existing reserve force levels can be maintained. Alternative manning tables and re-examination of missions will be necessary. Hence, test programs restructuring units and analysis of reserve missions are essential.

The problem of inadequate collective training has been mentioned. The establishment of Maneuver Commands to assist Army reserve components in group, brigade and division command post exercises was a useful first step. But, these units also need field exercises. Where would the American Army of World War II have been without Louisiana maneuvers? Another source would be greater inclusion in active force missions of rotating volunteer personnel.

The most innovative reserve training concept is the Marines VOTEC, a vocational education program which maximizes teaching by existing civilian instructional centers at low contract costs, thereby eliminating overhead. Examples of this arrangement include the maintenance and overhaul of diesel engines taught by a Texas technical institute and interpreter qualification training at a major university's language facility.

Obviously some improvements such as modern equipment require tax dollars. Further, substantial increases in reserve funding are unlikely. Therefore, planners must consider cuts to transfer funds. A possible starting point is the $1.4 billion (1974 dollars) savings to be gained through consolidation and the elimination of 300,000 excess paid reservists.[19] Such a policy would also narrow the equipment shortage gap. The basic features of that proposal were:

1 Merge training, recruiting and headquarters facilities of the Army Reserve with the Army National Guard and the Air Force Reserve with the Air National Guard.
2 Integrate reserve components into active force structures thereby somewhat reducing active duty manpower requirements.
3 Reduce IRR personnel and selected reserve units that could reasonably be expected to acquire skilled civilian personnel with transferable skills after mobilization began.
4 Alter the base year of retirement benefits from the year in which the annuity is drawn to the year in which the individual actually retires.

Recently, the Congressional audit watchdog, the General Accounting Office (GAO), has criticized inefficient reserve "layering". GAO urges the Army to eliminate the nine Army readiness and mobilization region offices and allow existing 19 Army Reserve Commands (ARCOM) to take over many mobilization functions—as does a state National Guard headquarters. The Defense Department has approved the elimination of these nine offices by FY86. Five CONUS-based field armies will coordinate training between the ARCOMs and overseas gaining commands and sponsors. Indeed, the "Capstone" program to align Army reserve units with gaining overseas commands or CONUS wartime command is one of the substantial improvements since 1978. Now some reserve units have designated assignments, help with training, and a chance to identify with a "real" mission. In 1983, nearly 10,000 Army Guardsmen will train in Europe, Korea, and elsewhere. Army reservists in Europe in 1983 could exceed 12,000.[20]

Refinements are possible. Although previous Guard-Reserve mergers have failed, the desirability of integrating the chain of command during peacetime cannot be denied. This option faces political problems even if President Carter were to back such moves. However, recognizing the desire of states to retain emergency forces, a possible solution is underway in California. An intensely trained emergency reaction force (like California's) could be left in state control with the remaining reserve and guard units being absorbed in a new Federal structure. Many states have para-military organizations—aside from the reserve units—such as state police forces or home guards that are available whenever the National Guard is employed elsewhere. Another option is to give Chiefs of Staff direct control over reserve policy decisions and reduce the duplication inherent in the National Guard Bureau and reserve Pentagon offices. Small, essentially policy staffs, could still represent "reserve opinions" to the Chiefs without the excess overhead. The premise is simple: an integrated staff for the "Total Force". Further, an internal emphasis on mission-oriented budgeting would sharpen the analytical focus of reserve assets. Dual basing of all mixed active-reserve units is desirable. Where a policy of dual basing is possible, this is the cheapest method.

Other cost savings come to mind. The "magic 48" drill periods could also be reduced for some units and personnel. The Army Reserve presently allows some medical doctors to drill as little as twelve assemblies and the Navy has units that drill twenty-four times annually. Certainly where the unit reflects civilian skills that are directly transferable—medical, building construction, legal, civil affairs, finance, some communication skills—a strong case exists that proficiency can be retained with fewer than 48 drills.

Personnel policy changes could also be advantageous. Reserve units frequently have senior commanders lacking active duty experience at their command level, and junior officers, who because they are ROTC graduates or State National Guard OCS graduates, lacking sufficient training. Senior officers would benefit from a lateral entry scheme that would emplace them in key operational slots for a year with active forces. Such an in-out program would incur minimal costs and richly reward participants through enhanced professionalism while also educating active duty personnel about reserve components. The Army recently reduced branch qualification courses for state OCS graduates from twelve to four weeks. While granting that more officers can attend such reduced training, they are certainly less competent platoon leaders. One solution is to adopt a modification of the Marine platoon leader program and establish urban centers utilizing advisor personnel and mobile training teams to provide instruction for a year prior to the young officer returning to his unit.

Deeper analysis about possible contingencies and the appropriate force structure and readiness is necessary. As a recent Congressional Budget Office staff working paper on the Army noted:[14] "The force structure that is evolving... is less well manned, less prepared for sustained combat and substantially more reliant on reserve component units than before."

Is this reliance sound? A recent report of the Defense Manpower Commission took note of a 1973 Secretary of Defense directive which said the "Total force is no longer a 'concept'. It is now the Total Force Policy..." But the Commission concluded that the policy "is still far from a reality".[15] This is the precarious state in which US defense policy rests. As threats and strategies change, organizational forms must also change.

Footnotes

1. *Hearings: Status of the Guard and Reserves*, 97th Congress, 1st Session (Washington: Govt. Printing Office, 1982) p. 12.
2. *ibid*, p. 1.
3. Jeffrey Record, *Sizing Up the Soviet Army* (Washington: The Brookings Institute, 1975) p. 47, and Professor John Erickson, "Soviet Ground forces and the Conventional Modes of Operations," *Journal of the Royal United Services Institute for Defence Studies*, June, 1976, pp. 45–59.
4. *The Washington Post*, 15 November 1976, p. 8.
5. Abbott A. Brayton, "The Transformation of US Mobilization Policies: Implications for NATO," *Journal of the Royal United Services Institute for Defence Studies*, March, 1975.
6. *Hearings: Merger of the Army Reserve Components*, 89th Congress, 1st Session (Washington: Government Printing Office, 1965).
7. *Hearings on S. 2115*, before the Senate Armed Services Subcommittee on Manpower and Personnel, 30 July, 1975.
8. William V. Kennedy, "Army to Revamp Its Reserve Components," *Armed Forces Journal International*, February, 1974, p. 26.
9. *Annual Defense Department Report, FY 1976 and FY 1977* (Washington: Government Printing Office, 1976) p. III–14.
10. Commander A. Babunek, USNR, "Fleet Observations from the Fleet," *US Naval Institute Proceedings* v. 102, n. 4 (April, 1976) p. 86.
11. Major Dick Crossland, "Task Force Reports IRR Is Hurting", *Army Reserve Magazine*, Winter 1982, pp 32–33.
12. BG Edwin I. Dosek, "Senior Officer Career Management Problems," *The Officer*, November, 1975, p. 18.
13. Cited in "Reserve Panel: Strength Up, But Equipment Still Short", *Army*, December 1982, p. 60.
14. *Hearings: Status of the Guard and Reserve, ibid*, p. 19.
15. BG Randall Peat, USAF, *ibid*, p. 23.
16. *Hearings: Fiscal 1973 Authorization for Military Procurement*, Part 3, p. 1623.
17. William K. Brehm, *Hearings on S. 2115* before the Senate Armed Services Subcommittee on Manpower and Personnel, 30 July 1975.
18. Legal complications arise in the National Guard and would require legislative changes or full-time Federal personnel from state missions.
19. Martin Binkin, *US Reserve Forces: The Problem of the Weekend Warrior* (Washington, DC: The Brookings Institute, 1974).
20. "Overseas Training For NG Expands", *Army Times*, December 13, 1982, p. 34, Larry Carney.
21. Edwin A. Deagle, Jr., *US Army Force Design: Alternatives for Fiscal Years 1977–1981* (Washington, DC: Congressional Budget Office, 1976) p. ix.
22. *Defense Manpower: The Keystone of National Security*, (Washington, DC: Government Printing Office, 1976) p. 98.

Left: Owing to being often literally on the spot, reserve forces play a major role in saving life and property in major disasters. Here men of the 107th Armored Cavalry, W. Virginia Army National Guard, clear up after a flood.

Facing page: Reserve forces, such as the 1st Battalion, 23rd Marines, were given up to a month's notice that they would take part in the NATO Exercise Display Determination in the Aegean and European Turkey in 1977. Three other NATO countries took part in the exercise which demonstrated, among other things, how quickly US reserve forces have to blend with regular units (of US and friendly forces), on foreign shores if necessary. They may not be given so much notice in actual conflict.

229

US Rockets and Missiles

Bill Gunston, Assistant Compiler of Jane's *All the World's Aircraft*; author of many technical books and papers on military affairs.

This catalogue includes the major rockets and missiles in service with the US armed forces and important projects under development. They are arranged in alphabetical order.

ALCM, AGM-86B

Origin: Boeing Aerospace Co. USA.
Type: Air-launched cruise missile.
Propulsion: One Williams F107-101 turbofan with sea-level rating of 600lb (272kg) static thrust.
Dimensions: With wings/tailplane extended, length 20ft 9in (6.32m); body diameter 24.5in (620mm); span 12ft (3.66m).
Launch Weight: 2,825lb (1,282kg).
Range: Max hi, without belly tank, 760 miles (1,200km).
Flight speed: Cruise, about Mach 0.65; terminal phase, possibly Mach 0.8.
Warhead: W-80 thermonuclear as originally developed for SRAM-B.

Today potentially one of the most important weapons in the West's inventory, ALCM (Air-Launched Cruise Missile) was presented by President Carter as a new idea when he terminated B-1 as a bomber; he even said B-1 had been developed "in absence of the cruise missile factor", whose presence in 1976 made the bomber unnecessary. This is simply not true. The cruise missile never ceased to be studied from 1943, and—apart from such USAF examples as Mace and Snark—it was cruise-missile studies in 1963-66 that led to AGM-86 SCAD (Subsonic Cruise Armed Decoy) approved by DoD in July 1970. This was to be a miniature aircraft powered by a Williams WR19 turbofan, launched by a B-52 when some hundreds of miles short of major targets. Like Quail, SCAD was to confuse and dilute hostile defenses; but the fact that some or all would carry nuclear warheads—by 1963 small enough to fit such vehicles—meant that SCAD could do far better than Quail. No longer could the enemy ignore the decoys and wait and see which were the bombers. Every SCAD had to be engaged, thus revealing the locations and operating frequencies of the defense sites, which could be hit by surviving SCADs, SRAMs or ARMs. SCAD was to be installationally interchangeable with SRAM, with a maximum range of around 750 miles (1,207km). SCAD ran into tough Congressional opposition, but the USAF

knew what it was about and in 1972 recast the project as ALCM, retaining the designation AGM-86A. SCAD had had only a secondary attack function but ALCM is totally a nuclear delivery vehicle, and like SRAM has the ability to multiply each bomber's targets and increase defense problems by approaching from any direction along any kind of profile. Compared with SRAM it is much easier to intercept, being larger and much slower, but it has considerably greater range and allows the bomber to stand off at distances of at least 1,000 miles (1,609km).

The original AGM-86A ALCM was interchangeable with SRAM, so that a B-52G or H could carry eight on the internal rotary launcher plus 12 externally, and an FB-111A four externally plus two internally (though the latter aircraft has never been named as an ALCM carrier). This influenced the shape, though not to the missile's detriment, and necessitated folding or retracting wings, tail and engine air-inlet duct. Boeing, who won SCAD and carried across to ALCM without further competition, based ALCM very closely on SCAD but increased the fuel capacity and the sophistication of the guidance, with a Litton inertial platform (finally chosen as the P-1000).

Opposite page, top: Mock-up AGM-86B cruise missiles hung on the external pylon of a B-52G in tandem triplets.

Right: The AGM-86B is the USAF's airborne cruise missile, but not the weapon commonly called "cruise" by protesters in the Western democracies.

Below: Wings have yet to flick open as an AGM-86B drops from a SAC B-52G on a test at White Sands range in October 1982.

AIAAM

Intended as a successor to AIM-54 Phoenix, the Advanced Intercept AAM is an in-house development by Raytheon which was revealed in the form of a one-third scale model at the US Navy League 1982 Convention. AIAAM has aircraft configuration, with one set of wings and tail controls for twist-and-steer manoeuvring. An inclined supersonic inlet under the belly feeds an advanced ramjet or hybrid propulsion system. One possible propulsion contractor is CSD, who also provides an integral ramjet for the Vought STM (Navy supersonic tactical missile) and ducted rockets for other

missiles. AIAAM thus has a wide choice of propulsion methods (indeed a company other than CSD could be selected as propulsion contractor), and is hoped to lead the way to the air-to-air member of the planned new family of air-breathing supersonic missiles offering enormously enhanced range and sustained high power of manoeuvre. Guidance will include mid-course and, it is predicted, active radar terminal homing. The US Naval Weapons Center at China Lake began a two/three-year technology validation programme in early 1982. This has involved simulations which are intended eventually to lead to hardware tests including trials with complete guided rounds.

and computer (4516C), updated progressively when over hostile territory by McDonnell Douglas Tercom (DPW-23). In 1976 the decision was taken to aim at maximum commonality with AGM-109 Tomahawk, but the guidance packages are not identical. The engine in both missiles is the Williams F107 of approximately 600lb (272kg) thrust, but in totally different versions; the ALCM engine is the F107-101, with accessories underneath and different starting system from the Dash-400 of AGM-109. The warhead is W-80, from SRAM-B.

AGM-86A first flew at WSMR on 5 March 1976. Many of the early flights failed—one undershot its target by a mile because its tankage had been underfilled!—but by the sixth shot most objectives had been attained and 1977 was spent chiefly in improving commonality with Navy AGM-109, in preparation for something unforeseen until that year: a fly-off against AGM-109 Tomahawk in 1979 to decide which to buy for the B-52 force. It was commonly said Boeing was told to make AGM-86A short on range to avoid competing with the B-1. In fact no more fuel could be accommodated and still retain compatibility with SRAM launchers, and in 1976 Boeing proposed an underbelly auxiliary fuel tank for missiles carried externally.

A better answer was to throw away dimensional compatibility with SRAM and develop a considerably stretched missile, called AGM-86B. This has a fuselage more than 30 per cent longer, housing fuel for double the range with a given warhead. Other changes include wing sweep reduced to 25°, thermal batteries for on-board electrical power, all-welded sealed tankage, improved avionics cooling and 10 year shelf life. President Carter's decision to cancel the B-1 in June 1977 opened the way for Boeing to promote this longer missile, which could still be carried externally under the wings of a B-52 but would not have fitted into the weapon bays of a B-1. From July 1979 Boeing's AGM-86B was engaged in a fly-off against GD's AGM-109. Results were hardly impressive, each missile losing four out of ten in crashes, quite apart from other mission-related failures, but after a long delay the USAF announced choice of Boeing on 25 March 1980. A month later it was announced that the USAF/Navy joint management was dissolved and that the USAF Systems Command would solely manage 19 follow-on test flights in 1980 and subsequent production of 3,418 missiles by 1987. The first two rounds assigned to SAC joined the 416th BW at Griffiss AFB in January 1981. Since then about half the 169 operational B-52G bombers have been converted to carry up to 12 rounds each, in two tandem triplets, and in 1982 President Reagan increased the buy to 3,780 missiles by 1990 to permit 96 B-52H bombers to be equipped also. From 1986 the internal bomb bays are to be rebuilt by Boeing-Wichita to permit each aircraft to carry a further eight rounds on an internal rotary launcher. Each B-52, after conversion, will have a permanently attached wing-root "strakelet", vissible in satellite pictures, as demanded by SALT II provisions. The pre-loaded wing pylons will be carried only in time of emergency.

The production B-1B will carry the same eight-barrel rotary launcher as the rebuilt B-52, and except for the first few aircraft will also carry a further 4 on eight external racks, making a total of 22. It is unlikely on present planning that any other aircraft in any NATO air force will carry the ALCM, though there would be no technical difficulty.

AMRAAM

Origin: Hughes Aircraft, Missile Systems Group, Tucson, Arizona, USA.
Type: Advanced medium-range AAM.
Propulsion: Advanced internal rocket motor, details and contractor not yet decided.
Dimensions: Length 145.7in (3.7m); body diameter 7.0in (178mm).
Launch Weight: 326lb (148kg).
Range: In excess of 30 miles (48km).
Flight speed: About Mach 4.
Warhead: Not yet announced, but may be expected to be lighter than 50lb (22kg).

Also called BVR (Beyond Visual Range) missile, the Advanced Medium-Range AAM is the highest-priority AAM programme in the United States, because AIM-7F is becoming long in the tooth and is judged urgently in need of replacement in the 1980s by a completely new missile. AMRAAM is a joint USAF/USN programme aimed at producing a missile having higher performance and lethality than any conceivable advanced version of Sparrow, within a package that is smaller, lighter, more reliable and cheaper. AMRAAM will obviously be matched with later versions of F-14, -15, -16 and -18 equipped with programmable signal processors for doppler beam-sharpening and with advanced IR sensors able to acquire individual targets at extreme range. The missile would then be launched automatically on inertial mid-course guidance, without the need for the fighter to illuminate the target, the final terminal homing being by a small active seeker. The task clearly needs a very broad programme to investigate not only traditional sensing and guidance methods but also new ones such as target aerodynamic noise, engine harmonics and laser scanning to verify the external shape and thus confirm aircraft type. Multiple-target and TWS will be needed, and AMRAAM will have a high-impulse motor giving rapid acceleration to a Mach number higher than 4, with subsequent maneuver by TVC and/or tail controls combined with body lift, wings not being needed. The original list of five competing groups was narrowed to two in February 1979, and at the end of 1981 Hughes was picked over Raytheon to build 94 test missiles, with options on 924 for inventory plus follow-on production (which, because the US buy alone is expected to exceed 13,000 for the USAF and 7,000 for the Navy/Marines, is expected to be split between two contractors, Raytheon probably becoming second-source). By late 1982 the AMRAAM (always-pronounced as a word) was well into firing trials, with fully guided rounds doing well against increasingly tough targets at Holloman and Pt Mugu. Mid-course guidance is Nortronics inertial, and the small Hughes active terminal radar now uses a TWT (travelling-wave tube) transmitter. In 1980 West Germany and the UK signed a memorandum of understanding assigning AMRAAM to the USA and ASRAAM to the European nations. Since then work has gone ahead on integrating the US missile with the RAF Tornado F.2, replacing Sky Flash, and the Luftwaffe F-4F (the latter possibly being refitted with APG-65 or improved APG-66 radar under the Peace Rhine programme). The Tornado Foxhunter radar may need a small L-band transmitter to provide mid-course updating. Testing of full-scale development rounds is due in 1984.

Below: This AMRAAM, one of the initial 94 for test firing, was launched from a Navy F-14A over the Pacific Missile range. AMRAAM will be matched by specially equipped later versions of F-14, -15, -16 and -18.

Asalm

Origin: No contractor selected, USA.
Type: Advanced strategic air-launched missile.

The US Air Force has for almost a decade recognized the size of the performance gap between existing strategic air-launched missiles and what is becoming possible, and in 1976 issued an RFP for the Advanced Strategic Air-Launched Missile, generally written Asalm, pronounced as a word. All the submissions featured ram-rocket propulsion (integral rocket/ramjet) giving a cruising Mach number in the region of 3.5 to 4.5. This is fast enough for body lift to support the missile and give adequate maneuvrability, so Asalm will probably have no aerodynamic surfaces except cruciform tail controls. Various arrangements of inlet and duct are proposed, a favored inlet being in the chin position with a retractable or blow-off fairing to streamline the missile during the rocket boost phase. In mid-1978 the industrial teams most likely to develop Asalm were Martin Marietta with Marquardt propulsion and McDonnell Douglas with CSD (UTC) propulsion. Rockwell and Raytheon are among probable guidance contractors. With a range of several hundred miles, flown in about 10 minutes, Asalm is to be effective against all forms of surface target including those of the highest

Above: Artist's impression of an Asalm showing the proposed wingless (body lift) configuration possible at about Mach 4.

degree of hardening; it is also to be able to destroy Awacs-type aircraft. In late 1979 CSD ran a simulated mission test of the Asalm combustor and silica/phenolic nozzle. Lack of funding is a problem.

Asat

For many years small offices within the US Department of Defense and USAF have studied Asat (anti-satellite) weapon systems. In 1979 these at last led to a program for operational hardware, with a $78.2 million contract award by the USAF to Vought Corporation for an Asat system to be deployed by about 1985. It will comprise an advanced intercepter no warhead being necessary. It will be launched by an F-15 aircraft (presumably following a pre-directed flight trajectory) and then boosted to orbital height by two rocket stages. The first stage is based on the SRAM, a Boeing Aerospace product, and Boeing will develop this stage, provide integration vehicle with guidance so accurate that it will destroy its targets by collision, services and manage development of the mission control center. The second stage will be Altair III, the Thiokol motor which for many years has been the fourth stage of Vought's Scout vehicle. McDonnell Douglas will modify the F-15 to serve as the launch platform. An $82.3 million contract was voted in 1980 and a further $268 million in 1981 to continue development through flight testing in 1984.

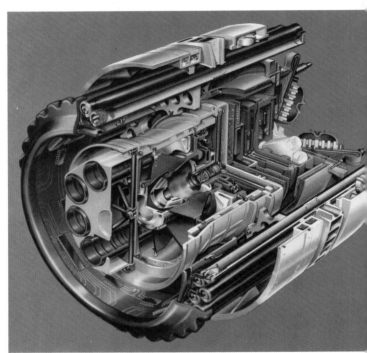

Left: Artist's portrayal of Asat launch from an Air Force F-15. The fighter acts merely as a launch pad, with guidance from ground stations only.

Above: This Vought interceptor has direct side thrust in any direction from 56 motors whose nozzles form a radial ring round the mid-section.

ADSM

Origin: GD Pomona, USA.
Type: Air-defense suppression missile.
Propulsion: Similar to, or derived from, that of Stinger: high-thrust launch motor and main-body sustain motor (see MLMS).
Dimensions: Not defined but rather longer and heavier than Stinger-POST (see MLMS).
Launch weight: About 30lb (13.6kg).
Performance: Not defined.
Warhead: Modified from that of BGT Viper.

ADSM is a further variant of the infantry-fired Stinger SAM, and uses the same helicopter of fixed-wing launch installation as MLMS. The missile itself differs in having an extended nose guidance section with the POST (passive optical seeker technique) modified to use two-color IR plus broadband RF aerials in two projecting probes extending well ahead of the glass seeker cover. The RF target designation system provides radar warning to the pilot of hostile radiating targets and cues the passive missile guidance on to that target. The complete dual-mode seeker had been fully tested by mid-1982, but funding for full development was still being sought. ADSM could be carried in groups of four by all tactical aircraft, a normal load being eight or 16.

Right, upper: The Hughes 500MD advanced Defender with mast-mounted sight is flying with twin boxes of ADSM with two superimposed launch tubes for use in the air-to-air role.

Right: Side elevation of ADSM showing warhead section.

ASMD/RAM

Origin: GD/Pomona, California.
Type: Anti-ship missile defense system.
Dimensions: Length 110in (2.79m); body diameter 5in (127mm).
Launch weight: 154lb (70kg).
Propulsion: Rocketdyne Mk 36 Mod 5 solid motor.
Guidance: Dual passive radar/IR homing with proportional navigation.
Range: 3 miles (5km).
Warhead: Similar to AIM-9L (WDU-17B blast/frag).

The ASMD (anti-ship-missile defense) system was studied throughout the 1970s and appears to have settled down as a close-range system using Sea Sparrow (if fitted) as primary weapon and a mix of RAM (Rolling-Airframe Missile) and the 20mm Phalanx gun system as combined last-ditch defence. RAM has been funded in partnership with Denmark and West Germany, and while it has much in common with Sidewinder it has no canards, rear control

Above: Bits of Chaparral Stinger and Sidewinder are all helping the ASMD/RAM project.

fins being used instead and driven by signals from the dual-mode seeker which depends on the target (a sea-skimming missile) emitting both IR and radio waves. The nose is based on that of Stinger. RAM can be fired from NATO Sea Sparrow launchers, five missiles to each cell, or from a new 24-tube launcher (16-tube model for very small ships). Sea firing trials were due in 1983.

Asroc, RUR-5A

Origin: Honeywell Aerospace and Defense Group, Minneapolis.
Type: Anti-submarine rocket.
Dimensions: Length 181in (4.6m); body diameter 12.8in (32.5cm); span 33.25in (84.5in).
Launch weight: 960lb (435kg).
Propulsion: Naval Propellant Plant solid tandem boost motor, basic missile is torpedo.
Guidance: Ballistic in flight.
Range: 6 miles (10km).
Flight speed: Transonic.
Warhead: Standard Mk 44/46 torpedo.

Operational since 1961, this elementary all-weather ASW weapon used sonar and fire-control computer to slew and elevate the launcher (Mk 46 or Mk 10 Terrier/Standard/Asroc launcher). The Asroc flies a ballistic trajectory to the vicinity of the target. The rocket is jettisoned after burnout, and a parachute decelerates the torpedo for a safe water entry, thereafter homing on the target in the usual way. As an alternative, the payload can be a nuclear depth charge, likewise lowered by parachute. Though obsolescent, Asroc is still operational aboard 27 cruisers, 87 destroyers and 65 frigates of the US Navy, and is being installed aboard each new DD-963 destroyer.

Above: Launch of Asroc from USS *Brooke,* a guided-missile escort. Asroc is an old weapon but has the advantage of compatibility with hundreds of existing magazines and launchers.

Assault Breaker

This broad research programme is the US Army effort to find the optimum munition for countering hostile armoured forces covering large areas at considerable distances, in the range 12 to 19 miles (20 to 30km). Though no decision had been made on hardware selection by 1983, the chief contenders are the SDV (Skeet delivery vehicle) and the T-16 and T-22 bus

vehicles. The latter are rockets respectively based on the Raytheon Patriot SAM and Vought Lance SSM, T-16 normally being air-launched by an F-111 or F-16 with Pave Mover radar, and the T-22 being fired from the ground. The Skeet is dispensed in a cloud and after being braked and set spinning begins ejecting pairs of "smart" submunitions each with an IR target sensor and SFF (self-forging fragment) warhead. Munitions failing to lock-on to a target burst at a preset low altitude.

Bullpup

Origin: Martin Marietta, USA (also Maxson).
Type: Radio command rocket missile family.
Propulsion: Prepackaged storable liquid rocket.
Dimensions: (AGM-12B) length 10ft 6in (3.2m); body diameter 12in (305mm); span 37in (940mm).
Launch weight: (B) 571lb (259kg).
Range: 7 miles (11.3km).
Flight speed: (B) Mach 2.4.
Warhead: Conventional 250lb (113kg) GP bomb.

During the Korean War the US Navy urgently needed a precision ASM capable of being launched by carrier-based aircraft, and RFPs were issued in 1953. Martin Orlando Division's offering was chosen in May 1954, and subsequently was developed as ASM-N-7 Bullpup. It comprised a 250lb (113kg) bomb inside a roll-stabilized airframe with Aerojet-General solid motor, fixed rear wings, four pneumatically actuated nose control fins and twin rear tracking flares. The operator in the launch aircraft acquired the target visually, fired the missile and used a radio command joystick to impart left/right and up/down directions whilst keeping the flares lined up with the target as seen through his gunsight. It became operational in April 1959.

The existence of this primitive weapon at a price near $5,000 resulted in very wide acceptance. In 1960 it was replaced in production by N-7A, with Thiokol prepackaged LR58 acid/amine motor, extended-range control and a new warhead. Re-styled AGM-12B in 1962, it was put into second-source production by W.L. Maxson, since 1963 US prime supplier for missiles, terminating at 22,100 rounds in 1970. Present carrier aircraft include the USN/USMC A-4, A-6, F-4, and P-3, and in Europe the F-4, F-5, F-100, F-104 and P-3.

In 1959 Martin Orlando developed an improved version for the Air Force with radio guidance that freed the operator from the need to align the target with his sight, allowing guidance from an offset position. This was produced as GAM-83A, and used by TAC. At the same time Martin developed two new versions. For the Navy ASM-N-7B (AGM-12C), Bullpup B, was a larger missile with 1,000lb (454kg) warhead, wings greatly extended in chord and Thiokol LR62 liquid motor; 4,600 were delivered. The Air Force

Above: Launch of a Bullpup from one of the right-wing pylons of a P-3 Orion patrol aircraft of the US Navy.

adopted GAM-83B (AGM-12D) using an airframe closer to the original but with an increased-diameter centre section able to house either a conventional or nuclear warhead. The TGAM-83 (ATM-12A/B/D) Bullpup Trainer developed by Martin's Baltimore Division was later replaced by firing surplus AGM-12Bs with inert warheads. The final model was AGM-12E, briefly (840 rounds) built for the Air Force by Martin, with an anti-personnel fragmentation warhead.

There were several derived missiles intended to supplement or replace the established models. Texas Instruments worked on Bulldog with EO (laser) guidance. Martin's AGM-79A Blue Eye competed with Chrysler's AGM-80A Viper, the former having a scene-correlation TV scanning system and Viper a strapdown inertial platform; both had the warhead detonated by radio altimeter before impact.

CASW/SOW

Origin: (vehicle) The Boeing Co. (payload, guidance and acoustics/signal processing) Gould Inc. (motor) Hercules Inc.
Type: Stand-off ASW weapon.
Data: Not disclosed but physical characteristics similar to Subroc.

The Combined Anti-Submarine Warfare Stand-Off Weapon uses a common vehicle propelled by a single-stage solid rocket motor arranged in tandem with a payload which may be either an ALWT (advanced lightweight torpedo),

a Mk 46 torpedo or a nuclear depth bomb developed by the Department of Energy. The missile will be compatible with vertical launch systems of the CG-47, DDG-51 and DD-963 class surface combatants. It will also be supplied in a submarine capsule for SSN-637 and 688 class attack submarines; the capsule will be fired like a torpedo, rise to the surface and release the vehicle for motor ignition. The Mk 46 Mod 5 torpedo will be a payload option for surface ships only. RDT&E costs are estimated at $550m at the start of development in 1980, and development authorizations climb steeply in 1982-85. CASW/SOW is expected to replace Subroc aboard 688-class submarines around 1988.

Chaparral, MIM-72C

Origin: Ford Aeronutronic Division, Newport Beach.
Type: Mobile surface-to-air guided missile system.
Dimensions: Length 114.5in (2.91m); body diameter 5.0in (12.7cm); span 25in (64cm).
Launch weight: 185lb (84kg).
Propulsion: Rocketdyne Mk 36 Mod 5 single-stage solid motor.
Guidance: Initial optical aiming, IR homing to target heat emitter.
Range; About 2.5 miles (4km).
Flight speed: About Mach 2.5.
Warhead: (MIM-72A) 11lb (5kg) HE-frag with pre-formed splinters; (MIM-72C) M-250 (Picatinny Arsenal) blast-frag.

Above: Planned as a temporary stop-gap because of the collapse of Mauler, Chaparral now has to take the place of Roland as well.

When the purpose-designed Mauler missile was abandoned this weapon was substituted as a makeshift stop-gap, the missile being the original Sidewinder 1C modified for ground launch. A fire unit has four missiles on a manually tracked launcher, carried on an M730 (modified M548) tracked vehicle, with a further eight rounds on board ready to be loaded by hand. Owing to the severe delay with the Americanized Roland, Chaparral has continued to fill the gap, and is now widely used by the Army and Marine Corps, usually with an equal number of Vulcan air-defense gun systems. The missile now in production is MIM-72C, which not only carries the better warhead noted above, but also has improved DAW-1 all-aspect guidance and the Harry Diamond Labs M-817 prox fuze. Though totally inadequate, Chaparral is having to remain the USA's forward-area low-altitude SAM system for at least the next decade instead of being replaced

by Roland. Urgent efforts were being made in 1980-82 to improve it with a blindfire radar, smokeless motor and Stinger IFF.

Below: A Chaparral launch at Fort Bliss, Kentucky, on 20 October 1970 by C Btry, 6th Bn, 67 Air Defense Arty, 1st Inf Div. Advantage of this missile system is experience and availability.

Copperhead, M712

Origin: Martin Marietta, Orlando.
Type: CLGP (cannon-launched guided projectile).
Dimensions: Length 54in (1,372mm); diameter 155mm.
Launch weight: 140lb (63.5kg).
Propulsion: Fired from gun.
Guidance: Laser homing.
Range: 1.9-10 miles (3-16km).
Flight speed: Supersonic.
Warhead: HESH (high-explosive squash-head) type, 49.6lb (22.5kg).

The tank is the the the dominant threat facing NATO forces in Europe. NATO has deployed large numbers of ATGWs (including the HOT, Milan, TOW, Dragon and Swingfire) to meet this threat, but ATGWs and tanks alone could not hope to halt a determined thrust by Warsaw Pact forces. Conventional artillery, when being used in the indirect fire role, has a 1-in-2,500 chance of killing a tank. The US Army started a high-risk program to develop a projectile which could be fired from a standard 155mm weapon (for example, the M109A1 self-propelled gun or the M198 towed howitzer) and hit targets over 12km away.

One of the problems was designing the electronics, as these would have to stand up to 7,000g when being fired. Basic research, however, proved that the project was possible and contracts were awarded to Texas Instruments and Martin Marietta. Each company built a small number of projectiles (or Cannon-Launched Guided Projectiles as they are called) which were tested at the White Sands Missile Range. The Martin Marietta CLGP

scored direct hits on both stationary and moving tanks at ranges of 8 to 12km. The projectile hit the target despite deliberate aiming errors of several hundred metres. In September 1975 a CLGP hit a stationary M48 tank 8km away while the target was being illuminated by a laser carried in a Praeire IIA RPV. The RPV located the target with a TV camera, focusing on the target, and signaled the artillery to fire a CLGP. As a result of these trials, Martin Marietta was awarded a contract for full scale development of the CLGP.

The basic idea is that a forward observer sees an enemy tank approaching. He then radios its approximate position to the artillery and one weapon fires a CLGP in the general direction of the target. Once the CLGP is on its way the forward observer illuminates the target with his Ground Laser Locator Designator (or GLLD), the CLGP senses the reflected laser energy and, by applying commands to its control fins, flies into the laser spot on the target. It can be steered into the target provided the nominal gun-aiming point is within about 0.7 mile (1.1km) of it. Copperhead is treated like any other gun ammunition, and trials have shown it is usable with guidance in European weather about 95 per cent of the time. Production was authorized in 1980, and fiscal years 1981 and 1982 respectively awarded $117.6m for 3,125 rounds and $141.1m for 4,550; 1983 was to fund 7,629 at a cost of $183m. The weapon achieved IOC in 1982, by which time a European co-production industrial group was slowly taking shape with companies in the USA (Martin Marietta), Germany, Britain, Italy, the Netherlands and Belgium.

Right: Despite prolonged troubles due to funding and politics, the Copperhead programme is so important that in 1983 it was at last moving ahead. This is a test with inert warhead on an M47 tank.

GBU-15, CWW

Origin: Rockwell International, USA.
Type: Guided bomb system.
Propulsion: None.
Dimensions: Length 154in (3.91m); body diameter 18in (457mm); span 59in (1,499mm).
Launch weight: 2,450lb (1,111kg).
Range: Variable with launch height and speed, but typically 5 miles (8km).
Flight speed: Subsonic.

The CWW (cruciform-wing weapon) is the modern successor to the Vietnam-era Pave Strike Hobos (homing-bomb system), of which GBU-8 (guided bomb unit) was the chief production example. Like GBU-8, GBU-15 is a modular system comprising standard GP (general purpose) bombs to which a target-detecting device and trajectory-control fins are added. The full designation of the basic production missile is GBU-15(V)/B, and it is also called a modular guided glide bomb (MGGB) or modular guided weapon system. Though the payload and structural basis may be the CBU-75 cluster munition, the normal basis is the Mk 84 2,000lb (907kg) bomb. To the front are added an FMU-124 fuze, a tubular adapter and either of two target-detecting devices, TV or IIR (imaging infra-red). At the rear are added an autopilot, displacement gyro, primary battery, control module and data-link module, and the weapon is completed by attaching four canard fins and four large rear wings with powered control surfaces on their trailing edges. (An alternative PWW, planar-wing weapon, by Hughes, is no longer active). GBU-15 is launched at medium to extremely low altitudes. In the former case it is guided over a direct line of sight to the target. In the latter it is launched in the direction of the target, while the carrier aircraft gets away at very low level. It is steered by a data-link by the operator in the aircraft, who has a display showing the scene in the seeker in the nose of the missile (TV is the usual method). The missile climbs until it can acquire the target, and then pushes over into a dive. The operator has the choice of steering the missile all the way to the target or locking-on the homing head. Extensive trials from F-4, F-111 and B-52 aircraft are complete and substantial deliveries had been made by early 1983.

Below: GBU-15 hung on an F-4E Phantom II of the USAF. Note Diseo EO sensor above the pylon.

CSW

Origin: No contractor yet selected, USA.

The proposed Conventional Stand-off Weapon is seen by many in the USAF as one of the best, if not the best, ways to destroy hostile anti-aircraft defenses and armor moving forward behind the FLOT (forward line of own troops, previously called FEBA). CSW is planned to be integrated with the Pave Mover synthetic-aperture SLAR (side-looking airborne radar) as now on evaluation in F-111 aircraft (competing radars are by Grumman/Norden and Hughes), and the PLSS (precision location strike system) is also available as an already deployed alternative carried in the TR-1 aircraft. In late 1982 there was still much argument over how best to engage distant armor, one of the major technical problems being how to give a radar such as Pave Mover the ability to discriminate between tanks and low-value trucks or even mobile decoys. No configuration for CSW has been announced, and the US Army is said to be undecided about offering participation or support. The USAF, however, sees CSW as a smaller and much cheaper back-up to MRASM (Medium-Range ASM), with especial value in defense-suppression, and was hoping to initiate competitive development before 30 June 1983.

Dragon, M47, FGM-77A

Origin: McDonnell Douglas Astronautics (second-source production by Raytheon and Kollsman).
Type: Infantry anti-tank/assault missile.
Dimensions: Length 29.3in (74cm); body diameter 5.0in (12.7cm); fin span 13in (33cm).
Launch weight: 13.5lb (6.12kg).
Propulsion: Recoilless gas-generator thruster in launch tube; sustain propulsion by 60 small side thrusters fired in pairs upon tracker demand.
Guidance: See text.
Range: 200 to 3,300ft (60-1,000m).
Flight speed: About 225mph (360km/h).
Warhead: Linear shaped charge, 5.4lb (2.45kg).

In service since 1971, Dragon comes sealed in a glass-fibre launch tube with a fat rear end containing the launch charge. The operator attaches this to his tracker comprising telescopic sight, IR sensor and electronics box. When the missile is fired its three curved fins flick open and start the missile spinning. The operator holds the sight on the target and the tracker automatically commands the missile to the line of sight by firing appropriate pairs of side thrusters. The launch tube is thrown away and a fresh one attached to the tracker. The Army and Marine Corps use the basic Dragon, while developments involve night sights and laser guidance.

Below: USA troops deploy roughly 250,000 Dragon missiles. According to the book, no harm can come to the operator, but the flame, debris and smoke make a launch look impressive!

Falcon

Origin: Hughes Aircraft, USA.
Type: Air-to-air guided missiles, various guidance.
Propulsion: Solid motor (various suppliers), some with boost/sustain charges.
Dimensions: See separate table of variants.
Launch weight: See separate table of variants.
Performance: See separate table of variants.
Warhead: Various 29.40lb (13.18kg) with proximity fuze (AIM-26A, 1.5kT nuclear).

First guided AAM in the world to enter operational service, Falcon was created with impressive assurance by a new team. In 1947 the newly created USAF asked for bids on a completely new radar-based fire-control system for manned intercepters, and a guided AAM for the following interceptor generation. To the surprise of most bidders both packages were won by Hughes Aircraft, lately diversified into advanced technologies and at that time of daily concern to Howard Hughes himself. By 1955 the family of fire-

Above: AIM-4H was a new missile in 1970 when it was photograph hung under a USAF F-4D Phantom II. Today it is seldom carried.

The Falcon Family

1947	1950	1962	Guidance	Length	Diameter	Span	Launch wt	Speed	Range	Production
XF-98	GAR-1	AIM-4	SARH	77.8in (1.97m)	6.4in (163mm)	20.0in (508mm)	110lb (50kg)	M2.8	5 miles (8 km)	4,080
—	GAR-1D	AIM-4A	SARH	78.0in (1.98m)	6.4in (163mm)	20.0in (508mm)	120lb (54kg)	M3	6 miles (9.7 km)	12,100
—	GAR-2	AIM-4B	IR	79.5in (2.02m)	6.4in (163mm)	20.0in (508mm)	130lb (59kg)	M3	6 miles (9.7 km)	16,000
—	GAR-2A	AIM-4C	IR	79.5in (2.02m)	6.4in (163mm)	20.0in (508mm)	134lb (61kg)	M3	6 miles (9.7 km)	13,500
—	GAR-2B	AIM-4D	IR	79.5in (2.02m)	6.4in (163mm)	20.0in (508mm)	134lb (61kg)	M4	6 miles (9.7 km)	4,000
—	GAR-3	AIM-4E	SARH	86.0in (2.18m)	6.6in (168mm)	24.0in (610mm)	150lb (68kg)	M4	7 miles (11.3 km)	300
—	GAR-3A	AIM-4F	SARH	86.0in (2.18m)	6.6in (168mm)	24.0in (610mm)	150lb (68kg)	M4	7 miles (11.3 km)	3,400
—	GAR-4A	AIM-4G	IR	81.0in (2.06m)	6.6in (168mm)	24.0in (610mm)	145lb (66kg)	M4	7 miles (11.3 km)	2,700
—	XGAR-11	XAIM-26	SARH	84.0in (2.13m)	11.0in (279mm)	24.4in (620mm)	200lb (91kg)	M2	5 miles (8 km)	c100
—	GAR-11	AIM-26A	SARH	84.25in (2.14m)	11.0in (279mm)	24.4in (620mm)	203lb (92kg)	M2	5 miles (8 km)	1,900
—	GAR-11A	AIM-26B	SARH	81.5in (2.07m)	11.4in (290mm)	24.4in (620mm)	262lb (119kg)	M2	6 miles (9.7 km)	2,000
—	GAR-9	AIM-47A	SARH/IRTH	126.0in (3.2m)	13.2in (335mm)	33.0in (838mm)	800lb (363kg)	M6	115 miles (213 km)	c80
—	—	XAIM-4H	ALH	c80in (2.03m)	6.6in (168mm)	24.0in (610mm)	160lb (73kg)	M4	7 miles (11.3 km)	c25

Genie, AIR-2A

Origin: Douglas Aircraft Co, USA.
Type: Unguided air-to-air rocket.
Propulsion: Thiokol solid motor, 36,600lb (16,600kg) thrust.
Dimensions: Length 116in (2,946mm); body diameter (except warhead) 17.5in (445mm); span (fins extended) 40in (1,016mm).
Launch weight: 822lb (373kg).
Range: 5-6.2 miles (8-10km).
Flight speed: Mach 3.3.

Though it is an unguided rocket, which flies a near-ballistic trajectory, this can certainly be classed as an AAM and the most powerful in the world because it has a nuclear warhead. Development was begun by Douglas Aircraft in 1955, as soon as LASL (Los Alamos Scientific Laboratory) could predict complete success with the special 1.5kT warhead. The first live missile was fired from an F-89J at 15,000ft (4,572m) over Yucca Flat, Nevada, on 19 July 1957. The rocket was detonated by ground command, and USAF observers standing unprotected at ground zero (ie directly under the burst) suffered no ill effects. During development this programme was called Ding Dong and subsequently High Card; its original designation was MB-1, changed in 1962 to AIR-2A. A training missile, with a white-cloud spotting charge instead of a warhead, was called Ting-a-Ling and is now ATR-2A. Genie is carried externally by the CF-101B and internally by the F-106, having earlier also armed the F-89J and F-101B. The Hughes MA-1, MG-10 or MG-13 fire-control tracks the target, assigns the missile, commands the pilot to arm the warhead, fires the missile, pulls the interceptor into a tight turn to escape the detonation, and finally triggers the warhead

Above: A few AIR-2A Genie nuclear rockets are still on the strengt of F-106 Delta Dart interceptor squadrons of USAF and ANG.

at the correct moment. Lethal radius is over 1,000ft (several hundre metres). Missile propulsion is by a Thiokol TU-289 (SR49) motor of 36,600 (16,602kg) thrust. Flick-out fin-tips give the missile stability, and correct ro and gravity-drop. Several thousand Genies had been built when productio ceased in 1962; the improved TU-289 motor remained in production t 1982.

Harm, AGM-88A

Origin: Texas Instruments Inc, USA.
Type: High-speed anti-radiation missile.
Propulsion: Thiokol single-grain (280lb, 127kg, filling of non-aluminized HTPB) reduced-smoke boost/sustain motor.
Dimensions: Length 13ft 8½in (4.17m); body diameter 10in. (254mm); span 44in (1,118mm).
Launch weight: 796lb (361kg).
Range: Variable with aircraft to about 11.5 miles (18.5km).
Flight speed: Over Mach 2.
Warhead: Fragmentation with proximity fuze system.

Neither Shrike nor Standard ARM is an ideal air-launched ARM and in 1972 the Naval Weapons Center began R&D and also funded industry studies for a High-speed Anti-Radiation Missile (Harm). Among the objectives were much higher flight speed, to lock-on and hit targets before they could be switched off or take other action, and to combine the low cost and versatility of Shrike, the sensitivity and large launch envelope of Standard ARM, and completely new passive homing using the latest microelectronic digital techniques and interfacing with new aircraft systems. In 1974 TI was selected as system integration contractor, assisted by Hughes, Dalmo-Victor, Itek and SRI (Stanford Research Institute). The slim AGM-88A missile has double-delta moving wings and a small fixed tail. The TI seeker has a simple fixed aerial (antenna) yet gives broadbrand coverage, a low-cost autopilot is fitted,

control systems had included the E-9, fitted to the F-89H, with a new computer and software for guns, FFARs or guided missiles. Subsequently the more advanced MG-10 followed for the supersonic F-102, the MG-13 for the F-101 and the semi-automated MA-1 for the F-106. All were matched to the missile Hughes created at Culver City and put into production at a new plant at Tucson in 1954. Called Project Dragonfly, and at first classed as an experimental fighter (XF-98, see table), it matured as GAR-1 Falcon, but was later re-styled AIM-4, and for clarity the 1962 designations will be used throughout.

AIM-4 was an amazing exercise in packaging. The airframe, about the size of a man, contained a large proportion of GRP construction. Accelerated at about 50g by a single-charge Thiokol solid motor, it had a hemispherical nose radome flanked by receiver aerials like small nose fins, giving SARH proportional navigation and steering by elevons on the trailing edges of the slender-delta wings. Most early installations were internal, three being housed in the tip pod on each wing of the F-89H and J and six fitting the weapon bay of the F-102A. Both reached IOC with Air Defense Command in mid-1956. Later that year the first IR Falcon, AIM-4B, entered service with a distinctive glass nose, followed by AIM-4A (radar) with improved manoeuvrability from larger controls carried well behind the wings. AIM-4C had a better IR seeker able to lock-on against a wider range of ambient (background) temperatures. The IR missiles were especially popular in permitting the interceptor to break away as soon as the missile(s) had been launched (though, as in the Soviet Union,it was common doctrine to fire one missile with each type of guidance to ensure a kill). The early Falcons accounted for three-quarters of the total production.

In 1958 deliveries began of AIM-4E, the first so-called Super Falcon, to meet the greater demands of the F-106A. It introduced a longer-burning motor, advanced SARH guidance with a new receiver behind a pointed radome of new material, long wing-root fillets and a more powerful warhead. In May 1959 the Tucson plant switched to the -4F with a new motor having boost/sustainer charges, improved SARH guidance with greater accuracy and airframe modifications including a white moistureproof sleeve over the forebody and a 4in (102mm) metal probe on the nose to form a weak oblique shock and improve aerodynamics. A few weeks later came AIM-4G with the -4F airframe and a new IR seeker able to lock-on to smaller targets at considerably greater ranges.

In 1960 came a dramatic development. AIM-26 was developed to give high SSKP in head-on attacks. IR was judged inadequate in such engagements, and because of the reduced precision of SARH it was decided to use a much more powerful warhead. AIM-26A was fitted with almost the same nuclear warhead as Genie, triggered by four active-radar proximity-fuze aerials almost flush with the body ahead of the wings. The body naturally had to be of greater diameter, and a larger motor was necessary to achieve the required flight performance. AIM-26B followed, with large conventional warhead, and this was exported as HM-55 and licence-built by Saab-Scania as RB 27. Today about 800 of the -26B model are the only Falcons left in USAF Aerospace Defense Command service.

In 1958 Hughes began work on a challenging fourth-generation fire-control and AAM system to arm the Mach 3.2 "Zip-fuel" North American F-108 Rapier intercepter. The ASG-18 radar was used for mid-course guidance and target illumination over ranges exceeding 100 miles (161km), and the missile, then called GAR-9, was also given IR terminal homing. Propulsion was by a Lockheed Propulsion Co storable liquid rocket giving hypersonic speed, so that the wings became mere strakes along the body. In 1959 this very large AAM, still called Falcon, was transfered to the proposed YF-12A "Blackbird" research interceptor with which it conducted much basic fact-finding in advanced interception techniques.

The final production Falcon was the AIM-4D of 1963. The only Falcon tailored for anti-fighter combat, it was a crossbreed combining the small airframe of early models with the powerful motor and advanced IR seeker head of the large -4G. The result is a very fast and effective short-range missile. More than 8,000 -4A and -4C have been remanufactured to this standard. In 1969 the AIM-4H was funded to improve the -4D by fitting an AOPF (Active Optical Proximity Fuze) with four laser pancake beams at 90° to the major axis. It was abandoned for budgetary reasons in 1971.

Harpoon, AGM/RGM-84A

Origin: McDonnell Douglas Astronautics, Huntington Beach.
Type: All-weather anti-ship missile (AGM, air-launched; RGM ship- or submarine-launched).
Dimensions: Length (AGM) 12ft 7in (3.84m), (RGM) 15ft 2in (4.58m); body diameter 13.5in (34.1cm); span 36.0in (91.4cm).
Launch weight: (AGM) 1,160lb (526kg), (RGM) 1,460lb to 1,530lb (662 to 694kg).
Propulsion: Teledyne CAE J402-CA-400 single-shaft turbojet rated at 660lb (300kg) static thrust; (RGM) in addition, Aerojet MX(TBD)B446-2 tandem solid boost motor for launch and acceleration to Mach 0.75.
Guidance: Pre-launch, parent platform target data and IBM computer; mid-course, Lear Siegler strapdown platform and radar altimeter; terminal, all active radar seeker.
Range: Up to 70 miles (113km).
Flight speed: About Mach 0.85, 645mph.
Warhead: Naval Weapons Center 500lb (227kg) blast type.

This important anti-ship missile became operational in 1977-78 after extended development. The simplest form is AGM-84A, launched by such aircraft as the A-6E Intruder, A-7E Corsair II, P-3 Orion and S-3 Viking. RGM-84A can be fired from surface-vessel Tartar/Terrier/Standard or Asroc launchers, or from a four-round lightweight canister for high-speed craft or a buoyant capsule fired from a submarine torpedo tube. After launch the missile turns toward its target, zooming down to sea-skimming cruise height, finally locking-on with terminal radar and climbing in the last seconds to dive on to the target. By 1983 some 2,000 rounds had been delivered

Above: An F/A-18A Hornet can carry four Harpoons as well as two Sidewinders and two Sparrows or AMRAAMs.

to the US Navy, with production continuing for a wide range of attack submarines and surface combatants including PHM hydrofoils.

and Motorola supplies an optical target detector forming part of the fuzing for the large advanced-design warhead. Carrier aircraft include the Navy/Marines A-6E, A-7E and F/A18, and the Air Force APR-38 Wild Weasel F-4G and EF-111A, with Itek's ALR-45 radar warning receiver and Dalmo-Victor's DSA-20N signal analyzer both interfaced. Proposed carriers include the B-52, F-16 and Tornado. Harm can be used in three modes. The basic use is Self-protect, the ALR-45 detecting threats, the launch computer sorting the data to give priorities and pass to the missile a complete set of digital instructions in milliseconds, whereupon the missile can be fired. In the Target of Opportunity mode the very sensitive seeker locks-on to "certain parameters of operation and also transmissions associated with other parts of a radar installation" which could not be detected by Shrike or Standard ARM. In the Pre-briefed mode Harm is fired blind in the direction of known emitters; if the latter are silent the missile self-destructs, but if one of them radiates, Harm at once homes on to it. Test flights began in 1976; redesign followed and following prolonged further tests delivery to user units began in early 1983.

Left: This General Dynamics proposal for a Wild Weasel version of the F-16 Fighting Falcon has flown with various weapons including (reading inwards from the wingtip) AIM-9J Sidewinder self-defence AAMs, AGM-45 Shrikes and AGM-88 Harm missiles. A Westinghouse ALQ-131 ECM pod forms the usual avionic load on the centreline pylon, leaving room for two drop tanks. Britain's Alarm weighs only half as much as Harm, using later technology.

Hawk, MIM-23B

Origin: Raytheon Company, Missile Systems Division.
Type: Transportable surface-to-air missile system.
Dimensions: Length 16ft 6in (5.03m); body diameter 14in (360mm); span 48.85in (1,190mm).
Launch weight: 1,383lb (627.3kg).
Propulsion: Aerojet M112 boost/sustain solid rocket motor.
Guidance: CW radar SARH.
Range: 25 miles (40km).
Flight speed: Mach 2.5.
Warhead: HE blast/frag, 120lb (54kg).

Above: Very large numbers of Improved Hawk missiles are still in global use; this was a 1975 firing at White Sands range.

Hawk (Homing All-the-Way Killer) was the world's first missile with CW guidance. When developed in the 1950s it looked a good system, but by modern standards it is cumbersome, each battery having a pulse acquisition radar, a CW illuminating radar, a range-only radar, two illuminator radars, battery control center, six three-missile launchers and a tracked loader, the whole weighing many tons. An SP version has ground-support items on wheels and towed by tracked launchers or loaders. Hawk became operational in August 1960 and is deployed widely throughout the Army and Marine Corps and 17 other nations. Improved Hawk (MIM-23B) has a better guidance system, larger warhead, improved motor and semi-automatic ground systems ("certified rounds" are loaded on launchers without the need for further attention). Further development is attempting to improve CW radar reliablity and improve pulse-acquisition speed by allowing automated threat-ordering of all targets that could be of importance. Since the early 1970s Hawk has been planned to be replaced by Patriot.

Hellfire

Origin: Rockwell International, USA.
Type: Laser-guided "fire and forget" missile.
Propulsion: Thiokol TX657 reduced-smoke "all-boost" motor.
Dimensions: Length 64in (1,626mm), body diameter 7in (178mm).
Launch weight: 98.86lb (44.84kg).
Range: Up to "several kilometers", "far in excess of present anti-armor systems".
Flight speed: Transonic, quickly builds to Mach 1.17.
Warhead: Firestone 20lb (9kg) 7in-diameter hollow charge.

A direct descendent of Rockwell's Hornet, this missile has applications against hard point targets of all kinds, though it is officially described as "the USA's next-generation anti-armor weapon system". Numerous development firings took place from 1971 before full engineering go-ahead was received in October 1976. It has semi-active laser homing with a very advanced seeker from Martin Marietta. The seeker has a Cassegrain telescope under the hemispherical glass nose sending signals to the electronics section with microprocessor logic. Steering is by four canard controls, and Hellfire can pull 13g at Mach 1.17. The US Under-Secretary of Defense, The Hon. William J. Perry, said "This missile most often goes right through the center of the bull's eye". The primary carrier is the AH-64A Apache helicopter (16 rounds) but Hellfire has flown on the Cobra and the A-10A Thunderbolt II fixed-wing platform. Numerous Hellfires have been launched without prior lock-on, some of them in rapid-fire homing on different multiple targets using ground designators with individual coding. The missile notices the laser radiation in flight, locks-on and homes at once. IOC will now be 1984, by which time this missile will probably also be developed with "launch-and-leave" IIR guidance. The first 680 rounds are being delivered before September 1984.

Above: Four quads of Hellfires form the primary armament of the AH-64A Apache armed helicopter. In fact it would also make a fine AAM, because its relatively slow speed enables it to turn much tighter than any manned aircraft, unlike today's AAMs.

Lance, MGM-52C

Origin: Vought Corporation, Michigan Division.
Type: Mobile tactical guided missile.
Dimensions: Length 20ft 3in (6.17m); body diameter 22in (56cm).
Launch weight: 2,833 to 3,367lb (1,285-1,527kg) depending on warhead.
Propulsion: Rocketdyne P8E-9 storable-liquid two-part motor with infinitely throttleable sustainer portion.
Guidance: Simplified inertial.
Range: 45 to 75 miles (70-120km) depending on warhead.
Flight speed: Mach 3.
Warhead: M234 nuclear 468lb (212kg, 10kT), W-70-4 ER/RB (neutron) or Honeywell M251 1,000lb (454kg) HE cluster.

In service since 1972, this neat rocket replaced the earlier Honest John rocket and Sergeant ballistic missile, with very great gains in reduced system weight, cost and bulk and increases in accuracy and mobility. Usual vehicle is the M752 (M113 family) amphibious tracked launcher, with the M688 carrying two extra missiles and a loading hoist. For air-dropped operations a lightweight towed launcher can be used. In-flight guidance accuracy, with the precisely controlled sustainer and spin-stabilization, is already highly satisfactory, but a future Lance 2 could have DME (Distance Measuring Equipment) command guidance. The US Army has eight battalions, six of which are normally deployed in Europe. Production was completed in 1980, but the T-22 derived vehicle is an important part of the Assault Breaker programme.

Right: Lance is the only Western missile (apart from the French Pluton) to counter many thousands of Soviet battlefield weapons in the same class. One is shown here being launched from the M752 SP erector/launcher. The black smoke comes from the spin motors.

Maverick, AGM-65

Origin: Hughes Aircraft, USA.
Type: Rocket missile with various forms of guidance.
Propulsion: Thiokol boost/sustain solid motor, from 1972 TX-481 and from 1981 TX-633 with reduced smoke.
Dimensions: Length 98in (2,490mm); body diameter 12in (305mm); span 28.3in (720mm).
Launch weight: (AGM-65A, shaped-charge) 463lb (210kg), (65A, blast/frag) 635lb (288kg).
Range: 0.6 to 10 miles (1 to 16km) at sea level, up to 25 miles (40km) after Mach 1.2 release at altitude.
Flight speed: Classified, but supersonic.
Warhead: Choice of Chamberlain shaped charge (83lb, 37.6kg, charge) or Avco steel-case penetrator blast/frag.

Smallest of the fully guided or self-homing ASMs for US use. AGM-65 Maverick was approved in 1965 and, following competition with Rockwell, Hughes won the programme in June 1968. An initial 17,000-missile package was fulfilled in 1975, and production has continued at reduced rate on later versions. The basic missile, usually carried in triple clusters under the wings of the F-4, F-15, F-16, A-7, A-10 and Swedish AJ37A Viggen, and singly by the F-5 and the BGM-34 RPV, has four delta wings of very low aspect ratio, four tail controls immediately behind the wings, and a dual-thrust solid motor.

In mid-1978 Hughes completed production of 26,000 AGM-65A Mavericks and for three years had no production line. The pilot selects a missile, causing its gyro to run up to speed and light a cockpit indicator. He then visually acquires the target, depresses his uncage switch to remote the protective cover from the missile nose, and activates the video circuitry. The TV picture at once appears on a bright display in the cockpit' and the pilot then either slews the video seeker in the missile or else lines up the target in his own gunsight. He depresses the track switch, waits until the cross-hairs on the TV display are aligned on the target, releases the switch and fires the round. Homing is automatic, and the launch aircraft at once escapes from the area. Unguided flights began in September 1969. AGM-65A has been launched at all heights down to treetop level. In the 1973 Yom Kippur war it was used operationally, in favorable conditions. It requires good visibility, and the occasional $48,000 A-model breaks its TV lock and misses its target—for example, because of overwater glint.

AGM-65B, Scene-Magnification Maverick, has new optics, a stronger gimbal mount and revised electronics. The pilot need not see the target, but instead can search with the seeker and cockpit display which presents an enlarged and clearer picture. Thus he can identify the target, lock-on and fire much quicker and from a greater slant range. AGM-65B was in production (at up to 200 per month) from May 1980 to May 1983. AGM-65C Laser Maverick was for close-air support against laser-designated targets, the lasers being the infantry ILS-NT200 or the airborne Pave Knife, Pave Penny, Pave Spike, Pave Tack or non-US systems. Flight testing began in January 1977, using the Rockwell tri-Service seeker. Troop training has established the method of frequency and pulse coding to tie each missile to only one air or ground designator, so that many Mavericks can simultaneously be homed on many different sources of laser radiation. AGM-65C was replaced by AGM-65E with "tri-Service" laser tracker and digital processing which sen-n 1982 was entering production for the US Marine Corps with heavy blast/frag warhead. Westinghouse tested Pave Spike with the Minneapolis-Honeywell helmet sight for single-seat aircraft.

Above: One of the first AGM-65B (Scene-Magnification) Maverick missiles to reach the USAF, photographed at White Sands Missile Range in 1976. Substantial numbers of this model are now in use.

In May 1977 engineering development began on AGM-65D IR-Maverick, with Hughes IIR tri-Service seeker. Consequently more expensive than other versions, the IIR seeker—especially when slaved to an aircraft-mounted sor such as FLIR, a laser pod or the APR-38 radar warning system—enables the Maverick to lock-on at at least twice the range otherwise possible in north-west Europe in mist, rain or at night. Of course, it also distinguishes between "live targets" and "hulks". Using the centroid seeker in place of the original edgelock optics, AGM-65D was tested from an F-4 in Germany in poor weather in January-March 1978. While Hughes continues to produce the common centre and aft missile sections, delay with the laser-seeker E-version means that AGM-65D got into pilot production first.

All AGM-65A Mavericks have the same 130lb (59kg) conical shaped-charge warhead, but different warheads are in prospect. The Mk 19 250lb (113kg) blast/fragmentation head is preferred by the Navy and Marines, giving capability against small ships as well as hard land targets, and may be fitted to CD versions with new fuzing/arming and a 4in (102mm) increase in length. Another warhead weighs 300lb (136kg), while in December 1976 the Air Force expressed a need for a nuclear warhead.

Hughes' Tucson, Arizona, plant is likely to be hard-pressed to handle TOW, Phoenix and residual Roland work on top of enormously expanded Maverick production. By far the largest numbers are expected to be of the IIR Maverick, AGM-65D, of which well over 30,000 rounds are predicted at a rate of 500 per month. Prolonged tests have confirmed the longrange, which at last matches the flight limitations of the missile itself, and AGM-65D is the standard missile for use with the Lantirn night and bad-weather sensor system now being fitted to F-16s and A-10s. The Navy is expected to procure AGM-65F, which is almost the same missile but fitted with the heavy penetrator warhead of AGM-65E, and with modified guidance software exactly matched to give optimum hits on surface warships. With this missile family Hughes has achieved a unique capability with various guidance systems and warheads, resulting in impressively large production and interchangeability.

Minuteman, LGM-30

Origin: Boeing Aerospace Company, Seattle (missiles were assembled at a plant near Ogden, Utah).
Type: ICBM deployed in hardened silo.
Dimensions: Overall length 59ft 10in (18.2m); body diameter (first stage) 72in (183cm).
Launch weight: Minuteman II, 70,116lb (31,800kg); Minuteman III, 76,015lb (34,475kg).
Propulsion: First stage, Thiokol TU-120 (M55E) solid rocket, 200,000lb (91,000kg) thrust for 60 sec; second stage, Aerojet SR19 solid rocket, with liquid-injection thrust-vector control, 60,000lb (27,200kg) thrust; third stage (II) Hercules solid rocket, 35,000lb (16,000kg) thrust, (III) Aerojet/Thiokol solid rocket, 34,876lb (16,000kg) thrust, plus post-boost control system (see text).
Guidance: Rockwell Autonetics inertial.
Range: (II) over 7,000 miles (11,250km); (III) over 8,000 miles (12,875km).
Flight speed: At burnout, over 15,000mph (24,000km/h).
Warhead: (II) Avco Mk 11C with single thermonuclear device (about 2MT) with Tracor Mk 1A penaids; (III) three (sometimes two) General Electric Mk 12 MIRVs (see text).

Minuteman was designed in 1958-60 as a smaller and simpler second-generation ICBM using solid propellant. Originally envisaged as a mobile weapon launched from trains, it was actually deployed (probably mis-takenly) in fixed hardened silos. Minuteman I (LGM-30B) became operational in 1963 but is no longer in use. Minuteman II (LGM-30F) became ▶

Right: Minuteman is the only Western missile (apart from France's SSBS) to counter thousands of Soviet strategic missiles which are mostly much larger. Photograph shows a Minuteman III launch.

► operational from December 1966 and today 450 are still in use, though replacement because of expired component-lifetimes cannot be long delayed. By 1978 all the re-entry vehicles were of the Mk 11C type hardened against EMP; consideration has been given to prolonging missile life, and improving accuracy, by retrofitting the NS-20 guidance used on Minuteman III (LGM-30G). The latter, operational since 1970, has a new third stage and completely new re-entry vehicles forming a fourth stage with its own propulsion, guidance package and pitch-roll motors; as well as several warheads, individually targetable, it houses chaff, decoys and possibly other penaids. Production of LGM-30G Minuteman III ended in late 1977, but the force is continually being updated, with improved silos, better guidance software, and the Command Data Buffer System which, with other add-ons, reduces re-targeting time per missile from around 24 hours to about half an hour, and allows it to be done remotely from the Wing's Launch Control Centre or from an ALCS (Airborne Launch Control System) aircraft or an NEACP (National Emergency Airborne Command Post). The latter comprise the E-4B (Boeing 747-200 derived), while the ALCS authority is vested in nine EC-135C aircraft which can monitor 200 Minuteman missiles and via improved satellite communications links retarget and launch any of these missiles even if their ground LCC (Launch Control Center) is destroyed. Missile updating is having to be planned to dates beyond those originally considered because of the continuing absence of any later ICBM. Installation of the Mk 12A RV began in 1979 and though most Minuteman III missiles still had the Mk 12 in early 1983 (usual payload three MIRV W-62 of 200 kT each), some 180 of a planned eventual 300 had received the Mk 12A. This has various advantages and carries the 330-kT W-78 warhead, but it is about 16kg heavier and this slightly reduces range and MIRV footprint. Another major change due to have been completed by June 1983 was conversion of 50 silos from M-II to M-III, making the future force 600 Mk III and 400 Mk II.

Right: Stylized representation of a Minuteman launch silo, within which the missile is supported on shockproof mountings. Not much shows above the ground, other than launch control center environmental stack, and silo surveillance system and concrete lid.

MLMS (Air-Launched Stinger)

Origin: General Dynamics Pomona Division, USA.
Type: Multi-purpose missile system.
Propulsion: Tandem Atlantic Research solid motors, high-thrust launch motor and longer-burn flight motor.
Dimensions: Length 60in (1,524mm); body diameter 2.75in (69.85mm); span (fins extended) 3.6in (91.4mm).
Launch weight: 22.3lb (10.1kg); with launcher 34.5lb (15.6kg); complete twin launch installation with electronics and cooling system 99lb (45kg).
Range: Up to 3 miles (4.8km).
Flight speed: Supersonic.
Warhead: Picatinny Arsenal fragmentation, 6.6lb (3kg).

From the well-known Stinger infantry SAM, GD Pomona is developing a range of other weapons, including the MLMS (multipurpose lightweight missile system) and also ADSM. MLMS uses either the standard Stinger, as now widely used by US troops, or the much more effective Stinger-POST (passive optical seeker technique) which replaces the simple IR homing by an advanced two-color (IR and UV) guidance using the latest IRCCM logic circuits and with a unique rosette scan which greatly enhances target detection. MLMS is intended for all battlefield helicopters, and since early 1982 studies have also included the A-10A and Alpha Jet fixed-wing aircraft. A fire-and-forget weapon, Stinger is issued as a certified round in its sealed launch tube and requires no attention between delivery and launch. The basic launcher houses the seeker coolant reservoir and modular electronics and can be stacked three or four deep, giving a total of 16 rounds. For high-speed aircraft a faired launcher is available, enclosing the twin missile tubes. The pilot has a reticle sight or HUD, control panel and a select/uncage/fire control on his cyclic stick, launch being made when the acquisition tone is heard in his headset. Originally a company initiative, MLMS received DoD funding from 1981; nevertheless, despite the clear need for MLMS, and interest from many quarters, the US Army had failed to approve the ROC (required operational capability) by October 1982.

Below: Closely resembling ADSM except for using the standard Stinger-POST missile, MLMS may fly with 13 types of tac aircraft.

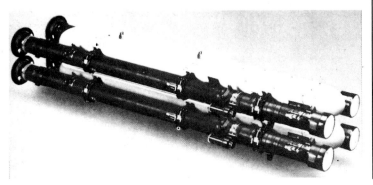

MLRS

Origin: (prime contractor) Vought Corporation, Dallas.
Type: Unguided battlefield-mobile free rocket system.
Dimensions: (rocket) length 13.1ft (4m); diameter 8.94in (227mm).
Launch weight: Not stated.
Propulsion: Atlantic Research solid rocket motor.
Range: Over 18.6 miles (30km).
Flight speed: Just supersonic.
Warhead: Dispenses payload of submunitions, initially about 660 standard M42 bomblets.

Known from 1972 until 1979 as the GSRS (General Support Rocket System), the MLRS (Multiple Launch Rocket System) is planned to be a standard NATO weapon. It has the same battlefield mobility as armored formations, being carried on a tracked vehicle weighing 50,000lb (22.7 tonnes) which can travel at 40mph (64km/h) but is not amphibious. It carries a trainable and elevating launcher which can be rapidly loaded with two six-round containers without the crew of three leaving their cab. Each box houses six preloaded tubes with a 10-year shelf life. The crew can ripple-fire from two to 12 rounds in less than one minute, the fire control re-aiming after each shot. The rocket is highly accurate and is intended to carry any of three types of submunition: M42 shaped-charge grenade-size, scatterable anti-armor mines, or guided sub-missiles. Each launcher load of 12 missiles is said to "place almost 8,000 submunitions in an area the size of six (US) football fields". The first production system was delivered to the Army in early 1982, by which time $317m had been voted for the first 112 vehicles and 6,210 rockets. Production is intended to rise to 5,000 rounds per month.

Below: MLRS could at last give NATO armies some real muscle!

MX (Missile-X)

Origin: Martin Marietta Denver Aerospace.
Type: ICBM for unspecified form of basing.
Dimensions: Length 70ft 10in (21.6m); diameter 92in (2.34m).
Launch weight: 195,000lb (8,845kg).
Propulsion: Intended to be cold-launched by gas pressure from canister, subsequently flying on four successive stages of advanced rocket propulsion. Stages 1, 2 and 3 use HTPB propellant, upper stages having extendible-skirt exit cones; stage 4 has hypergolic liquid propellants feeding a vectoring main chamber and eight small attitude-control engines.
Guidance: High-precision inertial.
Range: 6,900 miles (11,100km).
Flight speed: Typically about 15,000mph (24,000km/h).
Warhead: Intended to be ten Mk 12A MIRVs each of 330kT yeild.

Like the B-1 bomber this weapon system has consumed money at a prodigious rate for many years without making the slightest contribution to Western defence or deterrence. Though the need has been self-evident for many years, and there are no problems in producing the missile, arguments had raged for seven years by 1983 on how to base it. In 1974 a packaged Minuteman was pulled by parachute from a C-5A, and prolonged research has established the feasibility of an air basing concept. This remains one of the basing options, ideally using a purpose-designed CPA (continuous patrol aircraft) tailored to maximum flight endurance and lifting capability to heights around 20,000ft (6km) with no interest in speed or distance covered. Early in MX development (pre-1978) all interest centred on mobile deployment using road (curiously, not railroad) cars or various forms of transporter/launcher driven around underground rail networks, in most variations with the missile erected so that it would break through the surface in virgin terrain. The Carter administration favored the MPS (multiple protective shelter) scheme, but the Reagan administration found this faulty and announced in December 1981: ". . . initial deployment will be in existing Minuteman silos. At least 40 MXs will be deployed, with the first unit of ten missiles operational in late 1986. The specific location . . . will be determined in spring 1982 . . . In addition, the Air Force has initiated R&D to find the best long-term option . . . by July 1983 a decision will be made . . . The options include the following: ballistic-missile defense of silo-based or deceptively based missiles; DBS, deep-basing system, in underground citadels; and air-mobile basing . . . Congress approved $1,900m for Fiscal 1982 and some $2,500m has been spent to date. The cost to produce 226 missiles and deploy 40 in Minuteman silos is estimated at $1,800-1,900m in 1982 dollars." Next, the Senate Armed Services Committee rejected Minuteman-silo-basing and asked for a permanent basing plan by 1 December 1982. This resulted in other suggestions, notably DUB (deep underground basing) about 1km down in rock, with a self-contained tunnelling machine for each launch capsule and crew, and CSB (closely spaced basing). The latter, called "dense pack", relies on the so-called fratricide effect in that debris from each nuclear warhead is supposed to disable those following behind (it apparently being assumed that hostile warheads would be spaced only a second or two apart). President Reagan approved CSB in May 1982, for 100 missiles spaced at 500m intervals over a region about 6km across, but the validity of CSB was later doubted

Above: The first completely assembled MX is shown here in its vertical rig for strength testing at Martin Marietta at Denver.

by several authorities. Thus, though the first cold-launch pop-up test took place in January 1982, and the first MX flight test in January 1983, any actual MX force appears as far away as ever.

Patriot, MIM-104

Origin: Raytheon Missile Systems Division and Martin Orlando Division.
Type: Advanced mobile battlefield SAM system.
Dimensions: Length 209in (5.31m); body diameter 16in (40.6cm); span 36in (92cm).
Launch weight: Not disclosed, but about 1,500lb (680kg).
Propulsion: Thiokol TX-486 single-thrust solid motor.
Guidance: Phased-array radar command and semi-active homing.
Range: About 30 miles (48km).
Flight speed: About Mach 3.
Warhead: Choice of nuclear or conventional blast/frag.

Originally known as SAM-D, this planned successor to Nike-Hercules and Hawk has had an extremely lengthy gestation. Key element in the Patriot system is a phased-array radar which performs all the functions of surveillance, acquisition, track/engage and missile guidance. The launcher carries four missiles each in its shipping container, from which it blasts upon launch. Launchers, spare missile boxes, radars, computers, power supplies and other items can be towed or self-propelled. Patriot is claimed to be effective against all aircraft or attack missiles even in the presence of utter or intense jamming or other ECM. Fundamental reasons for the serious delay and cost-escalation have been the complexity of the system, the 1974 slowdown to demonstrate TVM (track via missile) radar guidance, and inflation. Unquestionably the system is impressive, but often its complication and cost impresses in the wrong way (for example each battery needs two 150kW turbo-generators and each launcher has a 15kW diesel generator), and the number of systems to be procured has been repeatedly revised downwards. The authorized development programme was officially completed in 1980, when very-low-rate production was authorized, but much remains to be done and instead of Patriot being AADS-70 (Army Air Defense System for 1970) it will be "AADS-84". In 1983 production was cautiously being stepped up after total expenditure exceeding $2.6 billion. The USA had hoped to buy 103 fire units and 6,200 missiles for a further $6 billion.

Above: One of the many test firings of Patriot, in this case from the production type quadruple box launcher.

Paveway LGBs

Origin: Texas Instruments, USA.
Type: Laser-guided conventional bombs.
Propulsion: None.
Dimensions: As for original bombs plus from 6 to 20in (152-500mm) length and with folding tailfins.
Launch weight: As for original bombs plus about 30lb (13.6kg).
Range: Typically within 3 miles (5km), depending on launch height.
Flight speed: Free-fall.
Warhead: As in original bombs.

This code-name identifies the most diverse programme in history aimed at increasing the accuracy of tactical air-to-surface weapons.This USAF effort linked more than 30 separately named systems for airborne navigation, target identification and marking, all-weather/night vision, weapon guidance and many other functions, originally for the war is SE Asia. In the course of this work the "smart bombs" with laser guidance managed by the Armament Development and Test Center at Eglin AFB, from 1965, were developed in partnership with TI, using the latter's laser guidance kit, to form an integrated family of simple precision weapons. The first TI-guided LGB was dropped in April 1965.

By 1971 the Paveway I family of guidance units had expanded to eight, in six main types of which the three most important were the KMU-388 (based on the 500lb, 227kg, Mk82 bomb), KMU-421 (1,000lb 454kg, Mk83) and KMU-351 (2,000lb, 907kg, Mk84).

All these bombs are extremely simple to carry, requiring no aircraft modification or electrical connection; they are treated as a round of ordnance and loaded like a free-fall bomb. Carrier aircraft have included the A-1, A-4, A-6, A-7, A-10, A-37, F-4, F-5, F15, F-16, F/A-18, F-100, F-105, F-111, AV-8A, B-52 and B-57. Targets can be marked by an airborne laser, in the launch aircraft or another aircraft, or by forward troops. Like almost all Western military lasers the matched wavelength is 1.064 microns, the usual lasers (in Pave Knife, Pave Tack or various other airborne pods) being of the Nd/YAG type. More recently target illumination has been provided by the Atlis II, LTDS, TRAM, GLLD, MULE, LTM, Lantirn and TI's own FLIR/laser designator.

In all cases the guidance unit is the same, the difference being confined to attachments and the various enlarged tailfins. The silicon detector array is divided into four quadrants and is mounted on the nose of a free universal-jointed housing with an annular ring tail. As the bomb falls this aligns itself with the airstream, in other words the direction of the bomb's motion. The guidance computer receives signals from the quadrants and drives four control fins to equalize the four outputs. Thus, the sensor unit is kept pointing at the source of laser light, so that the bomb will impact at the same point. Electric power is provided by a thermal battery, energised at the moment of release, and power to drive the fins comes from a hot-gas generator.

Above: Release of Paveway II GBU-16B/B (1,000lb Mk 83) by F-15.

Below: From top, Paveway II GBU-10E/B (Mk 84, 2,000lb); British Mk 13/18; GBU-16B/B (Mk 83); and GBU-12D/B (500lb Mk 82).

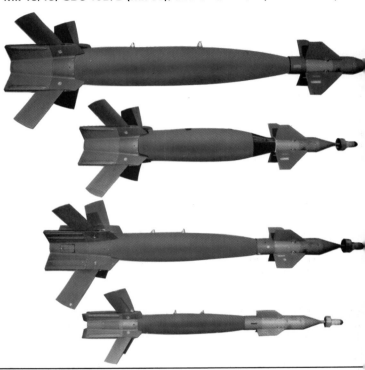

Pershing, MGM-31

Origin: Martin Orlando Division.
Type: Mobile tactical ballistic missile system.
Dimensions: Length 34ft 6in (10.51m); body diameter 40in (1.01m); fin span about 80in (2.02m).
Launch weight: About 10,150lb (4,600kg).
Propulsion: Two Thiokol solid motors in tandem, first stage XM105, second stage XM106.
Guidance: Army-developed inertial made by Eclipse-Pioneer (Bendix).
Range: 100 to 520 miles (160-840km).
Flight speed: Mach 8 at burnout.
Warhead: Nuclear, usually W-50 of approximately 400kT.

Originally deployed in 1962 on XM474 tracked vehicles as Pershing 1, the standard US Army long-range missile system has now been modified to 1a standard, carried on four vehicles based on the M656 five-ton truck. All are transportable in a C-130. In 1976 the four battalions with the US 7th Army in Europe were updated with the ARS (Azimuth Reference System) allowing them quickly to use unsurveyed launch sites, and the SLA (Sequential Launch Adapter) allowing one launch control center easily to fire three missiles. Pershing II is a proposed further improvement, using the same missiles. To replenish the inventory additional Pershing 1a missiles were manufactured in 1978-80. Since then the development effort has been entirely on Pershing II, which has been studied since 1969 and in full development since 1974. It mates the existing vehicle with Goodyear Radag (Radar area-correlation guidance) in the new nose of the missile. As the forebody plunges down towards its target the small active radar scans the ground at 120rpm and correlates the returns with stored target imagery. The terminal guidance corrects the trajectory by means of new delta control surfaces, giving c.e.p. expected to be within 120ft (36m). As a result a lighter and less-destructive warhead (reported to be based on the B61 bomb of some 15kT) can be used, which extends maximum range. Some problems were met in 1982 development firings but deployment with the USA in Europe was expected from late 1983. It is planned to replace Pershing 1a on a one-for-one basis, perhaps by refurbishing the original motor sections. Procurement in fiscal years 1982 and 1983 were respectively 21 missiles costing $193.7m and 91 at $498.3m.

Right: The white radar nose and external control fins identify this as a Pershing II, planned for Europe from 1983.

Phoenix

Origin: Hughes Aircraft, USA.
Type: Long range air-to-air missile.
Propulsion: Aerojet (ATSC) Mk 60 or Rocketdyne Flexadyne Mk 47 long-burn solid motors.
Dimensions: Length 157.8in (4.01m), body diameter 15in (380mm), span 36.4in (925mm).
Launch weight: 985lb (447kg).
Range: Over 124 miles (200km).
Flight speed: Over Mach 5.
Warhead: Continuous-rod (132lb, 60kg) with proximity and impact fuzes.

By far the most sophisticated and costly AAM in the world, this missile provides air defense over an area exceeding 12,000 square miles (31,000km²) from near sea level to the limits of altitude attained by aircraft or tactical missiles. But it can be fired only from the F-14 Tomcat and costs nearly half a million dollars.

Following the classic aerodynamics of the Falcon family, Phoenix was originally AAM-N-11 and Hughes Aircraft began development in 1960 to replace the AIM-47A and Eagle as partner to the AWG-9 for the F-111B. This advanced fire-control system was the most capable ever attempted, and includes a very advanced radar (derived from the ASG-18 carried in the YF-12A) of high-power PD type with the largest circular aerial (of planar type) ever carried by a fighter. It has look-down capability out to ranges exceeding 150 miles (241km), and is backed up by an IR tracker to assist positive target identification and discrimination. AWG-9 has TWS capability, and an F-111B with the maximum load of six Phoenix missiles could engage and attack six aircraft at maximum range simultaneously, weather conditions and target aspect being of little consequence. Indeed the basic interception mode assumed is head-on, which is one of the most difficult at extreme range.

Propulsion is by a long-burning Rocketdyne (Flexadyne) Mk 47 or Aerojet Mk60 motor, giving a speed to burnout of Mach 3.8. Combined with low induced drag and the power of the large hydraulically driven tail controls this gives sustained maneuvrability over a range not even approached by any other AAM, despite the large load of electrical battery, electrical con-

Below: Few enemy pilots will ever get this view of six AIM-54 Phoenix (and, unusually, two tanks) under an F-14A Tomcat.

Above: This was the launch, seen on ciné film by telephoto lens, of the third AIM-54C advanced Phoenix test round, from YF-14A No 157990 of the Pacific Missile Test Center in 1980.

version unit, autopilot, electronics unit, transmitter/receiver and planar-array seeker head (all part of the DSQ-26 on- board guidance) as well as the 132lb (60kg) annular blast fragmentation warhead with Downey Mk 334 proximity fuze, Bendix IR fuze and DA fuze.

Hughes began flight test at PMTC in 1965, using a DA-3B Skywarrior, achieving an interception in September 1966. In March 1969 an F-111B successfully engaged two drones, and subsequently Phoenix broke virtually all AAM records including four kills in one pass (out of a six-on-six test, there being one no-test and one miss), a kill on a BQM-34A simulating a cruise missile at 50ft (15m), and a kill on a BQM-34E flying at Mach 1.5 tracked from 153 miles (246km), the Phoenix launched at 127 miles (204km) and impacting 83.5 miles (134km) from the launch point. The first AWG-9 system for the F-14A Tomcat, which replaced the F-111B, was delivered in February 1970. Production of Phoenix AIM-54A at Tucson began in 1973, since when output averaged about 40 per month. By the third quarter of 1978 output had passed 2,500; it then slowed sharply and ended in 1980.

Since late 1977 production missiles were of the AIM-54B type with sheet-metal wings and fins instead of honeycomb structure, non-liquid hydraulic and thermal-conditioning systems, and simplified engineering. In 1977 Hughes began a major effort to produce an updated Phoenix to meet the needs of the 1990s. This missile, AIM-54C, has totally new all-digital electronics, more reliable and flexible in use than the analog unit, with a solid-state radar replacing the previous klystron tube model. Accuracy is improved by a new strapdown inertial reference unit from Nortronics, and ECCM capability is greatly enhanced. Another improvement is a new proximity fuze developed by the Naval Weapons Center. Hughes delivered 15 engineering models from summer 1980, the first firing (head-on against a QF-4, the missile being in the semi-active mode throughout) being successful on 2 June 1980. Then followed 30 pilot-production rounds in the second half of 1981, with full production following from mid-1982. There is a possibility that AIM-54A missiles may be updated.

Poseidon, UGM-73

Origin: Lockheed Missiles & Space Company, Sunnyvale, California.
Type: Submarine-launched ballistic missile.
Dimensions: Length 34ft 0in (10.36m); body diameter 74.0in (188cm).
Launch weight: About 65,000lb (29,500kg).
Propulsion: First stage, advanced solid motor by Thiokol and Hercules with gas-pressurized gimballed nozzle; second stage, Hercules motor with similar nozzle.
Guidance: Inertial, developed by MIT, manufactured by GE and Raytheon.
Range: See "warhead".
Flight speed: At burnout, about Mach 10.
Warhead: AEC (Lawrence Lab)/Lockheed MIRV system carrying ten W-76 50kT RVs for ultimate range of 3,230 miles (5,200km) or 14 for 2,485 miles (4,000km), in each case with full kit of penaids.

Resulting from prolonged studies of the benefits of later technology, Poseidon C3 can be carried by Polaris submarines after the installation of the Mk 88 fire-control system and minor modifications to the launch tubes. Compared with Polaris A3 it has at least equal range, carries double the payload and has roughly twice the accuracy (halved CEP), as well as much-improved MIRV and penaid capability. Of the original 41 FBM submarines the ten oldest remained operational with Polaris until their withdrawal in the early 1970s. The remaining 31 were converted to Poseidon in 1969-77, retaining 16 launch tubes each. In 1973-6 a major modification programme rectified various deficiencies, and the final modification was an improved INS (ship inertial navigation system) and General Electric Mk 88 fire control. In 1979-83 three squadrons (12 submarines) were converted to re the C-4 Trident, leaving 19 still operational with Poseidon as this book is published.

Above: Launch in 1970 from Cape Canaveral land pad of the last Poseidon development missile; many have been withdrawn.

Rapier

Origin: British Aerospace Dynamics, UK.
Type: Mobile air-transportable SAM system.
Dimensions: Length 88.2in (2.24m); diameter 5.25in (133mm); span 15in (381mm).
Launch weight: 94lb (42.6kg).
Propulsion: IMI Troy dual-thrust solid rocket motor.
Guidance: Optical target tracking (with blindfire radar), TV missile tracking and computer/radio command.
Range: 0.3 to 4.5 miles (0.5 to 7.25km).
Flight speed: Mach 2+.
Warhead: Crush-fuzed semi-AP, 1.1lb (0.5kg) charge.

By far the most successful close-range SAM of the modern era, Rapier was designed to have guidance so accurate that every round would actually strike its target. Thus the missile could be made very much smaller, since the warhead explodes inside the hostile aircraft without needing a proximity fuze. The system has been proved in several thousand firings, including many in the Falklands in 1982 after having endured treatment on ships and on land far more severe that the limiting design cases. In February 1981 the US DoD placed an initial contract (estimated at £140 million) for 32 complete fire units and eight blindfire radars, for the defence of USAF airfields in the UK: Alconbury, Bentwaters, Fairford, Lakenheath, Mildenhall, Upper Heyford and Woodbridge. These installations are to be manned by RAF Regiment personnel. Further contracts are being discussed, reportedly including fire units for USAF airbases in Federal Germany and possibly elsewhere. Rapier also exists in a fully mobile form, with eight rady-to-fire

Above: RAF Regiment firing crews will man the Rapier missiles which will defend US airbases in the United Kingdom; blindfire radar, not shown in the picture, will be included at all locations.

missiles on the amphibious M548 tracked chassis, but this has not yet been bought for US use.

Redeye, FIM-43A

Origin: General Dynamics/Pomona.
Type: Shoulder-fired infantry surface-to-air missile.
Dimensions: Length 48in (122cm); body diameter 2.75in (7cm); span 5.5in (14cm).
Launch weight: 18lb (8.2kg); whole package weighs 29lb (13kg).
Propulsion: Atlantic Research dual-thrust solid.
Guidance: Initial optical aiming, IR homing.
Range; Up to about 2 miles (3.3km).
Flight speed: Low supersonic.
Warhead: Smooth-case frag.

The first infantry SAM in the world, Redeye entered US Army service in 1964 and probably 100,000 had been delivered to the Army and Marine Corps by 1970. It has severe limitations. It has to wait until aircraft have attacked and then fire at their departing tailpipes; there is no IFF. Flight speed is only just enough to catch modern attack aircraft and the guidance is vulnerable to IRCM. Engagement depends on correct identification by the operator of the nature of the target aircraft. He has to wait until the aircraft has passed, aim on a pursuit course, listen for the IR lock-on buzzer. fire the missile and then select a fresh tube. The seeker cell needs a cooling unit, three of which are packed with each missile tube.

Right: Though it had severe shortcomings—to the point of being just a morale-raiser—Redeye was produced in quantity.

Roland

Origin: Developed by Euromissile (Aérospatiale, France; MBB, West Germany) and Americanized and manufactured by Hughes Aircraft, with major participation by Boeing Aerospace and others.
Type: Lofaads/Shorads (Lo-level forward-area air-defense system, Short-range air-defense system).
Dimensions: Length 94.5in (240cm); body diameter 6.3in (16cm); span 19.7in (50cm).
Launch weight: 143lb (65kg).
Propulsion: Internal boost and sustain solid motors.
Guidance: Initial IR gathering followed by semi-active radar command to line-of-sight.
Range: Up to 4.3 miles (7km).
Flight speed: Burnout velocity Mach 1.6.
Warhead: 14.3lb (6.5kg), contains 65 shaped charges each with lethal radius of 20ft (6m); prox fuze.

Originally developed as a mobile battlefield system with plain optical (clear-weather) guidance, Roland has from 1969 onwards been further developed as Roland 2 with blindfire radar guidance. The missile has folding wings and is fired from a launch tube on a tracked vehicle, the US Army carrier being the M109. Decision to buy Roland was taken in 1974, but the introduction to Army service has been affected by prolonged technical difficulties and cost overruns, and no American Roland was fired until the end of 1977. The cost of developing the US system escalated by several hundred per cent, and after prolonged delays the decision was taken not to cancel the whole programme but to restrict it to a single light battalion for use with the Rapid Deployment Force. Meanwhile, studies are in hand for adapting the system to direct the fire of other systems (Chaparral, Stinger) and to fire instead the small Stinger missile, ten of which can be housed in a single Roland fire unit, five per tube.

Above: There is little wrong with the Roland concept, but the Americanized version ran into technical/cost/time problems.

Sea Sparrow, RIM-7

Origin: Raytheon Company, Missile Systems Division.
Type: Semi-active homing ship-to-air missile.
Dimensions: Length 144in (3.66m); body diameter 8.0in (20.3cm); span 40in (1.02in).
Launch weight: About 500lb (227kg).
Propulsion: Aerojet Mk 53 Mod 2, Mk 65 or Hercules Mk 58 dual-thrust solid.
Guidance: CW semi-active homing.
Range: (7E) about 5 miles (8km), (7H) about 8 miles (13km).
Flight speed: At burnout, about Mach 3.
Warhead: (7E) 60lb (27kg) conventional, (7H) 66lb (30kg) continuous rod.

AIM-7E (see air-to-air section) is used almost unchanged as RIM-7E, the missile in the US Navy BPDMS (Basic Point-Defense Missile System), which became operational in 1969. It is used on many classes of surface vessel, including the attack carriers, fired from a modified eight-box Asroc launcher. The later RIM-7H has a higher performance and folding fins to fit a smaller launcher box. It is part of IPDMS (Improved PDMS) which also includes new radar and IR sensors. Because of basically limited performance Sea Sparrow was intended as an interim system, but it is obvious it will now have a very long life. It is installed in over 50 US ships and is the only weapon of the giant attack carriers. In February 1982 the second-source Sparrow

Above: The success of various forms of Sea Sparrow (here being fired from CVAN-65 *Enterprise*) spurred study of Sea Phoenix.

contractor, GD Pomona, was awarded a contract for 690 of the improved RIM-7M (AIM-7M) type missile (see Sparrow entry in AAM section).

Shillelagh, MGM-51A

Origin: Ford Aeronutronic Division, Newport Beach.
Type: Gun-launched guided missile.
Dimensions: Length 45in (114cm); body diameter 5.95in (15.2cm); fin span 11.4in (29.0cm).
Launch weight: About 60lb (27kg).
Propulsion: Amoco single-stage solid with hot-jet jetavators.
Guidance: Optical tracking and IR command link.
Range: Up to about three miles (4,500m).
Flight speed: High subsonic.
Warhead: Octol shaped charge 15lb (6.8kg).

Very large numbers of these advanced anti-tank missiles were supplied to the US Army in 1966-70, for firing from the 152mm dual purpose gun fitted to the General Sheridan AFV and M60A2 main battle tank. The gunner, who can fire a missile or a conventional round depending on the target, has only to keep the target centred in optical cross-hairs for the IR guidance to keep the missile centred on the line of sight. Firings were carried out from UH-1 helicopters, but an air-launched version is not in use. In 1976-78 trials were in hand of a proposed new guidance system using laser designators (either at the launch point or elsewhere) with a view to modifying the existing missiles, but no production followed.

Right: Despite severe technical problems, which reduce its operational effectiveness, Shillelagh is a widespread USA weapon.

Shrike, AGM-45

Origin: Naval Weapons Center (NWC), with production by TI, USA.
Type: Passive homing anti-radiation missile.
Propulsion: Rockwell (Rocketdyne) Mk 39 or Aerojet (ATSC) Mk 53 (polybutadiene) or improved Mk 78 (polyurethane, dual-thrust) solid motor.
Dimensions: Length 120in (3.05m); body diameter 8in (203mm); span 36in (914mm).
Launch weight: (Approximately, depending on sub-type) 390lb (177kg).
Range: 18 to 25 miles (29 to 40km).
Flight speed: Mach 2.
Warhead: Blast/frag, 145lb (66kg), proximity fuze.

Based in part on the Sparrow AAM, this was the first anti-radar missile (ARM) in the US since World War 2. Originally called ARM and designated ASM-N-10, it was begun as a project at NOTS (later NWC) in 1961. and in 1962 became AGM-45A. Production by a consortium headed by Texas Instruments (TI) and Sperry Rand/Univac began in 1963 and Shrike was in use in SE Asia three years later with Wild Weasel F-105Gs and EA-6As. Early experience was disappointing and there have since been numerous models, identified by suffix numbers, to rectify faults or tailor the passive homing head to a new frequency band identified in the potential hostile inventory. Carried by the US Navy/Marines A-4, A-6, A-7 and F-4, the Air Force F-4, F-105 and EF-111 and the Israeli F-4 and Kfir, Shrike is switched on while flying towards the target and fired as soon as the TI radiation seeker has locked-on. After motor cutoff Shrike flies a ballistic path until control system activation. The seeker has a monopulse crystal video receiver and continually updates the guidance by determining the direction of arrival of the hostile radiation, homing the missile into the enemy radar with its cruciform centre-body wings driven in "bang/bang" fashion by a hot-gas system. There were at least 18 sub-types in the AGM-45-1 to -10 families, with over 13 different tailored seeker heads, of which the USAF bought 12,863 by 1978 and the Navy a further 6,200. In the Yom Kippur war Israel used Shrike tuned to 2965/2900 MHz and 3025/3050 MHz to defeat SA-2 and SA-3, but was helpless against SA-6. In 1978-81 additional

Above: Initial experience with AGM-45 Shrike in the Vietnam war was little short of disastrous, but painstaking research led to a series of important weapons matched to many threats.

procurement centred on the -9 and -10 for the USAF to be carried by F-4G and EF-111A platforms, together with modification kits to equip existing rounds to home on to later SAM and other radars.

Sidewinder, AIM-9

Origin: Original design by US Naval Weapons Center, China Lake, commercial production by Philco (now Ford Aerospace) and later GE, today shared by Ford Aerospace (most versions, currently 9L and 9P) and Raytheon (9L and 9M).

Type: Close-range air-to-air missile with IR- or SAR- homing guidance.

Propulsion: Solid motor (various, by Rockwell, Aerojet or Thiokol, with Aerojet Mk 17 qualified on 9B/E/J/N/P and Thiokol Mk 36 or reduced-smoke TX-683 qualified on 9L/M).

Dimensions: See variants table.

Launch weight: See variants table.

Performance: See variants table.

Warhead: (B/E/J/N/P) 10lb (4.5kg) blast/fragmentation with passive IR proximity fuze (from 1982 being refitted with Hughes DSU-21/B active laser fuze), (D/G/H) 22.4lb (10.2kg) continuous rod with IR or HF proximity fuze, (L/M) 25lb (11.4kg) advanced annular blast/fragmentation with active laser IR proximity fuze.

One of the most influential missiles in history, this slim AAM was almost un-American in development for it was created out of nothing by a very small team at NOTS China Lake, operating on the proverbial shoe-string budget. Led by 'Doctor McLean, this team was the first in the world to attack the problem of passive IR homing guidance, in 1949, and the often intractable difficulties were compounded by the choice of an airframe of only 5in (127mm) diameter, which in the days of vacuum-tube electronics was a major challenge. In 1951 Philco was awarded a contract for a homing head based on the NOTS research and today, 28 years later, the guidance team at Newport Beach, now called Ford Aerospace and Communications, is still in production with homing heads for later Sidewinders. The first XAAM-N-7 guided round was successfully fired on 11 September 1953. The first production missiles, called N-7 by the Navy, GAR-8 by the USAF and SW-1 by the development team, reached IOC in May 1956.

These early Sidewinders were made of sections of aluminium tube, with the seeker head and control fins at the front and four fixed tail fins containing patented rollerons at the back. The rolleron is similar to an air-driven gyro wheel, and one is mounted in the tip of each fin so that it is spun at high speed by the slipstream. The original solid motor was made by Hunter-Douglas, Hercules and Norris-Thermador, to Naval Propellant Plant design, and it accelerated the missile to Mach 2.5 in 2.2 sec.

The beauty of this missile was its simplicity, which meant low cost, easy compatibility with many aircraft and, in theory, high reliability in harsh environments. It was said to have "less than 24 moving parts" and "fewer electronic components than the average radio". At the same time, though the guidance method meant that Sidewinder could be carried by any fighter, with or without radar, it was erratic in use and restricted to close stern engagements at high altitude in good visibility. The uncooled PbS seeker gave an SSKP of about 70 per cent in ideal conditions, but extremely poor results in bad visibility, cloud or rain, or at low levels, and showed a tendency to lock-on to the Sun, or bright sky, or reflections from lakes or rivers.

The pilot energized his missile homing head and listened for its signals in his headset. It would give a growl when it acquired a target, and if it was

Below: Though men can lift them, advanced weapons such as the AIM-9L and 9M need powered loaders managed with great finesse.

Above: Distinguished instantly by its long-span canard fins, the AIM-9L (and, now, the 9M) proved deadly in the Falklands.

nicely positioned astern of a hot jetpipe the growl would become a fierce strident singing that would rise in intensity until the pilot let the missile go. There were plenty of QF-80, Firebee and other targets that had early Sidewinders up their jetpipes in the 1950s, but unfortunately real-life engagements tended to have the wrong target, or the wrong aspect, or the wrong IR-emitting background. In October 1958, however, large numbers of Sidewinders were fired by Nationalist Chinese F-86s against Chinese MiG-17s and 14 of the latter were claimed in one day. This was the first wartime use of AAMs.

The staggering total of nearly 81,000 of the original missile was built in three almost identical versions which, in the new 1962 scheme, were designated AIM-9, 9A and 9B. Nearly all were of the 9B form, roughly half produced by Philco (Ford) and half by Raytheon. A further 15,000 were delivered by a European consortium headed by BGT, which in the late 1960s gave each European missile a new seeker head of BGT design known as FGW Mod 2. This has a nose dome of silicon instead of glass, a cooled seeker and semi-conductor electronics, and transformed the missile's reliability and ability to lock-on in adverse conditions.

By 1962 SW-1C was in use in two versions, AIM-9C by Motorola and -9D by Ford. This series introduced the Rocketdyne Mk 36 solid motor giving much greater range, a new airframe with tapered nose, long-chord controls and more swept leading edges on the tail fins, and completely new guidance. Motorola produced the 9C for the F-8 Crusader, giving it SARH guidance matched to the Magnavox APQ-94 radar, but for various reasons this odd man out was unreliable in performance and was withdrawn. In contrast, 9D was so successful it formed the basis of many subsequent versions, as well as MIM-72C Chaparral. The new guidance section introduced a dome of magnesium fluoride, a nitrogen-cooled seeker, smaller field of view, and increased reticle speed and tracking speed. The control section introduced larger fins, which were detachable, and high-power actuators fed by a longer-burning gas generator. The old 10lb (4.54kg) warhead with passive-IR fuze was replaced by a 22.4lb (10.2kg) annular blast fragmentation head of the continuous-rod type, fired by either an IR or HF proximity fuze.

AIM-9E was fitted with a greatly improved Ford seeker head with Peltier (thermoelectric) cooling, further-increased tracking speed and new electronics and wiring harnesses, giving increased engagement boundaries especially at low level. AIM-9G has so-called SEAM. (Sidewinder Expanded Acquisition Mode), an improved 9D seeker head, but was overtaken by 9H. The latter introduced solid-state electronics, even faster tracking speed, and double-delta controls with increased actuator power, giving greater maneuvrability than any previous Sidewinder as well as limited all-weather

The Sidewinder Family

Model	Guidance	Length	Control fin span	Launch wt	Mission time	Range	Production
AIM-9B	Uncooled PbS.25° look. 70 Hz reticle. 11°/sec tracking	111.4in (2830mm)	22.0in (559mm)	155lb (70.4kg)	20 sec	2 miles (3.2 km)	80,900
9B FGW.2	CO₂ cooling, solar dead zone reduced to 5°	114.5in (2908mm)	22.0in (559mm)	167lb (75.8kg)	20 sec	2.3 miles (3.7 km)	15,000
AIM-9C	Motorola SARH	113.0in (2870mm)	24.8in (630mm)	185lb (84.0kg)	60 sec	11 miles (17.7 km)	1,000
AIM-9D	N₂ cooled PbS, 40° look, 125 Hz reticle, 12°/sec tracking	113.0in (2870mm)	24.8in (630mm)	195lb (88.5kg)	60 sec	11 miles (17.7 km)	1,000
AIM-9E	Peltier-cooled PbS, 40° look, 100 Hz reticle, 16.5°/sec tracking	118.1in (3000mm)	22.0in (559mm)	164lb (74.5kg)	20 sec	2.6 miles (4.2 km)	5,000 (ex-9B)
AIM-9G	As -9D plus SEAM	113.0in (2870mm)	24.8in (630mm)	191lb (86.6kg)	60 sec	11 miles (17.7 km)	2,120
AIM-9H	As -9G plus solid-state, 20°/sec tracking	113.0in (2870mm)	24.8in (630mm)	186lb (84.5kg)	60 sec	11 miles (17.7 km)	7,720
AIM-9J	As -9E part-solid-state	120.9in (3070mm)	22.0in (559mm)	172lb (78.0kg)	40 sec	9 miles (14.5 km)	10,000 (ex-9B)
AIM-9L	Argon-cooled InSb. fixed reticle, tilted mirror system	112.2in (2850mm)	24.8in (630mm)	188lb (85.3kg)	60 sec	11 miles (17.7 km)	11,700+
AIM-9M	As -9L, better motor and ECCM	112.2in (2850mm)	24.8in (630mm)	190lb (86.0kg)	60 sec	11 miles (17.7 km)	3,500+
AIM-9N	As -9E plus part-solid-state	120.9in (3070mm)	22.0in (559mm)	172lb (78.0kg)	40 sec	9 miles (14.5 km)	7,000
AIM-9P	As -9N plus reliability improvements	120.9in (3070mm)	22.0in (559mm)	172lb (78.0kg)	60 sec	11 miles (17.7 km)	13,000

Above: This F-16A is carrying AIM-9L missiles on the wingtips and double-delta AIM-9Js just inboard; note ALQ-119 ECM pod.

capability. AIM-9J is a rebuilt 9B or 9E with part-solid-state electronics, detachable double-delta controls with greater power, and long-burning gas generator. Range is sacrificed for high acceleration to catch fast targets.

There are J-1 and J-3 improved or "all-new" variants. A major advance came with Sidewinder 9L, with which NWC (as NOTS now is) at last responded to the prolonged demands of customers and the proven accomplishments of BGT. The latter's outstanding seeker head developed for Viper was first fitted to AIM-9L to give Alasca (All-Aspect Capability), a great missile that was merely used by Germany as a possible fall-back in case 9L failed to mature. AIM-9L itself, in full production from 1977, has long-span pointed delta fins, a totally new guidance system (see table), and an annular blast fragmentation warhead sheathed in a skin of preformed rods, triggered by a new proximity fuze in which a ring of eight GaAs laser diodes emit and a ring of silicon photodiodes receive.

Above 16,000 of the 9L series were expected to be made by 1983, and at least a further 9,000 are likely to be made by a new BGT-led European consortium which this time includes BAe Dynamics and companies in Norway and Italy.

AIM-9M is a revised L. 9N is the new designation of J-1 (all are 9B or 9E rebuilds). 9P are rebuilds of 9B/E/J, and additional 9P missiles are being made from new.

Sidewinder Guidance Sections

	AIM-9B: 80,900 produced by Philco and GE and c15,000 by European consortium; 10,000+ updated by Ford.
	AIM-9C/D: 9C SARH model by Motorola (1,000+), 9D with better IR/speed/manoeuvre, 950+ by Ford for US Navy.
	AIM-9E: 9B rebuilt with new cooled wide-angle seeker, about 5,000 for USAF by Ford (Aeronutronic).
	AIM-9G/H: 9G improved 9D with off-boresight lock-on (2,120 Raytheon, USN); 9H solid-state (3,000 Ford AF).
	AIM-9L/M: 9L 3rd generation all-aspect (Ford and Raytheon, also Europe); 9M improved ECCM/motor (Raytheon).
	AIM-9J/N: J rebuilt B/E with new front end (Ford c14,000 for AF); N (formerly J1) further improved (c,7,000).
	AIM-9P improved B/E/J or new production, new motor/fuze and better reliability, c13,000 by Ford for USAF.

Sparrow, AIM-7

Origin: (AIM-7E, 7F, 7M) Raytheon Company, USA, with second-source production (7F, M) by GD Pomona and licence-manufacture (7F) by Mitsubishi, Japan.
Type: Radar-guided air-to-air missile.
Propulsion: (7E) Aerojet or Rockwell Mk 52 Mod 2 PB/AP solid motor, (7F, M) Hercules or Aerojet Mk 58 high-impulse solid motor.
Dimensions: Length (E, F) 144in (3,660mm), (M) 145in (3,680mm); body diameter 8in (203mm); span 40in (1,020mm).
Launch weight: (E) 452lb (205kg), (F, M) 503lb (228kg).
Range: (E) 28 miles (44km); (F, M) 62 miles (100km).
Flight speed: About Mach 4.
Warhead: (E) 66lb (30kg) continuous-rod warhead, (F, M) 88lb (40kg) Mk 71 advanced continuous-rod warhead, in each case with proximity and DA fuzes.

Considerably larger than other contemporary American AAMs, this missile not only progressed through three fundamentally different families, each with a different prime contractor, but late in life mushroomed into totally new versions for quite new missions as an ASM (Shrike) and a SAM (two types of Sea Sparrow).

Sperry Gyroscope began the programme as Project Hot Shot in 1946,

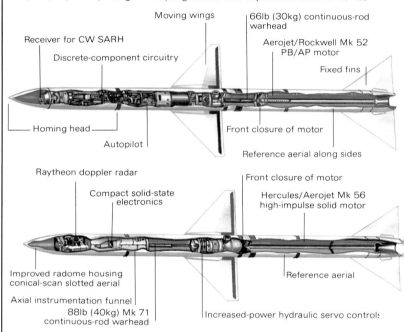

Above: Cutaways of AIM-7E (top) and AIM-7F/7M Sparrows.

under US Navy BuAer contract. By 1951 Sperry had a contract for full engineering development of XAAM-N-2 Sparrow I, and the suffix I was added because by that time there was already a Sparrow II. The first representative guided flight tests took place in 1953. This missile was a beam rider, with flush dipole aerials around the body, which picked up the signals from the fighter radar beam (assumed to be locked-on to the target) and drove the cruciform delta wings to keep the missile aligned in the centre of the beam. At the tail were four fixed fins, indexed in line with the wings. Propulsion was by an Aerojet solid motor, and missile assembly took place at the Sperry-Farragut Division which operated a Naval Industrial Reserve plant at Bristol, Tennessee.

IOC was reached in July 1956, and Sparrow I was soon serving in the Atlantic and Pacific Fleets, and with the Marine Corps.

In 1955 Douglas obtained limited funding for Sparrow II, as main armament for the proposed F5D-1 Skylancer. Amazingly, however, the company did not switch to SARH guidance but to fully active radar, and this was tough in a missile of 8in (203mm) diameter, a figure common to all Sparrows. In mid-1956 the Navy decided to terminate Sparrow II, but it was snapped up by the Royal Canadian Air Force as armament for the Arrow supersonic intercepter. After severe difficulties Premier Diefenbaker cancelled Sparrow II on 23 September 1958, and the Arrow itself the following February. ▶

Below: Launching a Sparrow from the seventh F/A-18A Hornet development prototype in 1980, with APG-65 radar guidance.

▶ Three years previously Raytheon had begun to work on Sparrow III, taking over the Bristol plant in 1956. Sparrow III uses almost the same airframe as Sparrow II but with SARH guidance. By the mid-1950s Raytheon had become of the most capable missile companies, possibly because its background was electronics rather than airframes. It built up a missile engineering center at Bedford, Massachusetts, with a test base at Oxnard (not far from Point Mugu), California; production of Sparrows was finally shared between Bristol and a plant at South Lowell, near Bedford.

Most of the airframe is precision-cast light alloy. Early Sparrow III missiles had an Aerojet solid motor, not cast integral with the case, and introduced CW guidance. AIM-7C, as it became, reached IOC in 1958 with Demons of the Atlantic and Pacific fleets. AIM-7D introduced the Thiokol (previously Reaction Motors) prepackaged liquid motor, and was also adopted by the Air Force in 1960 as AIM-101 to arm the F-110 (later F-4C) Phantom. All fighter Phantoms can carry four Sparrows recessed into the underside of the fuselage, with target illumination by the APQ-72, APQ-100, APQ-109, APQ-120, or APG-59 (part of AWG-10 or -11) radar. In the Italian F-104S Starfighter the radar is the Rockwell R-21G/H, and in the F-14 Tomcat the powerful Hughes AWG-9. The AIM-7D was also the basis for PDMS Sea Sparrow.

AIM-7E, the next version (also used in the NATO Sea Sparrow system), uses the Rocketdyne free-standing solid motor with Flexadyne propellant (Mk 38), which gives a slightly increased burnout speed of Mach 3.7. The warhead is of the continuous-rod type, the explosive charge being wrapped in a tight drum made from a continuous rod of stainless steel which shatters into about 2,600 lethal fragments. DA and proximity fuzes are fitted. Many thousands of -7E missiles were used in Vietnam by F-4s, but, owing to the political constraints imposed on the American fighters, were seldom able to be fired. Accordingly AIM-7E2 was developed with shorter minimum range, increased power of maneuver and plug-in aerodynamic surfaces requiring no tools. The AIM-7C, D and E accounted for over 34,000 missiles.

Introduced in 1977, AIM-7F has all-solid-state guidance, making room for a more powerful motor, the Hercules Mk 58, giving further-enhanced flight speed and range, as well as a larger (88lb, 40kg) warhead. Claimed to lock-on reasonably well against clutter up to 10db, -7F is compatible with CW PD radars (and thus with the F-15 and F-18), and has a conical-scan seeker head. In 1977 GD Pomona was brought in as second-source supplier and with Raytheon is expected to deliver about 19,000 missiles by 1985, split roughly equally between the Navy and Air Force, plus hoped-for exports.

In 1982 both contractors switched to AIM-7M, developed by Raytheon. This has an inverse-processed digital monopulse seeker generally similar to Sky Flash in giving greatly improved results in adverse conditions. GD's first contract was for 690, following 3,000 of the -7F type.

The Sparrow Faimly

1950 designation	1962	Guidance	Length	Span	Launch wt	Range	Production
AAM-N-2 Sparrow I	AIM-7A	Radar beam riding	140in (3.56m)	39in (0.99m)	310lb (141kg)	5 miles (8 km)	c2,000
AAM-N-3 Sparrow II	AIM-7B	Active radar homing	144in (3.66m)	39in (0.99m)	420lb (191kg)	?	c100
AAM-N-6 Sparrow III	AIM-7C	SARH CW	144in (3.66m)	40in (1.02m)	380lb (172kg)	25 miles (40 km)	2,000
AAM-N-6A/AIM-101	AIM-7D	SARH CW	144in (3.66m)	40in (1.02m)	440lb (200kg)	25 miles (40 km)	7,500
AAM-N-6B	AIM-7E	SARH CW	144in (3.66m)	40in (1.02m)	452lb (205kg)	28 miles (44 km)	25,000
—	AIM-7F	SARH CW solid-state	144in (3.66m)	40in (1.02m)	503lb (228kg)	62 miles (100 km)	3,000
—	AIM-7M	SARH CW solid state	145in (3.68m)	40in (1.02m)	503lb (228kg)	62 miles (100 km)	1,800 +

SRAM, AGM-69

Origin: Boeing Aerospace, USA.
Type: Fully maneuvrable self-guided wingless rocket.
Propulsion: Originally Lockheed Propulsion Co two-pulse solid motor; Thiokol is in low-rate production with a long-life motor with numerous improvements.
Dimensions: Length (with tail fairing for external carriage) 190in (4.83m), (without fairing) 168in (4.27m); body diameter 17.5in (444.5mm); span (three fins at 120°) each tip is 15in (381mm) from axis of missile.
Launch weight: 2,230lb (1,012kg).
Range: Very variable depending on launch height and selected profile) 35 to 105 miles (56 to 169km).
Flight speed: Mach 2.8 to 3.2.
Warhead: Nuclear W-69, 200kT, air burst and DA fuzes.

Throughout the 1950s nuclear warheads became ever smaller, and by 1960 studies showed that a missile that could be carried by a fighter could deliver a large nuclear warhead from a range exceeding 100 miles (161km). In the event the SRAM (Short-Range Attack Missile) has not been used by fighters, but by aircraft of SAC, primarily to neutralise potential hostile defenses such a radars, SAMs and other AA systems. The adjective "short-range" has taken on a new meaning, while the compact lightweight design of this high-performance weapon multiplies in dramatic fashion the number of targets that one bomber can engage. Boeing, the final prime contractor, began SRAM studies in December 1963, ahead of the drafting of SOR-212 in 1964 which resulted in the establishment of WS-140A. A keen competition followed in 1965, with selection in November 1965 of Boeing and Martin and final choice of Boeing (now Boeing Aerospace Co) on 31 October 1966. A dummy SRAM was dropped from a B-52 in December 1967, live flights began in 1969, and IOC was reached in early 1972. Production of 1,500 AGM-69A missiles was completed in July 1975, the missile then equipping 18 SAC bases operating the B-52G and H and FB-111A.

Below: This SAC FB-111A bomber is carrying a single SRAM on the left of the bomb bay, the four pylons not being fitted.

Above: Four triplets of SRAMs have long been a standard external load for SAC B-52s, this aircraft being a fan-engined H.

Originally there were to be different guidance systems, Sylvania supplying a radar-homing version and an IR-homer also being required. These were not procured, and AGM-69A has only inertial guidance by Singer-Kearfott, with a Delco on-board computer to command very varied flight profiles. Four basic trajectories are: semi-ballistic; terrain-following; pull-up from "under the radar" followed by inertial dive; and combined inertial and terrain-following. The small, almost perfectly streamlined missile is said to have a radar cross-section "about as large as a bullet". The B-52 can carry eight on a rotary launcher reminiscent of a revolver cylinder in the aft bomb bay (exceptionally, and at the expense of other loads, it can carry three such launchers internally), plus two tandem triplets on each former Hound Dog pylon, modified for SRAM compatibility, a total of 20 missiles. The FB-111A can carry up to six, four on swivelling wing pylons and two internally. The bombardier selects each missile in turn, checks the updating of the KT-76 inertial guidance and lets it drop. The motor accelerates it to about Mach 3, fast enough to fly and steer with body lift and three tail fins (there are no wings). Nearing the target the second propulsion stage is ignited.

About 1,300 missiles remain available to SAC's dwindling forces. AGM-69B, an improved missile with nuclear hardening throughout, the W-80 warhead, a completely new Thiokol HTPB-propellant motor and greatly increased computer memory, was almost ready for production for the B-1, which can carry 32; AGM-69B was cancelled in 1977 following discontinuance of the production programme for B-1. The remaining A-series missiles must, however, be fitted with the new Thiokol motor, because of ageing problems, and computer memory and nuclear-hardening improvements are also projected. There is no money for production of new missiles, despite attractions of large carrier aircraft such as the 747-200F which could carry 72 internally. Originally the size of SRAM dictated the dimensions of ALCM, but the latter is now much longer. There is no announced intention to produce extra SRAMs for the B-1B.

Standard ARM (RGM/AGM-78)

Origin: General Dynamics, Pomona (California).
Type: Anti-radar missile (AGM, air-launched; RGM, ship-launched).
Dimensions: Length 15ft 0in (4.57m); body diameter 13.5in (34.3cm); fin span 42.9in (109cm).
Launch weight: Basic 1,356lb (615kg), Mod 1 1,800lb (816kg).
Propulsion: Aerojet Mk 27 Mod 4 dual-thrust solid motor.
Guidance: Passive radar seeker by Maxson and GD/Pomona.
Range: 15 miles (25km).
Flight speed: Over Mach 2.
Warhead: Conventional, impact/prox fuze.

Announced in 1966, Standard ARM is a development of the Standard ship-to-air SAM. The first model used the TI seeker head of the Shrike ARM but improved guidance is now fitted. This missile has augmented, and is now replacing, Shrike in US Navy A-6 squadrons and USAF units flying the F-105, F-4 and possibly other aircraft such as the A-10; it has also been reported as carried by the Navy EA-6B Prowler EW aircraft and the E-2C Hawkeye AEW platform. Carrier aircraft can be fitted with TIAS (Target Identification and Acquisition System) to help the missile strike home despite the enemy radar being intermittently or permanently switched off; in the USAF Standard ARM is linked with the Wild Weasel system and would probably be carried by the EF-4E (F-4G) and EF-111A. (See HARM.) RGM-66D is an interim US Navy ship-to-ship missile which can hit radar-emitting targets beyond the horizon. It is fitted to two patrol gunboats (in

Above: AGM-78 hung under a Wild Weasel Republic F-105G Thunderchief at Holloman AFB in 1967; still active with ANG.

stern box launcher); RGM-66E is tailored to the Asroc launcher and is interim ARM on six DDGs and six FFGs. All Standard ARM production was completed in 1978.

Standard, RIM-66/67

Origin: General Dynamics/Pomona.
Type: Ship-to-air missile; also surface-to-surface, see text.
Dimensions: Length (MR) 15ft 0in (4.57m), (ER) 27ft 0in (8.23m); body diameter 13.8in (35.0cm); fin span (MR) 42in (107cm), (ER) 62in (157cm).
Launch weight: (MR) about 1,300lb (590kg), (ER) about 2,350lb (1,060kg).
Propulsion: (MR) dual-thrust solid, Aerojet/Hercules Mk 56 Mod 0; (ER) boost, Atlantic Research Mk 30 Mod 2, sustainer, Naval Propellant Plant Mk 12 Mod 1.
Guidance: Semi-active radar homing, varies with ship installation.
Range: (SM-1, MR) about 15 miles (24km), (SM-2, MR) about 30 miles (48.5km), (SM-1, ER) 35 miles (56km), (SM-2, ER) 60 miles (96km).
Flight speed: (MR) about Mach 2.5 (ER) over Mach 2.5.
Warhead: (SM-1) Usually Mk 90 (about 6,000 fragments, plus blast and incendiary) with Mk 45 proximity fuze.

RIM-66A (SM-1 MR) and RIM-67A (SM-2 ER) are Standard Missile 1 Medium Range and Extended Range, and were respectively developed to replace Tartar and Terrier as standard US Navy ship-to-air weapons, RGM-66D is a horizon-limited surface-to-surface version. Both are in US Navy use, and the same weapon was the basis of AGM-78 and RGM-66D Standard ARM described separately. RIM-66C, SM-2 (Standard Missile 2), is also being developed in MR and ER forms, the latter having a tandem boost motor as in the ER version of SM-1. SM-2 is a similar airframe but has totally different guidance and augmented propulsion, and forms part of the complex Aegis ship-defence system having capability against missiles and multiple threats. Guidance includes a new two-way link for mid-course

Above: Unusual land firing (from Point Mugu, Pacific Missile Test Center) of Standard MR from single overhead launcher.

command and terminal homing with higher ECM resistance. The Aegis system incorporates giant SPY-1A phased-array radars facing all round each ship, the first being CG-47 *Ticonderoga* which despite delays and massive cost-escalation, was expected to join the fleet in 1983.

Stinger, FIM-92A

Origin: General Dynamics/Pomona.
Type: Shoulder-fired infantry surface-to-air missile.
Dimensions: Length 60in (152cm); body diameter 2.75in (7cm); span 5.5in (14cm).
Launch weight: 24lb (10.9kg); whole package 35lb (15.8kg).
Propulsion: Atlantic Research dual-thrust solid.
Guidance: Passive IR homing (see text).
Range: Probably about 3 miles (5km).
Flight speed: Supersonic.
Warhead: Smooth-case frag.

Developed since the mid-1960s as a much-needed replacement for Redeye, Stinger has had a long and troubled development but is at last beginning to come into low-rate production with inventory delivery beginning in 1981. An improved IR seeker gives all-aspect guidance, the wavelength of less than 4.4 microns being matched to an exhaust plume rather than hot metal, though there is no indication of whether IFF is incorporated (so the operator may have to rely on correct visual identification of oncoming supersonic aircraft). It is hoped that about three-quarters of future rounds will have a new guidance system using a "two colour" seeker, one part sensitive to IR and the other to UV and thus defeating IRCM or optical countermeasures. To rescue something from the Roland programme Boeing has developed a container for four Stinger missiles which fits the Roland launch tube, though this had not entered production by 1983. In fiscal 1981 the first 1,144 missiles for the inventory were delivered at $70.1m, and totals for 1982 and 1983 were respectively 2,544 at $193.4m and 2,256 at $214.6m. Air-launched MLMS is described separately.

Above: Getting ready to engage an obviously very low-level target by Stinger of the 3rd Armored Cavalry at Fort Bliss.

Subroc, UUM-44A

Origin: Goodyear Aerospace, Akron.
Type: Submarine-to-Submarine rocket.
Dimensions: Length 20ft 5in (6.25m); body diameter (boost motor) 21.0in (53.3cm); span, no fins or wings.
Launch weight: 4,086lb (1,853kg).
Propulsion: Thiokol TE-260G solid tandem boost motor with four jetavator nozzles.
Guidance: Kearfott SD-510 inertial system.
Range: Up to 35 miles (56km).
Flight speed: Supersonic.
Warhead: W-55 nuclear (estimated 1kT, radius about 4 miles (6.4km).

Standard ASW weapon of US Navy attack submarines, Subroc is launched from a 21in torpedo tube in the conventional way. The missile arches up through the water and at a safe distance the rocket ignites, guiding the weapon towards its target both before and after breaking the ocean surface. Steering is accomplished by the jetavators during powered flight. At motor cutoff the warhead vehicle is separated and continues to its target guided by aerodynamic fins. Entry to the water is cushioned, after which the warhead sinks to the correct depth before detonating. Subroc has been operational since 1965. Attack submarines usually carry four to six missiles each.

Above: That's a startled seagull behind the Subroc which has just broken surface (at a typical angle) and ignited propulsion.

In 1979 Congress decided not to introduce a revised rocket motor and new digital guidance system, and instead to replace Subroc late in the decade with CASW/SOW.

Titan II, LGM-25C

Origin: Martin Marietta Corporation, Denver (Colorado) Division.
Type: ICBM deployed in hardened silo.
Dimensions: Length 102ft 8½in (31.30m); body diameter 120in (305cm).
Launch weight: 330,000lb (149,690kg).
Propulsion: First stage, Aerojet LR87 twin-chamber engine burning nitrogen tetroxide and Aerozine; second stage Aerojet LR91, similar but one smaller chamber (all chambers gimballed).
Guidance: Inertial, IBM/AC Spark Plug.
Range: 9,300 miles (15,000km).
Flight speed: Over 15,000mph (24,000km/h) at burnout.
Warhead: General Electric Mk 6 RV containing thermonuclear warhead (W-53, estimated 9MT) and penaids.

By far the biggest and oldest of America's surviving strategic missiles, Titan was begun in the mid-1950s as a later alternative to Atlas with the bold feature of a second stage that had to ignite in space. Titan II, operational since 1963, combined silo emplacement with hypergolic (self-igniting) propellants which reduced reaction time from hours to one minute. A total force of only 54 missiles was deployed, in three wings centred at Davis-Monthan, McConnell and Little Rock AFBs, but hypergolic-fuel explosions in 1978 and 1980 reduced this total to 52 missiles. In March 1978 work began on replacing the original guidance by the USGS (Universal Space Guidance System) used on the Titan III space launcher, chiefly to reduce maintenance cost from about $173 million to $101 million per year, and this was completed in 1981. Since 1980 there has been much rethinking on when to start dismantling this force, which is the only one in the West to offer anything like the range and throw-weight of the far more numerous Soviet ICBMs. Fortunately, in 1983 it was still intact.

Below: Launch of a Titan II in the missile's youth; today there are only 52 left and no replacement in sight on this scale.

Tomahawk (Sea), BGM-109A, B, C and E

Origin: General Dynamics/Convair, San Diego.
Type: All versions rocket-launched turbojet-propelled cruise missile for use by submarines or surface ships: (A) nuclear land attack, (B/E) anti-ship, (C) conventional land attack.
Dimensions: Length, loosely given as 252in (6.4m) with boost motor, but varies type to type; length in flight, typically 219in (5.56m); body diameter 21in (533mm); span 100in (2.54m) or 103in (2.61m).
Launch weight: All naval versions, typically 4,190lb (1,900kg).
Propulsion: One Williams F107-WR-400 turbojet rated at 600lb (272kg); launch by 7,000lb (3,175kg) Atlantic Research solid rocket motor.
Guidance: (A) INS/Tercom, (B/E) strapdown AHRS/active radar, (C) INS/Tercom+Dsmac.
Range: (A, C) 1,553 miles (2,500km), (B/E) 280 miles (450km).
Flight speed: 550mph (885km/h).
Warhead: (A) W-80 thermonuclear, (B/E, C) conventional, Bullpup type.

Since it was first developed in December 1972 the Tomahawk family has diversified so that, despite losing the big USAF buy of an air-launched strategic version to Boeing's AGM-86B, four variants remain active programmes: three for the US Navy described here, and one for the USAF for land mobile deployment described later. The three Navy versions are all basically similar and differ in fuel capacity, guidance and warhead. All have conventional light-alloy aircraft-type airframes, with a tubular body, pivoted wings which unfold to zero sweep after launch, four powered tail fins for trajectory control and a ventral inlet. In naval versions of the missile the tail fins and inlet also deploy after launch. The BGM-109A version is the TLAM-N (Tactical Land Attack Missile, Nuclear). It has inertial mid-course guidance updated by Tercom (terrain-contour-matching) guidance in the terminal phase, giving outstanding accuracy despite the fact that it has an extremely powerful warhead (thus, it can be used against hardened targets). It is expected to be deployed aboard submarines and surface warships. In the submarine mode it is delivered encapsulated in a stainless-steel container which provides environmental protection even at great ocean depths as well as control, communication and launch facilities including gas-drive cold launch. In the SSN-688 class attack submarines 12 vertical launch tubes are being built into the bow section outside the pressure hull (the original plan was to fire from existing torpedo tubes). Retired Polaris-type SSBNs are being studied as CMC (cruise-missile carrier) boats with up to 80 rounds. BGM-109B/E is the TASM (Tactical Anti-Ship Missile), with conventional Bullpup-type warhead, much less fuel and active radar homing based on that of Harpoon. It follows a pre-programmed flight profile and can be fired from submarine capsules or surface ships, vertical launch tubes being planned for CG-47, DD-963 and DDG-X class ships. Funding continues to support development of this variant, the ship installations and the required OTH (over the horizon) command/control systems. BGM-109C

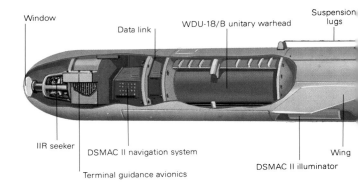

Window · Data link · WDU-18/B unitary warhead · Suspension lugs · IIR seeker · DSMAC II navigation system · Terminal guidance avionics · DSMAC II illuminator · Wing

Tank Breaker

Origin: Hughes Aircraft, Culver City.
Type: Fire-and-forget anti-tank missile.
Dimensions: Length 43in (1.09m); body diameter 3.94in (100m).
Launch weight: Complete system under 35lb (15.8kg).
Propulsion: Boost/sustain solid motors.
Guidance: Staring focal-plane array IR.
Range: Similar to Tow.
Flight speed: Transonic.
Warhead: Shaped charge.

One of the first weapons to use a focal-plane array, an advanced imaging IR seeker, Tank Breaker is a one-man portable missile which can be locked-on to a tank, helicopter, low-performance fixed-wing aircraft or other target, and fired. It will thereafter home by itself, the operator having previously programmed it either to fly a direct course or (against armour) plunge down from above. The "system weight" given above is that for the missile, throw-away launch tube and reusable sight/control unit. Development began in 1980, the seeker being field tested in late 1982.

Right: Tank Breaker has obvious features in common with its ancestor, Tow, but is a much newer and more compact weapon.

---

s TLAM-C, the conventional counterpart to BGM-109A and like other versions planned for both sea and land warfare, and its guidance will have the super-accurate Dsmac (Digital scene-matching area correlation), in which scenes ahead of the missile are scanned and analysed into digital information which is compared with information on the target approach terrain stored in the guidance system.

Tomahawk (Air), AGM-109

Origin: General Dynamics Convair Division, USA.
Type: Medium-range air-to-surface missile.
Propulsion: Modified Teledyne CAE J402-400 turbojet (660lb, 300kg, sea-level thrust).
Dimensions: Length (H, K) 234in (5.94m), (I) 192in (4.88m); body diameter 21in (533mm); span (wings extended) 103in (2.616m).
Launch weight: (H) 2,900lb (1,315kg), (I) 2,225lb (1,009kg), (K) 2,630lb 1,193kg).
Range: (Sea level, Mach 0.6) (H) 293 miles (472km), (I) 350 miles (564km), K) 316 miles (509km).
Flight speed: 550mph (885km/h).
Warhead: (H) 58 TAAM bomblet/mine payloads, 1,060lb (481kg); (I) WDU-7B or -18B unitary warhead, 650lb (295kg); (K) WDU-25A/B unitary warhead, 937lb (425kg).

The General Dynamics AGM-109 was one of the chief versions of the Tomahawk strategic nuclear cruise missile, first tested in air drops from P-3 Orions and A-6 Intruders in 1974. It differed from the ship/submarine/GLCM versions in having no rocket boost motor or launch capsule/box. Main propulsion, at first a J402, switched like other versions to a Williams F107 turbofan in competition with the Boeing AGM-86B as the ALCM for SAC. When the Boeing missile was chosen, Tomahawk was recast in different roles, and eventually in 1981 the naval versions were all terminated, chiefly on cost grounds. GLCM continued as a tactical weapon of the Air Force, and a completely new version, MRASM (Medium-Range ASM) was launched in 1981 as a non-nuclear cruise missile for wide use by the Air Force, arming many types of aircraft beginning with the B-52 and F-16. Though in early 1983 still not given a full go-ahead by Congress, which for two years has looked at alternative delivery systems, MRASM has been taken to a high pitch of development—interestingly enough with the original pure-jet engine, but in a much modified form able to fly 8-hour missions burning the new JP-10 fuel and with a positive oil storage, retapered turbine, oxygen start system and zirconium-coated combustor. The basic missile has been developed in three forms, differing in payload and guidance. AGM-109H is the baseline airfield attack missile, with DSMAC II (digital scene-matching area-correlation) guidance and carrying a heavy payload of 58 TAAM (tactical airfield attack missile) bomblets or mines, discharged from upward-facing tubes along the fuselage. This version is in competition with short-range or free-fall anti-airfield weapons, and justifies its high cost by the fact it is a launch-and-leave missile which eliminates the need for the carrier aircraft to come within 300 miles (483km) of the target. AGM-109I is a dual-role weapon proposed by the Navy for use by A-6E squadrons. It has a large unitary warhead and both DSMAC II and IIR (imaging IR) guidance for either anti-ship or land attack missions. AGM-109K is a pure sea-control missile with only IIR guidance; the scene-matching and large fuel-cell power plant are replaced by an enlarged warhead. GD states that all versions could have IOC in 1985.

Tomahawk (Land), BGM-109G

Origin: General Dynamics/Convair, San Diego.
Type: Rocket-launched turbojet-propelled cruise missile for use from land vehicle.
Dimensions: Length 236in (600mm); body diameter 20.5in (520mm); span 98.5in (2.5m).
Launch weight: 3,200lb (1,451kg).
Propulsion: One Williams F107-WR-400 turbofan rated at 600lb (272kg); launch by 7,000lb (3,175kg) Atlantic Research solid rocket motor.
Guidance: INS/Tercom + Dsmac.
Range: 1,550 miles (2,500km).
Flight speed: 550mph (885km/h).
Warhead: W-84 nuclear or thermonuclear (classified).

In most essentials BGM-109G is identical to the long-range naval versions of Tomahawk, but it has Dsmac (digital scene-matching area-correlation, see BGM-109C) guidance and the new W-84 warhead. Its mission designation is GLCM (Ground-Launched Cruise Missile), and it is assigned to the Air Force for deployment relatively close to potential trouble-spots, notably Europe. Under the desperately needed NATO TNF (theatre nuclear force) modernization programme a total of 464 GLCMs are to be stationed in NATO European nations under the management of TAC on behalf of SAC. Each missile is packaged with aerodynamic surfaces and engine inlet retracted inside an aluminium drum. Tanks are filled and guidance pre-targeted. The BGM-109G may then be left for many months without attention. For use the canister is loaded aboard the TEL (transporter/erector/launcher) vehicle, a GD product weighing 33 tons which carries four missile tubes in a single box which can be elevated to the desired launch angle. Each Combat Flight Group comprises four TELs (16 rounds) and two LCCs (launch control centers), the latter also being built into a vehicle, in this case weighing 36 tons largely because of the CBR protection for the crew. Thus the total force will comprise 29 Flights totalling 116 TEL vehicles. These are divided between sites in Britain, West Germany, Belgium, Italy and (possibly) the Netherlands. Britain will house four Flights (64 missiles) at Greenham Common and two Flights at Molesworth. Deployment of what the so-called peace movement calls "cruise" (ignoring the fact that most cruise missiles are Russian) has been made the subject of a gigantic campaign of opposition by European protestors who appear not to understand that, in any time of political crisis, the GLCMs would be driven many miles from their peacetime base to hidden locations in other parts of the host country. Thus, unlike the nuclear bombers which have been parked on NATO airbases for years, these missiles cannot invite retaliation because an enemy could not know their future locations. The scale of the Communist propaganda reaction is a fair measure of this missile's deterrent power.

Left: This cutaway drawing shows main features of the AGM-109I dual-role version of Tomahawk for use by Navy A-6E attack squadrons, with a large anti-ship warhead. Apart from the warhead and the IIR seeker the missile is the same as MRASM (AGM-109H) which dispenses 58 TAAM (tac airfield attack missile) bomblets or delay-action mines.

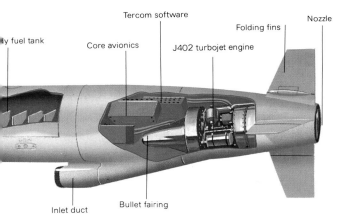

Tercom software · Folding fins · Nozzle · Core avionics · J402 turbojet engine · ly fuel tank · Inlet duct · Bullet fairing

Trident, UGM-93

Origin: Navy and Lockheed Missiles & Space Company, Sunnyvale.
Type: Advanced SLBM (submarine-launched ballistic missile).
Dimensions: Length 34ft 0in (10.36m); body diameter 74in (188cm); (Trident D5 same diameter but longer).
Launch weight: 70,000lb (32,000kg); (D5, about 110,000lb, 50,000kg).
Propulsion: Three tandem stages of advanced solid motors each developed jointly by Thiokol and Hercules, with thrust vectoring; studies by Thiokol (first stage), Hercules (second) and CSD (third) for alternative propellants and nozzle systems.
Guidance: Inertial.
Range: (Trident C4) 4,400 miles (7,100km), (D5) 6,800 miles (11,000km).
Flight speed: Similar to Minuteman.
Warhead: Eight Mk 4 (100kT each) MIRVs, with possibility of using Mk 500 Evader MARV (manoeuvring RV) later; (D5) not known.

Up to 30 extremely large submarines are being built to carry this larger longer-range SLBM system (see warships technical section). Each will have 24 launch tubes for Trident C4, the initial production version. This missile completed its programme of 18 flights from a flat pad on land in 1976-9 and was authorized for production in 1980 at the rate of 72 per year, costing $829m in fiscal year 1981, $906m in 1982 and $743m in 1983. C4 is very like an updated Poseidon making better use of the same size launch tube, and with higher-energy motors, lighter and more accurate guidance and new warheads. The only novel feature is that to reduce drag during the supersonic climb through the atmosphere a long spike is deployed ahead of the bluff nose. So far nine of the giant *Ohio*-class submarines have been ordered, plus long-lead parts for two more. Various factors delayed the lead boat and dramatically inflated its price, but it finally commissioned in November 1981 as SSBN-726, and fired C4 missiles at sea in 1982. To make up for this delayed class 12 existing submarines have been converted to the C4 weapon system at an accelerated pace, all being back in service by 1983.

For nine years a second-generation Trident, D5, has been the subject of intense study. In recent years this has also become known as Trident II, and it has been chosen by Britain to follow the Polaris/Chevaline programme, but in 1983 the D5 missile had not been finalized. Variables include range, throw-weight, warhead, length and diameter, the last two clearly affecting submarine design also. According to British estimates D5 will be both longer and of larger diameter than C4, but will fit the 42ft (12.8m) diameter tubes of the 726 *Ohio* class. The number of warheads has been given as 14 but official US sources insist that the whole programme is still in a

Above: The very first test launch of C4 Trident, from Cape Canaveral on 18 January 1977. Today D5 is becoming more important.

state of flux, despite the fact that IOC (initial operational capability) is hoped to be advanced from 1989 to 1988.

Tow, BGM-71

Origin: Hughes Aircraft, USA.
Type: Heavy anti-tank missile system for vehicles or aircraft.
Propulsion: Hercules K41 boost (0.05s) and sustain (1s) motors.
Dimensions: Length 45.75in (1,162mm); body diameter 6in (152mm); span (wings extended) 13.5in (343mm).
Launch weight: (BGM-71A) 46.1lb (20.9kg).
Range: 1,640 to 12,300ft (500 to 3,750m).
Flight speed: 625mph (1,003km/h).
Warhead: (BGM-71A) Picatinny Arsenal 8.6lb (3.9kg) shaped-charge with 5.3lb (2.4kg) explosive. See text for later.

Often written TOW (Tube-launched, Optically tracked, Wire-guided), this weapon is likely to set an all-time record in the field of guided-missile production.

Prime contractor Hughes Aircraft began work in 1965 to replace the 106mm recoilless rifle. The missile's basic infantry form is supplied in a sealed tube which is clipped to the launcher. The missile tube is attached to the rear of the launch tube, the target sighted and the round fired. The boost charge pops the missile from the tube, firing through lateral nozzles amidships. The four wings indexed at 45° spring open forwards, and the four tail controls flip open rearwards. Guidance commands are generated by the optical sensor in the sight, which continuously measures the position of a light source in the missile relative to the LOS and sends steering commands along twin wires. These drive the helium-pressure actuators working the four tail controls in pairs for pitch and yaw. In 1976 production switched to ER (Extended-Range) Tow with the guidance wires lengthened from 9,842ft (3,000m) to the figure given. Sight field of view reduces from 6° for gathering to 1.5° for smoothing and 0.25° for tracking. The missile electronics pack is between the motor and the warhead.

Tow reached IOC in 1970, was used in Vietnam and the 1973 Middle East war, and has since been produced at a higher rate than any other known missile. The M65 airborne Tow system equips the standard American attack helicopter, the AH-1S TowCobra and the Marines' twin-engine AH-1J and -1T Improved SeaCobra, each with a TSU Telescopic Sight Unit) and two quad launchers. Other countries use Tow systems on the BO 105, Lynx, A109, A129, 500MD and other attack helicopters.

Hughes has developed a mast-mounted sight (MMS) which uses the BAe Tow roof sight but with a TV down-tube, the whole mounted above the rotor hub of the 500MD. In late 1981 production began of the Improved Tow, with a new warhead triggered by a long probe, extended after launch to give 15in (381mm) stand-off distance for greater armor penetration. The shaped-chargehead, with LX-14 filling and a dual-angle deformable liner, is also being retrofitted to many existing rounds. By late 1982 Hughes

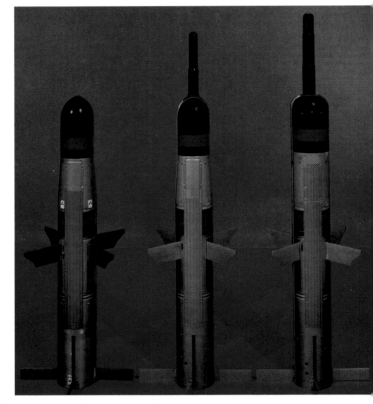

Above: From left, the three main members of the family, Tow, I-Tow (Improved) and the larger Tow 2 now entering production.

was near mass-production of Tow 2, which has several I-Tow improvements plus a new head with the same diameter as the rest of the missile with a mass of 13lb (5.9kg) and an even longer (21.25in, 540mm) extensible probe, calculated to defeat all tanks of the 1990s. Flight performance is maintained by a new double-base motor giving about 30 per cent greater total impulse. Both new missiles are for air-launch applications. By 1983 Tow output exceeded 320,000.

Walleye, AGM-62

Origin: Martin Marietta, USA.
Type: Glide bomb with TV guidance.
Propulsion: None.
Dimensions: Length (I) 135in (3.44m), (II) 159in (4.04m); body diameter (I) 12.5in (317mm), (II) 18in (457mm); span (I) 45.5in (1.16m), (II) 51in 1.3m).
Launch weight: (I) 1,100lb (499kg), (II) 2,400lb (1,089kg).
Range: (I) 16 miles (26km), (II) 35 miles (56km).
Flight speed: Subsonic.
Warhead: (I) 825lb (374kg), (II) based on Mk 84 bomb.

An unpowered glide bomb with TV guidance, AGM-62 Walleye was developed from 1963 by the NOTS at China Lake, assisted from 1964 by the Naval Avionics Facility. Intended to overcome the aircraft-vulnerability hazard of visual radio-command ASMs, Walleye quickly proved successful, and in January 1966 Martin was awarded the first production contract. This was later multiplied, and in November 1967 the need for Walleye in SE Asia resulted in Hughes Aircraft being brought in as second-source. In 1969 the Navy described this missile as "The most accurate and effective air-to-surface conventional weapon ever developed anywhere". Walleye I has a cruciform of long-chord delta wings with elevons, a gyro stabilized TV vidicon camera in the nose, and ram-air windmill at the tail to drive the alternator and hydraulic pump. The pilot or operating crew-member identifies the target, if necessary using aircraft radar, aims the missile camera at it, focuses it and locks it to the target using a monitor screen in the cockpit. The aircraft can then release the missile and turn away from the target, though it must keep the radio link with the missile. In theory the missile should glide straight to the target, but the launch operator has the ability to break into the control loop and, watching his monitor screen, guide it manually into the target. In 1968 the Navy funded several developments—Update Walleye, Walleye II, Fat Albert and Large-Scale Walleye among them—which led to the enlarged Walleye II (Mk 5 Mod 4) for use against larger targets. In production by 1974, Walleye II was deleted from the budget the following year and replaced by the first procurement of ER/DL (Extended Range/Data-Link) Walleye II (Mk 13 Mod O). the ER/DL system was originally planned in 1969 to allow a launch-and-leave technique at greater distance from the target, the missile having larger wings to improve

Above: Walleye I on test under an A-7 at China Lake in 1969. This missile has no propulsion but excellent guidance.

the glide ratio, and the radio data-link allowing the operator to release the missile towards the target and then, when the missile was much closer, acquire the target on his monitor screen, focus the camera and lock it on. Operations in SE Asia showed that it would be preferable to use two aircraft, the first to release the Walleye (if possible already locked on the approximate target position) and then escape and the second, possibly miles to one side, to update the lock-on point and monitor the approach to the target. Since 1978 about 1,400 Walleye I and 2,400 Walleye II missiles have been converted to ER/DL.

WAAM

Origin: Various company studies, USA.

Since the late 1970s the WAAM (Wide-Area Anti-armor Munitions) programme has been the greatest part of the USAF's largest basic research effort into future tactical weapons. It runs parallel to the USA's Tank Breaker, which—though airborne sensors and illuminators play a major role—is for missiles fired from ground launchers. WAAM, often written and spoken Vaam, comprises the Wasp missile, ERAM (Eram) and ACM. Eram, Extended-Range Anti-armor Mine, is an ambitious programme in which —at least until mid-1982—Honeywell and Avco were in competition. Most of the proposals are classified but in spring 1982 Avco was permitted to reveal its Skeet submunition, part of the Eram effort, clusters of which

are carried in the USAF SUU-65 dispenser, as well as in the Vought T-22 Assault Breaker bus vehicle. Each Skeet warhead comprises a cylindrical body with four curved stabilizer fins flicked open as the payload is separated from the delivery vehicle. At the same time an offset unstreamlined mass called a wobble arm is extended from one side of the body, causing an oscillating motion which makes the IR sensor in the nose sweep over an area "the size of a US football field". A microprocessor converts images into steering commands until the warhead is directly over an armored vehicle, whereupon the warhead fires straight down through the thin top armor. The transverse disc of explosive accelerates a lens of dense metal ahead of it so violently it is converted into an SFF (self-forging fragment) with a streamlined shape moving at some 9,000ft/s (2,750m/s) to pass straight through the armor. Any warhead failing to acquire a target switches into either a low-altitude airburst mode or a run-over mine on the ground.

Wasp

Origin: Hughes Aircraft, USA.
Type: Wide-area anti-armor munitions (see WAAM).
Propulsion: Solid boost motor with 1st burn through central nozzle, two solid sustainers with diagonal lateral nozzles, fired in sequence.
Dimensions: (approximate) Length 59in (1.5m); body diameter 8in (203mm); span (wings and fins when extended) about 20in (508mm).
Launch weight: 105lb (48kg).
Range: Several miles.
Flight speed: (Constant) high subsonic.
Warhead: Hollow charge of full forebody diameter firing jet through central hole in electronics/guidance unit.

By far the most advanced in timing of the various USAF WAAM research programmes, Wasp progressed to an industrial competition between Hughes and Boeing which was won by the former in March 1982. Described as "The first ASM ever developed with the ability to identify and aim itself at tactical targets" Wasp fills the vital requirement of being cheap enough to deploy in swarms (hence the name) in a fire-and-forget mode while the launch aircraft stays safely out of sight behind a hill and away from the land battle area. The missile has a classic configuration with large delta wings and rear rectangular control fins, but with the difference that all surfaces flick open after firing from a launch tube. The standard launcher is about the size of a 370-US gal drop tank, weighing almost 2,000lb (900kg). It has six tubes, each loaded with two missiles. That in the rear of each tube is protected by an exhaust deflector which diverts the boost-motor blast of that in front out through side ports. Clear of the tube, the missile climbs from treetop height to its cruise altitude at a steady high speed. It levels off and its millimetre-wave (94GHz) pulsed radar seeker sweeps up to 45° off-axis looking for metal targets. Trials with the homing head mounted in a pod under a Sabreliner at Eglin AFB in 1982 "showed that the seeker repeatedly found the targets while flying over strong ground clutter". All

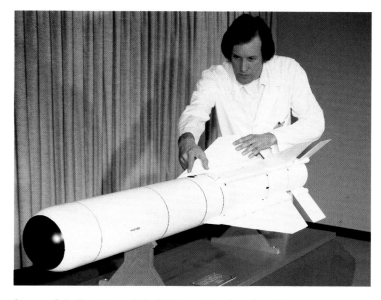

Above: A full-scale model of Wasp, showing that it has aerodynamic kinship with Falcon and Maverick missiles.

12 rounds in a pod can be fired in twos. The F-16 normally carries two pods, as can the Harrier, Jaguar, Mirage 5 and Alpha Jet; the F-111, A-10 and Tornado would normally carry four. Flight testing began in November 1982, and the program has been so successful that a production decision could be taken in late 1983.

The US-Soviet Balance

John M. Collins, **Senior Specialist in National Defense, Library of Congress.**

Research assistants: Thomas P. Glakas and Elizabeth Ann Severns.

AMERICAN military competence spanned a much larger functional and geographic sphere in support of security interests than Soviet armed services could cover for the Kremlin before the Cuban missile crisis in 1962. US forces have registered many improvements since that time, but their relative decline has been dramatic when compared with Soviet counterparts.

President Kennedy told Moscow in 1962 to remove its ballistic missiles from Cuba or face US military action. Soviet Premier Khrushchev complied. President Carter, who flatly stated that "the status quo is not acceptable", *asked* Moscow to remove its combat brigade in October 1979, and Soviet President Brezhnev refused. Those confrontations, of course, are not strictly analogous, but the shift in strength since the first showdown has clearly reinforced US risks around the world and reduced America's room for maneuver.

This chapter sketches the situation in 1960 before the Soviet buildup began, depicts the present balance, and identifies some significant issues for US defense decisionmakers.

Balance before the Cuban Missile Crisis

The US/Soviet military balance was not bad from the US standpoint in 1960. That country's deterrent threats and defensive contingents were credible in most respects.

America's main aim, called containment, accepted the status quo at that time. It lacked means to retake lost territory, but US military services, in concert with allies, were sufficient to safeguard the Free World from Soviet armed aggression.

Strategic Air Command (SAC) possessed unparalleled powers, when ballistic missiles on both sides were neither numerous nor very accurate. Its bombers could burst through the pervious Shield erected around Russia's rim but the small force of Soviet Bears and Bisons would have found US defenses-in-depth much more difficult. Medium-range Badgers could strike American targets on one-way suicide missions only if they flew high to conserve fuel. That shortcoming kept them vulnerable, in full view of US and Canadian surveillance systems. SAC's "short-legged" B-47s, which were forward-based or programmed for in-flight refueling, could make fairly lengthy low-level bomb runs beneath Soviet radar fans and below the best fields of fire for their surface-to-air missiles (SAMs).

Nuclear supremacy also underpinned US strategy in Europe. No pressing Soviet military threat was apparent in other theaters. Moscow could not employ medium- and intermediate-range ballistic missiles (MRBMs, IRBMs) against NATO's tempting center sector without risking retaliatory strikes against critical targets in Russia. NATO, conversely, could tolerate conventional inferiority in land formations, because theater nuclear weapons still could take up the slack.

Inflexible Soviet forces were clearly outclassed in every other category. US tactical air forces were far superior to Soviet Frontal Aviation, which promised poor support for fast-moving offensive operations if Red Army

logistics failed to fold first. Gorshkov's coastal navy could not yet contest US control of the seas. His submarines might have been able to cut American lines of communication to Europe, but with minor implications, because NATO's reinforcement and resupply requirements reputedly were of reduced moment. Massive nuclear retaliation could conclude any conflict quickly, according to US concepts, without resort to costly attrition in the air or on the ground.

In short, US armed services, assisted by allies, held Soviet forces in check across the conflict spectrum. Reserves were on tap to contend with contingencies where the Kremlin could not reach.

The Balance in 1983

Few trends that typify the US/Soviet military balance from America's perspective have been positive for the past two decades.

Strategic Nuclear Trends

US nuclear capabilities have passed through three distinct stages since 1960. Each was less adaptable than its predecessor.

The current version features far fewer realistic options than those evident 20 years ago, largely because the US now lacks any credible means of controlling escalation and can no longer protect either the American people or production base. US threats of massive retaliation comprised a believable brake when coupled with nuclear superiority. Bluff plays a much bigger part today.

US intercontinental ballistic missiles (ICBMs) and bombers are more vulnerable to attack than ever before. That condition erodes national security, even though no current combination of Soviet assaults could smother the two systems simultaneously. Soviet counterparts are comparatively secure, because the US subscribes to a second-strike strategy. Submarine-launched ballistic missiles (SLBMs) on both sides are still safe at sea, given the current state of the art in antisubmarine warfare (ASW), although that situation conceivably could change with little notice.

Intercontinental Ballistic Missiles

The present and projected balance between US and Soviet ICBMs creates two central consequences. One involves the pre-launch survival of undefended American missiles. The other concerns comparative capabilities to attack and destroy land-based ICBMs.

Pre-Launch Survival Prospects

Most authorities agree that Soviet ICBMs pose substantial threats to Titan and Minuteman missiles in the 1980s. The key questions are not *whether* the Soviets could eventually crush them with a first strike, only *when* they could achieve that capability, and how seriously that situation affects US security.

Installing more US ICBMs would prove impractical, because the Soviets could add hard-target warheads much faster than the United States could build silos and fill them with missiles, at a fraction of the cost. Reinforcing US silos faces finite limitations, even if tech-

Note: This chapter was originally published as Issue Brief No. IB78029 of the Library of Congress Congressional Research Service.

254

Far left: The Soviet soldier is a conscript; hardy, tough, well-trained in a limited field, and well disciplined. He will fight with great determination for a cause he believes to be correct, especially in defense of his Motherland. On the other hand the Soviet Army suffers from all the problems of conscription, allied to the complications posed by the USSR's multi-ethnic, multi-lingual composition.
Left: The US soldier is a regular, and is also capable of being as tough and as hardy as any in the world, if properly led and motivated. His training, especially in the technological field, is superior.
Below: The overall balance is probed, with varying degrees of sublety, every day, on land, or on under the sea, and in the air.

nical problems attendant to "super hardening" can be solved. Launch-on-warning would improve survivability only if the US alert system remained intact. Should it fail for any reason, including Soviet action, chances are slim that any decision to launch could be made, much less implemented, in the few minutes available.

Substituting some sort of deceptive, semi-mobile land-based missile system for all or part of US stationary ICBMs, therefore, is under active advisement. Costs would be considerable, but, because mobile missiles are more difficult to hit than those in silos, there would be no need to replace Minutemen on a one-for-

Left: The missiles of the USA's strategic forces. The mighty Titan II has a 9MT warhead, but has been in service for many years; only 52 remain and these will be replaced in the next few years. Minuteman I was the progenitor of the current fleet but is now used only for test purposes, the US having standardized on the Minuteman II and III, of which 1,000 are in service. The Mark 12A warhead for Minuteman III has 3 MIRVs, each with a 350KT yield and a CEP of 0. The picture above shows Minuteman ICBMs being launched from silos.

Below: The two types of US SLBMs in service are the Poseidon C-3, and Trident C-4. Poseidon mounts 10 50KT MIRVs, and Trident 8 of 100KT. Accuracy is much less than that of land-launched warheads, and CEP is 0.3nm making them counter-value weapons.

Titan II   Minuteman I   Minuteman III   Poseidon   Trident

SS-9 Scarp

one basis. Closely-spaced (dense pack) basing that depends on "fratricide" effects for prelaunch survival, is another candidate.

Deterrent properties of all concepts under consideration proliferate, rather than remove, aim points. Rivals, faced with prospects of expending huge numbers of nuclear weapons without assurance of preventing US response, presumably would find risk-versus-gain ratios poor. Should that assumption, however, prove false, the side effects of saturation attacks, especially fallout, could create more problems than they solve.

The search for a faster, cheaper, more

Left and below: Soviet missiles are generally much larger than those of the USA, because the Russians have tried to make up for a lack of accuracy by more powerful warheads. There are very few SS-9s left, but some 570 SS-11s, each with 3 MRVs, are still deployed. The main Soviet ICBM force is now more or less standardized on SS-17 (150 in service), SS-18 (308) and SS-19 (310). SS-16 is still something of an enigma as it was a fully mobile ICBM and caused great alarm in US strategic circles. The Soviets agreed at SALT-II not to deploy it, although the top two sections are used as SS-20. Soviet SLBMs include SS-N-6 and SS-N-8; nobody in the West has seen SS-N-17/18.

SS-11 Sego   SS-N-6 Sawfly   SS-16   SS-17   SS-N-8   SS-18   SS-19

Above: The Tupolev Tu-22M (Backfire) is a capable aircraft, but does not seriously affect the strategic nuclear balance.

effective fix thus may remain in the offing. Fresh looks at free mobility models, land, sea and air, could be among the options.

Countersilo Capabilities

America's ICBMs, constrained by a second-strike strategy, could not match Moscow's countersilo capabilities, even if the United States deployed bigger missiles, more multiple independently targetable reentry vehicles (MIRVs), and greater accuracy.

Should the Soviets, after conducting a first strike, choose to launch reserve ICBMs on warning, US warheads could not destroy them before they took flight. Such action actually could invite additional devastation in the United States. Catching a few Soviet reserves in their silos and preventing refirings from "cold launch" facilities would afford slight comfort in such circumstances. "Essential equivalence", in short, would remain elusive even if US and Soviet ICBM holdings were precisely the same in quantities and technical characteristics at this exact moment.

Strategic Air Power

The US accent on strategic air power is still strong. Soviet stress has been slight since the Cuban missile crisis, although supersonic Backfire bombers, which began to deploy in 1975, cause increasing controversy. The present

Below left: When Titans are withdrawn from service only six ICBM fields will remain unless MX basing issues are resolved.
Below right: Strategic bomber and tanker airfields are more widely dispersed.

bomber balance affects US force requirements in two significant ways: one concerns perceptions; the other concerns security.

Backfire Bombers Related to US Bombers

Soviet Backfire bombers may have some bearing on US needs for improved air defense, but are unrelated to reciprocal offensive force requirements. Backfire squadrons, which currently contribute less to Soviet strategic nuclear capabilities than forward-based fighters add to that of the United States, could double in number or disappear without diluting any advantages that accrue from Strategic Air Command's aircraft. Manned bombers may indeed be a legitimate leg of the US triad, but maintaining superiority, essential equivalence, or any other balance with Backfires would serve some symbolic purpose, nothing more.

Bombers Replaced by Cruise Missiles

President Carter on June 30, 1977, disclosed his decision to cancel prospective production of B-1 bombers, which were scheduled to strengthen the US triad in the 1980s. The Pentagon anticipates converting 151 B-52Gs to carry 20 air-launched cruise missiles (ALCMs) apiece, for a total of 3,020 weapons. Only about 75 B-52s will be modernized to improve penetration probabilities against future Soviet surface-to-air missiles (SAMs) and interceptor aircraft.

Implications of that determination are subject to debate. Cruise missile technology tactics are still uncertain. Proposed B-52 modification programs present many problems. Most important, abilities of US ALCMs to penetrate Soviet defenses-in-depth is in dispute.

In the final analysis, therefore, US security will be well served by substituting ALCMs for aircraft only if satisfactory capabilities can be deployed at acceptable costs in time to support

stated strategy. If not, America's deterrent could suffer. (The Reagan administration has decided to put 100 B-1Bs into SAC inventory from 1986; see entry in aircraft section. — *Editor.*)

Strategic Defense Problems

CONUS (Continental United States) defense plays no serious part in US nuclear strategy. Deterrence depends almost entirely on powers to survive preemptive strikes, then savage the aggressor. The Soviets conversely seek to develop credible safeguards. A "vulnerability gap" of disputed proportions consequently grows.

Analysts at one end of the spectrum contend that Soviet air and civil defense abilities, abetted by detailed plans, psychological conditioning, and physical preparations, already degrade US deterrence and place America in peril. Some noted US specialists speculate that crisis relocation procedures would limit Soviet fatalities to 4 or 5 per cent during a general war, under worst-case conditions. Official estimates indicate that almost half the American people would die, and another 35 million would require medical attention. If those casualty ratios were even close to correct, US capability to deter attack would indeed be "a myth", as some claim, since US deterrence is predicated on an "assured destruction" capability, meaning the ability to inflict unacceptable damage on an aggressor.

Skeptics draw less drastic conclusions. Most concede that the Kremlin stresses city defense, but doubt that US deterrence is in danger. One faction, for example, sees this as a spurious issue. Its followers believe that nuclear blasts can break through the best protection. Others, whose opinions are widely shared, suspect that Soviet defensive capabilities, while significant, are overstated. US over-reaction, they contend,

ICBM Missile Fields in the USA

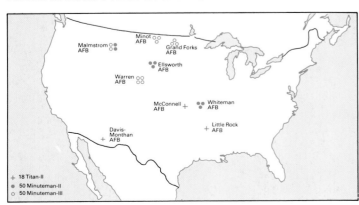

+ 18 Titan-II
● 50 Minuteman-II
○ 50 Minuteman-III

Strategic Aircraft Bases in the USA

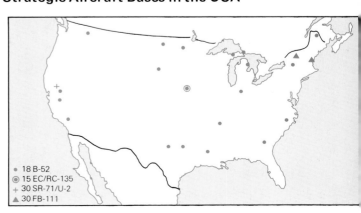

● 18 B-52
◉ 15 EC/RC-135
+ 30 SR-71/U-2
▲ 30 FB-111

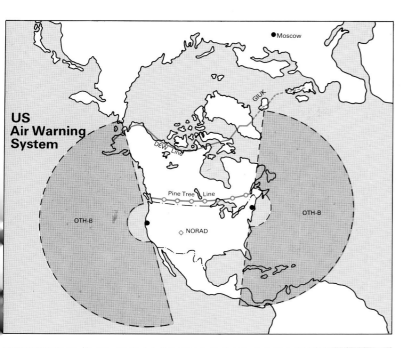

US Air Warning System

Left: Because Soviet bombers flying at low altitude could probably penetrate undetected through radar coverage gaps in Canada and the ocean approaches the US DoD is experimenting with Over-the-Horizon-Backscatter (OTH-B) radars. Funding has been planned through 1982–86 with IOCs in 1984 and 1986. The gaps are in the Pine Tree Line long-range radars and it is considered that the aging DEW-line stations could also be bypassed. Options for improvement being considered are an enhanced Distant Early Warning Line (EDEW) and a northwards-looking OTH-B although the Aurora Borealis may well cause insuperable electro-magnetic problems. AWACS aircraft will, of course, have a vital role to play in giving early warning of air intruders.

Below left: US satellites over the Indian Ocean would give warning of Soviet ICBM launches within 90 seconds of blast-off, but would lose sight of missiles before the penetration aids separated, where BMEWS would take over to track and identify re-entry vehicles coming in from the North. PARCS would warn of the number of RVs and estimate their impact points. Satellites and PAVE PAWS would warn of SLBM attack and there is improved coverage of the threat from the Caribbean and FOBS attack from the south. The US Navy's Space Surveillance System (SPASUR) stretches across the southern USA.

Below: One of the great and unceasing battles fought every day in peace takes place under the oceans. It is not just a rehearsal for what might happen in war; it is essential in establishing submarine deployment patterns to give warning of any variations which might indicate warlike intent. In this, the USA has an undoubted advantage over the USSR in that it has more friendly bases, and more allies prepared to cooperate in this ASW activity. Ocean-floor sonar arrays are used to cover the east and west seaboards of the USA and to cover the major choke points in the Caribbean, the north-west Pacific and in the GIUK gap. The considerable coverage given by these systems is increased by the ASW aircraft of the USA and its allies. It must not be thought, however, that this all gives a complete and thoroughly effective submarine warning and detection system. In reality the oceans are a curious medium whose behaviour is both variable and, in many instances, little understood. Vast sums are spent on oceanographic research and on ever-more sophisticated and expensive monitoring systems, but the great breakthrough in ASW has yet to be made. Indeed, some would argue that, so long as ASW is imprecise and SSBNs cannot be detected, then the balance of terror will be maintained.

US Missile Warning System

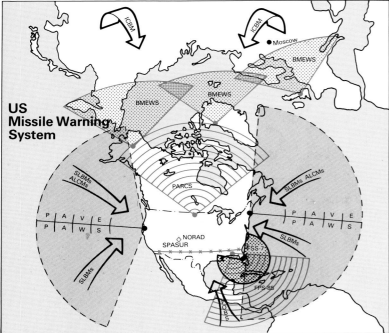

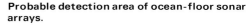

Estimated location of US and allied ocean-floor sonar arrays.

Probable detection area of ocean-floor sonar arrays.

Estimated additional coverage given by US Navy P-3 Orion ASW aircraft.

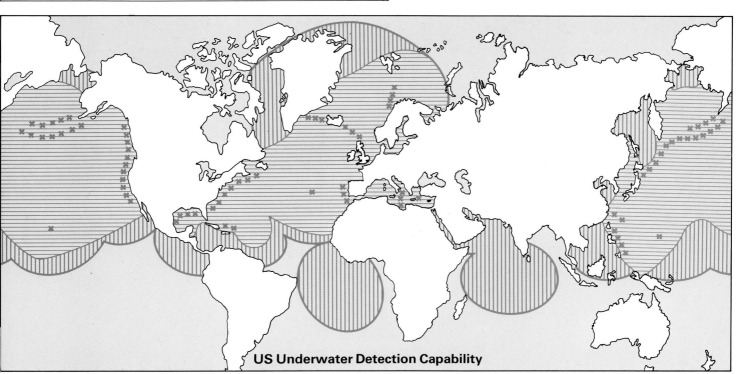

US Underwater Detection Capability

259

could be just as ruinous as complacency.

Nevertheless, students of the subject seem to agree that Soviet active and passive defenses in combination *are* beginning to create a survivability imbalance that favors the Soviets. Assertions that they soon could survive a general war appear premature, but long-term consequences could be severe if the trend proceeds too far. Civil defense would assume a completely different connotation, if accompanied by Soviet breakthroughs in antisubmarine or antiballistic missile warfare. Active defense in that case would become the primary shield. Civil defense, as part of a strategic defensive triad, would simply serve as a backstop.

Any amalgam that allowed the Soviets to evade "assured destruction", while America still could not, would, in fact, allow them to satisfy the true aim of strategy, which is "not so much to seek battle as to seek a . . . situation so advantageous that if it does not of itself produce the desired decision, its continuation by a battle is sure to achieve this".

Stated succinctly, the side that solves defensive equations first would attain true nuclear superiority, expressed in terms of survival prospects despite the rival's raw destructive power. Supremacy without defense appears to be unattainable regardless of offensive numbers, as long as each side can devastate or destroy the other.

General Purpose Force Trends
US general purpose forces have developed quite differently from Soviet counterparts.

Soviet leaders, who implicitly prefer a principle of war called "mass", rarely reduce force levels, and winnow out stocks only when they cease to serve useful purposes. US defense decisionmakers are partial to "economy of force". Quality, not quantity, has been considered essential. America's armed services consequently are cut severely after every war. Outmoded weapons customarily retire when new ones enter the inventory.

Soviet strength thus dilates, even when US strength declines. US quality at this stage can no longer compensate completely for the lack of flexibility caused by quantitative inferiority.

Huge conscript ground forces are the traditional source of Soviet general purpose force strength. Other services are subsidiary, despite the emergence of a modern air force and navy. The much smaller US Army and Marine Corps currently consist of volunteers. Quantitative gaps that favor the Soviet Union are great in nearly every category.

US Strengths
The US Army has access to firepower unprecedented in the past. Tanks with stabilized turrets and night sights can attack targets on the move, in daylight or darkness. What they see, they can generally stop. TOW antitank weapons not only exceed the range of Soviet tank cannons, but possess penetration powers that outpaced opposing armor by the mid-1970s.

Improved artillery ammunition can cause up to four times as many personnel casualties per round as conventional high explosives could in past conflicts. Projectiles with time-delay submunitions extend suppression capabilities for protracted periods after impact. Laser range finders for forward observers reduce target estimation errors from 400 meters to about 10, hugely increasing probabilities of first-round hits. Response times have been cut from minutes to seconds. Precision-guided artillery projectiles, when perfected, should cause a quantum jump in destructive power. Land mine lethality has increased dramatically in the last decade.

US Shortcomings
There are points, however, beyond which mass matters more than excellence. The US Army has just 16 active divisions. The Marine Corps has three. A fourth of the Army divisions lack one regular brigade. Others lack one or more active maneuver battalions. Readiness is reduced, even though reserve component "roundouts" train part time with Regular Army divisions. Only a few of those 19 divisions can be made available for contingency purposes without slighting commitments and spreading the force very thin.

Eight Army National Guard and one Marine Corps Reserve divisions complete the US complement of major maneuver units. Six to eight weeks would be needed to bring armored and mechanized divisions up to minimum combat standards and otherwise ready them for deployment following calls to Federal service in a national emergency, which can be designated only by the President or Congress. Consequently, they are poorly prepared to participate in any "come as you are party", such as those contemplated by the US Rapid Deployment Force (RDF).

Soviet ground forces, in contrast, retain a comfortable cushion of reserves that could create multiple contingencies on call. Six airborne divisions in first-class shape afford special flexibility. US decisionmakers would find it difficult to determine priorities if the Politburo brought things to a boil around Berlin, encouraged a crisis in Korea, and simultaneously made military motions toward the Middle East. Successful feints could spoil US plans to support friends under fire, or forestall action until too late, if the US President and his advisers feared that premature commitment of divisions in strategic reserve would expose the true point of decision.

Soviet Air Defences

★ Air Force Div/Reg HQs   PVO Concentrations   ● Space/Missile Complexes

Above: The USSR has the largest air defense system in the world, but it also has by far the largest area to cover.

Deployment of Soviet ICBMs

Above: There are about 30 missile fields in the USSR which generally follow the line of the Trans-Siberian railway.

Doctrinal Dilemmas

Few forces, coupled with second-strike, selective containment policies, dictate a defensive doctrine for the US Army at the onset of any conflict against numerically superior Soviet forces or the Warsaw Pact. US commanders until recently were advised to concentrate winning combinations at proper times and places, "using reserves from the rear" and forces "from less threatened flanks", which would remain lightly covered. Should concentration occur at the wrong spot, the mission was to redirect mobile elements immediately. Delaying actions, the most difficult of all ground combat operations, would have been in demand.

Critics, who deplore doctrinal accommoda-tions of that sort, suggested that US decision-makers would do well to "redesign . . . our military force posture and possibly our diplomatic commitments", rather than encourage a "can-do" attitude in the Army that risked almost certain defeat if committed against massed Soviet forces in Europe or the Middle East. Instead, the US Army and Air Force are developing a new doctrine called AirLand Battle, which calls for interdiction operations deep in Soviet rear areas. The intent is to destroy, disrupt, or delay Soviet second, third, and successive echelons before they can expand initial penetrations. Whether the wherewithal will be available by 1986 (the tentative implementing date) is open to dispute.

Tactical Air Force Problems

America's tactical air combat assets furnish flexibility not available to the Soviet Union, whose Frontal Aviation (roughly equivalent to US Tactical Air Command, US Air Force Europe, and Pacific Air Force) is largely confined to the Eurasian land mass. A clear US qualitative edge is still evident in most respects, although the gap is closing.

Small size, however, creates an "Achilles heel" for America. A fairly small proportion of its active forces remain unfettered. Reserves can respond in most cases only after congressional approval. US tactical air combat power consequently could cope with a single large-scale conflict against any non-Soviet foe, but critical interests elsewhere could start to become uncovered.

Quantitative shortages could prove critical in a showdown with the Soviet Union, since "many-on-one" seems to be Moscow's rule. The few US aircraft, compared with Frontal Aviation, will find it increasingly perilous to compete if current trends continue. Soviet mobile air defenses further undercut US capabilities.

Projected US procurement programs will do little to brighten the picture before the mid-1980s at best.

General Purpose Navy Problems

Sea power is a necessity for the United States. Soviet naval needs, by and large, are less compelling.

Commerce, always a US tradition, assumes a salient role as dwindling natural resources increase dependence on other countries for critical supplies. Petroleum products are most

Left: The recent order for the B-1B armed with ALCMs will cause the USSR to look again to its air defense systems, and has already generated new developments in fighter, missile and radar coverage.

Below: The nightmare that haunts every US strategist: an incoming Soviet ICBM bus starting to deploy Multiple, Independently Targetted Re-entry Vehicles (MIRVs) on a first-strike attack against the USA.

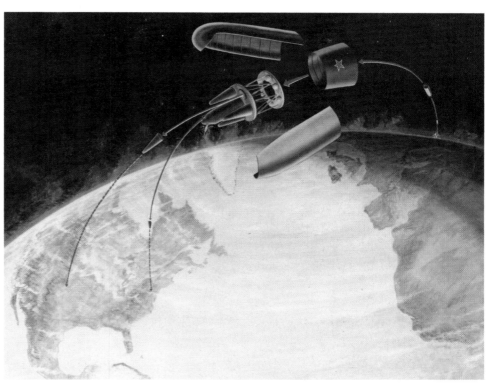

publicized, but foreign minerals are also important to America. Routes must therefore be secured for friendly merchant ships under adverse conditions. Essential sea lines of communication must also be kept open in wartime to ensure the free flow of military forces and logistic support between America, its allies, and/or contested areas.

The Soviet Union, with far fewer requirements for foreign raw materials and intrinsic interests that center on the Eurasian land mass, has only recently begun to break out of its continental cocoon. Its Navy is still cast as a spoiler that emphasizes negative sea denial, rather than positive sea assertion capabilities.

The "New" Soviet Navy

The modern Soviet Navy is an innovative Service consciously designed to serve Soviet purposes rather than match its US counterpart. Its focus since the early 1960s has shifted from coastal defense to sea-based deterrence in peacetime and power projection in event of nuclear war. Such a transformation in such a short space of time is close to unprecedented.

The "new" Soviet Navy suffers from several chronic shortcomings that it shares with the "old". All Soviet surface ships, for example, would have to contend with lack of air cover if they swept far from friendly shores. Land-based bombers for area defense are poor substitutes for defenses-in-depth that feature carrier-based fighters, disallowing some specialized circumstances.

Soviet naval forces are also short on stamina, except for late-model ships such as *Kirov*. *Kiev*, *Kara*, and *Krivak*. Small surface combatants, lacking large fuel capacities or nuclear power, have limited ranges. Restricted space for rations, ammunition, and other stores prohibit prolonged operations without resupply. Merchant tankers routinely refuel Soviet ships at sea, and trawlers serve some logistic purposes, but underway replenishment procedures are substandard compared with US skills. Lengthy, large-scale operations would be risky in sea areas remote from friendly port facilities.

Strengths, however, may well outweigh those weaknesses.

Tactical strike capabilities of the new Soviet Navy center on cruise missiles, which Fleet Admiral Sergei G. Gorshkov feels are "practically unstoppable" against floating targets. As he sees it, not even well-screened, nuclear-powered aircraft carriers could withstand assaults "delivered by a group of ships armed with cruise missiles".

Soviet attack submarines outnumber US contingents by more than 3:1. Most are diesel-powered, and many are well past their prime, but 68 were fitted to fire anti-ship cruise missiles in January 1982. Tubes totalled 538. Papa and Charlie classes can shoot from submerged positions. All classes carry torpedoes for close combat. Forty-four US submarines mounted 176 Harpoon launchers. They are substantially outranged.

Cruise Missile Threat to US Surface Navy

More than 20 sorts of Soviet surface warships, submarines, and aircraft carry at least one kind of cruise missile. Soviet strategy seems designed to seize and secure initiative with a single killing salvo. Missile-carrying surface ships, submarines, and aircraft, moving without tactical formation, could trigger surprise, preemptive strikes on signal, converging on targets from many directions, and perhaps from point-blank range.

US sea control tactics traditionally try to

Above: SS-N-3 Shaddock was the first effective sea-launched cruise missile in the Soviet Navy; it has a nuclear warhead with a yield in the kiloton range.

Right: Bow shot of a Soviet Navy Kashin-class "large ASW ship". The heavy armament and comprehensive electronic outfit are clearly seen, but should not be considered superior to those of an equivalent warship of the US or other Western navies.

destroy enemy weapons before they endanger friendly ships. First strike assaults by Soviet cruise missiles, launched at close range, could make that approach obsolete.

The US Navy as yet has no satisfactory solution under less stringent circumstances. Current ship-launched SAMs would be essentially ineffective against concerted attacks. The time from detection to target engagement is excessive and coordination among missile batteries on different ships will remain poor until cruisers armed with the Aegis replace present systems. These difficulties are compounded by SAM vulnerability to electronic counter-measures. Even Phoenix-armed F-14s, which can engage six targets simultaneously, are subject to saturation unless they catch attacking

Left: Charlie class SSGN running on the surface. The latest version has a new cruise missile (SS-N-9) with a range of more than 60nm (111km).

Below: A Nimitz-class nuclear-powered attack carrier underway. These warships carry what amounts to a small tactical air force; the Soviets have nothing so far to compare, though 60,000-ton carriers are now building.

enemy aircraft before missile loads are launched. The three-layered defense-in-depth designed to improve US posture substantially will not be in place for several more years.

Threats to Merchant Shipping

Successful ASW operations depend on abilities to find, fix, and finish enemy undersea raiders before they can wreak heavy damage. Prospects for US success are more favorable than they were a few years ago, but breakthroughs in detection are still in the blueprint stage. Beyond that, the small size of America's specialized force causes concern. ASW is mainly a time-consuming matter of attrition, in which numbers count more and more as friendly losses mount. Some authorities conclude that America might at most sink 20 per cent of all opposing submarines before the Soviets took serious toll among merchantmen. Consequently, Soviet capacities to interfere with US lifelines at sea could prove to be low-cost, low-risk operations under certain circumstances, at least as long as a "Mexican standoff" persists at strategic nuclear levels.

The Upshot

America's Navy, which matches a three-ocean mission with a one-and-a-half-ocean capability, is marginally capable of carrying out its mission in support of national strategy. Its forces are stretched so thin that further peacetime forward deployments could be attained only at great expense to personnel and equipment by drawing down reserves to a dangerous extent or uncovering existing commitments. Wartime attrition is an unpropitious prospect.

Serious students of naval strategy sum up the current situation with one succinct statement: the US Navy had entered an era of reduced options and reinforced risk by the mid-1970s.

Amphibious Abilities

The US Marine Corps, with a total personnel strength slightly exceeding 190,000, comprises three active and one reserve divisions, together with associated air wings and combat/service support. The closest Soviet counterpart, six naval infantry regiments, contain approximately 2,000 men each, with minimum fire support.

Above: The battlecruiser *Kirov*, a heavily armed and flexible ship, and a deliberate challenge to the US Navy. The Soviets, however, have had little experience of naval strategic operations compared to the US.

Above left: Soviet aircraft carrier *Kiev* with four Hormone ASW helicopters and a single Yak-36 Forger aircraft aft. Unlike US carriers these Soviet ships are heavily armed surface warships in their own right.

Comparative power projection possibilities, however, are not quite as lopsided as that picture seems to paint.

US amphibious assault abilities are strictly abridged by the shortage of specialized sealift. Current assets are confined to 61 ships, of which 15 per cent are normally in overhaul. That level is sufficient for short-notice landings by battalions and brigades, but a single Marine division/wing team would absorb all but four operational ships, which are scattered from Manila to the Mediterranean. Lead times for assembly would be long, and combat losses

irreplaceable. Prepositioned supplies on ships alleviate lift requirements to some extent, but are no substitute for amphibious assault capabilities.

Amphibious sealift for Soviet naval infantry features coastal landing craft, along with the *Ivan Rogov* (an LPD) and 25 LSTs. That shortcoming makes long-distance operations unfeasible for the full force, but the combination is well suited for commando-style raids and amphibious assaults close to Soviet flanks. Reinforcements, if required, could arrive on merchant ships.

Mobility Trends
Intercontinental lift over open oceans is a US essential. Russian requirements thus far have been more regional. Dissimilar demands, coupled with policy peculiarities and geographic circumstance, consequently foster mobility force structures that are quite different in size as well as composition.

US Airlift Problems
America's air mobility means are still peerless, in large part because the Defense Department has accentuated "airlift enhancement" programs since the early 1960s. Soviet counterparts are improving, but present capabilities are comparable only along that country's periphery.

Still, 70 C-5As, the only aircraft that can carry outsize cargo (209,000lb/94,800kg maximum load), constrain US abilities to meet NATO reinforcement/resupply schedules or to support Rapid Deployment Forces, say, in the Middle East. They are complemented by 234 C-141s. A "stretch" program, completed in July 1982, increased payload capacity from 53,600 to 91,380lb (24,310 to 41,450kg). All C-5s and C-141s now can be refueled in flight. US decision-makers plan to procure 50 C-5Bs during the period 1983–87, but no additional C-141s. Losses from combat attrition or maintenance failures thus will remain irreplaceable as long as assembly lines stay "cold".

US tactical airlift assets, long the world's best, are showing signs of age. Nothing now in the mill will improve that posture appreciably.

US Sealift Problems
US sealift consistently gets short shrift. Interest in the 1960s centered on quick reaction instead of sustained support, but few funds were forthcoming for forces afloat, even for that purpose. Assets, which reached their apogee during World War II, consequently have been on a downhill slide for three decades.

The conversion has been from many ships to few; from military ships to civilian carriers; from US ships to foreign flags; from general cargo to container ships; from small, adaptable ships to large ones whose applications are limited. America's "mothball" fleet, which served well during the Vietnam War, is seriously depleted. Those trends in combination make it unfeasible for Military Sealift Command (MSC) and the US Merchant Marine to satisfy large-scale contingency requirements without massive aid from allies. Sealift "dehancement" continues as a long-term trend.

The balance between Soviet strategic airlift and sealift is precisely opposite. Moscow's merchant fleet, already much larger than US competition, is increasing capabilities at a rapid rate. Ship characteristics are chosen carefully to serve politico-military as well as economic purposes, especially in areas where large, specialized vessels cannot conveniently venture.

Above: An Ilyushin Il-76 (Candid) at Tyumen airfield in Siberia. Like all Aeroflot aircraft it has a direct military role and will be made available for military use whenever required. It has a very good short/rough field performance.

Comparative Flexibility
Composite Soviet mobility forces are sufficient to influence a range of low-key contingencies in widely-separated areas, from Angola to Afghanistan, but airlift/sealift shortages are still strong limiting factors for major military operations almost anywhere outside the home country or contiguous satellites.

Quick and efficient logistic support for allies is a US airlift specialty. MAC's squadrons also afford laudable (although limited) means of reinforcing forward deployed forces rapidly or

Below: An Antonov An-22 coming in to land. As far as is known this massive aircraft can airlift any mobile item in the Soviet Army inventory, including the T-72 and T-80 tanks. Such aircraft confer a new intervention capability on Soviet forces.

shifting sizable combat power anywhere in the world. Apparent flexibility, however, is conditioned by the dearth of merchant shipping, which makes it almost impossible to sustain major efforts without allied assistance. That combination calls for caution under most conceivable circumstances. since aid is not assured.

Overarching Policy Problems

Two overarching policy problems inhibit solutions to US shortcomings just described.

The price tag for US manpower dedicated to defense has been the dominant budgetary factor influencing the configuration and flexibility of America's conventional forces during the past decade, given fiscal constraints imposed by official policy. Inflation, coupled with attempts to compete with domestic pay scales, caused most of the problem. A retiree population

expanding exponentially also contributed. The biggest budgetary boost came in Nov. 1971, to start an All-Volunteer Force (AVF) off on the proper foot. Pay and allowances alone (including civilians) absorbed more than half of DoD's money for several years, before that proportion subsided somewhat. Percentage expenses for manpower, including outlays devoted to recruiting, construction, and dependent care, have stabilized, but costs continue to climb in response to periodic pay raises. (Pay for an entry-level enlisted man or woman now is

Below: The world's largest aircraft, a C-5A Galaxy. The overall US airlift capability still exceeds that of the USSR, but the lead is steadily diminishing, and the tactical airlift force, especially the C-130 Hercules, is showing signs of age.

Above: Soviet motor gunboats on the deck of a freighter, being delivered to a Third-World customer. The USSR is now the largest exporter of weaponry, which is giving them influence and creating a dependency in areas not previously in any way friendly to the Soviet Union.

$573.60 a month, as opposed to $21 for counterparts in the pre-World-War-II AVF. Soviet recruits receive an amount roughly equivalent to $5.50 a month.)

Inescapable expenditures for non-manpower-related operations and maintenance (O&M) approximated 15 cents more during the same 10-year period, a percentage that proved inadequate, given budgetary restrictions. US readiness to implement contingency plans still is subject to serious criticism as a consequence.

Above: The 25,000-ton Typhoon class strategic ballistic missile submarine is now under trial. It is armed with 20 forward-mounted SS-N-20 4,500-mile SLBMs.

The remaining third must be split between procurement programs, which shaped present US posture, research and development (R&D) which, in large part, determines US strength tomorrow, and military construction. The implications are inimical, because the Soviet Union devotes a much smaller proportion of its defense budget to manpower than the United States. Perhaps 20 per cent is a fair approximation. Moscow, therefore, could afford a larger force and modernize at more rapid rates if its total defense budget were exactly the same as that of the United States, since a much greater share of its money can be spent on machines.

A fragile US consensus that the United States should strengthen national security permitted the Reagan Administration to begin bolstering defense budgets in 1981. Whether that trend will persist is speculative, considering calls by many influential American blocs for scaled-back defense spending.

Declining Defense Technology

The United States starts with the world's richest reservoir of scientific resources. Constant feedback between civil and military markets encourages entrepreneurism and technological chain reactions not remotely equalled by Russian rivals. As a result, options still closed to the Soviets are completely open to America.

US predominance, however, shows signs of perishability that makes many intellectuals lament its lack of momentum.

Causes include uncertain goals that make it troublesome to chart a sound course for defense technology. Insistence on practical products is pronounced. Fund requests for abstract research are frequently cut or cancelled. Sharp fiscal caution extends to other R&D sectors. Consequent tendencies to tolerate few failures sometimes impede rapid progress.

Basic Research

US superiority in basic research still seems substantial. America clearly excels in 24 bellwether programs, the Soviets in 14:

Present Status

United States Superior		Soviet Union Superior	
Lead solid	13	Lead solid	14
Lead shaky	11	Lead shaky	0
	—		—
Total	24	Total	14

Statistical Summary (January 1960)	US	USSR	US Standing
Manpower	2,476,000	3,623,000	−1,147,000
Strategic nuclear			
Offense			
Bombers			
Long-range	540	160–190	+350–380
Medium-range	1,775	1,000	+775
Cruise missiles[1]	30	A few	About +30
Ballistic missiles			
ICBMs	12	Under 50	About −38
SLBMs[2]	48	48	Par
Warheads	60	Under 100	About −40
Defense			
ABM	0	0	Par
Interceptor aircraft[3]	2,700	5,000	−2,300
Surface-to-air missiles[3]	4,400	4,800	−400
Theater nuclear			
MRBM/IRBM[4]	51	200	−149
Other	Many	A few	+Many
Land power			
Manpower			
Army/Ground Forces	873,000	2,250,000	−1,377,000
Marines/Naval Infantry	170,600	A few	+170,600
Divisions			
Army/Ground Forces	14	136	−122
Marines/Naval Infantry	3	0	+3
Tanks[5]	12,975	35,000	−22,025
Tactical air forces			
Fighter/attack			
Land-based[6]	1,805	4,000	−2,195
Carrier-based	1,300	0	+1,300
Medium-range bombers[7]	0	1,000	−1,000
Naval forces			
Aircraft carriers	23	0	+23
Cruisers[8]	13	23	−10
Destroyers	226	124	+102
Frigates/other escorts	41	13	+28
Attack submarines	111	404	−293
Amphibious ships[9]	113	0	+113
Land-based bombers[10]	0	500	−500
Mobility forces			
Airlift[11]	1,725	1,065	−660
Sealift	954	873	+81

Notes

1. Short-range Soviet SS-N-1 cruise missiles deployed on Kilden and Krupny destroyers were primarily anti-ship weapons, but also had a nuclear capability against shore targets. US cruise missiles were in a Snark squadron at Presque Isle, Maine. Their range was about 5,500nm.
2. Six Soviet Zulu-V submarines, with two SS-N-4 SLBMs apiece, were deployed in the late 1950s. Ten Gulf-I and two Hotel-I companions, each with three SS-N-4 missiles, had been commissioned by 1960. All had to surface for firing.
3. US figures include interceptor aircraft and SAM systems in Army and Air Force reserve components.
4. Includes two Jupiter squadrons in Italy (total 25 missiles) and one in Turkey (26 missiles). Excludes Thor IRBMs, sent to Great Britain, because they passed to Royal Air Force (RAF) control after becoming operational.
5. US tanks included 12,500 Army and 475 Marine.
6. US fighter aircraft included 1,180 Air Force and 625 Marine.
7. The same Soviet medium-range bombers show in strategic nuclear and tactical air force categories.
8. Khrushchev's plan to scrap cruisers, resisted by Fleet Admiral Gorshkov, was still in gestation when the 1960s started. Retirements reduced the total to 19 by 1964.
9. Soviet naval infantry, which saw service during World War II, were nonexistent in 1960. Small regiments were reactivated in 1961–62. Landing Craft Utility (LCUs) were the largest available lift.
10. Soviet land-based naval aircraft, which exceeded 1,000 in the late 1950s, reduced rapidly after fighter squadrons shifted subordination to the PVO (air defense). Those shown above are all anti-ship bombers.
11. Excludes US Civil Reserve Air Fleet (CRAF) and Soviet Aeroflot. Includes active, reserve, strategic, and tactical airlift. Soviet aircraft are 140 AN-12 Cubs, 150 AN-8 Camps, and 775 LI-2s.

America's temporary purchase, however, is no cause for complacency. The US lead is solid in only slightly more than half of those cases (13 out of 24). Opposing scientists, who are closing the gap in 11 cases, protect Soviet primacy in every instance.

Relative US/Soviet ranks would reverse if straight-line projections of those trends continued:

Projected Status

United States Superior		Soviet Union Superior	
Present lead solid	13	Present lead solid	14
Subsequent gain	0	Subsequent gain	11
Total	13	Total	25

Soviet enterprise would take the technological lead by 25 to 13, where it now lags by much the same margin. Assuming that six entries currently carried as "parity" or "uncertain" shifted in US favor, the United States still could not reach Russia's level in basic research (19 to 25).

Applied Technology

It is sometimes difficult to distinguish fundamental superiority (a function of creativity) from design philosophy and restraints imposed by funds when assessing applied technology. This study makes no attempt to differentiate. It concentrates instead on practical products that now, or soon could, influence the US/Soviet military balance. *Supremacy that might have been has no practical value.* Each nation either applies technology effectively, or it does not.

Soviet forces presently deploy a smorgasbord of brand-new systems based on technology well known in the West, but slightly exploited. Significant samples include intercontinental ballistic missiles (ICBMs) with "cold launch" capabilities; mobile air defenses that can move with ground troops; satellite intercept and surveillance craft; armored vehicles and surface ships engineered expressly to operate in chemical/biological warfare environments; rapid-fire rocket launchers; and fire-control systems unmatched either by America or other NATO members.

US preeminence is undisputed in 35 signal instances, the Soviets in 28, but the situation promises to become increasingly unstable as the 1980s progress, given opposing prospects:

Present Status

United States Superior		Soviet Union Superior	
Lead solid	18	Lead solid	23
Lead shaky	17	Lead shaky	5
Total	35	Total	28

America's present lead is solid in about 50 per cent of the cases (18 out of 35). The Soviet side, gaining relative strength in the remaining 17, safeguards its top-flight ratings in all but five instances.

US/Soviet ranks would more than reverse if straight-line projections of those trends continued:

Projected Status

United States Superior		Soviet Union Superior	
Present lead solid	18	Present lead solid	23
Subsequent gain	5	Subsequent gain	17
Total	23	Total	40

Above: Basic and applied research are vital to maintain a technological lead over the USSR, but non-defense claims are given higher priority in the USA. The USA has shown through programs such as Apollo that given the determination and the financial resources it can achieve almost anything. That determination is, however, sometimes lacking and Congress finds pure research programs difficult to justify.

Below: Boeing NKC-135A with an airborne laser weapon fitted in the hump above the fuselage. This weapons system has been tested against both aircraft and missiles to see whether there is any future in this form of defense. A breakthrough in laser development seems imminent and when it happens the day of the beam weapon will have arrived, although space use seems more likely for a few decades yet.

Above: This chapter started with pictures of an American and a Soviet soldier side-by-side, and it is appropriate that it should end the same way. This US Army soldier is dressed for chemical warfare but NATO pays little more than lip service to a form of fighting which few seriously consider could actually happen, or could it?

Moscow would take the technological lead by 40 to 23, where it now lags by much less than that margin. Assuming four entries currently classified as "parity" or "uncertain" crossed into US columns, the United States still would be behind by 40 to 27.

Capstone

It is possible to quibble about classifications in the foregoing assessment, contesting whether proper categories have been included. Conclusions drawn are debatable at best, because one weakness may outweigh a dozen strengths, or vice versa. Some lags on each side are deliberate, caused at least as much by different missions and developmental styles as by asymmetries in competence or failures to foresee demands.

Still, if Soviet skills are overstated by, say 25 per cent, the day has passed when the United States could be smugly sure of unquestioned scientific and technological superiority, which has sustained it in the past and is the key to future capabilities.

Positive steps will be required to retain the present US stance, let alone improve its posture. Gray matter is more important than money when it comes to closing gaps. Success depends on strategists who understand the competition working in tandem with technologists to pick priorities that make research and requirements match, while reducing blind leads that waste time and resources. Perhaps most of all, the *potential* for superiority will prove meaningless if America fails to compete.

Culminating Comments

Quantitative changes since the Cuban missile crisis favor the Soviet Union. US *qualitative* superiority, less pronounced than in the past, is slipping away.

Nuclear Capabilities

Two legs of the US strategic nuclear triad are shaky. SLBMs, according to widespread belief, may become the only secure mainstay for some interim period, until some acceptable substitute replaces Minuteman missiles in silos and air-launched cruise missiles enter the US inventory in large numbers about the mid-1980s. (SAC had 16 B-52s armed with 12 ALCMs each – 192 total – in mid-December 1982.)

US nuclear strategy disregards defense. The American people and production base are exposed completely to ballistic missile attack. Their ability to survive a full-scale nuclear assault by the Soviet Union is nearly nil.

Resultant vulnerabilities drastically reduce the credibility of US promises to provide a nuclear "umbrella" for allies. The United States no longer could unleash assured destruction strikes against the Soviet Union to defend NATO or Asian friends without risking reciprocal devastation.

US theater nuclear weapons were practical deterrent and defensive tools two decades ago, when the United States could clamp a lid on local escalation by threatening to level the Soviet Union if its leaders employed counterpart systems. NATO allies in particular would have little to gain and a lot to lose today if we turned loose the theater nuclear genie, since war would take place largely on their home territory, where both people and possessions are unprotected.

Statistical Summary (January 1982)

	US	USSR	US Standing
		Current Status	
Strategic nuclear			
Offensive/retaliatory systems			
ICBMs	1,052	1,398	−346
Ballistic missile submarines[1]	(32)	(85)	(−53)
SLBMs	512	1,017	−505
Bombers[2]	376	235	+141
Total launchers	1,940	2,650	−710
Nuclear weapons			
ICBMs	2,152	5,302	−3,150
SLBMs	4,976	1,433	+3,543
Bombers[3]	2,534	325	+2,209
Total	9,662	7,060	+2,602
Strategic defensive systems			
ABM launchers[4]	0	32	−32
SAM launchers[4]	0	9,400	−9,400
Interceptor aircraft[5]	282	2,650	−2,368
Total	282	12,082	−11,800
Land power			
Armies/Ground Forces			
Active military manpower[6]	537	1,800	−1,263
Deployable[7]	781	2,882	−2,101
Total[8]			
Divisions			
US active, Soviet Cat. I-II			
Armor/tank	4	25	−21
Mechanized/motor rifle	6	48	−42
Infantry	4	0	+4
Air Assault	1	0	+1
Airborne	1	6	−5
Total	16	79	−63
US Natl. Gd., Soviet Cat. III			
Armor/tank	2	21	−19
Mechanized/motor rifle	1	82	−81
Infantry	5	0	+5
Airborne	0	1	−1
Total	8	104	−96
Grand total	24	183	−159
Tanks			
Heavy, medium	10,778	49,000	−38,222
Light[9]	1,560	1,600	−40
Total	12,338	50,600	−38,262
APC/AFV[10]	15,600	66,000	−50,400
Artillery	4,332	20,800	−16,468
Antitank guided missiles	14,577	25,500	−10,923
Heavy mortars[11]	2,691	7,800	−5,109
Tactical ballistic missiles[12]	229	1,370	−1,141
Tactical air defense			
Missiles	1,225	3,450	−2,225
Guns	564	9,300	−8,736
Marines/Naval Infantry			
Active military manpower[6]	101	13	+88
Deployable[13]	155	13	+142
Total			
Divisions			
Active	3	0	+3
Reserve	1	0	+1
Total	4	0	+4
Tanks			
Medium	550	0	+550
Light	0	200	−200
Total	550	200	+350
Armored carriers			
LVTPs[14]	853	0	+853
APC/AFV[10]	0	750	−750
Total	853	750	+103

Notes:
1. Includes 14 Soviet G-class diesel submarines.
2. Strategic bombers include B-52, FB-111, Bear, Bison, and Backfire (less those assigned to Soviet Naval Aviation).
3. US bomber loads are based on an average of 2 bombs per FB-111; 4 bombs per B-52, plus a variable number of SRAMs (1,150 from 1976–81). One large bomb or air-to-surface missile (ASM) per Bear and Bison; 2 ASMs per Backfire.
4. All Hawk and Nike Hercules SAMs number zero as of Apil 9, 1979.
5. US interceptor aircraft include Air National Guard.
6. Manpower figures are in thousands.
7. US Army deployable manpower includes mission-oriented base operating support. Soviet strengths exclude command and general support.
8. US Army manpower excludes strategic nuclear forces. Soviet strengths exclude paramilitary Border Guards and internal security troops, which total 438,000.
9. US light tanks include Sheridan armored assault vehicles.
10. US entries exclude wheeled vehicles. Soviet figures include them, since the characteristics are quite different.
11. Includes US 4.2-inch, Soviet 120mm and 240mm.

| | Current Status | | |
	US	USSR	US Standing
Artillery	604	0	+604
Antitank guided missiles	1,107	90	+1,017
Heavy mortars	0	180	−180
Naval forces (general purpose)			
Active military manpower[6]	521	415	+106
Surface combatants			
Aircraft carriers			
Attack	12	0	+12
Antisubmarine warfare	0	2	−2
Helicopter	12	2	+10
Total	24	4	+20
Cruisers			
SSM	22	27	−5
Other	5	9	−4
Total	27	36	−9
Destroyers			
SSM	47	13	+34
Other[15]	44	56	−12
Total	91	69	+22
Frigates[16]			
SSM	58	29	+29
Other	22	140	−118
Total	80	169	−89
Small combatants[17]			
SSM	1	155	−154
Other	1	500	−499
Total	2	655	−653
Attack submarines			
SSM	44	68	−24
Other	47	213	−166
Total	91	281	−190
Naval aircraft			
Afloat			
Fighter/attack	720	60	+660
ASW			
Fixed wing	110	0	+110
Helicopter	168	150	+18
Ashore			
Bombers			
ASW	0	460	−460
Fixed wing	220	195	+25
Helicopters	0	205	−205
Total	1,218	1,070	+148
Tactical air forces			
Active military manpower[18]	452	425	+27
Fighter/attack[19]			
Air Force	2,858	4,000	−1,142
Marine	440	0	+440
Total	3,298	4,000	−702
Bombers	259	565	−306
Grand total	3,557	4,565	−1,008
Helicopter gunships	1,082	1,000	+82
Airlift			
Strategic[20]	304	200	+104
Tactical			
Active	223	400	−177
Reserve	352	0	+352
Total	575	400	+175
Utility/cargo helicopters[21]	4,970	2,100	+2,870
Sealift			
Merchant cargo ships[22]			
Active	276	1,300	−1,024
Reserve	180	0	+180
Total	456	1,300	−844
Tankers[20]			
Active	563	400	+163
Reserve	16	0	+16
Total	579	400	+179
Grand total	1,035	1,700	−665
Amphibious ships[23]	61	81	−20

12. Tactical ballistic missiles include US Pershing, Lance, and Honest John, Soviet FROG, SCUD, Scaleboard, SS-21, and SS-22.
13. US Marines exclude air wings.
14. Landing Vehicle Tracked Personnel (LVTP).
15. US destroyer figure counts 8 in Naval Reserves.
16. 58 US frigates were armed with Harpoon missiles as of January 1981.
17. Soviet small combatants include Nanuchka and Sarancha SSM boats, and Grisha and Pots. US figures exclude 120 Coast Guard cutters and patrol boats.
18. Air Force manpower figures for both sides *exclude* strategic nuclear forces and *include* airlift forces.
19. Includes Air Force Reserve, Air National Guard, and Marine Corps Reserve.
20. Excludes 6 US KC-10 tanker aircraft that have cargo capabilities.
21. US cargo/utility helicopters include 4,569 Army and 401 Marine.
22. US merchant cargo ships and tankers include those in Military Sealift Command, the rest of the US Merchant Marine, the Effective US Controlled Fleet, and National Defense Reserve Fleet.
23. US amphibious ships include 12 helicopter carriers. Soviet figures count 55 air cushion vehicles.

Above: A Soviet soldier in a CW suit. The Soviet Army has actual combat experience of using chemical agents in Afghanistan and its client states have used them in Laos and Kampuchea. CW drills are tested far more regularly in the Soviet Army, which possesses huge stocks and gives every impression of intending to use them.

Plans predicated on nuclear options in the absence of effective defense for the United States or affiliates thus fail to inspire desired degrees of confidence at any employment level.

Chemical/Biological Warfare Capabilities

America's chemical/biological warfare (CB) capabilities, never considerable, are now next to nonexistent. No offensive forces in that medium might make the Kremlin fear starting a fray it could not finish. US defense is diffident.

Conventional Capabilities

Quantitative asymmetries are important when similar systems on each side (such as divisions) compete with each other in combat. Quality counts, but a prudent statistical balance must be maintained, because there are points beyond which mass matters more than excellence. Land, sea, and air forces alike lack flexibility if numbers are too few compared with competitors and commitments.

America's All-Volunteer Force (AVF) is too small to dispose of even one extensive contingency without reducing the required CONUS rotation base and/or uncovering commitments in other regions. It cannot absorb many more tanks, ships, and planes, because members are scarcely sufficient to maintain and operate machines now in service. The number of US divisions, aircraft squadrons, and carrier task forces would remain close to constant if the AVF were filled to authorized capacity with high performance personnel.

Attrition could take its toll quickly in all four US military services and the US Merchant Marine, which is also at a low level. Planned employment of Army reserve components or the National Defense Reserve Fleet to reinforce active strength and replace combat casualties early in any high-intensity conflict appears impractical, given depleted ranks and rather low states of readiness.

In short, current trends curtail US freedom of action. The upshot abridges abilities of US armed services to deter attacks on the United States, defend that country effectively if deterrence should fail, and safeguard associates whose security is closely linked with its own.

Those trends will be hard to reverse because:

High manpower costs inhibit force modernization much more in the United States than in the Soviet Union.

US technological supremacy shows signs of perishability that results more from policies than potential.

Most corrective options are politically and economically *unattractive*, but some current courses could prove *unacceptable* in the absence of change.

Step One in the process of obtaining a better balance between American and Soviet military strength is to ascertain true requirements, based on imperative US interests, objectives, and commitments. Step Two is to reshape US strategy. More money to operate, maintain, and refurbish US armed forces seems essential, but bolstering budgets will produce fewer defense benefits than desired unless US leaders improve their plans.

Sound conclusions would allow the Congress and the Executive Branch in concert to chart a course that assures America's ability to deter and, if need be, defend successfully against any sort of Soviet armed aggression into the Twenty-first Century.

Index

Illustration Credits

The publishers would like to thank wholeheartedly all the organizations, agencies, companies and the many individuals who have scoured their collections and so helped us to illustrate this book in the best manner possible. Most of the photographs in this book are official US Defense Department photographs supplied by the audio-visual services of the United States Air Force, Navy, Army and Marine Corps, and of the Department of Defense Office of Public Affairs. In addition, the Photograph Libraries of the State Department and The White House also provided photographs.

Many of the photographs which appear in the weaponry sections (and elsewhere) were supplied by the manufacturers of the weapons and systems described.

Certain photographic agencies and other organizations also supplied photographs and other illustrations, as follows:
10-11 (bottom) Gettysburg National Military Park (via Weidenfeld and Nicolson). **12:** Orbis Picture Library; **13:** Radio Times Hulton Picture Library. **14:** (top): Robert Hunt Library. **124, 127, 148** (warship profiles): *Jane's Fighting Ships* (© A.D. Baker III). **135** and **139** (warship profiles): © John Jordan. **196, 201** (colour profiles of aircraft): © Pilot Press Ltd. **258** (top): Royal Swedish Air Force photo.